PARENTHOOD
A Psychodynamic Perspective

THE GUILFORD PSYCHIATRY SERIES
Bertram J. Cohler and Henry Grunebaum, Editors

PARENTHOOD: A PSYCHODYNAMIC PERSPECTIVE
REBECCA S. COHEN, BERTRAM J. COHLER, AND SIDNEY H. WEISSMAN, EDITORS

In preparation
AGING AND SCHIZOPHRENIA
GENE COHEN AND NANCY E. MILLER, EDITORS

PARENTHOOD
A Psychodynamic Perspective

EDITED BY

REBECCA S. COHEN

*Michael Reese Hospital and Medical Center
and University of Chicago*

BERTRAM J. COHLER

University of Chicago

AND

SIDNEY H. WEISSMAN

*Michael Reese Hospital and Medical Center
and University of Chicago*

FOREWORDS BY
E. JAMES ANTHONY AND DANIEL OFFER

THE GUILFORD PRESS

New York   London

LIBRARY OF CONGRESS CATALOGING IN PUBLICATION DATA

Main entry under title:

Parenthood.

(The Guilford psychiatry series)
Outcome of the Conference on Parenthood as an Adult Experience held in March 1980 at
Marriott Hotel, Chicago, and sponsored by the Dept. of Psychiatry, Michael Reese Hospital.
Bibliography: p.
Includes index.
1. Parenthood—Psychological aspects—Congresses. I. Cohen, Rebecca S. II. Cohler, Bertram
J. III. Weissman, Sidney. IV. Conference on Parenthood as an Adult Experience (1980: Chicago,
Ill.). V. Michael Reese Hospital. Dept. of Psychiatry. VI. Series.
[DNLM: 1. Parent–child relations. 2. Parents—Psychology.
3. Psychoanalytic interpretation. WM 640.5.P2 P228]
HQ755.8.P378 1984   649'.1   82-18370
ISBN 0-89862-225-5

TO OUR SPOUSES AND
CHILDREN

CONTRIBUTORS

Jeanne Altmann, PhD, Biology Department, University of Chicago, Chicago, Illinois

Sol Altschul, MD, Faculty, The Institute for Psychoanalysis, The Barr–Harris Center for the Study of Separation and Loss during Childhood, and Department of Psychiatry, Northwestern University, Chicago, Illinois

E. James Anthony, MD, FRCPsy, DPM, William Greenleaf Eliot Division of Child Psychiatry, Washington University School of Medicine, St. Louis, Missouri

Helen Beiser, MD, Faculty, The Institute for Psychoanalysis, The Barr–Harris Center for the Study of Separation and Loss during Childhood, and Department of Psychiatry, University of Illinois, Chicago, Illinois

Paul Bohannan, DPhil, Division of Social Sciences and Communication, University of Southern California, Los Angeles, California

John Bowlby, MD, ScD, Department for Children and Parents, Tavistock Clinic, London, England

Andrew M. Boxer, MA, Laboratory for the Study of Adolescence, Department of Psychiatry, Michael Reese Hospital and Medical Center, and Committee on Human Development, University of Chicago, Chicago, Illinois

J. Alexis Burland, MD, Department of Psychiatry and Human Behavior, Jefferson Medical College of Thomas Jefferson University, and Philadelphia Psychoanalytic Institute, Philadelphia, Pennsylvania

Rebecca S. Cohen, MA, Department of Psychiatry, Michael Reese Hospital and Medical Center, and School of Social Service Administration, University of Chicago, Chicago, Illinois

Bertram J. Cohler, PhD, Departments of Behavioral Science (Committee on Human Development), Education, and Psychiatry, and the College, University of Chicago, Chicago, Illinois

Muller Davis, JD, Jones, Baer and Davis, Chicago, Illinois

Miriam Elson, MA, Faculty, Teacher Education Program, The Institute for Psychoanalysis, School of Social Service Administration, University of Chicago, and Chicago Child Care Society, Chicago, Illinois

Sherman C. Feinstein, MD, Bennett Laboratory for Child Psychiatry Research, Department of Psychiatry, Michael Reese Hospital and Medical Center, and Department of Psychiatry, University of Chicago, Chicago, Illinois

James Fisch, MD, Department of Psychiatry, Michael Reese Hospital and Medical Center, and Department of Psychiatry, University of Chicago, Chicago, Illinois viii

Benjamin Garber, MD, Department of Psychiatry, Michael Reese Hospital and Medical Center, Department of Psychiatry, University of Chicago, and Child Analysis Faculty, The Institute for Psychoanalysis, Chicago, Illinois

Jerome M. Grunes, MD, Department of Psychiatry, Michael Reese Hospital and Medical Center, and Latter Half of Life Program, Northwestern University Medical School, Chicago, Illinois

Gunhild O. Hagestad, PhD, College of Human Development, Pennsylvania State University, University Park, Pennsylvania

Florence Halprin, MA, Committee on Human Development, University of Chicago, Chicago, Illinois

Michael B. Hoffman, MD, Department of Psychiatry and Pritzker Children's Hospital, Michael Reese Hospital and Medical Center, Chicago, Illinois

Laura Lein, PhD, Wellesley College Center for Research on Women, Wellesley, Massachusetts

Abner J. Mikva, JD, U.S. Court of Appeals, District of Columbia Circuit, Washington, D.C.

Hyman L. Muslin, MD, Department of Psychiatry, University of Illinois College of Medicine, Chicago, Illinois

Daniel Offer, MD, Department of Psychiatry, Michael Reese Hospital and Medical Center, and Department of Psychiatry, University of Chicago, Chicago, Illinois

Anne C. Petersen, PhD, Department of Individual and Family Studies, College of Human Development, Pennsylvania State University, University Park, Pennsylvania

Mary J. Rogel, PhD, Young Adult and Adolescent Decision Making about Contraception Project, Department of Psychiatry, Michael Reese Hospital and Medical Center, and University of Chicago, Chicago, Illinois

John Munder Ross, PhD, Division of Child and Adolescent Psychiatry, Department of Psychiatry, Downstate Medical Center, and Department of Psychology in Psychiatry, Cornell Medical College, New York, New York

Leo Sadow, MD, Faculty, The Institute for Psychoanalysis, and Department of Psychiatry, University of Illinois College of Medicine, Chicago, Illinois

Donald D. Schwartz, MD, Faculty and Committee on Child and Adolescent Analysis, The Institute for Psychoanalysis, Chicago, Illinois

Michael A. Smyer, PhD, College of Human Development, Pennsylvania State University, University Park, Pennsylvania

Albert J. Solnit, MD, Departments of Pediatrics and Psychiatry, School of Medicine, and Child Study Center, Yale University, New Haven, Connecticut

Brenda Solomon, MD, Department of Psychiatry, Michael Reese Hospital and Medical Center, Chicago, Illinois

Karen Stierman, BS, College of Human Development, Pennsylvania State University, University Park, Pennsylvania

David Terman, MD, Department of Psychiatry, Michael Reese Hospital and Medical Center, Department of Psychiatry, University of Chicago, and Faculty, The Institute for Psychoanalysis, Chicago, Illinois

Sidney H. Weissman, MD, Department of Psychiatry, Michael Reese Hospital and Medical Center, and Department of Psychiatry, University of Chicago, Chicago, Illinois

ACKNOWLEDGMENTS

In a volume such as this, we must begin with an appreciation for the childhood experiences with our own parents during which were laid down the baselines for adult capacities, but especially, for our own experiences as adult parent persons. The continuity of the generations is demonstrated as we consider ourselves the linkage between our own parents' generation and the generation we have and continue to parent. Therefore, to both generations we express our gratitude.

Our volume is the outcome of a Conference on Parenthood as an Adult Experience held in March 1980, sponsored by the Michael Reese Department of Psychiatry. Dr. Daniel Offer, Chairman of the Department, who supported us in planning that Conference, and who generously offered his guidance and the resources of the Department in working on the book, was a "parent" and friend throughout both projects. To him, we are deeply indebted for all that he gave, but, particularly for the steady encouragement to continue when obstacles arose. We also want to thank the people, too numerous to acknowledge here, who helped make the Conference successful so that our present volume could emerge. We must give special thanks to the members of the interdisciplinary Michael Reese Department of Psychiatry Workshop on Parenthood who collaborated with us in conceptualizing the Conference and the book. These colleagues, Harold Balikov, Mark Gehrie, Doris Gruenewald, Paula Kliegman, Mark Levey, Mark Oberlander, Louise Saltzman, and Monica Schwartz, must be accorded great credit for nourishing our initial efforts in this work. We deeply appreciate the ardor and commitment of Ruth Strawder and Josephine Wright to the administrative and clerical tasks involved. Additionally, Ms. Wright's comments on the content were most helpful in our editorial work.

Finally, we want to thank those people who have shared marital and parenting alliances with us and have had a large part in the fortunate life circumstances out of which this volume grew. Anne Cohler, Julie Weissman, and Martin Cohen contributed greatly in supporting our work by their deep understanding of the demanding nature of the task we undertook. They gave of themselves unstintingly, and they have our deepest gratitude.

R.S.C.—B.J.C.—S.H.W.

FOREWORD

E. JAMES ANTHONY

In older times, child rearing was one of those menial and mediocre occupations that was relegated to women in the remoter parts of the household away from the male quarters where the serious and significant business of life was transacted. Once the young were regarded as sufficiently domesticated, and taught to be seen but not heard, they were gradually introduced to the menfolk, who then condescended to instruct them further in the arts of civilized living. The degree of segregation of fathers from children varied with class and culture. In the latter half of this century behavioral scientists began to take a closer look at child rearing. They rapidly concluded that parenthood was too important a matter to be left only to the parents, and more particularly to the mothers, grandmothers, and aunts. Parenthood was clearly a phenomenon open to investigation like other phenomena. One of the first questions asked was whether it was innate or acquired. If parenting was instinctual, then accumulated evidence would suggest that something was radically awry with the human instinct, since it often appeared to function deficiently, irregularly, and disturbingly.

According to some, man was paying a price for his apical position in evolution. His cortex had hypertrophied and the instinctual life had been largely taken over by the mind. It was not so much that his instincts had attenuated but that their operations were no longer adequate to the task of preparing a human being for a human habitat. The extraordinary grasp of consciousness, the equally extraordinary and mysterious grasp of self-consciousness, the capacity to think both retrospectively and prospectively, and the capacity to represent the world internally, downgraded the importance of instinctual life and favored the higher processes of learning and being taught. One could no longer count only on thoughtless automatic action and consequently that one had to learn everything anew. Since we were seen as less controlled by instinct, we could do things differently, try out different procedures, and strive to make human parenthood and human upbringing a specifically human experience. Depending on environmental circumstances, the parental functions could be adapted to what was needed.

Today we are aware of new, more complex understanding of the instinctual or biologic foundations of parenthood as well as of the complex psychological foundations of parenthood. The life experiences which support parenthood begin in infancy. Indeed, the child is the father to the parent. Early attachment behavior demonstrates in both parent and child (the next generation) the biologic or instinctual foundations of parenthood. Separation anxiety, surrogation problems, sibling experiences, and the triangulation of the mother, infant, and father relationship are all experiences which relate to either or both the biologic and psychological factors which will affect the child's eventual capacity to become a parent.

In the past when asked to recommend a textbook on parenthood, other than my own, I always came up with the classical exposition on the subject, Butler's *The Way of All Flesh*. The lack of focused literature about parenthood, other than my own, left Butler's classical work as a statement of the pitfalls of parenting which could be contrasted with those experienced by the modern parent. Butler tells parents what to do and what not to do if the well-being of the children is to be given prime consideration. The Pontifex children had all the material advantages of life: They ate and drank well, slept in comfortable beds, had the best doctors to attend them when they were ill, and the best education that could be had for the money. If they missed something that was warm and loving, they never knew it because they had never experienced it. As Butler put it, "Young people have a marvelous faculty for either dying or adapting themselves to circumstances." Even if the children are unhappy, they can be prevented from finding this out for themselves since the parents often make it clear to them that they have no reason for being unhappy, and that it would be absurdly illogical to be so.

Looking at my earlier work, and Butler's, we can now ask how we might today organize our present-day understanding and observations regarding the phenomenon of parenthood. First of all, we see it as a very dynamic state in which conflict and ambivalence are often crucially at work. Secondly, we see parenthood passing through "developmental phases" with the anlage of parenthood beginning in infancy and emerging in adult life. Thirdly, we observe mutual interactions between the parent and the child, so that the child evokes old feelings in the parent, and the parent new feelings in the child. Finally, parenting is no longer seen as shut off from the father. He is seen and experienced as an integral part of the child-rearing process through all stages of the child's development. A balanced amount of mothering and fathering is conducive to good mental health; too much of one or too much of the other creates problems and generates psychopathology.

This volume provides further clarification and expansion of our knowledge concerning the phenomenon of parenthood. Each of the above mentioned areas is addressed and elaborated upon. The editors address as well a number of other areas unique to the modern family and parent, and force us to reexamine many of our previously trusted assumptions. This volume serves as a welcome addition to the literature on parenthood.

FOREWORD

DANIEL OFFER

Parents have been the subject of universal interest since the beginning of time. Although they represent the origin of us all, their position vis-à-vis their offspring was always so tenuous that the fifth commandment in the Bible states explicitly to: "Honor thy father and thy mother as the Lord thy God commanded thee." And, on the other hand, the sacrifice of children to pagan gods is part of recorded (i.e., relatively recent) history.

Were we to focus only on the hostile–destructive aspect of the relationship between parents and their children we could not capture the intensity of the relationship. The love between the generations is often described in ancient times, one of the most famous examples being the mother who chose to give up her baby in Solomon's Court so that the baby would not be cut in half. Yet, deep-rooted ambivalence is so commonplace that it is universally observed among all cultures with which I am familiar. We see it in the historical battles for power between fathers and sons or in the once renowned fictionalized stories about generational battles, compromises, and true affection. It is not important, from our point of view, whether the stories are historically correct or whether they date from such remote periods that we are unable to determine whether such a person(s) existed. Legends, or myths, were created by man's fertile mind, always having one leg in the real (historical) world and the other in his imagination.

The behavior of the younger growing generation is a good indicator of the psychodynamics of the older generation. The unfulfilled dreams and wishes the adults have had for their own lives are only too often powerfully transferred to the behavior of their children. In addition, the young also represent to their parents their own (i.e., the parents) inevitable demise. As Freud (1913) has speculated in *Totem and Taboo*, the conflict between the generations is a continuous one, although it manifests itself in a variety of forms and intensities at different historical periods. To the children, the older generation represents a clear obstacle. They have to wait before they can acquire power, prestige, and leadership, and they are forever beholden to their parents. In addition, adolescents feel sexually and physically superior to their parents and make no secret of it.

The love and affection between the generations which is so clearly present seems also to be continuously in a state of flux. Children can bring out extremely positive feelings in their parents, and once established in one direction they are mirrored and reciprocated. In other words, the children learn to love and respect their parents, and so it goes on.

In no area is this complex, ambivalent relationship more apparent than when man lets his imagination run. Thus, Freud (1939) comments in *Moses and Monotheism* that in ancient times there was a continuous, murderous, battle between the leader–father and the young, growing sons. It was only with the "invention" of morality (i.e., religion) that these killings stopped. We have also the obvious examples of Sophocles's *Oedipus Rex*, Shakespeare's *King Lear* and *Hamlet*, and many others. It is of interest to note that the majority of the fictional representations deal with the conflictual aspects of the relationships between the generations.

Another universal mirror which allows us to see ourselves as we really are, albeit in an exaggerated form, is in fairy tales. It is not my purpose here to critically analyze this most fascinating literature. However, let me take the fairy tale of *Little Red Riding Hood*[1] as one example. From a psychological point of view, the mother sends Little Red Riding Hood off to "get lost." The directions to the grandmother's house were not clear enough, for whatever reasons, and the child did, indeed, get lost. Another mother figure, who should be reliable, turns into a wolf and threatens the girl. Only a "neutral" hunter rescues the girl from the complicated maternal figures. In the tale, the girl wants only to enjoy the beautiful flowers which are all around her. The possible psychodynamic explanations for this particular version of the intriguing fairy tale are numerous. I have only wanted to illustrate the complex ambivalent relationship between the generations as depicted in the above example. One might be tempted to ask why the fictional images point to conflict, aggression, and violence and rarely depict the positive aspects. Is that a statement about a universal, built-in, inevitable, natural conflict? Since every child will (or could) eventually become a parent, are hostility and envy really parts of the human condition? Are both parties equally involved, or are the parents the initiators of the process? If they did initiate the process, why?

During the past 100 years psychology, psychoanalysis, and psychiatry have entered the mainstream of scientific inquiry. Whether through experimental situations, clinical settings, or group psychology, many diverse forms of normal development and/or psychopathology have been investigated. We understand considerably more today about the individual and a large number of complex situations than we did during last century. Also, during the past three decades much progress has been made in the study of the disturbed family. Consequently, family therapy as a major form of psychotherapy has been well established. More

---

1. I am using only one example of the fairy tale; many other versions exist.

recently, Walsh (1982) has edited a book summarizing what is known about the functioning of the normal family.

A review of the clinical literature of the past three decades indicates clearly that families with disturbed children and adolescents have been described as disturbed social systems. The inability to communicate basic values, beliefs, and affect within the family has long been thought to be a corollary of mental illness and deviant behavior. Most of the research in the area of family functioning, however, has been on disturbed families. The assumption has been that well-functioning families are the antithesis of those with overt psychopathology. Only recently has there been a systematic attempt to discuss the normal family. Obviously, an understanding of normal family processes is essential to the understanding of families with disturbed children and adolescents, since there is a continuing need for the diagnosis and treatment of mentally ill children, adolescents, and their parents. If mental health professionals do not become more aware of what normal family processes are, it will be difficult, indeed, for them to determine what is psychopathological.

In a recent study my colleagues and I (Offer, Ostrov, & Howard, 1982) examined in great detail the relationship between parents and their adolescent children and the mental health of those adolescents. We examined, also, the extent of agreement between parents and adolescents regarding the adolescent's self-image. One hundred and six intact, middle-class, suburban, mostly white families (both biological parents) participated in the study. The study of the adolescents and their parents took place within the same time period, in 1980. These adolescents were between 15 and 17 years old.

Our results demonstrated that there was a high correlation between parent–child communication and the quality of the adolescent's mental health. In general, better parent–child communication is associated with more positive mental health in adolescents. This association indicates that in smoothly functioning family systems, there is good parent–child communication and positive self-perceptions among adolescents and children.

The association between parent–adolescent communication and adolescent self-image is consistent with the line of research begun by Singer and Wynne (1965) and more recently pursued by Doane, West, Goldstein, Rodnick, and Jones (1981). These studies have demonstrated that the more communication deviance there is among individuals in a family, the greater the risk for children in those families to develop severe psychopathology. Taken together, the results of these studies show that parents agree with their children's generally positive self-perceptions. They also show that the more parents agree with each other and with their adolescent child's self-perceptions, the healthier the adolescent's self-image. It seems reasonable to conclude that in a smoothly functioning family system, members of the two generations communicate with each other about their feelings, perceptions, and goals. However, it is not my purpose here to describe the studies, their methodology, and results. Suffice it to say that more studies like these are necessary before we can truly comprehend the full range of parenting behavior.

Parenthood as a specific psychological event for *both* generations has been an extremely difficult phenomenon to observe and/or study. There have been studies on the impact that being a parent has on parents, and many more on how parents influence their children. However, we do not have, to date, direct observational studies on reciprocal relationships between children and their parents and how the nature of the interaction influences mental health or mental illness in the parent and/or child. From an experimental research point of view, then, parenthood remains as elusive a phenomenon as it was in years gone by. Before we can seriously embark on new ventures in raising children and improving the parent–child relationship, it is incumbent upon us to find methods which will enable us to study the parenthood experience and parenting. These methods are needed in order to help us determine what went wrong and why in a particular family. For example, how do certain children grow up to be relatively healthy despite a disturbing familial environment? Once we understand better the complexities of the present situation, we should be able to raise a generation that can cope more effectively with modern life than did their parents.

This volume is a clear and concise statement about what is known currently in the field. The editors have assembled a group of distinguished investigators who share with the reader their vast clinical and scholarly knowledge about parenthood. I believe that mental health professionals and behavioral scientists interested in life-course study and in children and their parents will find this book fascinating. In addition to presenting the current state of our knowledge, it paves the way for expanding and integrating the study of parenthood with adulthood.

REFERENCES

Doane, J. A., West, K. I., Goldstein, M. J., Rodnick, E. H., & Jones, J. E. Parental communication deviance and affective style. *Archives of General Psychiatry*, 1981, *38*, 679–685.

Freud, S. Totem and taboo (1913). *Standard Edition, 13*. London: Hogarth Press, 1964.

Freud, S. Moses and monotheism (1939). *Standard Edition, 23*. London: Hogarth Press, 1964.

Offer, D., Óstrov, E., & Howard, K. I. Family perceptions of adolescent self-image. *Journal of Youth and Adolescence*, 1982, *2*(4), 281–291.

Singer, M. T., & Wynne, L. C. Thought disorder and family relations of schizophrenics: IV. Results and implications. *Archives of General Psychiatry*, 1965, *12*, 201–212.

Walsh, F. (Ed.). *Normal family processes*. New York: Guilford Press, 1982.

CONTENTS

PARENTHOOD
A Psychodynamic Perspective

I

DEVELOPMENTAL PERSPECTIVES

Across the past two decades, there has been a significant shift in the study of personality development from consideration only of infancy and early childhood, to a study of continuing development across the life course. As a consequence, the field of adult development has become an important source of findings regarding adjustment to major roles, including the process by which adults are socialized into these roles. Central to much of this discussion is the concept of developmental crisis, task, or issue. First discussions of adult development, such as Erikson's (1963), provided the outline for understanding the series of challenges to persons across the course of adulthood. Depending upon the mode of response to such challenges as that of generativity versus stagnation, more or less favorable outcomes could be expected for resolution of subsequent crises, such as that of ego integrity versus despair.

Subsequent discussion raised the question whether these challenges should be viewed strictly as crises, or whether it would be better to view them as tasks, similar to those confronted earlier in life, without assuming that major psychopathology would be the consequence of a less than complete resolution (Rossi, 1968). Much of the more recent discussion of such adult challenges as parenthood has employed the concept of the developmental task as used in the fields of education and human development. Perhaps the best statement of this concept is provided by Havighurst, who observes:

> A developmental task arises at or about a certain period in the life of the individual, successful achievement of which leads to happiness and success with later tasks, while failure leads to unhappiness in the individual, disapproval by society, and difficulty with later tasks. (1953, p. 2)

Within the fields of psychoanalysis and psychiatry, the concept of developmental task was first discussed by Freud (1905). In attempting to explain the basis of the perversions, Freud realized it was necessary to consider the process of development of the sexual instincts starting with early childhood. Beginning in the 1915 revision of the *Three Essays on the Theory of Sexuality*, and continuing through revisions during the years 1921–1924 which proposed the concept of the Oedipus complex, Freud delineated a series of stages or phases in early childhood in which, as a result of the experiences of stimulation of sensitive

1

zones or modes, the instinct was modified in particular ways through interaction with the caretaker. Abraham (1921, 1924) systematized Freud's thinking about the developmental process and noted that

> each new product of development possesses characteristics derived from its earlier history. . . . Psychoanalysis . . . has demonstrated that the close connection that character-formation has with the psychosexual development of the child in especial with the different libidinal stages and with the successive relations of the libido to its object . . . even after childhood the character of the individual is subject to processes of evolution and involution. (1924, p. 416)

This epigenetic perspective on the life cycle, in which events taking place earlier in life continually influenced the outcome of later events, was later enlarged by Erikson (1963) who translated the earlier libidinal formulation of epigenesis, into terms more acceptable in the contemporary idiom. However, neither Abraham nor Erikson denied the continuity of psychological development *over the course* of the life cycle. Events taking place in adulthood were given weight merely equal to those of childhood in understanding the vicissitudes of later personality development. This epigenetic perspective on personality development suggests only that there are a number of phases across the life cycle, each marked by some unique "core" conflict between the self and significant others which, as Bibring has noted, represent

> developmental phenomena at point of no return between one phase and the next, when decisive changes deprive former central needs of their significance, forcing the acceptance of highly charged new goals and functions. (1959, p. 116)

DEVELOPMENTAL TASK AND PSYCHOSOCIAL ADAPTATION

Depending upon the manner in which the core conflict is resolved which is associated with each of these phases along the cycle, more or less successful future adaptation may be realized. More appropriate resolution of nuclear conflicts associated with the several preadult and adult stages of personality development described so clearly by Erikson (1963) renders adults more immune to crisis and regression during periods of stress. When stress is experienced regarding the demand for more differentiated and complex modes of relating to others characteristic of adulthood, such as is represented by marriage, parenthood, or work, there is regression toward those preadult phases of personality development at which there has been either the greatest unresolved conflict or the greatest amount of previous satisfaction. This process of development and regression is consistent with Freud's (1911, 1913, 1915–1917, 1917) position on personality development and psychopathology, as well as with the subsequent formulations of Nunberg (1932), Fenichel (1945), and Nagera (1964).

Understood as a major adult developmental task, parenthood has a unique capacity to initiate such regression. Successively, across the years of active parenting, care of children may revive parents' conflicts or concerns related to their own childhood, leading to reactivation of earlier conflicts, and even regression to earlier phases in development such as is seen in serious psychopathology accompanying resolution of issues in child care. The guiding hypothesis for this view of parenthood as a developmental phase was first stated by Deutsch (1945) in her classic study of motherhood. As she observed:

> Every mother brings into [motherhood] certain emotional factors and conflicts, that is, a certain psychodynamic background partly determined by her life situation, partly by her inner disposition due to her whole psychological development. From this, we can understand that while the beginning of motherhood poses the most mature task of femininity, it will also tend to revive all the infantile conceptions of pregnancy and motherhood and childhood emotional reactions. (1945, p. 14)

In her paper "Parenthood as a Developmental Phase," Benedek (1959) extended this observation to the entire life cycle, considering not only the parents of young children, but parenthood during the school years, through adolescence and adulthood, and throughout the years after the children are grown, through grandparenthood and greatgrandparenthood.

As children grow older, subsequent experiences and the vicissitudes of the parent–child relationship continue to revive salient parental personality conflicts (Rangell, 1955; Anthony, 1970a, 1970b). Courtship, engagement, and marriage also stir up relevant parental developmental conflicts (Kestenberg, 1970, 1976). With the advent of parenthood, both generations of parents experience renewed conflicts. For the grandparental generation, observation of adult children with their own children evokes memories of their own child-rearing experiences, including concern that they may not have been good enough parents. Among adult offspring, discomfort may be evoked by realization that, as parents, they may be saying and doing the same things with their children which had in their own childhood caused them to experience feelings of anger and resentment.

DEVELOPMENTAL TASK AND SOCIAL TIMING

Viewed from a psychodynamic perspective, the concept of developmental task refers primarily to intrapsychic processes. However, this concept may also be understood from a normative perspective, in which parenthood is viewed in terms of expectable timing, together with other expected and eruptive life events (Neugarten & Hagestad, 1976). From this perspective, the task of parenthood becomes one of providing care for a dependent child in such a manner that the needs of each generation may be met. Failure to adapt to the relevant developmental task leads to conflict with other adult roles, and may prevent those changes in the parent–child relationship which are expected as children grow to adulthood.

In contrast with such developmental tasks as bereavement and grief, which, most often are not expected (Lindemann, 1944), the timing of parenthood is expectable in this society, and is based on a socially shared sense of timing, including changing definitions across successive cohorts. As Neugarten, Moore, and Lowe (1965) and Neugarten and Moore (1968) have demonstrated, there is a marked consensus regarding most appropriate timing in the attainment of appropriate adult roles. At the same time, changes do occur in perceptions of social timing as definitions change, both of markers of the life course, and of the most appropriate points for such role transitions. Daniels and Weingarten (1982) have shown that transition to the parental role, previously considered most desirable during the mid- to late 20s, is now more commonly defined as occurring during the late 20s to early 30s. Clearly, the experience of parenthood is quite different for women becoming parents just after completing school, than for couples assuming the parental role after several years of building both marital intimacy and solid careers.

Further, the nature of the social surround itself makes a difference. As Nydegger (1973, 1981) notes, assumption of the role of father in middle age might be more difficult for a man living in the suburbs, and having few other role colleagues, than for a man living in the city, acquainted with other middle-aged men who have recently become fathers: Having already attained a degree of career success and financial stability, these middle-aged fathers may be able to devote more attention and time to child care than their younger counterparts.

Timing of grandparenthood is as significant an issue as transition to parenthood, and even less well studied. As Rosow (1967) has noted, grandparenthood is not a role which persons themselves elect, but into which they are inducted as a result of changes in the lives of others. Depending upon the age both of parents and grandparents themselves, expectations for assistance and advice, and geographic proximity between the generations, the experience of this role is quite varied. It is not uncommon in contemporary society for the same person to be the parent of children roughly the same age as grandchildren from an earlier marriage. Such variations in timing and family formation have a significant impact upon the experience both of grandparenthood and parenthood.

Finally, it should be noted that the nature of the social convoy (Kahn, 1979) in which parents find themselves as they move across the life course, together with occurrence of other expected and eruptive events, continually reshapes the meaning of parenthood for parents themselves. A woman unexpectedly widowed in her 30s, while her children are still young, will have a different experience of parenthood than a woman whose husband is available to help with the child care and housework, and also provide a source of emotional support for both wife and children. Divorce may shape the experience of parenthood in similar ways, although introducing the additional problem of the continuing need for negotiation in behalf of the children, often among persons with an active dislike for each other. The presence of other divorcées or widows among parents in the same community can provide a much needed source of support in the presence of these unexpected and, generally, adverse life events which provide a major threat to maintenance of positive morale.

CONTRIBUTIONS IN SECTION I

The chapters in this volume address parenthood as a developmental task in each of the two ways we have outlined, with the exception of Altmann's chapter, which discusses aspects of ethology and parenthood.

For Altmann, development is both social and biogenetic. Reviewing the primate literature in terms of her own experience with the Amboseli baboons of southern Kenya, she demonstrates the significance of ecology and the social surround as determinants of parental capacity to provide good care. Particularly significant is the relationship between baboon mothers and their genetic relatives who provide them with support and protection, such as against predatory foe. To a much larger extent than among human mothers, maternal care among monkeys and apes is determined by the actions of others in the band with whom they compete for food. Noteworthy is the shared condition among baboon and monkey families and many human families that mothers must be caretakers as well as providers for their young. In such circumstances, particularly where competition is a significant determinant of caretaking and social organization, in general, infants must adapt their behavior to that of the parents. (Empathy is not an issue, here!) If too much primal time is devoted to caretaking, there is insufficient time for the critical issue of maintenance activity—and the family organization disintegrates.

Anthony explores the concept of creativity in the sphere of parenting in terms of childhood origins which set the stage for later parenting. Capacity for mutuality between mother and child, including capacity for creating a shared illusion between them, depends upon the nature of developmental issues reactivated by the experience of parenthood. Success achieved in the development of this shared experience intermediate between mother and child plays a critical role in the child's subsequent capacity for recreating this illusory and playful space.

Other chapters in the first section focus more directly on issues of timing, as related to social context, although both the chapter by Boxer and his associates, as well as that by Cohen and Weissman, recognize the importance of parenthood as a developmental task and as a transition point in the adult life course. In particular, Boxer and his colleagues note the significance of the particular relationship between early adolescents and their parents upon the perceptions of the two generations. Both characteristics of the present age of the offspring, and also the nature of the parent's own adolescence, as reexperienced in the adolescence of their offspring, contribute to the degree of satisfaction experienced in the present. Cohen and Weissman assume the importance of the parents' past as an influence on the present, but focus much more on present implications of that past.

Always important as that component of the marital tie which involves the couple together in child care, the parenting alliance becomes particularly important, as, for example, when the social context is less facilitating. As already noted, the parenting alliance is of particular importance when there has been a divorce; this alliance enables each parent to transcend immediate feelings in maintaining concern for the child's best interests. Psychiatric or medical hospitalization of a child represent other situations in which the parenting alliance becomes important. Always the "silent accompanist" of the marriage, the parenting alliance is put into particular relief at such times of crisis, so often created by eruptive events, or timing issues.

Issues of social context and timing are of particular significance in Rogel and Petersen's chapter. Rogel and Petersen detail the problems of very early parenthood, and of the variations in the quality of the social convoy for mothers negotiating the parental role at a point earlier in the course of life than role colleagues (early "off time"). In her chapter, Lein addresses the parental role and other adult roles. She details the relationship between home and work, including the struggles of "dual-career" couples to make ends meet and also realize their responsibilities as parents.

Just as children grow to adulthood, there is a shift in the nature of responsibility and care within the family. If child care marks the early stages of parenthood, parent care marks the late stage of this relationship. As Grunes's chapter indicates, where, formerly, parents had cared for their children, now they find themselves cared for *by* their children. It is not uncommon for a middle-aged parent to have responsibility for the care both of his/her own young children, and also responsibility for the care of his/her own parents, and even grandparents. Within these families, persons in their 60s may be continuing to care for their own parents who may be in their late 80s. We have only just begun to come to terms with the meaning of such patterns of care across generations.

REFERENCES

Abraham, K. The first pregenital stage of the libido (1921). In *Selected papers on psychoanalysis*. New York: Basic Books, 1960.

Abraham, K. A short study of the libido viewed in the light of the mental disorders (1924). In *Selected papers on psychoanalysis*. New York: Basic Books, 1960.

Anthony, E. J. The reaction of parents to adolescents and their behavior. In E. J. Anthony & T. Benedek (Eds.), *Parenthood: Its psychology and psychopathology*. Boston: Little, Brown, 1970. (a)

Anthony, E. J. The reaction of parents to the oedipal child. In E. J. Anthony & T. Benedek (Eds.), *Parenthood: Its psychology and psychopathology*. Boston: Little, Brown, 1970. (b)

Benedek, T. Parenthood as a developmental phase: A contribution to libido theory. *Journal of the American Psychoanalytic Association*, 1959, 7, 389–417.

Benedek, T. Parenthood during the life-cycle. In E. J. Anthony & T. Benedek (Eds.), *Parenthood: Its psychology and psychopathology*. Boston: Little, Brown, 1970.

Benedek, T. Discussion of parenthood as a developmental phase. In *Psychoanalytic investigations: Selected papers*. New York: Quadrangle Books, 1973.

Bibring, G. Some considerations of the psychological processes in pregnancy. *Psychoanalytic Study of the Child*, 1959, *14*, 113–121.

Daniels, P., & Weingarten, K. *Sooner or later: The timing of parenthood in adult lives*. New York: Norton, 1982.

Deutsch, H. *The psychology of women* (Vol. 2). New York: Grune & Stratton, 1945.

Erikson, E. *Childhood and society* (Rev. ed.). New York: Norton, 1963.

Fenichel, O. *The psychoanalytic theory of the neuroses*. New York: Norton, 1945.

Freud, S. Three essays on the theory of sexuality (1905). *Standard Edition, 6*, 125–248. London: Hogarth Press, 1953.

Freud, S. Psychoanalytic notes upon an autobiographical account of paranoia, dementia paranoides (1911). *Standard Edition, 12*, 3–84. London: Hogarth Press, 1958.

Freud, S. The predisposition to obsessional neurosis (1913). *Standard Edition, 12*, 311–326. London: Hogarth Press, 1958.

Freud, S. On transformations of instinct as exemplified in anal erotocism (1917). *Standard Edition, 17*, 125–134. London: Hogarth Press, 1955.

Freud, S. Introductory lectures on psychoanalysis (1915–1917). *Standard Edition, 15–16*. London: Hogarth Press, 1961–1963.

Havighurst, R. *Human development and education*. New York: Longmans-Green, 1953.

Kahn, R. Aging and social support. In M. Riley (Ed.), *Aging from birth to death: Interdisciplinary perspectives*. Boulder, Colo.: Westview Press, 1979.

Kestenberg, J. The effect on parents of the child's transition in and out of latency. In E. J. Anthony & T. Benedek (Eds.), *Parenthood: Its psychology and psychopathology*. Boston: Little, Brown, 1970.

Kestenberg, J. *Psychoanalytic studies of development*. New York: Aronson, 1976.

Lindemann, E. Symptomology and management of acute grief. *American Journal of Psychiatry*, 1944, *10*, 141–148.

Nagera, H. Arrest in development, fixation, and regression. *Psychoanalytic Study of the Child*, 1964, *19*, 222–239.

Neugarten, B., & Hagestad, G. Age and the life-course. In R. Binstock & E. Shanas (Eds.), *Handbook of aging and the social sciences*. New York: Van Nostrand Reinhold, 1976.

Neugarten, B., & Moore, J. The changing age status system. In B. Neugarten (Ed.), *Middle age and aging*. Chicago: University of Chicago Press, 1968.

Neugarten, B., Moore, J., & Lowe, J. Age-norms, age constraints, and adult socialization. *American Journal of Sociology*, 1965, *70*, 710–717.

Nunberg, H. *Principles of psychoanalysis* (1932). New York: International Universities Press, 1955.

Nydegger, C. N. *Late and early fathers*. Paper presented at Annual Meeting of the Gerontological Society of America, Miami Beach, Fla., November 1973.

Nydegger, C. On being caught in time. *Human Development*, 1981, *24*, 1–12.

Rangell, L. The return of the repressed "oedipus." *Bulletin of the Menninger Clinic*, 1955, *19*, 9–15.

Rosow, I. *Growing old*. Berkeley: University of California Press, 1967.

Rossi, A. Transition to parenthood. *Journal of Marriage and the Family*, 1968, *30*, 26–39.

1

SOCIOBIOLOGICAL PERSPECTIVES ON PARENTHOOD

JEANNE ALTMANN

INTRODUCTION

In this chapter I consider the nature of parenting within the life cycle of monkeys and apes, as affected by their social milieu and physical environment. We share with these anthropoid relatives an unusually large brain, offspring that require long periods of gestation and parental care, and an extended period of postinfancy immaturity. In what follows, I shall consider these and other similarities to us, and some differences, as they relate to parenthood. However, this is not a dichotomous comparison, us and them, but in many areas a varied rainbow of "thems" living out their lives in a range of physical and social worlds. First, then, we need to consider the variety of family structure and parenting. After that we can turn to the nature and divisions of the primate life cycle, the extent to which the social group provides a mother with additional stresses or with support, and, finally, the nature of environmental stress for parents. I shall present here a perspective that draws on diverse fields. The utility of this eclectic perspective has become apparent to us in our longitudinal study of wild savannah baboons in Amboseli National Park in southern Kenya, and I shall return repeatedly to the findings of that project throughout the present chapter. Whenever recent reviews of particular topics are available, I refer the reader to those rather than repeating them in detail.

FAMILY STRUCTURE AND SYSTEMS OF PARENTAL CARE

Mating Systems: A Cross-Sectional View

In considering the mating systems and family structure of nonhuman primates, one point should be kept in mind: A mating system is labeled according to the

Jeanne Altmann. Biology Department, University of Chicago, Chicago, Illinois.

predominant form, say polygyny, that is observed to occur. This is in contrast to anthropological classifications of human societies in which a society is often labeled by the maximum number of wives or husbands that an individual is allowed to have simultaneously. Thus, a human society may be labeled polygynous even if most men have a single wife, whereas a monkey mating system is usually considered to be polygynous only if most of the individuals that have any mate have more than one.

Polyandry is rare or perhaps nonexistent among mammals, including primates (Kleiman, 1977). In addition, monogamy in mammals is relatively rare and is associated almost exclusively with a few special circumstances (Kleiman, 1977). With the primary exception of gibbons, the monogamous primates are among the smallest. They show little or no difference in size between the sexes, and live in habitats in which only a single female and her young can sustain themselves in a territory. Moreover, twin births, and occasional triplets, are the norm among these primates as is a parental care system in which the father and older siblings provide almost all the infant care other than nursing. Several years ago Katherine Ralls provided an excellent synthesis of this complex of traits both in primates and in other mammals (Ralls, 1977). In this system the social unit consists of a single breeding male and female, with their immature offspring, both of whom share in defense of their territory against conspecifics. Young of both sexes must disperse as adults to establish their own territory and become reproductively active (Kleiman, 1977).

Gibbons, and their close relatives the siamangs, are the one group of large primates that are monogamous. They differ from most of the monogamous monkeys in several ways—they usually bear only a single young and although there is more paternal care than in most nonmonogamous primates, the extent of direct care such as carrying is more variable (Chivers, 1972, 1975; Ellefson, 1974). Tenaza (quoted in Kleiman, 1977, p. 51) has suggested that the lower amount of direct paternal care in white-handed gibbons is a consequence of a greater need for these males to spend time in predator defense. The ability of a gibbon male to provide protection from predators would be reduced if gibbons had twins, with their greater requirement for direct parental care, rather than a single young. Thus, several physical and behavioral traits seem linked to produce a coherent suite of characters (Stearns, 1976).

Primates of most species are to varying degrees promiscuous or polygynous. Some of the polygynous species, such as African savannah patas monkeys (Hall, 1968), some Asian langurs (e.g., Sugiyama, 1967), and most hamadryas baboons (Kummer, 1968), live in single-male, multifemale social groups that are, spatially and socially, relatively isolated from other such groups most of the time. However, even here we find considerable variety. For example, single-male units of hamadryas baboons come together in large, spatially close but relatively noninteractive aggregations or herds at nighttime sleeping cliffs. Gelada monkeys, in contrast, form large herds while foraging during the day, but separate more distinctly into their single-male units on the cliff faces at night (Crook, 1970;

Dunbar & Dunbar, 1975). Hamadryas groups and those of gorillas sometimes include a second, younger male who may or may not have breeding opportunities and who may eventually "take over" the group. In some primate species, including savannah baboons (Hausfater, 1975; McCuskey, 1975) and hanuman langurs (e.g., Jay, 1965; Sugiyama, 1967), both single-male and multimale breeding units are found. Orangutans, those shaggy-haired Asian apes, provide us with the most unusual living and family structure among primates. These sparsely distributed animals usually live in social isolation. A mother with her dependent young are the only individuals that consistently sleep or travel together. Because orangutan youngsters grow up without the regular presence of adult males, peers, or even adult females other than their mothers, David Agee refers to them as the primates that grow up in a female world (Horr, 1977).

Mating Systems: A Lifetime Perspective

From the very few long-term longitudinal field studies of monkeys and apes we have begun to gain a life-cycle view of these animals. Not surprisingly, new insights are emerging that would not have been guessed at from the first short cross-sectional field studies. With respect to mating and family structure, it is becoming increasingly clear that even in single-male, multifemale groups, most females will, over their lifetime, have several different mates as successive replacements of males occur.

A more complex picture also emerges for primates that live in multimale, multifemale groups. Although one or a few, aggressively dominant adult males may have disproportionate reproductive access to the females of the group, these males, like those of the single-male societies, do not hold their position for long, and during a female's lifetime she will encounter a succession of males in the high-ranking position (Hausfater, 1975; Saunders & Hausfater, 1977). In these groups an adult female mates with several males, and similarly a male does the same with several females, but this mating is not at random nor is it selective only on the basis of dominance rank; long-term consistent mating partner preferences occur and these preferences sometimes persist despite changes in dominance rank (Hausfater, 1975; Altmann, 1980; Rasmussen, 1981); each adult mates with a small subset of the group's adult members of the opposite sex.

Implications for Parental Care and Infant Development

The consequence for primate parents and infants of these varied family structures is that for some species—the monogamous ones—parental care and infant development occur within small family groups that include full siblings and just two adults, the parents. For most other species, the social milieu is a more complex mixture of ages, of both sexes, and of a wider range of degrees of genetic relatedness. Within any particular type of family or group structure the nature of this milieu is further determined by rates of maturation, interbirth intervals, and other life-history characteristics, and it is to these that we shall turn next.

LIFE-HISTORY PATTERNS

Common Patterns and Sources of Variability

From longitudinal field studies we are learning that we are even more similar to monkeys and apes in life-history patterns than originally thought. It has long been recognized that monkeys and apes have longer gestation, fewer young, and a longer infant and juvenile stage than do other mammals of comparable size (see recent discussions in Sacher, 1978; Western, 1979); with respect to the length of the prereproductive period, humans have carried this trait to the extreme. In humans and other primates there is, however, considerable within-species variability in features such as interbirth intervals, age at menarche, and age at birth of first infant. For humans, the world-wide variability and the secular trend in age of menarche is one example (reviewed in Eveleth & Tanner, 1976; Wyshak & Frisch, 1982). Differences in postpartum amenorrhea and interbirth intervals, for example, between traditional Kalahari !Kung and well-nourished noncontracepting human populations is another (Howell, 1979; Lee, 1980).

For nonhuman primates most of the early life-history data came from well-fed and relatively inactive captive animals. We now know that wild primates have periods of postpartum amenorrhea and interbirth intervals that are about double those in captivity, that growth rates are lower, and that menarche and first reproduction come much later (Altmann, Altmann, Hausfater, & McCuskey, 1977; Mori, 1979; Packer, 1979; Pusey, 1980; Harcourt, Fossey, Stewart, & Watts, 1980; Altmann, Altmann, & Hausfater, 1981). The most extensive available data are for baboons, for which the ratio of the age at which developmental markers are reached in captivity to the age at which they are reached in the wild is approximately 3.5 to 5 (Altmann *et al.*, 1981). Finally, and not surprisingly, mortality in the wild is very high during infancy, as it is for all mammals, and adults die at a younger age in the wild than in well-managed captive colonies. No nonhuman primate species has been shown regularly to have menopause or a postreproductive period, although decline in reproduction sometimes occurs in very old animals and complete reproductive senescence has been recorded in several captive macaque individuals (Bowden, 1979).

In terms of an individual human or nonhuman primate's life stages, the consequences of a protected existence or of a high plane of nutrition combined with little activity are that a smaller proportion of life is spent in immaturity and dependency, a larger proportion as a reproductively mature individual who produces infants that are born at shorter intervals and that are more likely to survive. In addition, under these conditions adults are more likely still to be alive when their own offspring give birth (Keyfitz, 1977; Altmann & Altmann, 1979).

Consequences of Differences in Demographic Parameters

All of the life-history parameters discussed above have extensive ramifications. They affect the size of age cohorts, the age structure of the population, family size, age differences between successive siblings, whether parents are called upon to provide simultaneous care for more than one successive infant at a time, and virtually every other aspect of social behavior and of group structure (Crook, 1970; Altmann & Altmann, 1979; Dunbar, 1979). Moreover, for nonhuman primates we have little information on the extent to which acceleration of various aspects of physical development are ontogenetically coupled, that is, change at similar rates if any one is accelerated or delayed. Even less is known about the extent to which psychological and social development are accelerated when physical development is accelerated. Thus, when a baboon female in captivity produces her first infant at the age of 4 years instead of 6, is it at the same stage of her own growth? And what of social development? At the age of 4 years a female baboon in the wild has not yet attained her position in the adult female dominance hierarchy, whereas by age 6 she has (Walters, 1980; Hausfater, Altmann, & Altmann, 1982). Is this process accelerated in captivity? As an individual, has a female been able to accelerate the learning process, so that at 4 years of age in captivity she is as well prepared for adulthood (albeit in captivity) as is a 6-year-old female in the wild? We do not yet know.

SOCIAL STRESS VERSUS SOCIAL SUPPORT

Family System as a Determinant of Social Milieu

Primate females that live alone or in small, monogamous groups give birth and raise their young in the presence of only a few members of their own species. These conspecifics are genetically closely related to the infants—father and full-siblings in the case of the monogamous primates, full- or half-siblings in orangutans. These family members provide all the infants' playmates, role models, direct and indirect care. In monogamous species, with paternal care, mothers are relieved of more infant care than in any other primate social system and the other family members provide enough care so that in most cases the females are able to bear twins and to do so once or twice a year (Epple, 1975; Box, 1977; Kleiman, 1977; Ralls, 1977).

However, females of most primate species raise one infant at a time in a group that consists of several adult females and their young and plus one or more adult males. Interactions within these complex social groups range from care, mutual defense and support against predators or members of other groups, social grooming, and play, to usurpation of food, harassment, fights, and, occasionally, killing. To what extent and under what circumstances do mothers and infants reap the benefits of their social group or suffer from dangerous and stressful interactions within it?

Many studies of captive primates have demonstrated the effects on development and on adult sexual and maternal behavior of extreme social deprivation, particularly deprivation of mother or peers (see reviews in Suomi & Harlow, 1978; Suomi & Ripp, 1983). Less is known about the consequences for parenting of variations in experience and care that fall within the ranges normally encountered by wild animals. In addition, it is not just the social environment during a mother's infancy and development that is important but also the social environment at the time that she gives birth and is raising her own infant. At parturition, the social life of most group-living primate females changes dramatically as the female and her infant become a focus of interest within the group (see Hrdy, 1976; McKenna, 1979a; Nash & Wheeler, 1982, for recent reviews). However, the identity of the interactants and the types of interaction differ both among and within primate species (Rowell, 1967; Crook, 1970), to a considerable extent because of the differences in group composition outlined in the previous sections of this chapter.

Peers and Other Immature Animals

Other infants and young juveniles provide an infant with playmates, sources of social learning through imitation, and companions in exploration. They reduce the extent to which the infant focuses its activities on its mother and vice versa (Mason, 1965). Experimental studies in which captive mother–infant pairs were isolated from conspecifics have shown that under these conditions mothers are less protective (e.g., Rowell, 1968) and more punitive of their infants (e.g., Jensen, Bobbitt, & Gordon, 1967). In these situations, mothers exhibit greater differences in their treatment of male and female infants and the infants develop sex differences in behavior earlier than has been reported for socially living mothers (Jensen et al., 1967; Rosenblum, 1974). All these effects are exaggerated when the infants are deprived of physical as well as social alternatives to interaction with their mothers.

For the majority of primate mothers living and raising their infants in multifemale groups, their infants' young associates are the offspring of several different adult females. These adult females are usually members of one or a few matrilines because, with a few notable exceptions such as gorillas, chimpanzees, and hamadryas baboons, males but not females of most primate species migrate from their natal group at maturity (Wrangham, 1980). As a result, the adult females of a group are often closely related, and an infant's age cohort of potential playmates are its maternal cousins. In addition, in those groups with only one reproductive adult male or in which one or a few of the males monopolize the matings each year, many of those same playmates are paternal half-siblings (Altmann, 1979). Consequently, although the degree of relatedness between an infant and its young associates is not as great in multifemale groups as it is in single-female groups, it will usually be greater than the average relatedness in the population or even in the social group as a whole. Such family structuring within a population probably sets limits to the evolution of certain harmful behaviors among young playmates within the group and enhances mutualistic or cooperative ones (see, e.g., Wade 1978).

Adult Males

What is the role of other adults in the group vis-à-vis the mother and infant? Hrdy (1976) provided a comprehensive review of the literature up to that time on the care and exploitation of primate infants. More recently, Snowden and Suomi (1982) update earlier discussions of care of primate infants by adult males and they point out that no single factor is a good predictor of the extent of male care in a species. Even within the macaques one finds among the species a range of paternal care despite similarities in group structure and mating system. Nor is care of infants by adult males greater in single-male, multifemale groups than in multimale, multifemale groups, despite the greater certainty of paternity in the former groups, suggesting (Snowden & Suomi, 1982) that sociobiological predictions of primate care cannot be based solely on this factor.

Infanticide occurs at least occasionally in a number of primate species (reviewed in Hrdy, 1979) and is most often associated with an adult male forcefully replacing the resident male in a single-male group. In single-male groups the father of the infant in effect protects his offspring against other males by maintaining his position as the male of the group. No further protection against males is needed in daily interactions within the group. In contrast, infants of multimale groups are in regular close proximity both to males who are likely to be their father and to others who are not. This system of moderate uncertainty of paternity within a social group may simultaneously produce a degree of danger to infants from males unlikely to be their father and also a level of attention and protective behavior from males likely to be their father. In this way, the need for protection from other males counterbalances the lower certainty of paternity between single-male and multimale groups and may be one reason no simple relationship exists between relative certainty of paternity in a species and the degree of paternal care in that species.

Adult Females

Despite the dramatic nature of infanticide and the fact that most primate infanticide is probably perpetrated by adult males, most social stress that primate mothers experience is caused by other females, just as most aggression directed toward adult females in other contexts emanates from other females. Consequently, relationships among adult females are important determinants of a mother's social experience.

Primate mothers' behavioral interactions have traditionally been classified primarily on the basis of presence or absence of threats or overt aggression by the actor. On this basis, various authors refer to the mother's avoidance of "friendly" approaches. Handling, grabbing, and pulling of the infant were usually considered "interest" rather than "aggression." However, if we wish

DEVELOPMENTAL PERSPECTIVES

to understand the experiences of motherhood and infancy and to predict the consequences of these experiences, it is surely more fruitful to consider interactions from the standpoint of the mothers and their infants rather than primarily from the standpoint of their interactants (Bronfenbrenner, 1979; Altmann, 1980; Cohler & Grunebaum, 1981).

A baboon mother is often harassed by other adult females, particularly those that are higher in dominance rank than the mother, as these females try to gain access to the infant. The mother clutches her infant, cowers, and gives other ''fear'' gestures and vocalizations (Altmann, 1980). The mother's stress is obvious, and I think we would agree that in some sense psychological harm is done to the mother by these interactions. Moreover, there is a complete gradation from visual inspection of infants through handling, pulling, and even kidnapping, which occasionally results in the death of the infant (Strum, 1975; Quaitt, 1979; Altmann & Shopland, in prep.). These intrusive interactions are potentially a form of reproductive competition (see, e.g., Hrdy, 1977, 1981; Silk, Clark-Wheatley, Rodman, & Samuels, 1981). Mothers respond to the threat of such interactions by being more protective and restrictive in their care of young infants.

Studies of langurs and of macaques suggest two factors that result in less social stress for females in general and mothers in particular. Under conditions in which large maternal kinship groups can form, as in expanding populations in which reproductive rates are high and/or mortality is low, females can and do associate primarily with close genetic relatives. Danger from kidnapping seems to be lower and mothers are less protective and restrictive of their infants (Berman, 1980). In langurs, where infant-sharing is common (e.g., Jay 1963), authors have suggested that the single-male mating system results in high genetic relatedness among the females (e.g., Hrdy, 1977). McKenna (1979b) and Wrangham (1980) have also proposed that dominance is less important in colobine monkeys such as langurs because as leaf eaters the animals eat large quantities of easily available food for which there is no advantage to competition.

The Social Environment of Baboon Mothers

Two major variables in our study of baboon mothers were clearly correlated with maternal dominance rank, the rate of expression of fear or distress, and the rate of being supplanted, primarily from resources. For the most part maternity exaggerated the effects of dominance rank, but by maintaining a close relationship with an adult male, low-ranking mothers were able to avoid or buffer some of these interactions. Most baboon mothers frequently associated with a particular adult male, usually the male with whom she mated when her infant was conceived (Altmann, 1978, 1980). Although the male sometimes overtly threatened away animals who came close or harassed the mother and infant, more often the male reduced harassment just by his presence: Other animals did not venture close to mother and infant. Other types of assistance are also subtle, but these subtle forms of aid are probably more common, and perhaps in the long run more important, than more obvious and dramatic behavior such as sometimes occur during predator attacks. Within a group, care is disproportionately provided by a male to those infants that he fathered.

The picture of mothers' social milieu that emerged from the research on baboon mothers was a complex one. Some behaviors and relationships were essentially independent of the existence or age of a female's infant: The rate of overt aggression and of noninteractive approaches and the direction of dominance–subordinance relationships were all of this sort. However, other dramatic and time-consuming behavior became much more common soon after parturition and remained infant-dependent: behavior indicative of fear or distress, described above, being approached and interacted with, and being the recipient of grooming. These increased dramatically in the first 2 months after a female gave birth. The increase was due to other animals, not to the new mothers, who themselves maintained or decreased levels of initiation of behavior.

The increased and time-consuming social life that is imposed on baboon mothers entails increased exposure to disease and perhaps to feeding competition because of the increased amount of time spent in close proximity to many other animals, but it may also provide additional predator protection and an increase in the benefits provided by social grooming. However, even nonharmful interactions take time and even small amounts of time per interaction add up to a considerable total. For the baboon mothers this increased social life probably involves approximately 10% of the daytime for grooming and at least 4% for other interactions (Altmann, 1980). As we shall see, below, this additional time must be fitted into a day already heavily committed to maintenance activities.

ENVIRONMENTAL STRESS AND DUAL CAREERS

Making a Living

Just as most studies of human parenting have been conducted among middle-class Europeans and Americans, so quantitative studies of nonhuman primates have depended heavily on the anthropoid equivalent of suburbia—cages or corrals with food and medical care provided.

Recently, quantitative studies both of ecology and of parental care and infant development have been conducted on unprovisioned wild animals. The results of these studies dramatically demonstrate the intimate relationship between parenting and ecological or economic aspects of life. The existence of these relationships will come as no surprise to ecologically oriented cross-cultural anthropologists (e.g., Whiting, 1964; Whiting & Whiting, 1975; Draper, 1976). I shall indicate here some of the ways in which environmental factors affect primate parenting and infant development.

It has become increasingly clear that in the wild, in the absence of food provided by humans, individuals of most primate species spend the majority of their day "making a living"—feeding, searching for food, and moving among food locations (Clutton-Brock & Harvey, 1977). As little as 25% of the day usually remains for resting, socializing, or any other activities (Slatkin, 1975;

Altmann, 1980). As a consequence of these time-budget constraints, any factor that appreciably increases the time needed to obtain an adequate diet presents the animals with potentially major problems. Although unusually harsh seasons or years may occur from time to time, pregnancy and infant care are regular, essential phenomena that provide added demands. Because most primate females are "dual-career" mothers who provide for both themselves and their infants, factors that ameliorate these stresses have probably been important throughout primate history.

Birth Synchrony and Seasonality

One of the most basic effects of different environmental conditions on females is to alter rates of conception. This may come about through reproductive sensitivity either to social partners or through direct environmental changes such as in photoperiod, in general food supply, or in specific components in food (reviewed in McClintock, 1983). In many primates the result is that mating and births are restricted to narrow seasons (Lancaster & Lee, 1965). Other primates, such as savannah baboons (Altmann, 1980) and humans (Jorde & Harpending, 1976), exhibit much weaker, but still demonstrable, environmental effects on conceptions and consequently on births. The degree of sensitivity seems to depend on the variability in the environment and the regularity or predictibility of that variability, on the ability of a species to shift to different foods under different conditions, and on the importance and temporal availability of "weaning foods." Treatments of these issues can be found in Jorde and Harpending (1976), Klein (1978), Mosher (1979), Altmann (1980), and Lee (1980), but relatively little is known about the significance of these potential sensitizing factors. For our present purposes, it is more important to consider the consequences of these environmental effects.

When births are synchronized, most adult females are caring for infants of about the same age at the same time. Moreover, if a male fathers the infants of more than one female, any paternal care must be apportioned among these infants if births are relatively synchronous. Some forms of paternal care, such as anti-predator behavior, may not be harder to provide for several infants than it is for one, but for other forms of paternal care such as carrying or food sharing this is not likely to be the case. Synchrony of births also provides each infant with a group of age peers with which it can play, explore, and learn about its environment. In contrast, where there is no synchrony, or where, as in Amboseli baboons, synchrony is imperfect, some infants will, by chance, be born with virtually no others close in age, whereas others will be members of large age cohorts.

If environmental effects on births also increase the probability that many infants reach weaning age at times of good food availability, as seems to be the case in baboons and vervet monkeys of Amboseli (Klein, 1978; Altmann, 1980), then stress of weaning should be reduced for these infants; we are currently investigating this in baboons.

Ecological Constraints on Parent–Offspring Relationships in Baboons

Ecological constraints affect parent–offspring relationships in baboons in several important ways (Altmann, 1980). In addition to a partial seasonality of births that seems to reduce the nutritional stress on mothers and infants, I found that the extent of an infant's independence during any day was affected by the foraging activities of the group, which varies seasonally and even from day to day within a season. Not surprisingly, this effect is seen not in the youngest or oldest infants, but rather in those who are at intermediate stages of development and who spend appreciable portions of the day riding on their mothers, and also appreciable portions on their own. These infants spend more time on their mothers on days when the group feeds far from the sleeping groves and spends much time traveling. Conversely, these youngsters play and explore on their own more on days of little travel.

An even finer effect of the mother's subsistence activities was found when I examined the relationship between a mother's activity and whether her infant was in contact at that moment. Young infants, up to about 4 months of age, were disproportionately out of contact when their mothers were resting or engaged in grooming interactions, and disproportionately in contact when their mothers were walking. For infants over 7 months of age, the relationship was just the opposite: Infants were much more likely to be in contact when their mothers were resting or grooming than when their mothers were walking. Another way of viewing this reversal in contingency is to examine the probabilities that a mother was engaged in various activities, at times that her infant was in contact. For mothers of older infants the probability was over 90% that the mother was resting or grooming if her infant was in contact, this despite the fact that mothers spent less than 25% of their total daytime in these activities. Nancy Nicolson has recently found a similar result for suckling in anubis baboons (Nicolson, 1982).

We are currently investigating the proposition that these contingencies are imposed upon the infant, that is, that the infant must adjust its behavior to that of its mother rather than vice versa. The young infant learns not just that it can be out of contact sometimes but that it can be out of contact at particular times that are determined by its mother's activity. If I am right, this enforced change in contingencies may be one of the earliest forms of socialization for an infant baboon and may provide the social sensitivity on which later social integration depends. One of the first areas of infant trauma seems to involve the reversal in these contact contingencies. Older infants must take advantage of their mothers' rest time for any contact and nursing that they want rather than using that time for play and exploration (Altmann, 1980). At the level of immediate behavior this ontogenetic change is a reversal. At another level, however, maternal rest time remains the same: it is the time to do the "unusual." However, the unusual is lack of contact for young infants and contact for older ones.

Why should a mother's maintenance activities so affect basic patterns of contact and interaction with her infant? In Amboseli baboons, as in most mammals whose populations are not expanding, infancy is the period of greatest mortality (Caughley, 1966; Altmann, 1980) and adult females are at greater mortality risk when caring for young infants than during other reproductive stages (Altmann, 1980). Moreover, a dependent infant's survival is contingent on its mother's survival. Consequently, factors that decrease a mother's feeding efficiency or her ability to detect predators, or that would otherwise increase the environmental stress that she experiences, probably will increase the chance that neither she nor her infant will survive. So, for example, during feeding, attention needed to watch a very vulnerable young infant that is not in contact, or the need to feed by reaching over and around a very large, older infant would each result in a loss of efficiency that mothers on a "tight time budget" (Altmann, 1980, 1983) cannot afford. Consequently, there has probably been considerable selective pressure for development of cooperation and compromise within primate mother–infant pairs. Although the evolutionary potential for parent–offspring conflict has been emphasized in recent sociobiological work, it will be necessary to incorporate and evaluate countervening pressures for compromise and cooperation in order to develop meaningful models of primate family interactions.

CONCLUSION

Mating systems and group structure, rates of birth, death, and maturation, all affect the milieu in which parents raise their offspring. These factors in turn are highly variable both within and between primate species, partially because of ecological conditions. The result is that parents and infants are provided with different stresses and opportunities to which they in turn respond with a degree of flexibility. Much is yet to be learned about the extent of this flexibility and the long-term consequences of parenting and development under diverse conditions.

Environmental impact also has immediate consequences for parent–offspring interactions because wild primates spend most of their time "making a living" and because mothers are "dual-career" mothers, providing both for themselves and for their infants. The result is pressure for parent–offspring compromise and cooperation, and for infants to modify their own behavior to accommodate that of their mothers in order to reduce potentially lethel stress on their mothers. This pressure has probably been widespread among primates over a long period of evolutionary history.

ACKNOWLEDGMENTS

Financial support has been provided by the Spencer Foundation, the Harry Frank Guggenheim Foundation, and the National Institute of Child Health and Human Development. Stuart Altmann provided valuable comments on an earlier draft and Deborah Malamud assisted with manuscript preparation.

REFERENCES

Altmann, J. Infant independence in yellow baboons. In G. Burghardt & M. Bekoff (Eds.), *The development of behavior: Comparative and evolutionary aspects*. New York: Garland, 1978.

Altmann, J. Age cohorts as paternal sibships. *Behavioral Ecology and Sociobiology*, 1979, *6*, 161–164.

Altmann, J. *Baboon mothers and infants*. Cambridge, Mass.: Harvard University Press, 1980.

Altmann, J. Costs of reproduction in baboons (*Papio cynocephalus*). In W. P. Aspey & S. I. Lustick (Eds.), *Behavioral energetics: Vertebrate costs of survival*. Columbus: Ohio State University Press, 1983.

Altmann, J., Altmann, S. A., Hausfater, G., & McCuskey, S. A. Life history of yellow baboons: Physical development, reproductive parameters and infant mortality. *Primates*, 1977, *18*, 315–330.

Altmann, J., Altmann, S. A., & Hausfater, G. Physical maturation and age estimates of yellow baboons (*Papio cynocephalus*) in Amboseli National Park, Kenya. *American Journal of Primatology*, 1981, *1*, 389–399.

Altmann, J., & Shopland, J. *Socially induced mortality in savannah baboons*. In preparation.

Altmann, S. A., & Altmann, J. Demographic constraints on behavior and social organization. In E. O. Smith & I. S. Bernstein (Eds.), *Ecological influences on social organization*. New York: Garland STPM Press, 1979.

Berman, C. M. Mother–infant relationships in rhesus monkeys. *Animal Behaviour*, 1980, *28*, 860–873.

Bowden, D. M. *Aging in non-human primates*. New York: Van Nostrand Reinhold, 1979.

Box, H. O. Quantitative data on the carrying of young captive monkeys (*Callithrix jacchus*) by other members of the family groups. *Primates*, 1977, *18*, 475–488.

Bronfenbrenner, U. *The ecology of human development*. Cambridge, Mass.: Harvard University Press, 1979.

Caughley, G. Mortality patterns in animals. *Ecology*, 1966, *47*, 906–918.

Chivers, D. J. The siamang and the gibbon in the Malay Peninsula. In D. M. Rumbaugh (Ed.), *Gibbon and Siamang*, 1972, *1*.

Chivers, D. J. The siamang in Malaya: A field study of a primate in tropical rain forest. *Contributions to Primatology*, 1975, *4*.

Clutton-Brock, T. H., & Harvey, P. H. Species differences in feeding and ranging behavior in primates. In T. H. Clutton-Brock (Ed.), *Primate ecology*. London: Academic Press, 1977.

Cohler, B. J., & Grunebaum, H. U. *Mothers, grandmothers, and daughters: Personality and child care in three-generation families*. New York: Wiley, 1981.

Crook, J. H. The socio-ecology of primates. In J. H. Crook (Ed.), *Social behaviour in birds and mammals*. London: Academic Press, 1970.

Draper, P. Social and economic constraints on child life among the !Kung. In R. B. Lee & I. DeVore (Eds.), *Kalahari hunter–gatherers*. Cambridge, Mass.: Harvard University Press, 1976.

Dunbar, R. I. M. Population demography, social organization, and mating strategies. In E. O. Smith & I. S. Bernstein (Eds.), *Ecological influences on social organization*. New York: Garland STPM Press, 1979.

Dunbar, R. I. M., & Dunbar, E. P. Social dynamics of gelada baboons. *Contributions to Primatology*, 1975, *6*.

Ellefson, J. O. A natural history of white-handed gibbons in the Malayan Peninsula. In D. M. Rumbaugh (Ed.), *Gibbon and Siamang*, 1974, *3*.

Epple, G. Parental behavior in *Saguinus fuscicollis*, ssp. *Folia Primatologica*, 1975, *24*, 221–238.

Eveleth, P. B., & Tanner, J. M. *Worldwide variation in human growth*. London: Cambridge University Press, 1976.

Hall, K. R. L. Behavior and ecology of wild patas monkey. *Journal of Zoology*, 1965, *148*, 15–87.

Harcourt, A. H. D., Fossey, D., Stewart, K. J., & Watts, D. P. Reproduction in wild gorillas and some comparison with chimpanzees. In R. V. Short & B. J. Weir (Eds.), *The great apes of Africa*. Cambridge, England: Journals of Reproduction & Fertility, Ltd., 1980.

Hausfater, G. Dominance and reproduction in baboons: A quantitative analysis. *Contributions to Primatology*, 1975, 7.

Hausfater, G., Altmann, J., & Altmann, S. A. Long-term consistency of social relations among female baboons. *Science*, 1982, *217*, 752–755.

Horr, D. A. Orang-utan maturation: Growing up in a female world. In S. Chevalier-Skolnikoff & F. E. Poirier (Eds.), *Primate bio-social development: Biological, social, and ecological determinants*. New York: Garland, 1977.

Howell, N. *Demography of the Dobe area !Kung*. New York: Academic Press, 1979.

Hrdy, S. B. Care and exploitation of non-human primates by conspecifics other than the mother. In D. S. Lehrman *et al.* (Eds.), *Advances in the study of behavior* (Vol. 6). New York: Academic Press, 1976.

Hrdy, S. B. *Langurs of Abu*. Cambridge, Mass.: Harvard University Press, 1977.

Hrdy, S. B. Infanticide among animals: a review, classification, and examination of the implications for reproductive strategies of females. *Ethology and Sociobiology*, 1979, *1*, 13–40.

Hrdy, S. B. *The woman that never evolved*. Cambridge, Mass.: Harvard University Press, 1981.

Jay, P. Mother–infant relations in langurs. In H. L. Rheingold (Ed.), *Maternal behavior in mammals*. New York: Wiley, 1963.

Jay, P. The common langur of North India. In I. DeVore (Ed.), *Primate behavior*. New York: Holt, Rinehart & Winston, 1965.

Jensen, G. D., Bobbitt, R. A., & Gordon, B. N. Sex differences in social interaction between infant monkeys and their mothers. *Recent Advances in Biological Psychiatry*, 1967, *21*, 283–292.

Jorde, L. B., & Harpending, H. C. Cross-spectral analysis of rainfall and human birth rate: An empirical test of a linear model. *Journal of Human Evolution* 1976, *5*, 129–138.

Keyfitz, N. *Applied mathematical demography*. New York: Wiley, 1977.

Kleiman, D. G. Monogamy in mammals. *Quarterly Review of Biology*, 1977, *52*, 39–69.

Klein, D. *The diet and reproductive cycle of a population of vervet monkeys (Ceropithecus aethiops)*. Unpublished doctoral dissertation, New York University, 1978.

Kummer, H. *Social organization of hamadryas baboons*. Chicago: University of Chicago Press, 1968.

Lancaster, J. B., & Lee, R. B. The annual reproductive cycle in monkeys and apes. In I. DeVore (Ed.), *Primate behavior*. New York: Holt, Rinehart & Winston, 1965.

Lee, R. B. Lactation, ovulation, infanticide, and women's work: Hunter–gatherer population regulation. In M. N. Cohen, R. S. Malpass, & H. G. Klein (Eds.), *Biosocial mechanisms of population regulation*. New Haven, Conn.: Yale University Press, 1980.

Mason, W. A. The social development of monkeys and apes. In I. DeVore (Ed.), *Primate behavior*. New York: Holt, Rinehart & Winston, 1965.

McClintock, M. K. Pheromonal regulation of the ovarian cycle: Enhancement, suppression, and synchrony. In J. G. Vandenbergh (Ed.), *Pheromones and reproduction in mammals*. New York: Academic Press, 1983.

McCuskey, S. A. *Demography and behavior of one-male groups of yellow baboons*. Unpublished master's thesis, University of Virginia, 1975.

McKenna, J. J. Maternal care among primates. *Yearbook of Physical Anthropology*, 1979, *22*, 250–286. (a)

McKenna, J. J. The evolution of allomothering behavior among colobine monkeys: Function and opportunism in evolution. *American Anthropologist*, 1979, *81*, 818–840. (b)

Mori, A. Analysis of population changes by measurement of body weight in the Koshima troop of Japanese monkeys. *Primates*, 1979, *20*, 371–398.

Mosher, S. W. Birth seasonality among peasant cultivators: The interrelationship of workload, diet, and fertility. *Human Ecology*, 1979, *7*, 151–181.

Nash, L., & Wheeler, R. L. Mother–infant relationships in non-human primates. In H. E. Fitzgerald, J. A. Mullins, & P. Gage (Eds.), *Child nurturance* (Vol. 3: *Primate behavior and child nurturance*). New York: Plenum, 1982.

Nicolson, N. *Weaning and the development of independence in olive baboons*. Unpublished doctoral dissertation, Harvard University, 1982.

Packer, C. Inter-troop transfer and inbreeding avoidance in *Papio anubis*. *Animal Behaviour*, 1979, *27*, 1–36.

Pusey, A. E. Inbreeding avoidance in chimpanzees. *Animal Behaviour*, 1980, *28*, 543–552.

Quaitt, H. D. Aunts and mothers: Adaptative implications of allomaternal behavior of nonhuman primates. *American Anthropologist*, 1979, *81*, 310–319.

Ralls, K. Sexual dimorphism in mammals: Avian models and unanswered questions. *American Naturalist*, 1977, *111*, 917–937.

Rasmussen, K. L. *Consort behavior and mate selection in yellow baboons (Papio cynocephalus)*. Unpublished doctoral dissertation, Cambridge University, 1981.

Rosenblum, L. A. Sex differences, environmental complexity and mother–infant relations. *Archives of Sexual Behavior*, 1974, *3*, 117–128.

Rowell, T. E. Variability in the social organization of primates. In D. Morris (Ed.), *Primate ethology*. London: Weidenfeld & Nicolson, 1967.

Rowell, T. E. The effect of temporary separation from their group on the mother–infant relationship of baboons. *Folia Primatologica*, 1968, *9*, 114–122.

Sacher, G. A. Evolution of longevity and survival characteristics in mammals. In E. L. Schneider (Ed.), *The genetics of aging*. New York: Plenum, 1978.

Saunders, C., & Hausfater, G. Sexual selection in baboons (*Papio cynocephalus*): A computer simulation of differential reproduction with respect to dominance rank in males. In D. J. Chivers & J. Herbert (Eds.), *Recent advances in primatology* (Vol. 1: *Behaviour*). London: Academic Press, 1977.

Silk, J. B., Clark-Wheatley, C. B., Rodman, P., & Samuels, A. Differential reproductive success and facultative adjustment of sex ratios among captive female bonnet macaques (*Macaca radiata*). *Animal Behaviour*, 1981, *29*, 1106–1120.

Slatkin, M. A report on the feeding behavior of two East African baboon species. In S. Konda (Ed.), *Contemporary primatology*. Basel: Karger, 1975.

Snowdon, C. T., & Suomi, S. J. Paternal behavior in primates. In H. E. Fitzgerald, J. A. Mullins, & P. Gage (Eds.), *Child nurturance* (Vol. 3: *Primate behavior and child nurturance*). New York: Plenum, 1982.

Stearns, S. C. Life history tactics: A review of ideas. *Quarterly Review of Biology*, 1976, *51*, 3–47.

Strum, S. C. Life with the Pumphouse Gang. *National Geographic*, 1975, *147*, 672–691.

Sugiyama, Y. Social organization of hanuman langurs. In S. A. Altmann (Ed.), *Social communication among primates*. Chicago: University of Chicago Press, 1967.

Suomi, S. J., & Harlow, H. F. Early experience and social development in rhesus monkeys. In M. E. Lamb (Ed.), *Social and personality development*. New York: Holt, Rinehart & Winston, 1978.

Suomi, S. J., & Ripp, C. A history of motherless mother monkey mothering at the University of Wisconsin primate laboratory. In M. Reite & N. Caine (Eds.), *Child abuse: The nonhuman primate data*. New York: Liss, 1983.

Wade, M. Kin selection: A classical approach and a general solution. *Proceedings of the National Academy of Science, U.S.A.*, 1978, *75*, 6154–6158.

Walters, J. Interventions and the development of dominance relations in female baboons. *Folia Primatologica*, 1980, *34*, 61–89.

Western, D. Size, life history and ecology in mammals. *African Journal of Ecology*, 1979, *17*, 185–204.

Whiting, B. (Ed.). *Six cultures: Studies of child rearing*. New York: Wiley, 1964.

Whiting, B., & Whiting, J. W. M. *Children of six cultures*. Cambridge, Mass.: Harvard University Press, 1975.

Wrangham, R. W. An ecological model of female-bonded primate groups. *Behaviour*, 1980, *75*, 262–300.

Wyshak, G., & Frisch, R. E. Evidence for a secular trend in age of menarche. *New England Journal of Medicine*, 1982, *306*, 1033–1035.

2

CREATIVE PARENTHOOD

E. JAMES ANTHONY

As an addicted daydreamer who is, at the same time, introspectively vigilant, I have sometimes detected within myself an unusual variant of Freud's (1909) "family romance." I suspect that all theoreticians in the field of family psychology are unconsciously, preconsciously, and even consciously influenced by this two-family system rooted in reality and fantasy. Although blessed with good-enough parents, I have, on occasion, hankered for more creative ones. Let me, however, immediately correct any possible misconceptions. I am talking here of ordinary, everyday, and not extraordinary creativity. I am talking of a process and not of a product to be assessed artistically or scientifically. I have at no time, even at my most grandiose, wished for genius in my fantasized parents, being well aware of the high incidence of psychopathology among those so gifted (Andreasen & Canter, 1975). If one takes the case of Wagner (1849) as a striking example, the thought of him as a father is traumatic in itself. Imagine a parent capable of making the following statement: "I come to you to break all chains which bear you down; to free you from the embrace of death, and instill a new life into your veins. All that exists must perish; that is the external condition of life, and I, the all destroying, fulfill that law to create a few new existences" (p. 127). One can only sigh with relief at having escaped daily familial contact with such malignant narcissism. Or again, is it possible to conceive of Van Gogh as a parent during that short period of time when he cut off his ear, offered it to a woman in a brothel, and then painted what is generally considered his best self-portrait, in which attention is focused on the bandage where his ear used to be. It would certainly not help a 5-year-old boy to adjust to his Oedipal turmoil.

Highly intellectual individuals, as opposed to highly intelligent ones, are also apt to lay constraints upon the creative aspects of parenthood, since they leave very little to the imagination, less to intuition, and hardly anything to

E. James Anthony. William Greenleaf Eliot Division of Child Psychiatry, Washington University School of Medicine, St. Louis, Missouri.

feeling. The parenting person cannot risk isolating his emotions from his caring functions.

My own "family romance" reminds me of the remark made by Alfonso X, the very learned King of Castile in the 13th century. "Had I been present," he said, "at the creation of the world, I would have proposed some improvements." In my fantasy, this would have been rephrased as follows: "Had I been present at my conception, I would have suggested certain alterations, the principle one being that the begetting couple would be liberally endowed with everyday creativity."

Let me pursue the concept of everyday creativity as described by Winnicott (1958), and then by Schachtel (1959). Both of them saw creativity as the iridescent healthy end of a spectrum at the other end of which was the morbidity of "embeddedness," compliance and conformity.

Winnicott was concerned not with "successful or acclaimed creation," but with the type of creativity available to anyone—baby, child, adolescent, adult, or old person—who looked at things healthily, did them deliberately, and felt that life was worth living. This colored his whole attitude to external reality. The baby could make a mess with feces because it felt good, or prolong his act of crying because it made a nice musical sound, and the toddler could run naked through the house with excited pleasure because clothes were so restrictive.

What is different about the ordinarily creative parent is the way in which he can move about the house, touching it here and there like a painter, molding it in this way or that way like a sculptor, humming or singing to himself like an opera star, cooking up meals from mysterious leftovers like an alchemist, and counting out pennies from an empty jam jar like an economist. Given a parent of this kind, who not only constantly makes silk purses out of sows' ears, but is able, at the same time as he is cooking the potatoes to hold a crying child securely or facilitate the child's frustrated attempts to accomplish a simple task, one can expect the child to establish a "personal capacity for creative living" and a general enhancement of the creative impulse.

In the household with these sort of parents, the total environment is enriched and exudes spontaneity, joyousness, and a breath of freshness. The children are confident and trustful, share of themselves and their abilities, stimulated by the unfamiliar and novel, and ready, in the presence of their parents, to explore the unknowns of a stranger. In this type of milieu, there is a continuity of contact with significant caretakers, periodic relief from the strains of objective reality, and the availability of transitional "treasures" when human resources are absent or insufficient.

This theory of everyday creativity is closely related to the "intermediate area of experience" that Winnicott (1951) defined as a realm of illusion potentially existing between mother and infant, between inner and outer reality, and between subject and object, where play and the creative impulse reigned supreme. Within this intermediate area, the everyday creative parent helps the child to construct a world that is essentially his; to challenge the notion that things must be just so; to populate this territory with transitional objects, fantasies, and nonsense; and to interpret reality as idiosyncratically as one wishes. It is through this universe of play that the child comes to differentiate himself from others because, while engaged in it, he is not only uniquely himself but is also uniquely considered by both parents.

In contract, the uncreative home generates a sense of sickness: "All that is real and all that matters and all that is personal and original and creative is hidden and gives no sign of its existence" (Winnicott, 1958). Children are also indifferent, unadventuresome, compliant, conforming, and lacking in playfulness. There is a general sense of futility and staleness, and the "intermediate area" is reduced to nothingness.

For Schachtel (1959), the average parent is embedded in countless patterns of routine, convention, and automatic behavior within the family, at home, at work, in a circle of friends, in language, culture, and country. These everyday "institutionalized" patterns take the place of the instinctive behavior of animals and are often as rigidly maintained. To escape from these patterns a parent needs to develop an openness toward the world and a receptiveness and responsiveness to his children with whom he must become actively engaged in exploring and examining the surrounding environment with enthusiasms and without trepidation. According to Schactel, this "allocentric interaction" helps in the metamorphosis of the good enough into the creative. The parent who induces a state of embeddedness in his child generates an unproductive syndrome characterized by dependency, inactivity, unforthcomingness, and unconstructiveness. The child has nothing to give and waits to be given to.

THE PSYCHODYNAMIC BASIS OF EVERYDAY CREATIVE PARENTING

The critical psychodynamic elements that contribute to everyday creative parenting include the following: (1) a looseness of repression that puts the parent in touch with unconscious processes and therefore makes him unconsciously sensitive to the deeper and less expressible needs of the child; (2) allowing oneself to regress in the service of the child to the latter's different developmental stages. This controlled regression and the loosening of repression together enhance the parent's capacity for empathy. The experience of primary process thinking governed by some ego control not only makes for originality but renders the parent's thinking more accessible to the child.

The implication in the previous discussion is that the parent who is both creative and fosters creativity in his child is somehow always active. Yet one of the most significant factors which supports the child's creativity is the presence of security and safety and the continued and constant care of devoted parent figures whose basic supportiveness ensures the child that he can continue to create without being abandoned.

There is a Turkish fairy tale, in which the hero, Iskender, arouses the enmity of his mother who forces his father to put Iskender into a casket and set him adrift on the ocean. Iskender's helper is a green bird, which rescues him from this danger, and from innumerable others, each more threatening than the preceding one. Each time, the green bird reassures Iskender with the words: "Know that you are never deserted."

One sees the "green bird" functioning like a creative parental impulse in the lives of so many children in various human predicaments. Its presence is often enough to help the child find a creative solution to his/her problems. Perhaps the most creatively oriented of these "green birds" are the grandparents who, time and again, have rescued an abandoned child and set it on a creative path.

EVERYDAY CREATIVE PARENTS IN THE MAKING

As with other psychological and psychopathological reactions in adult life, the antecedents are often apparent in rudimentary form in children. The future parent begins behaving like a parent, and behaving like his own parents in early life. In many respects, such a child is more creative and resourceful than his adult counterparts since the child often only has to function on the level of fantasy, symbolism, and play. Through the powerful mechanisms of introjections and identification, the child takes in both creative and uncreative aspects of the parents, developing mental structures that constitute bridges between biology and personality. The primary motherliness of the girl and the primary fatherliness of the boy may begin to reflect the rhythms of the parent and infant interchanges; little girls and little boys both demonstrate primary motherliness, but very soon boys' responses seem to wear off and they begin to take over the traits of primary fatherliness (Anthony & Benedek, 1970).

Here is an example of a 6-year-old girl in play:

> "He's crying. He must be hungry. I'll feed him." She holds the doll tightly to her little flat chest. "He's had enough. Look, he is going to sleep. Good night, baby. Have pleasant dreams and don't wet the bed."

Here we have a primary model simulated through experience and observation with its sequence of need–hunger–frustration–feeding–satiation –sleep–dreams–excretion. The little girl is not only preparing herself for motherhood but for sensitive, empathic mothering, requiring a great deal of preoccupation and concern.

Next we have a vignette of a boy of 5 who has already been showing boyish activity and interests:

> "He's crying. I think he is wet. I'll change him. He'll feel better. He needs powder for his 'little thing' [the doll, of course, had no "little thing"]. He's still crying. I'll hold him over my shoulder. Now, I'll rock him. Perhaps I had better walk with him."

In this instance we have a primary pacification model in which discomfort–frustration–crying–diapering and various modes of pacification follow a logical sequence. Not only are the rhythms of life being assimilated, but different crying behavior is being differentiated and treated accordingly. Ordinary creative interactions between parent and child are manifested by specific parental behaviors as the child matures. Some of these behaviors are summarized below as we follow the parents' responses to the child from the first moment the mother to be learns she is pregnant.

ORDINARY CREATIVE INTERACTIONS BETWEEN PARENT AND CHILD DURING DIFFERENT STAGES OF DEVELOPMENT

1. When the mother to be learns she is pregnant, the ordinary creative mother is caught up in the mystery of what is happening inside her and of the world that is being gradually created for her and her child. The womb creates a perfect environment, virtually soundproof and sheltered. There, one is alone in the company of one's mother and the mother is in union with her child. After birth the mother is enthralled with her baby. What was part of her is now in some strange way still part of her. She attempts to recreate the perfect internal environment outside of her body.

2. In nursing, the mother and child have as near as one gets to closeness between two separate human beings. The mother is taking in the baby and the baby is taking in the mother in a mutual process. At the same time they are helping to create worlds within each other, the baby is being represented in mother's psyche and the mother is becoming the basic part of baby's psyche.

3. Kierkegaard (1938) describes the almost miraculous moment when an infant rises to his feet and takes his first steps forward.

> The loving mother teaches her child to walk alone. She is far enough from him so that she cannot actually support him, but she holds out her arm to him. She imitates his movements, and if he totters, she swiftly bends as if to seize him, so that the child might believe that he is not walking alone. The truly loving mother can do no more if she really intends for her child to walk alone. Yet, she does more. Her face beckons like a reward, and encouragement. Thus, the child walks alone with his eyes fixed on his mother's face, not on the difficulties in his way. He supports himself by the arms that do not hold him and constantly strives towards the refuge in his mother's embrace, little suspecting that in the very moment that he is emphasizing his need for her, he is proving that he can do without her, because he is walking alone. (p. 85)

In this delicate piece of insight, Kierkegaard crystallizes an episode of mutual creativity with each of the perambulating partners putting their share into it. Almost every nonhandicapped human child goes through this process, and what is described here is a part of everyday creativity and gives us a feeling of magical participation.

4. In toilet training, "His Majesty the Baby" (as Freud referred to him) is on his throne and his prime minister is having an audience with him. The baby is generously storing the products that he has created, presumably specifically for his mother, and she is accepting them with enchantment. The vitality of the experience can become an additional bond of warmth between parent and child.

5. The everyday creativity of parent and child is often reflective in its quality. The two live in a "hall of mirrors" and each sees himself in the other. "In the individual emotional development, the precursor of the mirror is the mother's face. The mother is looking at the child's face and what she looks like is related to what she sees there. The child looks and sees himself. It is only when the child is in trouble or aggressive or unsettled that the mother's face is not then a mirror. If the mother's face is unresponsive then a mirror is a thing to be looked at but not looked into" (Winnicott, 1958). Winnicott sees this mirroring as essentially creative:

> When I look I am seen, so I exist.
> I can now afford to look and see.
> I now look creatively and what I apperceive,
> I also perceive.

The mother's creative role here is to give the child back his self, and, as the child matures, he becomes less and less dependent on her doing this.

6. One of the most creative of everyday creative activities on the part of the parent is to provide a secure place, a safety nook, a launching pad from which one can propel onself into an exploration of the universe or into which one can retreat when external danger threatens.

7. The creative parent eases the child's passage from tears to smiles without manipulating. The universe that was previously black with thunder, all of a sudden undergoes a creative transformation into "a pattern of many colors," as Maxim Gorky puts it.

8. Every small child, girl or boy, wants to be creative like his parents. To the small child it may mean wanting to have a baby, and the wish can be acted out in play or experienced in fantasy. The creative parent facilitates but does not intrude upon the play. The mother can bring the wish for a child into close contact with the creative process of reproduction. If pregnant she can allow the child to feel the movements of the baby or even the beating of its heart. Playing with or facilitating a child's play is a major example of creativity by either parent. Through it, the past may be reenacted, the present is enjoyed, and the future can be rehearsed. The parents can, by playing or observing, foster a safe environment for the child's exploration and fantasy development.

9. The parents, in knowing when to leave alone a child of any age foster the child's growing development of a sense of himself. The child's capacity to be alone allows the child the opportunity to evolve his own fantasies, thoughts, hopes, and feelings, perhaps even to express them in poems or stories.

ILLUSTRATION OF CREATIVE AND UNCREATIVE INTERACTIONS
BETWEEN PARENT AND CHILD

On observing the everyday creative parent and the creative child, one is reminded of their openness. It almost seems, using Freud's expression, that the intellect has withdrawn and watches at the gate as the ideas rush pell-mell in. It is exciting to be with them and observe them bubbling over with not-too-carefully censored thoughts, feelings, and actions. One gets the impression of fullness and diversity.

Everyday creative parents are not restricted to the western world. If the child of the Senoi tribe, living in the mountainous jungles of Malaysia, has a nightmare about being attacked by a monster, he is encouraged by his parents to go back to that dream on the following night and this time to attack the monster. "Tigers," they say, "that you see in the jungle in the daytime can hurt you, and you may need to run; those you see in your dreams at night can only hurt you if you run away from them. They will continue to chase you only so long as you are afraid of them." These primitively creative parents are thus able to help the child to distinguish actual reality from psychic reality and master the terrors occasioned by the nightmare by redreaming the dream differently. Garfield (1974) has referred to this as "creative dreaming," and apparently the procedure appears to work in practice. The parents treat the nightmares by power of suggestion.

Another example of a parent acting both creatively and therapeutically comes from the case of a cheerful little 4-year-old boy who suddenly began to become cranky and weepy in the afternoons and to sleep more deeply that usual at naptime. At nursery school he was independent, friendly, and cooperative except at resttime. Finally, he one day mentioned to his mother that he always dreamed that someone was chasing him and was going to cut off his head. She told him that people didn't get their heads cut off anymore. A week later, he complained that he had been dreaming that someone was trying to cut off his thumb, and, on a sudden hunch, the mother put her arm around him and said that his daddy would protect him, too. The little boy repeated after her: "Daddy won't let anyone hurt me," and she found herself saying with considerable fervor, that Daddy would kill anyone who tried to hurt his little boy. The youngster blinked, smiled, squared his shoulders, and marched out of the room. It was as if Atlas's load had been lifted from his back. Soon he was heard singing to himself as he had not done for months. The little boy had not known what was bothering him and neither had his mother, but somehow he had managed to communicate enough of his anxiety for her to sense that what he needed was extra reassurance about the continuing devotion of both his parents. It was a case of everyday creative parenting (Redlich & Bingham, 1953).

Examples of noncreative parenting are not difficult to find, but the following vignette illustrates the parental oppression of creativity in a concealed form:

A latency-aged boy had taken up carving and had made a model boat. He showed the simple structure proudly to his father who said, "Fine, but now let's make it float." The boy reworked the boat until it floated evenly and brought it back to his father who said again, "Fine, but now let's make it sail." At this point, the boy gave up all work on the boat. In psychotherapy, he reported that it was not the effort involved but that the boat was no longer his; it had been "taken over" by his father. He had started out being creative for the fun of it and then he was asked, as he perceived it, to be creative for the sake of somebody else. He felt it was easier to be noncreative.

There are dangers to cultivating creativity as an end in itself. First, the parents may try to make too much of it and thereby belittle the everyday creativity of the child. Second, parents may want to take over and enhance the creative product, as in the illustration, thus depriving the child of the fruits of his own construction. Third, too much creativity may be equated with eccentricity, so that in time a child comes to avoid it rather than risk appearing as an oddball to his peers. These are the possible snags which the everyday crative parents must keep in mind as they encourage the child to exercise his creative impulse.

CONCLUSION

The creative impulse that we have discussed in relation to parents and children still remains only partially understood. There is even some slight evidence that I have not addressed that it may have to do with the functioning of the right brain which is nonverbal and almost inaccessible to conscious intervention. Under ordinary circumstances, the early emphasis on the left brain (as occurs with verbal learning) tends to inhibit right brain activity. According to Hogan (1975), "In terms of everyday creativity, much depends on whether the activities of the right brain are felt as threatening to the stability and control exercised by the left brain. The reason is that, just as the experiences of early infancy . . . may be placed in the limbic system, those of early childhood may be placed to a great extent on the right—play, for example. In terms of creativity, no activity in early childhood is more important than play, and much play depends on right brain function" (p. 31).

The factors which lead to creativity are probably derived from multiple sources, including the neurophysiological, the genetic, the early life experiences, the style of the parents' parenting, and the opportunities offered by the environment.

To end this chapter, it would be logical for me to treat you in the way that ordinary creative parents treat their ordinary creative children. In the words of Walt Whitman (1926):

> I seek not to introduce you to any *theme of thought*,
> but to take you into the atmosphere of the theme of
> thought, there to pursue your own flight.

REFERENCES

Anthony, E. J., & Benedek, T. (Eds.). *Parenthood: Its psychology and psychopathology*. Boston: Little, Brown, 1970.

Alfonso, X. Las Siete Partedas, 1250.

Andreasen, N., & Canter, A. Genius and insanity revisited. In *Life history research in psychopathology* (Vol. 4). Minneapolis: University of Minnesota Press, 1975.

Freud, S. Family romances (1909). *Standard Edition, 9*. London: Hogarth Press, 1974.

Garfield, P. *Creative dreaming*. New York: Simon & Schuster, 1976.

Gorky, M. *My childhood, in the world, my universities* (I. Schneider, trans.). New York: Citadel Press, 1949.

Hogan, P. Creativity in the family. In F. F. Flach (Ed.), *Creative psychiatry*. Geigy Pharmaceuticals, 1975.

Kierkegaard, S. *Purity of heart*. New York: Harper & Row, 1938.

Redlich, F., & Bingham, J. *The inside story*. New York: Vintage Books, 1953.

Schachtel, E. G. *Metamorphosis*. New York: Basic Books, 1959.

Wagner, R. *The creative force*. Berlin, 1849.

Winnicott, D. W. Transitional objects and transitional phenomena (1951). In *Collected papers*. London: Tavistock Publishers, 1958.

Winnicott, D. W. *Play and reality* (1958). London: Tavistock Publishers, 1971.

Whitman, W. *Leaves of grass*. New York: Doubleday, 1926.

3

THE PARENTING ALLIANCE

REBECCA S. COHEN
SIDNEY H. WEISSMAN

INTRODUCTION

In this chapter, we will present and develop the concept of the parenting alliance which is an experiential component of the adult parenthood process. As a concept, the parenting alliance is a paradigmatic self–selfobject relationship[1] vital to the evolving parenthood experience and other adult tasks. It encompasses interactions between spouses which pertain to child rearing, with the provision that these behaviors are appropriate to the developmental needs of children. It is a contributing process for the continuous mastery of developmental issues for the adults and children involved in it. The relationship which operates between the parental partners is the fulcrum about which family process evolves. The parenting alliance has been acknowledged subliminally both in psychoanalytic individual developmental theory and in family theories. The concept was derived operationally from clinical work with adolescents, their parents, and adult patients who are parents. We will present the theoretical underpinnings and heuristic value of our conceptualization of the parenting alliance as a significant subjective

1. The concept of the self–selfobject relationship was initially developed by Heinz Kohut to describe a specific transference relationship which he observed in the psychoanalysis of certain patients. As his observations continued, the psychology of the self was developed. The self–selfobject construct was extended to normal development. We now regard the intrapsychic operation in which one individual (object) sustains his/her self-esteem regulation and psychological intactness by use of another individual (object) in a specific situation or relationship as a self–selfobject relationship. The individual may or may not be aware of the importance of the other in maintaining his/her psychological equilibrium. For further clarification of this concept see Elson (Chapter 20, this volume), Goldberg (1980), or Kohut (1971, 1977).

Rebecca S. Cohen. Department of Psychiatry, Michael Reese Hospital and Medical Center, and School of Social Service Administration, University of Chicago, Chicago, Illinois.

Sidney H. Weissman. Department of Psychiatry, Michael Reese Hospital and Medical Center, and Department of Psychiatry, University of Chicago, Chicago, Illinois.

experience of adulthood and its import for development in adults and children. We will also provide clinical illustrations.

Before addressing the parenting alliance, we must acknowledge the significance of parenthood as a critical and ongoing experience of adulthood. In becoming a parent, the adult faces numerous contingencies for decision making; moreover, these decisions are made usually by an adult with another adult. Much has been written about the revival of earlier experiences with love, dependence, and helplessness which surface in the course of adult parenthood (Benedek, 1959; Anthony & Benedek, 1970). These revived or residual experiences may be experienced stressfully and differentially and mastered according to the particular phase of the life course in which the adult parent finds himself/herself. Parenthood is, therefore, a complex process which ushers in a course for development throughout adulthood (Michels, 1981). The uniqueness of the parenthood experience lies in the complexity of the possible regressions in drives, affects, and self-esteem regulations, and the opportunity it affords for reaffirmations of self-esteem and adult effectiveness. We hope to demonstrate that the parenting alliance, as a self–selfobject relationship, functions as a milieu for the resolution of the aforementioned reactivated developmental issues. This alliance plays a critical role in the continuous unfolding of the parenthood experience. It performs a sustaining function for the individual partners as each responds continuously to the developmental progression of the child.

Societal expectations may vary as each culture constructs different values and timetables by which growth and development are monitored. However, parental responsibility for the biologically and psychologically dependent child is universal. Whereas parenthood as a process may originate in procreative, libidinal forces (Benedek, 1959), once a child is anticipated, a new experience develops between the parents, and takes on a life of its own. In all human societies, parenting alliances develop, although the roles of each partner may vary. Nevertheless, a parenting alliance emerges when the decision is made to procreate, or from the awareness of becoming a parent. This alliance proceeds out of the anticipation of mutual bonds to the child. Each partner anticipates a shared experience which will facilitate the performance of the tasks of parenthood. The fluidity of the child's needs creates continuous challenges, inconsistencies, and contradictions; hence, the constant fear of regressive pulls. It is evident, therefore, that parenthood tests the capacity to endure frustration and delay. The parenting alliance is the significant aspect, or constituent, of the parenthood experience upon which an adult can rely for affirmation and predictability when stressed by seemingly endless frustrations and tensions which occur in the many contingencies of parenthood. Much of the parenthood experience which has been discussed in the literature identifies several of its aspects, including the dyadic relationship between parent and child, and even the triadic aspects of parent–couple and child. However, what has not been addressed is the meaning of the experience of the parenting alliance not merely for the child's triadic relationship capacities but for the continuous maintenance of this triadic relationship for the adult parent.

THEORETICAL AND CONCEPTUAL CONSIDERATIONS

The parenting alliance is that component of a marital relationship which is distinct from the libidinal object needs of the spouses for each other. However, it clearly involves the issue of self-esteem and its vicissitudes which can endanger the adult's feeling of competence, effectiveness, and well-being. The alliance consists of the capacity of a spouse to acknowledge, respect, and value the parenting roles and tasks of the partner. This capacity must be at once firm and resilient to permit the alliance to endure when one or both partners experience stress in the parenting sphere or in other pertinent aspects of life. The parenting alliance, as a construct, can be applied to family process when it is stable, or in flux, to determine or predict how parents and children will master or fail in response to family changes.

Unquestionably, the existence and aspects of the import of the interactions between the parents has been acknowledged in the writings of psychoanalytic and systems family process theorists (Bowen, 1976; Lidz, 1963, 1976; Meissner, 1978; Minuchin, 1974; Stierlin, 1977). The process as a construct has been acknowledged but addressed largely as a derivative of libidinal drives and their resulting ties within family process. Therefore, as a process it is not conceptualized consistently; nor is it assessed independently from the entire emotional matrix of the family as a compendium of the interacting personalities of both spouses. When attempts were made to observe "parental coalitions" (Lidz, 1976) as a distinct segment of family process, they could not be sustained because the underpinnings of most family theorists are rooted in, or informed by, the concepts of psychoanalytic drive theory. It was apparent to us that in order for this process, the parenting alliance, to be understood and utilized clinically, a differentiation has to be made between the marital relationship and the parenting relationship. The former is an experience of sexual and libidinal ties along with self–selfobject functions; the latter is a selfobject relationship between the parents which evolves as they engage in child rearing and encompasses the experiential and transactional aspects of self-esteem regulation. Psychodynamic family theorists have addressed the relationship between the parents within the frameworks of (1) the complementarity of their mutual needs, or (2) their intrapsychic levels of differentiation of self from others (internal objects). When examined, their constructs do not help in understanding many situations which we observe in our offices or in our lives. These are the many instances we know wherein the marriages are stable and, yet, children emerge with severe pathology. Conversely, we have observed marriages which are fragile and unsatisfactory and yet the children have emerged with capacities for competence and creativity. Family clinicians (Lidz, 1976) have observed, along with us, that when marriages dissolve, some parents are able to maintain a stable connection to sustain a mutual process of empathic parenting. In our construct, therefore, we have attempted to identify a part of the system which can, and does, continue to operate when the larger system and some of its components shift or change shape. We recognize that parents, either married or divorced, must have the capacity (or structure) for commitment to engage in the demands of the parenting process. This commitment, however, does not reside in the domain of the libidinal drives. We will present, in this chapter, an aspect of self psychology theory which does illuminate the parenting relationship between two adults.

The early shared experience of child rearing for both parents lays down a nidus from which the alliance evolves and becomes a discrete process within the family structure. This early experience includes both parents with their initial responses to the ongoing, changing demands of the child which cannot be delayed. Our concept requires recognition that motherhood and fatherhood develop simultaneously and that the parent–child dyadic transactions of each proceed within the context of the alliance. Therefore, fathers participate psychologically and behaviorally from the beginning. Rather than contributing to triangulation by intruding upon the mother–child symbiosis (Meissner, 1978), they perform an important affirming and sustaining function for the mother whose empathic capacities are likely to be strained by the time-consuming, intimate contact of immediate nurturing.

Parenthood requires the commitment of adults to parent in the face of the child's unempathic relatedness. Under the best of circumstances, and at all developmental levels, children have difficulty in maintaining a stable relationship with more than one adult at a time. And yet, they require the nurturing, empathic responses of both parents for the establishment of object ties, gender identity, self-cohesion, and drive integration. Empathy in parent–child interrelatedness flows in one direction. The child is essentially a nonempathic partner whose empathic capacities will become established in the future upon the completion of a long and complex developmental process (Weissman & Barglow, 1980). The parents' potential for self-esteem dysfunction and for other regressions in response to the impact created by the child's needs is ever present (Cohen & Balikov, 1974). The mutual support (external and internal) of the parenting alliance sustains the parenting process by promoting the regulation of heightened tensions inherent in the process of child rearing.

The parenting alliance can be observed and understood best, therefore, within the conceptual framework of recent advances in psychoanalytic theory. As indicated, self psychology (Kohut, 1971, 1977) has introduced the concept of self–selfobject relationships. The self–selfobject construct is useful in understanding the parenting alliance. Wolf (1980) describes a developmental line of self–selfobject relationships. These do not disappear with growth but become less intense, and are subject to substitution as maturation occurs. Wolf describes, further, a continuous feedback process between the self and its selfobjects. This process results in continuous modifications of both. The selfobject requirements become less archaic over time, and as Terman (1980) has indicated, they become nonobligatory. The uniqueness of the adult parenthood experience lies in its being located within a matrix of self and selfobject transactions between both parental partners and child. As a consequence, changes and expansions in the self are continuous for both parent and child, each in the phase-appropriate context.[2]

For the adult parent, the seemingly dyadic parenting alliance involves transactions regarding a third individual. Thus, on an intrapsychic level, it is always a triadic process with its baseline resting upon the parental transactions about a child whose needs are being attended. Moreover, the child serves a selfobject purpose appropriate to adulthood—affirmations of adult experiences of pleasure and competence which sustain self-esteem. In the initial Oedipal triadic relationship, the child is the small undeveloped member of a triad wherein his/her fantasies do not match his/her capacities. In the parenting relationship, the parent's experience in the triad is quite different. In addition to dealing with the various emotional and cognitive capacities which are brought to bear upon each parent's care of the child, the parent must support and interact with the other parent in this unique constantly evolving caretaking role. The child's growth and development arouse specific fantasies as the parent either relives old fantasies, resolves old problems, or experiences a new sense of self in responding to the constantly evolving relationship with the child. The relationship with the coparent, when husband and wife address issues of parenting, is not one of satisfying dependency needs, or, as we have indicated, obtaining sexual gratification. In the parenthood experience, adults contend with the product of their sexuality and their ongoing needs for mutuality. Consequently, this is a new set of experiences which in turn can lead to further psychological development of the adult in a new universe of operations. Without the existence of the parenting alliance, the uniqueness of this experience may be lost for the adult's further psychological development. (We believe that this is an area for further investigation.)

Cohler, in describing the concept from self-psychology of maintaining selfcohesion, indicates that in this process "each person becomes a historian of the self, creating an internally consistent interpretation of the life cycle, so that past, present, and future appear to become congruent" (1981, p. 160). We propose that in the parenting dyad, as the triadic parenthood experience is played out, the shared parenting alliance becomes part of each spouse's personal stance toward the future. As the life course proceeds within each partner, the parenting alliance becomes a part of his/her personal history. This connectedness to the coparent, within the parenting experience, if affirmatively maintained, can continue in the face of marital disruption. A parenting alliance, therefore, is not coterminous with a marital alliance.

The alliance begins prior to the arrival of the child. The psychological support and idealization by the father of the mother during pregnancy and the child's infancy are critical factors in this phase. In essence, each parent provides the other with support in the new experience of early parenthood. Currently, we

2. For a further conceptualization of this process, see Elson (Chapter 20, this volume).

see many mothers who return early to work. Here, the father's continued idealization of his wife as mother is as critical as the sharing of responsibilities. The
alliance may operate to sustain parents during the toddler's rapprochement phase
(Mahler, 1968) or the transitional selfobject phase (Tolpin, 1971) when the
contradictory signals and separations can be frustrating to either parent but particularly to the mother. We know well the adult-appropriate soothing functions
provided by the father for the distraught mother of the 18-month-old who is at
once discovering the delights of the world and collapsing with rage and exhaustion
because his/her competence is far below his/her reach. Clearly, each parent's role
has specific values for a particular child. Each, however, needs the suport of the
other when the child's appropriate developmental forays erode a parent's empathic capacities. The emotional connectedness of the parents may be essential
for creating an environment for the mastery of Oedipal issues. The Oedipal
experience of exclusion is mitigated by the child's reliance upon the continuity
of the parenting alliance. This alliance may be a significant facilitating force in
promoting ego-ideal formation during the latency years.

The parenting alliance is of special significance for the adolescent. As he/she
negotiates the psychological tasks and physiological shifts of adolescence, the
presence of the parenting alliance provides him/her with a framework of consistency and support upon which to rely. We suspect that some of the pathology
attributed to adolescents, such as splitting the parents, may stem from the absence
of a parenting alliance. As the adolescent integrates changes in his/her body,
explores the world, and attempts to map out a route of his/her own, the existence
of a parenting alliance makes it possible for him/her to acknowledge a variety
of perceptions of the world. These can be reconciled into meaningful coexistence
just as varied perceptions can coexist between the parents. In this milieu, the
adolescent can proceed to adulthood. We suspect that in families which have an
effective parenting alliance, the adolescent process evolves smoothly. In such
families, the adolescent is free to experiment with the range of his/her newly
acquired capacities undergirded by the coparent–child triad. Oedipal resolutions
in adolescence hinge upon the continuity of this parental couple–adolescent triad.

Let us consider some specific assets provided by the alliance for parents.
Psychological or physical problems in a parent may limit his/her effectiveness
in caring for his/her children. Such a parent is prone to suffer a loss of self-
esteem. The parenting alliance may be the critical factor for sustaining the
maximum parenting functions possible for the parent with such limitations. For
all parents, the alliance assures each a relationship with an adult who serves as
an ongoing selfobject in which to test his/her responses, perceptions, hopes,
fantasies, and ideals regarding the child.

The decisions made in raising one's children mobilize the totality of one's
fantasies and self-perceptions. Whereas the reality of one's life is experienced
in work and marriage, it is in the raising of children that one tends to experience
one's fantasies. In the relationship with one's spouse, when the focus is on child
rearing, one confronts these fantasies implicitly or explicitly. The parenting

alliance is the means by which two adults can communicate meaningfully and share these fantasies and differing perceptions of the world. During periods in which parents are particularly vulnerable to the stimuli of regressive fantasies, the parenting alliance may be the critical factor for maintaining cohesion. Restated, the parenting alliance provides a substrate for the psychological growth and development of the parents.

We do not mean that parenting does not occur in the absence of a parenting alliance which is brought about by death, divorce, or illness. We recognize, moreover, that some adults become single parents by choice. In the absence of the parenting alliance, however, the adult must deal with the demands and stimuli of child rearing in isolation. We suspect that closer examinations of single parenting will reveal that such individuals parent most effectively when they can establish parenting type alliances with a family member or friend to sustain them in their roles as parents and adults.

CLINICAL PRESENTATIONS

In the previous discussion, we described the theoretical foundation and heuristic value of the concept of the parenting alliance. We will proceed with clinical material to demonstrate the operational value of the concept. In the first case vignette, we describe the development of the parenting alliance in a divorced couple.

Case 1

The identified patient was a 13-year-old boy, who was living with his divorced mother. In the 6 months prior to the evaluation, the quality of his schoolwork had deteriorated seriously and he was not to be promoted into high school. In the month prior to the evaluation, his mother became frightened that he would lose control, strike out, and hurt her. She took the initiative in requesting the evaluation. In her first interview, she was concerned about her son's school failure and expanded upon her concern that he could lose control and hurt her. In the week prior to the consultation, the son had stopped going to school and she was afraid to be home alone with him.

The identified patient was a muscular boy who appeared to be his stated age. He made clear that he saw no reason for seeing a psychiatrist, that his mother made him come, and that there was nothing wrong with him. He told the therapist to talk to his father who "agreed with him that he did not have any problems." When reference was made to problems at school, he responded angrily that there were none. Reference to his failing grades was greeted by silence. Inquiry into his feelings about his parents' divorce made him become agitated, slightly, but he insisted that the divorce had no effect on him. He became increasingly angry during the interview and insisted that his father would help him so that he wouldn't have to put up with a psychiatrist. After the initial interview with the child and his mother, a subsequent interview was arranged with the father, an attorney. There was no reluctance on the father's part to meet with the therapist. During the interview, with some hesitation, he spoke about his divorce, but the major focus was on his son's behavior. He reported that he had acted in much the same fashion when he was a child. Although he tended to dismiss the boy's problems as inconsequential and to be the usual issues faced by children, he was concerned about his son and interested in the psychiatrist's view of the problem.

Following further evaluation of the son, the psychiatrist advised the parents in a joint session that their son needed hospitalization because of the real danger that he could attack and harm the mother. The mother was relieved by this recommendation and the father was baffled. He could not understand that his son's problems required hospitalization, but indicated that he would support the recommendation. In planning the son's treatment, the therapist arranged to meet biweekly in joint sessions with the parents to focus on the unique needs of the son.

The boy was quite angry at being placed in the hospital. During the first few days of hospitalization, he insisted that he was leaving and called his father to take him out. The father was confused. He did not believe, yet, that his son should be in the hospital, but wasn't totally convinced that his exwife was wrong in being frightened of him; and, moreover, he, too, was concerned about the son's school performance. With much difficulty, he told his son that he would have to stay in the hospital, at least for a few weeks. The boy stormed out of the joint session with his parents and therapist which had been planned to discuss the course of his treatment. He refused, soon, to see the therapist individually, although he became comfortable in the hospital school. The parents continued to meet with the therapist. The son continued to attempt to convince his father that there was nothing wrong with him. He presented to the father the hospital treatment as a plot in which the therapist had allied himself with the mother to get him out of her house. At each visit, he insisted that his father do something to get him out of the hospital. The father was inclined, initially, to support this request, but before taking any action brought his concerns to the therapist and his exwife. Each time, in turn, the father came to understand better that his exwife's concerns about their son were related not to the old wounds from the failed marriage, but that her responses were related more relevantly to the boy's developmental needs. As this occurred, the boy gradually gave up the attempts to provoke his father and became increasingly involved in the hospital treatment program. The therapeutic work with the parents focused solely on the developmental tasks faced by the son, and the issues they presented to him in their coping together with his needs. And yet, as the work continued their capacities increased to share with each other their experiences with their son.

About the 8th month of hospitalization, the psychiatrist and hospital team determined that a residential placement outside of the mother's home was the most suitable treatment plan for the boy. The father reacted to this plan much as he had to the original plan to hospitalize the boy. Why was this necessary, hadn't the hospital been enough? This was dealt with, once again, in the joint session with his exwife. With some difficulty, we were able to arrange a placement at a youth center in another state. The agreement was made that after the boy left the hospital, the parents were to continue to work with the therapist on a once-a-month basis.

The issues during the early months at the youth center were replications of the initial ones during the hospitalization. The patient again regarded the placement as a plot by the therapist and the mother to get rid of him. He attempted to enlist the father as an ally in his battle. Again, the consistent focus of the work with the parents was on the developmental issues faced by the boy and the reason for the placement. After a year, the boy settled down in the placement. He began to attend the off-campus public school near the youth center, where his schoolwork was clearly above average. When the father, who had remarried, planned a visit, he was able to talk to his exwife and the therapist about the advisability of visiting his son with his second wife. After discussing the issue with his exwife, he decided to visit his son alone, first, and talk to him about the remarriage. After 3 years in the center, the boy graduated from the local high school and enrolled in college. At that time, the joint sessions with the parents ended.

At the termination of the joint sessions, each parent had a clearer sense of the needs of the son. They were able to communicate with each other about these needs, in and outside of the joint meetings. Although the problems of an older daughter were not the focus of the work, they became better able to address these and develop strategies to assist her. The initially guarded communication was replaced by an openness and eagerness to hear what was happening with the son when he visited with the other parent. The parents agreed also on the choice of college and were pleased by their son's growth.

This case demonstrates that an individual can have serious interpersonal difficulties with a spouse but still maintain a relationship focused on the needs of children. Here, a therapist was essential to nurture the latent alliance in these parents who were unable to function as effective parents prior to this intervention. The child's experience of the parenting alliance in a protected environment led to his subsequent growth and development.

The parenting alliance, and the factors in the parents which allowed it to develop, can be identified clearly. First, each of the parents had an investment in the son, with some recognition of his needs. The mother had a clearer perception of her son's needs than the father, but did not know what to do. The father, although invested in the child, was not aware of his special needs. Second, each parent valued the importance of the other parent in fostering the growth and development of the child. This view was shared by both parents but the pain of the unsuccessful marriage and divorce prevented them from acting accordingly. The therapist, hospital, and youth center provided neutral ground for the parents to develop this area of the parenting alliance. Third, each parent began to respect and value the judgments of the other parent. The turmoil of the divorce had obscured their underlying capacities for mutual engagement. The mother communicated her investment in her exhusband as the son's father by wanting to involve him in the son's therapy and life. The father, at first, did not hear or believe what she said. However, with the support of the therapist, he shifted from defensiveness to supporting the treatment process as well as his exwife's position. As the treatment proceeded, the father and mother became able to respect each other's judgments regarding the needs of the child without the therapist. Finally, an ongoing means of communication which maintains the alliance around the needs of the child must be established whether the parents are divorced or not. These parents, at the time the treatment ended, no longer needed the neutrality of the therapist and his office to communicate with each other and develop plans for their son. The parenting alliance, with subsequently effective parenting, was sustained outside of the clinical situation. The therapist provided a context, with the support of the hospital and residential treatment center, for a framework by which the parents could turn the anlage of a parenting alliance into a vibrant parenting alliance.

Case 2

The second case is that of a professional man in his mid-40s who was referred to the therapist when his bright 8-year-old son entered treatment with a child psychiatrist. The child's problems were poor peer relationships, multiple anxieties, and considerable irritability. Treatment for both parents was recommended by the child psychiatrist but the mother refused. At the beginning of the father's therapy, he was concerned that he might interfere with his son's growth and development. His primarily personal reasons for obtaining psychotherapy were difficulties in being assertive at home and work. The patient presented a picture of his wife as a cold, angry, depressed woman in her 40s. (This view of her corresponded to the diagnostic impression of the child psychiatrist.) In fact, the patient was concerned that if he left his wife she could become suicidal. In the therapy, he uncovered a similar relationship, as a child, with his mother wherein he felt used as an "antidepressant." He felt that his anger to his wife and estrangement from her contributed to his having extramarital affairs.

With his children, the patient was able to respond to their age-appropriate needs. In addition to the 8-year-old, the patient had two older sons, ages 13 and 15. As treatment proceeded, with the passivity in focus, he was able to perceive subtleties in the children's needs and was able to facilitate growth along with provision for safety in setting limits and boundaries. As his ability to respond assertively to the childrens' needs expanded, he experienced increasing anger at his wife's detachment. He felt most assaulted by her depreciation of what she considered to be his increasing infantilization of the children. For example, she thought that his insistence on setting up reasonable hours for adolescents would keep them immature, and that their initiatives would be crushed. She implied, also, that he seemed to be clinging to the children whose growth would be stunted, supposedly, just as his had been by his mother's handling of him during his childhood and adolescence. The wife regarded the patient's passivity to be the consequence of having been raised as a "sissy." He reacted to the wife's depreciation of his parenting as an assault on his masculinity and self-esteem.

On another occasion, substance abuse became an issue with the older boys, particularly the 13-year-old. The parents had good reason to suspect that the boy was involved, in some way, with a group of adolescent drug users. The patient suggested to his wife that they inform the son of their concern so that they could have an open discussion, and let the boy know about their disapproval. The wife was as concerned as the patient, but she believed that to forbid drug use in the home would either drive away the boy or that he would become overly anxious and cautious. She regarded the patient's efforts as proof of his lack of sureness of himself as a man, and felt that he was being "an intrusive Jewish mother." The patient, nevertheless, did confront the boy who revealed considerable depression and anxiety. At this time, the boy was referred for therapy. Once the task was done, the wife was relieved that her husband's assertiveness was successful.

As the patient continued to deal with his children, he became aware of a desire to talk to his wife about his feelings as a parent. The wife responded by absenting herself from these attempted conversations. Although she could not involve herself with her husband in the subtle process of sharing experiences and expectations concerning their children, she was a concerned parent and supported treatment for the children. She had, however, no ability to invest in a parenting dyad within the context of a triadic relationship involving a child. The wife's detachment caused the patient to experience a lack of affirmation in his parenting role. The lack of feedback and of a continuous milieu in the parenting sphere wherein such interactions are necessary for the parenthood experience to be creative and expansive left him depleted and doubtful about himself as a parent. Outside of the parenting relationship, the patient admired his wife's commitment to her public life and they shared many common values, ideals, and pleasures in recreational activities. His wife admired his many talents and encouraged their development.

The treatment proceeded with twice weekly psychotherapy for 4 years. After termination, the patient returned twice to his former therapist. Each visit focused on parenting issues. One is of particular interest. The patient's older sons were approaching late adolescence during the days of the anti-Vietnam war demonstrations. Both parents approved of their planned participation in a march on the Capitol. Once the sons announced that they planned to attend the march, the wife was not interested in discussing their concerns. In the days immediately prior to the march, she refused to discuss the boys' fears and to participate with them and her husband in planning how they could cope with the potential dangers. The patient became outraged by his wife's response. He asked to see his former therapist for two sessions in order to affirm the appropriateness of his responses to his sons in the face of an absent alliance with his wife. He was concerned that possibly he had been overprotective of his sons, yet he did not depreciate their needs for parental support. Exploration of the events and activities involving him, his wife, and sons revealed a concern that the sons could be physically hurt. As a young man, he had also participated in demonstrations and had seen people hurt, and recalled his fears and his shame about them.

Although the patient and his wife approved of the sons' activities they could not mutually experience either pleasure or concern about their activities. In the absence of a parenting alliance with his wife, the father utilized the therapist for the necessary feedback in parenting tasks. This enabled him to assess, in a neutral setting, his concerns about his sons and to untangle his identifications with them from his own youth. The therapist's confirming supportive stance enabled him to counsel and support the sons in a more effective parenting role. The therapist served, transiently, in a parenting type alliance when his rage at his wife and self-doubt threatened his sense of appropriateness with his children. Perhaps the positive therapeutic outcome led this man to seek a substitute when he was unable to get from his wife a mutual pride as well as concern as his sons took on mature tasks. In addition to the therapist, he utilized colleagues for the needed reflection around parenting tasks.

In this case, we see how a parenting alliance can be established with a therapist. This need not be regarded as extraneous to the process of intensive psychotherapy if adult developmental needs are conceptualized appropriately. The case illustrates that as a parent becomes aware of the phase appropriate needs of children, and is able to disengage his needs from theirs, he continues to need a milieu for child rearing in which he can feel valued and affirmed in a feedback process. As this patient became more sensitive and empathic, he became invested increasingly in becoming an effective parent just as he had struggled to become more effective in his career. In order to achieve this ideal, he sought actively for the kind of milieu which would help him sustain the gains he had made. In the example above, the milieu was created most economically by a short return to his therapist. We suspect that many such short-term alliances are created when a parent meets with a child's therapist to provide developmental gains for the child.

Case 3

This case will demonstrate, also, the problems in a family where a parenting alliance did not exist. The identified patient was a 16-year-old boy who was referred by a school counselor for truancy from school, drug abuse, and minor delinquent activities. The boy came readily to the therapist's office. Early in the therapy, he described a disrupted family situation and estrangment from his father. He elaborated that his father was actually his stepfather, that his mother and father had divorced when he was an infant, and that he never knew his biologic father. He was adopted by his mother's second husband. He had a stepsister at home in addition to his parents. The patient insisted that there was nothing that he could do to please his father. He believed that his father cared about him only as long as he didn't get into any trouble and was no bother. The boy described himself as unhappy and said that he used drugs, that there was nothing significant about it, that all of his friends used drugs. He promised that if his parents gave him another chance he wouldn't get into any further trouble.

On the basis of the boy's involvement with his parents, and his desire for an improved relationship with them, and to learn more about the family, an appointment was arranged with the boy and his parents. At this meeting, the boy voiced his complaints about his parents and they, in turn, expressed their concern about his behavior. Father expressed his anger at the boy for disrupting the family. As they spoke about their problems, they interrupted each other and could not listen to what the other person said. At the end of the hour, when the therapist proposed a second meeting to look further into some of the family problems, the father said that he saw no need to come back. All he wanted was that his son not cause any trouble and that he wasn't going to become any more involved than necessary. After further discussion with his wife, who said that she felt that the meeting had been helpful and wished that he return, he repeated that he didn't care and saw no reason to do so. The session ended with the patient startled by the outcome, the mother in tears, and the father restating he didn't want to have any more to do with the boy.

Unlike in the first case, the foundation for a parenting alliance and the capacity of the parents to work jointly with their child regarding his difficulty did not exist. The father did not share the mother's investment in the boy and did not see himself behaving as a father. Nor did he value the mother's concerns or her request that he become involved with the boy. Essentially, the father devalued his wife's parenting role as well as his own.

Case 4

A final clinical vignette will demonstrate the import of the parenting alliance for the family and the therapist in determining the course of clinical interventions, particularly with adolescents. A young adolescent girl was referred with urgency because of the suspected turbulence in the home. The desperate concerns of the mother were the girl's "active" promiscuity and "widespread" drug abuse. Both parents had psychological sophistication commensurate with their high educational and social status. They had great expectations because of satisfaction with the outcome of an earlier therapeutic experience involving another child, a boy 3 years older than the referred patient. There was, also, a 6-year-old son.

From everyone's account (except the girl's) of her behavior and her tenacious involvment with a "bad crowd," the therapist expected to find a seriously disordered girl. Initially, the mother and daughter were seen together, then separately, with the girl being seen first. She was an attractive, sullen girl who knew about her parents' concern, and depreciated her mother for being overly anxious. Though guarded, she gave many indications of an intact personality structure. She knew she had to see the therapist because her parents didn't know what else to do with her. During the individual psychotherapy, the girl revealed her depression, obstinacy, and provocativeness and the rather narrow scope of the acting out. The mother, an attractive, dependent, and rigid woman, was devastated by fears that the girl's life was ruined. She revealed her many anxieties because of emotional problems in both her parents' families. She reported that the son's adolescence did not trouble the parents and that he had a good relationship with them. She conjectured that perhaps the daughter was missing the old times with father who was described as being currently very preoccupied with serious matters in his business. (This, the daughter had mentioned, too.) From the mother's perspective, the parents had a compatible marriage and had maintained a good parenting alliance in the past. The daughter's adolescence created a threat to the mother's equilibrium for which psychotherapy was recommended, eventually.

To clarify the family situation, the therapist saw the father alone for an evaluation. He appeared to be a caring, thoughtful, somewhat rigid man, successful in his business, but recently engaged in a critical expansion, to which he was devoting much time. He recognized his wife's exaggerated response to the girl's activities, and was supportively aware of the historical reasons. He regarded highly her parenting efforts and was pleased that the therapist had wanted to see him. He was pleased to feel needed and became accessible to a better understanding of the daughter's developmentally appropriate longing for him and her need for a more stable alliance between the parents. For obvious reasons, and others which cannot be presented here, the therapist believed that the girl required individual psychotherapy. To facilitate the girl's treatment and create a more benign family process, the therapist worked with the parents in three sessions for the specific task of promoting a better alliance. The therapist continued to work with the girl who soon became aware of how her anxieties, disappointments, and conflicts contributed to her acting out. She maintained responsibility for her twice weekly sessions and seemed able to deal with the parents without further intervention by the therapist.

In this case, both parents were invested in the child and with each other as parents. The parenting alliance was strained by the father's preoccupations, leaving the mother vulnerable to regression. Although there was disagreement about discipline, their mutual respect for their needs and judgment remained intact. Each wanted communication with the other, and both were amenable to dealing with the developmental needs of their daughter. The mother decided to reduce the intensity of her concern with the daughter by engaging in more community work, and was supported by the father. The girl felt affirmed by their reengaged parenting and became pleased by her mother's successful activities. The therapy became remarkably smooth, with only occasional flare-ups emanating from the mother's intrapsychic stress. Had psychotherapy for the mother been immediately recommended or had family therapy been instituted, we are doubtful that the family could have settled into dealing with the appropriate issues and achieving some relief.

The mother's anxieties, self-esteem problems, and close tie to the daughter could have interfered with the therapy and the family equilibrium without the reestablishment of the alliance. Clearly, the parenting alliance could not serve as the sole therapeutic agent for the mother's threatened intrapsychic disruption. It can be credited, however, with cooling down the family and shifting the imbalance, and for providing sufficient self-esteem support for the mother to seek her own therapy which she had considered for many years. By pointing out to the parents their responsibilities, the therapist laid the groundwork for permitting the girl to take responsibility for her behavior.

We suspect that a gap is created often by recommending therapy for the family, or the parent(s), and/or the adolescent without proper focus on the vicissitudes of the parenting alliance. With a good-enough parenting alliance, parents are freer to attend to intrapsychic issues for which they need time for mastery. With the alliance in place, an adolescent has an advantage which enables him/her to address developmental or intrapsychic problems in psychotherapy, as is demonstrated in this case.

CONCLUSION

We regard the parenting alliance as a process which is critical for the study of adult development. Up until recently it has not been possible to conceptualize it so as to understand its explanatory power. Largely, it has appeared in the literature to amplify clinical understanding of child development or of seriously disordered young adults. Indeed, the relationship between the parents has been noted frequently when it is in disarray, or absent. It is often the case that we note the existence of a structure or function only when it is absent. So it has been in our clinical work from which we derived the concept of the parenting alliance. The need for essential vitamins was discovered only after various deficiency diseases were noted. The British naval medical corps knew that some factor in limes cured scurvy without knowing what that factor was. Today, we know it as ascorbic acid or vitamin C. Only by its absence, and the observation of scurvy among sailors, along with the observation that somehow limes prevented the illness, was the relationship noted between the lime and scurvy.

To review, therapists can assist parents in establishing a parenting alliance only if (1) each parent is invested in the child; (2) each parent values the other parent's involvement with the child; (3) each parent respects the judgments of the other parent; and (4) each parent desires to communicate with the other.

We believe that the parenting alliance is an adult life-course process which both amplifies and is amplified by the self psychology concept of self–selfobject relationships. Moreover, it can identify factors which promote creative growth in adulthood. We recognize the danger of overloading the concept but propose it, nevertheless, as a significant, interpersonal and intrapsychic process in assessing adult development, family cohesion, and planning therapeutic intervention.

In closing, we offer an incident which one of the authors witnessed. A couple had been married 20 years prior to obtaining a divorce. The divorce occurred well before the two older children prepared to attend college. The divorced parents were dating and the father planned to remarry. Nevertheless, when the children's departure time for college arrived, both parents accompanied them for two nights to help them negotiate their college entry. The father's mother put it best: "They will do anything for the children. I used to think they would get back together, but now I guess they won't." Parenting alliances exist and can survive marital break-ups, and are acknowledged in many families. We believe that the issue of the parenting alliance is a substantive entry point for psychodynamic clinicians confronting family stresses.

REFERENCES

Anthony, E. J., & Benedek, T. (Eds.). *Parenthood: Its psychology and psychopathology*. Boston: Little, Brown, 1970.

Benedek, T. Parenthood as a developmental phase. *Journal of the American Psychoanalytic Association*, 1959, 7, 389–417.

Bowen, M. Theory in the practice of psychotherapy. In P. Guerin, Jr. (Ed.). *Family therapy: Theory and practice*. New York: Gardner Press, 1976.

Cohen, R., & Balikov, H. On the impact of adolescence upon parents. In S. Feinstein & P. Giovacchini (Eds.), *Adolescent psychiatry* (Vol. III). New York: Basic Books, 1974.

Cohler, B. J. Adult developmental psychology and reconstruction in psychoanalysis. In S. I. Greenspan & G. H. Pollock (Eds.), *The course of life* (Vol. III: *Adulthood and the aging process*). National Institute of Mental Health, 1981.

Goldberg, A. (Ed.). *Advances in self psychology*. New York International Universities Press, 1980.

Kohut, H. *The analysis of the self*. New York: International Universities Press, 1971.

Kohut, H. *The restoration of the self*. New York: International Universities Press, 1977.

Lidz, T. *The family and human adaptation*. New York: International Universities Press, 1963.

Lidz, T. *The person* (Rev. ed.). New York: Basic Books, 1976.

Mahler, M. S., & Furer, M. *On human symbiosis and vicissitudes of individuation*. New York: International Universities Press, 1968.

Meissner, W. W. The conceptualization of marriage and family dynamics from a psychoanalytic perspective. In T. J. Paolino, Jr., & B. S. McCrady (Eds.), *Marriage and marital therapy*. New York: Brunner/Mazel, 1978.

Michels, R. Adulthood. In S. I. Greenspan & G. H. Pollock (Eds.), *The course of life* (Vol. III: *Adulthood and the aging process*). National Institute of Mental Health, 1981.

Minuchin, S. *Families and family therapy*. Cambridge, Mass.: Harvard University Press, 1974.

Stierlin, H. *Psychoanalysis and family therapy*. New York: Aronson, 1977.

Terman, D. M. Object love and the psychology of the self. In A. Goldberg (Ed.), *Advances in self psychology*. New York: International Universities Press, 1980.

Tolpin, M. On the beginnings of a cohesive self: An application of the concept of transmuting internalization to the study of the transitional object and signal anxiety. *The Psychoanalytic Study of the Child*. 1971, 26, 316–352.

Weissman, S., & Barglow, P. Recent contributions to the theory of female adolescent psychological development. In S. Feinstein, P. Giovacchini, J. G. Looney, A. Z. Schwartzberg, & A. D. Sorosky (Eds.), *Adolescent psychiatry*. Chicago: University of Chicago Press, 1980.

Wolf, E. On the developmental line of selfobject relations. In A. Goldberg (Ed.), *Advances in self psychology*. New York: International Universities Press, 1980.

4

PARENTS AT HOME AND ON THE JOB

LAURA LEIN

Paid work and family life represent the two primary spheres of activity for most adults for much of their lives, in terms of emotional investment and time. Most adults, both men and women, make decisions about two major adult responsibilities, paid employment and parenting, during the same decade of their lives, their 20s and early 30s. This is an immensely exciting time in adult lives, a time of unleashed energy and creativity. Accompanying the excitement, however, are complexity and stress. Furthermore, the relative significance to men and women of these two major undertakings is quite different. In this chapter we review the patterns of paid work and family responsibilities in men's and women's lives, and the impact of paid work on family life and vice versa.

These two life activities, paid work and parenting, not only have an immense impact on each other, they also affect almost every other aspect of an individual's life. Paid work and family responsibilities shape the composition and activities of an individual's social network, the contributions made by an individual to community organizations and the political system, and an individual's financial and leisure-time resources.

Rosebeth Kanter (1977) points out that, until recently, sociologists, in their study of men's and women's life patterns, tended to divide life into spheres of activity: paid work, community, family, and so on. There was little recognition that for most men and women the spheres of their lives overlap considerably, each having a major impact on the others. Kanter calls for further studies exploring the interactions among these life spheres for individuals, and assessing the impact of each life sphere on the others. Her work draws heavily on an "open systems" approach, suggesting that family systems interact heavily with other institutional systems, and interactions among institutional systems have a considerable effect on individuals.

In tracing the impacts of employment and family responsibilities on men and women, this chapter draws on national survey data illustrated by intensive

Laura Lein. Wellesley College Center for Research on Women, Wellesley, Massachusetts.

interviews with family members to explore the impact of paid work and parenting, as mutually interacting activities, on adult lives. The interviews were accomplished in 1973–1975 by the Working Family Project (1974, 1976) and included a series of interview visits with 25 middle-income, dual-earner couples.

In selecting among paid work and family options men and women are always in the position of reacting to social stereotypes. The variety of decisions made by men and women in the two spheres of job and family need to be contrasted with the sex-based stereotypes suggested to them in our society. The impact of life decisions is highly dependent on whether or not they are in line with societal expectations.

The decisions men and women make about family life and paid work shape their entire adult lives. The effects of work and family choices remain with the individual long past the period of their direct impact. Choice of occupation affects the options available to men and women in terms of training and entry into other occupational areas, as well as advancement in the area of their original choice. Choice of family life-style affects not only one's family life during the child-rearing years, but also the number of children and grandchildren one can enjoy, depend on, and offer support to in one's old age.

Many of the life tensions experienced by men and women are the result of the multiplicity of demands on them arising from the dual tasks of job and family, and the long-term effects of the decisions they make. Paid work and homemaking are both conglomerates of large numbers of tasks, requiring organization and collaboration with other people, as well as specific skills. When men and women add paid work to the work of parenting, they face heavy, and often conflicting, demands.

It is not simply the weight of the number of demands that affects men and women as they combine paid work and family responsibilities. These two responsibilities represent the longest and strongest emotional commitments most people make during their lives. The responsibilities associated with them demand resources of tact and organization, stamina and emotional depth. It is these demands arising out of decisions about adult responsibilities that make decisions about paid work and family life milestones in adult development.

Men's and women's experience of family life is highly dependent not only on the choices made, but also on the timing of paid work and family responsibilities in their lives. Men's and women's decisions about marriage, children, and occupation and career not only form their life histories, but decisions in each realm affect their options in other arenas. Daniels and Weingarten (1981) point out that the timing of childbearing in a woman's life affects her entire career and job history, as well as her experience of young adulthood and the later years. Women who have children before starting their careers face a very different experience from those who interrupt their careers to have children later in life. This is true because women's traditional responsibilities for children in the family often constrain the job-related career development decisions they make during their child-rearing years.

It is not so obvious, but equally true, that men's employment decisions are affected by their family responsibilities. However, where women face clear conflicts between the demands of family and employment, men see advancement on the job and the rewards it can bring as one of their most substantial contributions to the family. For men, undertaking family responsibilities often carries with it a need to strengthen commitment to paid work. This pressure is shared to some extent by many women, particularly those who are the sole breadwinners in their family.

Much early work on paid work and family life concentrated on men and women with well-paid careers (Rapoport & Rapoport, 1976; Holmstrom, 1972). Parents with professional careers are in a minority, of course. In this article I concentrate on the issues of job and family as they emerge in the mainstream of middle-income American families. This approach is limited too. The experiences of single parents and of minority parents differ significantly from those of two-parent white couples. However, many of the same issues must be faced by all employed parents, although in different ways, considering different alternatives. The experience of responsibility for children is shared by all parents.

Notwithstanding the significance of each of the life spheres to the others, it is important to understand the meaning of both paid work and parenting to men and women as separate activities involving individual choices before we can explore the important ways in which they are interrelated parts of the adult experience. For this reason I will discuss men's and women's experience of paid work and parenting separately as well as the ramifications of each sphere of activity for the other in the family system. The issues for men and women facing these decisions include:

• Mobilization of personal resources to meet the demands of adult responsibilities. For both men and women, employment and family life represent substantial tests of their skills and abilities, as well as their stamina and commitment.
• Conflicting demands made by different life spheres. Employment and family responsibilities demand different skills and abilities, as well as time and energy commitments.
• Commitment for a number of years to activities and individuals making continuous demands.

CHILDREN

For most couples, the arrival of children, rather than marriage, intensifies issues around paid work and family life. Children create the most significant changes in day-to-day adult responsibilities. Alice Rossi (1968), in her article "Transition to Parenthood," suggests that the onset of parenthood is the major crisis for adults in family life. She describes it as a crisis, both because of the sudden onset of new responsibilities, and because the nature of the responsibilities that parents have toward their children requires new tactics for negotiating between spouses. The kinds of responsibility undertaken by adults on behalf of each other, and the kinds of negotiating these require, do not necessarily meet the demands of parenting.

These two issues, the work required and the negotiating skills needed by the parenting adults, are clearly related, but work issues and negotiation styles have somewhat different implications for the husband–wife team. The work required by children is continuous and difficult to control and contain, compared to most other aspects of homemaking. Now parents find that evenings, lunchtimes, times they are accustomed to spend on themselves or each other, are now occupied by the work of child rearing. Not only do parents have more work, but the time during which they can obtain rewards from each other is shorter, and more liable to interruption.

Work caused by the arrival of a new child not only takes time, but energy, and parents, emerging from interrupted nights and stressful days, often feel less fit that they might to deal with the requirements of daily parenting. Parental fatigue is not, of course, a new discovery. Fatigue, however, hampers the ability of parents to develop new styles of negotiating work and responsibility. Styles of negotiating and play that have developed between adults before the arrival of children often do not work out very well after their arrival. Parents cannot decide on the spur of the moment to go out and celebrate a new achievement; to put off cooking dinner to see a TV show; to have a long discussion about who will do a particular task (i.e., pick up the now-screaming baby). It is more difficult to keep relationships friendly while negotiating work allotments in the home under the pressures of children's needs and parental fatigue.

The ability of parents to meet family needs is deeply affected by their paid employment. First, the money and benefits available to families through the employment of parents affects the services families can mobilize on behalf of their children and themselves. This includes not only income, but possible benefits of medical coverage, insurance, child-care support, and paid vacation and holidays. Some employers are beginning to recognize the significance of benefits in meeting family needs and are developing interesting alternatives for families at different life-cycle stages.

However, income and employer-provided benefits are not the only issues for parents in analyzing issues around jobs. Parents must develop their own values and priorities around child rearing. They need to figure out what counts. Thus, parents interviewed have valued such qualities in their job as schedule flexibility, lack of responsibility for the performance of others, limited or no overtime requests, because these qualities in employment, although often linked to lower wages, provide the possibility of more time with families. These are not just women's issues. They are faced by both men and women torn between paid employment and family life.

Second, the security of the job has an important impact on families. Families with relatively secure earned incomes can engage in long-term planning and spend fewer resources developing protective strategies against the possibilities of lay-offs and unemployment. Furthermore, security on the job often enables parents to express more confidence in the stability of their family's life style. Third, pressures and irritations on the job often reverberate in family life. The psychological and physical demands of employment shape the demands that individual workers make on their families, not just in terms of scheduling and material services, but also in terms of needs for quiet and free time.

Furthermore, because women's labor force patterns have changed so dramatically during the last generation, mothers and fathers today have few models of successful combination of paid work and family life in either the dual-worker or single-parent family. Almost all parents report that it is impossible to prepare someone sufficiently for parenthood. The new work, the new responsibilities, and the new pressures, while more than outweighed by the joys of children for most parents, are almost overwhelming and completely unpredictable. Undertaking these new tasks with the additional burden of wives' paid employment can be particularly stressful as well as rewarding. Both men's and women's experience in the labor force is affected by their parenthood.

MEN'S PAID WORK

A number of facets of a job affect family life: These include, in addition to the financial rewards, the peer group and friends offered by the job to the worker, the scheduling and constraints of work on the job, and the pressure and tension of the job. Some occupations, such as firefighting and medical work typically provide men with tight-knit social groups that reach out to members of their families (Lein, 1979). Others provide either little social network or social ties that distance the worker from his family (LeMasters, 1975). It is not simply the nature of the work, its pressures and schedules, that affect family life. The values of the work-related peer group have an important impact on the family. The differences in employed-related peer groups are clearer for men. Few employment-related peer groups anticipate that women will allow an employment-based peer group to draw them away from family responsibilities.

Occupations such as police work typify employment of a high level of scheduling constraints combined with a high degree of tension and pressure on the job. Not only do difficult work schedules impact heavily on family life, but men and women under pressure on the job bring such pressure home with them (Piotrokowski, 1979). These constraints of paid employment clearly affect employed women as well as men. However, their impact on men is strengthened by the significance of the breadwinner role to men's contributions to the family. Men more often feel constrained to sustain the long-term pressures of a particular employment situation; furthermore they feel they owe their family such successful maintenance of the breadwinner role.

Traditional stereotypes in the United States suggest that men find most of their adult satisfaction in the context of their paid occupation. Indeed, most men, for most of their lives, are involved in paid labor. Recently, psychologists such as Joseph Pleck and Linda Lang (1978) have suggested that, for men as well as women, family life is the major focus of concern and the source of the greatest life satisfactions. In an analysis of national survey data, Pleck and Lang found that reports for both men and women of general life satisfaction are most closely related to the quality of their home life.

This finding appears to contradict older work beginning with that of Parsons and Bales (1955), who hypothesized that while women express the greatest concern about their performance of home or family-based work, men are concerned primarily with their performance in the sphere of paid work. Whereas women's self-esteem was viewed as based on their performance of work in the home, men's most often was related to success on the job. Women were characterized as concerned with the internal life of the family, men with the life of the larger society.

How Pleck and Lang's findings concerning the primary importance of family life for both men and women can mesh with the apparently contradictory earlier hypothesis about men's ties to the larger society and women's ties to the home is illuminated through analysis of intensive family interviews by the Working Family Project (1974, 1976) and Lein (1979), among other researchers. The Working Family Project reports that most of the men interviewed described paid work as the primary contribution they made to their family. Through their paid job they offered their family the financial support it required. For men, paid work is usually the avenue for their major contribution to family life.

The relationship between men's employment and their contributions to their families is not a simple one. Men do not perceive this as simply handing money over to their families for the purchase of goods and services. Their job not only supports the family, it gives status to the family, and associated benefits and rewards contribute to family well-being. The job is a direct support and it is also the symbol of the father's ability to support his family.

Men's concern with their performance on the job, largely construed, and their successful advancement in career is substantially motivated by their concern that they be adequate family-providers. Thus, the men interviewed by the Working Family Project did indeed invest heavily in job-related success. However, for men as well as women, paid work is perceived at least in part as a mechanism for major contributions to family life. Furthermore, they accurately perceive that not only the financial returns from the job, but also the stresses and advantages it offers, affect family life.

This interpretation is supported by an analysis of men's patterns of paid employment throughout the life cycle. Although there are few national survey data available to support these findings, the Working Family Project has found that men's attitudes toward paid work and their actual employment pattern changes, not so much with marriage, but with the birth of their first child. Although most men have been steadily involved in the paid labor force, usually full-time, before having children, their employment pattern is likely to have included considerable experimentation. They are likely to have changed employers frequently and to have explored both different kinds of jobs and work hour schedules.

However, shortly after the birth of the first child, the pattern of paid worl becomes more regular. Men tend to stay with the same employer for much longer periods of time. The choice of job, and concerns about advancement and experimentation with new job options, are controlled by concern for successful performance of the "breadwinner" role. Men experiment much less with job and career options after fathering children; they remain tied to the position in which they most adequately support their family.

The breadwinner role requires the provision of more than just money. It implies the maintenance of those job benefits that have become essential to maintaining the family standard of living. It includes maintenance of the social status given the family through the father's occupation. It includes the provision of security and continuity of support.

The particular decisions made by individual fathers vary, of course, with their personalities and the family constraints on them. However, there is a consistent concern among fathers with the relationship of the paid job to family responsibilities. One father, discussing his desire to experiment with a different kind of employment, explains that it is not now possible because of the risks to his family. He cannot afford any drop in income. Therefore, any explorations he might undertake become more constrained as he achieves more, and, because of seniority and growing experience, is paid more in his occupation.

> "I certainly feel that I have an obligation to provide the security that my family deserves. I wouldn't take a chance on something that would leave us short. If something did crop up and I wanted to try it, it would have to be moderately close to what I'm doing now as far as financial returns are concerned. I certainly wouldn't take a drastic change in income, since that would affect my family. They are uppermost, foremost, in my mind."

Not only income, but other aspects of the job—hours, benefits, training—are closely tied to family life. One father with preschool children explains that he determines his work hours according to the needs of his family.

> "I work 5 o'clock in the afternoon until 2 o'clock in the morning. So I'm here all afternoon and night. I get to bed at 10 o'clock, and I'm up by 4 o'clock. I don't get as much sleep now, because I can't go to bed at 8 o'clock. But it works out good. I enjoy it. I work harder now at work, and when I get out, I just want to get away and come home and relax. I really look forward to it . . . with this new shift I can do more things. I'm planning to join a bowling league in the fall, and I spend a lot of time with my kids. . . . In a few years when the kids are in school, I'll probably change my hours. I won't want to be home during the day."

Still another father explains a series of complicated career track and job changes he made in response to his family's growing financial needs.

"In high school I had hopes of being a professional baseball player and several scouts were watching me. But I broke my elbow and had to give up that ambition. Then I thought I might be a teacher–coach. I spent part of a year teaching school after college graduation. Then I was drafted and served in the army for several years. After the army I finished a year of teaching, but I needed more money because we were having children, so I went into sales. For twelve years I worked for a trucking company getting other companies to ship with my firm. Finally I changed jobs, because, with more kids, I wanted more job security, and the trucking firm didn't offer a lot of security to people in my position. I went back to teaching, taking a cut in pay in return for the security it offered."

All of these fathers express much of their life anxiety and concern around issues of their paid employment, but the motivation for the concern is most often family based. It is fed by concern for family stability and security, by the necessity of maintaining a certain standard of living, and by the recognition that the job represents a pivotal support of the family's social status. Concern for paid work cannot be separated from concern for the quality of family life, and for the father's ability to contribute to it. For husbands and fathers the spheres of family and paid work represent closely intertwined life goals. The pressures of responsibility for children interacts with the early employment experiences of men to give life-long impact to the decisions made during this period. Under the pressure of family responsibilities, men find it increasingly difficult to change their minds regarding their employment decisions.

WOMEN'S PAID WORK

The traditional stereotype of the "woman at home" taking care of her husband, home, and children no longer reflects the reality of the majority of American families. Due to the changing patterns of women's participation in the paid labor force, the unemployed housewife is becoming part of an evershrinking minority. Of families in the United States, only 7% have an employed father, a stay-at-home mother, and a couple of children (Hayghe, 1976). Of all married couples in the United States, only 25% include an employed male and an unemployed female. In 50% of the couples both are employed. The remaining 25% include retirees and couples both members of which are unemployed (Hayghe, 1976).

Unmarried women, both single parents and women with no dependents, have, as one would predict, even higher rates of employment than do married women. For single mothers, there is usually considerable pressure to earn a living. They are required to combine the breadwinning role and the parenting role.

Not only are women working at paid jobs in ever-increasing numbers, but the increase has been most marked among mothers of young children. In 1950 only 11.9% of mothers of preschool children (under 6 years of age) were employed. The figure now is fast approaching 50% (U.S. Bureau of the Census,

1978). Increasing numbers of women are working for pay, and mothers are more often combining paid work with the work of parenting.

Furthermore, the accelerated movement of women into the paid labor force is a matter of choice for only a small minority of women. Nearly two thirds of employed women are working for money out of clear economic need; that is, they are either the sole earner in their household or they are married to a spouse earning under $10,000/year (U.S. Department of Labor, 1980). Thus, women are participating in the "breadwinning" function because of their families' needs as much as out of choice. In fact, women's selection of both occupation and specific job are usually determined as much by family need as by personal choice.

One woman describes the family's need for her paycheck to support their standard of living.

> "Well, with my check it's easy to describe what it goes for. My check goes for paying my son's baby-sitter and buying some groceries, although it doesn't go far enough to buy all the groceries. So that's that. We don't put it in the bank. We just spend it. . . . It used to be that I could spend two or three dollars a day just on little things, like crayons for the kids or a new kind of shampoo. I can't do that any more. We really need the money for the grocery bill."

For women, in a different way than for men, the move into the paid labor force represents no diminution in the importance of family life to them. Women continue to consider family life their primary sphere of responsibility, and indeed continue to assume most of the responsibilities toward the family that have been traditionally assigned to women. Their family work and paid work, like that of men, is motivated by concern for and involvement in family life. Women are working not only out of a concern for their own development and experience in the paid labor force, but for what they can contribute to their families in terms of improved standard of living.

However, for women in two-parent families, paid work is not perceived as a primary contribution to family well-being. In particular, women, unlike men, do not plan and foresee their paid work as a primary contribution to family life. In one recent study almost half (49%) of a national survey of female high-school students either "agreed" or "mostly agreed" with the statement, "It is usually better for everyone involved if the man is the achiever outside the home and the woman takes care of the home and family" (Herzog, Bachman, & Johnston, 1979).

Even today, women's work patterns remain distinct from those of men. During their child-rearing years, when most men are employed full-time or close to it, women are more usually employed part-time. An examination of census figures indicates that only 20% of married mothers with children under 18 are employed full-time—full day, 50–52 weeks/year (O'Donnell & Stueve, 1980). These figures are, of course, different for single-parent mothers who are much more likely to work full-time. Intensive interviews by O'Donnell and Malson indicate that paid work is an "add-on" for most married mothers of young children, an additional contribution they can make to their family, but not the principal contribution (Families and Communities Project, 1981).

Thus, women, like men, see paid work as a means of contributing to family well-being. Women, unlike men, do not think of paid employment as the primary means at their disposal for making such a contribution. Therefore, they discuss their work, their work schedules, and their pay not as contributions in themselves necessarily, but as flexible parameters that must be made to fit around other demands of family life. Flexibility is an important quality in making a job likeable for a young mother. One woman describes how she selected her job, because the flexible work hours fit the constraints of her family's schedule:

"Where I worked before, one of the women had a son who was in personnel over at the hospital. When he found out they needed a secretary, she told me. I drove over and applied. I really like it. It's a job. The work, you know, nobody likes to work. I guess it's okay. You have to work more or less full time to get anything. I don't think there are many places that would let me work like I work now. I more or less make my own hours. Now that my husband's on this crazy schedule, he works late and sleeps late. I'm supposed to be in at 10 o'clock. But if I can't get in at 10, but get in at 11, nobody says anything."

For her, the job itself, job advancement, and self-improvement were not the issues. Rather this mother needed to contribute income through a job that would permit her to meet her other family obligations.

For some mothers, pay and flexibility are not the only issues. Aside from the money earned, women do look to other aspects of their job for contributions to family life, and to themselves. One woman explains how her occupation helps her family by helping her to be a more knowledgeable, more involved parent.

"When you have a part-time job, no matter where you are, you see a lot of the world, not just your little close-knit circle. Then, when your kids come home and talk to you, you at least know some things that are going on, even if you don't know too much about them."

Employed mothers are committed to their jobs, often because of intrinsic qualities of the job as well as for what they can contribute to their families through their paid work. For the majority of women this does not detract from their primary focus. Personal interest in the job itself does, for some women, change paid work into a vocation.

HOMEMAKING

Although there have been some significant changes in the last two decades, it remains the case that, employed or not, women contribute more than men to the work of caring for the house. Early figures by Walker and Woods (1976) indicate that employed mothers, on the average, worked 70 hours/week in the combination of home care and paid work, while their husbands on the average, contributed 55 hours/week. More recent work by Pleck and Rustad (1980) indicates that men's and women's contributions remain different from each other, but that the number of hours each contributes is declining.

Intensive interviews with family members by the Working Family Project indicate that negotiations about changing contributions made to household work by husbands and wives can be difficult. Changes in the psychosocial interior of the family caused by women's increasing participation in the paid labor force during the child-rearing years include the necessity for tighter scheduling of family responsibilities and activities; closer negotiation between husband and wife concerning their contributions to the home; and more difficulty in coping with the increased demands made by the presence of young children. For employed mothers and their families, homemaking has become more than the work of child care and home maintenance. It includes a significant amount of negotiation of a sensitive and time-consuming nature.

The necessity for continuing negotiations over the work of homemaking highlight the differing attitudes husbands and wives may have about contributions to family life. In one family discussions over the organization of contributions to family life illustrate the impact of the wife's paid work on both husband and wife. In this family both husband and wife agree that men's and women's responsibilities to the home are and should be substantially different. However, the wife's periodic participation in the paid labor force has put pressure in the past on all family members to change their contributions to the previously sex-segregated work of the home. The wife describes this process in her family, beginning with the period of their marriage before they had children.

> "I was working and earning money, and I thought I was very independent, and my husband hated that, hated that with a passion. I think we used to fight about that all the time. I would give him a lot of flip answers, and say, 'Well, I worked and. . . .' Not that we fought over money itself, it was just my attitude because I was out working. . . ."

Partly because of the difficulties involved, this wife dropped out of the labor force until her third child was school age. Now, she reports,

> "He feels very good about my job. He was glad I got it. I felt I was in a rut, and he felt I was in a rut. You get almost hibernated. . . . He thought it would be good for my morale to get out and meet other people and just broaden my whole world. So he was glad. He had no regrets that I took the job. . . . But I think if it was a case of my having to work financially, it would have bothered him very much."

Partly because her work is so removed from issues of family well-being, this mother's anxieties remain centered on her homemaking responsibilities:

> "When I was home I never let the house go—everything got done, but I still had that leisure time. That's what I miss. . . . The thing that bothers me most is the housework. . . . As far as the children go, I don't think they suffered

in any way, because I am here when they leave in the morning. I am here when they return in the afternoon.''

This woman's money buys extras but not necessities for the family. Her contribution to the "breadwinner" function is minimal, and pressures on the husband to contribute to homemaking are correspondingly small. This family has financial resources which permit them to place a minimum dependence on the wife's earnings.

Another family has arrived at something of an impasse in seeking a solution to the problems raised by the wife's employment. Because the wife is employed full-time, there is substantial pressure, both implicit and explicit, on the husband to contribute more to the household:

"She feels I should help her more around the house when she's working. Of course, I don't agree one hundred percent with her there. This is something we've never agreed on, and I don't think we ever will. . . .''

On her part, she reports,

"Well, he probably wouldn't admit this, but he's real old-fashioned in the way that a man should work and a woman should be at home. . . . I think he feels that if I am working, I am going to expect him to do certain things that in his mind a man shouldn't do . . . as much as he says he doesn't mind my working, I know he does.''

For both these families, attitudes toward the work of homemaking is affected by the husband's and wife's participation in the paid labor force. Although families emerge with different adjustments and solutions to the pressures of paid work and family life, the entry of the women into the paid labor force has highlighted issues of men's and women's roles in most families.

PAID WORK AND PARENTING: RESPONSIBILITY AND PRESSURE

Two kinds of pressure have acted to increase the stress on parents during the last several decades. One we have already discussed: more and more women are continuing their paid work outside the home during their childbearing and child-rearing years. Thus, husbands and wives together are facing a larger work load during the years they are responsible for young children. It is also the case that more single women and some single men are assuming responsibility for young children and the necessity of making a living as single parents. The necessity of combining paid work and family life during the years of responsibility for young children clearly places increasing stress on mothers and fathers.

Another kind of responsibility on parents is caused by the rising expectations our society has generated for what parents should be able to provide for their children. Staff of the Working Family Project were able to interview two generations of parents in several families. Their findings confirm a historical analysis about family life that indicates considerable changes in the work and care required for adequate child rearing.

Rising expectations of parents are evident in at least two kinds of attitudes toward the evaluation of parenting behavior. First of all, a combination of adequate physical care and love and emotional care is no longer considered sufficient. Parents are required to be active in encouraging the cognitive and social development of their child through the exercise of parenting skills. They are expected to relate, on behalf of their children, to a number of complex bureaucracies including schools, sports programs, and social and educational community programs.

Second, parents are evaluated by their peers, based not only on their performance as parents, but on the behavior and eventual success of their children. Today, there is little sense that some children are more difficult than others and "harder to parent." Children are perceived to be the product of their parents' skill in parenting. Under the pressure of these spiraling expectations, parents, meeting the demands of both home life and life on the job, frequently feel stressed.

Stress on parents is increased also by the needs for continuous negotiation between the parents. Under the stress of high expectations for parenting performance, and with an increased work load, parents are deviating from societal stereotypes of parental roles. Either trying to maintain traditional standards under a new work load or trying to deviate from societal standards of work load is difficult. Attempts to do either leave parents without a set of generally accepted standards for adequate performance. In the absence of generally acknowledged standards, parents turn to each other for acknowledgment, support, and the "working out" of what constitutes reasonable performance of parenting. This is a difficult and emotion-laden task for any couple and this is the task faced by dual-worker couples today.

REFERENCES

Daniels, P., & Weingarten, K. *Sooner or later*. New York: Norton, 1981.

Families and Communities Project. Funded by the National Science Foundation. L. Lein, principal investigator. Concluded December 1981.

Hayghe, H. Families and the rise of working wives—An overview. *Monthly Labor Review*, 1976, *99*(5), 12–19.

Herzog, A., Bachman, J., & Johnston, L. *High school seniors' preferences for sharing work and family responsibilities between husband and wife*. Ann Arbor, Mich.: Institute for Social Research, Monitoring the Future Project, Occasional Paper No. 3, 1979.

Holmstrom, L. L. *The two-career family*. Cambridge, Mass.: Schenkman, 1972.

Kamerman, S. B. *Parenting in an unresponsive society: Managing work and family*. New York: Free Press–Macmillan, 1980.

Kanter, R. M. *Work and family in the United States: A critical review and agenda for research and policy*. New York: Russell Sage Foundation, 1977.

Lein, L. Male participation in home life: Impact of social supports and breadwinner responsibility in the allocation of tasks. *The Family Coordinator*, 1979, *28*(4), October.

LeMasters, E. E. *Blue collar aristocrats*. Madison: University of Wisconsin Press, 1975.

O'Donnell, L., & Stueve, A. *Women, work and children's activities*. Unpublished manuscript, October 1980.

Parsons, T., & Bales, R. (Eds.). *Family, socialization and interaction process*. New York: Free Press–Macmillan, 1955.

Piotrokowski, C. *Work and the family system*. New York: Free Press–Macmillan, 1979.

Pleck, J. H., & Lang, L. *Men's family role: Its nature and consequences*. Wellesley College Center for Research on Women, Working Paper No. 10, 1978.

Pleck, J. H., & Rustad, M. *Husbands' and wives' time in family work and paid work in the 1975–1976 study of time use*. Wellesley College Center for Research on Women, Working Paper No. 63, 1980.

Rapoport, R., & Rapoport, R. N. *Dual-career families re-examined*. New York: Harper & Row, 1976.

Rossi, A. Transition to parenthood. *Journal of Marriage and the Family*, 1968, *30*, 26–39.

U.S. Bureau of the Census. *Nursery school and kindergarten enrollment of children and labor force status of their mothers: October, 1967 to October, 1976*. Current Population Reports, Series P-20, No. 318, 1978.

U.S. Department of Labor, Women's Bureau. *Twenty facts on women workers*. Washington, D.C.: U.S. Government Printing Office, 1980.

Walker, K., & Woods, M. E. *Time use: A measure of household production of family goods and services*. Washington, D.C.: American Home Economics Association, 1976.

Working Family Project: Paid work and family life. Final Report to the National Institute of Education, 1974.

Working Family Project. Final Report to the National Institute of Mental Health, 1976.

5

PARENTS' PERCEPTIONS OF YOUNG ADOLESCENTS

ANDREW M. BOXER
BRENDA SOLOMON
DANIEL OFFER
ANNE C. PETERSEN
FLORENCE HALPRIN

INTRODUCTION

"There are few situations in life which are more difficult to cope with than an adolescent son or daughter during the attempt to liberate themselves" (A. Freud, 1958, p. 278). This statement characterizes the current theoretical vantage point of most clinicians working in the mental health field. The theory is based on considerable experience with clinically disturbed adolescents. It is extended to normal development by most of the leading developmental theorists who use psychoanalytic theory as the basis for their understanding of personality development. From the vantage point of parenting, this perspective on adolescent development is no less apparent. As Rossi (1980a) has observed, a number of investigators have found that marital satisfaction reported by couples during the

Andrew M. Boxer. Laboratory for the Study of Adolescence, Department of Psychiatry, Michael Reese Hospital and Medical Center, and Committee on Human Development, University of Chicago, Chicago, Illinois.

Brenda Solomon. Department of Psychiatry, Michael Reese Hospital and Medical Center, Chicago, Illinois.

Daniel Offer. Department of Psychiatry, Michael Reese Hospital and Medical Center, and Department of Psychiatry, University of Chicago, Chicago, Illinois.

Anne C. Petersen. Department of Individual and Family Studies, College of Human Development, Pennsylvania State University, University Park, Pennsylvania. Previous address: Laboratory for the Study of Adolescence, Department of Psychiatry, Michael Reese Hospital and Medical Center, and Department of Psychiatry, University of Chicago, Chicago, Illinois.

Florence Halprin. Committee on Human Development, University of Chicago, Chicago, Illinois.

years of active parenting decreases with the birth of subsequent children and remains low during the years when there are adolescents in the home, increasing with the departure of young adult children from the "nest" (Campbell, Converse, & Rodgers, 1976; Gove & Peterson, 1980; see also Cohler & Boxer, 1983). A common interpretation of these changes is that adolescents, as a volatile and difficult group, contribute to their parents' lowered morale (Rossi, 1980a). However, parents have their own developmental concerns which may be a contributor to adolescent stress or may interfere with parents' abilities to parent their adolescent children; parents may be preoccupied with age-related changes that are occurring in their own lives. Others (e.g., Colman, Bremner, Clark, Davis, Eichorn, Griliches, Kett, Ryder, Doering, & Mays, 1974; Spacks, 1981) have noted the ambiguities inherent in adolescence as a social role, with unclear guidelines for behavior and often conflicting sets of expectations, thus facilitating the projection by parents of their own fears, desires, and memories onto their adolescent children, particularly with regard to sexual fantasies and behavior (Anthony, 1969; Giovacchini, 1970; Petersen & Boxer, 1982).

To examine the concerns that parents express about their adolescents, we report on a nonclinical population, in a study of the psychosocial experience of young adolescents and their parents. To provide a conceptual framework for understanding parents and young adolescents we will consider three importantly related, yet conceptually distinct, areas: (1) the nature of the parent–child relationship as part of a family system; (2) the adolescent as a developing individual undergoing a complex set of biological, social, and psychological changes; and (3) the parent as an individual with a unique set of preoccupations and concerns as a developing and changing adult.

PARENT–CHILD RELATIONS DURING ADOLESCENCE

While we assume that during adolescence there are a number of changes in parent–child relationships, relatively little is known about the particular sequences of events which may characterize them. Even less is known about how parents themselves may be affected by these changes. Recent attention has been focused on the need for a greater understanding of the processes involved in the mutual accommodation of developing individuals and the systems that contain them (Bronfenbrenner, 1977; Lerner & Busch-Rossnagel, 1981; Riegel, 1976). Nonetheless, there are few studies which have systematically investigated both parents and their young adolescents over time (see Hill, 1980; Rossi, 1980a).

As stated in the introduction, most accounts of adolescent development have been framed stereotypically within the dimensions of a conflict and crisis model (Blos, 1962; Erikson, 1959; Freud, 1958). Empirical studies of normal adolescents (Block & Haan, 1971; Grinker, Grinker, & Timberlake, 1962; Heath, 1965; Offer & Offer, 1975; Vaillant, 1971) indicate that the characterization of adolescence as necessarily entailing tumult is inaccurate, although it has been suggested that early adolescence may be a particularly difficult phase (Hamburg, 1974; Offer, 1969). Likewise, parent–child relationships during adolescence have also been characterized by conflict, rebellion, and general strife. A number of studies have challenged this assumption as well, and have documented the ways that groups of adolescents and their parents enjoy positive family relationships, as these have been reported by parents and adolescents (Douvan & Adelson, 1966; Kandel & Lesser, 1972; Offer, 1969). Most current research has refuted the notion of a strong youth culture distinct and different from that of the generation of parents of these adolescents. Several investigators (Flacks, 1971; Haan, Smith, & Block, 1968; Kandel & Lesser, 1972; Offer & Offer, 1975) find a continuity of values and ideals extending across generations and continuing into young adulthood as well (Troll, Neugarten, & Kraines, 1969; see also Nassi, 1981).

In studies in the Laboratory for the Study of Adolescence we are collecting baseline data which examine parent–child relationships over time, the kinds of changes which characterize them, and their association with growth patterns of young adolescent boys and girls.

THE EARLY ADOLESCENCE STUDY

While it has been demonstrated that, in general, women show more mental illness than men in adulthood (Bradburn & Caplovitz, 1965; Gove & Tudor, 1973; Meile & Haese, 1969), the differences between the sexes in the onset of psychological difficulties are first apparent at adolescence. The sex differences may be related to a number of factors, including biological transformations, different expectations from society, different expectations from parents, and changes in peer structure. Recent investigations have delineated asynchronies amongst all of these dimensions as especially stressful for young adolescent girls (Simmons, Blyth, Van Cleave, & Bush, 1979). The Early Adolescence Study is focusing on some of these factors in an attempt to begin to explain the development of psychological differences between the sexes, in particular, and to provide baseline data not currently available on biological, social, and psychological development in early adolescence, in general.

Early adolescence seemed to be an essential time to study development from the biopsychosocial perspective. The limited data available regarding influences on human development at this stage of life suggest: that most forms of mental illness become apparent no earlier than adolescence, with adolescence recapitulating any earlier difficulties (Anthony, 1970; Blos, 1967; Grinker & Holzman, 1973); that sex differences in a variety of psychological problems reverse during adolescence (Gove & Herb, 1974) and sex differences in cognitive functioning first appear at the time (Maccoby & Jacklin, 1974); that adult forms of cognitive and self-reflective capacities begin to develop at adolescence (Elkind, 1967; Offer, 1969); and that early adolescence may be the phase of life most predictive of adult functioning (Livson & Peskin, 1967; see also Livson & Peskin, 1980).

Since factors such as socioeconomic status, race, geographical location, and family structure may influence psychological development (see Petersen, Offer, & Kaplan, 1979), we have attempted to control some of this variability by studying a relatively homogeneous group, and have focused on middle-class youth as the majority group in our society.

In the remainder of this chapter we focus primarily on preliminary findings which relate to the mental health characteristics of the parents of the normal adolescents in our sample. Parenthood is not a unitary phenomenon and we cannot do justice here to the complex biopsychosocial characteristics which contribute to the end product we call "parenting." Rather, we will present selected mental health variables which we believe contribute to the quality of parenting in our sample. Specifically, we shall discuss how this group of parents view their own young adolescent children, and the quality of the relationship the parents have to their children and to each other. Further, we asked these parents about important dimensions of their own early adolescence. Finally, we shall consider these two sets of perceptions, of past and present, that is, (1) the parents' current relationship to each other and to their own child, and (2) the reconstructions of their own memories of early adolescence and some of the ways that these perceptions may relate to transactions between parent and young adolescent in the family.

Methods

Subject Selection

With community and school cooperation, the participants for this study were randomly selected from two middle-class, Midwestern, suburban school districts.[1] All sixth graders in these two districts were administered a new version of the Offer Self-Image Questionnaire (the Self-Image Questionnaire for Young Adolescents; Petersen, 1980a). The original questionnaire measures 11 areas considered relevant to adolescent life and has been used with thousands of subjects in the United States and in several foreign countries; its reliability and validity are well established (Offer & Howard, 1972; Offer, Ostrov, & Howard, 1977; Offer, Ostrov, & Howard, 1981a). The new version is especially appropriate for young adolescents. From each community, 100 subjects were randomly selected and contacted for participation. This process was repeated during a second year with another cohort of sixth graders. Every subject is interviewed twice yearly, from the sixth through eighth grades, with a semistructured interview conducted at school, in addition to being given a number of paper-and-pencil assessments which measure several relevant social, psychological, and cognitive dimensions. In addition, there is a retest control group drawn from the eighth-grade population, and a dropout control group. For the first cohort, almost

1. Some details have been altered to protect the confidentiality of the participants.

20% of the adolescents or parents contacted refused to be in the study, leaving a sample of 188 young adolescents.

Parents of the study subjects are interviewed twice in the study, once when their child is in the sixth grade and again during the eighth grade. The interviewers of the parents are different from those who interview the young adolescents. Each parent is interviewed individually, in the parents' home. In addition, parents are asked to complete a number of paper and pencil assessments, including the Offer Parent–Child Questionnaire, a measure which assesses the parent's perceptions of various aspects of his/her child, matched to be roughly equivalent with the child's version of the self-image questionnaire. Parents also complete the Lowman Inventory of Family Feelings (Lowman, 1971) designed to assess feelings of bondedness and attachment toward members of the nuclear family.

The Interviews

While many questions in the interview are precoded, interviewers also take extensive notes during the interviews and code the responses according to a set of variables developed in pilot studies. These pilots studies have shown us that the interviewers are trained to see and hear similar things in the interview and to record them in a standard procedure on the protocol. A random 10% of the interviews were initially tape-recorded and coded by a trained research assistant to assess the extent to which we are coding similarly and to provide a basis for corrective feedback should any of us begin to shift from the coding baseline.

Sample Characteristics

The findings presented here are from the sixth-grade interviews with the first cohort of parents. We have generally found these parents to be interested, cooperative, and eager to participate in the study. By the end of the first interview, the interviewers were impressed by the openness of the parents, their eagerness to talk about their children, their high degree of self-disclosure with regard to their own concerns, reminiscences of their past, and their present preoccupations of adult life. All parents expressed a willingness to give a second interview during the child's eighth-grade year. Thus, we have been able to establish a research alliance (Offer & Sabshin, 1967) with these adults.

In this group of parents there are 347 adults, 48% of who are fathers and 52% mothers. Twelve percent of our families are headed by single parents, owing to divorce, separation, or widowhood. The parents as a group are roughly matched between parents of boys (45%) and of girls (55%).

These parents are generally a young group, with the median age of fathers being 42 and that of mothers being 39 years. We do have a wide age range represented, with the youngest parent in our sample being 30 years of age and the oldest being 64 years. Seventy-four percent of the fathers and 50% of the mothers have at least a bachelor's degree or advanced professional training.

These respondents are somewhat better educated than most members of their birth cohorts.[2] As a group the sample would be classified as middle- to upper-middle class. One third of the mothers work full-time outside of their homes, one third are full-time housewives, and one third work in some type of part-time job. It should be noted that a number of the mothers indicated a current transition in their work status; some returning to a full-time job, and others beginning to work part-time for the first time since marriage.

Findings

Over three fourths of the parents assessed their marital relationships as either good or excellent. Over half of these parents said that they did not anticipate that their marital relationships would be affected as a result of their child entering adolescence. One father said: "I don't think there will be a change in our personal relationship. There is the realization that we are aging, but that doesn't affect our relationship." Another father put it this way: "I'm sure it will be influenced, but only to the extent that we were with Martha's older sister. There could be more emphasis on my wife and I having to deal with things together more than prior to adolescence. Before I left things more up to Martha's mother." Many parents stated that previous experience with an adolescent child helped prepare them for the present child. Another of our female respondents put it this way: "There are always new problems to deal with, but I don't think it will affect my relationship with my husband. We always have to direct our parental roles to new endeavors with the kids growing up."

One third of the parents interviewed thought there might be a change in their own relationship as a result of their child entering adolescence. Such changes include increased marital tensions over conflicting views of child rearing and disagreement about age-appropriate behavior for an adolescent. However, most of the parents who anticipated change thought that it would be positive. Only a small group (10% of the total sample) anticipated negative changes. The reason for the negative expectations usually had to do with parental disagreement on child-rearing issues. For example, the mother of one adolescent girl wanted to increase her daughter's privileges with regard to spending time at her friend's house; the father, on the other hand, believed it was necessary to institute more rigid controls on his daughter to avoid conflicts which might arise when she begins to go out on dates. On the whole, the majority of parents present a picture of smooth and stable marital relationships. Within such families it seems easier for parents to anticipate jointly the varieties of normal adolescent behavior.

Pubertal changes are just beginning for this group of young adolescents. The sex differential in development is readily apparent. One third of the boys' parents, contrasted to over three quarters of the girls' parents, report some

2. Comparisons based on Current Population Reports, Series P-20, No. 314, *Educational Attainment in the U.S., March 1977 and 1976*. Washington, D.C.: U.S. Government Printing Office, 1977.

physical changes in their children associated with puberty. For the small group of boys, the most frequent change is the appearance of body hair. For girls, the most frequently reported change is breast development, reported by about three quarters (74%) of the fathers and mothers, and a growth spurt reported by one third of the girls' parents. Seventeen percent of the parents report the occurrence of menarche in their daughters. The parents' reports of pubertal changes in their children are quite similar, with fathers and mothers reporting about equally the same kinds of changes. These reported changes are consistent with stages of pubertal development as they have been described in growth studies of adolescents (e.g., Tanner, 1962; 1972).

In a recent analysis which examined convergence of reports from mothers, fathers, and their daughters, within families (Petersen, 1983), 77% of the girls (at sixth grade) in cohort one agreed with both parents about their menarcheal status, 6% stating that menarche had occurred and 71% stating that it had not yet occurred. In another 12% of the cases, the fathers didn't know but the mothers and daughters agreed (9% no and 3% yes). In the remaining 10% of the cases, there was a discrepancy between the daughter's report and that of the mother and father. Of these 9 girls, 3 were cases where the parents both said menarche had not occurred while the daughter either refused to respond or said that she didn't know if any pubertal change had occurred.

The six girls who denied menarche when in fact it had occurred are an interesting group and are discussed in greater detail elsewhere (Petersen, 1983). Generally, however, across our sample, parental agreement, with regard to observations about pubertal change, is quite high.

Half of the boys' parents and slightly over half of the girls' parents (58%) state that their relationships with their children have undergone changes in the last year. These changes include psychological dimensions. One of the mothers in our study put it this way with regard to her son: "He still kisses me goodbye, but he wants to make sure no one sees him. He is more circumspect now." One of our female respondents said about her daughter: "The older they get the more understanding they are, and the more tolerant of you. Our relationship is better now, these days." And a middle-aged father told us about his son: "It's gotten better. We do alot of things together. Yet, I am not his buddy. I'm his father. He helps me a great deal. He's a valuable assistant." The direction of the perceived changes are characterized by these parents as positive ones. Only 16% of the mothers of boys, as contrasted with 28% of the girls' mothers discuss these changes in relationships in terms of negative or ambivalent feelings. One mother, discussing her daughter, told us: "In ways our relationship is better and in ways I have to work a little bit harder. She's maturing and opening up in some ways and closing in others. She was a very quiet person and now I think she wants a relationship with an adult and she's putting forth a little bit more effort than she used to. Although I have to work harder at it too, and she can back off a bit and close herself off."

On the whole, these parents expressed positive aspirations for their children.

They were certain that their children would attend college, though very few parents ventured to guess what their child would choose as an occupation or career. Many parents would tell us about a particular strength or skill of their child, such as acumen with interpersonal relations, or particular talents such as drawing or writing. Obviously, the parents have high expectations for their children, although they did not spell them out in detail.

The parents whom we interviewed are very happy with the way their sixth-graders' lives are going thus far. The 11% who stated they were not happy with the life course of their children are a group worth watching. It would be of interest to determine whether these children will have more problems in the years ahead than the rest of our sample.

About half of our parents consider themselves to be stricter disciplinarians than other parents they know. One third of the parents say they are on the lenient side. While styles of disciplining children may vary across and within households, the withdrawal of a privilege is the most common method of discipline. Parents' arguments with their children typically center around rules and demands made by parents on their children—cleaning up their rooms, taking out the garbage, and other household chores. These differences do not usually produce great arguments or fights between the parents and children. One of the mothers told us: "Sometimes I ask Jim to do something around the house—like mowing the lawn at the house we care for next door. He wants to do it later. I want him to do it at the time I ask him." Another mother told us about her daughter: "Sarah tells me what to do—let's go shopping downtown. I tell her, I can't go right now. We argue about what she wants to do at the time and what I want."

Concerns of Parents about Their Young Adolescents

When asked what they thought was their child's main concern in life at the present time, most parents had to think twice before responding. One father said: "He probably thinks his biggest concern is that we won't send him to this summer camp he and all his friends want to go to. It is the 'in' thing. It's too expensive. He considers it a big problem. He also thinks he should have his own room and that for however much it costs, we should add on a room to the house."

In an analysis of these data, Wilen (1980) found that when asked about their main concern in life, 75% of the young adolescents reported school, friends, and family, while concerns with school and academically related concerns were the most frequently reported ones. While parents underestimate the frequency of the child's concern with school, they overestimated their children's family concerns. Parents may be unaware of the pervasive influence of school on their children's lives. As Wilen (1980) pointed out, parents see their children as developing *within* the context of the family and may not realize the pervasive extent to which school is a primary concern to their children.

When asked about their own current concerns with regard to their adolescent children, only concern with orderliness and completing tasks was reported by over half of the parents of both boys and girls. Table 5-1 produces a frequency distribution of parents' concerns for their young adolescents. The young adolescents were also asked what they thought concerned their parents, currently, about themselves. Analyses of variance on these items produced significant main effects for the sex of the child on only three items. Parents of boys are more concerned with cleanliness of their young adolescents that those of girls. In addition, while more mothers of boys are concerned with the schoolwork of their sons than mothers of girls, both boys and girls overestimate the extent of their parents' concern with school. They also tend to overestimate their parents' concern with their eating habits. Not surprisingly, excessive telephone use is an expressed concern by more parents of girls than of boys.

To examine agreement on endorsement of items within each family, alpha coefficients were computed by concerns for family agreement (Table 5-2). On the items of orderliness, schoolwork, choice of friends, and completing tasks, agreement among families with boys and girls is quite evenly distributed. Agree-

TABLE 5-1. CONCERNS EXPRESSED BY CHILDREN AND PARENTS

	Percentage expressing concern					
	Boys	Mothers	Fathers	Girls	Mothers	Fathers
Eating habits	50	30	31	45	34	38
Staying out late	28	7	3	30	3	2
(Single dating)[a]	3	0	1	1	2	1
Clothing	23	33	20	28	41	23
Orderliness	42	55	56	52	54	55
Cleanliness	21	34*	34*	19	15*	12*
Choice of friends	37	20	15	34	19	18
(Being too independent)[a]	7	26	15	15	11	16
Not telling everything	28	39	31	27	36	20
Schoolwork	62*	43*	35	44*	24*	25
Respect elders	21	8	10	22	12	11
Amount/quality of social life	14	21	23	15	32	33
(Physical sports)[a]	18	13	14	16	10	3
Completion of tasks	43	56	54	46	54	56
(Smoking)[a]	20	4	1	11	4	1
Excessive phone use	12*	10*	10*	38*	20*	28*
Manners	29	26	26	34	18	20
13 concerns α	.74	.52	.69	.66	.48	.51
n	70	74	70	91	91	84

[a]Items in parentheses deleted from alpha coefficient because of the limited number of respondents who endorsed these items.
*ANOVA main effect/sex of child: $p < .03$.

TABLE 5-2. ALPHA COEFFICIENTS FOR FAMILIES BY CONCERN

	Boys + parents	Girls + parents
Eating habits	.38	.46
Staying out late	.46	.16
Single dating	−.05	−.04
Clothing	−.32	.13
Orderliness	.62	.60
Cleanliness	.34	.32
Choice of friends	.49	.45
Being too independent	.17	−.06
Not telling everything	.39	.19
Schoolwork	.62	.55
Respect elders	.21	.29
Amount/quality of social life	.44	.37
Physical sports	.40	.10
Completion of tasks	.48	.45
Smoking	−.22	.01
Excessive phone use	.48	.61
Manners	.51	.07

ment may reflect shared perceptions that a given concern is a problem, or may also reflect that all family members share no concern about a given item (and thus Table 5-2 should be read against Table 5-1 in order to assess the saliency of a given item).

To examine agreement within dyads in these families, correlations were computed by items among fathers, mothers, and their young adolescents (Table 5-3). Clearly there is more agreement about concerns between parents than between any one parent and their young adolescent. The moderate correlations between the boys and girls and their fathers and mothers reflects the fact that within families the extent of shared perceptions about concerns may be limited, and dyad-specific, that is, limited to a given pair in the family constellation. Note, however, most of the respondents did not report a great many concerns. Thus, the extent of concerns for sixth graders as perceived by both parents and the young adolescents themselves is limited. As other studies of the behavior problems of both normal and disturbed children have demonstrated, age, socioeconomic, and clinical status are important mediators for the problems and concerns of young adolescents (Achenbach & Edelbrock, 1981; MacFarlane, Allen, & Honzik, 1954). Whether the number of concerns and extent of family agreement changes over time is a question we shall address in future analyses.

That children overestimate the concern of their parents with regard to school work deserves further attention. Nearly two thirds of the boys stated that their parents were concerned with their schoolwork, while 44% of the girls reported such parental concern. A recent longitudinal analysis of the grade and achieve-

TABLE 5-3. FAMILY AGREEMENT LEVEL

	Boys			Girls		
	/Father	/Mother	Father/mother	/Father	/Mother	Father/mother
Eating habits	.21					.36
Staying out late	.28		.38		.29	
Single dating						
Clothing	−.26					.29
Orderliness	.27	.29	.49	.26	.21	.52
Cleanliness			.49			
Choice of friends		.28	.28		.24	.27
Being too independent			.34			
Not telling everything			.23			
Schoolwork	.30	.28	.46	.20	.30	.37
Respect elders		.34				.27
Amount/quality of social life		.23	.28			.32
Physical sports			.42			.37
Completion of tasks			.48			.39
Smoking						
Excessive phone use	.23		.40	.33	.49	.21
Manners		.37	.28			.33

Note. Only correlations above .20 or below −.20 are reproduced here.

ment data of these boys and girls (Kavrell & Petersen, 1983) does not support the extensive sex difference in concern with school. While girls tended to do better in school than boys (across 3 years, from sixth through eighth grade), there were no significant sex differences in achievement test scores. Thus, perceptions and preoccupations with schoolwork are quite different from the reality of school performance. The boys may be displacing their own concerns about school work onto their parents. Clearly fewer of the boys' parents were concerned with their schoolwork than the number of boys reporting their parents' concern. Sex-role constraints may be operating here, with boys giving expression to the need for achievement which presages their future adult attainments. Hill and Lynch (1983) have discussed "gender-intensification" at this age as a possible mechanism whereby gender-related role expectations intensify with increased emphasis on social prescriptions for sex-typed appropriate behavior. The factors which may influence this process are not entirely clear. The parents' concerns with orderliness and completing tasks for both boys and girls may also reflect anticipations of adolescence and young adulthood for their children. As these sixth graders enter puberty and adolescence, they are no longer regarded as children but are not yet adults either. However, parents express concerns that their children develop the necessary skills and competence to live up to the requirements for the attainment of future life goals.

The Best and the Worst in Their Children's Development

We asked parents to discuss their children's development and to consider which period in the children's lives had been the most troublesome and which they had enjoyed the most. About 40% of the parents said some trouble had occurred during the first 5 years of grade school, between kindergarten and fifth grade. The reason for this trouble varied—sometimes owing to a social problem, such as the parent who told us: "John hated his fourth-grade teacher. Then his grades began to slip."

Other problems stemmed from illness, accident, or general difficulties in meeting a child's needs and demands: "Mitchell used to like to play hide-and-seek all around the neighborhood. I was constantly worrying about where he was."

About one third of the parents stated emphatically that there had never been one period which had been most troublesome. Over half of the parents told us that the current sixth-grade year, was the best in their child's development. Often this was explained by the parent because: "He's a real person now. You can talk to him like a person and carry on a real exchange. He is growing and I can enjoy him more."

The Parents' Recall of Their Early Adolescence

We asked the parents to recall their own early adolescence, when they were about the age of their child. Most parents' recalled this time as being fairly to moderately smooth. About one third (38%) of the girls' mothers recalled some turmoil, contrasted to both mothers and fathers of boys and fathers of girls in which there were remarkably fewer recollections of any turmoil or unhappiness.

One third of the fathers recalled their own mother as having poor coping abilities with them in adolescence, while a number of mothers also responded that their mothers had not dealt with them well.

In attempting to assess the process of relationships over time, the parents were asked to evaluate their present relationships with surviving parents and compare them to the relationships they had had with them during adolescence. Both parents' relationships with their fathers over time were relatively stable, while one third of the fathers reported improved adult relationships with their mothers. Half of the mothers reported similar improvement over time.

We asked each parent to recall the person to whom he/she felt closest back in early adolescence. Approximately one quarter of the mothers and fathers felt closest to their mothers. The majority of mothers valued friends as the person closest to them much more frequently than did fathers.

We also asked the parents who understood them best ("You may know who understands you best but not necessarily feel closest to that person"). About one tenth of the fathers and 8% of the mothers replied that no one understood them then. Forty percent of the fathers replied that their mothers understood them best, and small percentages reported that their fathers did, or friends and adults other than grandparents understood them best. Thirty-seven percent of the mothers believed that they were most understood either by friends, grandparents, or relatives other than parents. Less than a third of the mothers (29%) reported that their mothers understood them best. We find then, that a large group of mothers report that they found understanding outside of the nuclear family.

DISCUSSION

These empirical data were obtained from in-depth interviews with the parents. As we have demonstrated in our review of the literature, very few empirical studies of young adolescents and their parents exist. Most statements in psychological, psychiatric, and psychoanalytic texts stress the serious problems that a parent encounters when he/she attempts to rear an adolescent child. Our preliminary data question that assumption. Most parents enjoy having an young adolescent child and do not get into momentous battles with him/her. Parents are able to anticipate and cope with the everyday problems associated with rearing their young adolescent children. The clinician will wonder whether children of these parents have at all begun in the long and complex task of adolescent individuation. Perhaps we are dealing here with a group of "latency adolescents" who have not begun to experience the psychological changes associated with adolescence, even though many have begun to experience biological changes. We cannot answer this question here. However, judging from our empirical studies of these adolescents, it appears that we are indeed dealing with mentally healthy young adolescents, drawn randomly from a school population in which there is generally no great psychopathology discernible (Offer & Petersen, 1982).

As we have pointed out elsewhere, mental health professionals have problems conceptualizing and understanding normal development (Offer, Ostrov, & Howard, 1981b; Offer & Sabshin, 1974, 1983). The theory concerning normal development needs to be built from data collected from nonpatient populations. The clinician can contribute understanding of the internal world of people and, by using interview skills on normal individuals, should be able to add to our knowledge of normal development. Clinicians often shy away from studies of nonpatients because they believe, erroneously, that the resistance will be so intense that the information gathered will be worthless. We have demonstrated that it is indeed possible to use the interview as a meaningful data collection device with normal individuals.

With regard to our results, we wish to emphasize that most of these parents do *not* expect upheaval with their children in adolescence. They cope well with their internal and external environments and expect to cope well with their children in the future. It may well be that the parents' *expectations* of their children's adolescence are a powerful force played out in the particulars of their adolescents' development. A certain degree of self-confidence in parenting has already been established and this may contribute to a sense of continuity in one's ability to successfully parent an adolescent.

Adolescence is marked by change in the parent–child relationship (see Anthony, 1969; Cohen & Balikov, 1974; Lidz, 1969). This may be initiated by developmental changes occurring in the adolescent, as well as by parents' reactions to their adolescents and to their own developmental changes. A change in the quality of the parent–child relationship may result, as well as quantitative changes in such things as the amount of time parent and adolescent spend together. The processes involved in the mutual accommodation of individuals within a family system are particularly important at adolescence (see, e.g., Steinberg, 1981), and especially relevant to an understanding of the modifications in the young person's family. We are pursuing studies of these changes in the parent–child relationship over time, examining adjustment in the adolescent and the nature of the tie to the parent (Wilen, 1981).

Although there is much speculation about how a parent's own adolescence influences his/her parenting of adolescent children, there are few systematic studies which have investigated these issues. Notions about this include the idea of a continuity of parenting styles across generations. Others have suggested that such continuity may function as a transference response (Benedek, 1959; Anthony, 1970), with parents enacting a set of repetitive responses to their child, drawn from their own earlier experience as adolescents.

As the adolescent becomes more adultlike in appearance, the parent is more likely to identify with the offspring. One of the interesting conclusions of the Offers' study (1975) was that there appeared to be a strong relationship between the parents' view and experience of adolescence and their sons' experience of adolescence. Parents who enjoyed adolescence assumed that it would be an enjoyable period for their children; parents who experienced difficulties in adolescence tended to expect their children to have troubles during this time. Parents may create a double-bind for the adolescent by admonishing him/her against particular behaviors at the same time that they clearly expect these behaviors to occur, frequently because they themselves engaged in these behaviors as adolescents. The adolescent will generally live up to this expectation, yet also experience the guilt, thus replicating the parental pattern.

Parents may also envy their adolescent children, particularly in our society which places a high value on youthfulness. A parent may envy the adolescent offspring's increasing opportunities as the parent perceives his/her own opportunities to be decreasing. This envy is frequently sexually laden; the parent may envy the increasing sexual attractiveness of the developing adolescent. As Rossi (1980a) and others (e.g., Anthony, 1969) have noted, the parents of adolescents may be "winding down," dealing with such issues as menopause for women and fears of decreasing sexual potency for men, while young adolescents are "winding up."

There may also be a sexual component on the adolescent side of this relationship. Anna Freud interpreted the youthful rebellion at adolescence as being a function of the resurgence of infantile sexuality, empowered with adult sexual urges and capabilities, which makes the former emotional attachment to parents feel dangerous to the adolescent. The emerging sexual adult in the former child may confuse parents as well. Cuddling that was once nonsexual to the parent may now be accompanied by sexual feelings and lead to embarrassment or acting out on the part of the parent.

In our interviews with parents we have investigated the parents' own retrospections of their adolescence, or what Cohler (1981, 1982) calls the "personal narrative" or life script, and we shall be investigating how these narratives may change as their children move through adolescence. It would appear that chronological age, along with its subjective meanings and developmental concerns of parents, are all affected by and have impact upon relations with adolescent children. There is some research evidence which indicates that middle-aged persons, in contrast to older and younger individuals, make use of their memories in a different fashion; they draw on and select from the past in the solution of current problems (Cohler, 1981; Revere, 1971; Revere & Tobin, 1980–1981). One of the central issues for middle-aged persons has been characterized as the resolution of time mastery versus time capitulation (Neugarten, 1967). Studies in our laboratory are attempting to delineate the ways in which parents recast and restructure their past in relation to the problems and concerns they have with their developing adolescent children. The longitudinal design of our study allows us to examine changes in the retrospections of these parents with regard to their own life history and in relation to changes in their perceptions of and relationships with their adolescent children (Boxer, 1981).

In our sample of parents slightly more mothers than fathers recalled their own adolescence as turbulent. Yet some fathers as well as mothers stated that their own mothers were not able to cope with them well during puberty. Men in general may recount their adolescence as less affected by mothers than women do. Many of the mothers in our study recounted being understood best by significant people other than their own mothers, and report improved relationships with their mothers in the present as compared to their early adolescence. Mothers of girls, in particular, tended to recount their early adolescence as less smooth than mothers of boys. Mothers of girls may be better able to affectively recall their own adolescence because their daughters have begun to move into adolescence, while mothers of boys are less likely to do so, especially since boys are not as physically mature at this point. Physical changes of puberty are an important mediator of change in family process, as some recent investigations demonstrate (e.g., Steinberg, 1981). It is our belief that the difference between parental affective response to the adolescent child is gender determined. Our young adolescent boys were not as developed physically as the young adolescent girls; it is conceivable that as the boys grow the mothers' responses will change. However, we believe that the gender differences are psychosocially determined.

Chodorow (1978) and others (e.g., Cohler & Grunebaum, 1981; Gilligan, 1979) have emphasized the importance of intimacy and attachment as salient developmental organizers for women, particularly as these are structured into the mother–daughter relationship. Others have characterized the mother–daughter relationship in young adulthood as one marked by cement and dynamite (Hagestad, 1977). Mothers and daughters express affects more easily than men and sons. Young adolescent daughters are more expressive of their feelings than young adolescent sons, and therefore may stir a special set of emotions and feelings in their mothers.

The central role of work as a developmental organizer in men's lives may be reflected in the large number of young adolescent males preoccupations with school-related concerns. The nature of men's intimate relationships have been characterized by a number of social-psychological constraints which may inhibit the expression of their nurturant and affective needs and feelings until the second half of life (Cohler & Boxer, 1983). Middle-class men tend to operate on what Hess (1979) calls the proposition of "all eggs in one basket"; they turn only to their wives, rather than to friends, to meet their intimacy needs. The reproduction of mothering (Chodorow, 1978) may thus be paralleled by the reproduction of fathering.

The nature of parent–child relations may also change in adolescence as a function of the child's new cognitive abilities. Hill and Palmquist (1978) have observed that there is a general lack of research investigating the effects of the onset of formal operations on parental behavior. Presumably, the child will now be able to compare actual parental behavior with possible parental behaviors. Peers may become more important where relationships with parents are weak or conflicted.

From the preliminary evidence and existing theoretical work, we hypothesize that identifications with both parents are important for the psychosocial development of young adolescents with some specific differences in the nature of cross-sex and same-sex identifications. Haan (1972) presented data on the mothers of girls in the Berkeley studies at the Institute of Human Development. Mothers were interviewed while the subjects were adolescents. The most satisfied, intelligent, verbal mothers produced girls who were rated in a high ego group (above the mean on both coping and defensive behaviors). Mothers with high energy but who were critical of their female (study) child produced girls who were high on coping behaviors and low on defensive behaviors as adults. Girls who later became defensive (with low coping skills) had mothers who were uncritical and were the least verbal and intelligent in adolescence. In a different vein, Hoffman (1977) reports that parental identification and support is important to the choice of a career for adolescent girls. Without a mother or father who encourages a career orientation, or other significant figures in the adolescents' social world, a girl is likely to choose an inappropriately low-status career or to defer the decision entirely.

Because of the importance of biological and social factors to psychological development in both young adolescents and their middle-aged parents, we take an integrated, systems theory approach to the study of development across the life span. Petersen (1980b) has outlined a model for biopsychosocial development and has applied it to the development of sex differences in cognition at adolescence (Petersen, 1979) and to the relations between puberty and psychological development (Petersen & Taylor, 1980; see also Tobin-Richards, Boxer, & Petersen, 1983). The evidence for biological and social influences on the self among both adolescents and parents suggests that such a framework is ideal, perhaps necessary, for an understanding of psychological development among parents and their young adolescents.[3] It seems that our project will enable us to shed some light on a number of important issues with regard to development. Can our data help explain the factors which contribute to continuities and discontinuities of development? We believe that as we follow our subjects certain patterns will emerge. Will those parents who recall a tumultuous adolescence raise adolescents full of turmoil? How will the memories of the parents concerning their own adolescence change as their children grow and change? What functions might these changes in the parents' narratives serve in structuring their perceptions about themselves as well as their children? We have offered in this chapter some preliminary data to help us in understanding the ways in which parents perceive and shape the past, present, and future, as these configurations give meaning to their lives and to the lives of their children. Parents and their young adolescents can be considered "consociates" (Plath, 1980), in a transactional process of development which changes over time.

ACKNOWLEDGMENTS

The research presented in this chapter is part of a larger investigation, Developmental Study of Adolescent Mental Health, supported by Grant MH30252 from the National Institute of Mental Health, Anne C. Petersen, PhD, Principal Investigator. Andrew M. Boxer is a predoctoral fellow, Clinical Research Training Program in Adolescence, National Institute of Mental Health Grant T32 MH14668. The authors wish to thank Dr. Bernice L. Neugarten for her critical comments and discussion of an earlier version of this chapter presented at the conference on Parenthood as an Adult Experience.

REFERENCES

Achenbach, T. M., & Edelbrock, C. S. Behavioral problems and competencies reported by parents of normal and disturbed children aged four through sixteen. *Monographs of the Society for Research in Child Development*, 1981, *46* (1), Serial No. 188.

Anthony, E. J. The reactions of adults to adolescents and their behavior. In G. Caplan & S. Lebovici (Eds.), *Adolescence: Psychosocial perspectives*. New York: Basic Books, 1969.

Anthony, E. J. Two contrasting types of adolescent depression and their treatment. *Journal of the American Psychoanalytic Association*, 1970, *18*, 841–859.

Benedek, T. Parenthood as a developmental phase: A contribution to the libido theory. *Journal of the American Psychoanalytic Association*, 1959, *7*, 389–417.

3. Rossi (1980b) has formulated hypotheses concerning the ways in which biological and psychological changes may interact in middle-aged individuals' development.

Benedek, T. Parenthood during the life cycle. In E. J. Anthony & T. Benedek (Eds.), *Parenthood: Its psychology and psychopathology*. Boston: Little, Brown, 1970.

Block, J., & Haan, N. *Lives through time*. Berkeley, Calif.: Bancroft Books, 1971.

Blos, P. *On adolescence: A psychoanalytic interpretation*. New York: Free Press–Macmillan, 1962.

Blos, P. The second individuation process of adolescence. *The Psychoanalytic Study of the Child*, 1967, *22*, 162–186.

Boxer, A. M. *The dynamic of adolescence in middle-aged adults*. Presentation to the seminar of the Clinical Research Training Program in Adolescence, Committee on Human Development, University of Chicago, December 3, 1981.

Bradburn, N., & Caplovitz, D. *Reports on happiness*. Chicago: Aldine Press, 1965.

Bronfenbrenner, U. Toward an experimental ecology of human development. *American Psychologist*, 1977, *32*, 513–531.

Campbell, A., Converse, P., & Rodgers, W. *The quality of American life: Perceptions, evaluations, and satisfactions*. New York: Russell Sage Foundation, 1976.

Chodorow, N. *The reproduction of mothering: Psychoanalysis and the sociology of gender*. Berkeley: University of California Press, 1978.

Cohen, R. S., & Balikov, H. On the impact of adolescence upon parents. In S. C. Feinstein & P. L. Giovacchini (Eds.), *Adolescent psychiatry* (Vol. III). Chicago: University of Chicago Press, 1974.

Cohler, B. J. Adult developmental psychology and reconstruction in psychoanalysis. In S. I. Greenspan & G. H. Pollock (Eds.), *The course of life: Psychoanalytic contributions toward understanding personality development* (Vol. III: *Adulthood and the aging process*). Washington, D.C.: U.S. Government Printing Office, DHHS Publication No. (ADM) 81-1000, 1981.

Cohler, B. J. Personal narrative and life-course. In P. Baltes & O. G. Brim, Jr. (Eds.), *Life-span development and behavior* (Vol. IV). New York: Academic Press, 1982.

Cohler, B. J., & Boxer, A. M. Settling into the world: Person, time and context in the middle-adult years. In D. Offer & M. Sabshin (Eds.), *Normality and the life cycle*. New York: Basic Books, 1983.

Cohler, B. J., & Grunebaum, H. *Mothers, grandmothers, and daughters: Personality and childcare in three-generation families*. New York: Wiley, 1981.

Coleman, J. S., Bremner, R. H., Clark, B. R., Davis, J. B., Eichorn, D. H., Griliches, Z., Kett, J. F., Ryder, N. B., Doering, Z. B., & Mays, J. M. *Youth: Transition to adulthood* (Report of the Panel on Youth of the President's Science Advisory Committee). Chicago and London: University of Chicago Press, 1974.

Conger, J. J., & Petersen, A. C. *Youth and society* (3rd ed.). New York: Harper & Row, in press.

Douvan, E., & Adelson, J. *The adolescent experience*. New York: Wiley, 1966.

Elkind, D. Egocentrism in adolescence. *Child Development*, 1967, *38*, 1025–1034.

Erikson, E. H. Identity and the life cycle. *Psychological Issues*, 1959, *1*, 1–171.

Flacks, R. *Youth and social change*. Chicago: Markham, 1971.

Freud, A. Adolescence. *Psychoanalytic Study of the Child*, 1958, *13*, 255–278.

Gilligan, C. Women's place in man's life cycle. *Harvard Educational Review*, 1979, *49*, 431–446.

Giovacchini, P. Effects of adaptive and disruptive aspects of early object relationships upon later parental functioning. In E. J. Anthony & T. Benedek (Eds.), *Parenthood: Its psychology and psychopathology*. Boston: Little, Brown, 1970.

Gove, W. R., & Herb, T. R. Stress and mental illness among the young: A comparison of the sexes. *Social Forces*, 1974, *53*, 256–265.

Gove, W., & Peterson, C. An update of the literature on personal and marital satisfaction: The effect of children and the employment of wives. *Marriage and Family Review*. 1980, *3*, 63–96.

Gove, W., & Tudor, J. Adult sex roles and mental illness. *American Journal of Sociology*, 1973, *78*, 812–835.

Grinker, R. R., Sr., Grinker, R. R., Jr., & Timberlake, I. Mentally healthy young males (homoclites). *Archives of General Psychiatry*, 1962, *6*, 311–318.

Grinker, R. R., & Holzman, P. S. Schizophrenic pathology in young adults: A clinical study. *Archives of General Psychiatry*, 1973, *28*, 168–179.

Gutmann, D. Parenthood: A key to the comparative study of the life cycle. In N. Datan & L. Ginsberg (Eds.), *Life-span developmental psychology: Normative life crises.* New York: Academic Press, 1975.

Haan, N. Personality development from adolescence to adulthood in the Oakland growth and guidance studies. *Seminars in Psychiatry*, 1972, *4*, 399–414.

Haan, N., Smith, M. B., & Block, J. Moral reasoning of young adults: Political–social behavior, family background, and personality correlates. *Journal of Personality and Social Psychology*, 1968, *10*, 183–201.

Hagestad, G. O. *Mothers and daughters: Cement and dynamite in intergenerational linkages.* Unpublished manuscript, Committee on Human Development, University of Chicago, 1977.

Hamburg, B. A. Early adolescence: A specific and stressful stage of the life cycle. In G. V. Coelho, D. A. Hamburg, & J. E. Adams (Eds.), *Coping and adaptation.* New York: Basic Books, 1974.

Havighurst, R. The social competence of middle-aged people. *Genetic Psychology Monographs*, 1957, *56*, 296–348.

Heath, D. *Explorations in maturity.* New York: Appleton-Century-Crofts, 1965.

Hess, B. Sex roles, friendship, and the life course. *Research on Aging*, 1979, *1*, 494–515.

Hill, J. P. The family. In M. Johnson (Ed.), *Toward adolescence: The middle school years* (The 79th Yearbook of the National Society for the Study of Education). Chicago: University of Chicago Press, 1980.

Hill, J. P., & Lynch, M. E. The intensification of gender related role expectations during early adolescence. In J. Brooks-Gunn & A. C. Petersen (Eds.), *Girls at puberty: Biological, social, and psychological perspectives.* New York: Plenum Press, 1983.

Hill, J. P., & Palmquist, W. Social cognition and social relations in adolescence. *International Journal of Behavioral Development*, 1978, *1*, 1–36.

Hoffman, L. W. Changes in family roles, socialization, and sex differences. *American Psychologist*, 1977, *32*, 644–657.

Kandel, D., & Lesser, G. *Youth in two worlds.* San Francisco: Jossey-Bass, 1972.

Kavrell, S. M., & Petersen, A. C. Patterns of achievement in early adolescence. In M. L. Maeher & M. W. Steinkamp (Eds.), *Women and science.* Greenwich, Conn.: JAI Press, 1983.

Lerner, R. M., & Busch-Rossnagel, N. Individuals as producers of their development: Conceptual and empirical bases. In R. M. Lerner & N. Busch-Rossnagel (Eds.), *Individuals as producers of their development.* New York: Academic Press, 1981.

Lidz, T. The adolescent and his family. In G. Caplan & S. Lebovici (Eds.), *Adolescence: Psychosocial perspectives.* New York: Basic Books, 1969.

Livson, N., & Peskin, H. Prediction of adult psychological health in a longitudinal study. *Journal of Abnormal Psychology*, 1967, *72*, 509–518.

Livson, N., & Peskin, H. Perspectives on adolescence from longitudinal research. In J. Adelson (Ed.), *Handbook of adolescent psychology.* New York: Wiley, 1980.

Lowman, J. *Development and field-testing of a self-administered measure of family functioning.* Unpublished doctoral dissertation, University of North Carolina at Chapel Hill, 1971.

Maccoby, E. E., & Jacklin, C. N. *The psychology of sex differences.* Stanford, Calif.: Stanford University Press, 1974.

Macfarlane, J. W., Allen, L., & Honzik, M. P. *A developmental study of the behavior problems of normal children between twenty-one months and fourteen years.* Berkeley and Los Angeles: University of California Press, 1954.

Meile, R., & Haese, P. Social status, status incongruence and symptoms of stress. *Journal of Health and Social Behavior*, 1969, *10*, 237–244.

Nassi, A. J. Survivors of the sixties: Comparative psychosocial and political development of former Berkeley student activists. *American Psychologist*, 1981, *36*, 753–761.

Neugarten, B. L. The awareness of middle age. In R. Owen (Ed.), *Middle age.* London: British Broadcasting Corporation, 1967. Reprinted in B. L. Neugarten (Ed.), *Middle age and aging.* Chicago: University of Chicago Press, 1968.

Offer, D. *The psychological world of the teenager.* New York: Basic Books, 1969.

Offer, D., & Howard, K. I. An empirical analysis of the Offer self-image questionnaire for adolescents. *Archives of General Psychiatry,* 1972, *27,* 529–537.

Offer, D., & Offer, J. B. *From teen-age to young manhood: A psychological study.* New York: Basic Books, 1975.

Offer, D., Ostrov, E., & Howard, K. I. The self-image of adolescents: A study of four cultures. *Journal of Youth and Adolescence,* 1977, *6,* 265–280.

Offer, D., Ostrov, E., & Howard, K. I. *The adolescent: A psychological self-portrait.* New York: Basic Books, 1981. (a)

Offer, D., Ostrov, E., & Howard, K. The mental health professional's concept of the normal adolescent. *Archives of General Psychiatry,* 1981, *38,* 149–153. (b)

Offer, D., & Petersen, A. C. Psychiatric research and the public: An 18-year perspective. *American Journal of Psychiatry,* 1982, *21,* 86–87.

Offer, D., & Sabshin, M. Research alliance vs. therapeutic alliance: A comparison. *American Journal of Psychiatry,* 1967, *123,* 1519–1526.

Offer, D., & Sabshin, M. *Normality: Theoretical and clinical concepts of mental health* (2nd ed.). New York: Basic Books, 1974.

Offer, D., & Sabshin, M. (Eds.). *Normality and the life cycle.* New York: Basic Books, 1983.

Peskin, H., & Livson, N. Uses of the past in adult psychological health. In D. H. Eichorn, J. A. Clausen, N. Haan, M. Honzik, & P. H. Mussen (Eds.), *Present and past in middle life.* New York: Academic Press, 1981.

Petersen, A. C. Hormones and cognitive functioning in normal development. In M. A. Wittig & A. C. Petersen (Eds.), *Sex-related differences in cognitive functioning: Developmental issues.* New York: Academic Press, 1979.

Petersen, A. C. *The self-image questionnaire for young adolescents.* Unpublished manuscript, Laboratory for the Study of Adolescence, Michael Reese Hospital and Medical Center, Chicago, 1980. (a)

Petersen, A. C. Biopsychosocial processes in the development of sex-related differences. In J. Parsons (Ed.), *The psychobiology of sex differences and sex roles.* New York: Hemisphere, 1980. (b)

Petersen, A. C. *Early adolescent development.* Invited presentation at the Departmental Meeting, Psychosomatic and Psychiatric Institute, Department of Psychiatry, Michael Reese Hospital and Medical Center, Chicago, February, 1981.

Petersen, A. C. Menarche: Meaning of measures and measuring meaning. In S. Golub (Ed.), *Menarche.* New York: Heath, 1983.

Petersen, A. C., and Boxer, A. M. Adolescent sexuality. In T. J. Coates, A. C. Petersen, & C. Perry (Eds.), *Promoting adolescent health: A dialogue on research and practice.* New York: Plenum, 1982.

Petersen, A. C., Offer, D. O., & Kaplan, E. The self-image of rural adolescent girls. In M. Sugar (Ed.), *Female adolescent development.* New York: Brunner/Mazel, 1979.

Petersen, A. C., & Taylor, B. The biological approach to adolescence: Biological change and psychological adaptation. In J. Adelson (Ed.), *Handbook of adolescent psychology.* New York: Wiley, 1980.

Plath, D. Contours of consociation: Lessons from a Japanese narrative. In P. Baltes & O. G. Brim, Jr. (Eds.), *Life-span development and behavior* (Vol. III). New York: Academic Press, 1980.

Revere, V. *The remembered past: Its reconstruction at different life stages.* Unpublished doctoral dissertation, Committee on Human Development, University of Chicago, 1971.

Revere, V., & Tobin, S. Myth and reality: The older person's relationship to his past. *International Journal of Aging and Human Development,* 1980–1981, *12,* 15–26.

Riegel, K. The dialectics of human development. *American Psychologist*, 1976, *31*, 689–699.

Rossi, A. Aging and parenthood in the middle years. In P. Baltes & O. G. Brim, Jr. (Eds.), *Life-span development and behavior* (Vol. III). New York: Academic Press, 1980. (a)

Rossi, A. Life-span theories and women's lives. *Signs: Journal of Women in Culture and Society*. 1980, *6*, 4–32. (b)

Simmons, R. G., Blyth, D., Van Cleave, E. F., & Bush, D. M. Entry into early adolescence: The impact of school structure, puberty, and early dating on self-esteem. *American Sociological Review*, 1979, *44*, 948–967.

Spacks, P. *The adolescent idea: Myths of youth and the adult imagination*. New York: Basic Books, 1981.

Steinberg, L. D. Transformations in family relations at puberty. *Developmental Psychology*. 1981, *17*, 833–840.

Tanner, J. M. *Growth at adolescence*. Springfield, Ill.: Charles C Thomas, 1962.

Tanner, J. M. Sequence, tempo, and individual variation in growth and development of boys and girls aged twelve to sixteen. In J. Kagan & R. Coles (Eds.), *Twelve to sixteen: Early adolescence*. New York: Norton, 1972.

Tobin-Richards, M., Boxer, A. M., & Petersen, A. C. The psychological significance of pubertal change: Sex differences in perceptions of self during early adolescence. In J. Brooks-Gunn & A. C. Petersen (Eds.), *Girls at puberty: Biological, social, and psychological perspectives*. New York: Plenum, 1983.

Troll, L., Neugarten, B., & Kraines, R. Similarities in values and other personality characteristics in college students and their parents. *Merrill-Palmer Quarterly of Behavior and Development*, 1969, *15*, 323–327.

Vaillant, G. Theoretical hierarchy of adaptive ego mechanisms. *Archives of General Psychiatry*, 1971, *24*, 107–115.

Wilen, J. B. *Current concerns of young adolescents and their parents*. Paper presented at the Annual Meeting of the American Educational Research Association, Boston, April 1980.

Wilen, J. B. *Adolescent adjustment and the parent–child relationship*. Paper presented at the Annual Conference on Adolescence of the Clinical Research Training Program in Adolescence, Michael Reese Hospital and Medical Center, Chicago, June 1981.

6

SOME ADOLESCENT EXPERIENCES OF MOTHERHOOD

MARY J. ROGEL
ANNE C. PETERSEN

Although we think of parenting as an adult experience, not all parents are adults. Growing numbers of teenagers, in many ways children themselves, are having children of their own. While both the birthrate and the actual number of births to adult women have been decreasing over the past 2 decades, the birthrate for 15- to 19-year-olds has not dropped as rapidly, and the birthrate for teenagers under age 15 has continued to rise (Baldwin, 1979). Apart from fluctuations in the birth*rates* for teenagers, the actual *numbers* of births have not decreased proportionately because of the absolute increase in the number of teenagers in the population (Baldwin, 1979; David & Baldwin, 1979). Nationally, about 17% of babies are born to teenagers (David & Baldwin, 1979), but in some communities the proportion is as high as one third (see, e.g., Illinois Department of Public Health, 1980). Because more and more of these adolescent parents are opting to raise their children by themselves (Baldwin, 1976; Chilman, 1978), more children are growing up in families that are "disadvantaged" and, hence, at risk in a variety of ways that we discuss later in this chapter.

Many studies have addressed the outcomes of adolescent pregnancy (e.g., Aznar & Bennett, 1961; Baizerman, Sheehan, Ellison, & Schlesinger, 1974; Dott & Fort, 1976; Duenhoelter, Jimenez, & Baumann, 1975; Hardy, Welcher, Stanley, & Dallas, 1978; Hassan & Falls, 1964; McGanity, Little, Fogelman, Jennings, Calhoun, & Dawson, 1969; Phipps-Yonas, 1980; Zackler, Andelman,

Mary J. Rogel. Young Adult and Adolescent Decision Making about Contraception Project, Department of Psychiatry, Michael Reese Hospital and Medical Center, and University of Chicago, Chicago, Illinois.

Anne C. Petersen. Department of Individual and Family Studies, College of Human Development, Pennsylvania State University, University Park, Pennsylvania. Previous address: Laboratory for the Study of Adolescence, Department of Psychiatry, Michael Reese Hospital and Medical Center, and Department of Psychiatry, University of Chicago, Chicago, Illinois.

& Bauer, 1969). Fewer have addressed the outcomes of adolescent parenting
(e.g., Baldwin & Cain, 1980; Card & Wise, 1978; Furstenberg, 1976, 1978;
Kinard & Klerman, 1980; Lorenzi, Klerman, & Jekel, 1977; Moore & Hofferth,
1977; Trussell, 1976). Fewer still have explored what the experience of being
a parent means to an adolescent (e.g., Hatcher, 1973; Rothstein, 1978; Smetana,
1980). In this chapter we explore the adult experience of parenting from the
perspective of the adolescent parent. Because the literature focuses almost exclusively on the teenage mother, our discussion effectively is limited to the
experiences of girls. Findings from the literature are augmented with data that
we have obtained in our own empirical investigation of adolescent girls' attitudes
about pregnancy and motherhood.

THE ADOLESCENT EXPERIENCE OF PREGNANCY

A discussion of pregnancy is germane to the discussion of parenting only to the
extent that the experience of pregnancy and the pregnancy outcome affect parenting. Therefore, our discussion of adolescent pregnancy will examine the ways
in which the physical and psychosocial correlates of pregnancy differentially
affect adolescent parents. In a later section we discuss the conflict between the
tasks of adolescence and the tasks of pregnancy, the perceptions of some adolescent girls about motherhood, and the implications of these for adolescent
parenting.

It is during pregnancy that the prospective parents begin to define themselves
as parents and to develop a relationship with their unborn child (Leifer, 1979).
The establishment of the parent–child bond may be impaired when the pregnancy
is unwanted, when there are health problems associated with the pregnancy,
when the social relationships of the pregnant woman are stressed, and when the
newborn baby has health problems (Klaus, Leger, & Trause, 1974; Mercer,
1974a, 1974b; Mosher, 1972). These conditions occur more frequently in the
pregnancies of teenagers than in the pregnancies of older women.

Medical Outcomes of Adolescent Pregnancies

The pregnancies of adolescents, compared to those of older women, are more
often characterized by serious health problems, such as toxemia of pregnancy,
high blood pressure, anemia, and prolonged labor (Roosa, Fitzgerald, & Carlson,
1980). These are likely to have a negative influence on the pregnant teenager
by making the experience of pregnancy unpleasant and worrisome. One who is
concerned about her physical ability to carry a pregnancy to its natural end will
be more reluctant psychologically to bond to the unborn child. The fact that the
babies of teenagers are more likely to be born prematurely and to be of low birth
weight complicates the picture. Small and premature babies are more susceptible
to health problems, and they evoke more tentative responses from adults. Pre-

mature infants appear more fragile, and persons not accustomed to handling them frequently are hesitant to do so. Obviously this has an effect on the bonding process.

Though teenagers do have more difficulties during their pregnancies, the negative outcomes apparently are not the direct consequence of their age, except in the case of the very young adolescent. Instead, the problems stem from inadequate prenatal care, poor nutrition, and inadequate living conditions (Dott & Fort, 1976; Duenhoelter, Jimenez, & Baumann, 1975; Hassan & Falls, 1964; Zackler, Andelman, & Bauer, 1969). Among teenagers who obtain adequate prenatal care, there are no apparent differences from older women; and in some studies the teenagers actually had better pregnancy outcomes (see Aznar & Bennett, 1961; McGanity et al., 1969; Roosa, Fitzgerald, & Carlson, 1980). However, most teenagers do not receive adequate care during their pregnancies and are susceptible to these negative health influences on their later parenting experiences.

Psychosocial Outcomes of Adolescent Pregnancies

Pregnant teenage girls are usually unmarried (Kantner & Zelnik, 1972), and their relationships with their boyfriends often falter as a result of the pregnancy or terminate naturally before or soon after the baby is born. Consequently, teenagers frequently do not have the emotional support of the baby's father during and after the pregnancy. Further, the pregnancy of a teenager often triggers negative responses from other persons who are important in her life. Parents are seldom overjoyed to learn that their daughter is pregnant, and some forcibly eject their pregnant daughter from the family. Such conditions put an obvious strain on the young parent.

Teenage mothers usually forego their educations; even those who return to school do not continue as far as their peers who did not become parents while teenagers (Card & Wise, 1978; Furstenberg, 1976; Moore & Hofferth, 1977; Trussell, 1976). Diminished educational attainment is directly related to lower earnings and greater job dissatisfaction and, frequently, to increased incidence of dependency on the state (Trussell, 1976). Teenage fathers who stay with their families suffer these same negative consequences, though usually not to the same degree as the teenage girls (Card & Wise, 1978). Those pregnant teenage couples who decide to marry suffer a higher incidence of divorce than their peers who decide to marry for other reasons than to legitimize a pregnancy (Lorenzi, Klerman, & Jekel, 1977). Finally, women who begin their families while still teenagers have larger completed families than women who begin their families at older ages (Card & Wise, 1978; Furstenberg, 1978; Moore & Hofferth, 1977; Trussell, 1976). Those teenagers who give birth in their early teens experience these negative outcomes to a greater degree than those who give birth after they have completed high school (Card & Wise, 1978).

While some intervention programs aimed at improving the pregnancy outcomes and parenting skills of adolescents are meeting with success (Bennett & Bardon, 1977; Schweitzer & Youngs, 1976), most adolescents do not have access to intensive intervention programs. Nor are there data available concerning long-term (e.g., 10-year) outcomes of the interventions. Consequently, we may say that the majority of teenage parents are susceptible to the negative psychosocial outcomes that have been associated with parenting as such a young age.

The outcomes for the children of teenage parents also tend to be negative, in part the consequence of the medical, social, and economic conditions cited above. The children of teenage parents suffer a higher incidence of child abuse (Johnson, 1974; Smith, Mumford, Goldfarb, & Kaufman, 1975); however, this relationship may be a function of poverty and disturbed family life rather than of becoming a parent while still a teenager (Kinard & Klerman, 1980). In addition, the children—particularly the male children—show deficits in cognitive development (Baldwin & Cain, 1980). The children of younger mothers tend to test more poorly and to be farther behind in school than the children of older mothers (Hardy, Welcher, Stanley, & Dallas, 1978). They may also experience negative outcomes in social and emotional development and school adjustment (Baldwin & Cain, 1980). In their review of the literature on the development of children of teenage parents, Roosa et al. (1980) conclude that teenagers are less than adequate parents, as they tend to be insensitive to their children's needs and inconsistent in their caregiving. However, they note that these negative qualities may be counterbalanced by the teenagers' interest in their children, their energy, and their enthusiasm for parenting.

THE ADOLESCENT EXPERIENCE OF PARENTING

Although it seems clear that not all of the negative outcomes associated with adolescent pregnancy and parenting are the direct effect of age, we wish to examine the effect of age on adolescent parenting. In particular, we focus on how cognitive development, identity formation, and the capacity for intimacy contribute to adolescent parenting experiences. While other factors affect parenting, we feel that these three are most salient to our discussion of adolescent parenting.

Cognitive Issues in Adolescent Parenting

The Piagetian focus on the quality of thought and how it changes with maturation (Inhelder & Piaget, 1958) is a good place to begin our exploration of developmental maturity and parenting. Progression through the four maturational stages (sensorimotor, preoperational, concrete operational, formal operational) described by Inhelder and Piaget (1958) is marked by several trends. Thinking becomes more flexible and future oriented, and the person begins to deal with problems ahead of time rather than after the fact. Secondly, the individual becomes more skilled at adapting to and solving problems. Finally, the individual becomes less and less dependent on the stimulus world, as control is transferred from external stimuli to internal mediators or schemes of thought (Flavell, 1963).

Most individuals enter adolescence in the stage of concrete operational thought. Concrete operations represent true logical thinking; however, concrete operational thought is bounded by concrete, physical reality. For an individual in the stage of concrete operations to represent something cognitively it must exist in reality; counterfactual things or events cannot be understood or represented mentally. This limitation colors the meaning of pregnancy to the concrete operational teenager. It is difficult for a concrete child to understand menstruation, conception, and childbirth because she cannot imagine the internal physiological processes associated with these experiences in the same way that an older woman can.

The concrete operational child is also egocentric, unable to distinguish between what is *thought* and what *is*. Thus, to the concrete operational person, the solution that he/she derives for a particular problem, such as an unplanned pregnancy, is the same as the true solution; alternatives cannot be considered. When contradictory evidence is presented, the individual simply reinterprets the opposing evidence to fit the "solution." A girl who is forced to accept someone else's solution to her unplanned pregnancy may have an extremely difficult time integrating this experience into her sense of self. In such a situation a girl will sometimes repeat the pregnancy in order to carry out her own solution.

The ability to think counterfactually, to see that reality and thoughts about reality are different, and to generate and recognize hypotheses about reality emerge with formal operational thinking. Research evidence concerning Piaget's theory of cognitive development suggests that formal reasoning is *one* style of mature thinking, not the only style (Dulit, 1972; Elkind, 1975). The extent to which any given individual develops and uses formal thought depends on cultural influences, schooling, and individual experiences. Thus, our discussion of formal thought must be tempered by the reality that not everyone uses formal thinking and that those individuals who do, do not necessarily use it in all problem-solving situations.

The adolescent early in the stage of formal operations is egocentric, but in a qualitatively different way from the egocentrism of the concrete thinker. The concrete child believes that his/her initial interpretations of the world are correct because they are the products of his/her own reasoning. In contrast, an early formal thinker can take the point of view of another person, but fails to differentiate between the object of others' thought and the object of his/her own thought. Therefore, the early formal thinking adolescent thinks everyone is concerned about the same things that concern her (Elkind, 1967).

One of the consequences of adolescent egocentrism is the adolescent's feeling of being "on stage." Teenagers can spend a great deal of time constructing an imaginary audience (Elkind, 1967) and envision that this audience "knows" what the thinker knows and is as self-critical as the thinker is. This may account for adolescents' desire for privacy and for their fear that everyone will know about their sexual activity if they use birth control.

Another aspect of adolescent egocentrism is the personal fable (Elkind, 1967), a construction complementary to the imaginary audience. Because the adolescent sees the self as being so important to so many people (in the imaginary audience), she comes to regard the self as special and unique—so much that no one else can know how she feels, or experience what she experiences. Further, the personal fable may encompass a sense of invincibility: Unfortunate things may happen to others, but I'm different. The thousands of pregnant teenage girls who thought that they could not get pregnant were operating with personal fables. The personal fable is also operating for those pregnant teenagers who believe that they will escape the negative consequences of teenage parenthood.

Thus, the experience of pregnancy is likely to be vastly different according to the level of cognitive maturity of the pregnant adolescent. Reality-based concrete thinkers are likely to have a very difficult time imagining their babies as unique individuals with identities apart from their own. The baby is an object that is part of them. In contrast, formal reasoners can appreciate the emerging individuality of their unborn children, as well as the subtle distinction between self and other that develops with pregnancy.

While there may be clear limitations to the cognitive capacities of adolescents, particularly young adolescents, it is important to recognize that the *capacity* to think abstractly does not always insure that an individual will be able to use this capacity in a specific situation. Gilligan and Belenky (1980) have shown that a traumatic situation can produce regression, not only in affective state but also in level of cognitive performance. The effect on cognitive as well as psychosocial development of pregnancy during adolescence remains a major unaddressed question.

Identity Issues in Adolescent Parenting

One's concept of self is linked to reasoning capacity. For example, formal reasoners are more facile than concrete reasoners in their mental representations of self. Regardless of its degree of elaboration, however, self-concept, or identity, may be discussed in terms of four content areas: physical self, social self, moral self, and psychological self.

Physical self includes all tangibles in one's possession, its major component being one's body. Because the body is continuously changing throughout pubescence, physical self-concept or body image are continually revised through adolescence (Hamburg, 1974). Pregnancy during adolescence alters this process since pregnancy requires its own adjustment of body image. The changes of pregnancy combined with the changes of adolescence may be stressful to the individual trying to assimilate both at the same time.

The social self consists of the roles the adolescent plays and evaluations of those performances. During adolescence one begins to try out possible adult roles, searching for those that are compatible with other aspects of the self. Adolescents, with their maturing powers of adult cognition, may fantasize about taking particular roles; such fantasies serve as experiments to help them decide which roles they prefer. Motherhood is one of the roles about which teenage girls fantasize. However, one who becomes a mother, rather than taking the role temporarily, as with baby-sitting, cannot easily postpone the responsibilities that come with the role or put the role aside when it becomes too cumbersome. Typically, adolescents are not prepared for the day-to-day responsibilities of motherhood and cannot conceive of themselves as full-time mothers. Indeed, many become even more dependent on their own mothers, after becoming mothers themselves, at a time when they are naturally moving toward increased independence and autonomy. In societies where it is expected that young girls will bear children, these developmental costs are balanced by social supports that directly or indirectly recognize adolescent limitations.

The moral self includes values and principles that govern and provide direction to one's life. Adolescents are in the process of building such a moral system. Some build a socially grounded moral system; others develop one that is more personally grounded (Haan, Smith, & Block, 1968). The particular moral system that an adolescent has, as well as its status at any given time, will serve as the basis on which an adolescent raises his/her child. A teenage parent who has a poorly developed or incoherent moral system will reflect this in the way the child is disciplined.

The psychological self is one's sense of inner self, which is composed of the thoughts, feelings, and attitudes one holds about the self. Changes in the psychological self occur with the emergence of formal thought and the capacity to consider the self as an object of reflection. Almost everyone has knowledge about the inner self, but not everyone "knows that she knows" about it. The adolescent identity crisis (Erikson, 1968) appears to involve this higher sense of self-awareness. New social roles affect the self-concept as well. In particular, becoming a parent while still an adolescent is likely to affect identity formation and how one thinks about oneself. Self-definition as well as feelings of competence, independence, and responsibility are affected by parenthood. An adolescent who does not have a firm sense of self is likely to feel threatened by the demands of parenthood and the newborn child. At a time when the adolescent needs to be attending to her own personal growth, the young mother is called upon to give of herself to a demanding, dependent infant who can reciprocate little of her care.

It is obvious, then, that pregnancy and motherhood can have a profound effect on identity and identity formation. Those adolescents who have dealt with most of their identity issues, particularly late adolescents, may find the experience of parenting a challenge toward positive growth. Those who take on motherhood while still immature themselves are likely to suffer as a result and will be unable to meet the demands of the role.

Intimacy Issues in Adolescent Parenting

Erikson (1963) considered the development of identity to be the central task of adolescence. After this foundation is laid, then the individual may move on to the task of establishing intimate relationships. This particular progression, however, has been questioned as more descriptive of male development than female development (Marcia, 1980). Male identity focuses on individual competence and knowledge while female identity focuses on relationships with others. Thus, in girls the development of identity is integrated with the development of intimacy in relationships.

The relationship between mother and child is such an intimate relationship. While it is understandable how one might clarify one's self-image in a relationship with a peer, it seems more difficult to do so in the unequal relationship of parent and child. Because the infant cannot mirror back information about the self as can a peer, the parent–child relationship must be seen as one-way and as demanding a particular level of maturity from the parent.

Thus, the adolescent parent may be faced with dual problems of intimacy. She is struggling to build intimate relationships with her peers and with her baby. Her sexual activity, which resulted in the pregnancy, may represent one attempt at establishing intimacy, or else one consequence. The relationship with a child is very different, calling for a giving of the self in a different way. Yet, in order to give of herself to her child, an adolescent must have some experience in personal giving and intimacy with peers. If she has not had these experiences (physical intimacy does not require psychological intimacy), she will be limited in how much she can provide for her child. This is true for teenage fathers as well. Indeed, in many cases it is more true for the teenage father because he typically must cope with the additional barrier of physical distance from his child and may be in an antagonistic relationship with the child's mother.

The Tasks of Adolescence and the Tasks of Pregnancy

Among the tasks of adolescence are cognitive growth, identity formation, and movement toward the establishment of intimate relationships. As the adolescent achieves these tasks, she/he becomes increasingly independent and autonomous from the family of origin and involved in extrafamilial relationships. The tasks of pregnancy, on the other hand, involve accepting and incorporating embryonic growth, and the body changes it occasions, into the pregnant woman's sense of self, and individuation of the fetus growing within her body as a unique person whose existence will be separate, ultimately, from her own.

Though the completion of such tasks is only an ideal toward which one strives, it would seem that the tasks of pregnancy presuppose the completion of the tasks of adolescence or progress toward their completion. Indeed, in her review of the tasks of pregnancy in relation to the tasks of adolescence, Klue (1980) noted that "the developmental tasks of adolescence . . . are conceivably all at risk when the adolescent becomes pregnant" (p. 23). We might also suppose that the developmental tasks of pregnancy are at risk when the pregnancy occurs during adolescence, particularly early or middle adolescence.

The natural course of pregnancy facilitates the acceptance of embryonic growth and individuation of the fetus. A woman knows that she is pregnant for several months before bodily alterations become apparent. During this period she has time to adjust to the fact of pregnancy. Knowing that she is pregnant and experiencing some of the early symptoms of pregnancy help her to incorporate her new image into her sense of self. During this time attachment to the fetus typically begins to develop. With quickening, there develops a sense of the fetus as another person, to be loved for its own sake. The process of personifying the fetus continues through pregnancy; with parturition, the reality of this other is revealed, and the other becomes externalized.

Leifer (1980) observed that baseline personality characteristics were predictive of adjustment to pregnancy, and that both personality and adjustment were predictive of attachment to the fetus and infant. Women who had not developed ties to the infant during pregnancy were emotionally distant and poorly attached to their infants in the postpartum period. Given the immaturity of adolescents, particularly early and middle adolescents, one might expect that they would have difficulty adjusting to pregnancy and attaching to their infants.

The research data tend to support these hypotheses. On the average, adolescents tend to deny their pregnancies and to be unconcerned about the developing fetus. They exhibit minimal investment in the pregnancy and have rather unrealistic ideas about what their babies will be like (Hatcher, 1973). Once the baby is born, adolescents can provide well for the physical needs, but they may have difficulty providing for social and cognitive needs.

Adolescent Perceptions of Motherhood

In our investigation of the attitudes and behaviors of teenage girls at high risk for pregnancy during adolescence, we interviewed 120 girls between the ages of 12 and 19 who had come to one of three clinics (Prenatal, Teen Family Planning, and Pediatric Acute Care) at the Michael Reese Hospital and Medical Center between April and August 1979. All participated in the study voluntarily and spoke with us about a variety of issues including their attitudes and experiences concerning sexuality, pregnancy, and motherhood. The girls were residents of the South Side of Chicago and lived in the economically depressed neighborhoods near the Medical Center. Almost all were black, and most lived in families headed by a single parent.

Of the 75 girls in our sample who had become pregnant, only 4 had wanted to become pregnant. The majority explained their pregnancies as the result of not using birth control. Once they did become pregnant, they experienced strong internal and external pressure to keep their babies. They perceived their families and boyfriends as wanting them to keep the baby even when they themselves would have resolved the pregnancy with abortion or adoption. However, very few girls considered alternatives to keeping the baby (Rogel, Zuehlke, Petersen, Tobin-Richards, & Shelton, 1980).

Not having other plans for the future was an important factor in the decisions of many of the girls to keep their babies. We noted with interest, however, that over 70% of the girls disagreed with the statement, "Having a baby makes a girl a real woman." Once the baby was born, 59% of the girls reported that they were the principal caretakers, 26% reported that their mothers cared for the baby, and 15% reported that some other person was the principal caretaker.

We asked the girls how they expected pregnancy and motherhood to affect their lives. Those who had never been pregnant were asked to imagine what would happen if they did become pregnant. Those who had already given birth were asked to compare how they had expected their lives to change with how things had actually changed after the birth. Though this comparison may be confounded by inaccuracies in recall of expectations prior to pregnancy, we report the comparisons, which are summarized in Table 6-1.

Of girls who had never been pregnant, 60% expected that cost would be a problem. Of those who had given birth, 44% had expected cost to be a problem, but only 23% reported that it actually was a problem. While it is likely that the babies were not yet old enough for the expenses to pile up, it is interesting to see the large discrepancies in the reports of the ever- and never-pregnant girls and in the expectations of those who had given birth compared to what actually happened. This latter difference, between expectation and reality, is statistically significant below the .001 level by sign test.

Expected changes in interpersonal relationships were also discrepant. Never-pregnant girls expected more negative consequences (32%) and fewer positive changes (9%) in their relationships with their parents, compared to the expectations of the adolescent mothers. Before their pregnancies, 25% of the mothers had expected that a pregnancy would harm their relationships with their parents, but this happened in only 12% of the cases. In contrast, 22% had expected the pregnancy to improve their relationships with their parents, and this actually happened in 26% of cases. These differences are not statistically significant.

Differences between the ever- and never-pregnant girls are rather dramatic concerning expectations about change in relationships with boyfriends. Among the never-pregnant girls, 28% expected a pregnancy to harm the relationship, and 20% expected a pregnancy to improve it. Before getting pregnant, only 6% of the mothers had expected a pregnancy to harm their relationships with their boyfriends, and 32% expected there to be an improvement. After the pregnancy, they reported that the relationship was harmed in 12% of cases and improved in 35%. The large discrepancy between the expectations of the ever- and never-pregnant girls before pregnancy is statistically significant ($\chi^2 = 11.246$, $df = 2$, $p < .01$) and suggests that the strength of the girls' expectations for change in that relationship may influence their willingness to risk a possible pregnancy. We should note, however, that a number of the never-pregnant girls also had not yet become sexually active, though most girls had boyfriends.

TABLE 6-1. RESPONSES OF EVER- AND NEVER-PREGNANT GIRLS TO QUESTIONS ABOUT HOW A PREGNANCY MIGHT OR DID AFFECT THEIR LIVES

	Never pregnant			Ever pregnant					
				Expected			Happened		
Cost a problem	No 40%		Yes 60%	No 56%		Yes 44%	No 77%		Yes 23%
	Harm	No change	Improve	Harm	No change	Improve	Harm	No change	Improve
Relationship with parents	32%	59%	9%	25%	51%	22%	12%	62%	26%
Relationship with boyfriend	28%	50%	20%	6%	61%	32%	12%	52%	35%
Relationships with friends	14%	81%	2%	4%	85%	6%	3%	84%	11%
Future life	68%	27%	4%	42%	46%	11%	26%	56%	16%
Feelings about self	34%	54%	11%	14%	54%	32%	16%	52%	30%

Note. Percentages do not always total 100% because some girls responded "don't know."

There were also some rather interesting but nonsignificant differences in the ways in which ever- and never-pregnant girls expected pregnancy to change their lives. The majority of never-pregnant girls (68%) believed that a pregnancy would have a negative impact on their future lives. In contrast, 42% of the mothers reported that they believed, before they became pregnant, that pregnancy would negatively affect their futures, and 11% said that they believed their futures would be improved. In actuality, only 26% said that the pregnancy had indeed harmed their lives, while 16% said that their lives had improved.

Concerning their feelings about themselves, 34% of the never-pregnant girls said that a pregnancy would make them feel worse about themselves, and 11% said that a pregnancy would make them feel better. Of the mothers, only 14% said that they had expected to feel worse, while 16% actually did feel worse; and 32% said that they had expected to feel better, and 30% actually did. The discrepancy in the expectations of the never-pregnant girls and the mothers is statistically significant ($\chi^2 = 9.897$, $df = 2$, $p < .01$).

In general, it seems that the never-pregnant girls expected more negative outcomes from pregnancy in their relationships with their boyfriends and in their feelings about themselves. Girls who had been pregnant reported fewer pre-pregnancy expectations of negative consequences. This discrepancy may, in fact, be a distortion created by hindsight, since these are retrospective reports. However, their reports may in fact be true. If so, expectations about the consequences of pregnancy, particularly how it may affect identity and intimate relationships, may serve as a deterrent to early pregnancy. Given the generally poor use of birth control in the sample, however, we may also speculate that those not yet pregnant may simply be the ''lucky'' ones.

While the ever-pregnant girls reported expecting fewer negative consequences from pregnancy than did the never-pregnant girls, they also reported that the actual consequences of the pregnancy were even less negative than they had anticipated. They seem to be communicating that teenage pregnancy is not a cause for concern. However, since a significant minority (41%) were not the principal caretakers of their children, it is likely that they did not experience negative consequences because they were only nominally the mothers of their children. They had the status of mother without the responsibility.

Though we cannot generalize from this sample to all adolescents, we may make some inferences that can be tested in other populations. More of the never-pregnant girls saw pregnancy as interfering with their development in terms of interpersonal relationships, independence and autonomy, and self-concept. In their retrospective views, fewer of the adolescent mothers saw pregnancy interfering in the same way, and even fewer reported that it actually had interfered. Though we do not know for certain, it is possible that the mothers had reevaluated their expectations for their lives in the light of their pregnancies and had incorporated their new social role into their emerging identities.

Analyses of other data from these same girls suggest that the experience of pregnancy may be affected by the progress of development. Klue (1980) examined the girls' reports of their mental pictures of their unborn babies. Girls who had already delivered were asked to describe how they had expected their babies to look while they were still pregnant. Responses were coded as negative, neutral, or positive, and as vague or specific. Few girls gave negative or ambivalent responses; equal numbers were coded as positive or neutral. Positive responses were associated with higher scores on self-esteem and autonomy but were not related to interpersonal relationships.[1] Almost twice as many girls gave vague rather than specific responses. However, specificity of response was not associated with these personality measures, though specificity did seem to be related to active resistance to dependence on familial ties. Girls who gave specific and positive responses seem to have progressed further in their development to maturity, given their higher scores on self-esteem, autonomy, and independence from family. Thus, data from the girls in our sample corroborate our expectations from the theoretical material discussed above and the data reported by others.

PROGNOSIS FOR ADOLESCENT PARENTING

Though a number of intervention programs have reported successful attempts to reverse the negative pregnancy and parenting outcomes that have been associated with adolescent parenting, the tasks targeted by these programs are broad and complex. The cognitive limitations of many early and middle ado-

---

1. Self-esteem was measured with the Rosenberg Self-Esteem Scale (1965). Autonomy was measured by four items combined in an additive scale ($\alpha = .34$): (1) "When you have a problem, do you do something to solve it or do you let it solve itself?" (2) "Would you say that you and your friends all think alike?" (3) "Would you describe yourself as someone who sticks with the group?" (4) Interviewer rating of behavior during interview.

Interpersonal relationships were measured with three additive scales. The Family Relations Scale ($\alpha = .38$) consisted of six items: (1) "How do you feel you get along with your family?" (2) "How would you describe your relationship with your mother?" (3) "If you want to do something that you think your parents might not approve of, what do you do?" (4) "Do you think the pregnancy has improved, harmed, or not changed your relationship with your parents?" (5) "Do you see your life in 15 years (when you're about 30 years old) as similar or different from your mother's?" (6) Interviewer rating: Was there obvious evidence of conflictual feelings in relation to questions about family? The Heterosexual Relationship Scale ($\alpha = .65$) was constructed with six items: (1) "Do you have a boyfriend?" or "Are you married?" (2) "How long have you known your boyfriend or husband?" (3) "How often do you see him?" (4) "How well can you talk to your sexual partner about sex and birth control?" (5) "Many factors might enter into a decision about what to do about being pregnant. Here are some things that are important to some people. Which were important for you?—My boyfriend's or husband's opinion. . . ." (6) Dating was or was not mentioned spontaneously as an after-school or after-job activity. The Friends/Activities Scale ($\alpha = .46$) was composed of five items: (1) Informal activities with friends were or were not mentioned spontaneously as an after-school or after-job activity. (2) "Do you and your friends discuss your problems together?" (3) "What did your friends want you to do about the (last) pregnancy?" Responses coded "didn't care/didn't consult/no opinion" versus any response indicating an opinion. (4) School or neighborhood clubs were or were not mentioned as an after-school or after-job activity. (5) Church functions were or were not mentioned as an after-school or after-job activity.

lescents and the need they have to focus upon themselves as they develop make it rather unrealistic to expect that one can truly intervene to make these children better parents, particularly in a complex culture such as ours.

It has already been demonstrated that adolescents can provide for the physical needs of their children (Epstein, 1980); and one can see how an intervention program can teach even preadolescents how to diaper and bathe a baby. However, the real challenge in parenting is to stimulate a child to perform in an age-appropriate fashion and to help that child through emotional crises in such a way as to enhance growth. These skills cannot be taught easily because they spring from the parent's own experience with the world (particularly the experience of being parented) and from the parent's ability to observe the child from the vantage point of superior cognitive skills. It is difficult to teach concrete operational adolescent parents consistently to imagine the world as it is seen by their infants or toddlers. They can learn to take the perspectives of their children but only in specific rather than general ways. The psychological world of the child of an adolescent is frequently impoverished because of the limitations adolescents bring to parenthood. The majority of pregnant teenagers do not have access to the parenting intervention programs that can ameliorate the negative outcomes of adolescent parenting.

We must qualify, in several ways, the negative picture that emerges from our exploration of adolescent parenting. Being an adolescent parent does not mean that one automatically will be an inadequate parent. The limitations that some adolescents bring to the parenting experience must be viewed in perspective. First of all, they are developmental limitations, which means that they are probably temporary. Secondly, they are limitations only in the context of a complex society that places certain demands on parents. Simpler societies typically do not view adolescent parenting as a problem.

There is a great range of individual variation among adolescents, just as there is variation among adults. As we noted earlier, the endpoints of development are not absolute. For example, not all adults show the capacity for formal operational reasoning. Yet most adults are parents. Therefore, it is conceivable that some adolescents may, in some ways, be better prepared for parenting than some adults. However, preparation for parenting is only part of the issue. Adolescents should not *have to* take on adult roles so early. They deserve the experience of adolescence.

For those adolescents who are thrust into the role of parent, their experience of parenting will depend on where they are in their own development. Older and more mature adolescents may benefit tremendously from parenting intervention programs, and some need no more ''intervention'' than older parents. It has been demonstrated that adolescents who have completed most of their own development to adulthood can use a pregnancy and the subsequent parenting experiences as a catalyst for further growth.

The parenting prognosis of immature adolescents, however, is somewhat grim. They are less likely to benefit from parenting interventions though they are most in need of them. Still children themselves, they deserve the opportunity to complete their own growth. It would be unrealistic and inappropriate to suggest that they all should have abortions or give their babies up for adoption. Yet, they cannot care for their babies without assistance. Perhaps the most appropriate intervention for the immature adolescent is to identify a responsible adult in the adolescent's environment who is willing to take primary responsibility for raising the child until the adolescent parent is able to take over primary responsibility. It is important that the adolescent be identified as the parent and be held accountable for as much of the parenting of the child as possible in order to facilitate the relationship between parent and child and to minimize future problems in that relationship.

The more satisfactory solution to the problem of inadequate parenting by adolescents is to prevent the problem in the first place. This, of course, is easier said than done. While adolescents are better contraceptors now than they were 5 years ago (Zelnik & Kantner, 1980), progress is slow, and pregnancies continue to occur. It is unrealistic to expect that we can persuade adolescents to refrain from sexual activity. Some may be willing to postpone first intercourse when they realize and accept that they do not have to be sexually active to be normal and when they learn how to deal with the pressures to become sexually active. Nonetheless, large numbers of adolescents will be coitally active before they are ready and able to be parents. Sex education programs must address not only the reproductive facts of life but also must explore with young people the values that lead persons to become sexually active, the responsibilities that come with being sexually active, and the tremendous giving of self that is required of parents. The information must be developmentally appropriate and must be provided at all age levels if we are to be successful in reducing the tragedy—for adolescents, babies, and society—of children having children.

ACKNOWLEDGMENTS

We thank the following staff of the Young Adult and Adolescent Decision Making about Contraception Project for their assistance in our investigation of the attitudes and behaviors of teenage girls at high risk for pregnancy during adolescence: Michelle Shelton, Maryse Tobin-Richards, and Martha E. Zuehlke, MD. Funding for this phase of the research was provided by the Michael Reese Hospital and Medical Center. Current funding is being provided by the MacArthur Foundation (Grant 80-64). We are grateful to Joyce Bonner and Shirley E. Wharton for their assistance in preparing the manuscript.

REFERENCES

Aznar, R., & Bennett, A. E. Pregnancy in the adolescent girl. *American Journal of Obstetrics and Gynecology*, 1961, *81*, 934–940.

Baizerman, M., Sheehan, C., Ellison, D. L., & Schlesinger, E. R. A critique of the research literature concerning pregnant adolescents, 1960–1970. *Journal of Youth and Adolescence*, 1974, *3*, 61–75.

Baldwin, W. P. Adolescent pregnancy and childbearing—Growing concerns for Americans. *Population Bulletin*, 1976, *31*(2).

Baldwin, W. P. *Adolescent pregnancy and childbearing—Rates, trends and research findings from the Center for Population Research, National Institute of Child Health and Human Development*. Bethesda, Md.: Department of Health, Education and Welfare, Social and Behavioral Sciences Branch, 1979.

Baldwin, W. P., & Cain, V. S. The children of teenage parents. *Family Planning Perspectives*, 1980, *12*, 34–43.

Bennett, V. C., & Bardon, J. I. The effects of a school program on teenage mothers and their children. *American Journal of Orthopsychiatry*, 1977, *47*, 671–678.

Card, J. J., & Wise, L. L. Teenage mothers and teenage fathers: The impact of early childbearing on the parents' personal and professional lives. *Family Planning Perspectives*, 1978, *10*, 199–205.

Chilman, C. S. *Adolescent sexuality in a changing American society: Social and psychological perspectives* (DHEW Publication No. (NIH) 79-1426). Washington, D.C.: U.S. Government Printing Office, 1978.

David, H. P., & Baldwin, W. P. Childbearing and child development: Demographic and psychosocial trends. *American Psychologist*, 1979, *34*, 866–871.

Dott, A. B., & Fort, A. T. Medical and social factors affecting early teenage childbearing. *American Journal of Obstetrics and Gynecology*, 1976, *125*, 532–536.

Duenhoelter, J. H., Jimenez, J. M., & Baumann, C. Pregnancy performance of patients under fifteen years of age. *Obstetrics and Gynecology*, 1975, *46*, 49–52.

Dulit, E. Adolescent thinking à la Piaget: The formal stage. *Journal of Youth and Adolescence*, 1972, *1*, 281–301.

Elkind, D. Egocentrism in adolescence. *Child Development*, 1967, *38*, 1025–1034.

Elkind, D. Recent research on cognitive development in adolescence. In S. E. Dragastin & G. H. Elder, Jr. (Eds.), *Adolescence in the life cycle*. Washington, D.C.: Hemisphere, 1975.

Epstein, A. S. New insights into the problems of adolescent parenthood. *Bulletin of the High/Scope Foundation*, 1980, *5*, 6–8.

Erikson, E. H. *Childhood and society* (2nd ed.). New York: Norton, 1963.

Erikson, E. H. *Identity: Youth and crisis*. New York: Norton, 1968.

Flavell, J. H. *The developmental psychology of Jean Piaget*. New York: Van Nostrand, 1963.

Furstenberg, F. F., Jr. The social consequences of teenage parenthood. *Family Planning Perspectives*, 1976, *8*, 148–164.

Furstenberg, F. F., Jr. *Burdens and benefits: The impact of early childbearing on the family*. Paper prepared for conference on Family Impact Perspectives toward Teenage Pregnancy, Washington, D.C., October 1978.

Gilligan, C., & Belenky, M. F. Crisis and transitions: A naturalistic study of abortion decisions. In R. L. Selman & R. Yando (Eds.), *New directions for child development: Clinical–developmental psychology*. San Francisco: Jossey-Bass, 1980.

Haan, N., Smith, M. B., & Block, J. H. Moral reasoning of young adults: Political–social behavior, family background, and personality correlates. *Journal of Personality and Social Psychology*, 1968, *10*, 183–201.

Hamburg, B. Early adolescence: A specific and stressful stage of the life cycle. In G. Coelho, D. A. Hamburg, & J. E. Adams (Eds.), *Coping and adaptation*. New York: Basic Books, 1974.

Hardy, J. B., Welcher, D. W., Stanley, J., & Dallas, J. R. Long-range outcome of adolescent pregnancy. *Clinical Obstetrics and Gynecology*, 1978, *21*, 1215–1232.

Hassan, H. M., & Falls, F. The young primipara: A clinical study. *American Journal of Obstetrics and Gynecology*, 1964, *88*, 256–269.

Hatcher, S. L. M. The adolescent experience of pregnancy and abortion: A developmental analysis. *Journal of Youth and Adolescence*, 1973, *2*, 53–102.

Illinois Department of Public Health. *Vital statistics in Illinois 1977*, April 1980.

Inhelder, B., & Piaget, J. *The growth of logical thinking*. New York: Basic Books, 1958.

Johnson, C. L. *Child abuse in the Southeast: Analysis of 1172 reported cases*. Athens, Ga.: Regional Institution on Social Research, 1974.

Kantner, J. F., & Zelnik, M. Sexual experience of young unmarried women in the United States. *Family Planning Perspectives*, 1972, *4*, 9ff.

Kinard, E. M., & Klerman, L. V. Teenage parenting and child abuse: Are they related? *American Journal of Orthopsychiatry*, 1980, *50*, 481–488.

Klaus, M. H., Leger, T., & Trause, M. A. (Eds.). *Maternal attachment and mothering disorders: A round-table*. Conference sponsored by Johnson & Johnson Baby Products, Sausalito, Calif., October 1974.

Klue, R. A. *The relation of pregnant adolescents' conceptualizations of their unborn children to selected aspects of ego development*. Unpublished master's thesis, Smith College School of Social Work, 1980.

Leifer, M. Psychological changes accompanying pregnancy and motherhood. *Genetic Psychology Monographs*, 1979, *95*, 55–96.

Leifer, M. *Psychological effects of motherhood: A study of first pregnancy*. New York: Praeger Scientific (Praeger Special Studies), 1980.

Lorenzi, M. E., Klerman, L. V., & Jekel, J. F. School-age parents: How permanent a relationship? *Adolescence*, 1977, *12*, 13–22.

Marcia, J. E. Identity in adolescence. In J. Adelson (Ed.), *Handbook of adolescent psychology*. New York: Wiley, 1980.

McGanity, W. J., Little, H. M., Fogelman, A., Jennings, L., Calhoun, E., & Dawson, E. B. *American Journal of Obstetrics and Gynecology*, 1969, *103*, 773–788.

Mercer, R. T. Mothers' responses to their infants with defects. *Nursing Research*, 1974, *23*, 133–137. (a)

Mercer, R. T. Responses of mothers to the birth of an infant with a defect. In *American Nurses Association Clinical Sessions*. New York: Appleton-Century-Crofts, 1974. (b)

Moore, K. A., & Hofferth, S. L. *The consequences of early childbearing: Research summary results from the national longitudinal survey of young women*. Contract No. N01-HD-62829 (Urban Institute Project No. 9-0999), December 1977.

Mosher, C. *A study to explore the relationship between the mother's perception of herself and her experience during pregnancy, the infant's behavioral response patterns, and the mother's perception of her infant*. Unpublished master's thesis, University of Washington, 1972. (Cited in Barnard, K. The process of maternal acceptance. *Proceedings of the First Maternal–Infant Life Conference: The First Week of Neonatal Life*, Oshkosh, Wisc., 1973.)

Phipps-Yonas, S. Teenage pregnancy and motherhood: A review of the literature. *American Journal of Orthopsychiatry*, 1980, *50*, 403–431.

Rogel, M. J., Zuehlke, M. E., Petersen, A. C., Tobin-Richards, M., & Shelton, M. Contraceptive behavior in adolescence: A decision-making perspective. *Journal of Youth and Adolescence*, 1980, *9*, 491–506.

Roosa, M. W., Fitzgerald, H. E., & Carlson, N. A. *Teenage parenting and child development: A literature review*. Unpublished manuscript, Michigan State University, Institute for Family and Child Study, Mother–Infant Project, Report 2, 1980.

Rosenberg, M. *Society and the adolescent self-image*. Princeton, N.J.: Princeton University Press, 1965.

Rothstein, A. A. Adolescent males, fatherhood, and abortion. *Journal of Youth and Adolescence*, 1978, *7*, 203–214.

Schweitzer, B., & Youngs, D. D. A new professional role in the care of the pregnant adolescent. *Birth and the Family Journal*, 1976, *3*, 27–30.

Smetana, J. G. *Adolescent pregnancy and abortion: Developmental concerns*. Paper presented at the Annual Meeting of the American Psychological Association, Montreal, September 1980.

Smith, P. B., Mumford, D. M., Goldfarb, J. L., & Kaufman, R. H. Selected aspects of adolescent postpartum behavior. *The Journal of Reproductive Medicine*, 1975, *14*, 159–165.

Trussell, T. Economic consequences of teenage childbearing. *Family Planning Perspectives*, 1976, *8*, 184–190.

Zackler, J., Andelman, S., & Bauer, F. The young adolescent as an obstetric risk. *American Journal of Obstetrics and Gynecology*, 1969, *103*, 305–312.

Zelnik, M., & Kantner, J. F. Sexual activity, contraceptive use and pregnancy among metropolitan-area teenagers: 1971–1979. *Family Planning Perspectives*, 1980, *12*, 230–237.

7

PARENTHOOD ISSUES IN
THE AGING PROCESS

JEROME M. GRUNES

The concept of role reversal has entered the psychological literature but has not been clarified with any precision. What is commonly meant is that adult children take on parental prerogatives for their aged parents who become the children of their children. The plaint usually arises from the burdened adult child and is heard frequently in the consulting rooms of psychotherapists. What is less often voiced or even listened to is the parents' complaints about their children. I shall endeavor in this chapter to air what older people want from their children, the impasses that frequently occur between aged parent and adult children, and attempt to suggest certain ways to resolve such conflicts. I shall also try to delineate some theoretical concepts which may be of help in understanding the aged and their special relationships with their adult children.

The population that I will draw upon are people usually of 75 years or over who have led reasonable lives with successes and failures and who have not suffered from major, crippling psychopathology. I chose this group out of familiarity with them as I have been a psychiatric consultant to a home for the aged for more than 25 years and it is this group who generally have the problem of becoming a child to their children. I have eliminated those people with major psychopathology early in life, not because they become worse as they age (this may not be true at all) but because their psychopathology has clearly affected their children and predisposed them to view their parents as ill, defective, and stigmatized and therefore prone to regression whether this is accurate or not. For this chapter, I prefer to look at the "normal aged" or the aged who present with psychopathology for the first time later in life.

The aged never truly become children because development is a dialectic concept. As Benedek has written, development "refers to the interaction between maturational processes and environmental influences which lead to higher struc-

Jerome M. Grunes. Department of Psychiatry, Michael Reese Hospital and Medical Center, and Latter Half of Life Program, Northwestern University Medical School, Chicago, Illinois.

turalization and to individual variations in the psychic apparatus" (1952, p. 63). Progress, the successful completion of an early stage, precludes a total regression to a previous stage. The toddler never becomes the crawler except when he/she reverts to crawling under specific circumstances, for example as with the birth of a new sibling, but even in such situations, the regression is time limited. So, too, parenthood renders the return to childhood impossible except under certain states which will be illustrated later in this chapter.

The classical theory of development focuses on psychic conflict and its resolution. As development is a stepwise process, it then is apparent that the solutions of earlier psychic conflict need to be reworked as the cycle of life progresses. Each resolution contains elements of previous conflict and solution as well as responses to new developmental tasks. At such times, there is increased danger of the elements of past conflicts being revived. Thus, one can look at development from the point of view of the repetition of old impulses and old defenses emerging from early conflicts and requiring resolution at intervals during the person's life; or, one can focus on the developmental tasks which are age specific and require adaptation albeit using defenses which were successful in previous psychic conflict. Sigmund Freud (1905) was the first to uncover the early developmental problems related to infantile sexuality. This pioneering work led to a tendency to interpret all behavior on the basis of early conflicts and their vicissitudes, and the trend to view current problems as the result of poor early solutions. When one is dealing with an aged person who has traversed more or less successfully infancy, childhood, adolescence, and adulthood, it seems reductionistic to focus only on early developmental periods. Surely the human psyche is more complex and the multilayering of structure cannot be seen as emerging from early conflicts alone. Thus, too, regression is never complete, usually time limited, and certainly not to the earliest stages of life.

I shall now report four clinical vignettes. Each relates to the problem of psychopathology developing for the first time in aged individuals and in each situation the adult children were of significance in the development and solution of the conflicts which emerged in the aged parent.

An 80-year-old woman came for consultation at the insistence of her two daughters because of persistent mild depressive symptoms. When she called for an appointment, she told me that she was depressed because she had lost the love of her life. When she came into the office, she said that she was referring to her husband who had died some 10 years earlier. The symptoms about which she complained were lethargy, an inability to mobilize herself to shop for clothes or spend money. She was somewhat frugal. She tended to avoid social activities, and wished to remain in bed all day although she would dress and remain at home. The depression could not have been of 10 years' duration, I reasoned, as this lady appeared alert, vital, and even somewhat seductive. She then discussed recent events, and I began to understand her symptoms. The patient was the fourth in a sibship of seven. In the last 5 years she had lost five of her brothers and sisters. She was now the oldest living sister. The repeated illnesses, deaths, and the ensuing mourning processes had sapped the energy of this unusually energetic woman. She had always found men interesting and interested in her, and after her husband's death, had several relationships with men and had taken trips with them. Suddenly, she had begun to feel old, and fearful that she was no longer attractive. In reality, at 80, she was still a handsome woman. Her daughters reacted to the changes in their mother by becoming "bossy" and controlling. The patient was fearful of expressing her displeasure with them. She was afraid that they would abandon her. Although she was in need neither of financial nor of physical care from her daughters, she nevertheless needed them to respect and admire her. As a result she became extremely cautious in expressing herself whereas before this, she had been generally outspoken and direct. Her rage at her daughters for not giving her what she required was great, but her fear of losing her daughters as objects whose love and respect she needed was greater still. She felt that she needed an ally to resist being infantilized, for without someone to help her, she could not reestablish her self-esteem. The children, rather than recognize the burden of the mourning reactions and the fears of their mother's aging, preferred her to be what she had always been to them, active and interested in life, and were not above interfering with the patient's autonomy under the guise of maintaining her previous level of adjustment.

The patient, in the course of psychotherapy, avoided the temptation of infantilization, with the consequent loss of self-esteem, and of an open break with her daughters. Using the therapist as an authority, she asserted herself with her children and reestablished her autonomy while regaining their respect and admiration. In this case the patient's temporary regression due to repeated mourning reactions was overcome and she did not become a "child" to her children.

The second vignette is that of an 82-year-old woman who fell ill with a depression following cataract surgery. The patient's only wish was to be with her children. At home with her husband, she would moan and call for her dead mother. She could no longer keep house, much to the chagrin of her husband who, at age 86 and for the first time, had to shop and cook. His efforts failed to please his wife and he began to show depressive symptoms as well. The significant history was that her mother died when the patient was 16 years of age. Her father immediately remarried and the patient could not get along with her new stepmother. She felt that father had betrayed her mother by the unseemly haste in remarrying. She arranged to leave her native country and migrate to America to live with an aunt. Alone and unprepared, she set sail for the United States deeply unhappy. The patient always felt that she had not had a proper childhood. As a youngster (although she was not the eldest daughter), she had been the confidante of her mother. While this gave her a special position in the family, it had burdened her prematurely. Her siblings teased her by calling her an old woman and she remembers being a "worrier."

When the patient fell ill, she longed to be cared for by her daughter as she had longed to be cared for by her mother who had been sickly and needed nursing care. The daughter responded appropriately to the patient's feeling of helplessness but resisted being infantilizing, that is, responding to the regression in a total manner. Treatment helped the patient remobilize her considerable resources. The husband improved as well. The patient's need to be infantilized was replaced by a realistic view of herself as we reviewed her life. The daughter and the other children were at all times supportive of the patient and helpful at points of regression, but also were encouraging and hopeful of the patient's recovery.

This case illustrates that regressive wishes from past unfullfilled hopes can be dealt with by the family and in the therapeutic situation. It would seem that for a parent to become a "child" requires both the regressive wish of the parent and the active acquiescence of the significant family members as well.

The third clinical precis is the situation of a 76-year-old man whom I knew many years ago when he was a resident of a home for the aged. He had entered the institution following the death of his wife some 5 years earlier. He had become totally immobilized by the loss and could not manage to live alone in the community. He had attempted to live with his daughter but both were uncomfortable with this arrangement. His son tried also to be of help but his aid was insufficient. Eventually both children acceded to the patient's wish to enter the aged home.

The patient was a thin frail man who was an isolate in the institution. He spoke rarely to the other residents nor did he participate in any of the social activities. I saw him once a week for about 1 year when the following incident occurred. The interviews were rather strange in that the duration and the content were controlled by the patient. Mr. C would ask me for a cigarette, light it, and remain with me until his cigarette was finished. Then he would bounce up and leave, although I might be in the middle of a sentence or he may have not completed a thought. The subject of our talks were of his early life, which would be interspersed with discussions of current events. He had been a youth at the time of the intellectual ferment in Czarist Russia and had been converted to progressive views. He had broken with his tyrannical father and had run away from home at the age of 14 to join a gang of wild boys on the road. Eventually, he came to the United States, learned a trade, married, and had two children. His wife and his mother were two subjects he would not discuss. I developed the habit of bringing him *The New York Times* Sunday section reviewing the events of the week. One day as his cigarette was burning low and I knew our ritualized session was coming to an end, I mentioned that Mr. C was wearing worn and cracked shoes. I commented that he needed a new pair and suggested that he ask the housekeeper who was in charge of clothing to buy him a pair. When I returned the following week, Mr. C looked very serious. To my question of how he was feeling, he told me that he had wrestled with the possibility of suicide for much of the week. I was taken aback. He said that when I had commented on his shoes, he had felt mortified. What had he done to himself to have fallen into such a state that a doctor had to remind him that he needed to take care of himself! If he was so inadequate, he felt he should die. He spent three sleepless nights wrestling with these thoughts and finally came to the conclusion that the world was an interesting place. He wondered if he would see the day when some of his political ideals would be realized. He then decided to live. Within a matter of weeks he left the home albeit with a paranoid attitude toward the staff (except me) as a defense against the passivity he had displayed. He was able to find both a room for himself, and a job, and continued to see me for the next half year as an outpatient.

I recall this case surely not for the brilliance of my interpretive powers. I was completely unaware at that time of the significance of my comment about his shoes on this regressed and passive man. What has always impressed me is that this childlike man could return to his previous functioning after 5 years of institutionalization. Perhaps, like many persons who experience depression, he had suffered enough and had appeased his primitive conscience. Yet, the matter of the "screen interpretation" needs to be considered. As I look back, I am aware that I dealt this man a narcissistic blow, and that somehow the mortification reverberated with the old conflicts with his father. The old solution was to leave and reconstitute a self based on ideals which were inimical to those of his father. So, too, he was in advanced age able to reconstitute a self which had fallen apart at the time of the death of his wife, and basing himself on his youthful ideals and hope in a future in which ideals and reality were intertwined, reintegrated his personality.

The fourth case I would like to report was that of an 83-year-old man whose daughter, with whom he lived, noted a change in his personality. This man had been a house painter in his earlier years and had long since retired. Suddenly, he began to paint a neighbor's house, would climb ladders, and generally was unresponsive to her warnings of the danger of such proceedings. He turned a deaf ear to her entreaties and would be gone from the house for many hours without explaining his absences. While he had always been a quiet man, now he was almost mute when at home. The daughter took him to an internist who declared him physically fit, but this merely emphasized his unexplained personality alteration. I saw the patient who could not understand the reason for the visit to a psychiatrist. Nevertheless he was compliant and cooperative. At first, he merely spoke of his need to return to some activity from which his daughter barred him. Gradually he let me know that he was interested in a widow in the neighborhood and it was for her that he was painting the house. He loved his daughter but felt that she was interfering with his life. There was no evidence of organic signs. I then saw the daughter and after confronting her with the information that the father had given me, she began to weep. She told me that she knew of his lady friend but thought it ridiculous for a man of his age to get involved. She had promised her mother to care for the father when the mother lay dying 10 years before. She herself had done everything to make her father happy even to the point of neglecting her own family. The father's behavior had only made her feel betrayed and abused by his inability to appreciate her sacrifices. After this interview, it was decided that the father should live with another child and that the daughter seek treatment for herself.

This is not an uncommon phenomenom. The patient turned out to be the daughter, whose old unresolved problem with her father had come to the surface when he no longer acted into her fantasies of being a good wife–mother to him. The father's behavior may well have been in response to the daughter's increasing need to enact an Oedipal triangle using her old solution.

Unresolved, or more accurately poorly resolved, problems in parents and children do tend to surface during the parent's aging. In this case, an unresolved Oedipal situation came to light when the father sought a different solution than the one his daughter had expected of him.

Erik Erikson (1951), writing of the final stage of man, constructed the polarity of ego integrity versus despair, that is, the core of a firm self against the meaninglessness and emptiness of life. The task in aging for Erikson is to assess one's existence and to recognize either that it could not have been lived in any other way or to give way to the feeling of wasted time and wasted opportunities. While one rarely finds pure clinical types of the polar opposites that Erikson postulates, he is to be credited with defining an ego task for aging and for the recognition that development proceeds throughout the life cycle.

From the vantage point of the study of aging one is aware that the self should be the focus in treating late-life psychopathology. The concept of impulse and defense may be less appropriate to the later stages of life than is the self subjected as it is to dangerous dislocations during the later years. This is not to imply that structural conflicts, that is, within the tripartite model of the mind, do not exist in late life, but that such conflicts are muted and of less significance to psychopathology in the aged than are the issues of self and its steadiness and the vicissitudes of normal and pathological narcissism. Thus self psychology (Kohut, 1971) may be the proper arena for studying the coming of old age. Perhaps a better and more apt comment would be that the therapist and patient must Janus-like look back on old structural conflicts and forward to the struggle for narcissistic supplies for the continued health of the individual. Sophocles in his 90s looked at Oedipus at Colonus and, from a certain perspective, saw that he was not much changed from the arrogant Oedipus Rex particularly as he deals with his rebellious and disrespectful son, Polyneices. Continuity, and yet gradations of change, seem to be the goal of psychological growth. Further, one must remember that the self requires objects, be they selfobjects as Heinz Kohut has described or love objects in the more familiar libidinal sense. Moreover, love objects over time take on selfobject properties as any observer may note in old married couples, and selfobjects can be invested with libido as anyone can attest who has been the object of an erotic transference of an aged person.

Children are always seen, in part, as extensions of the parental self. This kernel of normal narcissism can become the basis for special problems in old age. In aging the fear of loss of control over one's body and of one's mind create the conditions for which parents are apt to use their children as selfobjects. I would prefer to use Winnicott's (1958) term of "transitional object" since it stresses the effect (i.e., soothing and reparative) which the self requires rather than the process ("mirroring" in Kohut's term). Transitional object, however, has a developmental ring which sounds unidirectional while Kohut's nomenclature suggests a developmental line with its vicissitudes. Also the point I wish to emphasize is that older people try to preserve what Federn (1952) has called the "ich-gefuhl," that is, the feeling of the self, to which I would add, the sense of the historic self over time. The need for reassurance from those who are more self than others, that is, one's children, as well as from the outside world, are the responses to anxieties which impoverish the self in aging. At times children blame their aged parents for their own inability to respond adequately to the emotional requirements of their parents. To control one's children, that is, to get a proper response when one cannot control the rest of one's internal and at times external environment, is of significance beyond the "manipulation" of which parents are often accused. With other child–parent interactions, one can find that the sameness of the parent may be insisted on despite the obvious changes which have occurred. Both child and parent become coconspirators in this denial; the former for fear of awakening past structural conflicts and the latter to preserve the illusions of the historical self. At times the child's insistance itself can become a hindrance to the parent who must try to live up to an ideal state that has long since been abandoned as impossible. Psychotherapy is quite helpful in such situations for both parent and child.

In the next section of this chapter, I should like to outline some aspects of the symptom of role reversal in the interaction of parent and adult child.

The stereotypic view of the aged stresses external losses. Implicit in this concept is that aging is an inevitable response to external losses. It is as if the significant idea that objects are internal representations and not simply external phenomena has been discarded in dealing with the aged. The result is therapeutic nihilism when it comes to treating the aged. A bias exists which views all older people as helpless victims of external circumstances and to consider that they suffer from the same difficulties and therefore should be treated in the same way. Newer perspectives are being developed which focus on the potentials for growth in the latter half of life (see Grunes, 1981; Gutmann, Grunes, & Griffin, 1980). These studies based on late-blooming psychopathology have helped identify age-specific issues in aging which, incidentally, appear to be different for men and women.

The role of parenting is a complex one which has its own development and corresponds to the child's specific needs. It includes the caretaking of the first 9 months of the infant's life (which Benedek has labeled as the mother–child unit or symbiotic phase). It also involves the capacity of the parent to permit the child to experience optimal frustration and even graded amounts of anxiety in order for the development of autonomy to take place. Parenting also includes the permission for the child to separate and individuate from the parents. If we use such a model, then the concept of role-reversal must include different and even at times antagonistic functions. Reversal of roles is generally thought of when the children become the caretakers of their parents. While it is true that under stress and development, some functions are temporarily suspended for the aged, the mere taking over of them by the child does not constitute role-reversal. Since such regressions are usually time limited, it merely means that the child fulfills the absent functions. It should be understood, however, that if the adult child persists in this role beyond its necessity, he/she may be threatening the integrity of the parent. This is illustrated in the first case where the parent could not risk alienating the child, feared acquiesing and lapsing into a helpless state. Even when certain functions are lost due to profound psychopathology such as in the third case, such aspects of the personality may be revived during the psychotherapeutic process. The percentage of aged who require total care is relatively low and even such people may continue to demonstrate their unique personalities, express their defects in specific ways, and may continue to have a range of affective responses which is quite appropriate despite profound cognitive deficits.

Caretaking then is not the only aspect of parenting. It is merely lending functions, usually temporarily but sometimes permanently, to parents who require such assistance. That this can be difficult for the adult child is unquestioned, but the underlying source of such difficulties should be determined, particularly if the child's distress is excessive. Some adult children feel pulled by what they perceive to be the demands of their own children and the needs of their parents. This may hide unresolved or poorly resolved early conflicts, as illustrated by the fourth case. It may involve rivalry with siblings which takes the form of "who is doing most for our aged parent?," that is, the need to prove one's "goodness" and to show up the other siblings. It may represent a respite from a bad marriage. Thus by focusing on the needs of the aged parent, the child can avoid the more serious difficulties at home.

At times I have seen children exhaust themselves for their parents when their rival is a dead and idealized sibling. They long for the parent to tell them that they are preferred over their dead rival, but to no avail, particularly if the rival was a child who died in early adulthood. Another common dynamic is for the child to deny the parent's aging as a means of denying his/her own aging process.

For the parent, caretaking can be associated regressively with being loved. If certain autonomous ego functions are impaired, then the help of children who perform such tasks—for example balancing a checkbook, or paying bills, or even serving as a "memory bank"—is a way for the parent to deny the loss of function. By having the function executed by a child, who is always in part a narcissistic object, the pain of the dislocation of self may be relieved. When there is a good functional relationship between parent and child, the adult child takes on the assigned tasks willingly and does not feel depleted by the effort, nor does he/she require undue gratitude from the aged parent. The adaptive paranoia of old age is an extreme example of denial of loss of functions and the projection onto the environment of the negative aspects of the self thereby retains the positive side internally. It is adaptive in as much as it wards off depression and encourages an active struggle with the outside world. Such people may be difficult for their children to cope with as they can be extremely hostile, and are obviously unappreciative of any acts of kindness by their children. The paranoia is generally benign. The aged rarely act upon their delusions, and the symptom may even be life saving in the acute phase.

In summary, I have discussed and illustrated with case material the complexity of reactions of adult children to their aged parents, and the obverse. The concept of role reversal has been examined and found wanting. It is imprecise and inaccurate and contains a bias against the aged. It should not be used in the literature without exact definition. From the viewpoint of phenomenology, what seems to occur in middle old age and old old age (see Bernice Neugarten's [1979] definition), is that certain functions are either temporarily or permanently impaired. These generally fall within the sphere of what Heinz Hartmann has called "autonomous ego functions" and include memory, judgment, perception, and motor activity. Children are expected to, and most often do, take over such tasks. The sensitivity of the adult child and the manner in which he/she fulfills this role is of significance to the aged parent. The sense of sameness of the self is crucial to aged people as they struggle with the specific tasks of the aging process. Derailments in the bond between adult child and parent may occur because of old structural conflicts in the child, too great expectations that children will be the unlimited suppliers of narcissism by parents, or by failures by both parent and child to relinquish the special roles when the acute, time-limited loss of function ends. The tendency for stereotypic responses by both child and parent predispose toward the helpless collapse of the parent's self, and the overburdened adult child's complaint which heretofore has been called "role reversal."

REFERENCES

Benedek, T. Personality development. In F. Alexander & H. Ross (Eds.), *Dynamic psychiatry.* Chicago: University of Chicago Press, 1952.

Erikson, E. *Childhood and society.* New York: Norton, 1951.

Federn, P. Ego psychology and the psychoses (E. Weiss, Ed.). New York: Basic Books, 1952.

Freud, S. Three essays on the theory of sexuality (1905). *Standard Edition, 7.* London: Hogarth Press, 1953.

Grunes, J. Reminiscences, regression and empathy—A psychotherapeutic approach to the impaired elderly. In S. Greenspan & G. Pollock (Eds.), *The course of life* (Vol. 3). Washington, D.C.: National Institute of Mental Health, U.S. Government Printing Office, 1981.

Gutmann, D., Grunes, J., & Griffin, B. The clinical psychology of later life: Developmental paradigms. In N. Datan & N. Lohmann (Eds.), *Transitions in aging.* New York: Academic Press, 1980.

Kohut, H. *The analysis of the self.* New York: International Universities Press, 1971.

Neugarten, B. Time, age and the life cycle. *American Journal of Psychiatry,* 1979. *136,* 887–894.

Winnicott, D. Transitional objects and transitional phenomena. In *Collected papers.* New York: Basic Books, 1958.

II

PSYCHOSOCIAL PERSPECTIVES

In approaching the psychosocial dimensions of the parenthood experience, we recognize a confluence of the biological, the psychological with its components of affect and mentation, and the continuous input from the sociocultural–economic–historical surround at any given time. Thus, a psychosocial perspective can be widely inclusive, or it can serve as a viewpoint with which to observe some interfaces in the adult parenthood experience among the inner life, social role, and environmental opportunities. As Grinker (1979) has stated:

> It is a simple matter to enumerate the various sciences that are significantly involved in understanding human behavior. These would, in general, include genetics, general biology, anatomy, physiology, biochemistry, pathology, psychology, and all of the social sciences. This is a vast array of disciplines, all of which should be recognized as extremely important for some aspect of behavior, although obviously as a group they cannot possibly be mastered by anyone person or even by a group of reasonable size. (p. 57)

With these precepts in mind, we present the following chapters. They do not, of course, encompass all of the psychosocial aspects of parenthood. Rather, they deal with certain active and reactive parenthood experiences which shape the life course and command the current attention of the clinician and the behavioral scientist.

The psychosocial perspectives the papers identify are the sequelae of recent social changes which have significant import for the ways in which adults experience parenthood. The issues are complex, linking the parenthood experience to skewed social circumstances, to changes in family structure by loss of marital partners, and to the ever-changing role of the state in its pursuit "of the best interests of the child" (Goldstein, Freud, & Solnit, 1979). All of the parenthood experiences which follow are experienced as stressful by adults because of their vulnerable psychological integration or because of increased demands upon their coping mechanisms for accommodation to changing social roles. Parenthood has the ubiquitous capacity to create regression, or at the least, to initiate fear of regression. How adults cope or fail in the response to the expected or unpredictable in the parenthood experience is a significant component of the quality of their lives.

Cohler's chapter deals with the initial phase of the parenthood experience. He presents the dilemma of young women who have been socialized in myths of the unalloyed joys of motherhood when faced with the impact of an experience which can resemble a crisis. While many are the joys of parenthood, it has not been easy for young parents, particularly women, to experience the ambivalence about parenthood without shame and lowered self-esteem. Cohler postulates further that women are especially vulnerable, psychologically, because of life-long problems created by the historical socialization of women into the role of mother rather than to adulthood in general.

Contrary to current belief that young families live in relative isolation from their parental generation, Cohler and Grunebaum (1981) have shown that the multigenerational family is so closely bonded that this very bondedness may be experienced as a stress which tends to increase rather than decrease anxiety and depression upon assumption of the maternal role. In his chapter, Cohler demonstrates, further, that the unresolved dependency issues between the young mother and her aging mother create much stress for the young mother. In the vulnerable group, those who require psychiatric hospitalization, there is a clear association of the development of psychopathology with assumption of the motherhood role. In his review of the stresses and strains incurred by mothers known to have had psychiatric illness prior to child rearing, Cohler indicates that these are similar to those found in the family experience, though with less intensity, of "ordinary" mothers of young children. Although not optimistic about a handy resolution for the compounded problems for young mothers, Cohler carves out the dimensions of the problem and presents some remedies.

Cohler's suggestions for improving the motherhood experience are based on the type of psychological affirmations required by adults as described in the concept of the parenting alliance developed by Cohen and Weissman in Chapter 3 of this volume. Programs geared to sustain the course of self-selfobject relationships in adulthood can maintain self-esteem, and stem the potential for regression. Cohler presents a warning as well as a challenge to social policy and mental health professionals responsible for the design of community programs congruent with human needs.

Burland and Hoffman present variants of dysfunctional parenting. Burland addresses the parenthood experience of poor ghetto residents, predominantly young women, whose life experiences of deprivation are so similar to those of their own children that there seems to be little developmental generation gap. The mothers under consideration by Hoffman are seen in private practice and bring with them a range of social resources and options. We can assume that their social frameworks provide much opportunity to acquire ego strengths regardless of their childhood life experiences. Both, however, experience parenthood as stressful, though there are significant differences in how life is experienced.

Parenthood to Burland's dysfunctional parents cannot be experienced as a "second chance." Most parents are endowed with accumulated psychic resources which support their egos, as well as love for the child, which includes the ubiquitous hope that the child will fare better than the parent. Also, parents are motivated to help the children achieve their developmental goal. Although this is a conscious operation, a parent will rework his/her own unconscious conflicts which relate to the child's developmental task and achieve a new level of maturation.[1] Hoffman's parents can utilize interventions which sustain previously acquired competence and facilitate transformations from early and current experiences into a more integrated adulthood. Burland's group expects no growth, no mastery, but rather an opportunity to obtain narcissistic gratification. No wonder the rage and helplessness which occur when the incompetent infant fails to comply! Moreover, further insult is inevitable because these weakly attuned-to-baby mothers cannot elicit rewarding responses from the infant. Mother and baby are left to engage in a recycling of multigenerational early chronic depressions which pervade their lives. Hoffman's group, in bringing the child for help, expect, at least, better success in the parenthood experience.

Burland presents the mental health professionals who confront the dysfunctional ghetto parenting experience with a challenge. To provide services which can address the needs of the children in this population, a systematic program of interventions directed to the mothers must be designed so as to provide them with the emotionally necessary selfobject (real and transference) relationships they need so desperately. Burland, in an elegant use of countertransference, presents a moral dilemma. Because our own humanity tends to distance us from close engagement with this tragic mother–child dyad, we have been unable to develop urgently needed research programs which require an intense and empathic involvement with them. This tends to stretch and stress the limits of human capacity. Burland is firm, however, in his position that this is both a worthy and necessary humanistic and scientific endeavor.

Hoffman's operational model is based on a broader conceptualization of a parent's motivations and behavior and not just as the source of a history. Hoffman regards the parents' communications from the inner experience of parenthood—the wishes, fantasies, and aspirations for the child and himself/herself—as the interface for child, parent, and child therapist.

Implicit in Hoffman's view of working with parents is the stance of collegiality. He acknowledges that both therapist and parent have an investment in the child and the therapy. He places responsibility, however, for the management of the inevitable stress which envelops the encounter between the parent and child therapist upon the therapist. His integration of the adult experience, the injured parental narcissism and transference reactions to the child and his/her therapist is not limited to the potential for regression. Rather, he identifies the struggle of an adult for growth. Seemingly, the uniqueness of the encounter with

1. The concept of the "second chance" is derived from Benedek's discussion (Anthony & Benedek, 1970) of "processes which indicate that the reworking of childhood conflicts leads to resolving them, i.e., to intrapsychic changes in the parents" (p. 131). See Elson, Chapter 20, this volume, for a self psychology presentation of the "second chance."

the child therapist is the opportunity for the parent to improve self-esteem in the context of an adult self–selfobject relationship.

Much of the literature emphasizes parenthood as a normal developmental experience. Although parents must rework or complete earlier developmental tasks, we must not assume that this will become pathological. As has been noted, here, and elsewhere in this volume, however, the predominant risk for adults in the parenthood experience is its potential to initiate regression. Essentially, public policy which promotes ''the best interests of the child'' evolved in response to the social needs of children when illness or regression has caused parents to become dysfunctional. Mikva and Solnit believe that the activity of the law and the state should be restricted and used as emergency devices to preserve the primacy of the parenting function in the family. Where regression, no matter what the source, has occurred the law must be called upon to create stability in the environment of the child. Therefore, the effects of family disruption have been studied largely from the vantage point of the child.

The chapters by Bohannan, Garber, Feinstein and Davis, and Hagestad, Smyer, and Stierman deal with adults reacting to a major life stress—a failed marriage. Where there are children, the stresses in the failure of the marital alliance are compounded as the couple confronts parenting concerns. Those chapters which focus on the clinical situation demonstrate the failure of the parents to stem regression at numerous phases of the marital conflict and eventual divorce. Garber indicates, further, that even when the divorce is long past and the child is engaged in a psychotherapy, those parents whose regression was severe are continuously vulnerable to further regression. As long as the child needs their care, parenting remains the substrate for continuing their hostile interactions.

Feinstein and Davis present divorce mediation and arbitration as techniques which can abort or stem hostile interactions and thereby sustain higher level parental functioning. Bohannan's conviction that the parenting relationship between the divorced couple[2] endures wherever possible follows Feinstein and Davis in focusing on maintaining family operations, though they will be structured differently after divorce. Bohannan deals with a later configuration—the stepfamily. He also points to the need for a continuous coparent dyad for the successful negotiation of future tasks for the adults and children. Bohannan indicates that the complexity of relationships in a stepfamily can be mitigated by recognizing some of its similarities to the nuclear family and some of its uniqueness. He presents the hope that further research on the stepfamily will reveal more than we know now about the successful ones. Currently, we know most about those who come for therapeutic assistance.

Garber's clinical data will startle the reader because of the regressive quality of responses in parents, grandparents, and teachers to the child of divorce. By comparing the resources of that latter group to the more sustaining responses of

2. For further discussion of the relationship between the parents, see Cohen and Weissman, Chapter 3, this volume.

the parents, family, and school personnel to the child whose parent died, he indicates that we must consider that the death of a parent can be less traumatic for children than that of an ongoing battle between living, divorced parents. This suggests, once again, that the preservation of the parenting alliance for divorcing parents must become a critical aspect of sustaining programs and clinical interventions.

Mikva and Solnit present current thinking in family law. Here, judge and child psychoanalyst construct their arguments out of the conviction that as much conflict as possible be resolved within the family. Although their argument reflects optimism because the majority of family conflicts (including custody battles) are being resolved outside of the courts, they are mindful of the need to call in the mental health professional when parents and children become dysfunctional.

Life-course study reinforces the desirability of caution in predicting adult effectiveness from any particular developmental period in childhood. Although Garber's child patients who lost parents by divorce have far fewer dependable support systems than those bereaved by death of a parent, clinical study of the adult life course of the latter group shows that their adult parenthood experience can be stressful and dysfunctional. Psychoanalysis, both as a theory of how people think, feel, and behave, and as a clinical intervention, has directed much attention to understanding the meaning of childhood separations and losses for later adult functioning. Altschul and Beiser demonstrate that early parent loss can produce vulnerabilities for adults who parent, deficits in their parenting, or the need to avoid a parenting experience. Often, only a therapeutic experience will produce the necessary resolution of the conflicting issues leading to parental regression. They indicate that psychoanalysis or a more educationally directed therapy can be effective if applied differentially.

Hagestad directs our attention to the enduring and critical nature of the parent–child bond. She indicates that a divorce between a couple has intergenerational impact which creates much change in the shape and content of the parenting experience during later years as well as earlier ones. This moves us to consideration of the losses of self-esteem and regressive potential in the parenthood experience through the complete life span. Hagestad includes, furthermore, the effects of divorce on the experience of parenthood in later life and upon grandparenthood. She points up the deficiency in the study of the impact of divorce for adult offspring and upon the parents of a divorcing couple. This lack must be remedied, she argues, to improve our designs for interventions with families and individuals affected by divorce. Moreover, further study of the effects of divorce across the life cycle will provide the "significant building blocks" for theoretical work about the continuity of parent–child relationships and shifts in generational constellations. By enlarging our view of the longitudinal impact of divorce, we recognize, once again, the significance of the parenthood experience and its integral role in maintaining self-esteem throughout the adult life course.

REFERENCES

Anthony, E. J., & Benedek, T. B. (Eds.). *Parenthood: Its psychology and psychopathology.* Boston: Little, Brown, 1970.

Cohler, B., & Grunebaum, H. *Mothers, grandmothers, and daughters: Personality and child care in three-generation families.* New York: Wiley, 1981.

Goldstein, J., Freud, A., & Solnit, A. J. *Beyond the best interests of the child.* New York: Free Press–Macmillan, 1979.

Grinker, R. R., Sr. *Fifty years in psychiatry: A living history.* Springfield, Ill.: Charles C Thomas, 1979.

8

PARENTHOOD, PSYCHOPATHOLOGY, AND CHILD CARE

BERTRAM J. COHLER

Parenthood represents the cardinal social role and major developmental task of adulthood, beginning with the birth of the first child and continuing through old age. While clearly a source of satisfaction and joy, the advent of motherhood may also be a source of strains portrayed by Gutmann (1975) as a "period of chronic emergency." As children become adults, marry, and have children of their own, grandparenthood succeeds parenthood, and may evoke, once more, the same ambivalence experienced with the advent of parenthood. Across adulthood, parenthood continues as a major developmental organizer of personality, including the source of continuing conflict, as past unites with present in determining important attitudes and actions regarding the care of succeeding generations (Benedek, 1959).

As a social role, parenthood is central both to the family and the larger society. Clearly, the family represents the foundation of social life, and is the most elementary, self-sustaining social institution capable of maintaining the reproducing itself (Parsons, 1955) and, as a consequence, society as a whole. Important functions of the family are fulfilled through socialization, which refers to the means by which family members are taught, and by which they learn, aspects both of society, including status and role, and culture, including values and other symbolic meanings. Further, as a result of this socialization process, beginning with earliest infancy, enduring motivational dispositions and concepts of self are learned which comprise personality (Parsons, 1955). Both as a reflection of parental regard for the child, and as a result of the child's experience of the parents as sources of tension management and regulation of self-regard, the child evolves a sense of self.

Parenthood begins with the sudden shift from responsibility solely for self to the care of another. No prior preparation can fully anticipate the significance

Bertram J. Cohler. Departments of Behavioral Science (Committee on Human Development), Education, and Psychiatry, and the College, University of Chicago, Chicago, Illinois.

of becoming a parent, including both care for a dependent child, and also the particular skills which are required in order to understand and meet the child's needs (Rossi, 1968; Lopata, 1971). As a result, parents may experience a sense of helplessness in which demands for child care become merged with other developmental tasks experienced in adulthood, including the care of the parent's own aging parents. While a number of studies have shown that both parents experience the advent of parenthood as a crisis in their own lives, from the outset, the advent of parenthood is felt particularly as a crisis by women (LeMasters, 1957, 1970; Yalom, Lunde, Moos, & Hamburg, 1968; Jacoby, 1969; Russell, 1974; Gutmann, 1975; Bernard, 1975; Hobbs & Cole, 1976; Alpert & Richardson, 1980; Entwisle & Doering, 1981). As Lopata (1966, 1971) has noted in this regard, motherhood is a stage in the life cycle which, even for women without predisposition to mental illness, permits little preparation and arrives with shocking suddenness. Only widowhood or other losses by death evoke a greater sense of crisis for the wife and mother in contemporary society.

Although changes in definitions of sex roles for mothers and fathers over the past decade have meant that more of the task of caring for young children may be divided between the two parents, it is nevertheless still true that mothers still view themselves, and are viewed by others, as the primary caretakers for infants and preschool children (Hoffman, 1977). Given the ambiguity which is inherent in the woman's own socialization across the life cycle, the continuing expectation that women should serve as the kin-keepers, and the reality that women typically spend more hours at home with the children than men do, many of the role strains realized with the advent of parenthood are more strongly experienced by mothers than by fathers. While the advent of parenthood may lead to some lasting impairment in the mental health of each parent, it is particularly among mothers that this adverse effect has been noted (Campbell, Converse, & Rogers, 1976; Gove & Geerken, 1977; Gove & Tudor, 1977; Goldman & David, 1980). Further since mothers are still the primary caretakers in this society, impairment in maternal mental health, sometimes even resulting in psychiatric hospitalization, is likely to have a particularly deleterious impact upon the childrens' own adjustment.

The present chapter considers the impact of parenthood as a social role upon the adjustment of mothers of young children, including factors leading to the development of psychiatric illness in the first years after becoming a mother. This chapter considers parenthood from the perspective of the mother's own life, focusing upon some possible solutions for the problems encountered in maintaining a satisfactory adjustment among both well mothers and those formerly hospitalized.

BECOMING A MOTHER

Motivation for Parenthood

Over the course of the past decade, particularly as a result of rethinking women's roles in contemporary society, there has been increased interest in factors associated with the decision to have children (Hoffman & Hoffman, 1973), together with increased discussion of alternatives to what Russo (1976, 1979) has termed the "motherhood mandate." Particular interest has been shown in the phenomenon of voluntary childlessness, the decision on the part of otherwise fecund couples not to have any children (Veevers, 1973a, 1973b, 1979; Freshnock & Cutright, 1978). Since this decision contradicts one of the prerequisites for the existence of society itself, that of reproducing itself over time (Radcliff-Brown, 1952; Parsons, 1951), it leads to what is regarded as a deviant position in society.

Reviews by Pohlman (1970), Bram (1978), and Veevers (1979), together with national survey findings (Veroff, Douvan, & Kulka, 1981), suggest that only a small proportion of couples (1–3%) elect to remain childless, and that this decision is generally made by highly educated, late-marrying, nontraditional couples, each of whom has a high-income job. Although some feminist critics have suggested that the decision to have children is largely inspired by the husband's more traditional "pro-natalist" stance (Hare-Mustin & Broderick, 1979), most research suggests that women electing to remain voluntarily childless are motivated for such reproductive freedom principally by the opportunities of the labor market (Ritchey & Stokes, 1974). Houseknecht (1979) notes that, in addition, women electing to postpone having children have been raised by mothers who value achievement to a greater extent than women having children earlier in the marriage, while Veevers (1979) suggests these childless women are more often first-born or only children. Rabin and Greene (1968) report that students anticipating having children when married are more altruistic and less "narcissistic" than those anticipating childlessness. Comparing childless women choosing traditional contraception or tubal ligation, Kaltreider and Margolis (1977) report that women determined not to have children were not only less traditional in their values, but also less comfortable and certain of their own identity, and less able to report capacity for intimacy. However, Kaltreider and Margolis note a common fear among all women in their study electing childlessness of a fear of becoming increasingly like their own mother after having children.

While women electing voluntary childlessness may be less motivated to provide nurturance, and more concerned with their own personal and social advancement (Wyatt, 1967, 1971; Stewart, 1980), there is little evidence that this decision is, itself, associated with impaired mental health. On the contrary, several studies have reported that childless women are happier than their counterparts electing to have children (Humphrey, 1975; Malmquist & Kaij, 1971; Andrews & Withey, 1976). Findings from survey studies (Renne, 1976; Campbell, Converse, & Rodgers, 1976; Gove & Geerken, 1977) suggest that childless women report more positive morale than their counterparts with children, particularly during the years when there is at least one child under the age of 6. Studies reviewed by Veevers (1979) of marital morale among childless couples and those with children show that feelings of satisfaction with the marriage are likely to be greater where there are no children than where the couple have children, although, as Blood and Wolfe (1960) have noted, the major deleterious impact upon morale occurs where there are a large number of children. Findings of Campbell, Converse, and Rodgers (1976), Rollins and Galligan (1978), and Rossi (1980) suggest both morale and the quality of the marriage vary with place in the family lifecycle; both during the preparental phase, and after all children are teenagers, mothers and fathers experience a better marriage and greater life-satisfaction than when there are young children at home.

Transition to Motherhood

During pregnancy, a woman, her husband, and their parental families can prepare for the new role, but no preparation can anticipate the full reality of the event itself (Grossman, Eichler, Winickoff, & Associates, 1980; Entwisle & Doering, 1981). Time, energy, and emotional resources must now be shared, and even sleep is sacrificed for the baby's welfare. Although there is some controversy in the literature regarding the manner in which it is measured, systematic research suggests that most mothers do experience this transition as a crisis (LeMasters, 1957; Dyer, 1963; Meyerowitz & Feldman, 1960; Arasteh, 1971; Shereshefsky & Yarrow, 1973; Russell, 1974; Hill, 1978). Hobbs (1965) and Hobbs and Cole (1976) report that, while transition to parenthood is, indeed, experienced as a strain, the severity of the crisis is not as great as other studies purport to show. Much of the controversy in this area is affected by the manner in which the questions are asked and the scores are weighted (Jacoby, 1969; Hobbs & Cole, 1976); findings suggest that the advent of parenthood affects the new mother's self-esteem as well as the quality of her relationship with her husband (Ballou, 1978a, 1978b; Rollins & Galligan, 1978; Hoffman & Manis, 1978; Grossman et al., 1980).

Contrary to popular stereotype, stress associated with the transition to parenthood is associated less directly with pregnancy than with childbirth and the first postpartum months. Pugh, Jerath, Schmidt, and Reed (1963), in a careful epidemiological study of first admissions to Massachusetts psychiatric hospitals during one calendar year, find that the risk of mental illness is actually lower during pregnancy than would be expected by chance alone; significantly greater than chance for the first three postpartum months; lower than expected due to chance for the 4th through 6th months; and significantly greater than chance alone by the end of the first postpartum year. Similar findings have been reported by Paffenbarger and McCabe (1966). These studies show a clear association between assumption of the maternal role and the development of psychiatric illness during the postpartum period.

Some psychiatric symptoms are quite common in the months following childbirth, even among mothers who are not mentally ill, particularly among first-time parents (Entwisle & Doering, 1981; Cutrona, 1982). Jacobson, Kaij, and Nilsson (1965) report that depression, fatigue, and irritability were present in well over one third of the postpartum women in their sample. Yalom and his associates (1968) report that more than half the women in their normal postpartum sample showed signs of depression, including crying, during the first weeks after delivery. Yalom and his colleagues noted other evidence of postpartum emotional distress, including undue concern about the baby, fatigue, irritability, and insomnia. Melges (1968) notes a common syndrome in postpartum women, consisting of feelings of shame, helplessness, and confusion. Melges also notes that laboratory studies ruled out the possibility of endocrine factors as a determinant in this postpartum emotional distress. Especially interesting in the context of the present discussion, the same syndrome was noted among women adopting a baby as was noted among women delivering a baby. While this may represent modeling in conformity to culturally expected patterns of reacting to childbirth, it is clear that, even among women referred to by Middlemore (1941) and by Robertson (1962) as "ordinary devoted mothers," transition to motherhood is a unique developmental crisis in the life cycle (Cutrona, 1982).

A study by a group of Scandinavian investigators (Malmquist & Kaij, 1971) has used an ingenious twin design in examining this hypothesis. A sample was gathered consisting of monozygous twins, of whom one had married and had one child, and the other had not yet had a child. Twins and children showed a significantly greater number of psychiatric symptoms than those who had not yet had a child, and these symptoms were especially noticeable among younger women who, it was believed, felt especially burdened by the conflicting demands of marriage and parenthood. Even when both twins were married, the twin with children showed a greater number of psychiatric symptoms. Mothers with two children showed a greater number of symptoms than those with one child, suggesting the cumulative stress which occurs with increasing numbers of children.

MOTHERHOOD AND FAMILY BONDS

Recognizing the degree of life stress and role strain which is the effect of assuming the maternal role (Makosky, 1980; Radloff, 1980), it is widely believed that support provided within the family context could relieve some of this strain, but that the degree of geographic and social mobility characteristic of contemporary society militates against the use of family members in this way. However, studies of family life suggest that the presumed value of the family in supporting the mother of young children is much more complex than generally believed, and that the very relationship between the generations is as much a source of strain as of support.

A major source of strain in the maternal role is the belief prevalent in American society that aspects of maternal care represent the most important determinant of the child's later adjustment, even when, as is typical for assistance, it is believed not to be acceptable for the mother of young children to turn to her own family for help (Fischer & Fischer, 1963). After the first few postpartum weeks, parents are expected to manage the task of child care without the assistance of the extended family. Grandparents are often unenthusiastic about helping with child care (Cohler & Grunebaum, 1981). In the first place, grandparenthood is a role which grandparents themselves do not elect (Rosow, 1967). For many grandparents, assumption of this role is a clear sign of aging. Tension between the generations resulting from differences in child-rearing attitudes and practices further intensifies conflict between parents and grandparents. Partially as a result of the grandparents' own aging, partially as a result of the grandparents' own particular life experiences, and partially as a result of grandparents' particular place in the life cycle of the family, their advice tends to be more conservative and inflexible than is acceptable among parents of young children. Further, having raised their own children, grandparents are reluctant to assume once more the demands of caring for young children. Problems in realizing assistance from grandparents in contemporary urban society are due much more to conflict between the generations than to the physical availability of grandparents (Wood & Robertson, 1976).

Particular tensions arise between the mother of young children and her own mother which are inspired both by the nature of family structure in American society, and the process of preadult socialization of girls. This tension may lead to continuing ambivalence between these two generations of adult women which is further intensified by the daughter's assumption of the maternal role and increasing complementarity between her own life situation and that of her middle-aged mother.

Women and Asymmetry in Kinship Relations

Although it has been widely believed (Wirth, 1938; Parsons, 1949; Ogburn, 1953), that rapid urbanization and accompanying social and geographic mobility has had a detrimental impact on kinship relations within the extended family unit in contemporary society, several decades of research have shown that this stereotype does not correspond to the reality of family life (Sussman, 1959, 1965; Shanas, 1961a, 1961b, 1968; Reiss, 1962; Leichter & Mitchell, 1967; Adams, 1968, 1970). Indeed, available evidence suggests that the kind of extended family characteristic of preliterate traditional societies has never existed in America, and may not have existed in Western Europe either, at least since the Reformation (Demos, 1974; Laslett, 1965, 1977).

While kinship relations in American society are supposed to be governed by the principle of bilateral symmetry, there is, in fact, considerable asymmetry, with greater contact maintained between the wife and her parental family than between the husband and his parental family (Fischer & Fischer, 1963; Sweetser, 1963, 1964, 1966). Indeed, reviewing studies of intergenerational relations reported in the literature, two conclusions have been reported in nearly every such study:

1. The single most important family tie is that between mother and daughter,

which provides the basis for family continuity (Glick, 1957; Komarovsky, 1962; Aldous, 1967).

2. This tie is particularly pronounced across working-class famiilies, who show, in general, a greater degree of shared agreement in attitudes and values and more frequent contact in intergenerational visiting than is true within middle-class families (Young & Willmott, 1957; Sussman, 1960; Rosenberg, 1970; Rosenberg & Anspach, 1973; Fried, 1973; Lee, 1980).

These two conclusions obtain even when there is occupational and geographic mobility, and even moves across the country (Fried & Stern, 1948; Reiss, 1962; Robins & Tomanec, 1962; Komarovsky, 1962; Sweetser, 1963, 1964; Hagstrom & Hadden, 1965; Aldous & Hill, 1965; Farber, 1971; Bernardo, 1967; Leichter & Mitchell, 1967).

There are at least two reasons why the relationship between mother and daughter is particularly important in providing for intergenerational continuity. In the first place, it would be difficult for a woman to obtain as much consensus with her mother-in-law as with her own mother regarding desirable ways of caring for the house or raising children. Having lived with her mother for so many years, and having been socialized by her mother in her conception of her roles as housewife, wife, and mother, it is likely that a daughter will agree with her mother regarding fundamental aspects of family life.

In the second place, as Komarovsky (1950, 1962) and Robbins and Tomanec (1962) have shown, culture itself intensifies the continuing dependence of a woman on her own family during adulthood, with daughters expected to be more available than sons for family errands, for fulfilling kinship obligations, and for serving as "kin-keepers." As Young and Geertz conclude, on the basis of their cross-national survey:

> In all industrial countries, because of the similarities in their occupational structures, the tie between mothers and daughters is more strongly stressed than that between mothers or sons or between fathers and either sons or daughters, the strength or significance of the tie varying for social groups such as class. If we are right, daughters and mothers are the organizers of the wider family and the repositories of information about it, and form the central nerves of the loose but still highly important kinship network which is characteristic of modern society. (1961, p. 133)

As a result of socialization into culturally determined conceptions of appropriate feminine behavior, women within Western European and American society develop a greater need than men for affiliative relationships, and tend to value participation in extended family relationships to a greater degree than men (Parsons, 1955; Maccoby, 1968; Chodorow, 1974, 1978). Although it has been suggested that women are constitutionally more dependent and emotionally expressive than men (Diamond, 1965), most anthropological research suggests that cultural factors are of far greater significance (Mead, 1935; D'Andrade, 1966) in determining such sex differences.

Within our own culture, perhaps the most detailed description of the socialization of dependence found among women has been provided by Komarovsky (1950, 1962) and by Chodorow (1978) who suggest that women are socialized from early childhood into their role of kin-keeper and expressive leader within the family. She suggests that while parents encourage independence from the family among boys, they encourage dependence upon the family among girls. Boys are provided with greater incentive for activities which are independent of the family and are permitted greater privacy in personal affairs. Girls are encouraged to run errands and to help other family members, and are more likely than boys to be pressured into attending family rituals. Komarovsky suggests that this childhood socialization is functional in training boys and girls in their respective sex roles:

> The role of the provider, on the one hand, and of the homemaker on the other, call for different attitudes and skills. Competitiveness, independence, dominance, aggressiveness, are all traits felt to be needed by the future head of the family. Although the girl can train for her adult role and rehearse it within the home, the boy prepares for *his* outside the home, by taking a "paper route" or a summer job away from home. . . . The greater sheltering of the girl has, as unintended by-products, further consequences for kinship roles which are not perceived. (1950, p. 512)

This greater sheltering of the girl within the home, while it provides socialization into the "domestic" role, may also impair the young woman's ability to develop a more independent life outside the family and to adapt successfully to her role as wife and mother within her own marital family. While women may attempt to use the instrumental skills they were taught during childhood, both the asymmetry of the American kinship system and socialization into the dependent–expressive role within the family make it difficult for women to relinquish their ties to their own parental family. In addition, such continuing attachment to her own parental family means that additional conflict is created between a woman and her husband's parental family: Women typically choose to spend holidays with their own parental family, and are likely to place obligations to their own family above those to their husband's family (Cohler & Grunebaum, 1981). Wallin (1954) and Gray and Smith (1960) both report that, among young couples living some distance away from their own parents, wives were more homesick for their parents than husbands were for their parents. Stryker (1955) also reports that women are more attached than men to their own parental family.

This pattern of continued dependence on her own parental family for advice and assistance during the time the mother is caring for her young children is particularly striking within working-class families (Glick, 1957; Komarovsky, 1962). Fried (1973), in discussing this greater dependence of working-class women on their own parental family, suggests that working-class women experience with particular intensity the value upon close interpersonal relationships characteristic of working-class culture as contrasted with the emphasis upon technical mastery reflected by middle-class culture. Similar views have been expressed as a result of numerous comparative studies of middle-class and working-class families (Rainwater, Coleman, & Handel, 1959; Miller & Riessman, 1961; Dyer, 1963; Paterson, 1964; Rainwater & Handel, 1964; Aldous, 1967; Kohn, 1969; Kohn & Schooler, 1969).

Kin Keeping, Motherhood, and Mental Health

No single family member has as much contact with relatives on both sides of the family as the mother of young children, particularly within working-class families. According to the normative definition of the woman's role within the family, she is expected to be the "kin-keeper," and to provide the bridge between the generations. Such contact is maintained irrespective of extent of affectional bonds, but also exposes the mother to continuing conflict within the family. Her own efforts at socializing her mother into new ways of bringing up children according to the beliefs of her own generation further increase the extent of this intergenerational conflict.

Once married, although she may work for a period of time prior to the birth of her first child, a woman in our society is expected to become involved in the interpersonal world of the family. Consistent with Parsons's (1955) and Gutmann's (1975) characterization of the father's role within the family as the instrumental or task leader, national survey findings reported by Veroff, Douvan, and Kulka (1981) suggest that men and women perceive the parental role as most salient for women, and the role of worker as most salient for men. The woman's role within the family is primarily that of expressive or emotional leader, who provides support for her husband and children, in their struggles with work and children, even in the more than half of all families in which the wife and mother also holds at least a part-time job. In addition to this responsibility, the woman is supposed to be the "kin-keeper" in the family (Firth, Hubert, & George, 1970), maintaining contact with relatives, including both the woman's own parents and those of her husband. The priority which the wife is expected to give to her roles as mother and wife, may create a particularly high degree of role overload and conflict, and consequent feelings of strain, within what Rapoport and Rapoport (1971) have termed the "dual-career" family (Johnson & Johnson, 1977; Gilligan, 1979; Dunlop, 1981; Marecek & Ballou, 1981; Zaslow & Pedersen, 1981). Komarovsky (1962) and Chodorow (1974, 1978) have noted the extent to which women are socialized into the role of "kin-keeper" and "expressive leader" from earliest childhood. This expressive role, which becomes so much a part of the adult woman's life, particularly with the advent of parenthood (Hoffman, 1978; Cowan, Cowan, Coie, & Coie, 1980), especially within the working-class family (Rainwater, Coleman, & Handel, 1959; Komarovsky, 1962; Rubin, 1976), may also be a major source of role strain for the wife and mother within these tightly knit families (Bott, 1971; Cohler & Lieberman, 1980).

Ironically, it is this very closeness to relatives, including continuing inter-generational exchange of resources and assistance, which is the source of much of the strain which women report regarding their roles as mother and daughter. Socialized since early childhood into the role of "expressive leader" within the family (Parsons, 1955), women are exposed to greater role strain than their husbands who can escape family crises through increased involvement in their work. As a result of the role strain experienced by even the "ordinary devoted mother," many women with still dependent children experience lowered morale and feelings of sadness and lack of self-worth. These feelings of depression, common among mothers of newborns (Yalom, Lunde, Moos, & Hamburg, 1968), persist beyond the postpartum period, throughout the entire time that a woman is responsible for the care of still dependent children (Myrdal & Klein, 1956; Gavron, 1966). Gove (1972), Gove and Tudor (1972), and Goldman and David (1980) note that mental illness, particularly depression, is more common among women than among men, and that married women appear to be more at risk than single women. Systematic research by Brown, Bhrolchain, and Harris (1975), Brown and Harris (1975), and by Pearlin (1975) shows that women are particularly at risk for depression. Findings by Brown *et al.* (1975) and by Siassi, Crocetti, and Spiro (1974) suggest that the working-class woman is particularly likely to be depressed, even when class differences in stress levels are controlled. Similar conclusions regarding the increased vulnerability of women to depression are reported by Pearlin (1975), Radloff (1975, 1980), Ripley (1977), Belle (1980), Goldman and David (1980), Amenson and Lewinsohn (1981), Boyd and Weissman (1981), and, in unusually thoughtful and encyclopedic review articles, by Weissman and Klerman (1977) and Klerman and Weissman (1980). After considering the several alternative biological, sociocultural, and psychodynamic explanations for this greater prevalence of depression among women, these investigators conclude that explanations based on the nature of a woman's conflicting adult roles fit best with findings reported in the literature.

Weissman and Klerman's reviews of findings regarding prevalence of depression in women supports the model of "learned helplessness" (Seligman, 1974, 1975) in which dependency is learned as a mode of adaptation in preadult socialization. This learned helplessness is particularly salient among working-class women, who are particularly bound into a complex set of kinship obligations (Rainwater et al., 1959; Komarovsky, 1962; Rainwater & Handel, 1964; Rubin, 1976). Problems created by expectations of care for a large circle of relatives are compounded by increased tensions which women in working-class families may be expected to manage as a result of their husband's work. As Kohn (1969) and Kohn and Schooler (1969) have shown, working-class men are expected to be more conforming and subservient at work than their middle-class counterparts. As a result, feelings of resentment and hostility arise which cannot be expressed within the workplace. These feelings are then likely to be expressed within the home, leading to the increased hostility noted within working-class as contrasted with middle-class households.

Such problems have a particular impact upon the wife. In a study of working-class families reported by Siassi *et al.* (1974), working-class men were not found to express the alienation supposed by Marxist criticism of the division of labor. However, wives of these working-class men were found to be pervasively depressed, suggesting that the nature of the social relations within the workplace may have a significant impact upon the family because of the expectation that the wife and mother should become the repository of her husband's tensions and problems: If the blue-collar worker is not as troubled as might be expected, it is because he sheds these tensions at home which are then borne by his wife (similar findings have also been reported by Burke, Weir, & Duwors, 1980, regarding a middle-class group of families).

In addition to the feelings of futility and sadness which the wife of the blue-collar man bears as a consequence of her husband's relationship to his work, the wife in these families is continually confronted with demands for help and assistance from a large circle of relatives with whom she has life-long familiarity. A woman who is expected to care for her own young children and who, in addition, is expected to care for older parents or grandparents, whose child may be ill, and whose husband may be facing a periodic layoff at work, suffers serious role strain and overload (Goode, 1960). Consistent with suggestions of feminist critics who have suggested that homebound mothers of young children are particularly vulnerable to such depressive feelings, Kessler and McRae (1981) do find some effect due to return of women to participation in the labor force. Little additional variance is accounted for in these findings by having children in school. However, the major trend in women's symptoms was accounted for by an increase in men's symptoms, rather than by a decrease in women's symptoms.

Continuing conflict between this mother of young children and her own mother may further intensify her feelings of strain. Just as the mother of young children is burdened by conflicting demands on her time and attention, her own middle-aged mother is also faced with such demands. The daughter's expectation of help and support from her own mother may be denied, or met in such a manner as to further increase the degree of tension among these women in the two responsible adult generations of the family.

MATERNAL MENTAL ILLNESS AND PSYCHIATRIC HOSPITALIZATION

Findings from studies of preadult and adult socialization of women in contemporary society show both the asymmetry within the family in which kin keeping falls to the woman, and also the severe strain which may accompany the continuing relationship among relatives, particularly within working-class families. The irony is that in contrast with much earlier critical social science formulations of the role of the family in urban society, the problem may well be not that there is not enough contact between relatives, but that there may be too much contact, with accompanying mutual expectations, particularly among women within the family, which may intensify rather than reduce role strain and overload (Cohler & Lieberman, 1980; Cohler & Grunebaum, 1981).

These problems in the woman's adult adjustment are perhaps most clearly demonstrated among mothers who develop serious psychological impairment during the years that they are caring for their own young children. Particularly among those working-class women hospitalized for mental illness, the very factors which add to the development of the disturbance may also interfere with a satisfactory response to treatment, exacerbating problems in their posthospital adjustment.

Development of Psychiatric Illness among Mothers of Young Children

The role stress and strain which so many mothers in contemporary society report after the birth of the first child and, in many families, which is repeated with each addition to the family, is accentuated within families at risk, such as mothers of prematures (Caplan, 1960; Kaplan & Mason, 1960) and those already brittle women who typically show anxiety, emotional instability, and interpersonal isolation even prior to pregnancy. Assumption of the maternal role leads to additional strain, resulting in such psychiatric symptoms as the experience of unreality and depression, together with acute anxiety, characteristically requiring psychiatric hospitalization (Gordon & Gordon, 1958, 1960). As Gordon and Gordon (1965) have noted:

> Emotionally ill new mothers, 1) have usually suffered greater numbers of generally stressful experiences—events such as serious personal or familial illness or parental and personal divorce; 2) have had poorer preparation in the personal, economic, and social skills needed for coping with their responsibilities, and greater difficulty adjusting to their life roles. (p. 158)

These disturbed women lack the personal competence and social skills necessary for coping with the responsibilities and challenges of motherhood (Ginsparg, 1955; Grunebaum, Weiss, Cohler, Hartman, & Gallant, 1982).

As a result of conflicts with their parental family, intense marital conflict, and feelings of isolation from others, together with problems in establishing satisfying interpersonal relationships, some women become psychiatrically impaired after the first child, whereas others are able to manage with one child but, as a result of the increased strain which results from having two or more children to care for, either show increasing impairment after each child or, having had several children, suddenly become overwhelmed and require hospitalization.

Over the course of the past several years, a number of studies have been able to determine the contributions of life-event stress and role strain to the development of psychiatric illness. Brown and Birley (1968), Paykel, Myers, Dienelt, Klerman, Lindenthal, and Pepper (1969), Fontana, Marcus, Noel, and Rakusin (1972), and Jacobs and Myers (1972) all have reported that recently admitted psychiatric patients showed a significantly greater number of hazardous life events in the months immediately preceding admission than a group of well persons in the community. Further, these events seemed to be both noninde-pendent and additive, with later occurring events related to those taking place earlier in this period preceding hospitalization.

Such findings, particularly those based on the work of Brown, Sklair, Harris, and Birley (1973) and Brown, Harris, and Peto (1973), suggest that life-event stress appears to have more of a triggering than a causal relationship in the origin of severe symptoms and consequent hospitalization (although Doh-renwend & Egri, 1981, have challenged this interpretation of previous findings). However, even this triggering effect may disappear across multiple rehospital-izations (Birley & Brown, 1970). Finally, it appears that depressed patients are more directly adversely affected by stress than schizophrenic patients. Compar-ison of patients within these two categories shows that depressed patients are particularly likely to have reacted to a specific hazardous event prior to hospi-talization (Brown, Sklair, Harris, & Birley, 1973). This finding from the British research is supported by Beck and Worthen's (1972) report that the life-event stresses reported by schizophrenic patients are far more idiosyncratic and less normatively stressful than those reported by depressed patients.

Within the major psychoses, including both schizophrenia and unipolar and bipolar affective disorders, stress alone is clearly not enough to produce psy-chiatric symptoms of such intensity that hospitalization becomes necessary. Ge-netic factors clearly are integral in the origins of such disturbances, and most investigators currently accept some variation of the stress–diathesis hypothesis (Meehl, 1962; Kety, Rosenthal, Wender, Schulsinger, & Jacobsen, 1978; Kohn, 1972, 1976; Stabenau, 1977) in which both environmental and innate factors are required in order to produce such an incapacitating illness. This position is perhaps best stated by Zubin and Spring (1977), who observe:

> In the resilient person the "mini-episode" of coping breakdown [following life-stress] passes and after a temporary period of distress, routine coping strategies regain the field. In a highly vulnerable person, however, a temporary breakdown in adaptation may provide an occasion for more fundamental problems to man-ifest themselves . . . coping breakdown . . . provides an opportunity for vul-nerability to germinate into disorder.
>
> It seems likely that the person in a state of coping breakdown enters a period of rest, a state of lowered psychological resistance. If the individual's vulnerability is sufficiently low, this period will pass with relatively small consequence. On the other hand, if the vulnerability is high, such sensitive points are likely opportunities for vulnerability to develop in the expression of psychopathology. (pp. 112, 117)

In their reformulation of the origins of schizophrenia (their model might also be extended to include affective disorders) Zubin and Spring observe that recurrently hospitalized patients are not continuously schizophrenic between hos-pitalizations. Psychosis is not an enduring but, rather, an episodic state: A patient may maintain periods of satisfactory adjustment until a new set of life events call for coping responses which are beyond the patient's repertoire. At such times, there is a sense of increased distress and increased evidence of symptoms.

Both at the time of the initial hospitalization and, successively, as the patient is rehospitalized, additional stress is placed both on the patient and, as Hansen and Hill (1964) have emphasized, for the family as well. As true as this observation is for the family of the single male schizophrenic, typically studied in research on chronic (process) schizophrenics, it is even more true among psychiatric patients who are parents of young and dependent children (Cohler, Grunebaum, Weiss, Hartman, & Gallant, 1975). When the patient is the mother, the problem is particularly difficult, for the husband–father typically works during the day and is not available for child care (Grunebaum, Gamer, & Cohler, 1983). The task of child care most often falls to the mother's parental family, particularly her own mother. Both generations in the family experience increased strain as a result of the experience of hospitalization. The grandmother struggles not only with her own feelings of distress and confusion over her daughter's disturbance, but also with her feelings of guilty resentment as she contemplates the necessity of rearranging her own life in order to provide the necessary child care for her grandchildren during her daughter's hospitalization. Such conflict, in turn, may increase the intensity of emotional expressiveness within the family (Brown, Monck, Carstairs, & Wing, 1962; Brown, Birley, & Wing, 1972). This conflict within the family both increases the severity of the mother's illness and also further intensifies the very life stress which was at least a triggering event in the mother's original hospitalization.

Many mothers are recurrently psychotic in precisely the manner described by Zubin and Spring (1977) and Test and Berlin (1981), and, while there is little evidence that the role of life-event stress is different among women hospitalized for first as opposed to subsequent hospitalizations (Birley & Brown, 1970), the impact upon the family of such multiple hospitalizations is profound. As Rice, Ekdahl, and Miller (1971) have shown, each hospitalization further decreases the ability of the patient and her family to use community resources. As a result of such multiple rehospitalization, the family further isolates itself from helping resources in the community and makes increasingly desperate and haphazard arrangements for child care. At the same time that the family tries to cut its losses by increasingly isolating the mother from her responsibilities as housewife, wife, and mother (Dunigan, 1969), little effort is made at other kinds of arrangements. Her husband increasingly disparages her struggle to recover from her disturbance (Merrill, 1969; Grunebaum et al., 1983), and profound consequences are felt throughout the extended family, as the patient is increasingly relegated to a chronically ill position.

There has been relatively little study of these multiply hospitalized mothers of young children. Fontana, Dowds, Marcus, and Rakusin (1976) cite the importance in studies of rehospitalization of noting the manner in which the events surrounding the first hospitalization had been dealt with. Interpersonal conflicts arising from this, often terrifying, experience may become the source of subsequent conflicts, and additional stressfsl life events, which increase vulnerability and lead to the possibility of yet additional hospitalizations (Brown & Birley, 1968; Hoening & Hamilton, 1969). Findings reported by Deykin, Klerman, and Armor (1966) show that husband and own mother are among the relatives of hospitalized women least supportive of the patient during hospitalization and least cooperative with hospital staff, and yet it is precisely these two relatives whose cooperation is so vital if rehospitalization is to be prevented. This comparison is, in turn, dependent upon expectations of the patient regarding help she may be able to receive from her husband and her mother.

Scheurman (1972) reports that the feeling that the husband would "stand by her" and belief she could recover from her disturbance represented important predictors of the wife's posthospital adjustment, together with the wife's ability to find some additional support outside the marital relationship, such as friends or extended family members. Freeman and Simmons (1961) note that such contact between the family and the hospital is, at best, haphazard and unplanned. Pao (1979) notes that the extent of the mother's anxiety about her child's development is an important factor in her posthospital adjustment; mothers able to have someone to talk with regarding their fears were able to make a more successful posthospital adjustment.

Maternal Mental Illness and Posthospital Adjustment

Closely related to the question of factors associated with the initial decision to hospitalize a family member is that regarding the determinants of posthospital adjustment, including prevention of rehospitalization. Freeman and Simmons (1958, 1959, 1961, 1963) and Michaux, Katz, Kurland, and Gansereit (1969) have shown that the more that is expected of former patients in terms of instrumental performance, the more successful will be the patient's posthospital adjustment. However, some "low-level" performers do manage to avoid rehospitalization, largely because they live in their parental home where there are many other family members able to do the work which they are unable to do. Such patients are not expected to perform at very high levels, but it is also not really necessary for them to do so.

While familial expectations play an important role in determining the success of the patient's adjustment following psychiatric hospitalization, continuing contact with members of the patient's parental family, together with continuing involvement with them, may have an adverse effect on the patient's adjustment. In a series of papers from 1958 to 1972, Brown and his colleagues (Brown, Carstairs, & Topping, 1958; Brown, 1959; Brown et al., 1962; Brown & Rutter, 1966; Brown, Birley, & Wing, 1972) have shown that patients living in their parental home are rehospitalized in significantly greater numbers than patients living in marital families or even in boarding houses. Such increased risk appears to be a result both of the toleration and even encouragement which parents provide for the childlike and dependent behavior of their formerly hospitalized offspring, together with the intense conflict or "emotional expressiveness" which is so often present in these families (Vaughn & Leff, 1976, 1981). The effect of constant family conflict, in combination with tolerance of regressive behavior, is that the patient is driven back into her disturbance.

In the most recent research reported in this series of studies (Brown *et al.*, 1972), a curvilinear relationship was reported between family involvement and rehospitalization, with patients in those families characterized by high levels of emotional expressiveness or intrafamily conflict, and those patients living in the most isolated rooming houses, rehospitalized in greater numbers than patients having more benign contact with their parental family. Rose (1959) has reported essentially similar findings, in a much less rigorous study, and notes that rehospitalization most often occurs when relatives more distant from the patient, neighbors, or others in the community complain about the patient's actions. Only then, and with great reluctance, do relatives make arrangements for rehospitalization. Findings from a community study of women previously hospitalized for psychiatric illness (Angrist, Lefton, Dinitz, & Pasamanick, 1968) suggest that because of their roles as wife and mother, women intrinsically have continuing intense conflict with their own parental family following hospitalization. Further, their failure to enact their adult roles, particularly that of mother, is more visible within the community than among previously hospitalized men, further increasing the likelihood of rehospitalization (Davis, Dinitz, & Pasamanick, 1972, 1974).

Typically, more than half of mentally ill mothers are rehospitalized during the first year following discharge (Kreisman & Joy, 1974; Rosenblatt & Mayer, 1974; Erickson, 1975). In nearly all cases, when women are initially discharged from the hospital, they return home to their husband and children, assume once more all their adult roles, and immediately encounter high degrees of intrafamilial conflict (Abrahams and Varon, 1953; Lyketsos, 1959; Sampson, Messinger, & Towne, 1964; Jacobson & Klerman, 1966). While among men, marriage is associated with a better prognosis following hospitalization (Turner, Dopkeen, & Lebreche, 1970; Gove & Howell, 1974), among women, it is associated with a less favorable prognosis (Angrist, Lefton, Dinitz, Pasamanick, 1968; Test & Berlin, 1981). Among men, marital status is a sign of a higher level of premorbid social functioning, for greater instrumental activity is required in order for a man to get married. Typically, it is the man who actively seeks a marital partner; the woman is supposed to be more passive and acquiescent. For this reason alone, it is not necessarily true that married women will show the same high level of social competence as married men. Married, and the mother of young children, the hospitalized woman returns home to a life which is inherently more a source of conflict than among previously hospitalized men discharged from psychiatric hospitals, and functioning at equally problematic levels of social adjustment.

Even among more adequate formerly hospitalized mothers of young children, expectations of their performance of their adult roles repeatedly exposes them to precisely the same situations of intense family conflict on a day-to-day basis which was found by Brown and his colleagues (1962, 1972) to be associated with the greatest risk of rehospitalization. Finally, it should be noted that social class interacts with level of expectation in predicting posthospital adjustment among these hospitalized women. Lefton, Angrist, Dinitz, and Pasamanick (1962) report that middle-class husbands have fewer expectations regarding how well their wives could function following hospitalization than is found among working-class husbands. In addition, husbands' expectations were more closely associated with estimates by their wives of how well they could function after hospitalization among middle-class than among working-class husbands. This later finding suggests that among working-class women hospitalized for mental illness, already even more involved in the world of the family than their middle-class counterparts, the very high level of expectations held for these women further increases the level of role strain they feel, and further increases the risk for rehospitalization among these working-class women.

It should also be noted that, not only does the family have an adverse impact upon the posthospital adjustment of the psychiatrically impaired mother, but that the mother's illness, itself, has an adverse impact upon the family which, in turn, further affects the quality of the mother's adjustment following hospitalization. Not just in the origins of mental illness, but also in the process of initial hospitalization, subsequent outpatient treatment, and rehospitalization, the fate of the patient and the family are linked. In studies ranging from family dynamics and after-care (Brown et al., 1962, 1966, 1972; Mills, 1962; Hoenig & Hamilton, 1969), to achieving success in medication compliance programs (Goldberg, Schooler, Hogarty, & Roger, 1977), to success in independent living and remaining out of the hospital (Kohn & Clausen, 1955; Davis, Freeman, & Simmons, 1958; Dinitz, Lefton, Angrist, & Pasamanick, 1961; Dinitz, Angrist, Lefton, & Pasamanick, 1961; Freeman & Simmons, 1958, 1959, 1963; Brown, Parkes, & Wing, 1961; Schooler, Goldberg, Boothe, & Cole, 1967; Angrist et al., 1968; Michaux et al., 1969; Kreisman & Joy, 1974; Vaughn & Leff, 1976, 1981), the patient's role within the family, and the family's response to the patient's illness, is an important factor in the success of the patient's posthospital adjustment.

Among those families in which the mother of young children is recurrently rehospitalized, rehospitalization ultimately depletes the family's coping resources and has a deleterious impact upon the marital relationship, adjustment of the children, and the relationship between the patient and both her own parental family and that of her husband (Kaplan & Blackman, 1969; Rice et al., 1971; Grunebaum et al., 1983). The husband's need for assistance with housekeeping and child care during his wife's hospitalization, combined with the wife's own need for increased assistance after returning home from the hospital, lead to increased feelings of guilt and, on the part of other family members, increased feelings of resentment and anger which, in turn, increases that very conflict within the family which Brown and his colleagues (1962, 1966, 1972) have shown so adversely affects posthospital adjustment and which has been clinically documented by Musick, Stott, Cohler, and Dincin (1981).

CONCLUSION

Popular portrayals of the advent of motherhood suggest an image of radiant joy which, when not realized, only intensifies the feelings of depression which are experienced by many women after the birth of the first child. The births of later children further compound these feelings of futility and smoldering resentment regarding the roles of wife and mother. It is in the interest of society that couples should marry and have children; parents feel they are fulfilling their biological and social destiny. The failure to realize this destiny leads to the perception among otherwise fecund couples of a position of marked deviance and unwarranted self-entitlement. The normative expectation to fulfill a socially desired role is further intensified by such motivational factors as the wish to care for an infant, to continue the family name, or to insure the parents' own subsequent care in old age. While there are many enduring satisfactions which derive from the experience of parenthood, it is clear that, at least during the preschool years, and to some extent during the elementary school years as well, both parents experience their life as more burdened and unhappy than at any earlier or subsequent stage of adult life. This personal distress may be compounded by feelings of social isolation, and of feelings of lack of self-worth, due to the inability to acknowledge their ambivalent feelings regarding the care of their young children.

The picture which emerges from this review of personal and social factors associated with assumption of the maternal role, and subsequent psychological impairment, is not a particularly optimistic one. While the group of mothers succumbing to psychopathology of such magnitude as to require hospitalization represents a fraction of all mothers of young children, and, while these mothers are likely to have been predisposed to psychiatric impairment prior to having children, many of the factors associated with intensification of psychopathology during these first years of the family life cycle are found as well in less extreme form among "ordinary" mothers of young children. Life-long problems resulting from the socialization of women into the role of mother, rather than that of adult woman more generally, accompanied by the asymmetry present in American society which places the burden of kin keeping upon women, together with the failure to realize the personal and social satisfactions which can come with work, particularly during the years when there are very young children at home, all compounded personal conflict preceding childbearing. The belief prevalent in American society that the quality of the child's adjustment is directly a function of the nature of maternal care, further intensifies the feelings of distress which many women have during the years when their children are young. Indeed, findings from the national survey study reported by Veroff, Douvan, and Kulka (1981) suggest that their has been a change from 1957 to the present in the direction of an increasingly psychological orientation, particularly within middle-class families, which intensifies the soul-searching and feelings of inadequacy when difficulties arise in the course of caring for young children. It is not surprising to find, as shown in Boyd and Weissman's (1981) cross-national review, that American women show a greater lifetime risk of mood disorder (20–26%) than their European counterparts.

Finally, while it is believed that the problems of mothers of young children are compounded by the so-called isolation of the nuclear family in contemporary society, findings from a number of both survey research and intensive family studies show that, not only is the multigeneration family unit much more closely bonded than has often been portrayed, but also that this very bondedness may be an additional source of strain which may increase rather than decrease the feelings of personal distress accompanying care of young children. Both as a result of the mother's own unresolved ambivalent identifications with her own mother, and also as a result of her wish to continue an interdependent relationship which is perceived by her own middle-aged mother as an illegitimate demand, tension continues between these two generations of adult women as they maintain life-long ties.

While recognizing that this conclusion, based on findings from a large number of studies, is a sobering one, it does at least make clear the dimensions of the problem, and also suggests some possibilities for solution. Some aspects of this problem, like that regarding the nature of socialization of women, are to be found in the very nature of family life in our society. Although some critics like Chodorow (1978) suggest that complete shared child care between men and women would contribute to resolution of the present dilemma that women are socialized into motherhood, findings from crosspcultural research (D'Andrade, 1966) support the earlier claim by Parsons (1955) that instrumental–expressive differences in sex-role enactment are characteristic of relations among men and women and their family life across cultures.

Granted that, early in the family life cycle, women are expected to be the principal caretakers of young children, while their husbands work to support the family, much can be done to resolve the strains presently associated with the maternal role in the American family. In the first place, more can be done to encourage support among neighbors. Findings from Lopata's (1971) study suggest that neighbors represent an important source of support and assistance among mothers of young children. Findings reviewed by Cohler and Lieberman (1980) suggest that relations with neighbors provide much the same kinds of support, without the associated conflicts arising from expectations of interdependence, which might be provided by the woman's own parental family in adulthood. One of the many advantages of urban and suburban living, as contrasted with rural settings, is that contact among neighbors is so much more accessible. Formation of buying cooperatives, development of urban housing clusters with common areas, including play-areas for small children, and development of housing with shared entry ways, facilitating contact among neighbors, all can become important in supporting neighboring.

While the self-help movement has seen dramatic increase in interest among both mental health professionals and laymen over the past decade (Cohler &

Lieberman, 1980), there has been little attention to the development of self-help groups among the mothers of well young children similar to that reported among parents of children with illness or disability. Such self-help groups could provide a continuing source of support for women during the critical first years of the family life cycle and could contribute towards resolution of feelings of isolation and estrangement from friends which mothers of young children so frequently report.

Issues to be discussed within the framework of the self-help groups would include not just the ambivalent feelings regarding child care, but also feelings about the continuing relationship between mothers of young children and their own older mothers. The psychosocial interdependence between the two generations which, as Cohler and Grunebaum (1981) have suggested, results in less psychological differentiation between mothers and their own mothers than between fathers and their fathers, represents an important source of tension among women in each generation. This tension arises both as a result of the fact that continuing closeness is at odds with the prevalent value in contemporary society placed on psychological autonomy and independence, and as a result of personal needs created by the quite different position in the life cycle of women in the two generations.

Self-help groups, including both mothers and daughters, would also be an important means for reducing significant strains associated with the roles of wife, mother, and daughter. Sharing of experiences among a number of families helps to provide an important perspective for members of particular families. Hearing the experiences of others from each generation leads to increased understanding on the part both of mothers and grandmothers of the unique problems faced by each generation.

Advocacy of different housing patterns, of self-help groups, and of other innovative positive programs in mental health, represents a new direction for mental health professionals. There is good reason to believe that techniques developed in the consulting room and psychiatric hospital have generalizability within community settings if modified in ways appropriate for these settings. Understanding of meanings and intents, and of the satisfactions and problems inherent in adult life ought to result in the development of beneficial programs not just for those who are self-identified as patients, but also for the many mothers in the community with greater inner resources, who also struggle with similar problems regarding their present life during the first years after becoming parents.

REFERENCES

Abrahams, J., & Varon, E. *Maternal dependency: Mothers and daughters in a therapeutic group.* New York: International Universities Press, 1953.
Adams, B. *Kinship in an urban setting.* Chicago: Markham, 1968.
Adams, B. Isolation, function and beyond: American kinship in the 1960's. *Journal of Marriage and the Family,* 1970, *32,* 575–597.

Aldous, J. Intergenerational visiting patterns: Variation in boundary maintenance as an explanation. *Family Process*, 1967, *6*, 235–251.

Aldous, J., & Hill, R. Social cohesion, lineage type, and intergenerational transmission. *Social Forces*, 1965, *43*, 471–482.

Alpert, J., & Richardson, M. Parenting. In L. W. Poon (Ed.), *Aging in the 1980's: Psychological issues*. Washington, D.C.: American Psychological Association, 1980.

Amenson, C., & Lewinsohn, P. An investigation into observed sex differences in prevalence of unipolar depression. *Journal of Abnormal Psychology*, 1981, *90*, 1–13.

Anderson, E. W. A study of the sexual life in psychoses associated with childbirth. *Journal of Mental Science*, 1933, *79*, 137–149.

Andrews, F., & Withey, S. *Social indicators of well-being: Americans' perceptions of life quality*. New York: Plenum, 1976.

Angrist, S., Lefton, M., Dinitz, S., & Pasamanick, B. *Women after treatment*. New York: Appleton-Century-Crofts, 1968.

Anthony, E. J. The reaction of parents to adolescents and their behavior. In E. Anthony & T. Benedek (Eds.), *Parenthood: Its psychology and psychopathology*. Boston: Little, Brown, 1970. (a)

Anthony, E. J. The reaction of parents to the oedipal child. In E. J. Anthony & T. Benedek (Eds.), *Parenthood: Its psychology and psychopathology*. Boston: Little, Brown, 1970. (b)

Arasteh, J. Parenthood: Some antecedents and consequences: A preliminary survey of the mental health literature. *Journal of Genetic Psychology*, 1971, *118*, 179–202.

Ballou, J. *The psychology of pregnancy*. Lexington, Mass.: Lexington Books/D. C. Heath, 1978. (a)

Ballou, J. The significance of reconciliative themes in the psychology of pregnancy. *Bulletin of the Menninger Clinic*, 1978, *42*, 383–413. (b)

Beck, J., & Worthen, K. Precipitating stress, crisis theory, and hospitalization in schizophrenia and depression. *Archives of General Psychiatry*, 1972, *26*, 123–129.

Belle, D. Mothers and their children: A study of low-income families. In C. Heckerman (Ed.), *The evolving female: Women in psychosocial context*. New York: Human Sciences Press, 1980.

Benedek, T. Parenthood as a developmental phase: A contribution to the libido theory. *Journal of the American Psychoanalytic Association*, 1959, *7*, 389–417.

Bernard, J. *Women, wives, and mothers: Values and opinions*. Chicago: Aldine, 1975.

Bernardo, F. Kinship interaction and communication among space-age migrants. *Journal of Marriage and the Family*, 1967, *29*, 541–554.

Birley, J., & Brown, G. Crises and life changes preceding the onset or relapse of acute schizophrenia: Clinical aspects. *British Journal of Psychiatry*, 1970, *116*, 327–333.

Blood, R., & Wolfe, D. *Husbands and wives*. New York: Free Press, 1960.

Bott, E. *Family and social network* (2nd ed.). London: Tavistock Press, 1971.

Boyd, J., & Weissman, M. Epidemiology of affective disorders: A reexamination and future directions. *Archives of General Psychiatry*, 1981, *38*, 1039–1046.

Bram, S. Through the looking glass: Voluntary childlessness as a mirror of contemporary changes in the meaning of parenthood. In W. B. Miller & L. Newman (Eds.), *The first child and family formation*. Chapel Hill, N.C.: Carolina Population Center, University of North Carolina at Chapel Hill, 1978.

Brown, G. Experiences of discharged chronic schizophrenic patients in various types of living group. *Milbank Memorial Fund Quarterly*, 1959, *37*, 105–131.

Brown, G., Bhrolchain, M., & Harris, T. Social class and psychiatric disturbance among women in an urban population. *Sociology*, 1975, *9*, 225–254.

Brown, G., & Birley, J. Crises and life changes and the onset of schizophrenia. *Journal of Health and Human Behavior*, 1968, *9*, 203–214.

Brown, G., Birley, J., & Wing, J. Influence of family life in the course of the schizophrenic disorders: A replication. *British Journal of Psychiatry*, 1972, *121*, 241–258.

Brown, G., Bone, M., Dalison, B., & Wing, J. *Schizophrenia and social care*. London: Oxford University Press, 1966.

Brown, G., Carstairs, G., & Topping, G. Post-hospital adjustment of chronic mental patients. *Lancet*, 1958, *2*, 685–689.

Brown, G., & Harris, T. *Social origins of depression: A study of psychiatric disorder in women*. New York: Free Press–Macmillan, 1975.

Brown, G., Harris, T., & Peto, J. Life-events and psychiatric disorders. Part II: Nature of causal link. *Psychological Medicine*, 1973, *3*, 159–196.

Brown, G., Monck, E., Carstairs, G., & Wing, J. Influence of family life in the course of schizophrenic illness. *British Journal of Preventative and Social Medicine*, 1962, *16*, 55–68.

Brown, G., Parkes, C., & Wing, J. Admissions and readmissions to three London Mental Hospitals. *Journal of Mental Science*, 1961, *107*, 1070–1077.

Brown, G., & Rutter, M. The measurement of family activities and relationships: A methodological study. *Human Relations*, 1966, *19*, 241–263.

Brown, G., Sklair, F., Harris, T., & Birley, J. Life-events and psychiatric disorders. Part I: Some methodological issues. *Psychological Medicine*, 1973, *3*, 74–87.

Burke, R., Weir, T., & Duwors, R. Work demands on administrators and spouse well-being. *Human Relations*, 1980, *33*, 253–278.

Campbell, A., Converse, P., & Rodgers, W. *The quality of American life: Perceptions, evaluations, and satisfactions*. New York: Russell Sage Foundation, 1976.

Caplan, G. Patterns of parental response to the crisis of the premature birth: A preliminary approach to modifying mental health outcome. *Psychiatry*, 1960, *23*, 365–374.

Chodorow, N. Family structure and feminine personality. In M. Rosaldo & L. Lamphere (Eds.), *Women, culture, and society*. Stanford, Calif.: Stanford University Press, 1974.

Chodorow, N. *The reproduction of mothering: Psychoanalysis and the sociology of gender*. Berkeley: University of California Press, 1978.

Cohler, B. Character, mental illness, and mothering (1975). In H. Grunebaum, J. Weiss, B. Cohler, D. Gallant, & C. Hartman, *Mentally ill mothers and their children* (2nd ed.). Chicago: University of Chicago Press, 1982.

Cohler, B., & Grunebaum, H. *Mothers, grandmothers, and daughters: Personality and childcare in three generation families*. New York: Wiley, 1981.

Cohler, B., Grunebaum, H., Weiss, J., Hartman, C., & Gallant, D. Perceived life-stress and psychopathology among mothers of young children. *American Journal of Orthopsychiatry*, 1975, *45*, 58–73.

Cohler, B., & Lieberman, M. Social relations and mental health: Middle-aged men and women from three European ethnic groups. *Research on Aging*, 1980, *2*, 445–469.

Cowan, C. P., Cowan, P., Coie, L., & Coie, J. Becoming a family: The impact of a first child's birth on the couple's relationship. In W. Miller & L. Newman (Eds.), *The first child and family formation*. Chapel Hill, N.C.: Carolina Population Center, University of North Carolina at Chapel Hill, 1980.

Cutrona, C. Nonpsychotic post-partum depression: A review of recent research. *Clinical Psychology Review*, 1982, *2*, 487–503.

D'Andrade, R. Sex differences and cultural institutions. In E. Maccoby (Ed.), *The development of sex differences*. Stanford, Calif.: Stanford University Press, 1966.

Davis, A., Dinitz, S., & Pasamanick, B. The prevention of hospitalization in schizophrenia: Five years after an experimental program. *American Journal of Orthopsychiatry*, 1972, *42*, 375–387.

Davis, A., Dinitz, S., & Pasamanick, B. *Schizophrenics in the new custodial community: Five years after the experiment*. Columbus, Ohio: Ohio State University Press, 1974.

Davis, J., Freeman, H., & Simmons, O. Rehospitalization and performance level among former mental patients. *Social Problems*, 1958, *5*, 37–44.

Demos, J. The American family in past time. *The American Scholar*, 1974, *43*, 422–446.

Deykin, E., Klerman, G., & Armor, D. The relatives of schizophrenic patients: Clinical judgments of potential emotional resourcefulness. *American Journal of Orthopsychiatry*, 1966, *36*, 518–528.

Diamond, M. A critical review of the ontogeny of human sexual behavior. *Quarterly Review of Biology*, 1965, *40*, 147–175.

Dinitz, S., Angrist, S., Lefton, M., & Pasamanick, B. The posthospital functioning of former mental hospital patients. *Mental Hygiene*, 1961, *45*, 579–588.

Dinitz, S., Lefton, M., Angrist, S., & Pasamanick, B. Psychiatric and social attributes as predictors of case outcome in mental hospitalization. *Social Problems*, 1961, *8*,

Dohrenwend, B., & Egri, G. Recent stressful life-events and episodes of schizophrenia. *Schizophrenia Bulletin*, 1981, *7*, 34–42.

Dunigan, J. *Mental hospital career and family expectations*. Unpublished doctoral dissertation, Case Western Reserve University, 1969.

Dunlop, K. Maternal employment and child care. *Professional Psychology*, 1981, *12*, 67–75.

Dyer, E. D. Parenthood as crisis: A re-study. *Journal of Marriage and Family Living*, 1963, *25*, 196–201.

Entwisle, D., & Doering, S. *The first birth: A family turning point*. Baltimore: Johns Hopkins University Press, 1981.

Erickson, R. Outcome studies in mental hospitals: A review. *Psychological Bulletin*, 1975, *82*, 519–540.

Farber, B. *Kinship and class: A Midwestern study*. New York: Basic Books, 1971.

Firth, R., Hubert, J., & George, A. *Families and their relatives: Kinship in a middle class sector of London*. New York: Humanities Press, 1970.

Fischer, J., & Fischer, A. The New Englanders of Orchard Town. In B. Whiting (Ed.), *Six cultures: Studies of childrearing*. New York: Wiley, 1963.

Fontana, A., Dowds, B., Marcus, J., & Rakusin, J. Coping with interpersonal conflicts through life events and hospitalization. *Journal of Nervous and Mental Disease*, 1976, *162*, 88–98.

Fontana, A., Marcus, J., Noel, B., & Rakusin, J. Prehospitalization coping styles of psychiatric patients: The goal directedness of life-events. *Journal of Nervous and Mental Disease*, 1972, *155*, 311–321.

Freeman, H., & Simmons, O. Wives, mothers and the post-hospital performance of mental patients. *Social Forces*, 1958, *37*, 153–159.

Freeman, H., & Simmons, O. Mental patients in the community: Family settings and performance levels. *American Sociological Review*, 1959, *23*, 147–154.

Freeman, H., & Simmons, O. Treatment experiences of mental patients and their families. *American Journal of Public Health*, 1961, *51*, 1260–1273.

Freeman, H., & Simmons, O. *The mental patient comes home*. New York: Wiley, 1963.

Freshnock, L., & Cutright, P. Structural determinants of childlessness: A nonrecursive analysis of 1970 U.S. rates. *Social Biology*, 1978, *25*, 160–178.

Fried, E., & Stern, K. The situation of the aged within the family. *American Journal of Orthopsychiatry*, 1948, *18*, 31–54.

Fried, M. *The world of the urban working class*. Cambridge, Mass.: Harvard University Press, 1973.

Gavron, H. *The captive housewife: Conflicts of housebound mothers*. London: Routledge & Kegan Paul, 1966.

Gilligan, C. Woman's place in man's life-cycle. *Harvard Educational Review*, 1979, *49*, 431–446.

Ginsparg, S. *Post-partum psychoses*. Unpublished doctoral dissertation, Washington University, 1955.

Glick, P. *American families*. New York: Wiley, 1957.

Glick, P. Updating the life cycle of the family. *Journal of Marriage and the Family*, 1977, *39*, 5–13.

Goldberg, S., Schooler, N., Hogarty, G., & Roger, M. Prediction of release in schizophrenic outpatients treated by drug and socio-therapy. *Archives of General Psychiatry*, 1977, *34*, 171–184.

Goldman, N., & David, R. Community surveys: Sex differences in mental illness. In M. Guttentag, S. Salasin, & D. Belle (Eds.), *The mental health of women*. New York: Academic Press, 1980.

Goode, W. A theory of role strain. *American Sociological Review*, 1960, *29*, 483–499.

Gordon, R., & Gordon, K. Psychiatric problems of a rapidly growing suburb. *Archives of Neurology and Psychiatry*, 1958, *79*, 543–548.

Gordon, R., & Gordon, K. Social factors in prevention of post-partum emotional problems. *Obstetrics and Gynecology*, 1960, *15*, 133–138.

Gordon, R., & Gordon, K. Factors in post-partum emotional adjustment. *Obstetrics and Gynecology*, 1965, *25*, 158–166.

Gove, W. The relationship between sex roles, marital status, and mental illness. *Social Forces*, 1972, *51*, 34–44.

Gove, W., & Geerken, M. The effect of children and employment on the mental health of married men and women. *Social Forces*, 1977, *56*, 66–76.

Gove, W., & Howell, P. Individual resources and mental hospitalization: A comparison and evaluation of the societal reaction and psychiatric perspectives. *American Sociological Review*, 1974, *39*, 86–100.

Gove, W., & Tudor, J. Adult sex roles and mental illness. *American Journal of Sociology*, 1972, *78*, 812–835.

Gray, R., & Smith, T. Effect of employment on sex differences in attitudes toward the parental family. *Journal of Marriage and the Family*, 1960, *22*, 36–38.

Grossman, F., Eichler, L., Winickoff, S., & Associates. *Pregnancy, birth and parenthood*. San Francisco: Jossey-Bass, 1980.

Grunebaum, H., Gamer, E., & Cohler, B. The spouse in depressed families. In H. Morrison (Ed.), *Children of depressed parents*. New York: Grune & Stratton, 1983.

Grunebaum, H., Weiss, J., Cohler, B., Hartman, C., & Gallant, D. *Mentally ill mothers and their young children* (2nd ed.). Chicago: University of Chicago Press, 1982.

Gutmann, D. Parenthood: A comparative key to the life-cycle. In N. Datan & L. Ginsberg (Eds.), *Life-span developmental psychology: Normative crises*. New York: Academic Press, 1975.

Hagstrom, W., & Hadden, J. Sentiment and kinship terminology in American society. *Journal of Marriage and the Family*, 1965, *27*, 324–332.

Hansen, D., & Hill, R. Families under stress. In H. Christensen (Ed.), *Handbook of marriage and the family*. Chicago: Rand-McNally, 1964.

Hare-Mustin, R., & Broderick, P. The myth of motherhood: A study of attitudes toward motherhood. *Psychology of Women Quarterly*, 1979, *4*, 114–128.

Hill, R. Psychosocial consequences of the first birth: A discussion. In W. Miller & L. Newman (Eds.), *The first child and family formation*. Chapel Hill, N.C.: Carolina Population Center, University of North Carolina at Chapel Hill, 1978.

Hobbs, D. Parenthood as crisis: A third study. *Marriage and Family Living*, 1965, *27*, 367–372.

Hobbs, D., & Cole, S. Transition to parenthood: A decade replication. *Journal of Marriage and the Family*, 1976, *38*, 723–731.

Hoening, J., & Hamilton, M. W. *The desegregation of the mentally ill*. London: Routledge & Kegan Paul, 1969.

Hoffman, L. W. Changes in family roles, socialization, and sex differences. *American Psychologist*, 1977, *32*, 644–657.

Hoffman, L. Effects of the first child on the woman's role. In W. Miller & L. Newman (Eds.), *The first child and family formation*. Chapel Hill, N.C.: Carolina Population Center, University of North Carolina at Chapel Hill, 1978.

Hoffman, L., & Hoffman, M. The value of children to parents. In J. T. Fawcett (Ed.), *Psychological perspectives on population*. New York: Basic Books, 1973.

Hoffman, L., & Manis, J. Influences of children on marital interaction and parental satisfactions and dissatisfactions. In R. Lerner & G. Spanier (Eds.), *Child influences on marital and family interaction: A life-span perspective.* New York: Academic Press, 1978.

Houseknecht, S. Timing of the decision to remain voluntarily childless: Evidence for continuous socialization. *Psychology of Women Quarterly*, 1979, *4*, 81–96.

Humphrey, M. The effect of children on the marriage relationship. *British Journal of Medical Psychology*, 1975, *48*, 273–279.

Jacobs, S., & Myers, J. Recent life events and acute schizophrenic psychosis: A controlled study. *Journal of Nervous and Mental Disease*, 1976, *162*, 75–87.

Jacobson, L., Kaij, L., & Nilsson, A. Post-partum mental disorders in an unselected sample: Frequency of symptoms and predisposing factors. *British Medical Journal*, 1965, *1*, 1640–1643.

Jacobson, S., & Klerman, G. Interpersonal dynamics of hospitalized depressed patients' home visits. *Journal of Marriage and the Family*, 1966, *28*, 94–102.

Jacoby, A. Transition to parenthood: A reassessment. *Journal of Marriage and the Family*, 1969, *31*, 720–727.

Johnson, C., & Johnson, F. Attitudes toward parenting in dual career families. *American Journal of Psychiatry*, 1977, *134*, 391–395.

Kaltreider, N., & Margolis, A. Childless by choice: A clinical study. *American Journal of Psychiatry*, 1977, *134*, 179–182.

Kaplan, D., & Mason, E. Maternal reactions to premature birth viewed as an acute emotional disorder. *American Journal of Orthopsychiatry*, 1960, *30*, 539–552.

Kaplan, E., & Blackman, L. The husband's role in psychiatric illness associated with childbearing. *Psychiatric Quarterly*, 1969, *43*, 396–409.

Kessler, R., & McRae, R. Trends in the relationship between sex and psychological distress: 1957–1976. *American Sociological Review*, 1981, *46*, 443–452.

Kety, S., Rosenthal, D., Wender, P., Schulsinger, F., & Jacobsen, B. The biologic and adoptive families of adopted individuals who became schizophrenic: Prevalence of mental illness and other characteristics. In L. Wynne, R. Cromwell, & S. Matthysee (Eds.), *The nature of schizophrenia: New research and treatment.* New York: Wiley, 1978.

Klerman, G., & Weissman, M. Depression among women: Their nature and causes. In M. Guttentag, S. Salasin, & D. Belle (Eds.), *The mental health of women.* New York: Academic Press, 1980.

Kohn, M. L. *Class and conformity: A study in values.* Homewood, Ill.: Dorsey, 1969.

Kohn, M. Class, family and schizophrenia. *Social Forces*, 1972, *50*, 295–309.

Kohn, M. The interaction of social class and other factors in the etiology of schizophrenia. *American Journal of Psychiatry*, 1976, *133*, 177–180.

Kohn, M., & Clausen, J. Social isolation and schizophrenia. *American Sociological Review*, 1955, *20*, 265–277.

Kohn, M., & Schooler, C. Class, occupation and orientation. *American Sociological Review*, 1969, *24*, 659–678.

Komarovsky, M. Functional analysis of sex roles. *American Sociological Review*, 1950, *15*, 508–516.

Komarovsky, M. *Blue-collar marriage.* New York: Random House, 1962.

Kreisman, D., & Joy, V. Family response to the mental illness of a relative: A review of the literature. *Schizophrenia Bulletin*, 1974, 34–57.

Laslett, P. *The world we have lost: England before the industrial age.* New York: Scribners, 1965.

Laslett, P. Characteristics of the western family considered over time. *Family History*, 1977, *2*, 89–115.

Lee, G. Kinship in the seventies: A decade review of research and theory. *Journal of Marriage and the Family*, 1980, *42*, 923–934.

Lefton, M., Angrist, S., Dinitz, S., & Pasamanick, B. Social class, expectations, and performance of mental patients. *American Journal of Sociology*, 1962, *68*, 79–87.

Leichter, H., & Mitchell, W. *Kinship and casework*. New York: Russell Sage Foundation, 1967.

LeMasters, E. E. Parenthood as crisis. *Marriage and family living*, 1957, *19*, 352–355.

LeMasters, E. E. *Parents in modern America*. Homewood, Ill.: Dorsey, 1970.

Lindemann, E. Symptomology and the management of acute grief. *American Journal of Psychiatry*, 1944, *101*, 141–148.

Lopata, H. The life cycle of the social role of the housewife. *Sociology and Social Research*, 1966, *51*, 2–22.

Lopata, H. *Occupation housewife*. New York: Oxford University Press, 1971.

Lyketsos, G. On the formation of mother–daughter symbiotic relationship patterns in schizophrenia. *Psychiatry*, 1959, *22*, 161–166.

Maccoby, E. E. The development of moral values in childhood. In J. S. Claussen (Ed.), *Socialization and society*. Boston: Little, Brown, 1968.

Makosky, V. Stress and the mental health of women: A discussion of research and issues. In M. Guttentag, S. Salasin, & D. Belle (Eds.), *The mental health of women*. New York: Academic Press, 1980.

Malmquist, A., & Kaij, L. Motherhood and childlessness in monozygous twins. Part II: The influence of motherhood on health. *British Journal of Psychiatry*, 1971, *118*, 11–28.

Marecek, J., & Ballou, D. Family roles and women's mental health. *Professional Psychology*, 1981, *12*, 39–46.

McNeil, T., & Kaij, L. Obstetric complications and physical size of offspring of schizophrenic, schizophrenic-like and control mothers. *British Journal of Psychiatry*, 1973, *123*, 341–348.

McNeil, T., & Kaij, L. Prenatal, perinatal, and post-partum factors in primary prevention of psychopathology in offspring. In G. Albee & J. Joffe (Eds.), *Primary prevention of psychopathology*. Hanover, N.H.: University Press in New England, 1977.

Mead, M. *Sex and temperament in three primitive societies*. New York: Morrow, 1935.

Meehl, P. Schizotaxia, schizotypy and schizophrenia. *American Psychologist*, 1962, *17*, 827–838.

Melges, F. Post-partum psychiatric syndromes. *Psychosomatic Medicine*, 1968, *30*, 95–108.

Merrill, G. How fathers manage when wives are hospitalized for schizophrenia: An exploratory study. *Social Psychiatry*, 1969, *4*, 26–32.

Meyerowitz, I., & Feldman, H. Transition to parenthood. *Psychiatric Research Reports*, 1966, *20*, 78–84.

Michaux, W., Katz, M., Kurland, A., & Gansereit, K. *The first year out*. Baltimore, Md.: Johns Hopkins University Press, 1969.

Middlemore, M. *The nursing couple*. London: Hamish Hamilton Medical Books, 1941.

Miller, S., & Riessman, F. The working class subculture: A new view. *Social Problems*, 1961, *9*, 86–97.

Mills, E. *Living with mental illness: A study in East London*. London: Routledge & Kegan Paul, 1962.

Musick, J., Stott, F., Cohler, B., & Dincin, J. The treatment of psychotic parents and their children. In M. Lansky (Ed.), *Major psychopathology and the family*. New York: Grune & Stratton, 1981.

Myrdal, A., & Klein, V. *Women's two roles*. London: Routledge & Kegan Paul, 1956.

Ogburn, W. F. The changing function of the family. In R. Winch & R. McGinnis (Eds.), *Selected readings in marriage and the family*. New York: Holt, Rinehart & Winston, 1953.

Paffenbarger, R., Jr., & McCabe, L. The effect of obstetric and perinatal events in risk of mental illness in women of childbearing age. *American Journal of Public Health*, 1966, *56*, 400–407.

Pao, P. *Schizophrenic disorders: Theory and treatment from a psychodynamic point of view*. New York: International Universities Press, 1979.

Parsons, T. The social structure of the family. In R. Anshen (Ed.), *The family: Its function and destiny*. New York: Harper, 1949.

Parsons, T. *The social system*. New York: Free Press–Macmillan, 1951.

Parsons, T. Family structure and the socialization of the child. In T. Parsons & F. Bales (Eds.), *Family, socialization and interaction processes*. New York: Free Press–Macmillan, 1955.

Pasamanick, B., Scaroitti, F., & Dinitz, S. *Schizophrenics in the community.* New York: Appleton-Century-Crofts, 1967.

Paterson, J. Marketing and the working class family. In A. Shostak & W. Gomberg (Eds.), *Blue collar world: Studies of the American worker.* Englewood Cliffs, N.J.: Prentice-Hall, 1964.

Paykel, E., Myers, J., Dienelt, M., Klerman, G., Lindenthal, L., & Pepper, M. Life-events and depression: A controlled study. *Archives of General Psychiatry,* 1969, *21,* 753–760.

Pearlin, L. Sex roles and depression. In N. Datan & L. Ginsberg (Eds.), *Life-span developmental psychology: Normative life crises.* New York: Academic Press, 1975.

Pohlman, E. Childlessness, intentional and unintentional. *Journal of Nervous and Mental Disease,* 1970, *151,* 2–12.

Pugh, T., Jerath, B., Schmidt, W., & Reed, R. Rates of mental illness related to childbearing. *New England Journal of Medicine,* 1963, *268,* 1224–1228.

Rabin, A., & Greene, R. Assessing motivation for parenthood. *Journal of Psychology,* 1968, *69,* 39–46.

Radcliff-Brown, A. R. *Structure and function in primitive society.* New York: Free Press–Macmillan, 1952.

Radloff, L. Sex differences in mental health: The effects of marital and occupational status. *Sex Roles,* 1975, *3,* 249–265.

Radloff, L. Risk factors in depression: What do we learn from them. In M. Guttentag, S. Salasin, & D. Belle (Eds.), *The mental health of women.* New York: Academic Press, 1980.

Rainwater, L., Coleman, R., & Handel, G. *Workingman's wife.* New York: Oceana Publications, 1959.

Rainwater, L., & Handel, G. Changing family roles in the working class. In A. Shostak & W. Gomberg (Eds.), *Blue collar world: Studies of the American worker.* Englewood Cliffs, N.J.: Prentice-Hall, 1964.

Rapoport, R., & Rapoport, R. N. *Dual-career families.* London: Penguin Books, 1971.

Reiss, P. The extended kinship system: Correlates of an attitude on frequency of interaction. *Journal of Marriage and the family,* 1962, *24,* 333–339.

Renne, K. Childlessness, health, and marital satisfaction. *Social Biology,* 1976, *23,* 183–196.

Rice, E., Ekdahl, M., & Miller, L. *Children of mentally ill parents.* New York: Behavioral Publications, 1971.

Ripley, H. Depression and the life span-epidemiology. In G. Usdin (Ed.), *Depression: Clinical, biological and psychological perspectives.* New York: Brunner/Mazel, 1977.

Ritchey, P., & Stokes, C. Correlates of childlessness and expectations to remain childless. *Social Forces,* 1974, *52,* 349–356.

Robins, L., & Tomanec, M. Closeness to blood relatives outside the immediate family. *Marriage and Family Living,* 1962, *24,* 340–346.

Robertson, J. Mothering as an influence on early development. *Psychoanalytic Study of the Child,* 1962, *17,* 245–264.

Rollins, B., & Galligan, R. The developing child and marital satisfaction of parents. In R. M. Lerner & G. Spanier (Eds.), *Child influences on marital and family interactions.* New York: Academic Press, 1978.

Rose, C. Relatives' attitudes and mental hospitalization. *Mental Hygiene,* 1959, *43,* 194–203.

Rosenberg, G. *The worker grows old: Poverty and isolation in the city.* San Francisco: Jossey-Bass, 1970.

Rosenberg, G., & Anspach, D. *Working class kinship.* Lexington, Mass.: D. C. Heath–Lexington Books, 1973.

Rosenblatt, A., & Mayer, J. The recidivism of mental patients: A review of past studies. *American Journal of Orthopsychiatry,* 1974, *44,* 697–706.

Rosow, I. *Social integration of the aged.* New York: Macmillan–Free Press, 1967.

Rossi, A. Transition to parenthood. *Journal of Marriage and the Family,* 1968, *30,* 26–39.

Rossi, A., Life-span theories and women's lives. *Signs: Journal of Women in Society and Culture,* 1980, *6,* 4–32.

Rubin, L. *Worlds of pain: Life in the working-class family.* New York: Basic Books, 1976.

Russell, C. Transition to parenthood: Problems and gratifications. *Journal of Marriage and the Family,* 1974, *36,* 294–303.

Russo, N. The motherhood mandate. *Journal of Social Issues,* 1976, *32,* 143–153.

Russo, N. Overview: Sex roles, fertility, and the motherhood mandate. *Psychology of Women Quarterly,* 1979, *41,* 7–15.

Sampson, H., Messinger, H., & Towne, R. *Schizophrenic women: Marital crisis.* Chicago: Atherton–Aldine, 1964.

Schooler, N., Goldberg, S., Boothe, H., & Cole, J. One year after discharge. Community adjustment among schizophrenic patients. *American Journal of Psychiatry,* 1967, *123,* 986–995.

Scheurman, J. Marital interaction and post-hospital adjustment. *Social Casework,* 1972, *53,* 163–172.

Seligman, M. Depression and learned helplessness. In R. Friedman & M. Katz (Eds.), *The psychology of depression: Contemporary theory and research.* Washington, D.C.: V. V. Winston, 1974.

Seligman, M. *Helplessness: On depression, development and death.* San Francisco, W. H. Freeman, 1975.

Shanas, E. *Family relationships of older people.* New York: Health Information Foundation, Research Series No. 20, 1961. (a)

Shanas, E. Living arrangements of older people in the United States. *The Gerontologist,* 1961, *1,* 27–29. (b)

Shanas, E. *Old people in three industrial societies.* Chicago: Atherton–Aldine, 1968.

Shereshefsky, P., & Yarrow, L. *Psychological aspects of a first pregnancy and early post-natal adaptation.* New York: Raven Press, 1973.

Siassi, G., Crocetti, G., & Spiro, H. Loneliness and dissatisfaction in a blue collar population. *Archives of General Psychiatry,* 1974, *30,* 261–265.

Stabenau, J. Genetic and other factors in schizophrenic, manic-depressive and schizo-affective psychoses. *Journal of Nervous and Mental Disease,* 1977, *164,* 149–167.

Stewart, A. Personality and situation in the prediction of women's life patterns. *Psychology of Women Quarterly,* 1980, *5,* 192–206.

Stryker, S. The adjustment of married offspring to their parents. *American Sociological Review,* 1955, *20,* 149–154.

Sussman, M. B. The isolated nuclear family: Fact or fiction. *Social Problems,* 1959, *6,* 333–340.

Sussman, M. Intergenerational family relationships and social role changes in middle age. *Journal of Gerontology,* 1960, *14,* 71–75.

Sussman, M. Relationships of adult children with their parents in the United States. In E. Shanas & G. Streib (Eds.), *Social structure and the family: Generational relations.* Englewood Cliffs, N.J.: Prentice-Hall, 1965.

Sweetser, D. Asymmetry in intergenerational family relationships. *Social Forces,* 1963, *41,* 346–352.

Sweetser, D. Mother–daughter ties between generations in industrial societies. *Family Process,* 1964, *3,* 332–343.

Sweetser, D. The effect of industrialization on intergenerational solidarity. *Rural Sociology,* 1966, *31,* 156–170.

Test, M., & Berlin, S. Issues of special concern to chronically mentally ill women. *Professional Psychology,* 1981, *12,* 136–345.

Turner, J., Dopkeen, L., & Lebreche, G. Marital status and schizophrenia: A study of incidence and outcome. *Journal of Abnormal Psychology,* 1970, 76, 110–116.

Vaughn, C., & Leff, J. The influence of family and social factors on the source of psychiatric illness: A comparison of schizophrenic and depressed neurotic patients. *British Journal of Psychiatry,* 1976, *129,* 125–137.

Vaughn, C., & Leff, J. Patterns of emotional response in relatives of schizophrenic patients. *Schizophrenia Bulletin,* 1981, *7,* 43–44.

Veevers, J. The social meanings of parenthood. *Psychiatry,* 1973, *36,* 291–310. (a)

Veevers, J. Voluntary childlessness: A neglected area of family study. *The Family Coordinator,* 1973, *22,* 199–205. (b)

Veevers, J. Voluntary childlessness: A review of issues and evidence. *Marriage and Family Review*, 1979, *2(2)*, 1–26.

Veroff, J., & Feld, S. *Marriage and work in America: A study of motives and roles*. New York: Van Nostrand Reinhold, 1970.

Veroff, J., Douvan, E., & Kulka, R. *The inner American: A self-portrait from 1957 to 1976*. New York: Basic Books, 1981.

Wallin, P. Sex differences in attitudes to "in-laws." *American Journal of Sociology*, 1954, *59*, 466–469.

Weissman, M., & Klerman, G. Sex differences in the epidemiology of depression. *Archives of General Psychiatry*, 1977, *34*, 98–111.

Wilmott, P., & Young, M. *Family and class in a London suburb*. London: Routledge & Kegan Paul, 1960.

Wirth, L. Urbanism as a way of life. *American Journal of Sociology*, 1938, *40*, 1–24.

Wood, V., & Robertson, J. The significance of grandparenthood. In J. Gubrium (Ed.), *Time, roles and self in old age*. New York: Human Sciences Press, 1976.

Wyatt, F. Clinical notes on the motives of reproduction. *Journal of Social Issues*, 1967, *23*, 29–56.

Wyatt, F. A clinical view of parenthood. *Bulletin of the Menninger Clinic*, 1971, *35*, 167–180.

Yalom, I., Lunde, D., Moos, R., & Hamburg, D. Post-partum "blues" syndrome: A description and related variables. *Archives of General Psychiatry*, 1968, *18*, 16–27.

Young, M., & Geertz, H. Old age in London and San Francisco: Some families compared. *British Journal of Sociology*, 1961, *12*, 124–141.

Young, M., & Willmott, P. *Family and kinship in East London*. London: Routledge & Kegan Paul, 1957.

Zaslow, M., & Pedersen, F. Sex role conflicts and the experience of childbearing. *Professional Psychology*, 1981, *12*, 47–55.

Zubin, J., & Spring, B. Vulnerability—A new view of schizophrenia. *Journal of Abnormal Psychology*, 1977, *86*, 103–126.

9

DYSFUNCTIONAL PARENTHOOD IN A DEPRIVED POPULATION

J. ALEXIS BURLAND

Parenthood resists objective investigation; but the resistances are in themselves illuminating. Like such subjects as love and politics, it reverberates with deeply personal memories, affects, and attitudes within each of us; investigator bias is therefore inevitable. The sight of a functional—or dysfunctional—mother–infant dyad arouses strong emotions of one kind or another, and objectivity is compromised. Yet it is the subjective response that operates as an essential investigatory tool. As many have stressed, the mother–infant interaction is a communicative process (Spitz, 1965; Bowlby, 1969; Mahler, 1972; Mahler, Pine, & Bergman, 1975; Brazelton, 1981; Brazelton & Als, 1979), and any investigator must be capable of tuning in on it, of reverberating with it, to perceive and understand it. This skill goes beyond formal scientific training, reaching back to personal experiences from the investigator's past life. Many of us have attended conferences where films or videotapes of parent–child interactions are shown as part of a formal presentation, and hearing a roomful of scientists oohing, ahing, and giggling, or gasping in shock. Such responses are not to be dismissed as trivial or insignificant; they are important clinical clues as to the basic nature of the parenthood experience, and its investigation.

This presentation will describe and attempt to explain a particular variety of parenthood, one that is unpleasant to observe and unpleasant to experience. Over a decade ago, I began consultative work with inner-city foster care agencies. Parenthood is at the heart of foster care, for it is usually parental inadequacy that necessitates a child's placement in care. It is substitute, improved, or remedial parenting that is the service required; and, foster parent selection and supervision is centered on the aspirant's capacity for parenting. The world of inner-city foster care, in the broad meaning of that phrase, is depressing, at least

J. Alexis Burland. Department of Psychiatry and Human Behavior, Jefferson Medical College of Thomas Jefferson University, and Philadelphia Psychoanalytic Institute, Philadelphia, Pennsylvania.

to the adequately parented object-related adult who has expectations of a tender, empathic parent–child interaction (Burland, 1980). Through previously inadequate parenting, most children enter foster care inexperienced at, and often resistant to, that kind of interaction; and, for a variety of reasons I shall not go into, many of those who volunteer to serve as foster parents view parenting in terms of moral training rather than nurturance or empathic dialogue. Many children do not thrive in such a situation; for many, foster care alone is not enough, and responsible agencies find themselves, therefore, involved in dispensing or arranging for counseling, therapy, special education, temporary residential treatment programs, etc.

It took me several years to realize from my contacts with many of the children I saw in evaluation, or with whom I became indirectly involved as supervisor of their social worker or therapist, that there were certain basic communicative differences between us, differences because we operated interpersonally within different systems. These differences were not racial or ethnic; to a psychoanalytic developmentalist such as myself, they were clearly psychological and developmental. As a result, our interpersonal expectations and "vocabulary" were in varying degrees out of synchrony. It was, by the way, puzzling and disturbing to discover how many of my professional associates did not notice this dyssynchrony; this seemed to account for many of the service and therapeutic failures well known among those who work with this population. In ongoing dialogue with those fellow professionals who could perceive this dyssynchrony, and through the use of psychoanalytic developmental psychology, especially ego psychology, object relations theory, and self psychology, I began the process of explicating what I was able to see from the start as a syndrome secondary to maternal inadequacy. I treated in analysis an inner-city child suffering from this syndrome in order to gather analytic clinical data. And I accepted a position as consultant to a community mental health agency which offered parenting education to mostly young, single, inner-city mothers. It is the clinical data obtained from observing these mothers and their infants that will serve as part of the basis for this presentation. However, as is well known, there is an inner psychological continuity between the parenting children receive, their resultant psychological development, the variety of parenthood they then eventually experience, and, therefore, the kind of parenting they dispense to their children. Therefore, my clinical data on the subject of parenthood cover events both before and after the fact.

I will start with a description of the syndrome I first observed in the children, follow with my later observations of the early mother–infant interaction associated with the syndrome, and end with a description of the prototypical parenthood experience in this population. This is the sequence in which I collected and endeavored to understand the clinical data, and it has a narrative flow that I think aids exposition.

THE "AUTISTIC CHARACTER DISORDER"

"Mindlessness" was the term I first used in attempting to find a word for the syndrome that almost from the start I recognized as a vicissitude of maternal neglect (Burland, 1977). Such children are prone to action without any thought as to social expectations, propriety, safety, or consideration for the feelings of others. They are frequently labeled as "hyperactive," which is an appropriate adjective but all too often an inappropriate diagnosis; that is, they are often medicated as though they were suffering from what is now called "attention deficit disorder." Those words, too, are *descriptively* accurate, but medication is ineffective in this syndrome except for its placebo effect upon parents and teachers.

I found the developmental concept of "hatching" as explicated by Mahler (Mahler, 1975) a more useful way of thinking of these children. That is, they suffer from a delay in the development of a consistent and stable perceptual investment in external reality, a shift from the more inward directed preoccupation of the newborn to the perceptual responsiveness with the symbiotic mother, a shift that occurs usually in the middle of the first year of life. Their seeming "mindlessness," therefore, reflects a lack of contact with their social and physical surround and the kind of realistic and secondary process thinking which such contact fosters. Spitz termed this shift in the first year of life a move from a coenesthetic mode to a diacritic one (Spitz, 1965). It is my belief that this occurs as a direct result of the "good-enough" mother–infant dyad; that is, the adequate mother draws the infant's attention to her as the latter moves into a gratifying symbiotic relationship, and out of his/her interest in experiencing this relationship the perceptual equipment used to perceive its sights, sounds, smells, and feel is libidinized and therefore developed.

The strongest confirmation of this hypothesis came from the analysis of the inner-city child (Burland, in press). Some 14 months into it, to my surprise, he came in one day evidencing exactly the phenomenon so readily observable in the infant when he/she hatches; that is, he was suddenly bright-eyed, focused, goal directed, and perceptive of me and the office in a way he had not been before. Shortly thereafter, his performance in school improved, and he became interested for the first time in learning and mastering the rules of games. In the analysis, he began to replace dyadic issues with triadic ones. In retrospect, the analytic material made clear that it was his libidinization of the "good symbiotic mother," in the transference, which preceded and, I believe, made possible this delayed shift.

Indeed, I soon gave up the rather inelegant and not very scientific sounding term "mindlessness" and replaced it with "autistic character disorder" because of what I was discovering of the genetics and dynamics of the syndrome. In Mahler's conceptualization, the infant with a "good-enough" mother moves from the initial normal autistic phase into the symbiotic phase, which peaks at about 6 months. This developmental event has been observed and described by many observers, but has been given a variety of names. It is Bowlby's "attachment," infant psychiatry's and the ethologist's "bonding," Spitz's "establishment of the libidinal object," the difference among the terms usually reflecting variations in the dynamic or theoretical understanding of the phenomenon. It is, however, not an automatic accomplishment, but reflects directly upon parenting, primarily by the mother, and her ability to tune in on and interact responsibly with her infant. This communicative process, called the "dialogue" by Spitz, is what Brazelton and his co-workers are currently studying in its minutest detail in their fascinating research (Brazelton, 1981; Brazelton & Als, 1979). The capacity (or lack of capacity) to participate in this "dialogue" is, of course, an important part of the experience of parenthood but, also, of "infanthood." The newborn is an active participant as well as the parent. However, the physically intact "normal" infant in the first months of life, participates, more reflexively than intentionally, and the more controllable variable is, of course, the mother's participation.

In the syndrome I was uncovering, this developmental accomplishment is less than adequately achieved, and a good symbiotic interaction does not evolve. These babies do not grow to resemble the baby food bottle label babies. They reveal varying degrees of failure to thrive, and are fussy and inconsolable, or limp and lost looking. They do not evoke the joyful warm feelings that the average 6-month-old does. They are visibly unrelated, and remain so both affectively and cognitively (i.e., hatching is delayed). Their state reflects their part in the parent–child interaction, and is a clue, as I hope to show, as to the nature of their mothers' parenthood experience.

Unrelatedness, then, becomes a central symptom of this syndrome, which can be understood developmentally as inadequate movement out of the autistic and into the symbiotic phase; ergo the term "autistic character disorder." The inadequate "hatching" is a central explanation for the second symptom, namely, cognitive lag. With but a few exceptions, these children do not use their intellectual equipment to cope, perceive, learn, understand, or plan. There is little stimulus to do so, either from within or without. Their minds as reasoning instruments are not libidinized. Even the quality of their fantasy life is poor, fragmented, unelaborated, plotless fantasies, many of them with a content of no more than "smash, crash!"—as was the case early in the analysis of the inner-city child to whom I have referred. On intelligence tests these children rarely score above 80, even though as skilled psychologists can discern, their "true potential" is closer to average.

The third symptom is, not surprisingly, a preoccupation with primitive destructive aggression. Without adequate libidinal ties, and with the accumulation of memory traces characterized by unpleasure, negative introjects eventually predominate. Lack of socialization, and, as we shall see, a susceptibility to narcissistic rage reactions, further contribute to this. And, over time, those identifications, internalizations, and ego capabilities which make possible the neutralization of hostile aggression fail to develop. The destructiveness is seen both in its active form as violent behavior and fantasies and in its passive form as an almost panphobic and often paranoid retreat from a world viewed as exclusively destructive and threatening.

Pathological narcissism is the fourth and final cardinal symptom of the "autistic character disorder." The lack of empathic parenting, as the self psychologists have observed, makes the development of a cohesive and functional self difficult (Kohut, 1971). These children feel themselves to be real and in focus only when experiencing instant gratification, when being destructive, or when convinced by their own illusions of grandiosity. Boys, in particular, by age 2 throw themselves into aggressive phallic narcissism, clearly for its restitutive function in covering over a core of depression, loneliness, and fear. Otherwise, they collapse and fragment in an instant, and can, particularly in adolescence, appear psychotic. Indeed, many are diagnosed incorrectly as schizophrenic when they are brought to the emergency room in the middle of the night or on weekends, wild, incoherent, destructive and self-destructive, and "paranoid." They often reconstitute fairly promptly if one relates to them with even a modicum of empathy and support (medication, especially heavy medication, alone, is insufficient and can be counterproductive).

So, in summary, unrelatedness, inadequate "hatching" with its resultant cognitive deficit, a preoccupation with violence, and pathological narcissism, are the characteristics of this syndrome, all of it relating to the early mother–infant interaction and reflecting, therefore, characteristics of the parenthood experiences of the mother.

OBSERVATIONS OF RELEVANT MOTHER–INFANT INTERACTIONS

One can observe the syndrome unfolding before one's eyes, *if one looks for it*. To be sure, it is apparent to almost all observers in extreme cases with failure-to-thrive of sufficient intensity to necessitate hospitalization, or where the abuse is blatant. But any assessment of progress is based on a set of expectations, and it is remarkable how varied are peoples' expectations of infants, and mother–infant dyads, in the first year of life. Even many professionals place an almost exclusive emphasis upon such musculoskeletal developmental milestones as rolling over, sitting up, standing, and walking. It is not unusual to read a developmental assessment which states an infant is "average" or "doing well" because he/she can walk, with an added aside that there is "some delay in speech," or a chance note of the absence of smiling. Rarely is the mother–infant interaction even mentioned. Winnicott said, "there is no such thing as an infant," meaning what there *is* is a mother–infant dyad (Winnicott, 1960, p. 39, footnote). This, however, is not universally appreciated or acknowledged.

The mothers whom I will describe (and they will be from the more severely afflicted to aid exposition) have much difficulty observing their own parenting in the manner that the objectrelated, promaternal-adequacy oriented observer does. Most of these mothers believe, with some degree of sincerity, that they are adequate mothers; they are, after all, doing what they "should" be doing according to *their* psychosocial system. They are often either perplexed by, or in disagreement with, instructions as to an infant's need for attachment, empathic dialogue, or greater nurturance. A rich lore of myths exists concerning child development which supports neglect, punitive attitudes, and a perception of the newborn as an independent and self-contained, thinking individual to be held responsible for all of his/her actions; the concept of a selfobject, empathic, nurturant dyad is totally foreign. The failure of *education* to correct this speaks for it as being a problem far less of ignorance than of "blind spots."

It can also be said that the mothers' understanding of the infant development and parenthood, what we label myth instead of behavioral science, is perplexing to, and rejected by, the observer from a different system. This dyssynchrony, noted initially in my interactions with autistic character disordered children is here again in evidence. But on careful consideration it can be seen that the issue is not parenting per se; it is an underlying, implicit set of unspoken and in part unconscious assumptions, personal as much as (if not more than) acquired by book learning. Parenting, as an art, comes from within, from animal instinctual givens, and from ego structures and identifications which have evolved from infantile experiences; formal education, though it has its role, is of secondary importance in most instances.

When I am involved in an observational interaction with a mother from one of these dyads, though our focus is on how she and her infant interrelate, each of us brings to the confrontation a trunk full of expectations, memories, experiences, and affects. Furthermore, for the establishment of meaningful communications, these must be taken into consideration. Not surprisingly, our clinical experience at the community mental health parenting education agency has been that one must first bring the mother into a working relationship on the basis of her dissatisfactions with her life in general, and her chronically ungratified needs, part and present, before there can be informed and productive exchanges about her parenting.

The infants are another matter. As many observers have noted, the infant from birth is an active participant in the mother–infant dyad. Also infants are clear and unanimous in their expectations. By direct observation, one can "rediscover the wheel" and see what observers have noted for years: The infant reaches out to its mother and attempts with what equipment he/she has to extract empathic, tuned-in, loving mothering. Brazelton's research (1981) graphically demonstrates this, particularly in his split-screen videotapes of mothers interacting with their infants. The infant, even in the first days and weeks of life, communicates certain expectations. The adequate mother, or our object-related, pro-maternal-adequacy staffperson, gets the message and endeavors to respond, that response evoking more efforts at communication from the infant until his/her strength and concentration flags and he/she retreats for a rest.

But the mothers of whom I write do not perceive the infant's communications, and so do not respond.

This lack of response is often in evidence prior to the infant's birth. There is a lack of concern or involvement with the baby-to-be. Sometimes future parenthood is dismissed as nothing to be concerned about; more often, in contacts with friends and counselors the subject simply never arises. Or, what is said is negative. There is great and dysmorphic fear of the delivery. Expectations are that the baby will be "bad," or threats are voiced as to what will happen if the baby doesn't behave or is of the "wrong" sex (i.e., most often a boy). Often, the baby is seen as a means to an end, a way to get "my own check," to get out of the home, or to "get" the baby's father, or to relieve loneliness, or have someone "who loves me." Often the pregnancy is a focus of strife between the mother and her parents. They demand that the mother-to-be get an abortion or prepare to place the child in foster care or for adoption. The mother-to-be refuses, out of angry defiance, asserting the baby is "*mine.*"

After birth, there is a failure of attachment. The newborns try and respond steadily to staff or to other mothers who have difficulty attaching to their own babies. The mothers express their unrelatedness in a variety of ways. Some are fearful of and hostile toward the infant, pull back, are passive and inept in a way that suggests they feel threatened by the baby. They seek out things to criticize, or frighten themselves with a kind of projected hypochondria in the form of fantasies of a variety of physical illnesses or handicaps in their babies. They treat the infants as though they were autonomous beings, reading into their actions conscious intent. The crying newborn, for instance, is assumed to be bad to its mother on purpose, and is told to stop it, or is physically punished. Such physical needs as feeding or diapering are dispensed in a perfunctory way without using the occasion to "dialogue" or as an opportunity for eye contact. If the baby serves as a narcissistic support for the mother, she will seem to be appreciative. Many of our more rejecting and distancing mothers will overdress and bejewel their girl infants to show them off, or will swagger with pride when their baby boys, toward the end of their first year when they are developmentally able to, act "tough," "bad," or destructive. But their narcissistic rage explodes when the baby ceases to be the selfobject source of gratification they demand by acting in a manner the mother does not find rewarding.

One does not see a good symbiotic phase for these dyads, and hatching does not occur or is abortive. By the end of the first year of life the prototypical picture is of a tense, driven, joyless, destructive, overactive toddler, his/her face in a constant frown, running around creating havoc and wreckage, while mother, usually from across the room and often with her back turned, interrupts her activities with profane and hostile criticisms and orders to stop, all of which are ignored. When frightened, and these children tend to be very fearful, some of them cling to their mothers, but their reliance on autoerotism and autoaggression is far more prominent, just as Spitz described in a similar population years ago (Spitz, 1951). It is a chilling experience to be in a room with a group of mothers and their toddlers and to hear no laughter and see not one smile. The subjective response for the staff is both a great challenge to their professionalism and a graphic clue to the nature of the problem with which they have to deal; it is also emotionally draining.

In the second year the cognitive lag and pathological narcissism are increasingly in evidence, and the similarities between mother and child as to these are equally striking. The mother is as explosive and impulsive in her actions toward the child as the child is in his/her actions either toward the mother or toward any other equally inadequately libidinized part of his/her surround. And each demands total compliance from the other, raging when their grandiosity is not supported by instant gratification. I recall one moving moment: An impeccably and stylishly dressed mother and daughter were sitting on opposite ends of a couch, the mother looking in another direction, screaming profanities at her daughter, demanding she do what her mother said at once, as she was after all her *mother*, while the girl, about 2, stared straight ahead, tears streaming down her cheeks, serous discharge pouring out of her nose and over her mouth and chin, screaming inconsolably at no one; and that was not an unusual moment between the two. The girl, by the way, had spent several months in foster care, but was removed from foster care when her mother heard her call the foster mother "mother."

A word is in order about the ability of either member of this dyad to respond to an empathic, nurturant outsider. As mentioned above, in the first half of the first year of life, the infants respond quite readily. One very intelligent but very depressed, dependent, and remote mother, who was usually "high" or at least looked to be drugged, complained bitterly that her 4-month-old daughter was "limp." Indeed, her daughter was usually to be seen slumped in a baby chair with a blank, unfocused stare (not unlike her mother's, by the way). I picked her up, looked her in the eye, spoke baby talk to her, and bounced her gently but playfully on my lap. She was indeed as limp as a dishrag at first, but within 60 seconds she was smiling, gurgling, stiffening her legs in an effort to stand, wiggling her fingers in delight. From a limp and depressing baby, she became a charming one. With much support and instruction from me, the mother was helped to do as I did and got a similar response. The mother's response in turn was primarily one of great surprise, but with some pleasure. Within 2 or 3 minutes, however, the girl was back in her seat, slumped, and mother was again lying on the couch, staring at the television set, and over the following weeks, the mother's complaints about her baby continued.

It is increasingly difficult to elicit a responsive potential as time proceeds, but there are enough examples of its being achieved to suggest that given the right approach and opportunity the possibility remains. This is particularly evidenced in work with the mothers, and relates in fact to the one therapeutic maneuver that seems to be universally effective with this population. As has been reported by others, the mothers have to be "mothered" first before they can do the mothering (Burland & Cohen, 1980); that is, the therapist must first bring the mother into a dependent attachment, usually by means of a combination of material gratification (and food, of course, is a key element), empathy, support, interest, and tolerance; and is this not the evocation of a still dormant infantile receptivity? (See Spitz, 1956; Winnicott, 1956.) The child I saw in analysis revealed a capacity to resume 7 years later what resembled developmental processes usually allocated to the first year of life, doing this in response to my bringing him into a libidinized dyadic transference by means of a combination of interpretation and the impact over time of the real relationship. In other words, the capacity for the expression of what is, after all, an inherent biopsychosocial animal instinctual interrelatedness, suppressed by the experience of maternal inadequacy, can, under certain circumstances be reactivated; explicating the specifics of those certain circumstances is a subject for another presentation. One of those circumstances, by the way, is to be in the presence of a gleeful, excited, well-attached 5- or 6-month-old infant, something we have seen when some of our inadequate mothers are introduced to the thriving infant of an adequate mother; perhaps there is a therapeutic potential here that could be further developed.

DEFINITION OF THE POPULATION UNDER STUDY

It is difficult to draw a circle around this group of mother–infant dyads. Sociological definitions based on geography, race, and socioeconomic status seem inadequate to me. Such definitions have a certain utilitarian function in identifying target populations for social programs, but they lack clinical, psychodynamic, or developmental specificity. Though the majority of these mothers with whom I have come in clinical contact are black and poor and live in the inner-city, there are many exceptions. For one thing, not all black, poor inner-city mothers, even among those at our agency, are like the ones I describe. Further, a failure in the development of an adequate symbiosis is a phenomenon that occurs in other settings as well, of course. Among my more suburban, middle-class patient population, although the sociocultural support systems place a high value upon a nurturent and emotionally committed maternal stance, there are mothers who are unable to invest adequately in their newborns for a variety of reasons—that is, pathological narcissism, borderline personality organization, depression, etc. In such instances it is not unusual to see these children suffering later from interpersonal, behavioral, academic, and narcissistic problems not unlike those seen among the inner-city population of which I write. In personal communications from fellow professionals I am told one can see similar phenomena among poor rural white populations as well. None of this is surprising; an infant's needs know no geographical or social boundaries as far as we know, and no single group of mothers has an exclusive claim to maternal inadequacy, although, as my data suggest, within some populations (i.e., the inner-city poor) the failure rate may be higher.

All observers confirm the growing severity of the problem; the birth rate among this population of inadequate mothers is greater than that of the population at large. That it perpetuates itself is a truism to which I will later return. The incidence is unknown to me, but I am sure that in Philadelphia, a city of a little less than 2 million, the number of dyads such as those of which I write number in the thousands. At meetings of the Vulnerable Child Subcommittee of the Social Issues Committee of the American Psychoanalytic Association this subject has been discussed several times; it exists equally in all of the other major urban areas of this country that were represented. In other words, I am attempting to explicate what is a significant social problem and a large pool of self-perpetuating human misery.

As the reader will have undoubtedly noted, I have said nothing of fathers to date. A very small percentage of the mothers with whom I work have a stable relationship with the father of their child. They are what are euphemistically called "single mothers." I have seen too few fathers to allow for easy generalization or characterization. What we hear about them from the mothers focuses almost exclusively on their abuse, self-centered sexual demands, and neglect, although, at first, at the beginning of their relationship, they are generally overidealized. Parenthood seems for many of them primarily a confirmation of their potency and a support to their phallic narcissism, in keeping with the use of phallic narcissism in the boys we have observed, as a restitutive defense against an anaclitic depression. Only a very few are active in parenting per se. Their absence from the scene says much in and of itself.

THE EXPERIENCE OF PARENTHOOD IN THIS POPULATION

Parenthood is but one strand of the complex weave of life. What characterizes parenthood for any one individual probably characterizes many other life experiences. As the working-through process in the psychoanalytic situation demonstrates, to the psyche the infantile past, current reality, and intense relationships such as the transference are all of a piece. So what is right and what is wrong with one's experience of parenthood is probably what is right and what is wrong with one's life. These mothers are not successful as parents, but they are also not successful as people, and by and large for the same reasons and in the same way. When observed objectively they prototypically reveal the same four symptoms I had seen initially in many of the children in foster care and in my young analysand. They are unable to enter into stable, loving attachments, including with their children. They feel alone, unsupported, and often lonely. They seek without real success someone who loves them, but are far less interested in or capable of giving love. What relationships they do have are ambivalent at best or sadomasochistic. Some feel themselves to be the victims of a cruel world, many are paranoidlike in the organization and intent they read into the world's cruelty, many are masochistic in the way they get themselves into one bad relationship after another. Others are filled with rage they direct outwardly at parents, neighbors, peers, and their children, either through ongoing sadistic behavior or in episodic explosive outbursts. They reveal their inadequate hatching by being inattentive to their surroundings, maladaptive and asocial in their actions, self-centered in their perceptions, responsive to the affect-charged myths about conception, birth, parenting, and infant development while remaining totally unresponsive to objective facts. Their desperate narcissistic needs are almost painfully apparent; their grandiosity is evident more in their infantile self-centeredness than in a grandiose manner; they yearn for mirroring and they are prone to overidealize (rarely a professional deliverer of service, more often their boyfriend or rock stars).

Parenthood in this context can serve a variety of functions. Some of the mothers want their baby as he/she is "mine," or because they think he/she will love them, even though most of them only rage at and provoke *their own* mothers. But, of course, they are raging at the postrapprochement mother of separation for not being the symbiotic selfobject they yearn for her to be. It is the latter dyad they hope to recapture from their infants, it seems, and it is this yearning upon which a therapeutic relationship must be built and around which parenting skills have to be developed.[1]

1. A pertinent question to ask is: How can they yearn to recapture a symbiosis which, if my hypotheses are correct, they never adequately experienced? That had been a puzzle to me for a while; it was, in part Spitz who gave me the answer, coupled with direct infant observation. Spitz has stated that in the first year of life inherent maturational processes were more significant than experiences; thereafter, the latter grow in significance (Spitz, 1965). It is possible to identify a large gray area between completely adequate parenting and grossly inadequate parenting, a middle ground in which the mother's care is sufficiently attentive and benign to meet at least most of the infant's physical needs. The objective observer can see the situations in which the mother's perfunctory or distracted, and not emotionally involved parenting is simply not perceived by the infant; the infant out of his/her needs, and out of the subjective experience of at least token or material gratification, makes mother into a better mother than she really is. I suspect this holds true for all infants; is not the symbiosis more of a symbiosis for the infant than for the mother? Mahler's use of the term was not meant to imply what the biological meaning of the term implies, namely, a 50:50 arrangement between two equally dependent individuals; it is instead meant to convey what is hypothesized to be the infant's subjective perception. As Winnicott has said, the mother's task is to support that *illusion* and it takes consistently and blatantly inadequate caretaking to fail to do that *altogether*; when that does occur one sees severe failure-to-thrive, marasmus, and death. In other words, the "good mother" which these mothers long to recapture is indeed a mother who existed mainly as an illusion, an illusion necessary for survival; but again, that is probably more universal than not, and what we are discussing is in fact a matter of degree. It is with this in mind that I have referred to the autistic element of the autistic character disorder as an "autism built for two"—that is, included within the autistic shell is the illusion of a symbiotic partner who remains divorced from diacritic or externally perceived stimuli, and who therefore never becomes spontaneously externalized and from whom one therefore never separates or individuates. Developmental movement for these mothers as well as for the children is accomplished by offering them an object that they can accept for the externalization of this suppressed illusory selfobject; if they can be brought then into a dyadic transference, they can over time separate and individuate out of it. This is far too great a burden to place upon an infant, of course, which is why they fail as therapists for their mothers; it is difficult enough as a task for a professional.

The interaction with the infant, however, ends up all too often as the arena in which chronic narcissistically charged sadomasochistic power struggles continue to be played out. The infants are perceived as potentially threatening; in one instance, a mother grew terrified in her last trimester that her still unborn child was trying to cannibalize her from within, and she endeavored to induce labor with a knitting needle. She almost succeeded; however, the baby was born premature, heroic measures were used to save the baby's life, who then returned home with her, experienced failure-to-thrive, had to be rehospitalized, was finally placed in foster care. Whatever warmth the yearnings for the symbiosis that never was might have brought to soften this situation, it generally starts to fade within weeks, and is gone by 2 or 3 months. I assume that a role is played by the winding down of those biophysiological changes associated with pregnancy and delivery that stimulate maternal attitudes. We can perceive the infants' efforts at evoking responsiveness from their mothers and we ourselves can "dialogue" with them and maximize this activity; but the mothers' failure to do so results in the infants eventually becoming unresponsive with them and this undoubtedly contributes to the decline in what tender yearnings the mothers might initially have felt.

Increasingly the infant is felt as overwhelming, parenthood is experienced as a drain and a form of imprisonment, and the mother's actions and words become more exclusively accusatory and rejecting. The chronic conflicts with *their* mothers or their boyfriends (or their counselors) become focused now on the adequacy or inadequacy of their parenting. One mother stormed out of the house on a snowy day with her naked baby under her arm simply because her mother had angrily criticized the fact that the baby was inadequately dressed even while indoors; this young mother felt fully justified in what she did as her mother had been, after all, "unfair." Battle lines are often drawn around the mother's feeling a desperate need to escape, get out, return to her friends, parties, or return to the social contacts in high school, and her family's refusal, or reluctant and half-hearted willingness to babysit for them so they can do so.

It is the baby's *needs* that are his/her greatest fault, not surprisingly. In almost all of our mothers one can see an early phase where the baby's tearful hunger evokes fear in the mother, and a sense of being overwhelmed and unable to cope. But this is rapidly replaced by anger, and accusations that imply hostile intent on the part of the baby. One mother, with great righteous indignation and self-pity, declared that her 2-month-old son never cried for anyone else, and only let others comfort or feed him, and this was proof that he hated her and was out to get her; she assumed that he was "mean" just like his father, or perhaps, she could admit, like herself. The mothers can hardly wait for their baby to walk, and to be toilet trained, for then the babies are "on their own." There is talk of day-care in the first months of their baby's life even for those mothers who do nothing but sit alone in their homes or apartments all day. There is peace, therefore, primarily when the baby is independently entertaining himself/herself. The fear of the baby's dependency seems to be made up of several parts; competition for gratification (quite early we realized that if we were going to see to it that the babies were to be fed, we had to feed the mothers as well); fear of their own ambivalent oral incorporative wishes which are projected onto the baby; the narcissistic mortification that results from feeling, and being, and being told they are, inept, that is, unable to differentiate between types of crying, or unable to always instantly soothe the baby. There is little joy in giving for these mothers in any part of their lives.

The tensions and conflicts that arise within months of birth often peak by the second year of life, then decrease as the mother withdraws from parenthood. The children are placed in day care, or, as if often needed, therapeutic day nurseries, often by age 2. They are assumed by then to be fully self-motivated and self-reliant, and are expected to perform functions for their mothers, including now attending to the care of the younger siblings. It is not unusual to see 3-year-old children who are responsible for getting their own meals, as best they can. Many of these mothers will not even get up in the morning to get their children ready for the very day-care program they want them to attend, and they then rage at the child as though it is the child's fault that he/she was not outside, dressed and fed, and ready when the bus came by to get them. If the children are "impossible" in mother's view, they are often relegated finally to foster care.

Those mothers, marginal but not altogether inadequate, who do better do so primarily because some spark of maternal, empathic relatedness is kindled, sometimes by the child, sometimes by a sensitive counselor who can activate in the therapeutic relationship the tenderness needed for parenting. Almost like magic this spark brings to life the child, the mother, the dyad, and the counselor, and often other mothers in the vicinity who can perceive it. It is not unlike the oohs and ahs heard at scientific meetings to which I earlier referred, and it speaks to the affective and subjective core of parenthood.

CONCLUSIONS

One might ask what can be learned about parenthood from examining such an aberrant variant, but there are so many instances of information gleaned from pathology that such a question would have to be viewed as more visceral than reasonable. I was told by the author of a manuscript on life in the inner-city, that the publishers, in spite of the advance they had given him, were reluctant to publish the book as what he described of inner-city life was so unattractive if not repugnant. Although for a variety of reasons my presentation has not been that graphic, I assume, from experience, some who read it will be put off. Yet, in spite of this affective response to these mother–infant dyads, in this age of cultural relativity it can be difficult for some people to assert absolute standards about human behavior. Child-rearing practices are possibly the most sensitive of all human behaviors to cultural influence. In fact, an hypothesis I would see as confirmed by my data is that a subculture can be defined by the child-rearing practices which perpetuate it. The data I have briefly recounted clearly reveal this to be the case here; the phrase "subculture of maternal deprivation" seems applicable. But cultural patterns notwithstanding, is a subculture of maternal deprivation equal to but simply different from a subculture of maternal adequacy? The babies, and clinical practice, tell us otherwise. One can see the babies struggling to interact with the responsive mother for which their inherent reflexive systems are preset; and they submit to the neglectful mothers reluctantly. Further, one sees even within the mothers flashes of a buried and dormant readiness to respond, sometimes with infants, sometimes with their counselor. I believe one can say that symbiosis is the *natural* outcome of an adequate first six months of parenthood, and that failure in this is therefore *unnatural*, even when and where it is supported by subcultural behavior and tradition. The researches of Spitz, Bowlby, Mahler, and Brazelton (among others), alluded to earlier, all point to the same conclusion. There *is*, therefore, I believe, an absolute standard against which to measure any mother–infant dyad, and this should make possible for public education to take a much firmer stand on the matter of what is right and what is wrong parenting, who should parent, and who should not. The social ramifications of this are great, of course, and need not be elaborated here.

What the newborns struggle to actualize in the dyad with their mothers, and what needs to be rekindled for these mothers to move into counseling and improve in their parenting, is a subjective, affective, interpersonal, mutually gratifying, joyful, contagious, communicative experience, one that is rooted in inherent animal instinct. It is difficult to measure by objective means without thereby losing the existential heart of its nature. Cognitive processes are of secondary importance, so that "education" is less effective than most people hope. The sharing of the subjective dimensions of the experience are key elements in both enjoying the experience as a subject and in observing the experience for purposes of clinical research. It may be in part an oversimplification, but a thriving baby *feels* differently to the clinician than one that is failing to thrive, and the same can be said for an adequate mother–infant dyad as opposed to an inadequate one; and this difference in feeling can be diagnostic.[2]

The natural and subjective aspects of parenthood both make it a difficult topic for objective study and indicate at the same time the personal equipment of the investigator necessary in his efforts at explicating the various dimensions of the phenomenon. The behavioral sciences have long been caught between physics and philosophy, and the development of a scientific method for organizing subjective data is long overdue; perhaps research in this area will offer us an opportunity to do so. But meanwhile, one cannot help but be moved to philosophical speculation when confronted with clinical data such as I have sketched. Philosophy has long seemed to me to be the inheritor of the discoveries of the rapprochement subphase of the separation–individuation process (Burland,

2. The diagnosis of childhood autism can also be made on this subjective basis; this is not surprising as the defect in autism relates to similar interpersonal processes.

1975, 1976; Lax, Bach, & Burland, 1980); that is, when confronted with the gap between wish and reality, between inside versus outside, between the mother of symbiosis and the mother of separation, one way of coping is to elaborate a system of expectations of and judgments about reality. To see a dysphoric mother–infant dyad, and to share in the pain of it, is to rediscover the mother of separation and to have to therefore cope with her. It is not by accident, for instance, that at the parenting agency I have described much time is spent by the staff discussing "life." Witnessing the destruction wrought by some of these mothers on their children and upon themselves brings out a strongly negative reaction in even the most empathic and liberal minded, and that presents one of the greatest problems for those who endeavor to work with them. Such current social issues as abortion, for instance, take on a dimension that is probably absent for the much larger segment of the community that has no exposure to this population. One wonders how, in nature, there can be a child-rearing system that aims to destroy rather than preserve and perpetuate life; indeed, were it not for the intervention of multiple social services, this population probably would extinguish or at least diminish itself, something that creates great moral dilemmas for the humanist. I raise this point not to offer an answer, or even to share a personal philosophical solution, but again to point to the personal reverberations that are a part of the study of parenthood, and which need to be acknowledged and utilized in our efforts at understanding it.

REFERENCES

Bowlby, J. *Attachment and loss* (Vol. 1: *Attachment*). New York: Basic Books, 1969.

Brazelton, T. B. *The first four developmental stages in attachment of parent and infant.* Paper delivered at the 12th Annual Margaret S. Mahler Symposium, Philadelphia, May 1981.

Brazelton, T. B., & Als, H. Four early stages in the development of mother–infant interaction. *Psychoanalytic Study of the Child*, 1979, *34*, 349–370.

Burland, J. A. Separation–individuation and reconstruction in psychoanalysis. *International Journal of Psychoanalytic Psychotherapy*, 1975, *4*, 303–335.

Burland, J. A. Conservatism and liberalism: A psychoanalytic examination of political belief. *International Journal of Psychoanalytic Psychotherapy*, 1976, *5*, 369–393.

Burland, J. A. *The syndrome of mindlessness in deprived children.* Paper presented at the Vulnerable Child Discussion Group of the American Psychoanalytic Association, Quebec, Canada, April 1977.

Burland, J. A. A psychoanalytic psychiatrist in the world of foster care. *Clinical Social Work Journal*, 1980, *8*, 50–61.

Burland, J. A. The vicissitudes of maternal deprivation. In R. Lax, S. Bach, & J. A. Burland (Eds.), *The development of object constancy.* New York: Aronson, in press.

Burland, J. A., & Cohen, T. Psychoanalytic perspectives on vulnerable and high risk children. In P. Sholevar, R. Benson, & B. Blinder (Eds.), *Treatment of emotional disorders in children and adolescents.* New York: Spectrum, 1980.

Kohut, H. *The analysis of the self.* New York: International Universities Press, 1971.

Lax, R., Bach, S., & Burland, J. A. *Rapprochement: Critical sub-phase of separation–individuation.* New York: Aronson, 1980.

Mahler, M. S. On the first three sub-phases of the separation–individuation process. *International Journal of Psychoanalysis*, 1972, *53*, 333–338.

Mahler, M. S., Pine, F., & Bergman, A. *The psychological birth of the human infant*. New York: Basic Books, 1975.

Spitz, R. The psychogenic diseases in infancy: An attempt at their etiological classification. *Psychoanalytic Study of the Child*, 1951, *6*, 255–275.

Spitz, R. Transference: The analytic setting and its prototype. *International Journal of Psychoanalysis*, 1956, *37*, 380–385.

Spitz, R. *The first year of life*. New York: International Universities Press, 1965.

Winnicott, D. W. On transference. *International Journal of Psychoanalysis*, 1956, *37*, 386–388.

Winnicott, D. W. The theory of the parent–infant relationship (1960). In *The maturational processes and the facilitating environment*. New York: International Universities Press, 1965.

10

THE PARENTS' EXPERIENCE
WITH THE CHILD'S THERAPIST

MICHAEL B. HOFFMAN

INTRODUCTION

In treating children, the sensitive area of working with the parents cannot escape the serious attention of the therapist. Although this can be confusing and demanding, I have found it important to listen very carefully to the parents. Not to do so may cause difficulty in the treatment of the child or prevent it altogether. It is important to resist the tremendous pressure to "do something" in response to the parents' demands and to ask first how we can better understand the meaning of their communications. The task is to conceptualize a point of view, a way of understanding the parents' request for help, that will broaden our understanding and therefore help us in our responses.

The chief complaint, the child's history, symptoms, and behavior, are vital information about the child. However, the method that yields additional critical information is the standard psychoanalytically informed technique of treating all communication as associations (mental connections among feelings, thoughts, and memories) including comments about parties not in the room. The most productive approach, then, is to use the parents' communications primarily, or at least equally, as information about the inner world of the experience as parent. With this mode, we attempt further to understand and respond to the *person* sitting in front of us. We are not just taking a history; we are interested also in hearing the parent's "dream." The dream is a composite picture made up of the parent's unconscious conflicts. The child will surely be an important character in the manifest content of the dream. It is necessary, however, to listen to a parent's broader presentation (the associations) in order also to understand the deeper inner meaning of his/her parenting experience. The characters in the dream can be self-representations (self-images) or projections of the parents, or

Michael B. Hoffman. Department of Psychiatry and Pritzker Children's Hospital, Michael Reese Hospital and Medical Center, Chicago, Illinois.

representations of different objects (persons) disguised as the dream character. Since the child's psychopathology is usually interwoven into the fabric of the parent's unconscious conflicts, the parents can also be in trouble.

Even if not aware of the extent their distress, parents are also looking for someone to help them. What is often desired is a new relationship wherein the parents can work to repair the difficulties experienced with current self and object representations. Frequently, part of the difficulty in the relationship with the child has been the parents' need to use the child in a reparative way for themselves (Miller, 1981). They often hope that the child therapist can provide the object relationship which they seek, consciously or unconsciously. The child's therapist must differentiate those parents who will need personal psychotherapy from those who can benefit from his/her (the child's therapist's) interventions.

The child, in trouble, may represent for the parents a "second chance gone wrong." This is related to the concept of parenthood as a developmental phase (Benedek, 1959) which presents, in part, a "second chance," or at least another opportunity to master unfinished developmental tasks as the parenting of a child proceeds. The parent may feel that he/she has failed once again to leap an old hurdle, and along with it, to gain hope of becoming a more successful person. Since parenthood is a critical adult experience, failure in the parenting experience contributes to feelings of failure as an adult. We are, perhaps, more familiar with humiliation, and guilt over hurting the child, as well as suspiciousness and jealousy of the therapist.

To provide the opportunity for a "second chance," the child therapist must gear his/her interventions to promote increased differentiation and ego expansion for a more realistic perception of the child to evolve. Our task is more than simply to advise. Giving advice presupposes a conscious psychology in which people can do anything they consciously think is reasonable (Spector, 1980). The child therapist makes interventions addressing the parents' pain and humiliation.

I believe there are many reasons why we don't listen to parents as we do to others who consult us. These reasons lie within the attitudes of the parents and the therapist. When a parent-as-person seeks individual help from a therapist there are anxieties, but prior to the initial contact there has been a long process of getting ready at a pace inwardly determined. Something was experienced, isolated, and observed as a problem. Even if it is something general, such as a sense of depression about which the person does not feel in control, the very fact of getting ready at one's own pace, coming, and describing a problem bespeaks some ego mastery. And, perhaps most importantly, the very act of coming is part of a contract to engage with the therapist in the exploration of the problem.

For that same person-as-parent to bring his/her child, however, the situation is very different. He/she is not organized or oriented toward a therapeutic process. Although there is the process of getting ready, often it is determined not by the parent's own need and pace but rather by the child's symptoms and the trouble it has caused. The parent is not ready personally and, therefore, he/she presents experience that is not yet fully mastered. Because the parenting function is so intimately tied up with the individual's entire personality, the parent may feel out of control. In addition, there is the realization that the therapist may hear from the child or spouse more than the parent is ready to reveal. The person may become increasingly anxious and defend against the assaults perceived both from within and from the external world. Part of the defense may be the implicit or explicit demand that no contract be made between the parent and the therapist to explore the anxiety in the room—only the anxiety about the person left at home with the baby-sitter. Consequently, the therapist is faced with an anxious person who is often highly defended and with whom there is, at least thus far, no contract. At the same time, the therapist knows that nothing can happen until a contract is made.

There are, additionally, the therapist's attitudes, his/her own dreams, transferences, and countertransferences. Ghosts of the past of all parties can invade the consulting room. Out of his/her identification with the position of the child, the therapist may react to the parents as representatives of his/her own parents, or therapists may identify with the parents, resonate with their anxiety, and avoid difficult issues to protect the parents and themselves in this identification. By working to understand the parents' anxiety, the way they defend themselves, and why they need to do so, we do not change anything immediately, except our own attitudes. By so doing, we gain more control in the countertransference area and can better proceed with the work (Fraiberg, Adelson, & Shapiro, 1975).

It is precisely because parents are so sensitive and defensive that child therapists refrain from attacking, criticizing, or judging. We help them toward cooperating in their own behalf by a nonthreatening attitude and the understandings we convey. This is, in fact, how we listen to our designated patients. Our purpose is to understand the child and the parents' dreams for the child and to be able to interpret the child to the parents. The aim is to help the parents permit the child to separate and grow. In some situations, there is an added benefit—more growth on the part of the parents, which may at times include personal psychotherapy.

We are aware that disorders in development in the separation–individuation stages prior to the achievement of object constancy cause particular difficulty between parents and children. This is prevalent in the parents and children we see who have predominantly borderline ego organizations. It may also be a problem for those with more fully developed personalities containing deviations or arrests. The following vignette is presented to illustrate such a situation.

CASE 1

Mrs. A consulted the therapist about 9-year-old Jill, her only child. This happened after repeated urgings by the school which believed that the child's difficulty in paying attention in class and general immaturity and irritability had an emotional basis in addition to the documented learning disabilities. At home, Jill alternated between being easily frustrated and contenting herself for long periods with doll play.

The mother's concern was that Jill would never achieve the maturity and competence to care for herself. Mrs. A was a bright but insecure woman who worked part-time as a freelance editor after several years of doing similar work full-time. Although she had achieved a high and responsible position she never felt prepared or adequate and always felt she was playing catch-up. She was determined to feel finally on top of her work and wanted the same for her daughter. That this was not happening was deeply disturbing to mother. For her, it was a failed dream. In addition she was concerned that therapy for Jill would only encourage further regressive and irresponsible behavior.

Mrs. A's anxieties developed understandably. She had been raised by a woman who came to this country as a teenager and retained traces of an accent and some discomfort with the language. The grandmother's general sense of inadequacy as a person and her insecurity, especially in intellectual matters, was denied and hidden behind the language impediment. The grandmother couldn't help the mother sufficiently with her dependent longings nor, as is often in such cases, tolerate her hostility. Mother's "dream" lay in her hope that there would be bliss and relief with her daughter. She hoped to recreate a mother–infant symbiosis in which she could be both the loving mother and, by identification, the loved child. However, the mother's unconscious conflict about her own dependency needs made her irritable with her daughter's helplessness. Her own needs were disavowed and seen as "bad," and projected onto Jill. Through this process of projective identification, mother confused her own needs with those of her daughter and remained somewhat withdrawn out of her discomfort. She was pleased and proud of the "independence" Jill displayed even as an infant when she amused herself in her crib until late in the morning, allowing mother to sleep. In a deeper way, mother had never felt confidence in her own mother or herself and thus could never convey to Jill the confident expectation that she would grow into a competent adult. Mother could only convey her hopes and fears through anxious demands.

The result was for Jill to develop precocious ego strength in some areas and a pseudoindependence that attempted to bind her affects and impulses in imaginative play, thus not burdening or threatening the needed relationship with her mother. The result was successful only partially. Jill remained in a state of nearly constant agitation, including substantial fearfulness of any impulse break-through. She could not integrate into her personality an awareness of how she really felt because she feared that her mother couldn't bear it or help her with it. This precluded any genuine freedom to grow, including in the charged in-tellectual and academic realm. Such developments have been discussed by Win-nicott (1965) in terms of a "false self-organization" and also in an elegant way by Alice Miller (1981).

The understanding of this "dream" was enhanced and enriched by trans-ference interactions in the therapy with Jill, who was an attractive, likeable girl. During one period in the treatment, Jill's attitude toward the therapist alternated between open involvement and imperious exclusion. She protested her compe-tence and self-sufficiency and regally interrupted the therapist's attempts to talk. The therapist said that it seemed he was supposed to be high on the list of people who were afraid of Jill. She loved it and allowed the therapist to demonstrate his fear both of her anger and of the infantile, dependent side as well. She began to listen to the interpretation that she worried that the therapist too, like mother, would be frigthened of her feelings and thus leave her alone.

Jill's imperiousness represented in part an identification with her mother at her most demanding self. This, however, is not unusual in children whose parents have been afraid of affects. In a defensive way, the child attempts to scare off any intimacy that could arouse painful affects. Often, intimidating children have been raised by intimidated adults.

As with Jill, the mother related to the therapist from an anxious distance. She was very cooperative and committed to Jill's well-being and appeared sat-isfied to have infrequent contact with the therapist. This seemed to be an ideal arrangement. However, the mother's own needs were experienced in other ways. Her desire for a dependent relationship was revealed in the anxiety that Jill would become too dependent. Her concern about her capacity as a mother manifested itself in her anxiety that the therapist would become too valuable to her daughter. Jill reflected this in her own anxiety about regressive needs and in her fear of having something mother needed. In time this became a formidable interference in that Jill did not feel the permission to engage herself fully in the treatment. The loyalty conflict and her fear of injuring her mother, Ekstein's (1971) "neg-ative megalomania," were not manageable. Since the mother declined the re-commendation for her own separate treatment, the therapist decided to see her on a regular basis every 6 weeks.

The purpose and content of the sessions with mother revolved primarily around the elucidation of Jill's issues. These included Jill's anxieties about her dependency needs and the fear of reexperiencing the painful affects associated with previous traumas; the fear of her impulses, especially the fear of hurting mother; the fears of feeling driven by unnamed and uncontrolled inner forces; and her concerns for the fragility of those around her. This, of course, captured many of the issues mother herself had disavowed. She was able, however, to tolerate the discussion of these affective issues because they concerned Jill. She was powerfully motivated to tolerate her anxiety because of her love for her daughter. Also, a discussion of these issues as they related to Jill was a sufficient displacement to make the intensity of the affects tolerable and thus require less defensiveness. In time, the mother was able to discuss the idea of her transfer-ences to Jill. She saw she had made Jill into a parent to serve her needs—that she needed Jill to be loving and accepting of her. This gave Jill the frightening power to withhold love. This is similar to the technique in psychotherapy or psychoanalysis of addressing material outside the direct transference of the patient to the therapist. This understanding of feelings about outside events and transferences to other objects can be enlightening, particularly as an initial approach to highly charged material.

The transference to the therapist was to someone who could understand and tolerate those affects without enormous fear. Experienced in this way, he functioned as the helpful new object. Here, too, the intensity of her own longing and affects was diminished to manageable levels by her recognition that the therapist was not a person there exclusively for her. In the context of this new relationship, the mother became less vulnerable and less narcissistically injured by the failings she perceived in herself and in her daughter. She was not just a bad mother; she was also a person with her own conflicts which she could address.

These factors enabled the mother to expand her awareness and increase her ego capacity. She could regard Jill better as a separate person with her own needs. After 1½ years of such meetings, the mother was able to tolerate the idea that such conflicts were also present in herself. Eventually, because of the lowered feeling of narcissistic injury, she was able to seek personal psychotherapy.

CASE 2

Another example, although more troubled and interfering, was Mrs. B who came for consultation regarding 8-year-old Nancy, the older of her two daughters. The mother complained that Nancy had uncontrollable temper tantrums, was inconsiderate and selfish, and did poorly in school. While the mother had nothing at all good to say about Nancy, she could only praise her younger daughter's loving nature. Mrs. B had a severe borderline character disorder with profound symbiotic needs. She could not tolerate the depths of her depression, insecurity, or rage, all related to the traumatic relationship with her own mother. These affects were repudiated and attributed to Nancy. The affectionate feelings were entirely separated and attributed to the younger daughter, through the processes of projective identification and splitting.

Mrs B did not want to see the therapist at all. There was no capacity for her to consider that any part of the situation or the affects and impulses had anything to do with her. She did call frequently in a rage about Nancy's destructiveness and vindictiveness. And at times she included the therapist as an enemy. For hours, and years, the therapist tried on the phone to be supportive of Mrs. B without confirming her projections. The therapist's failure to retaliate was the opposite of her internalized expectation. The contact with the therapist drained some of the intensity of the rage at her daughter, although there was little change. This shift was just sufficient to allow Nancy to form an alliance with the therapist strong enough to help her to separate and grow.

The model I have described is not one of simultaneous treatment of child and parents. It may be beneficial, however, to meet with the parents regularly, if not often. The frequency varies: The parents' unconscious conflicts, with resulting transferences and projections onto the child and the therapist, are occurring all the time, not just when the situation is labeled "treatment." It is the work with the parents that may permit enough resolution of these conflicts to allow the individuation of the child to proceed and treatment to continue. The additional benefit that accrues sometimes is genuine separation for the parents. This is evidenced by recognizing those aspects of the difficulties that are internal to themselves. Personal psychotherapy may be sought by some parents in response to achieving such insight.

In some ways, this technique parallels some models of psychoanalytically oriented supervision. Here, the supervisor helps the therapist understand the patient's experience, conflicts, and defenses. Also, within the specific focus of the therapist–patient relationship, the supervisor may point out countertransference difficulties that inhibit the development of the therapeutic relationship. In our work with parents, their countertransference to the child is central. We function as consultants to the parents and the parenting process.

In my experience much of the work with parents has to be done between them and the child's therapist, even if both parents have their own treatment. The parents' individual treatments will not necessarily focus on the child and his/her treatment. In general, working with the child's therapist offers the reality of the therapist's actual attitudes as a reassurance and correction of transference distortions. The work is a statement of the parents' importance in the treatment, and allows the parents to participate more as the competent parents they want to be and whom the child needs. It also gives the parents the opportunity to hear positive things about the child. This can contribute to lessening the estrangement between parent and child.

Probably of greatest importance is the fact that most parents are not in treatment, and are not prepared to undertake treatment with another therapist for issues which involve the child. Suggesting that they do so is often experienced as an assessment that the main difficulty lies with them. This is disturbing and bewildering precisely because they have not yet acquired an understanding of how their conflicts are connected to or separate from their evolving experience of the child. It is exactly this interrelationship that the child therapist addresses. A parent's decision to seek personal therapy for his/her involvement with a child is often accomplished in the work with the child's therapist. There will be, however, many situations in which the sole responsibility for parental work will remain exclusively with the child's therapist.

The parents' relationship with the child's therapist is certain to have repercussions in the child's treatment. They will wonder both about confidentiality and "who is this treatment really for, anyway?" But in some sense, the child is also reassured, because there can be no treatment if there is not an alliance between the therapist and the parents. Otherwise, the loyalty conflict will be unmanageable and the child will have to preserve the relationship with the parents at the expense of the treatment.

SUMMARY

A most important and difficult area in child therapy is working with parents. Their attitudes affect the child at home, and determine the atmosphere that will or will not make therapy for the child possible. This chapter suggests that we must listen to parents very carefully, just as we do with our patients, even though they do not come as such. We listen for the history, but understand most by hearing what the parents say as associations having meaning for themselves. Furthermore, the chapter suggests that in this way we hear a report of the parents' unconscious conflicts that is much like a dream. The subjective meaning of the child tends to be determined by the parents' unconscious conflicts which interfere with a more objective view. At the same time, this interferes with the parents' attempt to resolve unfinished developmental tasks. To put this another way, we are faced with the recognition that the "second chance" which should be afforded by the parenthood experience has gone awry.

This directs us specifically to where the parents are experiencing difficulty with the child, and wherein they desire assistance. They seek a new opportunity, or a new object relationship, in their effort to heal the difficulties with the child and themselves. We intervene by translating or interpreting the child to the parents, including elucidating the parents' roles and importance, as well as the child's struggles and pain. But as is often the case, a person can only hear about the pain of another with whom there is conflict if the person's own pain is understood. It may be that the child therapist is the first person with whom the parent has been able to acknowledge the grief involved in the relationship with the child, or the grief of his/her own life.

Our purpose is to help the parents better understand, both cognitively and affectively, themselves, the child, and the relationship between them. This is an act of mastery that increases self-esteem and helps rearrange the relationship between the generations. Child and parents are now freer to address their own developmental tasks, and freer to utilize treatment when indicated.

There are important reasons why we often do not listen to parents as we do to others. We are accustomed to the stance of one who presents himself/herself as needing help. The parent is often more anxious, more defended, and not prepared to make a therapeutic contract that includes self-examination. Both the parent's and therapist's reactions need to be considered by the therapist. We must keep in mind that most parents do not perceive themselves as patients in bringing the child to a therapist. This makes possible the nonthreatening and nonjudgmental attitude that will allow the parents to cooperate as fully as possible on behalf of their child and themselves.

REFERENCES

Benedek, T. Parenthood as a developmental phase. *Journal of the American Psychoanalytic Association*. 1959, *7*, 389–417.

Ekstein, R. *The challenge: Despair and hope in the conquest of inner space*. New York: Brunner/Mazel, 1971.

Fraiberg, S., Adelson, E., & Shapiro, V. Ghosts in the nursery: A psychoanalytic approach to the problems of impaired infant–mother relationships. *Journal of the American Academy of Child Psychiatry*, 1975, *14*, 387–421.

Miller, A. *Prisoners of childhood*. New York: Basic Books, 1981.

Spector, J. S. Personal communication, 1980.

Winnicott, D. W. Ego distortion in terms of true and false self. In *The maturational processes and the facilitating environment*. New York: International Universities Press, 1965.

11

THE EFFECT OF EARLY
PARENT LOSS ON FUTURE PARENTHOOD

SOL ALTSCHUL
HELEN BEISER

INTRODUCTION

The study of the effects of loss by death of a parent in childhood has been going on for approximately 30 years at The Institute for Psychoanalysis in Chicago. The original study began in the early 1950s when it was discovered that several student analysts in supervision with Dr. Joan Fleming had patients who had suffered such a traumatic experience (Fleming, 1963; Fleming & Altschul, 1963). In 1976, The Barr–Harris Center for the Study of Separation and Loss during Childhood[1] was established to work with families and children who had recently experienced the loss of one or both parents by death. In this chapter, we will present observations of the effects of loss in childhood of a parent through death on the parenting functions of adult patients who were studied during their psychoanalyses or intensive psychotherapies.

We are aware that there are a surprising number of ways in which a child may lose the care of one or both parents. Separations and losses occur because of wars, occupational shifts, desertion, illnesses and hospitalizations, suicide, murder, or imprisonment. Increasingly, a frequent type of loss is separation or divorce of the parents. Here, the change is in the loss of the home rather than the loss of a parent. Wallerstein and Kelly (1980) have been studying intensively

1. The Center was created by funds made available to The Institute for Psychoanalysis, Chicago, by George Barr and Irving B. Harris.

Sol Altschul. Faculty, The Institute for Psychoanalysis, The Barr–Harris Center for the Study of Separation and Loss during Childhood, and Department of Psychiatry, Northwestern University, Chicago, Illinois.

Helen Beiser. Faculty, The Institute for Psychoanalysis, The Barr–Harris Center for the Study of Separation and Loss during Childhood, and Department of Psychiatry, University of Illinois, Chicago, Illinois.

the complexity of the responses of children and parents to divorce, which may be one of the most complex experiences to which a child may have to adapt.

Although any loss of a parent during childhood may be experienced as a trauma, it is well known that its effects are not directly proportionate to its type or intensity. To some it is devasting, to others a challenge. Many famous people have lost parents in childhood. For example, Lincoln's loss of his mother and tendency to depression is well known (Clark, 1933). On the other hand, loss of a parent early in life has been acknowledged as a significant issue for mental illness and adjustment in adulthood, particularly with regard to depression (Hilgard & Newman, 1959; Roy, 1981).

VARIABLES THAT INFLUENCE THE EFFECT OF LOSS

In order to discuss how adults who lost parents in early life experience their child-care role, we will begin by considering the variables which influenced the effect of the loss in childhood. Although there are many possible outcomes and adaptations, the circumstances surrounding the loss in childhood may have considerable significance. Some of the specific issues are whether the death was expected or not. What were the child's involvement in the death or grief process? Did the child have someone whom he/she could question or to whom he/she could express feelings? Was he/she permitted grief or anger, was he/she permitted to see the grief of others? To what extent was the child allowed to participate in rituals? Or was there denial?

The age of the child at the time of the parent's death is critical. The preverbal child reacts to changes in the caretaking environment with awareness that something is missing. Possibly, he/she may react more to the distress of the surviving parent than to the loss. At this time, the loss of the mother may be felt more than the father. However, by 5 or 6, the child has a clearer sense of a specific person, although the function may still be the important loss. In the late Oedipal and early latency period (5 to 8 years) the death may represent an Oedipal victory or defeat depending on the sex of the child and that of the dead parent. The early latency child seems to suffer most overtly. During this period, the dead parent was a very real person, and a model for the child of the same sex. Additionally, the child may suffer intense grief at a time when he/she has not yet developed supportive type peer relationships. Hilgard, Newman, and Fisk (1960) found that adults who suffered parent loss at 10 years or older made the best adaptation as adults. In our cases, we have observed that preadolescents and adolescents seem resentful of the disruption of their lives brought about by the death. They seem angry and to want to continue their established relationships and activities. They may not fully feel the loss until they experience another significant loss in adulthood.

Other considerations of the impact of childhood parent loss upon adults should be noted. The quality of the relationship with the dead parent must be examined for understanding subsequent fantasies and identifications. Similarly, the relationship with the surviving parent must be evaluated to determine how supportive the child's ongoing relationship is with that parent. This is relevant for understanding how the child will adapt and proceed with his/her course of development. For example, can the parent reveal grief and allow the child to do so? Does the parent's dependency need overburden the child and catapult him/her into premature adulthood? Also, one should assess the resources in the family and community and how the surviving parent used these and/or permitted the child to use them. Finally, the temperamental, intellectual, and physical endowment of each child must be considered. Only continued study can enable us to evaluate and weigh the many variables which affect the child who experienced early parent loss and its significance for subsequent adult parenthood. This brief overview was presented to lay the groundwork for our next section which will describe adults who sustained early parent loss, and the adult experience of parenthood as observed in the clinical situation.

CLINICAL EXAMPLES

From a clinical point of view, one can expect to observe a variety of reactions and potential difficulties in the parenting function in those individuals who have a history of suffering a loss of a parent or parents in childhood. Reactions can range in such individuals from inability to marry or marrying and choosing not to have children, to having children and adequately performing the job of parenting. Between these extremes are those individuals who marry, have children, and then experience significant difficulties in the parenting function.

We have already enumerated the many types of losses that are possible, but we will present only examples of individuals who suffered a loss by death of one or both parents during the formative years. We do this because our study to this point has been primarily with individuals whose loss has been by death, and because loss by death provides case material where the developmental tasks and the effect on parenting can be more clearly delineated.

It has been our experience from work with adults who experienced a loss by death of a parent in childhood that the greatest personal difficulties occur when the loss happened during the latency period and the deceased parent is of the same sex as the child. It would seem that this configuration is also important for those individuals who subsequently have difficulty in their parenting function. Children in this developmental stage present a combination of being advanced far enough in their development so that the loss has a profound effect on them, while their capacities to deal with the loss have not yet reached an optimal point to master the loss. Our experience indicates that when problems in the subsequent parenting by these bereaved children arise, they have their roots in two major areas: (1) the types of identifications with the dead parent and their child, and (2) the impact of the lack of experience with the dead parent in developmental stages that go beyond the point of loss. Handling of developmental struggles with one's own children makes one fall back on experiences that one had with one's own parents during the same or similar struggles in the parent's development. Benedek (1959) pointed out how developmental struggles are reactivated in the parent as the child goes through the various developmental phases. The parental historical experiences can thus be called upon consciously and unconsciously to foster or hinder development in their own children. We will proceed to discuss individuals who have suffered losses that affect their subsequent parenting function.

Effect of Father Loss on a Man

Mr. A presents an informative example of problems in parenting because he shows both of the aspects that produce difficulties in parenting and also demonstrates the effect of differences due to gender. Mr. A was the youngest of three children with two much older female siblings. His parents were in their late 30s when he was born, and his mother was extremely attentive to him to the point of intrusiveness. His relationship to his father was more obviously ambivalent. They enjoyed time together and his father regaled the young boy with stories of his adventures. On the other hand, the father often disappointed the youngster by promising excursions which he failed, with excuses, to carry through. Mr. A remembers being extremely angry at these times and literally striking out at the father. Mr. A was not aware of any great difficulties in the parents' relationship, but there was no affection expressed between them. Both older siblings had left the home and were working and planning marriages of their own. They seldom visited and were not important figures in the family constellation during his latency years. In retrospect, Mr. A wonders what was wrong with the parents' marriage, remembering how almost nightly he would get into bed with them and notice the physical and emotional distance between them. The parents were also erratic and in conflict with each other in their treatment of Mr. A, and seemed to take alternating positions of permissiveness and strictness. Rarely were they able to present an agreed-upon, coordinated stance with the child. In addition, Mr. A realized that he got much more affection from each of them than they gave to each other. All of this served to give Mr. A an exaggerated feeling of power and importance in his family constellation. Later, this contributed to his unconscious attitude about the relative power and influence of his son in the family as compared to that of his daughters.

In spite of these feelings of importance, Mr. A considered himself an unhappy child. His father's inconsistencies bothered him greatly and he was excessively stimulated by his mother's undue attention and intrusiveness. He was a stubborn child who was prone to minor destructive acts such as destroying others' belongings and marring household items. He was difficult to punish and the parents were intimidated by him and often threw up their hands in despair. It was in this angry atmosphere, after another promised excursion and disappointment, that the father committed suicide, when Mr. A was 9 years of age. Mr. A had many complex and contradictory feelings surrounding the loss. Initially, Mr. A responded to the tragedy with shock and disbelief. He cried briefly and felt some sadness and grief, but also felt some sense of pride as though he was now the man of the house as, indeed, he had been encouraged to feel by visiting mourners. Of course, these feelings faded rapidly when the impact of the loss descended upon the household. Anger toward both parents emerged. The mother's grief and helplessness increased Mr. A's anger and led to a prolonged sense of disillusionment with her.

As the years went by, Mr. A never fully faced the reality of the loss. Part of him functioned as though father was just temporarily ill and would soon return to the family circle. Another part of him felt deeply guilty and responsible for father's death, remembering his angry feelings toward father and feeling responsible for the conflict between the parents and father's despair. In therapy, Mr. A began to verbalize, for the first time, what a terrible deed (the suicide) his father had perpetrated on him and his mother and how disillusioned he must have been at the time of the death. Yet, at the same time, he realized that he was afraid that he, too, would end his own life, both as a punishment for the father's death and an identification with father in this tragic act.

Life was very difficult for Mr. A after his father's death and he suffered through many hardships. His brilliant mind allowed him to get through his schooling, although his record was extremely erratic, depending on the emotional climate at any particular time.

Important for our discussion of parenthood was Mr. A's relationship to women, seemingly delineated largely by his needs to be the caretaker. In his teens, when he began heterosexual activity, he entered into a series of erratic relationships with women with whom he would have brief, intense, unsatisfying interludes. In these relationships, he did a great deal of caretaking, stimulated by and similar to what he had experienced with his mother, who became depressed and almost nonfunctioning after his father's death. In his 20s, he married one of these women and a son was produced by this union. The marriage was stormy due to the immaturity of both partners and increasing difficulties of the young wife. She turned out to be an extremely volatile, emotional woman whose affects and behavior were so labile and erratic that she was basically unable to provide steady, secure caretaking of their son. Mr. A, feeling identified with the child's needs and also needing to shield his wife, began to make decisions about the child's upbringing and became the main source of emotional support for the child. Mr. A took over such support willingly and often provided the physical care of the child as well. In general, he seemed to be very much in tune with the young child's needs and conflicts. A divorce took place after about 5 years of marriage. Following a brief stay with the mother, the child took up permanent residence with Mr. A and his new wife. Mr. A's second marriage was a much improved, enduring relationship which produced two daughters.

An essential point for discussion was the difference in Mr. A's parenting functions as observed in his two families. These were affected markedly by the sex of the children and Mr. A's identifications. The relationship to his son was the most complex and stormy. The identifications between Mr. A, his son and the deceased father were so interrelated that unconsciously Mr. A had difficulty differentiating his son from his own representation as a boy and himself as a person. Thus, Mr. A expected his son to feel and behave as he had as a young child and was overly sensitive to issues of competition and power in the child. He began to feel threatened by the child as he imagined his father had felt about him. He could also empathize with the child's struggles to assert himself, but, at the same time, he feared unconsciously that the child would displace him and be the cause of the violent death that he was sure awaited him. This was especially true as he and his son approached the ages he and his father had been at the time of the father's suicide. These complex identifications and misidentifications produced the following kinds of impasses. Discipline was a serious problem for both father and child. Mr. A loved his son but feared him because of his own complex unconscious feelings toward his father and the expectation that the child was enraged at him as once he had been toward his father. He wanted to give the child a better chance in life than had been his, and, in particular, to keep promises even when the child stubbornly disobeyed and needed restraint. Mr. A would, therefore, at times overindulge the child and then impose severe restrictions on his activity and movements. This was much like the inconsistencies both his parents had displayed toward him. Also, during this time, Mr. A was preoccupied with fantasies of his own death and belief that he would not survive beyond age 40. The forms of fantasied death varied, but most often was a form of suicide. The marked ambivalence toward the child was intensified as the child grew, and, in fact, developed many of the traits and characteristics that Mr. A had shown when he was a child, thereby, increasing the mutual identification.

At adolescence, Mr. A was at a complete loss as to how to deal with his son's beginning heterosexual interests. He continued to treat his son as though he were a latency child and the only way he could imagine to show his interest and affection was to offer the son trips and excursions that were no longer appropriate. It was clear that the son no longer wished to participate in such plans, preferred the company of his peers, and wished to pursue outside interests. Seemingly, Mr. A was able to be sensitive and alert to the needs for comfort, closeness, and encouragement in a latency-age boy, but at a loss to deal with the more independent, growing adolescent.

With his daughters, Mr. A was far less conflicted and was able to feel loving toward them, but yet remained somewhat cool and distant. He left their care almost completely to his wife. He participated in leisure activities with his wife and daughters, but never made plans for any special activities with them. His daughters did well in school and socially, but Mr. A avoided them to a significant degree. He confided to the therapist that he did not want them to become too attached to him because they would feel too much grief and suffer too much if he were to die. Since Mr. A unconsciously did not expect to survive very long, he tried to protect his daughters by minimizing his significance to them. Of course, the effect of this attitude was to deprive the children of the expected supplies which all parents provide as an integral aspect of parenting. The case of Mr. A demonstrates clearly interference in the parenting function. With his son, complex identifications with both the son and dead father, along with the lack of experience with parents in adolescence, have led to severe problems in the parenting function that have contributed to problems of growth and development in the child. With his daughters, Mr. A identified with the potential grief and feelings of loss that they might experience, but he could not appreciate that his withdrawal itself produced deprivation. While the parenting function in regard to his daughters is probably more benign, nevertheless, it poses problems for the daughters' development.

Effect of Mother Loss on a Woman

In another case, we have a woman who lost her mother by death at age 7. This was a natural death due to a chronic illness in which mother was incapacitated to varying degrees. In general, Mrs. B's early life seemed to have been content. In the first few years of her mother's illness, the symptoms were not severe and did not produce any noticeable effect in the household. Mother was ambulatory and was warm and loving to Mrs. B and was able to perform the major caretaking functions. Mrs. B remembers many happy occasions with her mother with the exception of mother's profound anxiety when the whereabouts of Mrs. B were unknown to her. During the last year of the mother's life, the mother became increasingly symptomatic, but still was able to carry on most of her caretaking and household duties. Other relatives, however, began to participate in Mrs. B's care. It was only in the last few months of the mother's life that she became bedridden and was unable to care for her child. It was also at this time that some of mother's symptoms became extremely obvious and played a part in Mrs. B's later somatic complaints. It later became clear that, in spite of the mother's warm and considerate concern for her child, her illness and death had a profound effect on Mrs. B and contributed to Mrs. B's fearful image of herself as she grew and became a woman, wife, and mother.

Upon the mother's death, a short, hectic period followed in which Mrs. B was farmed out to relatives. At this time, Mrs. B was unempathically scolded by a relative because she seemed not to respond to the death, but continued to play with her friend in a "business as usual" fashion. It was about a year before the father could arrange to have his daughter live with him. Life with father took on a completely different tone than it had when mother had been the primary caretaker. Father was erratic, volatile, and inconsistent. He imposed irrational rules upon the child which, at times, bordered on the bizarre. Because of the inconsistencies, Mrs. B never knew what would offend father and bring forth a storm of rage. On the other hand, father often indulged Mrs. B with expensive clothes and outings. Being an only child, Mrs. B was generally lonely and frightened. Because of father's rules, she never brought children into the home and rarely visited other children. Father never remarried.

In adolescence, Mrs. B began to blossom, became popular with boys, did extremely well in school, and began to show artistic talent, so that her writing and drawing won school honors. She won a scholarship to a major university and so was able to leave home and get away from the stifling atmosphere of her home. While Mrs. B was delighted with her new-found freedom, she began to develop a multitude of somatic symptoms that at times incapacitated her and seriously interfered with the utilization of her many talents. Sometimes, she was bedridden for weeks with respiratory symptoms, joint pains, or gastrointestinal complaints. Repeated physical examinations brought forth no specific diagnosis, but, in retrospect, the symptoms reminded her of some of mother's chronic difficulties. In spite of these hindrances, Mrs. B was able to finish school and begin to work, but she could not make use of her special talents to further a career. She met a young man at work whom she consciously chose because he was the opposite personality to her father; that is, he was quiet and passive. After a brief courtship they married and had a daughter within a few years.

Mrs. B was quite pleased with her daughter and had a warm, intimate, loving relationship with her, and the daughter thrived. Mrs. B, however, began to have increased somatic complaints and the marital relationship became distant and unsatisfactory to both partners. When the daughter was about 6, Mrs. B began to change more toward herself and the child. She began to have fears of developing a fatal illness and dying. Her somatic complaints increased markedly and she began to take to her bed more often. She became quite irritable with the child and was fearful about the child's welfare. She began to impose severe limits and restrictions on the daughter's activities, worried constantly about the child's welfare, and was almost in a panic the minute the child was out of her sight. Within the next year, Mrs. B found herself imposing more and more irrational limits on the child, so that the child began to be timid and frighened and do poorly in school. Mrs. B was aware of the irrational aspect of her behavior and the effect on her child, but was unable to make any changes in her behavior. It was at this point, when her daughter was about the age that she had been when her mother died, that Mrs. B sought treatment. Although her symptoms had started in adolescence, the marriage and birth of her daughter seemed to stimulate difficulties in the parenting function to such a degree that Mrs. B felt obliged to seek help for these problems as well as for her own anxieties.

In psychotherapy, Mrs. B was able to focus on the complicated and contradictory views she had about parenting. The first few years of her child's life were pleasant and secure because Mrs. B had as a model the warm, close, loving relationship with her own mother and Mrs. B was sure of her role. However, as the child grew older, Mrs. B began to identify with her own mother's illness, and she feared for her own existence. She became less sure of how to guide and counsel her daughter except by imposing restrictive limits on the child's interests and movements as her father had done. Her view of parental function as well as her role had shifted to that which she had experienced with her father. As her child grew and entered early adolescence, Mrs. B felt helpless and at a loss as to know how to relate to her daughter's struggles with issues of self-esteem regarding attractiveness, makeup, dating, etc. She had had to handle alone such experiences in her own adolescence and she now seemed ignorant as to how to communicate about such concerns with her daughter.

While issues of identifications were obvious problems for Mrs. B, the lack of experience with her own mother beyond the age of 7 deprived Mrs. B of a model for the mother–daughter interrelation that was so vital for her role of mother to a teenage daughter. Earlier identifications with both mother and father were important for the development of good, secure, early mothering functions. The disturbing shift to father as the parental model stemmed from identifications with him from her own latency period. Mrs. B's parenting function also suffered from both problems in identification and the absence of a mother during her own adolescence.

Effect of Father Loss on a Woman

Another woman, Mrs. C, whose father had died in an automobile accident when she was 5, did quite well, in general, raising four children. Her mother had kept her own family intact and served as a figure of a strong, capable woman throughout Mrs. C's growth and development.

It is interesting to note that from all observable data, Mrs. C did an admirable job of raising four children. However, there was a subtle but significant difference in attitude toward her sons and daughters. She had an unconscious attitude that men were weak and unreliable, while women were strong, capable, and reliable. Thus, she had the utmost confidence and trust in her two daughters, but she always had some doubt and never could really believe that her two sons could carry on effectively. While all four children did well, her sons did suffer from feelings of inadequacy and unsureness about their abilities.

SUMMARY

Psychoanalytic experiences with patients who lost a parent by death as children have directed our attention to the effect of various types of childhood separation on adult functioning. The range of effects can be truly remarkable, and the variables almost unending. One effect may be an interference with the functions of parenting, or an avoidance of parenting. These problems seem most severe in persons who suffered an early loss of the parent of the same sex. They not only lack the experience of having been parented by that parent in the later stages of childhood, but often suffer confused identifications with the dead parent and their child, particularly those of the same sex. Such identifications may need intensive psychoanalytic treatment, but it is possible that ignorance of appropriate parenting functions, especially those necessary during a child's early years and adolescence, can be relieved by a more educationally oriented therapy.

REFERENCES

Benedek, T. Parenthood as a developmental phase: A contribution to the libido theory. *Journal of the American Psychoanalytic Association*, 1959, *7*, 389–417.

Clark, L. P. *Lincoln: A psychobiography*. New York, London: Scribner's, 1933.

Fleming, J. Evolution of a research project in psychoanalysis. In H. Gaskill (Ed.), *Counterpoint*. New York: International Universities Press, 1963.

Fleming, J., & Altschul, S. Activation of mourning and growth by psychoanalysis. *International Journal of Psycho-Analysis*, 1963, *44*, 419–432.

Freud, A., & Burlingham, D. T. *War and children*. Westport, Conn.: Greenwood Press, 1943.

Hilgard, J. R., & Newman, M. F. Anniversaries in mental illness. *Psychiatry*, 1959, *22*, 113–121.

Hilgard, J. R., Newman, M. F., & Fisk, F. Strength of the adult ego following childhood bereavement. *American Journal of Orthopsychiatry*, 1960, *30*, 788–798.

Roy, A. Role of past loss in depression. *Archives of General Psychiatry*, 1981, *38*, 301–302.

Wallerstein, J. S., & Kelly, J. B. *Surviving the breakup*. New York: Basic Books, 1980.

12

PARENTING RESPONSES IN DIVORCE AND BEREAVEMENT OF A SPOUSE

BENJAMIN GARBER

INTRODUCTION

Comparison of the traumatic effects of divorce and the death of a parent on the child (Garber, 1980) showed that the responses of the child to both types of losses are quite different in terms of the intrapsychic shifts as well as the resultant clinical phenomena. I have found also that the response of the immediate environment of the child is quite different toward the child of divorce compared with the child who lost a parent by death. Upon further examination of the psychiatric literature as well as my own clinical material it became even more evident how basically different our responses and countertransference reactions are toward children who have experienced the death of a parent contrasted with those who have experienced divorce.

The emergence of a clinical syndrome is the end product of a series of interactions between the organism and the environment. The resultant pathology may be the culmination of a lengthy process which has had its origins in certain predisposing factors in the child as well as his parents. Conceivably, one could argue that children of parents who later divorced were constitutionally different from children whose parents died. Indeed, one could say that the parents themselves were constitutionally different in terms of their strengths, weaknesses, and above all their emotional stability. One may assume that the intrafamilial interactions in families where the parents were divorced were different generally from the interaction in families where a parent died.

The general impression is that the family in which a parent died was generally more stable and less dissonant then the family in which the parents were divorced (Rutter, 1971). An exception to this generalization is the situation

Benjamin Garber. Department of Psychiatry, Michael Reese Hospital and Medical Center, Department of Psychiatry, University of Chicago, and Child Analysis Faculty, The Institute for Psychoanalysis, Chicago, Illinois.

wherein a parent had a chronic illness for a long time prior to the death. In such an instance, it is conceivable that there was much depression and unhappiness prior to the death which may have created a grossly pathogenic environment for the child.

In comparing the nature of the loss in death and divorce, one must emphasize the difference in the types of mourning reactions experienced by the child (Garber, 1980). The differences appear strikingly in the type of process involved, its intensity, the distribution of the affects, and the content of what is mourned. The type of preloss images that must be hypercathected and then relinquished are quite different in both types of losses. In this chapter, I will focus on the final link in the sequence of clinical events which has to do with how the important adults in the child's surround react to the child of divorce as compared to the child whose parent has died. Just as there are differences in the preloss life situation, and the significance of the type of loss, there are also striking differences in the postloss adaptation. I am proposing that the postloss adaptation of the child is in large measure determined by the reactions of the important adults in his life. It is indeed possible that these postloss responses of significant adults shape the child's stability as well as his psychopathology. Since the reactions of significant adults differ markedly toward children of divorce and children whose parents have died, perhaps then, the outcome and resulting adaptation of the child is also quite different—for better or for worse.

The long-term effects on the child of loss through death have been reported in the psychiatric and psychoanalytic literature in great depth and detail (Miller, 1971; Furman, 1974). The long-term effects of parental divorce on the child is a subject that has come under careful study and scrutiny in the past 10 years (Wallerstein & Kelly, 1975).

Michael Rutter (1971), in his thoughtful work entitled "Parent Child Separation: Psychological Effects on Children," compared the effects of divorce and death on the child. His work was a meticulous attempt to assess the effects of permanent separations on the child as they manifested themselves in subsequent delinquent behavior. In all studies reviewed Rutter found that the delinquency rates were nearly double for boys whose parents were divorced or separated as compared to normals; but for boys who had lost a parent by death the delinquency rate was only slightly higher. In other studies, also, findings indicated that delinquency and conduct disorders are associated with parental divorce or separation, but not with parental death. This suggests that it may be the discord and disharmony rather than the break-up of the family, as such, which led to antisocial behavior.

Earlier delinquency studies seemed to indicate that there was a slight increase in delinquency rates in boys after the death of a parent. The differences noted, however, were small and not statistically significant. An important factor may have been the grief of the surviving parent which often lasts as long as several years (Rutter, 1971). The conclusions about broken homes are surprisingly straightforward. Although parental death may play a part in the pathogenesis of some disorders, delinquency is mainly associated with breaks which follow parental discord rather than with the loss of a parent as such.

Rutter (1971) goes on to note that there are other factors which should be considered for a more complete linkage of cause and effect. For example, all of the studies cited were of boys only, since they seem to be more vulnerable to psychological stress, especially loss. Also, Rutter did not study the personalities of the parents, the temperament of the children, nor the fit or lack of it between surviving and/or custodial parents and children. All these variables aside, one could be tempted to arrive at the conclusion that a child might be better off losing a parent by death than by divorce. Certainly neither is desirable. Moreover, children do not make the choices.

Hetherington (1972) in some excellent comparative research found intensified seductive behavior in adolescent girls who lost their fathers through divorce. This emerged when they were compared with girls whose fathers died, and with those who were part of intact families. In the presence of males, the daughters of widows exhibited restraint, shyness, and inhibition while the daughters of divorcées manifested attention-seeking behaviors.

If one were to view the research of the two types of losses from a strictly clinical perspective, one would notice a fairly consistent thread. The pathology of the child whose parent died appears to be more inner directed. On the surface, the children seem to be more depressed, in keeping with the adultlike descriptive syndrome of depression. They appear very sad, lonely, withdrawn, and preoccupied with something within themselves. On the other hand, children whose parents have been divorced are more likely to be in conflict with their environment. Although they may also exhibit periods of sadness and inner-involvement, their pain seems to be more outward directed. They are more hostile, resentful, and acting out; in essence, it seems that their trauma is expressed often in a variety of antisocial behaviors. Although to the clinician such a difference may not be crucial in the day-to-day work with the child, yet, if one considers the long-range adaptation of the child, such a clinical differential may be highly significant.

It is only in the past 10 years that some of the initial work on the subject of divorce and its effects on the child has begun to emerge, whereas there is a rather extensive body of research dealing with the effects of the death of a parent on the child. In the psychoanalytic literature such influential researchers as Furman (1974) and Lopez and Kliman (1979) believe that almost every child whose parent has died is in need of some type of therapeutic intervention. They believe also that therapy with such youngsters will facilitate some type of mourning experience and in turn promote normal developmental processes. Wallerstein and Kelly (1980) in their extensive longitudinal study on children of divorce concluded that divorce was highly beneficial for many adults; there is, however, no comparable evidence regarding the experience of the children. There is no supporting evidence from their study, at the 5-year mark, for the commonly held notion that the divorce is better overall for the children then an unhappy marriage.

Research on children of divorce has confirmed that the child sees himself as a part of, and influenced by, two parents.

Although it is somewhat premature to draw conclusions about the effectiveness of therapeutic intervention with children of divorce, it appears that some of the initial results are not overly optimistic. One would imagine that perhaps with more clinical data and long-term follow-up, more precision will be established in the treatment offered to such youngsters. Yet, the trend in the literature does seem almost to imply that the child who has lost a parent by death is better off, emotionally, in the long run, than the child whose parents have been divorced or separated. That being the case, one would wonder how much of the outcome may relate to how the immediate milieu of the child reacts to both types of losses. I will address this issue of the differential adaptation of the child as a result of the trauma of the death of a parent and the trauma of divorce, and I will relate to certain variables in the day-to-day experience of the child with significant adults in his environment. I believe that from a clinical perspective these significant daily interactions may be critical for the outcome and the ultimate adaptation of the child to each type of loss.

I will focus on how the *significant caretaking* adults respond to the child who has experienced a loss through death and the child who has experienced divorce. Although the connecting thread of this chapter will be the emerging psychopathology of the child, the main focus will be on how the important adults in the milieu of the latency-age child experience and react to him. Consequently, I will examine first how the surviving as well as the custodial and noncustodial parents interact with the child. Secondly, I will discuss how other important adults, specifically grandparents, teachers, and therapists, perceive, and in turn, impinge on the functioning of the child who has experienced each type of loss. As already stated, it is my contention that the responses of the above individuals may be one of the pivotal determinants that shape the outcome of the traumatic effects of the loss on the two groups of youngsters.

PARENTAL RESPONSES TO THE CHILD

The nature and complexity of the child's interactions with parents is a topic that has received extensive scrutiny from the child's as well as from the parents' perspective. To focus on the myriad interactions between parent and child, to follow them over time, and then to refocus on them after the death of parent, or after a divorce is beyond the scope of this chapter. The nature of the parents' relationship with the child can be scrutinized from two vastly different perspectives. The first has to do with what the parent does for or to the child. The second perspective is more evanescent and it deals mainly with what the parent is to the child: In other words, what kind of a model does the parent present? The former perspective, wherein the parent is actively doing something to the child who is relatively passive, is the model with which we are most familiar as it is the easier one to describe and study. Although we do pay attention to the parent as a model, we are constantly searching, in our diagnostic evaluations, for the actions on the part of the parent which have been traumatic or injurious to the child. Very often, one is faced with a diagnostic evaluation in which the child's pathology is reduced to one traumatic event at a vulnerable period in his life. Although such reductionistic thinking makes for neat psychodynamic formulations, one hopes that the clinician's thinking is more sophisticated in matters of *cause and effect*. Any traumatogenic situation between parent and child is a process involving a series of interactions that ebb and flow over a particular time span. When a parent dies, the subsequent interactions between the child and the surviving parent will become different, quantitatively and qualitatively. For example, the parent and child may be able to mourn together, or they may go through a lengthy period of cautiousness and hesitation in each other's presence before they find that, indeed, it is permissible to reminisce together about experiences before the parent died (Garber, 1981). The parent and the child may have to find out that various events from the past have different meanings to each of them. For example, a birthday party for a child may have been an exciting, happy, and memorable event, but for the parent that same birthday party may have been a harrowing, painful experience. Consequently, the surviving parent and the child may recall the same experience in different ways and mourn the experience in different manners.

When parents divorce, not only do the quantities and qualities of the experiences between parent and child change, but, more importantly, there is a change in the complexity of every interaction. For example, the parent–teacher conference, or the child taking a trip with his father and the latter's new girl friend may bring forth maneuverings of such complexity that unraveling, let alone negotiating them, is beyond the scope of ordinary reckoning. Previously routine occurrences become unsurmountable obstacles in the daily functioning of the child and the parent. I will now discuss the complexities inherent in these matters, how the parents attempt to deal with these, and how these may affect the child. Specifically, I will focus on parental empathy for the child, the parents' responses to the child's identifications, and the dilemma of divided loyalties.

Why is it that many parents seem to be constricted in empathy toward their children's experience around divorce? One answer seems to be in the insufficient attention they give to their own emotional histories, for example, the accumulation of experiences and feelings that have brought them to their present modes of adapting to events. The parents' silences, their failures to revivify past experiences, moments of doubt, guilt, or grief and to share fully in these recollected feelings may be repetitions of similar silences on the part of their own parents. When a parent has to deal with the child around death there is, often, a storehouse of generational myths, experiences, and anecdotes on how members of one's own past dealt with death. Here, there tends to be a historical precedent with a reawakening of memories of earlier losses through death, real and fantasized. It is this historical precedent in the life of every individual that helps to ease the pain, and allows the parent and other adults to be empathic or identify with the loss experienced by the child.

There is somewhat limited historical precedent for the parent involved in divorce. For although a family experience of divorce is accumulating, it is of recent vintage with limits in mythology and folk-lore. Because of this void a concerned parent seeks books and presents highly intellectualized explanations, which have little emotional impact on the child. These explanations may be bolstered by the testimony of "experts" in the field; the experts, however, because of the lack of a significant body of research, are also struggling in a morass of uncertainty.

The parent may be bolstered by the best of knowledge and noble intentions and still find it extremely difficult to explain to the child how two people can love one another for many years and all of a sudden, for no apparent reason, stop loving each other and, in fact, may proceed to hate each other. If the child accepts the rationale for such an occurrence, he may have to accept, also, that the parent can stop loving him suddenly and for no apparent reason. Highly intellectual explanations about blood ties and biology may seem plausible to the parent; they have very little meaning and significance for a child's understanding of causality.

The parents' inconsistent and confusing explanatory stances may create confusion in the mind of the child. If, indeed, the child is confused he may not discuss the issue with anyone; he may proceed to make up his own story which may contain more primitive explanations in an attempt to explain the events around him. This chain of events is completed when the parents become aware of the inappropriateness and bizarreness of the child's explanations. Perhaps with the passing of time, a more thorough, historically rooted understanding of divorce based on an integration of individual family histories and objective scientific findings will emerge. Then, perhaps the parents' ability to understand the child's experience will improve.

Parents often observe, with concern, that growing up seems accelerated today, and that children know more than they, the parents, did at the same age. Seemingly, parents in the early phase of parenthood want to slow down things. to slow the tempo of that externalization which characterizes growth during the latency period. The opposite may be true in the case of divorce, where the parent wants to speed things up, to hurry the child through developmental sequences by condemning regressive behavior. Additionally, parents may impose excessive responsibility for daily routines on the child as well as for those of a sibling or often the parent himself. This hurrying along of the child deprives him of the chance to consolidate forward developmental positions via going back and re-working the same issues at a more leisurely pace. This may strain the adaptive capacities of the child. As a result, one may see the clinical picture of a hyper-mature youngster in areas of day-to-day negotiations and self-reliance, and yet be brittle under the impact of undue stress. Very often, these children may appear quite intact under the impact of stress or a crisis, but tend to "fall apart" when the environment is relatively stable and predictable. The parent, in a depressed state, may need a mature, self-sufficient child for the purposes of sharing intimacies, and relieving loneliness. An illusion of closeness and intimacy is created and the parent can maintain his seeming adequacy to the external world.

Let me illustrate: Hilary, age 10, told me with great pride how she and her recently divorced mother were buddies. She described numerous incidents of going shopping with her mother for clothes, going out to dinner to fancy restaurants, and attending plays and concerts. There was much excitement and pride in her voice when she said that ''I am probably my mother's best friend.'' After a long pause, she said somewhat wistfully, ''I wish my mother had more friends because sometimes I just want to be her daughter.''

One of the most crucial elements of the surviving or custodial parent's interaction with the child revolves around the child's identification with the dead or absent parent. Children show a variety of identificatory phenomena with the absent individual. One may see very massive and gross identifications which appear suddenly after the death of a parent. We have described these in more detail in our observations of children who experienced the sudden loss of a parent by death (Garber, 1980). At the other extreme, one may see a variety of subtle changes in the child which are more often related to the length of absence of the parent as well as the degree of ambivalence in the preloss relationship. Although there are multiple determinants that promote an identificatory process, most significant is the sex of the child and the sex of the dead or absent parent. The most commonly described identifications are those of the boy with his absent or dead father, although we assume that the less striking identifirations with the parent of the opposite sex are equally crucial for stable and rich personality formation.

It would seem that when a child shows massive, or even more gradual and subtle identifications with the dead parent encouragement came from the surviving parent. When the child is of the same sex as the dead parent, the identifications are in keeping with the parental expectations that he become the man of the house as a replacement for the absent parent. Striking examples of such expectations are when the parent encourages the child to sleep in the same bed or the same room as the parent to relieve parental loneliness. This is rationalized as preventing the child from being afraid. Such encouragement may be reassuring initially to the child because it allows him to use the identifications to defend against and perhaps even diminish the trauma of the loss. With the passage of time, the need to maintain such an identificatory posture may become too burdensome for the child, and one may see a massive regression. The child's identifications with the dead parent are generally viewed in a positive light by members of both families. The identifications of the child with the dead parent may be used also as a stimulus for reminiscing and recalling various activities and memories about the person who died.

Although in the early postloss period the surviving parent may encourage such identifications, problems may arise when the parent finds a replacement;

here, the previously encouraged behavior of the child may cause the parent much guilt. A mother may feel badly about kicking her son out of her bed or interrupting him at each effort. Particular difficulty arises if she had encouraged such practices when the father was alive, and the son recalls these episodes. As the mother of one 10-year-old boy who was sleeping with her nightly told me, "the days are not bad because I manage to keep busy and so I forget the pain; it is possible to sort of push it out of my mind. But the nights are horrible; it feels as if something deep inside of me is pulling at me, tugging at me and I just cannot close it off. When that happens I know only one thing—I have to have someone next to me, someone living and breathing, just to be there and I don't care who it is."

Perhaps not as massively, but in an ongoing way with more subtlety, the child identifies also with the absent parent in divorce. Such identifications probably emerge over a long time as the loss is not final nor sudden. The custodial parent realizes slowly and almost imperceptibly that the child has become the absent parent in miniature. Should the child continue to function well at home and at school, the custodial parent may be willing to overlook or even deny the changes. However, if the child has problems or shows unacceptable behavior and character traits, the custodial parent engages in a subtle and often not so subtle pointing out that the negative features stem from the child's development into just as bad, stupid, irresponsible, dishonest, etc., a person as the noncustodial parent. Since identification is basically an unconscious process, the child will become bewildered and confused by such accusations as he does not experience himself as being different than before.

This type of interaction between parent and child is one of the most difficult to detect and to bring out into the open, for here the parent is not so much reacting to what the child does, but more importantly, to what the child is or seems to be. Consequently, the parent's behavior toward the child is an ongoing process as the child becomes more and more like the absent parent.

The divorced mother of a 14-year-old boy told me with great puzzlement that the older her son becomes, the more he looks and acts like his father. She also confessed that, at times, she became frightened that she might kill him even though she knew that he did not do anything to elicit such hate. The relationship between mother and son had escalated to such a pitch that the police had to be called, once, to separate them. This outburst had led to the diagnostic referral. Only after several months of treatment did the woman become aware of the displaced rage.

A painful dilemma for the child of parent loss by death or divorce is that of loyalty conflict. Externally, the child has to deal with the caretaking adult's expectations of behavior toward a replacement for the dead or absent parent. More important, however, is the internal meaning of the loss to the child, who is burdened also by the external reality. Because of the immaturity of the psychic apparatus, the younger latency-age child is in an either/or position since he tends to have little capacity to accommodate to shadings in his thinking. Typically he longs intensely for a ready replacement and becomes prey to feelings of guilt and disloyalty to the lost parent.

This conflict is augmented by the latency-age child's limited ability to interact comfortably in triadic relationships. The most stable of children have difficulty in sustaining a balance in feelings of love and loyalty toward two individuals. To accept a replacement, the child must relinquish a highly cathected object. Should he have been ambivalent to the lost object, or should a surviving parent require premature relinquishment, the child is prone to experience much guilt. At the Barr–Harris Center,[1] we have observed that surviving parents have terminated child treatment when their mourning was completed and were ready to move into new relationships. Often, because of the immaturity of the psychic apparatus, the child is not able to keep pace and retains hypercathected, fixated memories of the dead parent. By removal of the child from treatment, the parent eases his guilt and hopes to remove references to the loss.

Surviving parents who come for help are troubled, often, by their children's intense attachments to memories of the dead parent. In fact, they tend to distract the child, or provide for a replacement, or to design excessive activities to fill the void. The message seems to be to get on with family life, "for life has to go on." It may be transmitted that mourning can be done at a future time. The child senses from this that his mourning must be subdued, hidden, and held secret. The unconscious is timeless and only in the conscious life do tasks supersede one another. The child, with reinforcement from the surviving parent, must turn feelings and memories inward. This makes for the excellent functioning and surface adaptation we see in such children. There remains, nevertheless, an inner core of longing, sadness, and a feeling of loss. These may surface later in life, particularly during developmental shifts or at times when subsequent significant losses occur.

The surviving parent, having completed a suitable period of mourning, attempts to prepare himself and the child for a replacement. The parent may seek a replacement in order to provide a more complete family life for the child. He may try vigorously to please the child by finding a likeable candidate, and by elaborate planning of outings and events. When the child's typical distancing or anger toward the replacement is revealed, the parent, in turn, becomes confused, enraged, and feels unappreciated for all of his efforts to improve the child's life. Moreover, the parent may blame the child for creating a dangerous threat to the "improved family situation," presumably wanted by the survivor and child. The ultimate fear of the parent is the destruction of the new marriage.

I saw the mother of an 8-year-old boy who was guilt ridden because of her fear that her son would chase away his new stepfather by constantly comparing him to his father who died 2 years ago. This mother had been beside herself because she felt that she could not stop her son from talking about his father,

---

1. The Barr–Harris Center of The Institute for Psychoanalysis, Chicago, is a facility for the treatment and study of children who have experienced parent loss through death and divorce.

but at the same time sensed that her husband was becoming more aloof and starting to avoid and withdraw from her son. She felt hurt and confused, for after all, the reason, in part, for her remarriage was to provide a new father for her depressed son. Torn between her loyalty to her husband and love for her child, she became severely depressed.

While many aspects of the loyalty conflict may be internalized by the child whose parent has died, often the child of divorce is not afforded such an opportunity. Because of the inherent nature of divorce one can observe and deal with almost every issue and interaction from the loyalty perspective. Whether the child wants to or not he is required, often, to choose from the very beginning. When parents begin to consider divorce, the issues of choice and loyalty are constant companions in every family interaction. A younger child may be asked to choose privately, and sometimes in public. We assume that parents are thoughtful, considerate, and respectful of the "child's rights" when they suggest or even demand that the child make the choice. Also assumed is that a child has the necessary intellectual equipment to make a choice once presented with all the facts.

Although this is not the parents' intent, the burden of choice strains the emotional capacities of the child. Here, parents seem unable to sustain empathic understanding of the child's vulnerability. The choice the child is asked to make is critical because it involves his future relationship with grandparents and other relatives. It impinges upon his living conditions, school, friends, and perhaps far-reaching commitments about his future. The older adolescents we see who seem unable to make vocational choices as well as marital decisions may have been burdened excessively with decision making too early in their development.

Loyalty is the paramount source of taxing interactions which emerge from the visiting between the child and noncustodial parent. There was no model for this relationship when the family was intact. This raises the question of what are the responsibilities of the visiting parent. How much of a role does he play in setting behavioral and moral standards; how does he express approval; how does he enforce discipline or doing homework? There are no safeguards and rituals of intact family life which soften the frustrations and anger from the inevitable conflicts which permeate all parent–child relationships. Therefore, there is little opportunity to clarify and relieve misunderstandings and hurt feelings. Fathers are usually the visited parent. And, they are left with a high level of confusion and uncertainty about their expected roles.

Fathers who may have been accustomed to commanding their children tend to experience a new sense of impotence and frustration. Those who become depressed after the divorce may find visiting painful. Those rejected by their wives expect the same from the children. Their lowered self-esteem, shame, and guilt create a sense of expendability and, thusly, they need their children to boost their self-esteem. When this is not forthcoming, these fathers feel more hurt and disappointment; defensively, they may sustain irregular visiting and withdraw completely.

Another reason for avoiding the complexities of the visiting process is the guilt many fathers feel, particularly if they had initiated the legal proceedings. They may withdraw because of the blame they expect from their children or their guilt may lead them into a flurry of activities and presents which cannot be sustained.

Research findings indicate that almost half of divorced men studied are fearful of the disapproval and anger of their children (Wallerstein & Kelly, 1980). Here, the child becomes the parent and the conscience of the man. These fathers respond in several ways. The depressed ones deal with these fears by avoiding the child for lengthy periods. The subsequent visits become laden with tension. Fathers may use reaction formations by extravagant gift buying and providing highly stimulating activities to present themselves as "superdads." Others may react with angry defensiveness, particularly if they feel they have been wronged. In the early postdivorce period, the Santa Claus role is the most comfortable because it enables the father to handle guilt by restitution. This may strain him financially and emotionally. Of course, the custodial parent who cannot match this on a daily basis becomes angry.

The psychological equilibrium of the father usually determines the emotional and frequency aspects of the visiting. The latter seems to have little to do with the state of the child. The father's conflicts, especially the feelings about the divorce, determine the crucial interactions with the child. Visiting problems have very little to do with the father's love or lack of love for the child.

Just as visits to the cemetery and anniversary reactions replay the events of the parent's death, the visit with the noncustodial parent frequently replays the anger, jealousy, love, mutual rejection, longing, and sadness between the divorcing adults. Except there is one crucial difference—the visits to the cemetery or even the relatives of a deceased parent have a certain proscribed pattern, ritual, and set of stable expectations. Within the confines of that ritual, child and parent may feel comfortable in showing their longing and grief or they may choose to remain aloof and detached with the child showing a facade of hypermaturity. The way they behave will depend, in large part, on previous interactions and what is ritualistically appropriate. There are no such clear-cut patterns or rituals surrounding visits with the noncustodial parent. Consequently, child and parent are left to their own devices, to follow a course of uncertainty punctuated by trial and error. There is no clearly visible historical precedent for how a child and a noncustodial parent should behave with each other.

Occasionally, a mother and stepfather may demand that the child renounce his love for the father as the price of acceptance and affection within the reconstituted family. Or, a child may be scapegoated, especially if there is a striking physical or emotional resemblance to the father. This is a reflection of the remarried mother's neurotic need to banish the father from her life.

In most divorcing families seen clinically, one or both parents consciously and unconsciously requires or even demands that the child align with one of them. This demand, especially when exerted on a vulnerable youngster, can produce feelings of despair, anger, and depression. Some children, especially older ones, have developed a relatively cohesive sense of self so that they, indeed, will make a conscious and reasoned loyalty choice—while unconsciously they may continue to pay the price for years to come. Others develop an "as if" quality to their interactions, in order to walk a thin line of appearing loyal to both parents. This may result in a short-term adaptation. In the long run, we may see a strain imposed on the adaptive capacities of the child's psyche. This type of adaptation may contribute, ultimately, to shallowness and superficiality in the child's relationships with peers and later with adults. Finally, we see a group of children on whom the demand for total loyalty creates an overwhelming conflict which can put the child in a state of total paralysis in daily functioning on one end of the spectrum, and to frantic acting out on the other end. Either behavioral response seems better than to have to make a conscious guilt inducing choice demanded by one or both of the parents.

In their work with divorced parents, Wallerstein and Kelly (1980) found that a high number of men and women sought some type of therapy. They recommended, as part of their follow-up project, various forms of therapy to one third of the women and to somewhat fewer of the men; a large number of both actually sought help. One fifth of the men in their study sought therapeutic interventions, mostly in the form of individual therapy. The length of contact for both men and women varied from brief interventions to more prolonged therapeutic relationships. Although the stimulus to the parents for seeking help came partly from the research project in which they participated, it is possible, nevertheless, that in large part the stimulus for doing so may have come from the notion that they are flawed or damaged. Consequently, there arose an imperative need to get professional help to cover over or repair this defect, or perhaps to be reassured that there is none at all.

Although there are no known comparable data from populations where a parent has died, one wonders if the percentage of parents seeking help is equally high. When a child whose parent has died is referred for an evaluation, it is usually the parent's intent to "check out" if everything is all right. The surviving parent wants to know how the child was affected by the death and if the parent himself is parenting well. Once reassured on that score, very few parents are motivated to return for follow-up, or, for that matter, treatment. One gets the impression that the parent has a sense of conviction that once the intensity of the mourning work diminishes or a replacement is found, everything will proceed normally, just as before. One does not sense such optimism in the parents who have been divorced, for there may be always the anxiety that remarriage could bring back the same problems.

The nature of their loss caused the bereaved to view themselves differently than the divorced or separated. The separated tend to regard themselves as misunderstood, betrayed, stigmatized and, perhaps, personally flawed. The bereaved are more likely to view themselves as both victims and survivors in relation to their spouses. Compared with the separated, the bereaved appear less self-doubting, and more hurt; in consequence, they are quicker to resent awkward or clumsy attempts to help.

THE RESPONSES OF GRANDPARENTS, TEACHERS, AND THERAPISTS WHO INTERACT WITH PARENTS AND CHILDREN OF DIVORCE AND BEREAVEMENT

Grandparenthood in some ways may be seen as a new lease on life because grandparents can relive the memories of the early phase of their own parenthood in observing the growth and development of their grandchildren. Grandparenthood is parenthood but one step removed, since grandparents are relieved from the immediate stresses and the responsibilities of motherhood and fatherhood. Grandparents appear to enjoy their grandchildren more than they enjoyed their own children. Since they do not have the responsibility for raising the child toward an unconscious goal, their love is not as ambivalent nor burdened by anxieties as it had been toward their own children (Anthony & Benedek, 1970). The love of grandparents is undemanding and gives the child a sense of security of being loved without always having to earn it. In return, the grandparents may receive a loving glance, an actual appeal for help, and sometimes the message that they are needed and wanted just the way they were by their own children a long time ago.

How does this ideal grandparenthood change when the grandparent is called upon to assume the role of parent in a parent-loss situation. Initially, the grandparent may experience pleasure and excitement that the "new lease on life" is not just a fleeting illusion, but indeed an all-encompassing reality. There may reemerge a certain youthfulness, a certain zest, and a fountain of energy that has been long absent. Grandparents may now see the chance to do all the things that they may have silently criticized their sons or daughters for not doing all these years. If the grandparent has been intrusive this may be indeed a dream come true. However, there sets in also a feeling of guilt, especially toward the parent who died or has left because of divorce. As much as the grandparent may rationalize this type of involvement on the basis of the "child needs me now" there is the ever-present suspicion that perhaps the grandparent had hoped for just such a moment. Such may exist in a situation where a parent had died, but more often it occurs under circumstances where the grandparents had opposed the marriage.

In a situation where a parent died, the grandparents will more than likely transfer the idealized aspect of a child unto the grandchild. Consequently, if the child should not do well, this may be a crushing blow to the grandparents' self-esteem and confront them with their own ambivalence and disappointment in their child who died. Usually during divorce, grandparents blame "the other parent" for deficits or disappointments in a grandchild.

In many ways, a stable supportive relationship with an involved grandparent can be exceptionally helpful and growth promoting to the child. We assume, generally, that as far as child-rearing practices are concerned, the grandparent has nothing to prove anymore. Their developmental tasks as a parenting adult have been completed so that they are free to deal with other issues and conflicts related to old age. Consequently, the unconscious conflicts they may experience would tend not to interfere with the developmental conflicts of the child. A grandparent can be potentially helpful in an unambivalent way to help promote the developmental progression of the child. The child's presence does not interfere, usually, with the grandparent's task of mastering the conflicts of old age. However, there are situations where grandparents are fixated in their need to prove that they can produce the perfect offspring. These are individuals, often grandmothers, who are invested intensely in helping raise the grandchildren with advice, provocations, bribes, and general interferences. These needs exist often in persons whose opportunities to prove their parenting capacities have been unrewarding. Such a grandparent may be eager to undo the failings of previous attempts. Divorce, more than any other situation, lends itself to such interference. Since there is an implicit assumption that the divorcing individuals are "flawed" in some way, it would only stand to reason that their child is also "flawed." But, the grandparents see the child as someone whose flaws they can correct —which they could not do with their own children.

Often grandparents are heard to say "what that kid needs is a good kick in the pants," or "what the kid needs is some love," or some other unempathic recommendation for emotional health. Grandparents who had given such prescriptions may see opportunities to carry these out when divorce occurs. Just as often, one may see the opposite; for when the grandparents have to put these prescriptions into practice, they may experience anxiety and panic and consequently withdraw.

For clinicians who work with children whose parents have died, one of the prime considerations in helping the child to deal with the loss is to mobilize the components of a supportive network. In assessing the extended family, one looks for grandparents who can often assume the initial caretaking responsibilities. Grandparents may not be available, however, if it is their child who died. Still, the grandchild becomes even more important in such a situation. As depressed as the grandparent may be, given another chance to raise the child, his depression may diminish by the mobilization of a sense of purpose.

Little help seems available to mothers of divorce. Wallerstein and Kelly (1980) found, with only few exceptions, that in divorce situations, grandmothers, or other extended family members, were not available for assistance such as baby-sitting at unusual times when the mother had to work or attend classes. Friends and neighbors rarely shared in household routines. Mothers worked late into the night taking care of household chores after a regular job or school attendance. A sense of aloneness was experienced, as though the mother had to prove against all odds that she could and would make it alone.

Wallerstein and Kelly (1980) found further that although most of the families had lived in the community for several years, few resources outside of the immediate family were of help to the child during the crisis period. Approximately three-quarters of the children were not helped by grandparents, uncles, or aunts, many of whom lived in different parts of the country. In the few situations where grandparents, who lived close by, did care for children these children were very responsive and appeared to benefit considerably from the special concern and care.

School seems to be the focus and often the place of earliest appearance of the outwardly visible signs of psychopathology in the child. Since school is less tolerant than home of deviant behavior, the school is the first place where problems tend to appear. As the child spends an increasing portion of his waking life at school, it stands to reason that next to his home, the school environment, particularly the teacher, becomes the most important individual in his daily routine. When a child begins to manifest difficulties in school the immediate reaction of the teacher is: What is the child responding to in me or in the class to make him unhappy? This response is in keeping with the egocentric focus that we all have vis-à-vis another person. This implies that another person's happiness or unhappiness is in some way related to or influenced by what I am or am not doing. Having exhausted all the in-classroom possibilities, the teacher may eventually consider other sources of conflict, such as the home.

When a child loses a parent by death, the teacher will learn about it from a variety of resources—newspapers, classmates, etc. Such news will elicit various appropriate and inappropriate responses. When the father of one of my daughter's 6th-grade friends died, a number of classmates got together on their own initiative and visited the bereaved family. This kind of activity was encouraged probably by the parents and supported by the teachers. When the child missed several days of school because of the funeral and related mourning rituals, the teachers were equally understanding in scaling down and postponing the demands for routine classroom obligations. One considers that the responses to the child may have included some inappropriate reactions, such as perhaps having regarded the child as more vulnerable than he really was or embarrassing him with special attention in front of his peers. Nevertheless, the general outpouring of empathy and consideration was probably more than helpful in giving the child the opportunity to assimilate certain aspects of his loss while having to function in the school setting.

One would expect, also, that upon seeing the child as preoccupied or sad, any teacher possessing a modicum amount of empathic capacity would respond appropriately. Eventually, each teacher will decide, based on his own unique history with loss, as to how long he will maintain an optimum empathic stance toward the bereaved youngster. One would assume that most teachers would remain generally sensitive, sympathetic, and probably empathic toward the child whose parent has died.

The teacher's reactions to a child whose parents are or have been in the process of divorce are quite different from those to the child whose parent died.

Although the teachers' responses are determined by their personal histories, and the personality of the child and his parents, there are certain global reactions that constitute an integral component of every response or the lack of it.

The initial reaction has to do with how the classmates and teachers find out that the child's parents are getting a divorce. Usually, it is not advertised; in fact, I have seen a general tendency on the part of parents and children to be secretive about it. Usually, other children will find out indirectly when the child talks about a visit with his father or mother. Occasionally, a child may experience an intense emotional reaction in and around some school activity and blurt out that his parents are getting a divorce. A common pattern emerges which reveals a conspiracy of silence involving the parents, the child, his peers, and the teacher. Teachers, as a rule, will not ask even if they suspect such a possibility. Although this is rationalized under the cloak of respecting the child's privacy, more often it may be the result of the teacher not knowing what to ask or say. Just as often, it results from the teacher's covert disapproval of the selfishness of the parents who are not concerned about "the best interests of the child." Should the divorce affect the child's behavior and school performance, most teachers would experience overt and covert anger toward the parents which may be displaced to the child. This resentment may be mitigated if parents can be open and appraise the teacher of the situation and how the child is reacting. For it seems, that in spite of the divorce, the parents still share a common concern for the child's welfare. However, if the parents do not contact the teacher about the child's current life situation, in essence, everyone remains silent, and behaves as if nothing has happened while the child may continue to deteriorate.

Parents may rationalize not telling about an impending divorce when they believe that the teacher may become prejudiced toward the child and judgmental toward them; such parental fears are often justified. Most parents and teachers expect the child to continue to function well in school in spite of the turmoil at home. Teachers may actually become impatient when the child daydreams or falls behind in his work. Parental divorce is, therefore, generally not accepted as a valid excuse for doing poorly in school. These inappropriate expectations of the child by parents and teachers probably stem from two sources. The latency-age child is idealized by the adult because he seems to embody the essence of childhood. The latency-age child is seen as devoid of instinctual conflicts and one whose total energy is focused on learning. Consequently, he is expected to function, academically, in spite of a collapsing environment. The second reason for the high expectations is the adults' need to deny the profound impact of the divorce on the child. The child's good school performance is considered to mean that the child is not experiencing the trauma of the divorce which in turn diminishes the parental guilt. It seems reasonable that the more teachers know about what goes on in the life of the child, the more helpful and supportive they can be. It is critical for the teacher to know about the status of the visiting. Frequently a child returns from a weekend with a noncustodial parent in a state of overstimulation. The child may be unable to function on Monday, but may settle down later on in the week. Here, teachers can be helpful to the child who manifests this behavior. Also, the teacher can be prepared for the sullen and disappointed child whose noncustodial parent failed to visit.

One of the more fascinating current phenomena related to school and divorce occurs at open house, special school events, and parent–teacher conferences. This involves a child who has two sets of parents, or a parent and a current boyfriend and/or girl friend who may attent school functions; several months later, there may be a different parenting couple. The result is that many more people are attending school-related functions. Another result is the emotional one. Teachers often become confused and overwhelmed by the task of trying to sort out which groups of parents belong to which children, and what to say, and what to withhold from any one of them.

Wallerstein and Kelly (1980) found that school is a good support system for those children who were of above average intelligence, who do well academically to begin with, and are psychologically stable. It seems that younger children, who are able to show their pain in more open and direct ways, were able to elicit nurturance, support, and solace from a caring teacher. Although this may have been helpful in school by diminishing anxiety in the learning situation, it is doubtful whether there was any carry-over effect into the home. But, this, perhaps, is expecting too much from a school situation and the best of teachers.

In dealing therapeutically with the child who has experienced divorce, the therapist's role becomes murky, involuntarily. Frequently, there is a threat of a custody battle in which the therapist may be called upon to participate. There is also danger that one parent will not support the treatment and refuse to pay, which may involve further court proceedings. Often, one parent will attempt to elicit information from the therapist about the other, and in turn withhold meaningful information. One parent may try to use the therapist to exert financial pressure on the other when dealing with the issues of fees and frequency of visits. Even the choice of therapist may become a focus for the parents' economic and sexual concerns.

From the inception of the diagnostic evaluation of the child whose parents are getting divorced, the therapist has to devote much time to the repetitive complaints of the parents about each other and their parenting capabilities. Attempts to short-cut this process by being directive or interpretive are futile. Both parents feel compelled and driven to present long lists of complaints. Many issues involving the parents' antagonisms to each other emerge in the diagnostic or planning of treatment phases and can cause delays. The child may become the ignored outsider and be in severe distress. Once treatment begins, he may be sullen, negativistic, angry, and unsure about who will make the important decisions in his life. His feelings of hopelessness, negativism, and passive–aggressive behavior are bound to elicit hopelessness and anger in the therapist. The therapist may see the worst of each parent in the child and react just as to one of them. Thus, the pathogenic situation which brought him into therapy is repeated as the child elicits the same responses from the therapist as from his parents.

In my experience all of the aforementioned issues which surface on the diagnostic and beginning phase of the treatment of every child are magnified by the hurt, angry, and distrusted feelings divorced parents present to the child's therapist. Neither the passage of time nor remarriage seems to diminish these feelings. Wallerstein and Kelly (1980) found in their follow-up after 5 years, that one third to one half of the parents expressed these same feelings. The child's therapist can expect, also, that he may be used as a source of information by a hurting parent. One mother of a 10-year-old boy called me periodically to learn about the father's life and travels "to keep her son informed about his father." Not being able to reply, I became, in her mind, the father's ally. This led to repeated threats to terminate the treatment. Similarly, the child may be drawn into a parent's need to maintain a secrecy which excludes the therapist and may prejudice the therapy.

The therapist's fee can become an issue when a father feels displaced and unimportant, and uses the fee as a way to reassert his position in the child's life. If payment is stopped, the therapist faces the uncomfortable dilemma of terminating or continuing, anticipating lengthy court proceedings to require the father to pay. And so, the therapist experiences also a narcissistic injury and practical deprivation with probable resentment for finding himself in the messy situation.

Mothers I have seen tend to use the child's therapist as an ally in extracting more benefits for a child. This may occur when a father plans remarriage and a new family. The mother may expect that her child will lose out because of the father's additional financial responsibilities. She may request the therapist's assistance in getting more material things (private school, summer camp, etc.) "in the best interest of the child." Again, the therapist confronts a dilemma. In refusing to comply with such requests, the therapist risks the child's regarding him as the father's ally. The most frequent accusation leveled at the therapist is that he is being misled by the other parent as well as the child.

Another issue exists when divorcing parents bring the child for treatment for correction of the flaws in the product of their flawed marriage. They may expect, unconsciously, that with this achievement, the destructiveness in the marriage will be eradicated and that the next one will be better. Should the therapist comply with this implicit wish, he will discover that there was no therapeutic alliance. When the magic is not forthcoming, the parents may take the child to another therapist with the same unrealistic goals in mind.

How do the aforementioned interactions affect the nature of a therapist's work with the child? For the therapist who is a parent, difficulty is in store. The therapist has trouble refraining from shifting among identifications with the individual parent(s) and the victimized child. The therapist will react most negatively to the most interfering one. He may also attempt to maintain an empathic stance toward both. Since he may not be able to deal with each parent around interferences, his rage may mount and though he may attempt to deal with it, it may be deflected and directed subtly toward the child. With the rationalization of utilizing a neutral therapeutic stance, he may engage in a cold withdrawal. Warmth, consideration, and empathy will not be available because the anger is most likely to interfere.

Research findings on the effects of divorce on children are scanty. There has been no research on the effects of therapy for children whose parents are involved in divorce. The general clinical impression is that short-term crisis intervention during the process seems to be helpful to the parents and in turn to the child. This seems to be the case whether interventions are geared toward exposng conflicts or toward a guidance approach. One wonders, however, whether long-term therapy with children and parents involved in complicated divorce can produce long-term benefits to the participants. The mutual hurt, anger, resentment, distrust, and consequent lack of cooperation are so huge and complex that they can defy the skills of the most competent and well-intentioned of therapists.

The role and experience of the therapist with the child whose parent had died parent had died is quite different. The task is straightforward and the work is mainly to facilitate the child's mourning activity in keeping with his developmental level. Children who have experienced the death of a parent can elicit intense, compassionate empathic responses from therapists. These responses are rewarding but can be so emotionally exhausting that no therapist should be expected to treat more than two or three such youngsters at a time. A common countertransference problem is the failure to work with the child's anger toward the dead parent and to focus only on the longing and sadness. Nevertheless, the task is made easier than with divorce because the external and practical issues are stable and few. The work can proceed with an internal orientation, for example, the memories, fantasies, images, and their accompanying affects. An issue for consideration always, is that the child may harbor the fantasy that the therapist will replace the dead parent. This is common in the younger latency child and also if the therapist is of the same sex as the dead parent. The fantasy may be shared implicitly with the surviving parent. When, in the course of the therapy, the child learns that he must relinquish the fantasy, he may experience disappointment, anger, and feelings of betrayal. On occasion, this may interfere temporarily with the treatment, and sometimes permanently.

CONCLUSION

A review of the psychiatric literature on the effects of parent loss on the child seems to indicate that the effects of loss by divorce are more pathogenic to the child's adaptation than loss by death. This outcome is related, in part, to the types of interactions between the child and significant adults prior to and after the loss. In comparison, the responses of the important adults toward the child whose parent died are quite different from those to the child whose parents are engaged in divorce.

1. The parental responses to the child of divorce are inconsistent and unclear, in part, because there can be gaps in family mythology to guide the parent during this difficult period. With the death of a parent there tends to be historical precedent in every culture to help the adults and the child to deal with the loss. Very often, the children of divorce, whom we see, must create their own explanations about the surrounding events because of parental silence and embarrassment.

2. The surviving parent tends to support a child's identification with a dead parent. When the mutual angers do not abate, parents in divorce tend to project these onto each other. Moreover, we have noted that the custodial parent may denigrate the other parent.

3. In both death and divorce loyalty conflicts may emerge. Loyalty conflicts tend to surface in case of death when the surviving parent accepts a substitute. In divorce, we see pathogenic effects when both parents impose loyalty issues. The younger child who has not consolidated a firm sense of self is particularly vulnerable.

4. Grandparents can be and have been very helpful in the immediate situation when a parent died. They have been available minimally during the crisis period in divorce. Where grandparents have taken an active caretaking role, the child was helped considerably.

5. Teachers often ignore obvious signs of a child's malfunctioning in reaction to divorce. This may reflect their condemnation of parents who seek divorce. In instances of parent loss, teachers are usually empathic and supporting during the acute period.

6. Therapists find it extremely difficult to work with children of divorce. The parents' overt conflicts and needs tend to intrude. This burdens child and therapist. Acting-out parents tend to elicit helplessness and rage in the child's therapist. Consequently, the therapist becomes prone to act out or block, in other ways, the effectiveness of the treatment. Therapists who work with children whose parents died are more empathic and able to help the child deal with the loss as an interference to normal development. Most often, he has continuous parental sanction for the work.

In conclusion, it seems that the environment of the child, as represented by parents, grandparents, teachers, and therapists, is much more empathic and appropriately responsive toward the child whose parent died than to the child whose parents are divorced. Consequently, the outlook for children whose parents died seems to be more optimistic than for children of divorce. At least, this seems true for the children who come to our offices and the few we have studied.

REFERENCES

Anthony, E. J., & Benedek, T. *Parenthood: Its psychology and psychopathology*. Boston: Little, Brown, 1970.

Furman, E. *A child's parent dies*. New Haven and London: Yale University Press, 1974.

Garber, B. *The effects of the death of a parent and divorce on the child: A clinical comparison*. Unpublished manuscript, March 1980.

Garber, B. Mourning in children: Towards a theoretical synthesis. *Annual of Psychoanalysis*, 1981, *9*, 9–19.

Hetherington, E. M. Effects of father absence on personality development in adolescent daughters. *Developmental psychology*, 1972, *7*, 313–326.

Lopez, T., & Kliman, G. Mourning in the analysis of a four year old. *Psychoanalytic Study of the Child*, 1979, *34*, 235–272.

Miller, J. B. M. Children's reactions to the death of a parent: A review of the psychoanalytic literature. *Journal of the American Psychoanalytic Association*, 1971, *19*(4), 697–719.

Morrison, J. H. Parental divorce as a factor in childhood psychiatric illness. *Comprehensive Psychiatry*, 1974, *15*, 95–102.

Rutter, M. Parent child separation: Psychological effects on children. *Journal of Child Psychiatry and Psychology*, 1971, *12*, 233–260.

Wallerstein, J. S., & Kelly, J. B. The effects of parental divorce—Experiences of the preschool child. *Journal of the American Academy of Child Psychiatry*, 1975, *14*, 600–616.

Wallerstein, J. S., & Kelly, J. B. *Surviving the breakup*. New York: Basic Books, 1980.

13

STEPPARENTHOOD: A NEW AND OLD EXPERIENCE

PAUL BOHANNAN

A STEPFAMILY MYTH

The King and Queen of Thebes, Laius and Jocasta, became unbearable in one another's eyes. After much bickering and hatred, they were divorced. Their son Oedipus was 4 years old. Following the rule of the patriarchal society in which they lived, Oedipus was obliged to stay with his father, while his mother left to make a life elsewhere. Oedipus was given a lot of freedom and became quite autonomous. His inner dream was that his parents would get back together so he could be whole again.

A few years later, Laius found a young new queen and presented her to Oedipus with the comment, "This is your new mother." She opened her arms and Oedipus fled. The new stepmother fawned on Oedipus one moment, was too strict with him the next because she was convinced that the poor motherless child was undisciplined. She demanded that he love her instantly. Oedipus found this situation intolerable, so he ran away to live with his mother.

Jocasta, after the divorce, had suffered a nasty loss of status. She had taken up with a shepherd, whom she later married. So, at his mother's house, Oedipus was not a prince but just another shepherd. Since he felt himself to be a prince, every time his stepfather told him to do anything, he brusquely refused: "You aren't my real father!" Because there was no way he could identify with the shepherd, he came to hate his mother because she actually seemed fond of this unworthy man.

One night, the shepherd had been drinking a little. Oedipus baited him repeatedly and the shepherd finally struck him. In a rage, Oedipus slew the shepherd on the spot. He fled from the house, back to the palace to make up with his father.

Paul Bohannan. Division of Social Sciences and Communication, University of Southern California, Los Angeles, California.

Laius told Oedipus not to worry about it—after all, the man was nothing but a sheepherder. But the stepmother now noticed that Oedipus had grown into a beautiful young man. She saw in him a younger version of his father, and forthwith seduced him.

Oedipus, in great anguish, ran away yet again. In a fit of despair and rage, he blinded himself, after which he wandered aimlessly through the countryside until he perished of unrequited guilt.

THE SOCIAL STRUCTURE OF STEPFAMILIES

Stepfamilies are, in some ways, very much like ordinary natural families. But in some other ways they are very different. Many people who enter stepfamilies are unprepared for this combination of sameness and differentness. They could handle either total similarity or complete difference. In the past there has been little they could learn ahead of time about just what is the same and what is different. Therefore, all people who get involved in stepfamilies—and all the rest of us as well—should know more about them: how they are the same, and even more importantly, how they are different. In order to examine such points, we shall first examine the social similarities and differences, and then proceed to some psychological factors: first, the matter of loss and mourning as the basis for the stepfamily, then, on to the many identifications within it, and then, to a word about stepfamily romances. Finally, we shall examine the vicissitudes of parenting in a stepfamily and the insights we can derive for creating better popular models of the stepfamily.

As a social group, the stepfamily is immensely more complex than the nuclear family. The nuclear family contains eight roles and eight possible dyadic relationships, if one defines roles and relationships by the kinship terms recognized in English. These relationships are husband–wife, father–son, father–daughter, mother–son, mother–daughter, brother–brother, sister–sister, and brother–sister. Other languages and other cultures may present slightly different dyads: There may be a term for parent or child of opposite sex and another for same sex; there may be a distinction between older and younger siblings, and there may be a distinction between siblings of opposite or same sex. Given the fact of different language and different cultural values, the number of dyadic relationships in the simple family may vary from 6 to 10, but the number is always within that range. It is indeed true that the relationships may be given different content when they are named differently—or even when they are not. But it is also true that the number of relationships is manageable and that the syndrome of relationships contains few built-in contradictions.

With the death of a parent, a number of interesting things may happen to the household (and household and family are to be kept distinct in our minds). In our own society, the household is likely to become a "single-parent household." There are vacant roles and absent dyads. Indeed, in the single-parent household, there are (using English terminology) only five roles and five dyads. Such a household is understaffed.

When the surviving parent remarries, there may be a sense of "reconstitution" of the nuclear family household, provided of course that the new mate was never married or else was widowed. The point to remember is that in households that are reconstituted after the death of a spouse/parent, there are no "outside parents." Such simple stepfamilies have been common in Europe and America, as elsewhere, for centuries—they are "simple" not in the sense of their internal construction (there may be 18 dyads instead of the classic 8), but rather because they "stand alone" as a nuclear family does, unencumbered by the demands or the images of surviving natural parents.

On the divorce of parents, the situation leads to more complex stepfamily types. In the family of divorce, there are seven dyads present instead of five dyads. The only relationship that is absent is the husband–wife relationship. And, in fact, *that* isn't exactly absent, but has merely been redefined into an exhusband–exwife relationship. Some aspects of the husband–wife relationship can be "canceled"—the coparent aspect, however, cannot. It can be repudiated, but it cannot be canceled. So the family of divorce actually retains the eight relationships in the *family*, but the *household* dimension may undergo considerable perturbation.

To put it another way, at divorce the structure of the *family* is not much changed, for all that its operation is immensely perturbed: it merely becomes a "divorced family" instead of a "nuclear family." It is the *household* arrangement that changes. If one set of parent–child relationships is repudiated, the result may resemble the stepfamily created by death, but usually neither parent totally repudiates responsibilities, for all the important changes occur in the context in which the responsibilities are carried out.

Therefore, one problem in the divorced family is which members are inside and which are outside which household. The divorced family in all cultures that practice neolocal residence (i.e., the married pair form the basic unit around which the household is built) usually has *two* residences: his and hers. From the standpoint of the children, that makes the residence pattern one that Ahrons (1979) calls "binuclear." Normally, a "nuclear" family lives in a single dwelling; the divorced or "binuclear" family lives in two dwellings.

If a child spends all his/her time in one household of the binuclear family, the result is an appearance of an "outside parent." When custody goes to one parent or the other, this is the way it feels. However, when custody is given jointly to both parents, the child may feel differently about it: the child has two houses, two places to sleep, two sets of toys.

Statistically, in our society today, it is still most common for children of divorce to live with their mother, in her custody. In such a case the binuclear family may *feel* like a household containing five dyads (two parent–child dyads and three sibling dyads) with three "outside relationships"—coparents and the other two parent–child dyads. If the children are split between two households, the structure is more complicated.

Some families prosper in the various binuclear situations. The health or lack of it in such family forms is apparently not related to the structure as much as it is to the personal characteristics and attitudes of the parents and their capacity to communicate with one another and to let the children "have" the relationships with the other parent on terms worked out by the other parent and the children.

When divorced parents remarry, a much more complicated structure is created. Now there are not merely two interlocked households in a binuclear family, but each household may become the scene of a stepfamily household. As a result, a whole set of stepfamily households are strung together by binuclear families so that a sort of chain results—what I some years ago (Bohannan, 1970) called "divorce chains."

When a divorced couple each remarries new spouses who already have children, there is a total of 22 possible dyadic relationships. Some types of these relationships appear in all the households. Others do not—the relationship between a woman's husband and her former husband, for example, is seldom lived out within the same household for all that it may be a salient point of the structure of the whole. Former husbands participate in the stepfamilies at one remove, because of their position in the linked binuclear families.

The child of a binuclear family is a more or less regular participant in two households—thus forming a link. The coparents, now each remarried and living in different households, nevertheless must communicate minimally about the movements of the children and make decisions about the children. These two households may have very different cultures, and the expectations and standards of behavior may be very different in them. What studies have been made (Ahrons, 1979; Steinman, 1980) seem to indicate that children can adjust to the binuclear family *if* the two natural parents are comfortable with the situation and allow the children to create their own relationship with the other parent on the terms worked out by that parent and the child. The major difficulties would seem to arise when one parent seriously criticizes or badmouths the other parent and the way that other parent's household is run.

There is a possibility, then, of 18 relationships in *each* of the two stepfamily households. Each relationship is necessarily given a somewhat different content, and even more important, a different emotional tone. Obviously, the age of the siblings and stepsiblings has something to do with that content and tone, and halfsiblings are usually marked by a greater age disparity than either stepsiblings or full siblings.

There are, however, four relationships among the adult members of the two binuclear families that are almost always external to the stepfamily household: (1) the relationship of exhusband–exwife; (2) those between a woman's husband and her exhusband; (3) a man's wife and his exwife; and (4) the relationship between an exhusband's present wife's exhusband and his exwife's present husband's exwife (this relationship may be an important stabilizing factor in a few cases, especially if they can communicate when their respective spouses cannot communicate with one another; such people have been known to marry, which complicates all this even further).

All external relationships have one quality in common: they are outside the orbit of planning of any household. Their position "out there" means that when one of them performs kinship obligations or makes binuclear family demands, the plans of the stepfamily household may have to bend in order to avoid conflict. Said more plainly, plans have to be made in both the binuclear family and the stepfamily. Sometimes conflict results for those who are members of both. Some money, in the form of child support, is likely to flow along lines of the binuclear family, sometimes creating trouble in the stepfamily. "Your children's father" or "your children's mother" may become the ghost that rules the stepfamily household if care is not taken to be absolutely open.

Thus, socially the stepfamily—and its accompanying household—is complex. It contains family relationships, but also contains relationships never found in intact nuclear families. Cultural standardization of many of these "new" relationships—that is, a commonly understood view of what the relationships ought to mean for the people in them, from which individual relationships can vary, or a set of standards with which they can compromise—is not clearly drawn. It seems, from the outside, to be chaotic. Indeed, it sometimes seems even more chaotic from the inside.

One further attribute makes this type of household different: It contains in-laws—what the anthropologists call affinal kinsmen. We all know that a mother-in-law in the house is likely, in Western cultures, to create strain. But stepchildren and stepparents are in-laws in precisely the same way—they are just in the younger generation rather than the older generation. Without these shared affinal links, there would be no relationship between them. There is no culturally recognized way in the Western world to deal with the discomforts of affines in the home.

One of the mistakes that people make repeatedly is to downplay or banish the differences and try to make everything in a stepfamily household work like things in a nuclear family household. Obviously, as long as the stepfamily is beset by the image of the nuclear family, it can't be made to work.

THE PSYCHOLOGICAL STRUCTURE OF THE STEPFAMILY

Emily and John Visher (1979) have pointed out that all stepfamilies are built on loss. Not only have the protagonists experienced a series of losses of object relationships, but also a series of shifts and losses in the identifications that are an important dimension of the ego and superego, and of the self.

The spouses, on divorce (or, of course, on being widowed) have had to adjust to a loss of primary relationships, as well as to the loss of their individual objects (some divorced people object to calling this loss "mourning" because they aren't "sorry" it happened). Some also mourn the loss of a specific role or status. Some indeed have struggled desperately with guilt, trying to keep from turning the mourning into melancholia.

Children, at the time of divorce, suffer a dual blow: Not only do they have to make a major social adjustment—to a completely new relationship with each parent (and the relationships with the external parent may be attenuated or sometimes completely lost)—but they have suffered a narcissistic blow in that the relationship of which they are a product has been severed. They, indeed, have at one level been cut in half. The identification of self as a part of their parents *as a unit* has been lost or mangled.

Parents at the time of divorce are likely to be psychologically busy with their own adjustments and thus to have little empathy with the children or may exhibit a more simplified and stylized regard for the child's situation than is in fact called for—indeed less than even they themselves might have shown in a calmer situation. Not only is the child's development knocked temporarily off-course, but the parent's capacity to parent may be directly affected.

IDENTIFICATION IN THE STEPFAMILY

It was Therese Benedek (1959) who brought together the first tenets of what she called "parenthood as a developmental phase." In order to understand the psychological dimensions of any forms of family found in our society it is well to begin with Benedek's views on the impact of marriage and parenthood on the psyche. The stages that she posited begin with falling in love, which she describes as an exchange of ego ideals. That is to say, each partner finds in the other some aspects of her or his own ego ideal that have been repressed but that might be expressed if one's secondary sexual identification (not being the sex that one is not) had not required those repressions. With sexualization of the relationship, there is an accommodation of the two ids, as well as of the two superegos, so that each ego takes into account the id and the superego of the object as well as of the self (Lidz, 1968).

At the next phase of growth of the relationship, an identification of spouses occurs: Each perceives the other as not only an extension of self, but also as a criterion by which third parties judge one; that is, I am myself, at least in part, because I first won and now keep this spouse. Thus, my spouse has become my ambassador.

The identifications become more numerous and complex with the birth of children. Each parent, in her/his own way (and this varies with the sexes as well as with individuals) identifies with the children. If one identifies with one's child, that means that one comes to identify the spouse with one's parent of opposite sex (if that has not already happened in earlier stages). One then identifies the spouse's spouse (oneself) with the parent of the same sex—that is, one's identification with one's parent of the same sex is reinforced and strengthened.

When a marriage is ended, either by death or by divorce, the work of mourning includes adjusting these many identifications to the new reality. When mourning has proceeded—or, indeed, as a means of speeding it up—one begins the processes of identification over again, with new objects. Severing one's identification with the exspouse is probably never complete, if for no other reason (and usually there are many other reasons) than that exspouses remain coparents, and the children are constant reminders. Presumably, and perhaps in altered form, a person maintains to some degree the identifications of the ex-spouse with his/her parent of the opposite sex, but the situation seems never to have been studied. No literature connects these points, just as there is no literature on the impact of divorce on dreams, although the divorced analysands I have talked to indicate fascinating mixtures of the images of their objects. Obviously, divorce cancels, as it were, the reality on which some aspects of such identifications are based, but it does *not* cancel the reality of other aspects. Therefore, one proceeds into the next relationship trailing clouds either of glory or of ignominy, or both.

For the remarried parent in a stepfamily, the following identifications (at very least) would seem to be present in some form or another:

1. Identification with each child.
2. Identification at a new level with the exspouse. This may be denied, but it cannot be totally stamped out. Instead of being the partner who maintained that relationship, one has become in one's own view (and may think the world concurs) the partner who did not or could not maintain it. That is, either you had the ego strength to break a bad relationship or else you did not have it, or would not even admit the relationship was bad, and so suffered the humiliation of being left. The latter situation is most often called "failure." The identification with the exspouse comes to be "he/she is that part of me that doesn't like me."
   a. But your exspouse is still the coparent of your child. Therefore, the identification between the exspouse and the parent of opposite sex undergoes some changes. But which ones?
   b. The identification of yourself, as parent, with your own parent of same sex (or, indeed, of opposite sex) may also undergo vicissitudes in this process.
3. Identification with a new lover or spouse may not be a problem—indeed, it may seem to be an experience of finally discovering your "real" self in the new lover. However, for some people, the identification with the exspouse seems seriously to interfere with, or at least color, the new relationship. Some people apparently have problems that arise through identifying the self with the new spouse's exspouse. It may be difficult to foresee the degree to which the new spouse merges into one's parental identification.
4. Now comes the most difficult part: *There is almost certainly no identification at all with the children of the new spouse.* That has to be consciously built. How do you do it? Or do you?

For the child of a remarried parent, the identifications are even more complex:

1. The child identifies with both parents. After the divorce, these identifications have to be split into separable parts. The child himself/herself becomes the primary vestige of an identification that presumably once existed between his/her parents. Indeed, most children would seem to assume that identity as an unstated premise.

2. Identification with siblings—a sort of "coidentification," as it were—may be strengthened or weakened depending on the reaction to the new threats to one's total identifications.

3. Identifications are expected with the stepparent. Certainly that takes time.

  a. If the identification with a stepparent threatens the identification with a parent, the child will probably resist the new identification. There is no empty cell in his/her perception of self.

  b. Identification with the remarried parent must be altered because the remarried parent seems to be a different person—and we have already seen the justice of such a view, because the parent herself/himself has a whole new set of identifications. Identifying with one's mother as one's father's wife is somewhat different from identifying with one's mother as some "stranger's" wife. If there is a struggle between father and stepfather, the identification with the mother is certainly going to get some reverberations.

4. The age-specific processes of psychological growth at the time a child must do all this work obviously affect the processes of identification.

Might it not be that after all this work is done effectively, and after the conflict has been reduced, the person who has had to do it, who now has many more identifications, is a more expanded self, for all that something may have been lost?

There is no literature on these identifications in stepfamilies. Yet, the social science literature is emphatic that, taken statistically, the adjustment of stepchildren to school and peers and family households is as good as the adjustment of natural children (Bernard, 1956; Wilson, Zurcher, McAdams, & Curtis, 1975; Bohannan & Erickson, 1978). Obviously, the stepchild has taken a very different route to success than has the child living in an intact household who has never undergone these various experiences. How is it done? In the absence of case material, it is difficult to say much.

I am going to suggest that children's identifications with parents are most often what Kohut (1971) has called "gross identifications." He points out that, in the psychoanalysis of some narcissistic character types, the "pattern of identification" changes and becomes "not gross and indiscriminate anymore, but . . . selective—increasingly focusing on features and qualities which are indeed compatible with the analysand's personality" (1971, p. 167). It seems to me to be precisely this process that is different in stepfamilies: Although one may find some examples of "gross identification" which can then become selective, nevertheless, the identification with the stepparent would seem most often to begin with massive resistance to any identification, then "focusing on features and qualities which are indeed compatible" with the child's personality, and (as a final stage) some recognition, perhaps with some surprise, that an identification has indeed taken place. A university junior whom I interviewed some years ago told me that all his good characteristics derived from his stepfather, while all his bad characteristics came from his father. He seems still to have been his mother's boy.

If, as Freud suggests (1923, pp. 32–34), the resolution of the Oedipus complex (for boys) involves identification with the father and giving up the mother as object in favor of the father, then the divorce of parents at any age (including adulthood) is likely to upset the Oedipal adjustment. Mother is, in one sense, available—at the same time that the identification with father is strained because he has foregone the relationship that you went through the Oedipal solution to allow him to preserve.

So much, however, is not the worst part: Father, after divorce, is a direct competitor for other women. He may become a model in a different way from what he was in the intact family. Moreover, mother is now a much more overtly sexual creature—it is possible to repress knowledge of, or interest in, mother's sex life when she is married to father, but far more difficult to suppress them about her relationships with other men.

And even *that* is not the worst part. The identification with father may be derailed by father's identification with his new wife. Norman Mailer, who has good reason to know, said somewhere that being married to two different women was like living in two different countries. Father's identification with his new spouse is likely to call up different dimensions of his personality than did his identification with his old spouse, your mother. That means that, to the child of the first marriage, the remarried parent may appear to be a "different person." Moreover, a boy's object relationship with mother, reactivated, has to be given up *again* at the time she remarries—to someone with whom the boy in all likelihood has no identification and to whom he may have a genuine, reality-based, antipathy.

The Vishers say that, based on their clinical evidence and their wide experience in conducting workshops for stepfamilies, the most difficult relationship in the stepfamily is that of stepmother–stepdaughter. Identifying with mother as the woman who rejected father (whom you gave up in order to identify with mother) may be hard enough. But to have to replay the rejection of father and identification with a woman whom you don't even *like* may be impossible!

In summary, the remarriage of a parent is difficult—one calls one's identification with the remarrying parent into question simply because the object of the parent-with-whom-I-identify is *not* the object that *I* have more or less successfully given up (either in the positive or negative Oedipal solution) and certainly is not somebody with whom I can instantly or fully identify.

STEPFAMILY ROMANCES

The vicissitudes of the family romance in situations of divorce, remarriage, and stepfamily seem to be unexamined in the literature. Because the family romance is so common a means for youngsters to begin the processes of dissociation from the parents, it would be astonishing if the stepfamily did not alter it markedly.

Before we speculate about the family romance of the stepchild, it is well to review the "normal" family romance in the intact family. Freud's account of the process runs:

> [The child] gets to know other parents and compare them with his own, and so acquires the right to doubt the incomparable and unique quality which he had attributed to them. Small events in the child's life . . . make him feel dissatisfied [and] afford him provocation for beginning to criticize his parents. . . . Other parents are in some respects preferable to them. (1909, p. 237)

He continues:

> The child's imagination becomes engaged in the task of getting free from the parents of whom he now has a low opinion and of replacing them by others. (1909, pp. 238–239)

Freud then discusses the relative rank of the families, which may or may not be relevant in today's cases (certainly rank means something different for today's America than it did for Freud's Vienna). The argument then undergoes a change of direction:

> When the child comes . . . to realize that *pater semper incertus est* . . . the family romance undergoes a curious curtailment: it contents itself with exalting the child's father, but no longer casts doubt on his maternal origin. (1909, p. 239)

Freud calls this a "second stage of the family romance." It sometimes happens that, with only this much information, the child imagines his mother in "situations of secret infidelity and . . . secret love affairs" (1909, p. 239). Freud finishes by telling us:

> In fact the child is not getting rid of his father but exalting him . . . [to the] vanished days when his father seemed the noblest and strongest of men and his mother the dearest and loveliest of women. . . . His phantasy is no more than the expression of regret that those happy days are gone. (1909, pp. 240–241)

But for the adopted child or the stepchild, reality is very different. Hence the myths and attitudes must be different.

A few sources do concern the family romance in cases of adoption, of which I found Blum (1969) the most useful. He discusses "the prolongation of the family romance and its fixation in the adopted child." He continues:

> The family romance fantasies then have the function of attempting to master the trauma of separation, the reality of having been rejected by the natural parents, and the possible associated unpleasant reality of being ambivalently accepted by the adoptive parents. . . . Since the adopted child really has two sets of parents, he cannot use the family romance as a game. (1969, pp. 897–898)

Wieder makes a comment about adoptees that can be taken to heart when we deal with stepchildren.

> A toddler *doesn't need to know he is adopted*; he needs to know he belongs to the people he experiences as parents. (1978, p. 799; original emphasis)

It is almost surely needing to know that one belongs that will be found to be paramount in the stepfamily romance.

Wieder also gives us a rubric for adoptees from which we may be able to make some deductions about stepchildren:

> The paradigm family romance was described in blood-kin children with knowledge of only one set of parents. The family romance of adoptees is built around the knowledge of two sets of parents who do in fact exist. The content of family romance fantasies was, along with their function, considerably modified in all my patients. The fantasy of adoption is the blood-kin child's illusory mastery of aggressive and sexual conflicts. The actuality of adoption is the *fait accompli*, the cause, underlying many of the adoptee's problems. The adoptees wish is to *deny* adoption, establish fantasied blood ties to the adoptive parents, and thereby erase the humiliation that adoption implies to him. (1978, p. 808)

Given this much, we can begin the process of asking about the family romance and associated identity problems of stepchildren. Can the stepchild use the family romance as a game, as natural children can but adoptive children cannot? If so, how? What does the stepchild do about rejection? How does the stepchild handle whatever humiliation being a member of a stepfamily might bring?

Surely the stepchild's family romance centers around an intact family—the old family that is different from what it is in actuality. We know, for example, that one reason many children resent their parents' remarriages, and their stepparents in particular, is that the marriage represents a barrier to the child's fantasy that the natural parents will remarry. Indeed, the fantasy of parental remarriage, as the family romance of stepchildren, may be one of the major blocks to their adjustment to a binuclear family.

Obviously, all these questions can be answered only on the basis of clinical material. It is, in my view, urgent for the comfort of stepfamily members that such material be gathered and published.

Meanwhile, one more suggestion by Wieder is instructive:

> The knowledge of having an unbroken genetic and historical attachment to past, present, and future family members is an important element in the adolescent's self-image. The identity confusion of many adolescent adoptees is aggravated by the knowledge of having genetic links to people about whom they know little or nothing. The resolution of their resulting disturbing phatasies or obsessive questioning about these people often rests on the adoptee's acquisition of new and realistic information about them. (1978, p. 809)

SOME VICISSITUDES OF STEPPARENTING

As a model for this segment of this article, I shall take the stages of parenting from Ellen Galinsky's *Between Generations, the Six Stages of Parenthood* (1981). Galinsky says little about stepfamilies, although a number of her examples are taken from them as well as from single-parent households. Her primary points are that stages of parenthood are determined by the developmental phases of the child, and that at every stage, parents have what she calls "images" of how they themselves and their children should develop and behave. It is the same phenomenon that Levinson (1978) calls "the dream." If reality coincides with their images—with the dream—they feel pleasure. If it does not, they get depressed and angry. These points are at least as important for stepfamilies as they are for nuclear families.

In order to explain her data and experience, Galinsky has divided parenthood into six stages: (1) image-making stage; (2) nurturing stage; (3) authority stage; (4) interpretive stage; (5) interdependent stage; and (6) departure stage. Parents, through identification with the children, are lead through the six stages. The parent not only experiences being the parent but at the same time vicariously experiences being the child, remembering his/her own history and difficulties.

The first phase is the *image-making stage*. In the natural family, it coincides with the period of the pregnancy. For stepfamilies, however, the image-making phase occurs during the courtship of the child's natural parent and the "stepping in" of the stepparent. During such times, both natural parents and stepparents prepare for the changes that will occur in themselves and in their relationships. They begin to pull together their ideas about what kind of parents or stepparents they will be, and how being a parent will affect their relationship with the spouse, with their own parents, with colleagues. In the process, these "image-making" parents are likely to fantasize about what the child will do at the same time that they think about what they themselves are doing. These images, if they accord well with reality, can be of immense help. If they do *not*, the parent may have considerable difficulty. If the stepparent-to-be has considerable contact with the stepchild-to-be, the stepparent may be able to get these images fairly clear. But it would seem that many stepparents do not. Perhaps the most difficult point is the negative folk-image of stepparents, particularly stepmothers. Many stepmothers have difficulty even pronouncing the word "stepmother," let alone so identifying themselves.

Parenthood enters the *nurturing stage* with the birth of a child in the natural family and lasts until the child learns to say "No." The major parental task is to cement an attachment to the infant and reconcile the real infant with the imagined child. A lot of difficulty may arise if the child does not in fact "live up to" the image. The image has to be redefined. There may be a period of greater or lesser mourning for the image, even as it is successfully replaced.

For stepparents, the nurturing stage comes in different rhythms. Whereas nuclear parents have been exchanging rhythms with the child ever since the child was born or before, in the stepfamily the child already has established habits and rhythms to which the stepparent must adjust. Neither the stepparent nor the stepchild is likely to be ready for this sudden change. There is also an identity problem that may arise at this stage if the child resembles the natural parent, just as there is sometimes difficulty for natural parents if the child resembles a disliked kinsman. Such assessments of physical resemblance to other people often color attitudes to the child. In stepfamilies they may create serious problems.

When the child learns to say "No," the parents enter the *authority stage*. As the child enlarges his/her environment, the primary parental responsibilities are to keep the child out of danger while still allowing enough leeway, and instilling the requirements of the parents and of the society. A parent at this stage is a hate object as well as a love object. Some parents have difficulty being hate objects; others do not grasp the nature of authority, confusing all authority with dictatorship. How does the parent enforce limits? How does he/she handle the child's conflicts?

In this phase, particularly as the child begins to talk, the parents' skill in understanding the child takes on a new dimension. The parent must listen not only to the child's speech but also to the child's body English and other non-linguistic communications. Some parents who have "listened" to nonlinguistic communication when the child was an infant, no longer notice it after the child learns to talk, but rather they go entirely on the child's spoken words.

The major task of this phase is avoiding battles of will (added to the two demands that run through all the phases—understanding the child and changing as the child changes). One serious trap during this stage is thinking of the child as the ambassador of the self—the child's actions are made a narcissistic extension of the parent's sense of self. The natural question, "How have I done as a parent?" is answered by reference outside the family instead of inside. If the child's actual behavior and the parent's image are too far apart, the parent may try to force the child to change. The parent's definition of the child's behavior is important at this stage of the child's creation of its own identity. The parents begin to assign motives to the child, and a child's self-opinion may be vastly influenced by the definition the parents give to the child's behavior. They tell children "you are" such and such when they discipline them, rather than merely telling the child what behavior is expected.

The task of establishing authority is much more diffuse in the stepfamily—and it crosses all the stages. A study of stepfathers by Phyllis Stern (1976) suggests in fact that authority is the gravest problem that stepfathers face. Often the wife/mother has an image of the stepfather taking considerable authority, but she is not always prepared to relinquish any of her own position of authority.

The *interpretive stage* of parenthood is the period, more or less during the child's latency, in which the parent's major task is to explain the cultural and physical world to the child, so that the child, at the end of it, has absorbed his/her parent's cultural view of society and the world. As usual, this stage is triggered by the growth of the child, and the parent's task is to keep up with the child.

Galinsky (1981) makes an important point here: The way in which the parents interpret the world is not merely culture-bound, imparting the standard cultural view, but is specific for each child—the culture is interpreted a little differently for each child, reflecting both the parent's age and his/her view of the particular child. Parents also begin in this phase to interpret themselves to their children. Children form images of what parents should be and do. Sometimes the child's images are "out of sync" with the parents' images.

The interpretive stage presents stepparents with special difficulties: the child may be getting a different set of interpretations from an external natural parent. Therefore, everything one says about the nature of the world and of society may be checked out with the child's "real" parents. The child tallies the stepparent's evaluations with those of the natural parents. The child is likely to opt for the natural parent's evaluation, thus creating strain and distance in the stepparent relationship.

The *interdependent stage* begins shortly before the child's puberty. At this stage, the parents have to renounce two images: their image of themselves as parents of a child they are helping to form, and their image of what the child is. The "need to get away" on the part of the adolescent must not be misunderstood by the parent. Parents in this phase have to stand up to their teenagers' criticisms of them as parents. The child is almost fully grown; punishment modes and even discussion modes have to change. The parent's problem with images is great here, because the teenager they see in front of them may be neither the child they have known nor the adult they will have ultimately to "settle" for.

One of the most difficult factors in a stepfamily with adolescent children—with parents, thus, in the interdependent stage—is that the children are pulling away from the family to establish their own identities. If the adolescents are urged to get back into the family, their resistance may be to junior status rather than to the stepparent: that is, not to the stepfamily as such, but rather to being treated in a way they consider suitable only for younger children.

The sixth stage is the *departure stage*. Natural parents all too often have an image of their own relationship with one another returning to what it was before children were born. They are thus likely to build images of themselves that are seriously out of phase with reality. The parent is also likely to think that when the child leaves home, "that is that." None of these images is likely to prove true.

The comparable trap for stepparents is thinking that as soon as the kids leave, their relationship can begin to be what they wanted it to be all the time—without any proof that it is the children who were making it what they did not want it to be.

Parenting an adult child, let alone parenting an adult stepchild, is something on which there is little research.

Finally, says Galinsky, "when images are not reached in reality, parents look for a place to place the blame: 'I gave too much,' 'I didn't give enough,' and 'the schools didn't give enough' are the three explanations that I heard most frequently" (1981, p. 313). In short, the parents are bringing their images into line with the actual personality of the grown child. Again, this period provides stepparents with a different challenge: Could I have done my stepparenting any better or was the damage done before I arrived on the scene?

Parents during all phases have to set "behavioral standards." This applies to stepparents as much as to natural parents. The parent in the nuclear family has, for example, to define physical relationships—how much touching, how much wrestling, and the like. Stepparents often feel at a grave disadvantage here because the last thing they want to do is distance a stepchild from themselves or distance stepsiblings from one another. Yet, not doing so may interfere with their own notions of propriety.

It has been said that stepparenting an adolescent is the most difficult of all stepparenting, especially if the stepping-in occurs at that time. The identity of the teenager is well along, but is likely to be very tentative and insecure. The task of creating new kinds of ties at the same time that greater distance is allowed and encouraged is difficult even in the nuclear family and is a very touchy situation for the new stepfamily.

It would seem that the major difference between parenting in nuclear families and in stepfamilies is the form that the challenges take. In stepfamilies, many of the tasks seem not to be phase-appropriate—therefore there are no secure "rules" about how to go about them. It may be, thus, that the images within the stepfamily may be more difficult to deal with than the images our culture supplies for its nuclear families. There are no ready-made images for stepparents except the cruel ones. In the absence of images, stepparents fall back on the images of themselves as natural parents and the images the culture does indeed provide to natural parents. When these images don't stand up—and they usually don't in the stepfamily—people need some new sets of images to work with. In light of the estimate that one of three children in the next decade will experience the stepfamily, it behooves us to begin undertaking research about and giving some help to the imaginative people who establish stepfamilies and make them work.

REFERENCES

Ahrons, C. R. The binuclear family. *Alternative Lifestyles*, 1979, 2(4), 449–515.
Benedek, T. The emotional structure of the family. In R. N. Anshen (Ed.), *The family: Its functions and destiny* (Rev. ed.). New York: Harper, 1959.

Bernard, J. *Remarriage: A study of marriage.* New York: Dryden Press, 1956.

Blum, H. P. A psychoanalytic view of who's afraid of Virginia Woolf? *Journal of the American Psychoanalytic Association,* 1969, *17*(3), 888–903.

Bohannan, P. *After divorce.* Garden City, N.Y.: Doubleday, 1970.

Bohannan, P., & Erickson, R. Stepping in. *Psychology Today,* 1978, *11*, 53ff.

Freud, S. Family romances (1909). *Standard Edition, 9,* 235–241. London: Hogarth Press, 1959.

Freud, S. The ego and the id (1923). *Standard Edition, 19,* 12–66. London: Hogarth Press, 1961.

Galinsky, E. *Between generations, the six stages of parenthood.* New York: Times Books, 1981.

Kohut, H. *The analysis of the self.* New York: International Universities Press, 1971.

Levinson, D. J. *The seasons of a man's life.* New York: Knopf, 1978.

Lidz, T. *The person: His development throughout the life cycle.* New York: Basic Books, 1968.

Steinman, S. *The experience of children in a joint custody arrangement: A report of a study.* Unpublished paper, 1980. (Available from the author, Jewish Family Services, San Francisco, Calif.)

Stern, P. N. *Integrative discipline in stepfather families.* Unpublished doctoral dissertation, University of California, San Francisco, 1976.

Visher, E., & Visher, J. S. *Stepfamilies: A guide to working with stepparents and stepchildren.* New York: Brunner/Mazel, 1979.

Wieder, H. On when and whether to disclose about adoption. *Journal of the American Psychoanalytic Association,* 1978, *26*(4), 793–811.

Wilson, K. L., Zurcher, L., McAdams, D. C., & Curtis, R. L. Stepfathers and stepchildren: An exploratory analysis from two national surveys. *Journal of Marriage and the Family,* 1975, *37,* 526–536.

14

JUDGES AND
OTHER PEOPLE'S CHILDREN

ABNER J. MIKVA

It has been fairly common for state legislatures to use their infinite wisdom to help children to grow up. Thus, most state codes contain provisions specifically directing teachers what to teach, what not to teach, and how to teach it. Some codes tell the children, also, that they are to love animals, to respect the flag, not to read dirty books, and not to stay out past a certain hour. These legislative directives, enforceable in the courts of law, have often drawn ridicule from enlightened critics. Clarence Darrow made notorious fun of the Tennessee law which told teachers how not to teach the world's creation. One author collected a list of all of the books that had been banned for children, which came to quite a tidy collection, starting, of course, with various disapproved versions of the Bible.

Yet, some of the same critics who object to the states' involvement at the teaching and reading level, seem to be championing more state involvement in the family situation. Concerned about child abuse and neglect, and unhappy about the trampling of children's rights and preferences, they have thrust some troublesome questions about how to raise children onto the courts.

Over the last decade or so, there has been a tremendous increase in the extent of judicial involvement in family life. More and more today—and I think much more than we would like—judges are being asked to make parental choices for other people's children.

I do not want to suggest that interventionists are all bad. But I think we have to keep reminding ourselves that they are not all good either. We ought to look at each proposal for intervention with an appropriate critical eye.

An area that typifies this situation is the Supreme Court's handling of the conflict between parents and children over the most sensitive of all contemporary disputes—abortion. In considering the problem of defining precisely the rights

Abner J. Mikva. U.S. Court of Appeals, District of Columbia Circuit, Washington, D.C.

of children to have abortions when their parents object, the Court has become enmeshed in the complex fabric of parent–child relationships and has been asked to place in its stead a simplified code of judge-made rights—whether those be the rights of children to act independently of their parents, or the rights of parents to control the conduct of their children. It may be time now for us to begin to rethink the wisdom of that entire enterprise.

In 1976, the Court was asked to rule on the constitutionality of a Missouri statute that made it illegal for a pregnant teenager to have an abortion unless she could obtain her parents' consent. The Court concluded that the Missouri statute gave parents what the Court called ''an absolute, and possibly arbitrary, veto'' over the child's abortion decision. For that reason, it declared the law unconstitutional.

In 1979, the Court was asked to pass on the constitutionality of a Massachusetts statute that also attempted to regulate parent–child relationships in the area of abortions. That statute was a masterpiece of legalism. It took several years of judicial proceedings just to figure out what it meant! As ultimately interpreted, the statute required that a pregnant minor who wanted an abortion must get the consent of both her parents, but the law also provided that if parental consent were denied, the child had a right to go to court and get a court order permitting her to have an abortion. Under the statute as interpreted, there was no way an adolescent girl could get an abortion without her parents knowing about it. The Court realized that this absolute notification requirement would be disastrous in some cases. Primarily for that reason, it declared that the statute was unconstitutional.

Four of the Justices were not content, however, to let the matter rest there. They undertook to make some general comments on how this conflict between parent and child might be managed by the legal system. Their solution? Send it to a judge. Justice Powell, joined by three other Justices, suggested that what was needed was a statute that would allow a judge to decide not only whether a child should be allowed to have an abortion, but also whether the parents of the child should be involved in that decision.

Some concerned parties may applaud that proposal as a victory for children's rights. Some may see it as one more incursion on parents' rights. All, I suspect, might be somewhat at a loss to understand how this intensely personal problem came to be fit for judicial resolution. Neither the advocates of children's rights nor the defenders of parental authority would be happy with a legal system in which the crucial decisions are being made by neither the child nor the parent, but are being made by a judge. Yet, that is what the Supreme Court recommended.

That brings us to the last of this small series of cases, decided in 1981. This case involved an attempt by the State of Utah to deal with the same problem that had confronted Missouri and Massachusetts. Utah's solution was to make it illegal for a physican to perform an abortion on a minor unless the physisican gave prior notice to the minor's parents. The Utah Supreme Court reasoned that the statute did not give parents a veto over the daughter's abortion decision; rather it gave them the option to "respond and consult" with the child and her physician. On that understanding, the Utah Supreme Court ruled that the statute was constitutional. The U.S. Supreme Court upheld the Utah statute. Antiabortionists hailed it as a great victory; advocates of free choice lamented it as a sad defeat. No one asked whether the legislature and all the courts had sufficient expertise to decide this intensely thorny problem of child–parent communications.

If we take just a minute to step back from this problem and to approach it from a commonsense point of view, the issue takes on more manageable proportions. The question is: Should parents have an opportunity to consult with their daughter before the daughter decides whether or not to have an abortion? The answer is obvious and clear: "Maybe—sometimes yes and sometimes no." If you ask, instead, for a single answer to handle all possible situations, you must necessarily simplify what by its nature is not simple. For example, even if you believe that daughters should, as a general rule, consult with their parents before having an abortion, do you think that such consultation should be required even when the child's father is the father of her child? It taxes the limits of human ingenuity to think that you could formulate a single rule that would do justice in all these cases.

There is, perhaps, an even more basic consideration. Before judges and legislators attempt to make pronouncements in such a sensitive area of parent–child relations, they at least should consider whether they should say anything at all. When parents and children (or perhaps more precisely the advocates of parents and children) come to the lawmakers with questions like this, the preliminary question to be addressed is: Why are you asking us? Is not this the kind of question that should be settled by parents and children themselves, with the guidance of physicians, religious leaders, and mental health professionals? Why do people insist on bringing such problems to lawyers, and why do they then complain because the answers they get are too legalistic to be of much human use? What, after all are the judges' and lawmakers' special insights into this delicate area?

Although it is most stark in the abortion context, the tendency to overlegalize parent–child relationships is much more widespread. It involves questions of parental control over a child's access to birth control information and contraceptive devices. It involves whether parents must be notified or must consent before a mental health professional can provide psychological counseling for minors. It involves whether parents can confine their children in mental hospitals over their children's opposition. It involves whether runaway children can be compelled to return home when they decide that the home they left is no longer hospitable to their needs. It involves whether children must conform to the lifestyles their parents choose in exchange for their parents' continued financial support.

One recent case brings this problem into sharp relief. It seems that a Colorado teenager was suspended from school for smoking and selling marijuana. As punishment, his parents required that he cut backyard weeds. Then the conflict escalated. The son withdrew from 10th grade, and his parents sent him to school abroad. Ultimately, there came an ultimatum: The parents said—either go back to school or get a job, or no more money from us. Did the teenager comply? Did the teenager call his parents' bluff? He did neither: He took his parents to court. He sued his parents under a tort theory that lawyers call "the intentional affliction of emotional distress."

Personally, I am not shocked by the idea that a child should accuse his parents of being bad parents. That is the opposite side of what parents have been doing for years. If parents can get a court to label their kids as "incorrigible," then I suppose it is only fair that kids can get courts to label their parents as tyrranical. The crucial mistake, I want to suggest, is to ask the courts to do either. Children frequently clash with their parents; parents frequently collide with their children. These conflicts are inherent in that most precious and most difficult societal institution—the family. Seeking the redress of the law and the judicial system is not good for the family or the law.

We all know, intuitively, that there are no bad parents with good kids or good parents with bad kids. There are only troubled families. But when troubled families bring their troubles to the judge, the label of troublemaker will affix to one side or the other. The unavoidable consequence of seeking a "decision" from an arbiter is that one family member will be compelled to bear the whole blame for family problems. As soon as a family accepts that a judge should serve as umpire for their disputes, they lose just about all hope that they may reach some sort of mutual accommodation among themselves. Courts are uniquely incapable of rendering sensitive, therapeutic verdicts when a case is presented to the court. Courts cannot give advisory opinions, or even propose temporary, tentative solutions. And yet those prohibitions may very well be the touchstones of the "right" solutions to family problems.

If schools can seek to make it official government policy to be allowed to inflict corporal punishment on the children, the child should obviously be allowed some recompense. Chicago's great political philosopher, the late Findley Peter Dunne, had Mr. Dooley sum up his view on how the state should raise children, as follows: "Spare the rod and spoil the child," said Mr. Hennessey. "Yes," said Mr. Dooley, "but don't spare the rod and you spoil the rod, the child, and the child's father."

When you come to the law to solve human conflicts you will invariably get answers that speak of rights and wrongs, of obligations and prerogatives. More specifically, when you bring such a problem to a judge, you will get a decision that someone has won, and someone else has lost. You will divert attention away from what is most meaningful to the parties, and will focus instead on what is most likely to persuade the judge. You will get a decision imposed on the parties from the outside, a decision that may be very different from what the parties would have come to if they had been allowed to—or in some cases, forced to—work out an accommodation by themselves. It would be like using psychiatrists to impose decisions about interpersonal disputes.

In dealing with parent–child disputes we might be well advised to shift our focus in a way recently suggested by Professor Robert Burt. We should not look at the law as a way of resolving parent–child conflicts, but as a way of structuring the conflict and of channeling the dispute in a way that forces the parties to reach some accommodation among themselves. As Professor Burt reminds us, the child in any family dispute is likely to view himself/herself in one of two ways: either as *alienated*, and outside the family unit and estranged from it; or as *aggrieved*, which suggests an underlying commonality of interests and sets the stage for mutual redefinition within the context of the family. A judge who attempts to resolve such disputes, whether judging in favor of parental authority or of children's liberty, must know that the psychological effect of making any judgment at all is to increase the parties' sense of their estrangement from each other. If the child is already alienated, the final order will etch the breach into hard rock. Even if the alienation is not yet complete, the final decree can rub the wound to a new rawness. Law suits are fights to a decision; there are winners and losers. There is no provision for backing off, or kissing and making up. Even the notions of "winning" and "losing" are hostile to good family relations. Members of good families do not judge each other as "right" or "wrong." The idea that some disputes simply are not fit for judicial resolution is not alien to our system of laws. In fact, that assumption is the bedrock of the American law of labor relations.

When the Congress attempted to fashion a federal labor law in the 1930s, there was one point upon which all sides agreed: a national labor court would be a bad idea. There was concern about the growing economic warfare in industry between labor and management, and there was a consensus that the way to deal with that was to force the parties to resolve their disputes between themselves and to fashion, without outside interference, an agreement with which both sides could live. It was, and it is, a basic tenet of American labor law that no one is to dictate to the parties what that agreement contains. The law requires that labor and management sit down and bargain in good faith. What they agree on in good faith is what the law will enforce—nothing more, nothing less. The role of the judge is to monitor the collective bargaining process to make sure both sides play by the rules, to enforce the agreement the parties arrive at, and in a few cases, to guarantee that the union lives up to its responsibilities to the workers it represents. But in no case can a party hope to get from a judge a better deal than it could wrangle from the other side. Sometimes the process breaks down, and the public must suffer from tactics of economic warfare, like strikes. But even then, the main focus of the law is to force the parties back to the bargaining table. It is better in the long run that the public suffer those inconveniences than that it attempt to dictate to workers and managers what the rules of the workplace should be.

If we substitute "psychological conflict" for "economic warfare," an analogy between labor–management relations and parent–child relations is not hard to find. In both cases, the judge must refrain from pronouncing judgment, from telling one side it is right and the other side it is wrong. In both cases, it is a mistake to force the parties into a premature resolution of their dispute. In both cases, the function of the law is not to resolve disputes but to avoid the resolution—to ensure the process, but not the result, to compel the parties to deal with one another on a basis of mutual dignity and respect. In both cases, the legitimate objectives of the law are satisfied when the parties are willing to accept—however grudgingly or reluctantly—some sort of accommodation: not a resolution that gives one side all it wants and the other nothing at all, but an agreement to which both can accommodate. There is no decision announcing that one side has won and the other side has lost. The parties may claim victory or complain of defeat, but there is no official decree proclaiming such a result.

There is one more comparison that needs to be stressed. Federal labor law did not get off the ground until there was a clear statement that unions have a right to exist, that they may legitimately represent workers in dealing with management, and, most important, that management must bargain in good faith with any union selected by the workers to represent them. In the area of parent–child relationships, there needs to be a corresponding statement of legitimacy. The law must say that a child's grievances are real and cannot be ignored or denigrated by parents, judges, or psychiatric experts. The law must recognize—to borrow a phrase from a popular Saturday morning TV show—that kids are people, too. That judges must refrain from passing judgment over other people's children must be balanced by the recognition that the law cannot allow parents or child-care experts merely to run roughshod over an adolescent's gripes. It is not good enough that the parents and the experts and the judges all agree on what is "in the best interests of the child." There must be, and the perception must be, that there is *some* input from the child into the decisions that affect his/her life. How much control the child should have, of course, will depend on many factors: the child's age, his/her emotional maturity, the nature of the decision to be made, and the general tenor of the family relationship. In each case, however, it must be recognized that the child's concerns should be given their due.

The most obvious application for this proposed judicial restraint would be the divorce situation and custody battles. I can envision a system in which judges would never determine custody except with the agreement of the parties and appropriate input from the child. And if the parties could not agree? Then the court would not decide custody—maybe the court would not grant the divorce. The nonsolution I propose is no different from when two parents disagree on how a child should be raised in a nondivorce situation. Unless there is physical abuse of the child, the courts do not intervene and decide which parent is "right." So too with custody in a divorce situation. There may be some side-effects—more split-custody agreements worked out by the parties, less divorces—side-effects that may be very beneficial to all concerned.

Today, the family is in trouble. I do not think courts created the trouble. But, we do not help by giving judges greater power to make choices for other people's children. Nor can we ignore the reality of parent–child conflict and hide behind a romantic and unhistorical vision of parental authority and family harmony of days gone by. We must accept that between parent and child, and especially between parent and adolescent child, there will often be an ongoing tension as each tries to redefine his/her relationship to the other. Our challenge is to devise methods by which the participants in that conflict can reach some accommodation between themselves and to avoid simplistic responses that merely subject both parents and children to the power of a stranger to their relationship—that is, to someone like a judge.

15

PARENTHOOD AND CHILD ADVOCACY

ALBERT J. SOLNIT

INTRODUCTION

Parenthood taps the adult's inner yearnings for historic continuity and for close-ness with a child. These yearnings lead to self-fulfillment and confidence in oneself as a parent, which crystallize out of the day-to-day care of the infant and young child. Out of this experience the adult becomes bonded to the child who is developing a firm primary attachment to the parent. These primary mutual relationships are unfolded as the parent's empathic responses become refined and adjust to the maturing, developing baby, and as the baby becomes able to cling and hold on to the parent, at first physically and then psychologically, moving from need-satisfying responses to the capacity for object constancy.

Self-fulfillment and a sense of competence is achieved in parenthood through launching a child into a progressive development, one that enables the child to utilize a parental nurture, protection, and guidance. This leads to a continuity of the adult's sense of self and of family. At the same time the child is becoming a unique person who is on the pathway to adult autonomy and self-realization. The parents react to the child's ongoing and evolving needs by developing specific advocacy responses in addition to the earlier nurturing activities. In this chapter, I will give specific attention to the meaning and implementation of the parents' advocate roles.

THE DEVELOPING CHILD

Children are born helpless; the personal relationships that are optimal for their physical and social development are rooted in their biologic immaturity at birth.

Albert J. Solnit. Departments of Pediatrics and Psychiatry, School of Medicine, and Child Study Center, Yale University, New Haven, Connecticut.

The biological factor is the long period of time during which the young of the human species is in a condition of helplessness and dependence. Its intra-uterine existence seems to be short in comparison with that of most animals, and it is sent into the world in a less finished state. As a result, the influence of the real external world upon it is intensified and an early differentiation between the ego and the id is promoted. Moreover, the dangers of the external world have a greater importance for it, so that the value of the object which alone can protect it against them and take the place of its former intra-uterine life is enormously enhanced. The biological factor, then, establishes the earliest situations of danger and creates the need to be loved which will accompany the child through the rest of its life. (S. Freud, 1926, pp. 154–155)

This is underscored by the fact that the human child remains dependent on adult care for a longer period of time than any other species. If a newborn infant is not fed, kept warm and dry, protected from noxious environmental agents, stimulated and soothed emotionally—that is, taken care of totally—he/she will die. As the child's biological stability is established and he/she progresses in development, the adults who do care for the child become a presence that can be known in increasingly specific ways. The parents' value preferences can also have a marked formative influence in terms of shaping the child's future adult personality and values.

What begins as biological helplessness leads to social and psychological attachment as a result of the interaction of the infant and maternal person or persons. The infant progresses from biological dependency to psychological and social attachment in which the child craves affection, approval, and predictable, dependable responses from the caretaking adults. This craving, or "social addiction," is the "stuff" out of which social development emerges as a result of positive and negative identifications. Through these close relationships, the child acquires and internalizes parental attitudes and expectations. In turn, these identifications become the core of the unique personality of each child.

In healthy development, these identifying processes proceed from imitative behavior to the internalization of parental attitudes and expectations. Gradually, this enables the child to separate and individuate as the attachment to the dependable, guiding parental person matures. Now the child is prepared to have short separations from the parents because his/her mental and emotional capacities have enabled him/her to have the parents with him/her psychologically when the child and the parents are physically separated. The child has now achieved ·a significant level of object constancy. Such children can separate from their parents and form secondary relationships with teachers, peers, and others as their progressive development enables them to socialize, learn, play, and move along through the toddler, latency, and adolescent phases. Thus, they carry with them the internalized, reassuring, guiding psychological presence of their parents as they become increasingly independent. In this connection, especially in our pluralistic society, there are differing styles of child rearing preferred by the parents. However, child rearing starts with nurturance in the home and becomes child advocacy when the child develops needs (e.g., for education or health care) which the parent meets from sources outside the home.[1]

Throughout development, the need for continuity with the same primary love objects is crucial as the child defines himself/herself against parents, siblings, and later on peers, teachers, and others. Each young child attributes to the primary or psychological parents the omnipotence and omniscience that early on become the basis for feeling secure with, and later awed by, these parents in the family setting. As maturation and development proceed, these attitudes and expectations undergo gradual change. The child's sense of himself/herself becomes clear and confident as he/she perceives reality more accurately and develops the capacity to think logically.

Gradually, then, children undergo a disillusionment about their parents as advocates. The parents lose their mantle of omniscience and omnipotence, "revealing" their human imperfections as the child is able to give up the need to feel that parents are all-powerful and all-knowing. Normatively, as the disillusionment is worked through, children perceive their parents more realistically. This enables children and parents to become closer friends and companions as a consequence of the rapid maturation and development which follow the rebelliousness associated with puberty and adolescence.

Throughout, the child and adolescent are storing up their future adult capacities to nurture, guide, rear, and be the advocates for their own children. If children lose their primary parents or have multiple and changing parents, there is the risk that these children will persist in relating to parental figures at an immature level. They may be fixated at the level of infantile magical thinking, in which adults in authority are viewed as omnipotent and omniscient.

PARENTS, CHILD, AND FAMILY

Parenthood has been accepted implicitly as an essential part of the life cycle. Although strictly speaking, the generative phase of adulthood may be expressed in many ways, in most instances it involves conceiving, giving birth to, and raising children. Parenthood is that phase of adulthood in which one is a mother or father caring for children from infancy through adolescence, and beyond.

1. In this chapter the advocacy function of parents refers to the protecting, buffering, sheltering activities of the adult caretakers. Dictionary definitions of "advocacy" or the "advocate" are not very satisfactory in conveying this meaning currently attributed to these functions and persons in the United States. For example, in *Webster's Third Unabridged International Dictionary* (Springfield, Mass.: G. & C. Merriam Co., 1961), "advocacy" is defined as the "profession or work of an advocate, the action of advocating, pleading for or supporting." In the same dictionary an "advocate" is defined as "one that pleads the cause of another: defender, counselor, and "to advocate" is defined as "to plead in favor, of, to defend an argument before a tribunal or the public: to support or recommend publicly." A number of other dictionaries do not vary significantly from these definitions, although the *Shorter Oxford English Dictionary* (London: Oxford University Press, 1952) does add in regard to an advocate, "One who pleads, intercedes or speaks for another."

"Parenthood as a psychobiologic process ends only with the death of the parent" (Benedek, 1970, p. xviii).

Courtship, lovemaking, conception, pregnancy, and giving birth to the child are powerfully influential experiences that can become a sound psychological preparation for parenthood. Ironically, the biologically mature human being is also capable of rejecting or may be forced to reject the opportunity to become a parent by giving up the child despite the dramatic experiences that characterize child bearing. There is no instinctual, inborn, inherited biosocial reflex to assure that the newborn will be wanted and kept well by his/her biological parents. "Parenthood in our age, as it evolves in individuals raised in our culture under the pressure of our civilization, often appears to be far removed from its biologic source, so much so that it is not infrequently discussed in clinical terms as if some pathogenic conflict had replaced the biologic process of parenthood" (Anthony & Benedek, 1970, p. 185).

The vicissitudes of parenthood include vicariously experiencing the repetition of one's own past as the child grows and develops. This indirect review and reexperiencing of the past, even in normative healthy parenthood, usually satisfying and self-fulfilling, also is often painful, frustrating, and uncomfortable. As the child masters his/her own developmental tasks, the parent can find satisfaction, not only in acquiring competence in nurturing, protecting, guiding, teaching, and disciplining the child, but also in achieving a sense of his/her own historical continuity from childhood to adulthood.

Parenthood as a cognitive and emotional review, of, or a visit to, one's own past becomes a validation of the adult's sense of himself/herself as a worthwhile, authentically unique person. In turn this validation fosters the parent's confidence in his/her own integrity and future. Thus, in nurturing and representing the dependent child, parents fulfill vital needs of the child and at the same time they have the opportunity to continue the unfolding of their own adult development. This mutuality, of course, arises not so much from what is originally associated with the blood tie, but more out of the hour-to-hour, day-to-day care of the child by the parents and the response of a child to the parents. These interactions establish resonating bonds and affectionate, empathic attachments that constitute the primary psychological relationships between parents and their children.

These primary child–parent psychological relationships are the essential ingredients of the family which is the basic social unit for transmitting from generation to generation certain cultural attitudes, values, and customs. In fact, the family has been repeatedly rediscovered and reaffirmed because it serves basic human needs at the same time as it expresses fundamental human motivations which surface in a variety of ways in different cultures throughout the ages. The family as a basic social unit is inextricably associated with survival for children and with the satisfaction of persistent adult yearnings for closeness and affirmation. In the functioning family, regardless of structure, we can see the expression of a universal search for an extension beyond the boundaries of one person's limitations.

The law "without explicitly defining 'family' assumes that 'family' is an essential component of the 'good' society and the 'family,' like law, is one of the basic processes for the control of human behavior" (Goldstein, 1977, p. 10)—a part, in Hartmann's terms, of each person's "average expectable environment." Mr. Justice Harlan pointed out [dissent in Poe v. Ullman (367 U.S. 497, 551–556, 1961) and later in Griswold v. Connecticut (381 U.S. 479, 499, 1952)] that the family and its integrity has been understood by the courts to have constitutional protection.

THE PARENT AND CHILD ADVOCACY

Anna Freud has observed that a "privilege of childhood is to be sheltered from direct contact with the law and to have society and the state's demands and prohibitions filtered by way of the parents' personalities. The parents thus not only represent the law to the child, but are also his representatives before the law" (A. Freud, 1979). Indeed, a crucial index of the "success" or "failure" of parents in fulfilling their tasks and in finding satisfaction in their own competence is reflected by how the children in internalizing the nurturing care and advocacy of their parents develop internal mechanisms of control sufficient for each of the offspring on becoming an adult to be "a law unto himself, but not above the law" (Goldstein, 1976).

This concept again gives recognition to what has been a value preference as well as an application of psychoanalytic theory: that children have the best opportunity to realize their potential as members of a family in which the desired integrity and intimacy of the family is assured by parents functioning as relatively autonomous adults in charge of their own family. "An integral part of the autonomy of parents is their authority and presumed capacity to determine whether and how to meet the legal care needs for their child—just as they do with regard to his medical care needs." This is based on the acknowledgment "that parents or those they select, are the exclusive representatives of their children before the law, even though the needs of individual family members differ" (Goldstein, Freud, & Solnit, 1979b, p. 112).

In most societies, parents are responsible for the dependent needs of their children in two ways: they nurture them; and they assume the advocacy responsibilities for guiding and planning for them and protecting them from the state and others. The nurturing functions include affection, continuity of care and attachment, dosing of frustration and gratification, and being an adult with whom the child can identify and in relation to whom the child can be different and unique. The advocacy functions are those of planning and making decisions that regulate the child's involvement in his community and society. These functions include the choice of education, health care, disciplinary influences, religious beliefs, and affiliation, and to some extent the mode of social and political expressiveness that is rooted in the parents' background and in their personal preferences. The latter include the decisions about who may visit, care for, and educate the child, including the role of siblings, grandparents, aunts, uncles, neighbors, and family friends in these activities.

This distinction between nurturance and advocacy is based on the assumption that the closeness of parent–child interaction is enhanced when it is accepted in custom and law that until disqualified the parent should be supported in both nurturing and advocacy functions; and that the parent should be protected by law from intrusions into those functions. In other words, the young child needs autonomous parents who are in charge of their family. "So long as the child is a member of a viable family his own needs and interests are merged with those of other members of the family" (Goldstein, Freud, & Solnit, 1979a).

THE CLINICAL EXPERT AND CHILD ADVOCACY

Professionals concerned with the care of children usually agree that children's interests and needs should be paramount. In this era their training and code of ethics should enable them to respect the rights of parents to develop their own style of family living and child rearing, no matter what the professional has "inherited" or selected for his/her own life-style.

The role of clinical experts in child placement conflicts has been generally conceptualized in terms of being an *advocate* for the best interests of the child, but has not been sufficiently examined in terms of its specific functions and limitations. As with other adversarial processes, lawyers will try to use clinical experts in the service of winning the case for one client or the other. In adjudications and dispositions concerned with child placement, there are usually two adults in conflict about the child's custody or placement. The adults may be parents, or representatives of the state or a private agency, and the biological or foster parents. Because of the simultaneous search for the best interests of the child and for equity between adults, the clinical expert is regularly invited and tempted to attend to what is fair for the adults (those who are verbal and able to be their own advocates), and then to express an opinion about which of the available alternatives would be in the best interests of the child.

The clinical expert faces certain temptations. He/she is tempted to become a detective in child abuse cases, in which the allegations of abuse are denied by the parent or parents. The clinical expert may attempt to decide the case himself/herself rather than to answer the court's questions, and yield to the temptation to become judge. If the court's questions are not clear, it is appropriate to ask for clarification. It is the expert's obligation to describe the child's relationship and tolerances in connection with the alternatives available to the child, as well as how these alternatives can be related to the child's current psychological relationships and needs.

Such clinical interviews and evaluations of children and of the conflicting adults, when part of an adversarial process, are of limited value for three major reasons:

1. They are not confidential since reports must be made available for the courts;

2. They are conducted primarily for adversarial, not therapeutic reasons; and often they are coercive, having been ordered by the court; and

3. The sample is a small one, one or two interviews, perhaps as many as three or four. The validity of such a sample in a nonconfidential, adversarial setting is limited.

If the limitations of the clinical expert's methods and knowledge in assessing the child's best interest in placement conflicts were understood and accepted, there might be less pressure to use clinical interviews and assessments. Also, their use would be more sharply focused on specific questions; for example, what is the nature of the child's relationship to each of his/her parents?

The acceptance of such limitations could become the basis for better use of the expertise of the clinician in response to more appropriate questions about placement, for example, available psychological child–parent relationships, limits of continuity, and short-term predictions about the alternatives available. Throughout, the clinical expert should emphasize how the child's development status (chronological age and maturity of functions) is kept in mind as the assessment is carried out. For example, the child's tolerance for separation from the parent at the age of 2 is much less than that of an 8-year-old child.

At the outset, the clinical expert and others should make it as clear as possible that the child's preference or wishes will be taken into account, but that the child will not be the one who decides. The decision will be that of the authorized adult, namely that, of the parents, or, if they cannot agree, a judge. The paramount feature is that the decisions are up to the adults, and should not become an unfair burden for the child. Advocacy for children is based on such assumptions about adult responsibilities and authority.

ISSUES IN DIVORCE AND CHILD ADVOCACY

The "best interests of the child" concept ordinarily does not become activated or emerge as a guiding principle in decisions regarding a child until, and unless, parental autonomy and the integrity of the family have ceased to be protective and have failed to provide the nurturance and advocacy which our society expects from parents. For example, this occurs when the child has been abandoned. In connection with divorce, however, "best interests of the child" as a principle does not become guiding unless the parents cannot agree on the custody assignment. Because the parents who have been his/her advocates are unable to agree, the child is left without an advocate until the court decides which parent shall become the custodial parent. In such instances, the court should assign an independent legal counsel to children whose divorcing parents cannot agree about who is to be the custodial parent (Goldstein *et al.*, 1979b). Such parental dis-agreement, at the point of separation and divorce, temporarily disqualifies par-ents, at least in regard to who will continue on as the custodial parent.

When the court appoints an independent legal counsel for the child because the divorcing parents cannot agree about custodial assignment, it takes on briefly the role of custodial parent. The legal counsel will use experts to provide knowl-edge that will assist him/her in seeking the least detrimental alternative custodial assignment for the children.

A recent case[2] illustrates the need for such advocacy. After 12 years of marriage, a 37-year-old woman separated from her husband because of increasing incompatibility. Both parents sought custody of the children, a 10-year-old girl and a 5-year-old boy. Initially, the mother, an artist, moved out because she wanted the separation, whereas her 39-year-old husband, a businessman, was still strongly attached to his wife and wanted to preserve the marriage. For the next 9 months, efforts at reconciliation failed. The children remained in the family home, and the mother visited them daily. She remained, also, involved in their school and health care activities as she had been before the separation. The father, a hard-working businessman and a busy community leader, hired a reliable housekeeper. He supported the open, flexible visitation that evolved during the separation. Initially, the mother had suggested a compromise as follows: the boy would stay with his father and the girl would live with the mother. Soon, the mother changed her mind, realizing that the children would gain more and lose less by remaining together, regardless of the custody decision. A competent child psychiatrist conducted a clinical evaluation in order to de-termine who would be the best custodial parent in serving "the best interests" of the children.

By a narrow margin the child psychiatrist decided that the father would be the least detrimental alternative as the custodial parent. The mother did not accept this and a court date was set. The mother asked for another opinion by another expert, to which the father agreed. The second expert, a senior consultant, was asked to see the children. The second expert refused, saying that the observations of the first expert were more than adequate and that children should not be required to have multiple psychiatric interviews. He suggested that, if everyone agreed, he would review the entire situation and discuss it with the first expert consultant and determine if he had anything to add or question.

This suggestion was acceptable. The second clinical consultant reached the opinion that the difference between the parents as to who was more fit or who was less fit was not sufficient to make a recommendation. He based this con-clusion on the limitations of our knowledge and methods when psychiatric in-terviewing is used, not for diagnosis or treatment, but for helping to decide about the placement of children when parents dissolve their family. The consultant recommended that the parents, realizing how fit each was, how human each

2. A recent New England case based on a composite of several cases.

was, how imperfect each was, should not allow a stranger, the judge, to decide who should have the custody. He pointed out how much better it would be for the children's sense of security and of worth if they knew that the parents on whom they were dependent, would decide for them. At that point, the recommendation was not successful and a court hearing was held. When the judge heard that the senior clinical consultant had tried to help the parents reach a decision, rather than to leave it up to him, he was incredulous. He wondered if the expert's credentials were authentic since, he assumed, "surely everyone knows that no one can get warring parents in a custody conflict to agree." The judge insisted that the clinical expert must realize and know in his expert heart-of-hearts that he preferred one parent over the other. Finally, he did allow the expert to explain why it would be much better for the children if the parents could decide, despite their conflicts, which parent could best serve the children's needs and best interests. The expert told him that both parents were devoted, conscientious, and above average—that he found the mother's sensitivity and intuitive responses more tuned in to the children, and that he found the father's ability to arrange for a secure and orderly reality in the everyday life of the children a bit more reliable and practical than the mother's ability in those areas. Therefore, the consultant said that he was glad to describe the strengths and weaknesses of each of the parents but that from a clinical point of view he could not find one parent more suitable than the other as a custodial parent. The consultant concluded that it was of crucial importance for the parents to improve the alternatives for their children by reaching their own decision, and not leave it up to the judge, a stranger to the children, no matter how wise, sensitive, and concerned he was, to make the decision.

There was a midday interruption in the hearing. When it resumed the parents, through their attorneys, advised the judge that in a lunch meeting they had agreed as to which of them would be the custodial parent. They had also agreed about visitation arrangements. The court approved their agreements. In this case the consultant assisted the children's attorney in supporting the parents in assuming their natural roles as their children's advocates. By doing this, the children experienced their parents and not the court in their natural role as their advocates.

Although there are no precise figures about the percentage of divorces complicated by custody conflicts, there is general agreement that the majority of divorces are carried out, because of practical reasons, without a conflict about the custody of children. In the minority of divorce cases, with associated conflicts, no one is satisfied that our present system is trouble free, especially in regard to visitation. The child's need for a parent who has the authority and responsibility for being his/her representative before the law, for sheltering him/her from direct contact with the law, and, especially to have society and the state's demands and prohibitions filtered by way of the parent's personality, is even greater after a divorce. In regard to visitation it has become the custom to deprive the child of such advocacy by permitting the court to place the noncustodial parent's right to visitation ahead of the child's need for visitation as interpreted and arranged by his/her only legitimate advocate, the custodial parent.

It is my conviction that the noncustodial parent should be encouraged and helped to work out plans for visitation with the custodial parent, rather than the court having the responsibility and authority for the control of visitation if parents are unable to agree about such decisions. When parents cannot agree, the assignment of legal counsel to represent the child or group of siblings should assure respect for the child's sense of time and a voice for children's best interest, that is, the least detrimental alternative. This conviction rests on two prior requirements: (1) that significant weight be given in resolving the custody conflict to estimating, all other things being equal, which of the contending parents is more likely to encourage and to support visitation by the noncustodial parent in a constructive and sustained manner; and (2) that once the court's decision is made about who will be the custodial parent, the grounds for change of custody would be no different for a divorced custodial parent than for the custodial parents in an intact (nondivorced) family.

These conditions could provide a different and more promising climate from the child's point of view for resolving custody conflicts and for promoting visitation on a sound and useful basis. Of greater importance would be the expectation that noncustodial parents would be more likely to seek visitation arrangements directly and in a more conciliatory manner. Current practices foster the use of the courts as an instrument of aggression against the custodial parent.

No system will completely protect the highly desirable goal of sound, sustained, nurturing visitation by noncustodial parents. These recommendations attempt to maximize the use of visitation in support of children's needs, development, and best interests; and to minimize the destructive efforts of conflicted, hostile visitation in which the courts are used by divorced parents to continue their battles and to avoid accepting a least detrimental alternative for their children. In addition, as we have stated elsewhere (Goldstein et al., 1979a), this practice would leave to the courts what they can and should do; it would encourage the state to curb access to the courts, which implies a promise of supervision that courts cannot and should not be allowed to make.

CONCLUSION

In the past, parents' right to be advocates of their children was associated, at times, with absolute power over their children (Pollack & Maitland, 1898). Starting in the early 1800s in this country, the state, acting in the role of *parens patriae*, began to limit parental power in certain areas in which the interests of children and society were believed to need protection or preference (Solnit, 1976).

For example, the enactment of Compulsory Education Laws limited the parents' previously boundless power to determine the manner of their child's education by eliminating the option of "no education." The child is not the mere creature of the State: those who nurture him and direct his destiny have the right, coupled with the high duty, to recognize and prepare him for additional obligations.[3] The parents' right to the child's services and earnings was limited by the enactment of the Child Labor Laws. In *Prince v. Massachusetts*, the Supreme Court stated: "But the family itself is not beyond regulation in the public interest. . . . Acting to guard the general interest in youth's well being, the State as *parens patriae* may restrict the parents' control by requiring school attendance, regulating or prohibiting the child's labor and in many other ways."[4] Child abuse legislation—designed to punish offending parents and protect victimized children—was enacted to try to curtail the more extreme methods of parental discipline (punishment).[5] Courts ordered life-saving medical treatments over the religious objections of parents despite the traditional parental prerogative to determine what type of medical care children shall receive."[6] (Gaballe, 1976, p. 12)

In spite of two centuries of encroachment and redefinition of parental power over children, our societal value preference is for minimal state intrusion of the family. Furthermore our psychoanalytic understanding is that children need a continuity of affectionate care in the intimacy of a permanent family, and require autonomous parents who are crucial in providing nurturance and in being advocates for their children. Children are crucial in stimulating most adult caretakers to achieve fulfillment as parents. At bedrock, the functions and needs of parents and children are mutually resonant and promising. We should do whatever we can to safeguard and foster harmonious resonances and well-kept promises minimizing interventions from the state.

REFERENCES

Anthony, E. J., & Benedek, T. Introduction. In E. J. Anthony & T. Benedek (Eds.), *Parenthood: Its psychology and psychopathology*. Boston: Little, Brown, 1970.

Benedek, T. Parenthood during the life cycle. In E. J. Anthony & T. Benedek (Eds.), *Parenthood: Its psychology and psychopathology*. Boston: Little, Brown, 1970.

Freud, A. Personal communication, 1979.

Freud, S. Inhibitions, symptoms and anxiety (1926). *Standard Edition, 20*, 154–155. London: Hogarth Press, 1959.

Gaballe, S. *The evolution of children's legal rights*. Unpublished research paper, Yale University Child Study Center.

Goldstein, J. On being adult and being an adult in secular law. *Daedalus*, 1976, Fall, 56–70.

Goldstein, J. *Psychoanalysis and a jurisprudence child placement*. Paper presented at the University of Chicago Lecture Series on Psychoanalytic Perspectives, April 13, 1977.

Goldstein, J., Freud, A., & Solnit, A. J. *Beyond the best interests of the child* (new ed. with Epilogue). New York: Free Press–Macmillan, 1979. (a)

3. Pierce v. Society of Sisters, 268 U.S. 510, 535 (1925).

4. 321 U.S. 158, 166 (1944).

5. See, for example, Conn. Gen. Stat. Rev. 1738–38a *et seq.* (1975).

6. See Annot., 30 A.L.R. 2nd 1138 (1953).

Goldstein, J., Freud, A., & Solnit, A. J. *Before the best interests of the child*. New York: Free
    Press–Macmillan, 1979. (b)
Pollack, F., & Maitland, F. *The history of English law* (2nd ed.). Cambridge: Cambridge University
    Press, and Boston: Little, Brown, 1898.
Solnit, A. J. Child rearing and child advocacy. *Brigham Young University Law Review*, 1976, *3*,
    723–733.

16

THE PARENTAL
COUPLE IN A SUCCESSFUL DIVORCE

SHERMAN C. FEINSTEIN
MULLER DAVIS

INTRODUCTION

Radical changes in psychosocial values in the last few decades have resulted in differing attitudes toward marital and family roles. One growing solution to the problem of dissatisfaction with a marriage is separation and divorce. In 1979, the most recent year statistics are available at the time of writing, there were over 1 million divorces involving more than 1.2 million children. It is estimated that over 10 million children live in fatherless homes having intermittent or no contact with the father (Schwartzberg, 1981; Jellinek & Slovik, 1981). The fatherless home may result in a serious threat to normal child development not only because the children are deprived of a role model but also because early fantasies of the absent father dominate their concept formation and deform the relationship between mother and child (Lasch, 1979).

To counter the threat of emotional impoverishment consequent to separation and divorce on children, the legal and behavioral professions have a responsibility to be aware of the complications of the process and to institute measures to avoid pathologic reactions. Among the most creative approaches to this problem is divorce mediation, in which a trained mediator—usually a judge, lawyer, or mental health specialist—works with the couple to resolve the technical aspects of the divorce without the traditional adversarial procedure. This approach is not without danger, however, and many attempts at mediation fail as the couple goes on to develop severe antagonism and hostility.

We will explore the states of antagonism and hostility that arise between

Sherman C. Feinstein. Bennett Laboratory for Child Psychiatry Research, Department of Psychiatry, Michael Reese Hospital and Medical Center, and Department of Psychiatry, University of Chicago, Chicago, Illinois.

Muller Davis. Jones, Baer and Davis, Chicago, Illinois.

a couple or in a family in a divorce, and trace them to their legal and dynamic sources. We hypothesize that the ability to maintain healthy parenting responses can help avoid many of the dilemmas of the shift in behavior as a reaction to the loss of attachment bonds and a resultant loss of self-esteem.

At first the decision to divorce may appear to arrive as a logical solution to irreconcilable differences. From a cognitive point of view it would seem that a fundamental abandonment of previous marital goals—love commitment to a spouse, the maintenance of intimacy with that individual, and stability of the marital unit—make marriage no longer possible or necessary. Since these characteristics also define the achievement of adulthood (Erikson, 1950) and reflect developmental accomplishments, the failure of the marriage to thrive may bring on a serious loss of self-esteem and precipitate a radical disturbance. Earlier magnanimous offers of equality and reasonableness may be soon forgotten or denied.

It is critical at this juncture for the divorcers to realize the psychological power of the divorce and that it will demand extensive renegotiation of one's life-style along with the maintaining of a parental alliance.[1] Certain inevitabilities of financial obligation and continuing generativity toward the children and former spouse are and will remain important considerations. Marital or family therapy can be helpful at this stage of disruption to encourage continued communication and problem solving. The function of therapeutic intervention is to engage the various principals in an uncovering and synthesizing process that should facilitate processing the conflicts to be resolved, and to develop a mediation mode and prevent a shift to hostile retaliation. The alternative to this resolution is the intrusion of the judicial system into the family and parent–child relationship.

LEGAL ASPECTS OF DIVORCE

At the time of a divorce, the law defines custody, visitation, support, education, and also concerns itself with any extraordinary circumstances, such as the serious illness of a child. These matters can either be agreed upon by the parents, subject to approval by a court, or they can be argued in a public courtroom and decided by a person with no connection to the particular family. An examination of the various legal stages of divorce that particularly affect children will more concretely illustrate how parents and lawyers can constructively contribute to the well-being of children in divorce.

Child Custody and Visitation

In most divorce cases, both the mother and father have a positive attitude toward the child they created, despite the souring of their emotions about each other.

---

1. For a discussion of the parenting alliance, see Cohen and Weissman, Chapter 3, this volume.

But divorce may distort one spouse's perception of the other. Most child-custody disputes are understood by one parent as a necessity to protect the children from the malign influence of the other parent. The myopia in the ability of one spouse to appreciate the relationship between the children and the other spouse is frequently compounded by one or both spouses actually manipulating their children in an effort to get back at the other for what he/she has done.

Child-custody disagreements can be resolved by agreement, by the intervention of a third, nonjudicial party, or by a court, but, regardless of how they are eventually decided, the threshhold problem is to differentiate between genuine custody issues and issues which are really between the husband and wife because they are getting a divorce. Many lawyers, because of their experience and training, are skillful in separating these issues, defining them for their clients, and often deflecting a spouse's anger from its focus on a child as a weapon against the other spouse, to a less fragile instrument, such as money. But because lawyers are preoccupied with the legal side of divorce, aggravated cases where children are caught up in the violence of divorce should be cared for by mental health professionals.

The best fashion in which to determine custody and visitation issues (with the least injury to all concerned) is through negotiation and agreement. Imaginative attorneys can often facilitate agreement by suggesting different arrangements to suit particular parents and children. Custody issues should never be straitjacketed by a slavish adherence to some formula, for example, an undue preference for sole custody as opposed to joint custody. Different combinations work for different parents and their children.

Custody can be either sole, joint, or shared. The frequent battles over these words are almost always misplaced and give an exaggerated importance that they do not deserve. The problem is not how to characterize a custody plan, but how to define it. For some parents it may be sufficient to state in an agreement that the children shall live with the mother, that the father shall have reasonable visitation with the children, and allow the parties and the children to work out the times and places. For others, schedules should be drawn. Participation by both parents in the children's lives should always be encouraged. Almost all agreements should provide that the parents will consult jointly on important subjects which concern the children, such as health and education.

Many fathers believe that their influence over the children is circumscribed by the words "sole custody to the mother." Joint custody, which also specifies where the children will live is, then, a possible solution. The arguments against joint custody that portray the desperately ill child held outside the operating room because the doctor was unable to obtain consent from joint custody parents is entirely specious. Any lawyer can provide for what is to happen in cases of emergency in order to implement joint custody. Different formulas solve different problems: For some, allowing a child to move back and forth between homes may be a proper solution; for others, an agreement to appoint an arbitrator (a lawyer or mental health specialist) who can make the final determination around a controversy may be a creative solution. The most important goal is to encourage rational compromise and thereby to avoid disputes which may flare into combats that injure children more than any particular resolution benefits them.

Stubborn disagreements over children that do not easily yield to negotiation and compromise can often be resolved if they are referred for mediation. Mediation specialists, in a nonadversarial manner, can interview the parents and children in depth, identify and analyze problems, and make recommendations for custody, visitation, and the development of future relationships. If both parents participate in the choice of a mediation specialist it is more likely that each will have sufficient confidence to abide by professional decisions. The attorneys can then translate the recommendations into an agreement between the parties.

Custody litigation, although proliferating today, should only be undertaken as a last resort in extreme situations, and almost never without first consulting mental health specialists. The danger is that the litigation will damage the children and their relationships with their parents, result in psychological, social, and economic consequences which disrupt and diminish parenting, and lead to impoverishment of the children's capacity to develop normal, intimate relationships in their adult lives (Wallerstein & Kelly, 1980).

A full custody trial is time consuming, expensive, and frustrating, but it is finally only a judge who can order the parents and children to do anything. The attorneys for the mother and the father present adversarial evidence through the parties, the children themselves, guardians appointed for the children, psychiatrists, experts, investigators, friends, and others in an attempt to persuade the court that it is in the best interests of the children that one or the other parent have their custody. Incidents, which should more properly remain private, are commonly described minutely in evidence. Young children are often interviewed by the judge, frequently in chambers, but in other instances they are compelled to testify in the public courtroom. Once the trial court has ruled, the decision may be appealed, thus leaving the children's custody undecided for years.

Whether finally determined by a court after litigation, or by agreement between the parties approved by a court, custody, visitation, support, and other issues concerning children are never permanent, but can always be reviewed and modified by a court if the circumstances on which the original decision was based change. For example, if custody of the children is initially given to the mother, but she subsequently becomes incapable of caring for the children, the father may then obtain their custody through a postdecree hearing using expert testimony.

CHILDREN AND THE FINANCIAL ISSUES IN DIVORCE

Money is inanimate and fungible; children are neither. Divorced spouses can almost always earn more or spend less. Court litigation over money and property, even over children's support, is therefore invariably safer for children than is litigation over their custody. Children and their relationships with their parents are less intimately bound up in money issues than they are in custody disputes. Given their choice, however, children would still prefer settlement to trials of financial disputes. Protracted litigation, even over money and property, tends to further estrange parents, makes it difficult for parents to later communicate on matters concerning the children, and often draws the children unnecessarily into the conflict. Unfortunately loss of money often symbolizes a loss of self-esteem and results in depressive reactions.

Monetary expectations in a divorce must be scaled to what is available in the family. Almost no income is great enough to provide as well for two households after a divorce as it did for one during the marriage. Therefore, neither spouse nor the children can anticipate continuing their life-styles at exactly the same standard, unaffected by the increased costs of living separately.

The particular financial arrangement which will best serve the children of divorce is one that fairly distributes the burdens of divorce. Since there will be more expenses, both spouses should share in the necessary restrictions. If the children are not very young and the mother can contribute income by working, she should do so. But, by the same token, it is foolish to expect her to match her husband's earnings and fully support herself. When the children go to college, each of the divorced parents will have to make additional sacrifices, as would have also been necessary had they stayed married.

Both sides must have full information concerning the resources of the family before a financial arrangement can be made intelligently, whether by negotiation or by a court. It is advisable for the spouse who is to be supported to prepare a detailed budget of anticipated expenditures in order both to apprise her husband of expected needs and to educate herself as to where she will be required to spend money. The allocation of support between alimony and children's support is often more dependent on tax and state law considerations than on the division of expenses between mother and children. Support is commonly reduced upon the remarriage of the spouse receiving it, after a period of time allowed for rehabilitation, and also upon a child reaching majority.

Provision should be made for the payment of unexpected extraordinary medical expenses of the children and for the maintenance of life insurance on the life of the spouse providing support. If the parties have accumulated property during the marriage, it is commonly allocated according to such equitable principles as contribution to the property and to the marriage. In community property states, division is more arbitrary. Property is seldom sufficient to replace support, but its allocation is taken into account in determining the amount of support required.

The typical divorce involves the marital home as the only significant asset plus income from employment. Although neither spouse may want to relinquish interest in the home, the home may represent the least expensive place for the mother and the children to live at first. Moreover, not requiring the mother and children to move upon the divorce allows the children to remain in their own rooms and in the same school with their friends. A solution is for the couple to retain their investment in the home, but to permit the mother and children to live in the house until the children go to college or the mother remarries.

Although it is generally better to resolve as many issues as possible during the divorce, where parties cannot agree, an issue can be fruitfully postponed until it actually has to be confronted; for example, how will the major expense of college be paid. Delaying this determination has the advantage of enabling the parents to examine their relative financial abilities at the time the expenditure must be made.

While divorce is almost always motivated by the individual concerns of the husband and wife rather than by a belief that divorce is in the best interests of their children, it does not follow that children are either better off in unhappy homes in which parents stay together or that their welfare cannot be protected during and after a divorce. Once the decision to divorce has been made, the welfare of the children depends upon keeping them apart from the conflict, properly providing for them, and making it possible for them to maintain a dignified, individual relationship with each parent.

CLINICAL EXAMPLE

This case will demonstrate how a therapist can nurture and sustain the parenting alliance in a divorce and serve as a mediator and eventually as an arbitrator in a conflictual situation.

The couple first met in college when the man was completing his education and the woman was a year behind. He was a shy, inhibited person who had rarely dated. She was a bright, warm, and capable person who had experienced much isolation as a child. She accepted her husband's advances because he seemed kind and generous as well as needy. A decision to marry was a great relief to both parties as the man struggled with loneliness and saw the woman as an adequate person; she was thrilled to find a sensible solution to her feelings of isolation and was relieved that she could be married to what appeared to be a fine person from a good background.

Within a few weeks of their marriage it became clear to both members that the original mutuality was not functional. They were both secretly disappointed in their mates. He, who had had little sexual experience, found her unappealing. He could function sexually only with great difficulty as he was repulsed by her short, squat body, although she was responsive to him. She found him aloof, withdrawn, and totally protective of his own needs for self-satisfaction. The couple's feelings were denied and repressed for many years while they completed their education, had several children, and began accumulating reasonable resources.

Following the birth of their first child, a brief trial of marital therapy was undertaken. The husband admitted his dislike of his wife's difficulty controlling her weight and his obsession with thinness, but continually protested his love and commitment. The wife acknowledged feeling rejected and isolated. Short of indicating their problems, they were not able to resolve them in the marital therapy. The wife continued individual treatment while having a second child and finishing up a graduate degree.

A suicidal gesture by their older child as a young teenager suddenly focused the family on the enormous strain under which they were operating. At this point, the wife resumed individual treatment. The husband attended occasional joint sessions and from time to time would see the same therapist around his own needs. He reiterated his great respect and affection for his wife, but confided his persistent discomfort with her physical appearance and revealed the recent assumption of an affair with his secretary. This relationship, he assured his therapist, was only to help him prove his own adequacy which he had come to question in recent years; the profound age, cultural, and educational differences made any possibility of continuity unlikely.

The therapist could observe that the careful balance maintained over the years was beginning to erode. The child's suicide attempt was a manifestation of the family strife. The couple reported increased confrontations and overt arguments. The wife had decided to go back to work in order to meet her own needs. Divorce was being continuously mentioned by her, but was rejected by the husband as unnecessary.

The suicide attempt of their child demanded a mutuality of support in order to help the child deal with the fear of impending loss of family unity. The long-standing polarization made joint efforts impossible, and since both parents projected the responsibility on the other this led to increased alienation and a splitting of efforts. The parenting alliance became completely fragmented and it became clear that a dangerous stage for the needs of the child was approaching. At this point, with the assistance of the therapist, both parents decided that a divorce was the inevitable solution and agreed to try to work out a joint custody arrangement instead of entering into litigation.

For the mediator this may be a period of great stress. Emergency sessions and long phone calls may be necessary. Efforts should be continuously made to correct cognitive distortions. Any change or compromise may be easily seen as a loss with a depressive reaction. The calm, constant insistence by the arbitrator on continuing the negotiations toward a mutual settlement is of prime importance.

After some months of struggle at this level of conflict, the parental couple finally developed enough trust in their newly redeveloped parenting alliance to begin realistic plans for separation and individuation of their own lives and the creation of a new family form, recently described by Bohannan (1981) as a "binuclear family." Some months after their divorce became final and they had secured residences close enough to each other so that the children could easily take advantage of their two homes, they set up a conference call to discuss a matter with their therapist who had agreed to function as an arbitrator in matters of controversy.

The divorced couple was planning the confirmation of the younger child. They decided along with their children that they would like to have a joint party at the mother's home. Many friends and relatives, however, were aghast at their plan, and some were particularly upset that the father's fiancée would be included. From the ensuing discussion it became clear that the parenting alliance was showing the mediator how well the plan was working and that a reasonable mutuality with its own creative identity was being formed. While the couple was unable to have a successful marriage, they were at least achieving a successful divorce and successful roles.

CONCLUSIONS

When a marital relationship begins to break down, the potential loss may result in destructive reactive, affective responses. The threat of loss to the integrity of the ego may be profound and may easily result in the assumption of hostile and antagonistic behaviors. In order to have a successful resolution to a decision to divorce, therapeutic mediation can aid in the avoidance of regressive responses to perceived loss and help establish a workable parental alliance without the need for intimacy in the partners. Arbitration by agreement is another technique that can be used in specific areas to enhance decision making, either prior to or after a divorce, and to avoid affective breakdown.

The ability to properly fulfill the developmental achievements of adulthood, and as a result function comfortably as a parent, provides fulfillment for both the children and adults in a family. Abandonment of a position of commitment and autonomy with subsequent intrusion of judicial structures into the family may lead to impoverishment and skepticism. The legal and mental health professions should make maximum efforts to preserve and encourage the use of healthy parenting responses.

REFERENCES

Bohannan, P. The binuclear family. *Science*, 1981, *81*, 28–29.
Erikson, E. H. *Childhood and society*. New York: Norton, 1950.
Jellinek, M. S., & Slovik, L. S. Divorce: Impact on children. *New England Journal of Medicine*, 1981, *305* (10), 557–560.
Lasch, C. *The culture of narcissism*. New York: Norton, 1979.
Parens, H. Parenthood as a developmental phase. *Journal of the American Psychoanalytic Association*, 1975, *23* (1), 154–165.
Schwartzberg, A. Adolescent reactions to divorce. *Adolescent Psychiatry*, 1981, *9*, 119–132.
Wallerstein, J. S., & Kelly, J. B. *Surviving the breakup*. New York: Basic Books, 1980.

17

THE IMPACT
OF DIVORCE IN MIDDLE AGE

GUNHILD O. HAGESTAD
MICHAEL A. SMYER
KAREN STIERMAN

INTRODUCTION

Recent changes in family size and spacing of children, combined with increased general life expectancy, have made four- and five-generation families a common occurrence. Because of such demographic change, the parent–child relationship now typically lasts four to six decades. For the greater part of its duration, it will be a relationship *between adults*, and most individuals will spend a considerable number of years when they occupy both the roles of parent and offspring. During middle age, people are likely to find themselves in a *bridge generation*, between two generations of adults: maturing children and aging parents. Because of this bridge function, one would expect divorce in the middle generation to have powerful consequences not only for the individuals experiencing the marital dissolution, but also for two more generations of adults. Past work on divorce has generally focused on marital breakup in early adulthood and has neglected two significant categories of significant others: adult offspring and the parents of the divorcing couple.

The present chapter argues that it is important to remedy these gaps in current knowledge on divorce. New knowledge is essential for intervention with individuals and families affected by divorce, and may provide significant building blocks for theoretical work on parent–child relationships across individual life spans and shifting generational constellations.

After a brief review of gaps in past work on divorce and parent–child relationships, findings from an exploratory study of divorce in middle age are

Gunhild O. Hagestad, Michael A. Smyer, and Karen Stierman. College of Human Development, Pennsylvania State University, University Park, Pennsylvania.

presented. Finally, implications for dynamic views of parent–child bonds and intergenerational relations are discussed.

PAST WORK ON DIVORCE

The dramatic increase in divorce rates over the last decade has resulted in considerable research on the process of marital breakup, as well as its causes and consequences (e.g., Bohannan, 1970; Levinger & Moles, 1979). However, as it now stands, this work has some distinct limitations. Scholars with an interest in parent–child relations should be concerned about two gaps in past work. First, it generally neglects the ages and family stage of the divorcing couple. Most of the work deals with individuals in the early stages of family development, when divorce is most likely to occur. Second, it neglects the effects of divorce on other family members, with the exception of young children.

The Young Adult Bias

The key social-psychological works on divorce deal with individuals under the age of 40 (see Bohannan, 1970; Goode, 1956; Levinger & Moles, 1979). This is to be expected, since 8 out of 10 dissolutions of first marriages occur while the spouses are in their 20s and 30s (U.S. Bureau of the Census, 1976). One of the few researchers who have examined divorce after age 40, Chiriboga (1979), has pointed to the importance of seeing marital dissolution from a life-course perspective, but little research has done so. A recent Canadian investigation (Deckert & Langelier, 1978) studied couples who divorced after 20 or more years of marriage, but focused more on the quality of the marital relationship than on how the event of divorce was related to developmental issues in later adulthood. A similar focus was found in a small-scale study of 70 volunteers (Hayes, 1976).

At a national conference on the older woman, convened by the National Institute of Aging (NIA) and the National Institute of Mental Health (NIMH) in September 1978, researchers from a variety of fields concluded that no information could be found on divorce in later life. In the Riley, Foner, Moore, Hess, and Roth (1968) comprehensive review of research on aging, divorce did not appear in the index. Ten years later, a 1978 issue of *The Family Coordinator*, devoted entirely to the topic of family and aging, did not include a discussion of divorce. Thus, it seems that Troll, Miller, and Atchley (1979), in a recent review of research on families in later life, are entirely correct when they state that divorce in the second half of adulthood is "one of the most neglected areas of research in social gerontology" (p. 80).

Neglected Significant Others: Parents and Grown Children

When researchers have moved beyond the couple in studies of the impact of divorce, they have repeatedly concentrated on young children. The two best-known recent studies on children of divorce are those by Hetherington, Cox, and Cox (1977, 1979) and Wallerstein and Kelly (1980), both of which have rich and complex data spanning 4–5 years. The first project concentrated on preschool children. The second study included children of various ages, but the oldest were young adolescents. Studies of kin contact and help patterns following divorce, again, has tended to focus on young parents and their children (e.g., Anspach, 1976; Spicer & Hampe, 1975). Psychological work on how parental divorce affects offspring appears to end at adolescence.

Furthermore, divorce research has taken a limited and outdated view of interdependencies among lives in the family. There is recognition that parents and children are important to one another, but the assumption seems to be that the bond is more important for the child. It appears that unidirectional views of the developmental influences between parent and child still dominate research surrounding divorce (Levitin, 1979). A further indication of this shortcoming is the fact that no research has looked at *parents of divorce*—middle-aged and old people whose children have gone through marital disruption. In sum, we have not carried the assumption that parents and children are important to one another to its logical extension: that the parent–child bond is important to *both* sides of the relationship.

Past work has recognized that parental divorce interferes with children's developmental timetables, because they lose material and emotional resources when one of the parents is not available on a day-to-day basis. However, it has not recognized that because of the very nature of family bonds and relationships, this experience may be shared by two other categories of individuals who have been neglected in past research: grown children, whose parents are divorcing after a lengthy marriage; and parents, whose adult children are divorcing. Thus, it appears that divorce research is out of step with current conceptualizations of life-span development and the nature of parent–child relationships. In particular, it shows an almost complete neglect of the complex interdependencies among developing individuals in the family. In part, however, this shortcoming characterizes the state of conceptual and empirical work on parent–child relations in general.

THE STUDY OF PARENT–CHILD RELATIONS

Alpha and Omega

Past work on parents and children does not adequately reflect recent demographic changes outlined earlier. A recent review of 1970s research on parent–child relationships (Walters & Walters, 1980), concludes that even in most recent work, the main focus is overwhelmingly on young children and their parents. The analytic focus is on the early phases of a long relationship career, and many life stages and generational combinations are neglected. The focus is on the

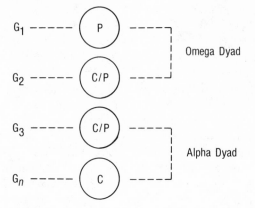

FIG. 17-1. A MULTIGENERATIONAL VIEW OF PARENT–CHILD RELATIONSHIPS.

alpha of such bonds. A second body of research, commonly not subsumed under the heading of parent–child relations, focuses on older people and their middle-aged offspring. This *omega* focus is typically not included in discussions of parent–child relations, but will be found under such headings as "older families," "families in later life," and "kin relations."

The alpha phase of the research is tilted toward the offspring; the omega research tends to be focused on the parent. Little or no effort has been made to link these two, either through cross-sectional or longitudinal research.

Hagestad (1982) has proposed a framework for linking them, by viewing parent–child relations within a multigenerational, dynamic perspective (Figure 17-1).

The oldest living generation in a family lineage, G_1, is the only one who occupies just the role of parent and not that of child. At the other end of the generational spectrum, which may be anywhere from one to six links removed, are lineage members who occupy only the role of child. Individuals in the connecting links are both children and parents. Among middle-aged parents, some are in the omega position, with none of their own parents living. Others may have two generations above them. One would expect such contrasts in generational contexts to have powerful ramifications for patterns of resource exchanges, sense of personal vulnerability, and the experience of age and finitude. They are also likely to influence relationships with offspring significantly. Very little work on middle age has considered generational location.

Parent–Child Relations in Middle Age

After a period of research which commonly referred to "the loss of the parent role" we recognize that there is no retirement from that role. One is a parent as long as one has living offspring. There is the "launching period," a time of *renegotiation*, when mutual expectations between parents and children are reviewed and reshaped. Particularly for women, grown children are likely to become a considerable interpersonal resource, both for emotional support and influence (Hagestad & Snow, 1977). Thus, the growing independence of the children not only spells increased freedom from day-to-day parent responsibilities, it may also represent new resources to pull from. We no longer argue, as was previously common, that the departure of children constitutes loss and crises for the parents, particularly the mothers. Indeed, recent research suggests that it is when the children *do not* leave on time and do not make normal progress into adulthood that parents show signs of stress and threats to personal well-being (Nydegger & Mitteness, 1979; Wilen, 1979). Such findings remind us of the intimate interconnections between lives of parents and children, throughout the entire duration of their relationship. They are what Plath (1980) calls *consociates*, with contingent life careers. Children count on a period of strength—almost invulnerability—in their parents, up to old age. Events which upset such expectations represent more severe crises than when they come as expected, on time. Parents also build strong developmental expectations regarding children. A sense of security and accomplishment in the second half of adulthood depends on the knowledge that offspring have "turned out right" and are "on track" in their adult progress. Indeed, the knowledge that children have been successfully launched into adult roles gives parents the freedom to attend to *their own* developmental concerns. A major part of what Blenkner (1965) calls filial maturity—the readiness to accept a new dependence from parents—builds on a successful transformation of the relationship with the third generation. Aged parents turn to middle-aged offspring for emotional and other types of support, and patterns of interdependence are again reshaped. The extent to which increased "parent caring" constitutes strain and overload for the middle-aged may often depend on how the third generation, their children, are doing.

An exploratory study by Smith (1983) found that when middle-aged women experienced a sense of overload in caring for aged parents, they tended to have young adult children who were "off track" in *their* life-course development. For example, they had a son in his late 20s, still without a job, or a daughter whose marriage had failed, who had moved back into her old room. Thus, it is essential to examine the stresses and strengths of middle-aged individuals within a multigenerational framework (Hill, Foote, Aldous, Carlson, & MacDonald, 1970; Hagestad, 1981). Very little work has done so. Beyond descriptions of visiting patterns, rates of contact, and the exchange of goods and services, we know little about the social-psychological and psychological significance of parent–child ties among adults. We have barely begun to ask what expectations members of such relations hold for one another, and what the consequences are when expectations are left unmet. We know, however, that because of the complex interconnections of lives in the family, critical life events create "countertransitions" (Riley & Waring, 1976) and challenges for significant others whose *own* life-course expectations have been upset. Thus, voluntary life decisions and transitions by one family member may create involuntary changes for others. Marriage by one member creates in-law status for others. Parenthood creates grandparenthood and great-grandparenthood. Divorce creates exrelationships and role loss for family members other than the couple. The complexity of such "developmental reciprocity" (Klein, Jorgensen, & Miller, 1979) has not been given the attention it merits in the fields of adult development and family development, or in substantive work on divorce.

We feel that research on divorce and its ripple effects may shed new light on this issue. By studying family members whose life-course progress has been interrupted through marital disruption, we may gain significant insights into how lives are interwoven and how expectations among family members are contingent. Divorce in middle age presents a unique opportunity to do so, because individuals in this stage of life are likely to be in a bridge position, between two other generations. Let us try to illustrate some of these points by discussing some findings from an exploratory study of such divorces.

A STUDY OF MIDDLE-AGE DIVORCE

Methods

To assure a sizable population of middle-aged individuals who had been divorced, a major metropolitan area was chosen as a research site. Names were drawn from the public records of divorce decrees, using cases from one court term. Individuals who met the following criteria were included in the original study population: (1) They were between the ages of 40 and 59 at the time of the divorce; (2) they had been married to the last spouse for 16 years or more; and (3) they had at least one child aged 16 or older. Of the people who met the criteria and who could be contacted by mail or phone, 57% of the men and 78% of the women agreed to be interviewed. The sample consisted of 43 men and 50 women. The interviews, carried out by social workers with extensive clinical experience, took place between the fall of 1979 and the winter of 1980. The average interview time was 2½ hours. The interview included both open-ended and structured items. In addition, the protocol had several standardized measures such as the well-being index developed by Campbell, Converse, and Rogers (1976) and the Beck Depression Inventory (Beck, Ward, Mendelson, Mock, & Erbaugh, 1969).

Characteristics of the Respondents

The men and women we interviewed ranged in age from 41 to 61, with a mean of 50 for men and 48.6 for women. Prior to the divorce, they had been married from 16 to 37 years, with an average marriage duration of about 25 years.

Our respondents came from all walks of life, with a wide range of income and educational backgrounds. Among the men, nearly 50% had a high-school education or less, while about the same proportion had a college degree or more. Among the women, 60% had a high-school education or less, and only 8% had a college education.

It is important to consider the historical context of these people's lives. The oldest among them had their childhood years affected by the Great Depression, either by experiencing it in their early years or by growing up in small families as a result of declining fertility rates during that era. About 13% were only children. Many of our respondents were young adults during World War II, and some of the men were veterans of that war.

Generational Context

Our respondents bore their children during the postwar baby boom. All of them had children. On the average, they had three children, while 40% had four or more. Roughly 25% of the sample had offspring under 16. However, the majority of the respondents (approximately 75%) were in the "empty nest" phase of the family cycle. About 25% of them were grandparents.

Roughly 60% of our respondents (56), had one or both of their parents still living. As would be expected, more of them had mothers than fathers. These parents ranged in age from the 60s to the 80s. Nearly half of the parents lived in the same metropolitan area as the respondent, and more than 80% of them lived in the same region—within weekend driving distance. As one would expect from previous research (e.g., Shanas, 1979), about one half of these men and women had face-to-face contact with their parents once a week or more; two thirds of them visited parents monthly or more often.

We now turn to a discussion of how these men and women talked about the divorce process and how it affected their children and parents. Finally, we discuss implications of their reports for intergenerational relations among adults in three generations.

DIVORCE AND YOUNG ADULT CHILDREN

The Divorce Process

Considering the fact that so many of our interviews provided narratives of chronically troubled or lukewarm marriages, we were surprised to find that only slightly over 50% of our respondents saw their children as having had an effect on the divorce timing. In most of these cases, the breakup was postponed until the children were grown. However, there were also cases in which the children actively encouraged parental divorce. Most commonly, this occurred in families where alcoholism and physical abuse were long-term problems, and the children provided support for the mother to leave the marriage. In one household, a 22-year-old son prevented his father from striking his mother and cried: "Up until today I thought I had a father and a mother. Now I know I only have a mother."

Men and women drew quite different time frames in describing the process of marital breakup. Forty-two percent of the women said more than nine years lapsed between the first open recognition of a possible divorce and the actual decree. Only 28% of the men reported such a long time span. Similar sex differences emerged when we asked what was the most difficult point in the divorce process. One half of the women, as contrasted to one fourth of the men, said the time prior to the final separation and before any final decision had been made about the divorce was most painful. For men, trauma was often reported *after* some movement toward divorce.

These findings most likely reflect long-term differences in adult role patterns of men and women. Work on family and intergenerational relations has suggested that women are "family monitors." Throughout their adulthood, particularly in these cohorts, women have had a strong family focus, both in terms of investments of time and energy, and their sense of self. Conflicts and problems in this sphere are not only more commonly recognized by women, but also likely to affect them more than their husbands. Thus, they may have gone through "anticipatory separation" long before the divorce process started. Our data seem to fit Chiriboga's (1979) finding that women reported being significantly less satisfied with their lives five years prior to separation than was the case for men. Thus, we have to allow for the possibility that women tax their informal support systems at an earlier stage of the divorce process than do men.

Indeed, our data suggest that women may also prepare the children for the possibility of a marital breakup—which is seldom the case for men. The majority of women in the study (two thirds) reported discussing their marital problems with the children. Only one fourth of the men said they had such talks. Both among the male and female respondents, the *wife* was the most frequently reported person to inform the children of an impending divorce.

The differences between mothers' and fathers' relationships with the children in the period preceding the divorce may account for some striking differences in their perceptions of the children's reactions later, when the divorce became both a personal and a legal reality.

Reactions to the Divorce

The respondents rated a number of family members' reactions to the divorce on a continuum, ranging from 1 (very negative) to 5 (very positive). On both these measures, men perceived children as more negative and concerned than did women. When we combined ratings for all the children in the family, 56% of the women reported *all of them* to have a positive response (3 or higher). Men described the children's reactions as much more mixed, and only one fourth of them saw all children as having favorable reactions.

On a checklist of divorce-related concerns among children, women tended to say that the children expressed few concerns, while men were likely to say the children had experienced a number of them. Both men and women agreed that children worried about how the divorce would affect their own and their parents' future. However, on items dealing with family unity and cohesion, there were marked contrasts between men and women. Men perceived their sons and daughters as fearing that they would not have a family any more, worrying about holidays and special occasions, and feeling that the parents should stay together. The item most commonly checked by women was one describing children as experiencing *relief*. As one woman quoted her daughter's reaction: "You should have gone sooner and saved me a lot of pain."

Children as Sources of Support

Not only did the women appear to have kept the children informed about marital difficulties and the possibility of a divorce, they also reported relying on their children for various forms of support before and after the divorce. For example, we asked the respondents to identify the people who were the most helpful during the worst part of the divorce process. Nearly one fourth of the women named a child—only 5% of the men did so. Repeatedly, we heard women say "I never would have gotten through this without my children!" Not infrequently, we encountered a child who was a protective "spokesperson" for the mother, and we had some difficulties gaining access to her. Thus, we would concur with Lopata's (1979) conclusion from her study of widows: Children are often the linchpin of a mature woman's support system.

Our data suggest that women, more often than men, approach maturing children as adult equals, to whom they can turn for advice and support. One 43-year-old father looked back on the divorce process and acknowledged misjudging his children:

"I underestimated the children. You don't realize the intelligence of children. I didn't think they had any comprehension for divorce—that they had any way of knowing. I think children should be consulted because they do understand. I think they want to be involved. I think there's a little resentment because they're not brought into it. I don't know. I just figured they were kids. Even the older ones. They're young men—but I thought, what the hell do they know—they're kids. . . ."

The women's reliance on family supports also showed up in discussions of finances. Nearly half of them said they would turn to a relative if they were in a money crunch. Only 12% of the men said they would do so. Their own resources or financial institutions were most frequently mentioned by men. The interviews also suggested that a number of women received indirect financial support from children. One third of the women had children over the age of 23 living with them. In most of these cases, the children helped with rent or mortgage payments and other household expenses. A number of these children had moved in with their mother since the divorce, and there were clear indications that some of them felt a responsibility to be with her.

A number of the women saw this as a double bind; a situation which was *not right*. Often, they expressed concerns over what we might call "accelerated filial maturity" in their children. A woman whose well-educated, 24-year-old daughter had moved back home, said pensively: "She is helping me make ends meet . . . she buys me clothes . . . I could not keep the house without her help. . . . But you know, it isn't fair. . . . She should have her life." This woman was trying to put into words a dilemma of interdependence. On the one hand, she felt that the support she was receiving was earned through years of caregiving, chauffering, and girl scouts. On the other hand, she knew that by caring for her, her children may have their own adult life career disrupted, which again would lessen *her* sense of accomplishment as a mother.

Effects of the Divorce on Ties with Children

When asked if the dissolution of their marriage had changed relationships with their children, men and women again gave quite different responses. Ninety percent of the women said the divorce left their relationship with their children unchanged or improved; 58% of the men said so. More than one third of the men said their relationship with one or several of their children had deteriorated. A 51-year-old crane operator put it this way: "It hurts me being close by . . . they'd say 'Dad, I'll come up to clean the house' . . . they will if I pay them. A birthday gift you don't want . . . you want them . . . they're too busy. If they do come up, what is there to do but talk a bit and then leave." One man angrily exclaimed: "Just at the time when I was ready to be with my family, I found that I didn't have one!"

Likewise, one third of the men said the divorce had made them *less effective* as a parent. Some of them felt that the children had turned against them and wanted little or nothing to do with them. On the contrary, only 4% of the women felt their effectiveness as parents had been reduced. Although several women described single parenting as exhausting, 92% of the women said their effectiveness as parents was the same or improved following the divorce.

Years of mothering seemed to have given these women an unshakable faith in the strength of their ties with children—a faith that nothing can threaten them. There was almost the message "of course the children will still have a family—I AM family!" Thus, for the women in this sample, time and energy invested in family relationships appeared to pay off in times of crisis. They seemed to have the expectation that they could count on their children, and in most cases, their expectations were met.

To sum up our discussion so far: Women were likely to see marital dissolution as a long, difficult process; men tended to see it more as a sudden event. Women turned to children for support, while men relied more on other resources. Men reported more negative reactions to the divorce among their children. While both men and women shared concerns about the future of the individuals involved, men also voiced concerns about the viability of bonds between parents and children. A similar trend emerged when our respondents discussed their aged parents.

DIVORCE AND AGING PARENTS

Reactions to the Divorce

When asked about their parents' reactions to the marital breakup, men again reported concerns regarding family unity. They, considerably more than women, saw their parents as troubled about how the divorce would affect the grandchildren and their own contact with them. "Worrying about the effects on the kids" was checked by 76% of men with parents living; 44% of women. "Worrying about losing contact with grandchildren" was seen as a parental concern by 52% of the men; 8% of the women. Men also reported parents as concerned about the loss of a daughter-in-law, and feeling that married people should "stick it out."

A 43-year-old man described his widowed mother's reactions by saying, "It was difficult from the standpoint of my own mother. The difficulty was one of change at 80 and having to shift gears. It was a security factor. She looked to the stability of the family being there when she got older." Significantly fewer women saw their parents as having had such concerns and a sizable proportion of them described parental reactions as one of relief.

Both men and women agreed that aged parents worried about the future of the child experiencing the divorce, the respondent. A nurse described her mother's reaction: "Mother is very concerned to see that I am remarried before she dies. She no longer talks about not being able to be remarried in the Church."

Parents as Supports

Among the respondents who had parents living at the time of the marital disruption, nearly half of the men and three fourths of the women said that they discussed marital problems with their parents. When they did *not* talk to the parents, it was typically because they expected disapproval or lack of understanding from the parent. One woman said: "I am ashamed to say it, but at 50 I am still afraid of what my mother thinks—she intimidates me. I was divorced almost a year before I told her—until finally she asked me. I hope my children don't feel that way about me!" A few admitted that the divorce had been delayed because of anticipated reactions by parents. On the other hand, many of the people who had feared parental disapproval found unexpected support. One woman recalled what her father said at the time of her wedding: "You make your bed—hard or soft—you'll have to lie in it." She added: "It turned out to be awfully hard." When her marriage crumbled, she turned to her father: "And you know—he told me to come home—where I belonged!'' Particularly among men, a sizable number did just *that*. About one third of the men who had parents living ''went home to Mom'' at some point in the divorce process. A man who moved in with his parents spoke of how his mother was ''a shoulder to cry on . . . company for lonesome times. She was supportive and helpful the way mothers should be.''

Although a sizable number of our respondents received some kind of help from parents during the divorce process, only *one* named a parent when asked ''who was the most helpful during the most difficult period?''

Impact of the Divorce on Parent–Child Ties

Looking back at the period of marital breakup, the majority of the respondents, men and women, said that the divorce had not seriously affected the relationship with their parents. Approximately two thirds of both men and women said that it remained unchanged. When there was a change reported, it was more likely to be an improvement than a negative change. About one fourth of the men said they had grown closer to their parents as a result of the marital breakup, about 15% of the women said so. The few cases in which the relationship had taken a turn for the worse were all reported by women (about 20%)—and mostly in dealing with their mothers.

Of course, all of our information came from the middle-aged child. We can only speculate about what the parents' own reactions would be.

Nearly a fifth of our respondents were only children. That means that the elderly parents may have been faced with ''countertransitions'' in the form of role loss, losing active role involvement both as parents-in-law and grandparents. For about one third of the parents, the divorcing child was their only son or daughter, which means that the divorce faced them with the possible loss of contact with their only son- or daughter-in-law.

For older people with middle-aged daughters going through divorce, our data suggest that not only may they face a child who has weakened material and emotional resources; the parents may also have new demands placed on their own resources. Indeed, it is possible that the cases of strained relationships between middle-aged women and their mothers reflect conflict over *who can be needy*. The mother may, like the middle-aged woman, *her* daughter, expect support and understanding, and not be ready for a reversal of the flow.

DIVORCE AND GENERATIONAL CONTEXT

Our study looked at divorces in which three generations of adults often were affected. From the accounts of middle-aged divorcées, it appears that the lives of young adult children considerably more than those of aging parents, are touched by the marital disruption. Even though parents were seen as having more negative reactions to the divorce than were children, the breakup was perceived as having more detrimental effects on the relationship with children, particularly among men. Furthermore, when family supports were relied on during the divorce process, children were both turned to more and seen as more helpful than parents, especially by women. Given our focus on parent–child relationships as part of intergenerational chains, we asked if those of our respondents who had no parents living (i.e., who were omegas) were more likely to turn to their children for support than those with parents. The results astounded us. We found a strong trend, particularly among men, for nonomegas to turn to children much more than omegas. Among men who had at least one parent living, 60% talked to children during the most difficult part of the divorce process. Among those with no parent living, 24% did so. The corresponding figures for women were 54% and 47%. The same contrast was found with regard to seeking support from siblings. Among men and women with parents and siblings living, 64% talked to siblings, compared to 47% among those who had no parents. Among men *with* parents living, 20% turned to neither a child nor a sibling. For men *without* parents, the corresponding figure was 53%. Thus, our data suggest that having parents still living appeared to make the middle-aged individuals, particularly men, more ready to turn to other family members, such as children and siblings during the process of marital breakup. Among those with no parents, there was less overall use of family supports.

These findings come from a small sample, but we find them intriguing and in need of further exploration. We have considered two possible ways to account for the trend we observed. The first would point to the importance of elderly parents, particularly mothers, in maintaining family cohesion. Such an explanation would seem reasonable in the case of siblings. As Young and Willmott (1957) described kin contact in East London: "The siblings see a good deal of each other because they all see a good deal of Mum." It would seem harder to extend the family cohesion argument to the relationship between the middle generations and their offspring. As we discussed, the contrast in frequencies of turning to children was particularly striking between men with and without living parents. One possibility might be that men relied on their wives to facilitate interaction with children prior to the divorce, and that parents assumed some of this function following marital dissolution.

On a more psychological level, a second way to account for the findings would relate them to a sense of personal vulnerability and a view of family ties as both precious and precarious. Discussions of middle age have suggested that the death of parents may contribute to a new sense of vulnerability, of being "next in line" (Neugarten, 1967), with no vertical family bond extending "up" generational lines. It is possible that the loss of such bonds makes the individual more hesitant to risk straining remaining family ties. Furthermore, men may define turning to children and siblings, particularly during a divorce process, more as interpersonal "risk-taking" than do women. One could advance this argument on two grounds. First, the experience of marital breakup often entails a profound sense of personal failure and loss of control. Given differences between male and female family roles, particularly among the cohorts we studied, acknowledging such feelings may be considerably easier for women than for men. Second, other work has demonstrated that overall, women are more likely to rely on kin, including children, as confidantes (e.g., Babchuk, 1978; Hagestad & Snow, 1977; Townsend, 1957). Thus, turning to family members during a difficult divorce process may represent more of a radical departure from past ways of relating and constitute more "interpersonal risk-taking" for men than for women. As we discussed above, men may also see family ties, particularly in relation to children, as precarious following marital breakup. This, combined with the lack of ties upward in generational links, may make them hesitant to jeopardize relationships.

Bengtson and Kuypers (1971) have discussed the concept of *developmental stake*, suggesting that parent–child relations are asymmetrical. They argue that as children mature, parents have more invested in the relationship than do the children, and will therefore be more "protective" of it than the offspring. Recent sociobiological perspectives on kin relations reach a similar conclusion. To our knowledge, Bengtson and Kuypers have not discussed the developmental stake within a multigenerational framework. Our preliminary findings suggest that when individuals are no longer children themselves; that is, they are no longer the "object" of a developmental stake, their stake in offspring may intensify. Particularly for men, this may lead to decreased readiness to seek support from children during times of crisis.

SUMMARY AND DISCUSSION

Our chapter has discussed findings from a pilot study of men and women who experienced divorce in middle age, after lengthy marriages. We have argued that research on this type of marital dissolution offers unique opportunities to study parent–child ties from a dynamic, multigenerational perspective.

The accounts in our interviews brought out a number of key points. First, they illustrated in a variety of ways the enduring nature of parent–child bonds. Even at the age of 50, the "children" were concerned about approval and support from parents. Even at the age of 80, the parents worried about the security and well-being of children. Even when adults had grown children who themselves had children, their own parents appeared to provide a source of "backing," simply by being there. Second, when both parents and children were available as potential adult supports, children were turned to considerably more than parents. Third, parents appeared to represent *indirect support*, facilitating the utilization of family resources during times of crisis. Fourth, men and women showed marked contrasts in their use of parents and children as interpersonal resources. Women turned to children and parents more during the process of marital breakup, and appeared to pull from family supports earlier in the process than did men. Furthermore, the absence of parents seemed to have a greater impact on men's ability to use family supports than was the case for women. The extent to which this would apply to other types of life crises needs to be investigated in further work.

Our data powerfully point to the importance of viewing parent–child relations in multiple links, across several generations. Contrary to the English proverb, our findings suggest that men and women remain sons and daughters, not all their lives, but as long as they have living parents. Once that changes, being mothers and fathers to the next generation in line takes on new meanings, particularly for men who are no longer sons.

We feel that these preliminary findings present exciting challenges to family research, developmental psychology, and intervention with individuals as well as families.

ACKNOWLEDGMENTS

This research was supported, in part, by a Research Initiation Grant from Pennsylvania State University, a grant from the Society for the Psychological Study of Social Issues, and a grant from the College of Human Development of Pennsylvania State University.

REFERENCES

Anspach, D. F. Kinship and divorce. *Journal of Marriage and the Family*, 1976, *38*, 323–330.

Babchuk, N. *Primary ties of aged men*. Paper presented at the Annual Meeting of the Gerontological Society, Washington, D.C., 1978.

Beck, A. T., Ward, C. H., Mendelson, M., Mock, J., & Erbaugh, J. An inventory for measuring depression. *Archives of General Psychiatry*, 1969, *9*, 295–302.

Bengtson, V. L., & Kuypers, J. A. Generational differences and the "developmental stake." *Aging and Human Development*, 1971, *2*, 249–260.

Blenkner, M. Social work and family relationships in later life with some thoughts on filial maturity. In E. Shanas & G. F. Streib (Eds.), *Social structure and the family*. Englewood Cliffs, N.J.: Prentice-Hall, 1965.

Bohannan, P. (Ed.). *Divorce and after*. Garden City, N.Y.: Doubleday, 1970.

Campbell, A., Converse, P. E., & Rodgers, W. L. *The quality of American life*. New York: Russell Sage Foundation, 1976.

Chiriboga, D. A. Marital separation and stress: A life-course perspective. *Alternative Lifestyles*, 1979, *2*(4), 461–470.

Deckert, P., & Langelier, R. The late divorce phenomenon: The causes and impact of ending a 20-year-old or longer marriage. *Journal of Divorce*, 1978, *1*(4), 381–390.

Goode, W. J. *After divorce*. Glencoe, Ill.: Free Press, 1956.

Hagestad, G. O. Problems and promises in the social psychology of intergenerational relations. In R. Fogel, E. Hatfield, S. Kiesler, & J. March (Eds.), *Stability and change in the family*. New York: Academic Press, 1981.

Hagestad, G. O. Adult intergenerational relationships: Parents and children. In L. E. Troll (Ed.), *Review of human development*. Wiley-Interscience, 1982.

Hagestad, G. O., & Snow, R. *Young adult offspring as interpersonal resources in middle age*. Paper presented at the Annual Meeting of the Gerontological Society, San Francisco, 1977.

Hayes, M. P. *Divorce in the middle years.* Unpublished doctoral dissertation, Oklahoma State University, 1976.

Hetherington, E. M., Cox, M., & Cox, R. The aftermath of divorce. In J. H. Stevens, Jr., & M. Mathews (Eds.), *Mother–child, father–child relations.* Washington, D.C.: National Association for the Education of Young Children, 1977.

Hetherington, E. M., Cox, M., & Cox, R. Play and social interaction in children following divorce. *Journal of Social Issues,* 1979, *35*(4), 26–49.

Hill, R., Foote, N., Aldous, J., Carlson, R., & MacDonald, R. *Family development in three generations.* Cambridge, Mass.: Schenkman, 1970.

Klein, D. M., Jorgensen, S. R., & Miller, B. Research methods and developmental reciprocity in families. In R. M. Lerner & G. B. Spanier (Eds.), *Child influences on marital and family interaction: A life-span perspective.* New York: Academic Press, 1979.

Levinger, G., & Moles, O. (Eds.). *Divorce and separation.* New York: Basic Books, 1979.

Levitin, T. E. Children of divorce. *Journal of Social Issues,* 1979, *35,* 1–25.

Lopata, H. Z. *Women as widows.* New York: Elsevier, 1979.

Neugarten, B. L. The awareness of middle age. In R. Owen (Ed.), *Middle age.* London: British Broadcasting Corporation, 1967.

Nydegger, C. N., & Mitteness, L. *Role development: The case of fatherhood.* Paper presented at the Annual Meeting of the Gerontological Society, Washington, D.C., 1979.

Plath, D. W. Contours of consociation: Lessons from a Japanese narrative. In P. Baltes & O. Brim, Jr. (Ed.), *Life-span development and behavior* (Vol. 3). New York: Academic Press, 1980.

Riley, M. W., & Waring, J. Age and aging. In R. K. Merton & R. Nisbet (Eds.), *Contemporary social problems.* New York: Harcourt, Brace, Jovanovich, 1976.

Riley, M. W., Foner, A., Moore, M. E., Hess, R., & Roth, B. K. *Aging and society: An inventory of research findings.* New York: Russell Sage Foundation, 1968.

Shanas, E. Social myth as hypothesis: The case of the family relations of old people. *Gerontologist,* 1979, 19:3–9.

Smith, L. *Meeting filial responsibility demands in middle age.* Unpublished master's thesis, Pennsylvania State University, 1983.

Spicer, J. W., & Hampe, G. D. Kinship interaction after divorce, *Journal of Marriage and the Family,* 1975, *37*(1), 113–119.

Townsend, P. *The family life of old people.* New York: Free Press–Macmillan, 1957.

Troll, L. E., Miller, S. J., & Atchley, R. C. *Families in later life.* Belmont, Calif.: Wadsworth, 1979.

U.S. Bureau of the Census. *Number, timing and duration of marriages and divorces in the United States, June 1975* (Current Population Reports, Series P-20, No. 297). Washington, D.C.: U.S. Government Printing Office, 1976.

Wallerstein, J. S., & Kelly, J. B. Children and divorce: A review. *Social Work,* 1980, *24*(6), 468–475.

Walters, J., & Walters, L. H. Parent–child relationships: A review, 1970–1979. *Journal of Marriage and the Family,* 1980, *42,* 807–822.

Wilen, J. B. *Changing relationships among grandparents, parents, and their young adult children.* Paper presented at the Annual Meeting of the Gerontological Society, Washington, D.C., 1979.

Young, M., & Willmott, P. *Family and kinship in East London.* London: Routledge & Kegan Paul, 1957.

III

CLINICAL AND THEORETICAL PSYCHOANALYTIC PERSPECTIVES

Contributions to our understanding of parenthood which stem from psychoanalysis are manifested clearly in the other sections of this volume. In this section, however, we will present work which will deal directly with either psychoanalytic, theoretical, or developmental perspectives on parenthood or on issues in the clinical practice of psychoanalysis and its relationship to parenthood.

Until the publication of Anthony and Benedek's *Parenthood: Its Psychology and Psychopathology* in 1970 the area of parenthood, as experience rather than technique or relationship with a child, was largely ignored by psychoanalytic contributors.[1] The probable roots for this neglect, we suspect, may stem from Freud's original work where issues of parenting were explicitly described but then ignored. In Freud's (1909) account of the genesis of a phobia in Little Hans, frequent references are made to the parenting technique of the parents. However, in order to present the argument that the infantile neurosis is a naturally occurring normal development in a normal child Freud does not pursue the potential impact of the parents on their child, the parents on each other, or the child on the parents.

However, Freud's account of the case provides data to address each of these areas. Freud indicates that the parents had formed and developed, at least, the beginning of a parenting alliance; ". . . they had agreed that in bringing up their first child they would use no more coercion in raising their child than might be necessary for maintaining good behavior" (1909, p. 6). After Little Hans is found by his mother with his hand on his penis she says, "If you do that, I shall send for Dr. A. to cut off your widdler [penis]. And then what'll you widdle with?" (1909, pp. 7–8). Although having described the parents as being prepared to raise their child with minimal coercion, we suspect that the mother's comment must be seen as not only coercive but frightening.

Later, when the boy develops a phobic symptom the father writes to Freud. He indicates his distress at Hans's symptoms that a horse will bite him in the

---

1. While there had been previous psychoanalytically informed studies of parenthood (Deutsch, 1945; Bibring, Dwyer, Huntington, & Valenstein, 1961), the work did not focus on the experiential aspects.

street, but he also attributes, partially, the development of this symptom to "sexual over-stimulation due to his mother's tenderness" (1909, p. 22). Here we can observe the clear presentation of some conflict which has not been resolved between mother and father, as well as the father's powerful transference to Freud who will enable him to cure his son's symptoms, and as we might state it today, help him to successfully parent his son.

At this point in the development of psychoanalysis the major thrust of Freud's work was finding substantiating data for his theory of the neurosis and, specifically, the infantile neurosis. Since the data offered ample evidence for Freud to make his case in this area, other potential views of the data were not explored and the parenting issues were ignored. The only potential reference is in the view that perhaps the treatment was successful because it was undertaken by the boy's father.

In the case of Dora, a similar avoidance of examining the parenting behavior of Dora's father can be observed (Freud, 1905). Here again, Freud is interested in elaborating his theory for the development of neurosis. Today, we would ask any number of questions regarding the parenting of Little Hans or Dora. We would inquire as to both the marital relationship between each set of parents and to the parenting alliance between them as well as to the meaning to them of the respective children.

Parenthood for Freud, after he renounced the seduction hypothesis for the development of neurosis, was not a major area of interest. Indeed, although the psychoanalytic literature has explored all kinds of diverse behavior, its contributions to understanding the psychology of parenthood are sparse. We can ponder if analysts since Freud have been reluctant to address an area assiduously avoided by the master after his experience with the seduction hypothesis.

In addition to the implicit inhibition by Freud in this area, one can ponder many other inhibitions to the exploration of the psychology of parenting. Have our concerns, and investments in our children, or the tensions with our spouses blinded us to a careful examination of their meanings to us, just as in an earlier time, tension regarding our sexuality blinded us to the initial insights Freud first made nearly 90 years ago?

Benedek, in 1959, began the first systematic psychoanalytic study of parenthood. Anthony and Benedek (1970) pursued the latter's early work with an examination of parenthood, utilizing the prevailing psychoanalytic drive defense model of behavior. The years immediately prior to the publication of that work and the years since have seen the elaboration of new psychoanalytic modes. The object relations school clearly deals with parent–child relationships but has not clearly elaborated upon this from the perspective of the parent. Mahler, Pine, and Bergman (1975) address issues of parenting in the mother's need for relief from the demands of the child and in the early triangulation in mother–child relationships supplied by father at 18 months but their major concern is the psychological growth of the child. Kohut, through the development of the concept of the self–selfobject, has offered another paradigm with which to assess parenthood.

The contributions in this section and elsewhere in this volume have utilized contributions from these schools and others to develop a more inclusive model of parenthood.

The contribution to this volume by Bowlby focuses on the intrapsychic issues presented to the parent and child in the process of parenting and being parented. Bowlby presents data which argue that the mother and child enter the parenting dyad with preprogrammed capacities which affect and facilitate parenting. These preprogrammed capacities facilitate what Bowlby refers to as attachment behaviors. Bowlby expands the concept of attachment behavior and implies that attachment behaviors relate to dependency needs which are manifest throughout life. Bowlby also presents data which supports the view that fathers are intimately involved with their children from birth and establish relationships with them which are unique and distinct from those of the mother.

This view is shared by Muslin in his chapter. Bowlby also addresses what Cohen and Weissman discussed as the parenting alliance. He sees parents as optimally involved with each other prior to the birth of their child and throughout the child's early development. Indeed, Bowlby views the parenting alliance as critical if not central for the child: "Looking after babies and young children is no job for a single person. If the job is to be well done and the child's principal caregiver is not to be exhausted, the caregiver herself needs a great deal of assistance."

In contrast to Bowlby's chapter which focuses on recent research on infants, children, and their parents, is the chapter by Sadow. Sadow explores the psychological experiences of the parent which lay the templates or are the precursors for his/her becoming an effective parent. Sadow divides the parent's life for purposes of his argument into three sections. The first is the parent's infancy, the second is his/her Oedipal period, and the third is later adult experiences. In describing the impact of experiences from infancy, Sadow refers to Monica, described by George Engel, who had to be fed as an infant in an upside-down position because of an esophageal atresia. As an adult, with her own child, Monica is observed feeding her child in exactly the same fashion as she had been fed. Indeed, she is holding the child in a position which is uncomfortable for her. When asked why she holds the child in that fashion, she gives a rationalization. Engel has assured us that Monica has never seen pictures of herself being fed. Sadow attaches this capacity of Monica's to an experience which occurred at the time of her development of sensory motor organization. Adding to Sadow's account, we offer the following: Monica as an infant is involved with her mother's and her own affective experience, and with her mother's and her own physical experiences in being fed. As a mother, when she experienced the new stimuli of caring for an infant, she is also simultaneously reexperiencing some of the same affects and physical experiences she initially felt in her early symbiosis or merger with her mother. She had, in addition to these experiences, the desire to optimally care for her child. The desire to appropriately care for the child in the affectively aroused situation of feeding the infant further heightened the reconnection of Monica to the merged boundless relation with her mother in infancy. The reconnection with this early period is to be in touch with experiences which are felt but not distinguished between self and object. Monica is in touch with her experience of her mother as part of herself. She then utilizes that recollection, which is a sensorimotor pattern, a nonverbal experience, to organize herself to feed her child. Essentially, she feeds the child just as she was fed.

Engel's account of Monica throws light on other instances from everyday life in which a parent replicates with his/her own children his/her early childhood experiences. We are all familiar with the young mother who sings to her child in the foreign language of her grandmother who died many years earlier. In any other than the situation of caring for her child it is difficult, if not impossible, for the mother to recall that song. The explanation for this behavior is not unlike that of Monica's feeding behavior. However, it poses the interesting question of how a person can reproduce, years later, songs heard in infancy, when at the time they were originally heard the child could not sing them.

A clear role for contemporary psychoanalytic theory building might be to develop a theory to account for these observations. Our present theory accounting for the procedure of how identification takes place is clearly inadequate. (Perhaps Terman's presentation, which we discuss below, points up the direction we might take in understanding these phenomena.)

In discussing the Oedipal period, Sadow utilizes a classical psychoanalytic framework to account for identifications with the parents. In the later stages, where he uses adult experiences that have an impact on the adult capacity to parent, Sadow suggests that adults frequently enter into selfobject relationships which have a structuring effect on their egos, which in turn may change their parenting modes from that of their parents. Sadow presents psychological data from these three periods of life to suggest that the anlage of parenthood is contained in all of life's experiences.

Elson addresses the psychological roots of parenthood in a different fashion. She constructs her explanation on the psychological percepts of self psychology. She views parenthood and the tasks of parenting as providing an opportunity for the constant evolution and transformation of the parent's narcissism as the parent responds to the narcissistic demands of the child. She proposes a double helix model. The age-appropriate narcissistic demands of the child trigger narcissistic experiences in the parent which lead to further transformation of narcissism of that parent. The capacity to parent in this model is built into the individual nuclear self. The experiencing of parenthood leads to changes in the parent's self. This model accounts for simultaneous development and integration in the self of the child and the self of the parent.

This view is implicitly shared by Muslin and Terman. Muslin, using the self psychology model, examines the relationship between father and child. He discusses the importance to parent and child for the father to be able to mirror the child and to serve as an idealizing object for him/her. He argues, further, that the child serves as an expression of the parent's narcissism so that the father does not need to look to the child for gratification of his narcissistic needs. Muslin also implicitly addresses the needs for the parenting alliance when he indicates that the coparents receive narcissistic supplies from each other and not their child.

Terman addresses the parent–child dyad and the affective stimuli involved. He is explicitly interested in how affect is integrated by the child into the self through appropriate selfobject relationships. Terman then examines what would appear to be identification in the parent with his parents. He postulates that what we call identifications are not such; rather what the parent does is mobilize structures which were laid down in his childhood. The process of structure building in the child through transmuting internalization (Kohut, 1971) leads the child to develop structures which are similar to the parents. Terman, although discussing parenthood, is also raising a significant issue in our understanding of the process of identification.

Fisch's chapter, although containing a clinical psychoanalytic ring, addresses a number of issues more central to parenting and to our understanding of the psychological growth in adults. Fisch argues that in the analysis of his patient, the focus on parenting issues created a context which aided the patient in developing a therapeutic alliance in her analysis. This alliance then permitted further growth to emerge in the analysis. A number of other views are possible to understand the success of Fisch's treatment. One view would be that the children served as narcissistic extensions of the patient and that in discussing the children, Fisch was, in fact, talking about the core issues and needs of the patient. Another view is that her growth occurred because parenting is so critical to the experiencing of the self that it, of necessity, must effect core experiences of the self. Her growth could be seen as not dissimilar to the growth reported in the clinical example in Sadow's chapter where the process of mothering appears to have facilitated major characterological changes.

The chapter by Schwartz is a classical psychoanalytic view of parenting. Schwartz makes the point which appears technical but is in fact critical that parenthood is a developmental process, not a developmental phase. He reports that Therese Benedek, after initially calling parenthood a developmental phase, later revised this, and suggested that it was a process. The distinction is that "phase" refers to the development in classic psychoanalytic theory of new psychological structures, while "process" does not. This view that parenting does not lead to the development of new structures can be regarded as being in conflict with the perspective of Elson, who, in utilizing a self psychology perspective, argues clearly that it does.

In his chapter on fatherhood Ross[2] presents the psychology of fathers both from a classical psychoanalytic stance and from the work of Margaret Mahler.

2. Ross presents a doubtful stance about the future of the American family; recent behavioral science studies (Cohler & Geyer, 1982) indicate greater stability. Clearly, this is an area for further investigation.

In contrast to Bowlby and Muslin who see the father as intimately involved with the parenting process from the beginning, Ross seems to place the father's role as a critical one in rescuing the child from the symbiotic attachment to the mother. Implicitly, this means that if left undisrupted, the child's development is impeded. Ross shares Muslin's view that the child clearly needs the father to idealize but his view of the meaning of idealization is clearly different. Muslin utilizes the concept from the perspective of self psychology, while Ross uses the term in its more classical psychoanalytic meaning within the context of the libidinal drives.

In conclusion, the chapters of this section address issues in understanding the psychology of parenthood from a number of psychoanalytic perspectives. The various contributions as a whole highlight the significance of parenthood in understanding adult growth and development and additionally present contemporary psychoanalysis as a vital discipline in creative ferment.

REFERENCES

Anthony, E. J., & Benedek, T. (Eds.). *Parenthood: Its psychology and psychopathology*. Boston: Little, Brown, 1970.

Benedek, T. Parenthood as a developmental phase: A contribution to the libido theory. *Journal of the American Psychoanalytic Association*, 1959, *7*, 389–417.

Bibring, G., Dwyer, T. F., Huntington, D. S., & Valenstein, A. F. A study of the psychological processes in pregnancy and of the earliest mother–child relationship. *Psychoanalytic Study of the Child*, 1961, *16*, 9–72.

Cohler, B., & Geyer, S. Psychological autonomy and interdependence within the family. In F. Walsh (Ed.), *Normal family processes*. New York: Guilford Press, 1982.

Deutsch, H. *The psychology of women* (Vol. 2). New York: Grune & Stratton, 1945.

Freud, S. Fragment of an analysis of a case of hysteria (1905). *Standard Edition, 7*, 7–122. London: Hogarth Press, 1953.

Freud, S. Analysis of a phobia in a five year old boy (1909). *Standard Edition, 10*, 5–149. London: Hogarth Press, 1955.

Kohut, H. *The analysis of the self*. New York: International Universities Press, 1971.

Mahler, M. S., Pine, F., & Bergman, A. *The psychological birth of the human infant*. New York: Basic Books, 1975.

18

CARING FOR THE YOUNG:
INFLUENCES ON DEVELOPMENT

JOHN BOWLBY

AN INDISPENSABLE SOCIAL ROLE

At some time of their lives, I believe, most human beings desire to have children and desire also that their children should grow up to be healthy, happy, and self-reliant. For those who succeed the rewards are great; but for those who have children but fail to rear them to be healthy, happy, and self-reliant the penalties in anxiety, frustration, friction, and perhaps shame or guilt may be severe. Engaging in parenthood, therefore, is playing for high stakes. Furthermore, successful parenting is a principal key to the mental health of the next generation. For all these reasons, mental health professionals need to know all they can, both about the nature of successful parenting, and about the manifold social and psychological conditions that influence its development, for better or worse. The theme is a huge one and all I can do in this chapter is to sketch the approach that I myself adopt in thinking about these issues. This approach is an ethological one.

Before I go into detail, however, I want to make a few more general remarks. To be a successful parent means a lot of very hard work. Looking after a baby or toddler is a 24-hour-a-day job 7 days a week, and often a very worrying one at that. And even if the load lightens a little as children get older, if they are to flourish they still require a lot of time and attention. For many people today these are unpalatable truths. Giving time and attention to children means sacrificing other interests and other activities. Yet I believe the evidence for what I am saying is unimpeachable. Study after study, including those pioneered by Roy Grinker (1962) and continued by Daniel Offer (1969), attest that healthy, happy, and self-reliant adolescents and young adults are the products of stable homes in which both parents give a great deal of time and attention to the children.

John Bowlby. Department for Children and Parents, Tavistock Clinic, London, England.

I want to emphasize also that, despite voices to the contrary, looking after babies and young children is no job for a single person. If the job is to be well done and the child's principal caregiver is not to be too exhausted, the caregiver herself needs a great deal of assistance. From whom that help comes will vary: very often it is the other parent; in many societies, including more often than is realized in our own, it comes from a grandmother. Others to be drawn in to help are adolescent girls and young women. In most societies throughout the world these truths have been, and still are, taken for granted, and the society organized accordingly. Paradoxically, it has taken the world's richest societies to ignore these basic truths. Man and woman power devoted to the production of material goods counts as a plus in all our economic indices. Man and woman power devoted to the production of happy, healthy, and self-reliant children in their own homes does not count at all. We have created a topsy-turvy world.

But I do not want to enter into complex political and economic arguments. My reason for raising these points is to remind you that the society we live in is not only, in evolutionary terms, a product of yesterday but in many ways a very peculiar one. There is, in consequence, a great danger that we shall adopt mistaken norms. For, just as a society in which there is a chronic insufficiency of food may take a deplorably inadequate level of nutrition as its norm, so may a society in which parents of young children are left on their own with a chronic insufficiency of help take this state of affairs as its norm.

AN ETHOLOGICAL APPROACH

I said earlier that my approach to an understanding of parenting as a human activity is an ethological one. Let me explain.

In reexamining the nature of the child's tie to his mother, traditionally referred to as dependency, it has been found useful to regard it as the result of a distinctive and in part preprogrammed set of behavior patterns which in the ordinary expectable environment develop during the early months of life, and have the effect of keeping the child in more or less close proximity to his mother figure (Bowlby, 1969). By the end of the first year, the behavior is becoming organized cybernetically, which means, among other things, that the behavior becomes active whenever certain conditions obtain and ceases when certain other conditions obtain. For example, a child's attachment behavior is activated especially by pain, fatigue, and anything frightening, and also by a mother who is, or appears to be, inaccessible. The conditions that terminate the behavior vary according to the intensity of its arousal. At low intensity, they may be simply sight or sound of mother, especially effective being a signal from her acknowledging his presence. At higher intensity, termination may require his touching or clinging to her. At highest intensity, when the child is distressed and anxious, nothing but a prolonged cuddle will do. The biological function of this behavior is postulated to be protection, particularly protection from predators.

In these examples, the individuals concerned are a child and his mother. It is evident, however, that attachment behavior is in no way confined to children. Although usually less readily aroused, we see it also in adolescents and adults of both sexes whenever they are anxious or under stress. No one should be surprised, therefore, when a woman expecting a baby or a mother caring for young children has a strong desire of her own to be cared for and supported. The activation of attachment behavior in these circumstances is probably universal and must be considered the norm.[1]

A feature of attachment behavior of the greatest importance clinically, and present regardless of the age of the individual concerned, is the intensity of the emotion that accompanies it, the kind of emotion aroused depending on how the relationship between the individual attached and the attachment figure is faring. If it goes well, there is joy and a sense of security. If it is threatened, there is jealousy, anxiety, and anger. If broken, there is grief and depression. Finally, there is strong evidence that how attachment behavior comes to be organized within an individual turns in high degree on the kinds of experience he has in his family of origin, or, if he is unlucky, out of it.

I believe that this type of theory has many advantages over the theories hitherto current in our field. Not only does it bring theory into close relationship with observed data, but it provides a theoretical framework for our field compatible with the framework adopted throughout modern biology and neurophysiology. Parenting, I believe can usefully be approached from the same ethologically inspired viewpoint. This entails observing and describing the set of behavior patterns characteristic of parenting; the conditions that activate and terminate each; how the patterns change as a child grows older; the varying ways that parenting behavior becomes organized in different individuals; and the myriad of experiences that influence how it develops in any one person.

Implicit in this approach is the assumption that parenting behavior, like attachment behavior, is in some degree preprogrammed and therefore ready to develop along certain lines when conditions elicit it. This means that, in the ordinary course of events, the parent of a baby experiences a strong urge to behave in certain typical ways, for example, to cradle the infant, to soothe him when he cries, to keep him warm, protected, and fed. Such a viewpoint, of course, does not imply that the appropriate behavior patterns manifest themselves complete in every detail from the first. Clearly that is not so, whether in human beings or in other mammalian species. All the detail is learned, some of it during interaction with babies and children, much of it through observation of how other parents behave. The process begins in the parent-to-be's own childhood and in the way his parents treated him and his siblings.

This modern view of behavioral development contrasts sharply with both of the older paradigms, one of which, invoking instinct, overemphasized the

1. An increased desire for care, either from husband or mother, has been reported in studies of representative groups of women by Wenner (1966) and Ballou (1978).

preprogrammed component, and the other of which, reacting against instinct, overemphasized the learned component. Parenting behavior in humans is certainly not the product of some unvarying parenting instinct, but nor is it reasonable to regard it as merely the product of learning. Parenting behavior has strong biological roots, thus accounting for the very strong emotions associated with it; but the specific form that the behavior takes in each of us turns on our experiences—during childhood especially, during adolescence, before and during marriage, and with each individual child.

Thus it is useful to look upon parenting behavior as one example of a limited class of biologically rooted types of behavior of which attachment behavior is another example, sexual behavior another, and exploratory behavior, and eating behavior yet others. Each of these types of behavior contributes in its own specific way to the survival either of the individual or his offspring. It is, indeed, because each one serves so vital a function that each of these types of behavior is in some degree preprogrammed. To leave their development solely to the caprices of individual learning would be the height of biological folly.

You will notice that in sketching this framework I make a point of keeping each of these types of behavior conceptually distinct from the others. This contrasts, of course, with traditional libido theory which has treated them as the varying expressions of a single drive. The reasons for keeping them distinct are several. One is that each of the types of behavior mentioned serves its own distinctive biological function—protection, reproduction, nutrition, knowledge of the environment. Another is that many of the detailed patterns of behavior within each general type are distinctive also: Clinging to a parent is different from soothing and comforting a child; sucking or chewing food are different from engaging in sexual intercourse. Furthermore, factors which influence the development of one of these types of behavior are not necessarily the same as those that influence the development of another. By keeping them distinct we are able not only to study the ways in which they differ, but also to study the ways in which they overlap and interact with each other—as it has long been evident that they do.

INITIATION OF MOTHER–INFANT INTERACTION

During the past decade there has been a dramatic advance in our understanding of the early phases of mother–infant interaction, thanks to the imaginative research of workers on both sides of the Atlantic. The studies of Marshall Klaus and John Kennell are now well known. Their observations of the behavior of mothers toward newborns when given freedom to do what they like after delivery are of special interest. Klaus, Trause, and Kennell (1975) describe how a mother, immediately after her infant is born, picks him up and begins to stroke his face with her fingertips. At this the baby quietens. Soon she moves on to touching his head and body with the palm of her hand and, within 5 or 6 minutes, she is likely to put him to her breast. The baby responds with prolonged licking of the nipple. "Immediately after the delivery," they noted, "the mothers appeared to be in a state of ecstasy," and, interestingly enough, the observers became elated too. From the moment of birth attention becomes riveted on the baby. Something about him tends to draw not only the mother and father but all those present to the new arrival. Given the chance, a mother is likely during the next few days to spend many hours just looking at her new possession, cuddling him, and getting to know him. Usually there comes a moment when she feels the baby is her very own. For some it comes early, perhaps when she first holds him or when he first looks into her eyes. For a large minority of primaparae who are delivered in the hospital, however, it may be delayed for up to a week, often until they are home again (Robson & Kumar 1980).

Phenomena of the greatest importance to which recent research has drawn attention are the potential of the healthy neonate to enter into an elemental form of social interaction and the potential of the ordinary sensitive mother to participate successfully in it.[2]

When a mother and her infant of 2 or 3 weeks are facing one another phases of lively social interaction ensue which alternate with phases of disengagement. Each phase of interaction begins with initiation and mutual greeting, builds up to an animated interchange comprising facial expressions and vocalizations, during which the infant orients toward his mother with excited movements of arms and legs. Then his activities gradually subside and end with the baby looking away for a spell before the next phase of interaction begins. Throughout these cycles the baby is likely to be as spontaneously active as his mother. Where their roles differ is in the timing of their responses. Whereas an infant's initiation and withdrawal from interaction tend to follow his own autonomous rhythm, a sensitive mother regulates her behavior so that it meshes with his. In addition she modifies the form her behavior takes to suit him. Her voice is gentle but higher pitched than usual, her movements slowed, and each subsequent action adjusted in form and timing according to how her baby is performing. Thus she lets him call the tune and by a skillful interweaving of her own responses with his creates a dialogue.

The speed and efficiency with which these dialogues develop and the mutual enjoyment they give point clearly to each participant being preadapted to engage in them. On the one hand is the mother's intuitive readiness to allow her interventions to be paced by her infant. On the other is the readiness with which the infant's rhythms shift gradually to take account of the timing of his mother's interventions. In a happily developing partnership each is adapting to the other.

Very similar alternating sequences have been recorded in other and different

2. See especially the work of Stern (1977), Sander (1977), Brazelton, Koslowski, and Main (1974), and Schaffer (1977). For an excellent review see Schaffer (1979). The state of heightened sensitivity that develops in a woman during, and especially toward the end of pregnancy, and that enables her "to adapt delicately and sensitively" to her infant's needs, is a process to which Winnicott (1957) has called attention.

exchanges between mother and child. For example, Kaye (1977), observing the behavior of mother and infant during feeding, has found that a mother tends to interact with her infant in precise synchrony with the infant's pattern of sucking and pausing. During bursts of sucking a mother is generally quiet and inactive; during pauses she strokes and talks to her baby. Another example of how a mother takes cues from her infant is reported by Collis and Schaffer (1975) in the case of an infant within the age-range of 5 to 12 months. A mother and her infant are introduced to a scene in which there are a number of large brightly colored toys which quickly seize their visual attention. Observation of their behavior shows two things. First, both partners as a rule are looking at the same object at the same time. Secondly, examination of the timing shows almost invariably that it is the baby who leads and the mother who follows. The baby's spontaneous interest in the toys is evidently closely monitored by his mother who almost automatically follows by looking in the same direction. A focus of mutual interest having been established, the mother is likely to elaborate on it, commenting on the toy, naming it, manipulating it. A sharing experience is then brought about, instigated by the infant's spontaneous attention to the environment but established by the mother allowing herself to be paced by the baby.

Another example (Schaffer, Collis, & Parsons, 1977) concerns vocal interchange between mother and child at a preverbal level. In a comparison of two groups of children, aged 12 and 24 months, it was found that the ability of the pair to take turns and to avoid overlapping was not only strikingly efficient but as characteristic of the younger as of the older infants. Thus, long before the appearance of words the pattern of turn-taking so characteristic of human conversation is already present. Here again the evidence suggests that in ensuring smooth transitions from one "speaker" to the other, the mother plays the major part.

My reason for giving these examples at some length is that I believe they illustrate some basic principles both about parenting and about the nature of the creature who is parented. What emerges from these studies is that the ordinary sensitive mother is quickly attuned to her infant's natural rhythms and, by attending to the details of his behavior, discovers what suits him and behaves accordingly. By so doing she not only makes him contented but also enlists his cooperation. For, although initially his capacity to adapt is limited, it is not absent altogether and, if allowed to grow in its own time, is soon yielding rewards. Mary Ainsworth and her colleagues have noted that infants whose mothers have responded sensitively to their signals during the first year of life not only cry less during the second half of that year than do the babies of less responsive mothers but are more willing to fall in with their parents' wishes (Ainsworth, Blehar, Waters, & Wall, 1978). Human infants, we can safely conclude, like infants of other species, are preprogrammed to develop in a socially cooperative way; although whether they do so depends largely on how they are treated. This is a view of human nature radically different from the one that has long been current in Western societies and that has permeated so much of the clinical theory and practice we have inherited. It points, of course, to a radically different conception of the role of parent.

ROLES OF MOTHERS AND FATHERS: SIMILARITIES AND DIFFERENCES

In the examples given so far the parent concerned has been mother. This is almost inevitable because for research purposes it is relatively easy to recruit samples of infants who are being cared for mainly by mother whereas infants being cared for mainly by father are comparatively scarce. Let me, therefore, describe briefly one of several recent studies which, together, go some way to correct the balance.

Several hundred infants have now been studied by means of the strange situation procedure devised by Mary Ainsworth (Ainsworth *et al.*, 1978) which gives an opportunity to observe how the infant responds, first in his parent's presence, next when left alone, and later when his parent returns. As a result, observers can classify infants as presenting a pattern either of secure attachment to mother or of one of two main forms of insecure attachment to her. Since these patterns have been shown to have considerable stability during the earliest years of life and to predict how a nursery school child in the age-range of 4½–6 years will approach a new person and tackle a new task (Arend, Gove, & Sroufe, 1979), the value of the procedure as a method of assessing an infant's social and emotional development needs no emphasis.

Hitherto almost all the studies using this procedure have observed infants with their mothers. Main and Weston (1981), however, extended the work by observing some 60 infants first with one parent and, 6 months later, with the other. One finding was that, when looked at as a group, the patterns of attachment the infants showed toward fathers resembled closely the patterns that were shown to mothers, with roughly the same percentage distribution of patterns. But a second finding was even more interesting. When the patterns shown by each child individually were examined, no correlation was found between the pattern he showed with one parent and the pattern he showed with the other. Thus, one child may have a secure relationship with mother but not with father; a second may have it with father but not with mother; a third may have it with both his parents, and a fourth may have it with neither. In their approach to new people and new tasks the children presented a graded series. Children with a secure relationship to both parents were most confident and most competent; children who had a secure relationship to neither were least so; and those with a secure relationship to one parent but not to the other came in between. Since there is evidence that the pattern of attachment a child undamaged at birth develops with his mother is the product of how his mother has treated him (Ainsworth *et al.*, 1978), it is more than likely that, in a similar way, the pattern he develops with his father is the product of how his father has treated him.

This study, together with others, suggests that by providing an attachment figure for his child, a father may be filling a role closely resembling that filled by a mother; although in most, perhaps all, cultures fathers fill that role much less frequently than do mothers, at least when the children are still young. In most families with young children father's role is a different one. He is more likely to engage in physically active and novel play than mother and, especially for boys, to become his child's preferred play companion.[3]

PROVISION OF A SECURE BASE

This brings me to a central feature of my concept of parenting—the provision by both parents of a secure base from which a child or an adolescent can make sorties into the outside world and to which he can return knowing that he will be welcomed, nourished physically and emotionally, comforted if distressed, and reassured if frightened. In essence this role is one of being available, ready to respond when called upon, to encourage and perhaps assist, but to intervene actively only when clearly necessary. In these respects it is a role similar to that of the officer commanding a military base from which an expeditionary force sets out and to which it can retreat should it meet with a setback. Much of the time the role of the base is a waiting one but it is nonetheless vital for that. For it is only when the officer commanding the expeditionary force is confident his base is secure that he dare press forward and take risks.

In the case of children and adolescents we see them, as they get older, venturing steadily further from base and for increasing spans of time. The more confident they are that their base is secure and ready if called upon to respond, moverover, the more they take it for granted. Yet should one or other parent become ill or die, the immense significance of the base to the emotional equilibrium of the child or adolescent or young adult is at once apparent. As I have already remarked, evidence is abundant from careful studies of adolescents and young adults, as well as of schoolchildren of different ages from nursery school up, that those who are most stable emotionally and making the most of their opportunities are those who have parents who, while always encouraging their children's autonomy, are nonetheless available and responsive when called upon. Unfortunately, of course, the reverse is also true.[4]

No parent will be able to provide a secure base for his growing child unless he has an intuitive understanding and respect for what I call the child's attachment behavior, and treats it as the intrinsic and valuable part of human nature I believe it to be. This is where the traditional term "dependence" has had so baleful an influence. Dependency always carries with it an adverse valuation and tends to be regarded as a characteristic only of the early years and one which ought soon

---

3. Recent studies of relevance are those of Lamb (1977), Parke (1979), Clarke-Stewart (1978), and Mackey (1979).

4. A review of these studies is contained in Bowlby (1973, Chapter 21).

to be grown out of. As a result, when attachment behavior is manifested in later years, it is not only regarded as regrettable but is often dubbed regressive. The ill-effects of this attitude on the way a parent treats his children needs no elaboration.

In discussing parenting I have focused on the parents' role of providing a child with a secure base because, although well recognized intuitively, it has hitherto, I believe, been inadequately conceptualized. But there are, of course, many other roles a parent has to play. One concerns the part a parent plays in influencing his child's behavior in one direction or another and the range of techniques the parent uses to do so. Although some of these techniques are necessarily restrictive and certain others have a disciplinary intent, many of them are of an encouraging sort. Examples are calling a child's attention to a toy or some other feature of the environment, or giving him tips on how to solve a problem he cannot quite manage on his own. Plainly the repertoire of techniques used varies enormously from parent to parent—from largely helpful and encouraging to largely restrictive and punitive. An interesting start in exploring the range of techniques used by the parents of toddlers in Scotland has been made by Schaffer and Crook (1979).

PERI- AND POSTNATAL CONDITIONS THAT HELP OR HINDER

So far in this chapter my aim has been to describe some of the ways in which the parents of children who thrive socially and emotionally are observed to behave toward them. Fortunately, much of this behavior comes naturally to many mothers and fathers who find the resulting interchanges with their children enjoyable and rewarding. Yet it is evident that even when social and economic conditions are favorable these mutually satisfying relationships do not develop in every family. Let us consider, therefore, what we know of the psychological conditions that foster their doing so and those that impede them.

At several points I have referred to the ordinary sensitive mother who is attuned to her child's actions and signals, who responds to them more or less appropriately, and who is able then to monitor the effects her behavior has on her child and to modify it accordingly. The same description, no doubt, would apply to the ordinary sensitive father. Now it is clear that, in order for a parent to behave in these ways, adequate time and a relaxed atmosphere are necessary. This is where a parent, especially mother who usually bears the brunt of parenting during the early months or years, needs all the help she can get—not in looking after her baby, which is her job, but in all her household chores.

A friend of mine, a social anthropologist, observed that in the South Sea island in which she was working it was the custom for a mother-to-be, both during and after the baby was born, to be attended by a couple of female relatives who cared for her throughout the first month, leaving her free to care for her baby. So impressed was my friend by these humane arrangements that when her own baby was born on the island she accepted suggestions that she be cared for in this VIP way, and she had no cause to regret it. In addition to practical help, a congenial female companion is likely to provide the new mother with emotional support or, in my terminology, to provide for her the kind of secure base we all need in conditions of stress and without which it is difficult to relax. In almost all societies an arrangement of this sort is the rule. Indeed in all but one of 150 cultures studied by anthropologists a family member or friend, usually a woman, remains with a mother throughout labor and delivery (Raphael, 1966, quoted by Sosa, Kennell, Klaus, Urrutia, & Robertson, 1980).

Turning to our own society, preliminary findings that, if confirmed, are of the greatest interest and practical importance have recently been reported by the Klaus and Kennell team from a study conducted in a hospital maternity unit in Guatamala (Sosa *et al.*, 1980). One group of women went through labor and delivery according to the routine practice of the unit which meant in effect that the woman was left alone for most of the time. The other group received constant friendly support from an untrained lay woman from the time of an individual's admission until delivery, one woman during the day and another at night. In the supported group, labor was less than half as long as in the other, 8.7 hours against 19.3.[5] Moreover, the mother was awake for a greater part of the first hour of the infant's life during which she was much more likely to be seen stroking her baby, smiling and talking to him.

Effects of a similar kind on the way a mother treats her baby as a result of her having had additional contact with him soon after birth are now well known. Among differences observed by Klaus and Kennell when the babies were 1 month old was that a mother given extra contact was more likely to comfort her baby during stressful clinic visits and during feeding, was more likely to fondle the baby and engage him in eye-to-eye contact. Differences of a comparable kind were observed when the babies were 12 months old and again at 2 years. In these studies the increased contact amounted to no more than an extra hour within the first three hours after birth, with a further 5 hours of contact each afternoon during the next 3 days (Kennell, Jerrauld, Wolfe, Chesler, Kreger, McAlpine, Steffa, & Klaus, 1974; Ringler, Kennell, Jarvella, Navajosky, & Klaus, 1975).

Confidence in the validity of these findings is enhanced by comparable findings by a Swedish team; although in that study, by De Chateau and Wiberg (1977), the extra contact was extremely brief, no more than 10–15 minutes. Almost immediately after birth and before the afterbirth had been delivered the baby was placed on the mother's abdomen and she was encouraged to suckle it. When the babies were 3 months old not only did the mothers given extra contact look at them full face and also kiss them almost four times more frequently

---

5. In a comparable study conducted independently by Goodman (1977) in California a reduction in length of labor for mothers given continuous personal care is also reported, as well as a reduction in the use of analgesics and anesthetics.

than did the control mothers, but the babies themselves were much less likely to cry and, conversely, were more likely to smile or laugh.[6]

Yet another recent study of the part these kinds of peri- and postnatal experiences play in either assisting a mother to develop a loving and sensitive relationship to her baby or impeding it is reported by Peterson and Mehl (1978). In a longitudinal study of 46 women and their husbands, interviewed and observed during pregnancy, labor, and on four occasions during the infants first 6 months, the most significant variable predicting differences in maternal bonding was the length of time a mother had been separated from her baby during the hours and days after his birth. Other variables that played a significant but lesser part were the birth experience and the attitudes and expectations expressed by the mother during her pregnancy.

INFLUENCE OF PARENTS' CHILDHOOD EXPERIENCES

There is, of course, much clinical evidence that a mother's feelings for and behavior toward her baby are deeply influenced also by her previous personal experiences, particularly those she has had and may still be having with her own parents; and, though the evidence of this in regard to the father's attitudes is less plentiful, what we have points clearly to the same conclusion.

In this area the evidence from systematic studies of young children is impressive: It shows that the influence that parents have on the pattern of caring that their children develop starts very early. For example, Zahn-Waxler, Radke-Yarrow, and King (1979) have found not only that aiding and comforting others in distress is a pattern of behavior that commonly develops as early as a child's second year of life but that the form it takes is much influenced by how a mother treats her child. Children whose mothers respond sensitively to their signals and provide comforting bodily contact are those who respond most readily and appropriately to the distress of others.[7] Not infrequently, moreover, what a child does in such circumstances is a clear replica of what he has seen and/or experienced his mother do. The follow-up of a group of children showing these early differences would be of the greatest interest.

Another line of evidence regarding the influence of childhood experience on how a woman mothers her child comes from studies undertaken in London. For example, a study by Frommer and O'Shea (1973) shows that women who, during their pregnancy, give a history of having been separated from one or both parents before the age of 11 years are particularly likely to have marital and psychological difficulties after their baby's birth and also to have trouble with

6. Since more recent studies, for example, Svejda, Campos, and Emde (1980), have failed to replicate initial findings of the effects of early mother–infant contact, the issue remains in doubt.

7. The role of close physical contact with mother during human infancy has been studied particularly by Ainsworth who finds that children who develop a secure attachment to mother are those who, during early infancy, are held longest in a tender and loving way (Ainsworth et al., 1978).

their infants' feeding and sleeping. Another study, also in London, by Wolkind, Hall, and Pawlby (1977) extends this finding by showing that women with this type of childhood history interact significantly less with their 5-month-old first-born infants than do women who have had more settled childhoods. These observations, which were carried out by an ethologist, extended over a period long enough to record 50 minutes of the baby's waking life, exclusive of any time taken to feed him. This usually necessitated the observer staying for the whole morning. Not only did the mothers from a disrupted family of origin spend on average twice as long as the other mothers out of sight of their babies, but even when one of them was with her baby she was likely to spend less time holding him, less time looking at him, and less time talking to him. Moreover, when asked the question "It takes a bit of time to begin to see a baby as a person—do you feel this yet?," mothers from a disrupted family were much less likely to say they did (Hall, Pawlby, & Wolkind, 1979). To date these investigators have reported few findings about how the children develop, though at the age of 27 months the children of mothers from disrupted families are found to have significantly poorer language development than the other children. The point I wish to emphasize here, however, is that the study already provides firm evidence that women whose childhood has been disturbed tend to engage in less interaction with their infants than do mothers with happier childhoods—at a period in their baby's life when the amount of interaction that ensues is determined almost entirely by the mother.

Some of the clearest evidence regarding the enormous part played by childhood experience in determining in later years how a parent treats a child comes from studies of parents known to have abused their children physically (see review by Parke & Collmer, 1975). A common picture includes a childhood in which parental care was at best erratic and at worst absent altogether, in which criticism and blame were frequent and bitter, and in which parents or stepparents had behaved violently toward each other and sometimes, though not always, toward the children. A feature that emerges from a recent study of mothers known to have abused a child physically (DeLozier, 1982) is the high proportion who have lived in constant dread lest one or both parents desert, and therefore of being sent away to a foster home or institution, and who were also threatened frequently with violent beatings or worse. Not surprisingly these girls had grown up to be perpetually anxious lest husband or boyfriend desert, to regard physical violence as part of the natural order, and to expect little or nothing in the way of love or support from any quarter.

Not every woman with childhood experiences of these sorts batters her child, however; nor indeed does a woman who physically abuses one of her children necessarily abuse the others. What accounts for these differences? Evidence suggests that individuals who, because of earlier experiences, are markedly prone to develop unfavorable parental attitudes are more than usually sensitive to what happens to them during and after their babies are born. For these women adverse experiences during this time, it seems, can prove the last straw.

In a study done at Oxford, for example, Lynch (1975) compared the histories of 25 children who had been physically abused with those of their siblings who had escaped. Children who had been abused were significantly more likely than their siblings to have been the product of an abnormal pregnancy, labor, or delivery, to have been separated from mother for 48 hours or more soon after birth, and to have experienced separations of other kinds during their first 6 months of life. During the first year of these children's lives, moreover, the abused children were much more likely to have been ill than were the nonabused siblings; and the mothers also were more likely to have been ill during the abused child's first year than during the siblings' first year. Since in this study the personalities and childhood histories of the parents were the same for the abused siblings as for the nonabused, the fate of each seems to have turned in large part on the mother's experiences with the child during the peri- and early postnatal periods. The findings of a study by Cater and Easton (1980) point to the same conclusion.[8]

Of the many other disturbed patterns of parenting that can be traced, in part at least, to childhood experience there is one that happens also to be well documented in studies of abusing mothers (e.g., Morris & Gould, 1963; Steele & Pollock, 1968; Green, Gaines, & Sandgrun, 1974; DeLozier, 1982). This is their tendency to expect and demand care and attention from their own children, in other words to invert the relationship. During interview they regularly describe how as children they too had been made to feel responsible for looking after their parents instead of the parents caring for them.

Most, perhaps all, parents who expect their children to care for them have experienced very inadequate parenting themselves. Unfortunately, all too often they then create major psychological problems for their children. Elsewhere (Bowlby, 1973, 1980) I have argued that an inverted parent–child relationship of this kind lies behind a significant proportion of cases of school refusal (school phobia) and agoraphobia, and also probably of depression.

HOW WE CAN BEST HELP

In this contribution I have given principle attention to what we know about successful parenting and to some of the variables that make it easier or more difficult for young men and women to become sensitive caring parents. In consequence, I have been able to say only a little about the many and varied patterns of deficient and distorted parenting that we meet with clinically. Another large theme omitted is how we can best help young men and women become the successful parents I believe the great majority wish to be. In conclusion, therefore, let me state what I believe to be the first principles for such work,

---

8. In interpreting the findings of these two studies caution is necessary because in neither study is it certain that in every case the child's mother was the abusing parent.

which are that we seek always to teach by example, not precept, by discussion, not instruction. The more that we can give young people opportunities to meet with and observe *at first hand* how sensitive, caring parents treat their offspring the more likely are they to follow suit. To learn directly from such parents about the difficulties they meet with and the rewards they obtain, and to discuss with them both their mistakes and their successes, are worth, I believe, hundreds of instructional talks. For a program of this kind, which in some places might be an extension of the mother's self-help groups now beginning to flourish, we would need to enlist the active cooperation of sensitive caring parents. Fortunately, there are still plenty of them in our society and I believe many would be willing and proud to help.

REFERENCES

Ainsworth, M. D., Blehar, M. C., Waters, E., & Wall, S. *Patterns of attachment: Assessed in the strange situation and at home.* Hillsdale, N.J.: Erlbaum, 1978.

Arend, R., Gove, F. L., & Sroufe, L. A. Continuity of individual adaptation from infancy to kindergarten: A predictive study of ego-resiliency and curiosity in preschoolers. *Child Development*, 1979, *50*, 950–959.

Ballou, J. The significance of reconciliative themes in the psychology of pregnancy. *Bulletin of the Menninger Clinic*, 1978, *42*, 383–413.

Bowlby, J. *Attachment and loss* (Vol. 1: *Attachment*) (1969). London: Hogarth Press; New York: Basic Books; Harmondsworth: Penguin Books, 1971.

Bowlby, J. *Attachment and loss* (Vol. 2: *Separation: Anxiety and anger*) (1973). London: Hogarth Press; New York: Basic Books; Harmondsworth: Penguin Books, 1975.

Bowlby, J. *Attachment and loss* (Vol. 3: *Loss: Sadness and depression*). London: Hogarth Press; New York: Basic Books, 1980.

Brazelton, T. B., Koslowski, B., & Main, M. The origins of reciprocity in mother–infant interaction. In M. Lewis & L. A. Rosenblum (Eds.), *The effect of the infant on its caregiver.* New York: Wiley-Interscience, 1974.

Cater, J. I., & Easton, P.M. Separation and other stress in child abuse. *Lancet*, 1980, *1*, 972.

Clarke-Stewart, K. A. And daddy makes three: The father's impact on mother and young child. *Child Development*, 1978, *49*, 466–478.

Collis, G. M., & Schaffer, H. R. Synchronization of visual attention in mother–infant pairs. *Journal of Child Psychology and Psychiatry*, 1975, *16*, 315–320.

De Chateau, P., & Wiberg, B. Long-term effects on maternal and infant behaviour of extra contact during the first hour post-partum. I: First observations at 36 hours. II: Follow-up at three months. *Acta Paediatrica Scandinavica*, 1977, *66*, 137–151.

DeLozier, P. Attachment and child-abuse. In C. M. Parkes & J. Stevenson-Hinde (Eds.), *The place of attachment in human behaviour.* London: Tavistock Publications; New York: Basic Books, 1982.

Frommer, E. A., & O'Shea, G. Antenatal identification of women liable to have problems in managing their infants. *British Journal of Psychiatry*, 1973, *123*, 149–156.

Goodman, M. P. *The effects of on-call staff and family participation in labor and delivery.* Paper read at Fifth Annual Conference on Psychosomatic Obstetrics and Gynecology, Point Clear, Ala., January 1977.

Green, A. H., Gaines, R. W., & Sandgrun, A. Child abuse: Pathological syndrome of family interaction. *American Journal of Psychiatry*, 1974, *131*, 882–886.

Grinker, R. R. "Mentally healthy" young males (homoclites). *Archives of General Psychiatry,* 1962, *6,* 405–453.

Hall, F., Pawlby, S. J., & Wolkind, S. Early life experiences and later mothering behavior: A study of mothers and their 20-week old babies. In D. Shaffer & J. Dunn (Eds.), *The first year of life.* Chichester and New York: Wiley, 1979.

Kaye, H. Infant sucking behavior and its modification. In L. P. Lipsitt & C. C. Spiker (Eds.), *Advances in child development and behavior* (Vol. 3). New York: Academic Press, 1977.

Kennell, J. H., Jerrauld, R., Wolfe, H., Chesler, D., Kreger, N. C., McAlpine, W., Steffa, M., & Klaus, M. H. Maternal behavior one year after early and extended post-partum contact. *Developmental Medicine and Child Neurology,* 1974, *16,* 172–179.

Klaus, M. H., & Kennell, J. H. *Maternal–infant bonding.* St. Louis: C. V. Mosby, 1976.

Klaus, M. H., Trause, M. A., & Kennell, J. H. Does human maternal behaviour after delivery show a characteristic pattern? In *Parent–infant interaction: Ciba Foundation Symposium 33* (new series). Amsterdam: Elsevier, 1975.

Lamb, M. E. The development of mother–infant and father–infant attachment in the second year of life. *Developmental Psychology,* 1977, *13,* 637–648.

Lynch, M. Ill-health and child abuse. *Lancet,* 1975, *2,* 317–319.

Mackey, W. C. Parameters of the adult-male–child bond. *Ethology and Sociobiology,* 1979, *1,* 59–76.

Main, M., & Weston, D. R. The independence of infant–mother and infant–father attachment relationships: Security of attachment characterizes relationships, not infants. *Child Development,* 1981, *52,* 932–940.

Morris, M., & Gould, R. Role reversal: A necessary concept in dealing with the battered-child syndrome. *American Journal of Orthopsychiatry,* 1963, *33,* 298–299.

Offer, D. *The psychological world of the teenager: A study of normal adolescent boys.* New York: Basic Books, 1969.

Parke, R. D. Perspectives on father–infant interaction. In J. D. Osofsky (Ed.), *Handbook of infant development.* New York: Wiley, 1979.

Parke, R. D., & Collmer, C. W. Child abuse: An interdisciplinary analysis. In E. M. Hetherington (Ed.), *Review of child development research* (Vol. 5). Chicago: University of Chicago Press, 1975.

Peterson, G. H., & Mehl, L. E. Some determinants of maternal attachment. *American Journal of Psychiatry,* 1978, *135,* 1168–1173.

Raphael, D. *The lactation–suckling process within a matrix of supportive behavior.* Unpublished doctoral dissertation, Columbia University, 1966.

Ringler, N., Kennell, J. H., Jarvella, R., Navajosky, R. J., & Klaus, M. H. Mother to child speech at two years: The effects of increased postnatal contact. *Journal of Pediatrics,* 1975, *86,* 141–144.

Robson, K. M., & Kumar, R. Delayed onset of maternal affection after childbirth. *British Journal of Psychiatry,* 1980, *136,* 347–355.

Sander, L. W. The regulation of exchange in the infant–caregiver system and some aspects of the context–content relationships. In M. Lewis & L. Rosenblum (Eds.), *Interaction, conversation and the development of language.* New York and London: Wiley, 1977.

Schaffer, H. R. (Ed.). *Studies in mother–infant interaction.* London: Academic Press, 1977.

Schaffer, H. R. Acquiring the concept of the dialogue. In M. M. Bornstein & W. Kessen (Eds.), *Psychological development from infancy: Image to intention.* Hillsdale, N.J.: Erlbaum, 1979.

Schaffer, H. R., & Crook, C. K. The role of the mother in early social development. In H. McGurk (Ed.), *Issues in childhood social development.* London: Methuen, 1979.

Schaffer, H. R., Collis, G. M., & Parsons, G. Vocal interchange and visual regard in verbal and preverbal children. In H. R. Schaffer (Ed.), *Studies in mother–infant interaction.* London: Academic Press, 1977.

Sosa, R., Kennell, J., Klaus, M., Urrutia, J., & Robertson, S. The effect of a supportive companion on length of labor, mother–infant interaction and perinatal problems. *New England Journal of Medicine*, 1980, *303*, 597–600.

Svejda, M. J., Campos, J. J., & Emde, R. N. Mother–infant bonding: Failure to generalize. *Child Development*, 1980, *51*, 775–779.

Steele, B. F., & Pollock, C. B. A psychiatric study of parents who abuse infants and small children. In R. E. Helfer & C. M. Kempe (Eds.), *The battered child*. Chicago: University of Chicago Press, 1968.

Stern, D. N. *The first relationship: Infant and mother*. London: Fontana Open Books, 1977.

Wenner, N. K. Dependency patterns in pregnancy. In J. H. Masserman (Ed.), *Sexuality of women*. New York: Grune & Stratton, 1966.

Winnicott, D. W. Primary maternal preoccupation. In *Collected papers: Through paediatrics to psychoanalysis*. London: Tavistock Publications, 1957.

Wolkind, S., Hall, F., & Pawlby, S. Individual differences in mothering behavior: A combined epidemiological and observational approach. In P. J. Graham (Ed.), *Epidemiological approaches in child psychiatry*. New York: Academic Press, 1977.

Zahn-Waxler, C., Radke-Yarrow, M., & King, R. A. Child rearing and children's pro-social initiations towards victims of distress. *Child Development*, 1979, *50*, 319–330.

19

THE PSYCHOLOGICAL ORIGINS
OF PARENTHOOD

LEO SADOW

INTRODUCTION

To speak of the psychological origins of parenthood is to immediately introduce a number of problems. Parenthood refers both to the choice to become a parent as well as to the kind of parent one becomes. The word "origins" suggests that factors quite early in development are central to the question of parenthood. But attitudes toward becoming a parent, as well as the specifics of parenting behavior, have undergone such profound alterations through history as to suggest that influences other than those stemming from the earliest periods of development play a very important role.

Attitudes about parenthood and attitudes toward children have changed many times through history. One has only to recall the Biblical image of God staying the hand of Abraham as he was about to sacrifice his son Isaac to realize that at one time the ritual sacrifice of a child was not uncommon. Closer to our own time children have been perceived as property, chattels subject only to the father's disposition. I suspect that this attitude is still at least covertly prevalent in some families. However, we think of it now as pathological. Then there are those striking Hogarth drawings of drunken children reveling with their drunken parents in 18th-century England—a pathetic view of children as small adults without the particular characteristics and needs we associate with childhood. This, too, one suspects is a vision of childhood which even today more or less molds the attitudes of some parents toward their children.

The change in attitudes toward both becoming a parent and the specifics of parental behavior cannot be explained by traditional psychological theory about the origins of parenthood. Central to such an explanation is an understanding of the mechanisms by which prevailing social attitudes may become struc-

Leo Sadow. Faculty, The Institute for Psychoanalysis, and Department of Psychiatry, University of Illinois College of Medicine, Chicago, Illinois.

turalized components of individual psychological organization in adults as well as in children. It is my purpose in this chapter to discuss the psychological origins of parenthood in the earliest as well as the later phases of psychological development and to suggest some of the psychological mechanisms by which the various developmental factors come together to produce a behavioral outcome.

STAGES IN THE ONTOGENESIS OF PARENTHOOD

There is no perfect way to design a meaningful developmental series which will encompass all the relevant factors that relate to the eventual choice to become a parent. Such a design inevitably reflects the bias of the designer and his/her understanding of the kinds of data which are relevant. So it shall be with what follows. The design which I believe to be most useful in considering the psychological origins of parenthood is one in which three fairly distinct but often overlapping developmental epochs or stages can be described.

The influence of the earliest stage pervades all subsequent parenthood development. This stage is synonymous with the earliest period in the psychological life of the individual, the period of the neonate and early infant. One might describe this period as characterized by the laying down of a template or pattern for future behavior which is not at all conscious. This template is based on the memory of being bodily handled—fed, changed, bathed, cuddled, held, rocked—and the memory of the smells, sounds, and visual cues associated with these kinesthetic and sensorimotor sensations. The psychological apparatus at this very early period is highly sensitive to sensorimotor stimuli—more sensitive than it is at later stages of life when organized language permits ideational–verbal memories to be laid down. While one hesitates to refer to human development in ethological terms, the early period does appear to have characteristics somewhat analogous to those described by Lorenz as *imprinting*. I do not mean to suggest that human infants can be trained to relate to the foot of the mother as a duck to the foot of the investigator, but the memory of being handled does influence action quite automatically and spontaneously at the appropriate time. It is reasonable to assume that infancy constitutes a so-called "sensitive period"[1] during which such sensorimotor experiences are readily internalized.

The evidence that such sensorimotor memories are indeed laid down and are automatically and spontaneously recovered, albeit without conscious awareness, is fairly good. It has been widely observed that children play with dolls in a manner remarkably similar to the way they themselves were handled as infants. Such behavior could have no other reasonable explanation than that it follows from a template laid down in the mind of the child which is based on

---

1. "Sensitive period" is an expression of the probability of certain forms of learning at certain times (Hinde, 1963).

the manner in which that child was handled by its mother (caretaker). A more striking piece of evidence can be observed in the remarkable films of Monica, who, you will recall, had a congenital atresia of the esophagus, and was followed by Engel (1957) from her birth through infancy, childhood, and, most recently, through her own motherhood. The film of Monica feeding her own baby is the case in point. Monica is pictured giving the baby a bottle while holding him on her lap, his head at her knees, his feet at her abdomen. She had precisely duplicated the film of some 20 years earlier showing her being fed through a tube inserted into her stomach through her abdomen. She, too, is lying head away from her mother who stands at her feet looking at the feeding apparatus and beyond it toward Monica's face. When Monica is asked by the nurse and by her mother why she holds her baby in such an awkward manner, she can only respond with the rationalization that her baby prefers to be held in this way. Engel tells us that Monica had not seen the pictures of herself as a baby being fed through the stomach tube. It is reasonable to assume that a sensorimotor memory was laid down and that it has no conscious verbalizable component, although it has the power to affect behavior decades into the future.

This evidence informs us as to the behavior of the once-baby toward its own future baby in terms of certain readily observable motor patterns. I would like to suggest an extension of these ideas. It seems entirely reasonable that just as motor patterns of behavior are laid down, so are somewhat broader behavior patterns relating to the handling of an infant. How the infant was handled, in sensorimotor terms, is somehow transmuted into a vaguely equivalent attitude toward handling an infant. By this I mean that to handle a baby feels right, good, pleasurable, if one was affectionately handled in one's own infancy and vice versa. Being parented is the first psychological step toward parenthood.

If this first psychological step were the exclusive or even the preponderant influence on parenthood, everyone would choose to become a parent and would perform the parenting functions precisely as they were experienced at the beginning of life. As this is obviously not the case, we are led to the next step in the ontology of parenthood.

The second stage in the psychological origins of parenthood is one which is most closely associated with psychological development as we have classically conceived and theorized about it. Perhaps the best place to start is with the concept originated by Winnicott (1953) who called attention to a primary sort of creative experience which is characteristic of the infant who has had what he referred to as "good enough mothering." Such an infant experiences an illusion of control over the body of the mother in such a way that there is an overlap between what the mother supplies and what the infant might conceive of the mother as supplying. It is an experience which is neither entirely of the thing offered by the mother—let us substitute parent—nor entirely an illusion of the infant; rather, the infant combines the experience of what might be called objective reality with an illusion which arises out of its own needs and constructions, to create, in Winnicott's language, a transitional phenomenon. We might also refer to this phenomenon as a coalescence of an external stimulus with an internal ordering. Through this coalescence the infant gradually creates the experience of self and of mother. As this vital developmental task proceeds within the context of the mother–child dyad, the child is internalizing (or learning, if you prefer) a scheme of prospective parenting behavior. The mother or caretaking individual is, of course, practicing a scheme of behavior and performing a set of functions learned by her in her own early childhood when she was the younger member of a mother–child pair.

Related to Winnicott's concept of transitional phenomena is the classical psychoanalytic theory of identification. It implies that certain qualities of mind or of behavior which characterize an individual become part of another individual by a psychological process which has not been very adequately explained. The process of identification implies neither mimicry of nor attachment to another (object). An identification is a trait or quality of mind of an individual which does not depend on the presence of the person who was the source. The trait enters deeply into the core of personality or the self, and the self is thereby permanently altered. Parenting behavior must be influenced by a myriad of qualities and traits passed from parent generation to child generation. The identifications are not only with the details of parenthood but with the whole idea of being like the parent by becoming a parent. The decision to become a parent is influenced by the identifications with one's own parents, by the conflicts in which those identifications play a part, and by the conflicting goals created by identifications which appear to be in opposition to one another. An example of identifications in conflict with one another would be a woman whose identification with the mothering functions of her mother is strong, but who has also significantly identified with certain nonmothering work or professional aspirations of her mother or of her father. Both sets of identifications may remain active with neither achieving a clear preponderance and without a satisfactory resolution.

A particular form of identification, the ego ideal, is probably of greatest importance for understanding the genesis of parenthood. The ego ideal is that part of the superego system which has acquired its content from the ideals of the parents. It is through this structure that the ideal of parenthood, of being a parent, and the pleasure in the accomplishment of this goal operates. Developmentally, the identifications which we refer to collectively as the ego ideal are introduced toward the end of the Oedipal period. Thus, while the earlier identifications involve mainly functions, behaviors, of parenthood, the ego ideal involves rather more abstract and potentially verbalizable or symbolic qualities.

The Oedipal period in general is a significant aspect of the second stage. For those whose development includes a significant Oedipal component the psychological configuration of this period has a profound influence on their later parenting behavior. The intense bonds of affection and hatred, the feelings of envy, guilt, and passion in both the positive and negative Oedipus provide the basis for a wide range of attitudes about parenthood. These ideas are so well known that I shall not pursue them here.

Taken together, all the developmental stages so far described would yield parenting aspirations, values, and goals in each generation which would be essentially equivalent to those of the preceding generation. There would be certain modifications of the high value placed on becoming a parent, as, for example, when it is not possible to resolve conflicting identifications in the traditional direction. But these would be relatively rare exceptions, expections which society has probably always experienced. What must be explained is the unquestioned fact that things are changing. The statistics which indicate a sharp decline in birth rate constitute compelling evidence. Even if we assume that a turnaround is possible or likely at some time in the future, we must still explain the psychological mechanism by which so profound a change, whether temporary or permanent, is effected. The situation can be argued in this fashion: if the mind is more or less completely structured by the time the ego ideal types of identifications have been introduced, then only these few individuals who are pathologically conflicted or who have been profoundly traumatized earlier—at the level of the first stage or early second stage of the ontogenesis of parenthood—would fail to consider parenthood as a goal of very high value. For all but these few, the experience of being the children of parents would dictate the choice to become parents. As such a goal has rather rapidly come under question by a significant portion of Western society, the assumption that early structuralizing experiences are of overriding significance in personality formation must be questioned. And, furthermore, the way in which other later influences acquire leverage on our behavior must be understood.

To explore how these later influences operate psychologically as well as to describe our third stage in the ontogenesis of parenthood, a shift of stance is required. We have been examining this developmental sequence from the traditional vantage point in which the mind and the individual are a psychological unit: coexistent. This frame of reference is extremely useful; it has yielded therapeutic capabilities and theoretical constructs of great value. However, we may also conceive of mind, of the psychological unit, as extending beyond the physical boundaries of the individual. Anyone who has ever experienced the profound impact of the "mind" of a mob on the behavior of the individuals who together constitute the mob will have no doubt that mind may indeed penetrate beyond the physical being of the individual.

Of course our third stage is not based on the psychology of the mob, but there are enough significant similarities between the impact of a mob, and the impact of tradition, of fads, of social pressures of all sorts, to suggest that similar psychological issues are involved. The thrust here in our third stage is to the group—the ideological group, the social group, the religious group—which is conceptualized as an extension of self. The effect of these extensions of self are such that group attitudes may deeply influence individual behavior in some cases. In some individuals, the effect of such seemingly extrinsic factors may be even more profound than the influence exerted by intrinsic structure.

To examine in greater detail how social pressures and influences are transformed, so to speak, into what might be called extended psychological structure, let us return to Winnicott. He addressed the issue of the gradual evolution of psychic structure and of self by postulating a matrix of external stimuli and the creative imposition of a fantasy on those stimuli. The new, resulting structure is called a transitional phenomenon. Modell used this idea to explain, in an unfortunately unprovable manner, the creation of primitive cave-wall drawings. In these early works of art, or magic, the artist makes use of the detailed qualities of the cave wall, the small elevations and depressions in it, to impose his/her drawing on a surface which was probably sacred, or became sacred. The new thing which is created, the bison drawing, is then subjected to ritualistic and fantastic manipulation, manipulation which may not have been very different from the manipulation of the actual beast. The created thing is experienced as somewhat separate, according to Modell (1968), but it has been penetrated and organized by the prepatterned perceptual apparatus. A new reality, psychic reality, is thereby constructed which is neither totally idiosyncratic nor yet a fully independent percept or object. The object is therefore inevitably a creation of the perceiver, and as such, is an aspect of self.

This concept was further advanced by Kohut (1971) who coined the term selfobject to express the rather widely understood idea that developmentally the infant cannot continue to exist without its being provided certain vital mothering functions; and that in some individuals, certain of these functions fail to become part of the self. Such individuals, and it is not unlikely that such individuals are all of us to some degree, continue to behave as if they perpetually require the provision by another of various functions. The self is incomplete; it requires an object to provide the missing something. And the object is stimulated by the spontaneous unconscious behavior of the child to provide the needed functions. In the mind of the child and/or in the mind of the parent, a new mental structure which transcends the individual is established.

In both the earlier Winnicott–Modell construction and the more recent Kohut construction, the self has penetrated beyond the constraints of the individual as a unit or physical entity. The intensity of the continuing need for the structuring attributes of another differs from person to person; but it is unlikely that anyone exists who is entirely free from such need. Given the ubiquity of parental transferences, we have a theory to explain how the group or the social order continues to exert a structuralizing effect on the individual long after the important Oedipal structures are laid down. How does this affect parenthood?

An example: A person who is quite needful of the support of a small group of friends finds that the price of the support is the adherence to the group ideal with respect to the issue of parenthood. The specific parenting position of the group may be antithetical to the position which that individual might otherwise take, but the group is of such paramount importance that any conflicting personal stand is repressed or renounced and thus prevented from exercising a compelling influence on behavior.

In other words, as long as the need to derive some functions or structuralizing qualities from others is powerful enough, the possibility exists for certain qualities which are quite secondary or not directly related to the needed function to exert a powerful influence. In effect, a Faustian bargain is struck in which the individual accepts a set of certain secondary constraints in order to obtain another set of more primary functions which are needed to achieve the comfort and pleasure of completion of self. What is important about both the primary and the secondary qualities is that both become to some extent structuralized; that is, the personality is more or less permanently altered by these influences which are introduced at an advanced, adolescent or adult, age.

An important motive for parenthood in some individuals is to achieve a sense of self-completeness which would not otherwise be possible. In others the compelling factor in completing the self is the molding of a child. That is, the self is experienced as incomplete, and a child is experienced as another part of self, a selfobject in Kohut's terms, which makes possible a more cohesive or whole self. It is not at all certain that such a motive is necessarily pathological: it is entirely likely that the wish to become a parent regularly entails an urge for completeness of self. The question of pathogenicity depends on the assessment of the observer. For example, a parent whose desire for a child is for the purpose of providing the parent with a caretaker presupposes such a reversal of generational responsibilities that it must be pathological. A vivid example of such a reversal is depicted in a painting by the surrealist, René Magritte, which hangs in the Tate Gallery, London, entitled *Maternity*. It depicts a giant baby holding a small mother in its arms, a portrayal which must represent an aspect of the artist's sense of his own existence. It stands in marked contrast to a Raphael Madonna and Child which transmits a powerful sense of loving unity of self and object.

To sum up thus far: The psychological development of parenthood may be described in three stages. First, there is a very early preverbal, presymbolic period which verges on the biological and which influences all individuals simply because everyone has been a baby and has had the experience of being parented, primarily mothered, deeply embedded in his/her mind. Second, there is a more symbolic, early verbal period wherein a variety of parenting identifications occur and an ego ideal which embodies aspects of parenthood is internalized. Finally there are late structuralizations, in adolescence and adulthood, which depend on the continuing need for others for structural completion or self-cohesion, the selfobject as an aspect of structuralization.

OUTCOME

How does this developmental sequence determine the choice of whether to become a parent and subsequent parenting behavior? In this section I will discuss the outcome of this developmental sequence. As previously noted, if the course of development, especially of the first and second stages, were to follow in a simple and direct fashion, the outcome would be predictable: Children of parents would always grow up to become parents except in those relatively few instances where trauma was so severe as to obstruct the otherwise inevitable course of action. To explain why the predictable outcome does not in fact necessarily occur requires a brief digression into developmental theory.

The very phrase, line of development, as it was coined by Anna Freud (1965) suggests that something begins, runs a certain course of development, and results in some behavior which is a direct consequence of the course of development. Two characteristics are generally implied in the idea of a line of development: (1) The psychological events depicted follow one upon the other in an orderly sequence which is repeated each time a particular line of development is examined, the order being linear; and (2) the outcome can be predicted if the early steps in the developmental sequence are known. Recent work in observational studies of child development, as well as a close examination of analytic work with adults, suggests that the situation is probably a great deal more complex than our theories about lines of development suggest.

In outlining three stages in the development of parenting, I suggested implicitly that the stages followed one another in an orderly sequence. While this is probably a reasonable assumption for a large part of the developmental process, it is not completely accurate. A tiny baby is not influenced by a group, but once it is possible for the third stage to be operative, the influences of this stage may overlap or interact with the first two. That is, psychological structures laid down in infancy and childhood, or the biological substrate, do not cease at a certain time to exert a powerful influence in the life of the individual. They may be altered in the course of time, but they continue to operate. Their relative influence on the final outcome of behavior, on parenthood in this case, is simply diminished as other influences play an increasingly important role.

But there are even more significant complications that must be considered in understanding any given bit of behavior as an outcome of a series of developmental stages. An attempt to predict an outcome based on a consideration of early developments will frequently fail (Emde & Harmon, 1982). It is far easier to explain outcome, once it has come about, as due to a certain series of antecedent events. Freud knew this, and the predictive limitations of developmental theory have again become an important consideration in the thinking of developmental workers. The implications for our subject are profound. If we cannot predict the outcome in terms of parenthood of various psychological events with any significant degree of confidence, how shall we use the knowledge gained from a study of development? I shall attempt to deal with this question shortly. But at this point it is important to call attention to the probability that our post hoc explanations are based on constructions which are consistent with our theoretical stands and our personal, idiosyncratic, understanding (Gedo, 1979). We can make a good case for the cogent story which seems to explain the history of behavior, but without predictive capability we cannot achieve a high level of certainty that our history is a true rendering of the actual developmental events.

The fact is that we cannot predict because at certain points development appears rather suddenly to alter direction, obfuscating prediction. Perhaps, as we gain more experience with our newer view of development, we shall acquire the data base on which to make better predictions.

If the outcome of a line of development with regard to the decision to become a parent, or with regard to the kind of parent one will become, cannot be made with confidence, how can we think about outcome? In his description of the unconscious as a system, Freud has provided a model which may be useful. Freud said that the unconscious is timeless (1900). That is, events which are widely separated in historical time may be associated in the unconscious in a manner which vitiates the temporal disparity. In a like manner, events from various developmental epochs may be associated in a nonlinear or nonsequential fashion. Once a psychologically significant experience has occurred, it may attach to, or become associated with, other related experiences or in some other manner enter the structure of mind. But however it exists as a structure of mind, it is thereafter available and may be brought into play whenever called for, but without any necessary reference to some specific sequence in historical time. Thus, sudden, unanticipated, and unpredicted change of direction observed by child development researchers as they view development from a vantage point early in the sequence toward future time may be explained in the intrusion of psychological factors unknown to the observer who is mainly concerned with a particular seemingly known line of development. Certainly by the time adulthood is reached so many possibilities exist that the behavioral outcome in terms of the question of becoming a parent may easily be influenced by psychological structuring which is acquired quite late in development and which may reinforce certain earlier influences without being a consequence of those earlier influences. That is, the decision to behave in a particular manner may arise naturally out of a given line of development as modified by the particular psychologically significant events of that person's life. Once the person proceeds in the behavior determined by his/her past history and establishes a stable psychological configuration around this new behavior (e.g., a structuralizing attachment to a person, a group, or an ideology), the newly acquired psychological structure will be a center of emotional influence which may promote, or reinforce, seemingly unconnected qualities already available to that person. The qualities so influenced will not be the ones which led to the new structure in the first place. Perhaps a better way of putting it would be to say that each of us has a repertory of responses which is created by the richness of our individual experiences in interaction with our personal capacities to relate to these experiences, to remember them, to collate them with other experiences, etc. These possible responses are available, but more or less dormant until activated by a contemporary stimulus. In some, the range of available responses is very great, and in others very small. The latter individuals we would diagnose as compulsive.

Perhaps an example would help clarify the last point. In the interest of confidentiality, the vignette will be kept to the minimum level of description necessary to make the point.

A young woman whose central sexual preference was homosexual married a somewhat isolated man of considerable wealth because she feared loneliness and poverty. The fear of poverty stemmed from the emotional poverty of her early life when neither parent was loving or supportive. Father was especially destructive, using his children as targets for his rather cruel, sadistic, and overtly seductive behavior. The mother was emotionally helpful only when the father's alcoholic bouts threatened the children physically. The understandable fear of men, together with the hoped for and rarely achieved support from mother, turned the young woman toward lesbian activities in which she was taken care of by her partners and, at times, took care of them. At a particular time when a partner let the young woman down, she turned to the somewhat feminine, isolated man who was selected because as a husband he would care for her without making too many demands. He did, however, require children of her. She reluctantly agreed, and so, into this loveless marriage of convenience, a number of children were born. You might expect that children in such a family would stand very little chance of developing normally. One of the children was regarded by this woman as a kind of ideal version of herself as a child and, fortunately, was treated with enough love and understanding to develop reasonably well. At the same time this woman's own development was enhanced as her depression lifted and her functioning improved.

The young woman in this example certainly had no wish to become a parent and became one only to avoid losing the support, emotional and financial (the financial being symbollic food of sorts) that her husband offered. As her real sexual interests could not be satisfied within the marriage, she continued to have occasional homosexual relationships. But once a child was born, she found herself reorganizing in such a manner as to become an interested, involved, and reasonably effective mother. Benedek (1959) has spoken of "parenthood as a developmental phase," a phase in which the parent has a new opportunity to rework, so to speak, aspects of his/her own development through his/her relationship to his/her child. In this vignette the unexpected turn to better-than-expected parenting behavior, as well as the unexpected progress in the woman's own development, represents a shift in behavior due to powerful psychological influences whose source lay in areas quite different from those out of which her severe sexual and character pathology arose.

It would be comforting, in a way, if we could say that parenthood, like other behavior, is derived from an easily traced line of development. But, as I have tried to demonstrate, this would not accord with the facts. Instead, parenthood or a decision against parenthood, as well as the specifics of parenting behavior, come about as a consequence of a complex dynamic flux. The details must be carefully teased out of a maze of intersecting, sometimes casually related, sometimes not casually related, developmental factors. These also interact with factors which are not ordinarily considered developmental because they occur so late in life, in adulthood. But we are now beginning to see these later influences as having structuralizing capacities much like the psychologically significant factors of early life.

PATHOLOGY OF PARENTHOOD

This is a huge topic about which I will make only a few remarks. To speak of a pathology of parenthood seems to imply that to become a good parent is a normal goal of an adult. Indeed, until just yesterday in historical time, this was the case. But just as our ontology of parenthood revealed new and complicated ways of thinking about the psychological origins of parenthood, so, too, does it complicate notions of a pathology of parenthood. Is it pathological not to become a parent? Let us assume an individual who has been reared in a manner analogous to Harlow's monkeys (Harlow & Seay, 1965). In that experiment a group of monkeys were removed from their mother and provided with a terrycloth covered wire frame from which issued certain good things associated with mother. These monkeys developed normally—or at least appeared to—except they would not mate and rejected babies placed with them. Aside from proving that one should not fool with mother nature, Harlow's experiment demonstrates that, at least with higher primates, a high level of trauma at the first stage is beyond repair. It is not difficult to conceive of equivalently traumatic circumstances which would produce a similar consequence in humans. An example would be a mother or mothering person or caretaker whose fear of injuring her infant is so great that she behaves in a wooden, clumsy, awkward, unspontaneous manner. In effect she is little different from a terry-cloth covered wire mother. In this event, then, a trauma of sufficient strength may interfere with parenthood in a manner that prohibits choice entirely because of its terribly constricting effects upon the personality. This we would call pathologic.

Earlier I cited an example of conflicting identifications. Let us simplify this example and say that a person identifies with the parenting functions of his/her own parents in a positive and loving manner. But this person also identifies with powerful vocational ideals which prohibit parenting, a priest or nun, for example. Here we might say that if the conflicting identifications are resolved with adequate sublimations—the priest becomes truly a "father" to his parishioners—there is a high probability that this person may be described as not psychologically ill. But if the choice against parenting results in continuing conflict and psychic pain, it is pathologic. Similarly, if a woman maintains a state of ambivalence about becoming a mother until she is no longer able to biologically become a mother, she may be said to have a disturbance about parenthood. It is not, then, the fact that one fails to become a parent that is pathological. It is the presence of an active torment about the issue or the fact that a choice is impossible because of the severity of the underlying trauma, or because the capacity to assess the reality of one's own biological state is defective.

On the other side of the coin, there are, of course, individuals whose parenting functions are disturbed. The fairly frequent kind of pathology exemplified by Magritte's weird painting is a case in point. There are many parents who expect their children to be their pals, to be calmed by them when the parent is anxious or excited; to control parental behavior in many possible ways; in short to be parent to the parent. There are others whose main interest is in the procreative aspect of parenting, in becoming a parent, but who have no interest in the myriad functions involved in being a parent. Still others use their children as outlets for their sadism, their frustrated sexual longings, as objects on whom to project their guilt. The list is, regretably, exceedingly long. All of these may justly be called pathologic because it is another person who is made an innocent victim.

SUMMARY

In sum, I have presented an ontology of parenthood in three developmental stages. The manner by which late structuralizations which may influence parenthood are introduced into the personality was discussed. The outcome in terms of becoming a parent and the kind of parent one will become was described as a function of the dynamic flux involving elements of all three stages. The idea that parenthood and parenting behavior can be traced as a sequential line of development was challenged.

REFERENCES

Benedek, T. Parenthood as a developmental phase: A contribution to the libido theory. *Journal of the American Psychoanalytic Association*, 1959, *7*, 389–417.

Emde, R. N., & Harmon, R. J. (Eds.). *The development of attachment and affiliative systems.* New York: Plenum Press, 1982.

Engel, G. L. Monica, an infant with gastric fistula and depression: An interim report on her development to the age four years. *Psychiatric Research Reports*, 1957, *8*, 12–27.

Freud, A. *Normality and pathology in childhood: Assessments of development.* New York: International Universities Press, 1965.

Freud, S. The interpretation of dreams (1900). *Standard Edition, 5*, 577. London: Hogarth Press, 1953.

Gedo, J. E. *Beyond interpretation.* New York: International Universities Press, 1979.

Harlow, H. F., & Seay, W. Maternal separation in the rhesus monkey. *Journal of Nervous and Mental Disorders*, 1965, *140*, 434–441.

Hinde, R. A. The nature of imprinting. In B. M. Foss (Ed.), *Determinants of infant behavior* (Vol. 2). London: Methuen, 1963.

Kohut, H. *The analysis of the self: A systematic approach to the psychoanalytic treatment of narcissistic personality disorders.* New York: International Universities Press, 1971.

Modell, A. H. *Object love and reality: An introduction to a psychoanalytic theory of object relations.* New York: International Universities Press, 1968.

Winnicott, D. W. Transitional objects and transitional phenomena: A study of the first not-me possession. *International Journal of Psychoanalysis*, 1953, *34*, 89–97.

20

PARENTHOOD AND
THE TRANSFORMATIONS OF NARCISSISM

MIRIAM ELSON

Parental love, according to Freud (1914, p. 91), "so touching and at bottom so childish, is nothing but parental narcissism born again, and, transformed though it be into object love, it reveals its former character infallibly."

Kohut has elucidated newer views of narcissism as a line of development separate from that of object love, rather than as a continuum, and thus enables us to understand the forms and transformations of narcissism in parenthood (Kohut, 1971, p. 6). He describes the evolution of narcissism from its most primitive form to its most mature, adaptive, and culturally valuable forms in empathy, creativity, wisdom, humor, and an acceptance of human transience. These transformations of narcissism are basic to parenthood and in this massive task the child assists the parent.

The newborn is an assertive, seeking, responsive being capable of cueing parents to needs and wishes by an array of signals and signs with which the newborn is endowed (Basch, 1976; Tolpin, 1971, 1980; Tolpin & Kohut, 1980). The older view of human development based on the taming of drives, each of which must be neutralized and sublimated as they achieve ascendancy; the older view of the human infant as a bundle of such drives which must come under the civilizing influence of caretakers, does not do justice to our current knowledge of neonates, the course of childhood, and the instructive role played by the infant for parents. In a process of mutual engagement, and in tune with the infant's capacity to accept mild frustration, parents perform a mirroring, confirming, guiding function, and they are the target of idealization.

Through this process of myriad interactions, the child transmutes the caretaking functions of selfobjects into a self and its functions. Tolpin (1971) has used the Goldilocks tale (not too much, not too little, but just right) to illustrate

Miriam Elson. Faculty, Teacher Education Program, The Institute for Psychoanalysis, School of Social Service Administration, University of Chicago, and Chicago Child Care Society, Chicago, Illinois.

the progressively optimal disillusionment through which parents as prestructural selfobjects facilitate the laying down of psychic structure. Through transmuting internalization, the selfobjects and their functions become uniquely the self-functions, continuous in time and space.

In this mutual interaction, the maturational thrust of narcissism within each parent quickens, deepens, and expands to include empathic responsiveness to the child's needs. As the child matures, the responsive mirroring, echoing, confirming, guiding function of parents as selfobjects is uniquely transmuted by the child into psychic structure, but it is a two-way process in which parental psychic structure also undergoes transformation. The child's unique response to their nurturant care, and their own experience of each other as parenting figures, instructs them and sets in motion maturing forms of narcissism. Applying the theory of self psychology to parenthood permits an enlarged understanding of this process.

In commenting on her original (1959) paper, "Parenthood as a Developmental Phase," Benedek (1975, p. 163), in an Annual Meeting of the American Psychoanalytic Association on the same subject more than 15 years later, used the term "developmental process" as more descriptive of parenthood. Parens, in his concluding comments at the same session, pointed out that "although the psychosexual line of development [made] a large contribution toward [an understanding] of total personality development, it [was] fruitful to distinguish the psychosexual development line from that of total personality development and specifically from the line of development pertaining to the *concept of the self*" (1975, p. 164, emphasis added).

Thus Benedek's (1959) original comment that parents repeat with each child in a different way steps in their own development and, in fortuitous circumstances, achieve further resolution of conflict, imbedded as it is in drive psychology, does not allow the broader experience of parenthood to be adequately understood. In her original paper and in her comments, she clearly foreshadowed the need of a psychology of the self to illuminate the experience of parenthood. Viewed from the psychology of the self, as each of the drives achieves ascendancy, the responsive mirroring, echoing, confirming, guiding function of parents as selfobjects is transmuted into psychic structure. When serious deficits within the parents do not permit adequate support to the forming self of the child, a particular drive, or certain aspects of a given drive, coalesce in any of the emotional and behavioral problems of childhood. The child cannot modulate typical stresses, fragments readily, lacks a sense of vigor and harmony (Kohut & Wolf, 1978). The energy of the drive remains outside and does not contribute to a cohesive, vigorous nuclear self.

Thus self psychology permits us to understand that parents may indeed experience with each child a reactivation of deficits or distortion in any phase of their development, but maturer forms of narcissism—as increased empathy with childhood needs, increased wisdom and creativity, and specifically the *ability to respond to the child as a center of perception and initiative*—now permit the parents to perform their caretaking functions without unempathic intrusion of their own conflicts. The parental self may be sorely taxed by intrapsychic or interpersonal events, but it is as parents offer themselves as precursors of psychic structure that the forming self of the child is supported and that parents may be able to fill in their own earlier deficits or distortions or manage more effectively with what they now learn about themselves.

The self has been defined operationally by Basch (in press) as the "uniqueness that separates the experiences of one person from those of all others while conferring a sense of cohesion and continuity on the disparate experiences of that individual throughout his life. The self is the symbolic transformation of experience into an overall goal-oriented construct."

Kohut views this self as bipolar. The child who is joyously received and mirrored lays down the rudiments of ambitions in one pole which is imbued with grandiosity and perfection. Permitted to merge with the idealized perfection and power of those who minister to emerging needs, the child acquires the rudiments of ideals and goals in a second pole. It is the relationship between these poles, the strength and harmony of their interaction, and the skills and talents which are elaborated through nature and nurture which define the cohesive nuclear self, continuous in time and space (Kohut & Wolf, 1978). Parents who are able to function in empathic merger with the forming self of the child, allow the use of their psychic organization as the child's own, and, at the same time, phase specifically in tune with the child's changing needs, accept the child's separateness, a center of perception and initiative. Thus, support of the forming and firming narcissism in the child is the developmental *task* of parenthood. The continuing transformation of their own narcissism is the developmental *process* of parenthood. Understood in this way, the forming and firming narcissism within the child and the further transformation of narcissism in the parents is essentially a twin process and may be best described as a double helix.

Unlike Freud (1914), Behrens (1954), and Benedek (1959), who viewed the attitude of fond parents toward their children as a revival and reproduction of their own long since abandoned narcissism, Kohut would view it as a reactivation through empathy of that grandiosity which fuels our ambitions, permitting a further transformation of narcissism. The capacity to fantasize for their child a limitless potential while performing a mirroring, affirming, and controlling function is the very hallmark of mature narcissism, of responsible parenthood.

As the tasks of parenthood grow ever more complex and demanding with each transitional phase through which the narcissism of the child finds expression in thought and behavior, permitting a further deepening and elaboration of self-esteem and ideals, the incentive for further transformation of parental narcissism intensifies.

It is not that parents, recognizing the experiences of their own childhood, seek to undo such experiences in their relationship with their children (Freud,

1914).[1] Such an approach would in effect intrude the parents' needs rather than serve to provide a response to the child's needs. It is that the parents now are empathically in tune with childhood needs. When they are specifically in tune with the child as a center of perception and initiative, parents can exercise the guiding and confirming relationship such needs dictate. In the process, there is implicit some humorous sadness in relinquishing a goal anticipated for one's child, some increase in wisdom in recognizing and supporting the direction of the child's goals, some acceptance tinged with sadness of one's own transience in relinquishing the position of centrality in the child's life. At work here is a simultaneous process in child and parents, a double helix of the formation, firming, deepening, and elaborating of narcissism in the child and the further transformation of narcissism in parents.

As would-be parents contemplate their unborn child, they experience a heightening of narcissism. The qualities one loves most about one's mate and oneself are externalized and reinternalized in fantasies about the unborn child. Those aspects one likes less, or thoroughly dislikes, are also scrutinized, and, when they cannot be overcome, accepted with resignation, at times with humor, and, at others, with a defiant this-is-how-I-am relish of one's own complexity. Even before conception, the thought of producing a child furnishes the impetus for the further transformation of parental narcissism, and, at the same time, exposes it to traumatic injury.

As they grow to adult years, would-be parents have had realtionships with brothers and sisters, nieces and nephews, children of friends, neighbors, and colleagues. The widening array of selfobjects have provided innumerable opportunities for preparenting practice, for deepening and broadening that capacity for empathy acquired in the earliest selfobject experience in having oneself been joyously received and parented (Anthony & Benedek, 1970; Benedek, 1959; Kohut, 1977; Wolf, 1980). Although broad experience may lend reassurance to couples who face parenthood, it is not necessarily the vital factor in their preparation. This lies, rather, in the capacity of each partner to increase modes of meeting the needs of the other.

The mother's health and vigor during pregnancy serves as a further confirmation of her power and beauty, but, at other times, bodily changes in the quickening tempo of gestation may also exert a draining ebb of energy and confidence. Like puberty or menopause, pregnancy is a profound maturational crisis which may lead to the revival and emergence of unsettled tasks from earlier phases of development (Bibring, 1959, 1961). Self psychology would view this not as faulty compromise of drive conflict but as an indication of specific earlier

---

1. There is more than a subtle difference between such a view of narcissism and that of Freud for whom the child is to fulfill "those dreams and wishes of parents which they never carried out" (1914, p. 91). Kohut does not view the parental longing for immortality as "the weakest point in the narcissistic position from which the ego flees—relentlessly pursued by reality—achieving security only in the child." Rather he views the acceptance of parental transience as a mature form of narcissism which the parent must achieve.

deficits arising from empathic failures of the parental selfobject milieu. A prospective mother may experience in the present a reactivation of specific vicissitudes of the self and an accompanying failure of confidence in her ability to nurture. Bibring's (1961) studies demonstrated that we could better understand the readiness with which equilibrium could be established by relatively brief supportive intervention if we recognized the disequilibrium typical of pregnancy as a maturational crisis. Self psychology would now understand this as the prospective mother's ability to transmute selfobject functions into self functions and to regulate self esteem. Preparing for motherhood, and with the anticipatory father as selfobject joined in preparing for their nurturant tasks, maturer forms of narcissism (enhanced empathy and an accretion of wisdom) may now emerge.

The father responds to his own part in the creation of another life and the changes in his wife's body often with a sense of heightened grandiosity, and, at other times, with some chagrin as he feels himself displaced from the center of her interest now to be shared with an unknown other. This is a task which faces the mother as well. Just as the wife's narcissism expands to include the developing fetus, the father's expands to include empathic protectiveness of her and of the expected child.

He, too, now experiences reactivation of the period of his forming self and his own vicissitudes in being parented as he now prepares for the extensive changes. Shortcomings in responsive empathy, each for the other, at times unavoidable, if not too great, permit further transmuting of selfobject functions of soothing and self-esteem regulation but now specifically in relation to prospective parenting. The shared experience of birth, common today, prepares both parents for special tasks. When inner vision and reality meet in the actual birth of the child, this mewling, stirring, small bundle, red-faced from its labors, inspires awe and wonder in the parents who already imbue it with limitless powers.

When Emerson (1885) wrote that "infancy conforms to nobody; all conform to it; so that one babe commonly makes four or five out of the adults who prattle and play to it" he was unaware of this behavior as a basic function of parenthood. Prattling and playing to it, mirroring, shaping, and giving affect to its sounds with playful intonations, stilling its cries, all these are the tasks of parenthood. And the experience of holding and comforting, changing, bathing, and feeding, affirms and expands a parent's sense of power and goodness.

This is not to suggest that there are no intense periods of doubt and anxiety as parenting skills are taxed through all the unavoidable vicissitudes of living. Minor breaks in empathy are a natural part of the process of parenting and are indeed essential in helping the child lay down the psychic structure of anxiety regulation. Healthy self esteem and ideals are acquired through, and are a history of, innumerable, infinitesimal incidents of optimal frustration, optimal disillusionment on *both sides* (Freud, 1914; Kohut, 1977; Tolpin, 1971). But young or new parents may be particularly upset by empathic failure in relation to each other's parenting tasks and to each other's needs. Parental narcissism matures in the forging experience of expanding and deepening tolerance of differences and the ability to reconcile these where reconciliation and resolution are crucial.

Through each developmental phase, child and parents inform each other. The factors impinging upon the parent–child relationship are reciprocal and complex. They are not just unidirectional. The child influences the parent to nearly the same extent that the parent influences the child (Cohler, 1980). This is the unique significance of the simultaneous ongoing process of the self experience in parents and children.

It is through such innumerable, infinitesimal transmuting internalizations that the child lays down the structure of a cohesive nuclear self. And it is in the further transmuting of earlier experiences of growth and development, understood now in the expanded cognition of previous life events, that the narcissism of the parent is further transformed. These processes in parent and child quicken and intensify at each significant developmental phase with its special demands on parent and on child.

But what of the experience when the birth of the child is flawed or when the couple is unable to conceive? The child born with congenital defects constitutes a profound narcissistic trauma and parents react to such children with a vast loss of self esteem. They face a period of sorrow and grief, not only initially, but with each developmental milestone in which once again they must face and respond to the child's deficits or their own. And yet, it is a triumph of the human spirit that many parents can enfold the child in their empathic warmth, tempering their own expectations and providing the child with such self esteem building and growth enhancing experiences as they and others can devise. The further transformation of their own narcissism, in certain instances, may also include the goal of helping others, of teaching, of writing.

There is, as well, the special parenthood of those who, failing to procreate, adopt the children of others. The response of adoptive parents to this initial narcissistic trauma involves a process through which they must absorb the grief and sorrow which the failure of their bodies stimulates. If the problem lies in the wife's failure to conceive, her loss of self esteem and confidence may be met by an increase in empathic enfolding by her husband. If the failure occurs because of the husband's inability to produce living sperm, the loss of confidence on his part may be met by an increase in understanding and empathic in-tuneness by the wife. But these experiences merit far more detailed discussion and are not the subject of this chapter.

Throughout the course of family life, then, there are periods of vibrantly intense joy parents and children alike experience when each enhances a sense of radiance and power in the other. There are equally intense periods of anger and despair. There may be times when the explosive force unleashed by the narcissistic needs and demands of one or both parents may be thoroughly distorting and destructive, giving rise to severe breaks in empathy. Parental behavior may become excessively punitive and counterproductive to the child's growth and development or unrealistic in relation to the child's interests and abilities.

Anxiety, guilt, and depression hamper the necessary search for understanding and resolution of the impasse. Parents may fail each other in providing support at a time when their need of such support is greatest and when the child's need of their understanding is keenest. Pathological forms of narcissism may perpetuate merger and control long after the child signals need for and capacity to forge a course and to use others in the expanding world of selfobjects for this purpose.

Disturbances in parental narcissism may be only mildly traumatic and a signal to the parent of necessary work in achieving a more mature form of narcissism. At one end of this spectrum one can set the humorous self-awareness of a physicist who replied to a friend's question as to what he would like his young son to become by saying that it was really up to his son: he himself really did not care what *branch* of physics the child went into.

Probably more illustrative of the manner in which parental narcissism must be transformed, however, is the letter which the elder Strauss, a horn player steeped in the classical tradition, wrote to his son, Richard, when he heard the first performance of the tone poem *Macbeth*. "One can accomplish the highest things without experimenting by setting great and noble thoughts in simple clothing, without highly colored instrumentation, and then it will be understood by all people in all times. Every great artist has in every period and in all forms of art accomplished the most artistic things with the simplest means . . . I counsel you, *although heavy hearted because I know it is useless*, revise Macbeth still once more with the greatest care, and throw out the excessive instrumental padding; and give the *horns* more opportunity to stand out" (Del Mar, 1962, p. 62; emphasis added).

The poignant sense of sadness in the father as he struggled ("heavy hearted because I know it is useless") to regain that central position in his son's life that he had once had is typical of the necessary process of further transformation of parental narcissism.

History is strewn with the locked combat of parents and children in this arena when the immaturity and rigidity of the parents' narcissism exacts behavior from the child which will exactly mirror the parents' needs. Unable to be free of a noxious merger, the child cannot elaborate skills and talents which will permit the expression of ambitions in realizable goals which stem from centrally perceived initiative.

Such a struggle from which the child ultimately freed himself is implicit in the story Eugene Ormandy tells of his childhood. A talented violinist, he was forced to practice in an office adjacent to his father's dental office. Whenever he stopped, his father rushed in to beat him. When Ormandy finally gave up the violin and became a famous conductor, he invited his father to hear a violin concerto he was to conduct and to witness the ovation his conducting received. At the conclusion, his father shook his head and commented, "If only I had beat you more, you would have been playing the violin and he would have been conducting!"

These illustrations focus on the efforts of these sons to find, explore, and pursue goals in fields of endeavor of their own choosing. They reflect, also, variations of normal and pathological forms of narcissism in the struggle of these fathers (intransigently in the elder Ormandy, poignantly in the elder Strauss) to cling to their sons as extensions, as instruments of their own narcissism.

The long process of the child's dependency taxes the cohesiveness and vigor of the bipolar self of each parent in relation to the child and to each other. Each developmental phase, beginning with the earliest experience of receiving that child into an empathic parenting environment, through early infancy, preschool years, latency, adolescence, and young adulthood, makes specific demands which are critical to the maturing narcissism of each parent. To these specific demands each parent responds uniquely, with varying degrees of empathic resonance. It may be fruitful to consider in greater detail problems encountered in this process. I shall use two cases for this purpose.

A 35-year-old mathematician sought treatment because he found himself responding with increasingly ungovernable rage to the behavior of his 6-year-old son. He was aware that the degree of his rage was totally out of proportion to the minor infractions of the child. Even though he believed that the child deliberately provoked these episodes, what troubled him was his incapacity to deal with the child in a reasoning manner as had been for the most part the quality of his parenting in the past.

The most recent incident had occurred on their way to the bus. The child knew that they had to make a particular bus so that each would arrive at his school in time. Just as the bus approached their stop, the child climbed to the top of a very high snow pile and perched there triumphantly. The bus took off without them. When the child slid down, the father shook him so violently that the boy fell to the ground. The father felt both horror at his loss of control and at the expression on his son's face as the child's eyes filled with tears. He experienced his son's humiliation and his own as a double burden; he could not shake off an intensifying depression.

He and his wife were both employed, for the most part sharing responsibility for the care of their son and their home. His wife had only recently returned to work and her sense of strain in proving her effectiveness in her job meant that more of their shared tasks fell on his shoulders. He did not object to this but he did experience increasing irritation generally and explosive rage specifically with his son. In his classes and with his graduate students, his usual zest and pleasure in challenging questions was lacking. With his colleagues on campus he found himself responding sarcastically and occasionally viciously. His usual manner was that of wry humor. He was a lively member of departmental conferences in which his wit had often been successful in defusing tension among his colleagues. Although his own scholarly work was of a high caliber, the question of tenure was looming; he had considerable doubt that the outcome would be favorable in view of the stringent financial outlook for the department. Brooding about this, he was frequently sleepless but reluctant to share these anxieties with his wife.

He expected that in revealing these problems to me I would in effect tell him that the conditions he was contending with were typical of the academic world, that he was too self-pitying, and that he ought to straighten up and control himself. Comments of this kind studded his own narrative and he seemed to seek such reproach from me. When, instead, I let him know that I could understand his unhappiness and depression, he revealed that part of his ebbing confidence was related to his wife's increasing interest in her own work and the loss of her enthusiastic response to his activities. It was not that she was uninterested but that there was not the same degree of absorption he had experienced before. Financially his wife's income was an assist at this time, and he rather admired the plucky way in which she had gone about re-equipping herself for her work after a substantial interval away. But the harmonious interplay of their life together seemed to have vanished. He could see the years stretching ahead in monotonous drudgery, which served to intensify his depression.

Memories began to surface of an earlier time when his own father failed to be made head of his industrial unit. Previously his son's warm admirer and teacher, father seemed to withdraw. His mother had gone back to teaching, and he was left with the responsibility for the after-school care of his younger brother and sister. When he would complain, he was sharply scolded by both parents for his selfishness and lack of understanding of what the family was going through. Only haphazard efforts were made to permit him the free time for his peers and school events which help an adolescent define himself, shape his abilities, deepen and expand his self-esteem. In his academic work, nevertheless, he continued to excel.

Although his father did later find suitable employment, their relationship never returned to the same depth it had once had. With his mother, her absorption in her work and in the younger children contributed to his feeling that his own needs were insubstantial and intrusive. He was left with the sense that, in effect, he wanted more than his share, that he had demanded too much from his family in the past and now in the present.

In the course of our work together, his earlier needs for affirming and confirming his ambitions, the further expansion and deepening of idealized goals, were reactivated, revealing the deficit resulting from the abrupt unavailability of his parents, particularly father. Turning from father to mother, he was met by rebuffs and accusation that he certainly was not the son she thought she was raising. His sense of continuity interrupted, he struggled with the usual adolescent problems in a lonely manner, subject to depressions which he handled by more intense involvement in academic work.

Families go through reverses and children are able to respond with an increase in competence and self esteem when the personality of the parents provides the selfobject support which is in tune with phase specific needs. But in this case, severe demands were made on him to shape up to his responsibility with the explicit and repeated reprimand that his behavior was childish and selfish. The specific impact of his father's failure and his mother's need to use him as an auxiliary parent were not alone in contributing to his feelings of depletion. The personality of the parents, their way of dealing with reverses in their own expectations, exerted a strong force on their adolescent son, particularly their inability to respond to the expanding horizon and hopefulness of his adolescence when contrasted with their midlife acute disappointments and more limited goals.

He managed well in his professional training and met and married his wife while both were graduate students. He had always been aware of a certain amount of easily aroused irritation usually effectively handled by wit. Praise of colleagues would trigger such irritation along with self criticism: he was above the need for such praise; he was not a child.

My recognition and acceptance of this painful period of his youth, and more importantly, the legitimacy of his needs at that time, brought into the main stream of his psychic life those longings for admiration from the selfobjects of his past. Through an empathic merger with me as a new edition of selfobject and selfobject functions, he could reveal his hidden fantasies of being a rare discoverer of newer theories. Current reality, the question of tenure, and his wife's return to work had exposed the need for further transformation of his ambitions and goals.

The sense of a bleak future, deadness, dullness, and sarcasm in his relationships, and particularly his explosive rage with what he viewed as his son's deliberately provocative behavior, gave way. Through my understanding and confirmation, he could accept the fact that his feelings were not childish, that he was going through a particularly trying period in his professional and emotional life. Its uncertainties had aroused similar feelings of the bleakness of the landscape of his early adolescence when events were not under his control, with an accompanying sense of vulnerability and fragmentation. His wife's return to work was not of the same mold as his mother's. It had always been their plan that she would return to work when their son reached school age and was not linked to his failure.

His son's dawdling over breakfast, playing along the way, his many intrusions when his father was at work, he could now understand not as deliberate provocation but as the legitimate needs of a 6-year-old child, the necessary "work" of childhood. The deferred experiences of childhood and youth, not understood at the time of their occurrence but comprehended only later (Cohler, 1980) could now be transmuted and integrated into a further transformation of narcissism. This more mature form enabled him to enter his son's play and his aspirations with renewed energy and pleasure. Recognizing that his son, as any child, could at times be a "pain in the neck," his own more moderate response, more creatively in tune with the child's needs, enabled his son to transmute selfobject functions into self functions, such as delay, imaginative planning, which permitted further elaboration of the child's very real gifts and skills.

The question of job tenure remained ambiguous, but other options were also available. He and his wife began to share more effectively their individual and mutual anxieties in their work and their future. The memory of his son perched triumphantly at the top of a snow pile often recurred to this father and served as a metaphor for his ability to protect the child from excesses while encouraging the child's efforts to fulfill appropriate goals.

Although this particular case is far richer in detail than I have elaborated here, the double helix in the work of father and son in the further transformation of narcissism seemed to me particularly instructive. Thus the tendency to repeat with one's children the negative experiences of one's own childhood can be better understood as exposing a deficit. Selfobject functions have not been transmuted into self functions; they are missing functions. And at the point at which these deficits are reactivated, the individual responds with failures in empathy.

The following case describes the manner in which the failure to have reflected a meaningful image of oneself may result in the repetition of such failure with one's child.

A 28-year-old mother of an 18-month-old girl could not account for a depression which seemed to be deepening. She had returned to graduate studies only recently. As she found herself in competition with classmates who had not interrupted their studies and contemplated those who, less talented than she, were where she would have been, there was an element of bitterness underlying her competitiveness.

Her manner was somewhat cool, and, though she was attractive, the severity of her style served to distance people from her. Perhaps more notable was the absence of warmth and pleasure in her discussion of her child or of her studies. She emphasized that she and her husband had both wanted a child; moreover, she had always planned to return to school when the infant reached 18 months. She was content with the adequacy of her child-care arrangements during her absence—a neighbor whose own child was now a toddler had offered to baby-sit.

She had always been subject to blue moods and was nicknamed "the grouser" by her brother, some 3 years younger than she. When she thought of her situation objectively, particularly now, it seemed that she had everything to be happy about; her child was a healthy little girl, her husband was very successful in his work, and very supportive of her. Though she certainly could have been further along in her own career, she was fairly confident that she would not encounter more difficulty than consistent work would overcome. She could not understand why she was "not jumping for joy." When she struggled to define her discontent, somehow a sense of unfairness was at the core of it.

She viewed herself as having had a reasonably comfortable childhood and adolescence. As a businessman, her father provided well for the family. Her mother was a lively woman with a flair for fashion. She herself had been something of a tomboy and an athlete in adolescence, and her struggles with her mother centered around this. Her mother would buy her inappropriate clothing, fussier than she liked. When she chose her own clothing, her mother always objected to the severity of the style and would compare her appearance unfavorably with that of cousins or daughters of neighbors who were "into the dating game." Her school interests were in debating and student government; her mother would have preferred that she go into drama and music. Never a great mixer, nevertheless she had friends among both girls and boys who shared her interests.

Her brother was always fun-loving and jolly so that people responded to him instantly. He was a "charmer," she was not. At the same time he experienced difficulty in his studies and there were family storms about this. She could recall her spontaneous efforts to help him, her sense that he had a good head but took little initiative in seeking information on his own. She herself could not remember a time when she was not really interested in ideas. It had been a special bond in her relationship with her self-educated father. Nevertheless as she reached her teens, it was an issue between her and both parents. "Why are you always with your books?" her father would tease, and this would trigger a sense of shame and humiliation along with a sense of unfairness. If brother evidenced the least intellectual curiosity, there was a higher level of responsiveness than to her own pursuits. At school events when she would win an award, her mother, by her presence in the audience, would indicate recognition but no real sense of joy in her achievement.

In her second undergraduate year, her father died suddenly of a heart attack. Even now she could savor the sense of loss; he wouldn't see her graduate, he wouldn't give her away in marriage, and he had not realized his hope of having grandchildren. Although she grieved and mourned his loss, it did not seem to be a part of her low moods. They were preexistent. It was a family joke that when her parents had returned with her baby brother, she had hidden behind a door in her mother's room and was found sucking her thumb. It was a story often told with much amusement in which she sometimes joined, but more frequently she experienced an undercurrent of shame, humiliation, and bitterness.

When she graduated from college she was awarded a prestigous fellowship. It was still a source of resentment and chagrin that when she telephoned her mother to tell her of the fellowship for further study, her mother burst into tears saying, "Now you'll never marry." Even though she knew she should have been prepared for her mother's reaction ("What did I expect? That she would turn cartwheels?") she felt a profound sense of loss followed by headache and nausea. She guessed she had just kept on hoping that mother would really rejoice with her, give her a pat on the back as various teachers had done all along the way. During her early graduate years, she met and married her husband, deferring further study.

This material would lend itself to the theory of Oedipal conflict, of pre-Oedipal strivings, to the theory that as a small child this young women had responded to the birth of her baby brother with penis envy. Her tomboyishness, her objection to fussy clothing, to dating, her "overinvolvement" in her studies, would lend impetus to an examination of her experience as a flight from competition with mother and brother. Although these aspects of her difficulty have validity, it was not the early experience of being displaced by her brother which accounted for her lack of zest in her life. It was that the expanded narcissism of the mother failed to undergo further transformation which would have enabled her to enfold her daughter in empathic warmth and to perform the function of mirroring and confirming her attractiveness and competence. It was the failure of further transformation of narcissism which permitted this mother to make a family joke of her little daughter's lonely isolation in response to her own joy in the birth of her son and, as the child matured, the repetitious use of the family joke at times of similar vulnerability.

We know little of the brother, described as a charmer who had considerable academic difficulty, and a continuing struggle to find some meaningful vocation. According to the sister's view, his choice was often interfered with or demeaned by the mother, but the vicissitudes of his development and relationship with her were not within the focus of therapy. It would seem that this mother retained a merger state with her children because of her own deficits, because of her own untransformed narcissism. Her children were to grow and develop, but their ambitions, their ideals, and goals were to be hers beyond the normal shaping of a child's interests which parenthood assumes.

The later course of our work together confirmed the flawed selfobject support of both parents. Although it was father who, particularly in early years, delighted in his little daughter's brightness, he became increasingly involved in his business activities, ready to defer to mother's aspirations for their daughter which indeed were also his. And the mother's needs, perhaps intensified by the father's increasing absences, were to bind the children more closely to her; they were to confirm her needs and wishes; they were to be her ornaments.[2]

With this mother, empathy with the needs of her children was seriously flawed. Her own needs intruded. Thus, although the daughter was successful, joyousness in motherhood and in her studies was lacking. For this young woman, the process of our work together allowed the reactivation of her earlier needs which could now be responded to in the present. Her sense of unfairness and a certain bitter tone, an accumulated reaction to repeated rebuffs covering over her wish to be loved for her unique qualities, began to recede and dissipate as reliable self esteem increased. In turn, she could enjoy the way in which her small infant wakened in her a sense of power to comfort, to protect, to respond to her needs. She was observant of the child's unique qualities and experienced particular delight and wonder in sharing them with me. The coolness of her manner and the severity of her dress, evidence of repeated disappointments in her efforts to have a meaningful image of herself reflected, and the twin need

2. Such an attitude could not be confused with that of Cornelia, a Roman widow of the second century B.C. Although she replied, "My children are my jewels" to a wealthy patrician boasting of her ornaments, history attests to the fact that she educated her children well and inspired them with a sense of civic duty and a desire for glory. One might speculate that even as she performed the task of enabling her sons, Tiberius and Caius Gracchus, to transform their narcissism into reliable self-esteem and ideals, her own narcissism was further transformed so that she could increasingly relinquish the intensity of her supervision.

to wall herself off from the merger and mirroring demands of mother, became more tempered.

At one point she commented that she had carried her mother inside her all these years and it was just too crowded. "She has her ways and I have mine"—an indication that the silent process of transmuting internalization was now reengaged in building reliable self esteem in a more cohesively functioning self related to her own very real abilities. More consistently, her depressed, bitter moods came under her cognitive scrutiny and their intensity was mitigated. As she experienced my acceptance of her ambitions and her goals as appropriate and legitimate, she functioned more resiliently and imaginatively in both work and leisure. With an increase in self-esteem she was able more effectively and appropriately able to allow the needs of her child to be central. In so doing she provided the conditions under which the child's healthy self-esteem could develop. These two cases illustrate the process of transforming parental narcissism into maturer forms which then support the child's forming or maturing narcissism.

The process of deepening self-awareness is most taxing for parents of adolescents, for it is at this phase that the necessary adolescent thrust toward a widening array of selfobjects threatens the sense of continuity in both generations. Benedek (Anthony & Benedek, 1970, p. 307) has likened the vastly divergent developmental paths between the generations as similar to those traversed by immigrant families and their first-generation children. Anna Freud (1958, p. 276) emphasized that "there are few situations in life more difficult to cope with than an adolescent son or daughter during the attempt to liberate themselves."

In the face of a broad sweep and quickening tempo of change within society, and intimate exposure to that change, parents who have been accustomed to anticipating and adjusting to new behaviors in their children, experience an even greater challenge to their values and beliefs. Maturing parental narcissism increasingly demands that parents relinquish their central position to a widening array of selfobjects, beliefs, or standards different from their own, vocational goals not within their own expectations. But rather than maturing forms of narcissism, regression to more primitive forms may ensue.

Some parents in their middle years, with a sense of stalemate in their relationship with each other, may be tempted to, and some do, experiment radically with new choices, new partners, preempting for themselves developmental tasks which their children face (Elson, 1964). It is here that self psychology offers newer understanding of the struggle, arising as it does less out of drive and earlier compromise formation than out of fragmentation and loss of vigor within the nuclear self. Deficits in the manner in which the energy of the drives had been integrated within the nuclear self may now be exposed. More primitive forms of narcissism may emerge as parents now experience competitive challenge, a need to bind the child more closely to their own ambitions and goals, or to abandon the role of parenthood while seeking solution to their own difficulties.

It is at the point of their children's adolescence that parents have the greatest need for flexibility and tensile strength in reviewing and expanding those enduring values and goals which are basic to a sense of continuity of the self in space and time. The profound upheaval which parents experience in this transitional phase has been less noted. In the light of newer societal norms, they must now examine within themselves the validity and importance of values, beliefs, and behaviors intrinsic to their own cohesive functioning.

There can be a refreshing and vigorous increase in the stream of ideas between the generations. In a vital, phase-appropriate thrust toward new selfobjects—peers, cult heroes, ideologies (Wolf, 1980; Gedo & Terman, 1972) —adolescents confront cognitively and affectively as if for the first time those values, ideals, and goals which have been laid down as psychic structure. Some they will jettison, others they will modify, and still others they will include more firmly and enduringly now as *their* values, *their* ideals, *their* goals.

This is a period when the double helix of the self experience in parents and children may be most vulnerable to enmeshment and distortion. Threatened by these changes, parents may enviously compete for the beauty, power, and opportunity of their adolescent children. In other instances they may misunderstand rebellious attitudes or behavior which often cover regression and retreat. The battle is joined interpersonally rather than intrapsychically as adolescents struggle against engulfment by the parents of their earlier years and as parents cling more tenaciously to their former encompassing central position in the lives of their children. The selfobjects adolescents seek to overcome this fear at times seem to, and may in reality annihilate those values which are central to parental self-esteem and have seemed to be central to that of their preadolescent children. In other instances, fearing separation and self definition, adolescents may linger in a merger which does not permit that quickening opportunity for differentiation which is the necessary task of these years. Parents, lulled by this continuity and relieved of the continuing task of transforming narcissism, may postpone the tasks which lie ahead for themselves—such tasks as the further deepening of certain cherished beliefs and goals, or acceptance of their transience and the need to test out and include newer values. They must endure the sadness this entails and the internal struggle which signals that necessary maturer forms of narcissism are in the process of emerging. Parents then grow in wisdom, engaging in effective, nondestructive dialogue or action, when this is feasible, or turning to newer creative outlets for their energy. The leavening of humor may help them accept a less central position in the lives of their children. It is not infrequent that in this context there now emerges and deepens an empathic awareness of similar critical periods which their parents traversed.

Thus, with each critical period in the lives of their children, the process of maturing narcissism within the parental generation, so intensely engaged in the adolescence of their children, continues. Each critical period may intensify the thrust toward maturer forms of narcissism or may precipitate fragmentation, enfeeblement, or disharmony within the parental self.

As their children face complex changes in vocational opportunities, newer forms of courtship, delaying marriage and parenthood, parental self-esteem and goals come under a powerful searchlight. An enlarged understanding of young adult years may emerge, and from that enlarged vision, an informed and responsive capacity is set in motion to accept the initiative and perception of their children as peers. This is especially tested by social norms of the current generation because of the tendency to delay marriage and family building. The transience of the parental generation, and now even the transience of their children's lives, add stress and must be mastered by accepting its reality more directly.

The experience, then, of becoming grandparents is not so much a "new lease on life . . . because grandparents relive the memories of the early phases of their parenthood in observing the growth and development of their grandchildren" (Anthony & Benedek, 1970, p. 200), but of the opportunity now through maturer forms of narcissism to offer joyous acceptance of a new generation and continuing empathic response to the new responsibilities of their children. As these children, in their turn, face the joys and sorrows of parenthood, grandparents can offer a depth of understanding and support leavened by increased wisdom. A final step in the transformation of narcissism is that in which an acceptance of fading powers conveys to the younger generation, where possible, administration and affirmation of their power and goodness.

More than three and a half centuries ago, Bacon commented, "The joyes of Parents are secret; and so are their griefes and feares: They cannot utter the one; nor they will not utter the other." But the self experience of parenthood requires that some joys be open, expressed, mirrored, and shared in a continuing dialogue with child, adolescent, and young adult, and that some grief and fear be silent.

It is part of maturing parental empathy, wisdom, and acceptance of human transience to be able to do so while moving toward a less central position in the lives of their children. Mirroring, confirming, guiding continue as parental functions but without that confining closeness which fails to recognize the increasing tempo of separateness, the validity and strength of self perception and initiative in the younger generation. In the course of myriad transmuting internalizations of parental selfobject functions, children have acquired as psychic structure the ability to take pleasure in their bodies, their relationships, their work, and parents do experience secret pleasure in the shape and vigor of that ability. Parental pride and pleasure in the work of family rearing, or in the work by which that family is sustained, also become the target of idealization in the younger generation. And parents silently savor (Muslin, Chapter 21, this volume) that sense of power and goodness which the long years of parental support to the forming and transforming self of the child have entailed.

And so with griefs and fears, it is a mark of parental empathy and wisdom to be able to share such experiential narcissistic deficits and injuries. This in itself further contributes to firming and elaborating reliable self-structure for esteem regulation, calming, soothing, repairing in the younger generation. But there is also that silent task of absorbing sorrow which recognizes deficits in one's self and in one's children which have resulted in poorer interpersonal relationships, lesser accomplishments in valued goals than one has hoped for. These are inevitable sequelae and contribute to that stream of inner experience through which further transforming of parental narcissism proceeds. And thus as in a double helix, the younger generation will be engaged in continuing the search for creative solutions to old problems and new. They will confront in newer forms and in other arenas those complexities parents have encountered. And they will deepen in empathy, increase in wisdom, and, in their turn, reach an acceptance of human transience.

REFERENCES

Anthony, E. J., & Benedek, T. *Parenthood: Its psychology and psychopathology.* Boston: Little, Brown, 1970.

Bacon, F. Of parents and children. In *The essays of Sir Francis Bacon.* New York: Heritage Press, 1944.

Basch, M. F. The concept of affect: A re-examination. *Journal of the American Psychoanalytic Association,* 1976, *24,* 759–777.

Basch, M. F. Toward an operational definition of the self. In B. Lee (Ed.), *Psychosocial theories of the self.* New York: Plenum Press, in press.

Behrens, M. L. Child rearing and the character structure of the mother. *Child Development,* 1954, *25,* 225–238.

Benedek, T. Parenthood as a developmental phase: A contribution to the libido theory. *Journal of the American Psychoanalytic Association,* 1959, *7,* 389–417.

Benedek, T. Discussion of parenthood as a developmental phase. *Journal of the American Psychoanalytic Association,* 1975, *23,* 154–165.

Bibring, G. Some considerations of the psychological processes in pregnancy. *The Psychoanalytic Study of the Child,* 1959, *14,* 113–121.

Bibring, G. A study of the psychological processes in pregnancy and of the earliest mother-child relationship. Part I: Some propositions and comments. *The Psychoanalytic Study of the Child,* 1961, *16,* 9–72.

Cohler, B. J. Developmental perspective of the self in early childhood. In A. Goldberg (Ed.), *Advances in self psychology.* New York: International Universities Press, 1980.

Cohler, B. J. Personal narrative and life course. In P. Baltes & O. G. Brim, Jr. (Eds.), *Life span development and behavior* (Vol. IV). New York: Academic Press, 1982.

Del Mar, N. *Richard Strauss* (Vol. I). New York: Free Press of Glencoe–Macmillan, 1962.

Elson, M. Reactive impact of adolescent and family upon each other in separation. *Journal of the American Academy of Child Psychiatry,* 1964, *3*(4), 697–708.

Emerson, R. W. *First and second essays.* Boston: Houghton Mifflin, 1885.

Freud, A. Adolescence. *The Psychoanalytic Study of the Child,* 1958, *13,* 255–278.

Freud, S. On narcissism (1914). *Standard Edition, 14,* 69–102. London: Hogarth Press, 1957.

Gedo, J., & Terman, D. On the adolescent process as a transformation of the self. *Journal of Youth and Adolescence,* 1972, *1,* 257–272.

Kohut, H. Forms and trasnformations of narcissism. *Journal of the American Psychoanalytic Association,* 1966, *14,* 243–272.

Kohut, H. *The analysis of the self.* New York: International Universities Press, 1971.

Kohut, H. *The restoration of the self.* New York: International Universities Press, 1977.

Kohut, H., & Wolf, E. S. The disorders of the self and their treatment: An outline. *International Journal of Psycho-Analysis*, 1978, *59*, 413–425.

Parens, H. Discussion of parenthood as a developmental phase. *Journal of the American Psychoanalytic Association*, 1975, *23*, 154–165.

Tolpin, M. On the beginnings of a cohesive self: An application of the concept of transmuting internalization to the study of the transitional object and signal anxiety. *The Psychoanalytic Study of the Child*, 1971, *26*, 316–352.

Tolpin, M. Discussion of the psychoanalytic developmental theories of the self: An integration by Morton Shane and Estelle Shane. In A. Goldberg (Ed.), *Advances in self psychology*. New York: International Universities Press, 1980.

Tolpin, M., & Kohut, H. The disorders of the self: The psychopathology of the first years of life. In S. Greenspan & G. Pollock (Eds.), *The course of life: Psychoanalytic contributions toward understanding personality development* (Vol 1: *Infancy and early childhood*). Washington, D.C.: Mental Health Study Center and U.S. Government Printing Office, 1980.

Wolf, E. On the developmental line of self object relations. In A. Goldberg (Ed.), *Advances in self psychology*. New York: International Universities Press, 1980.

21

ON THE RESISTANCE TO PARENTHOOD: CONSIDERATIONS ON THE SELF OF THE FATHER

HYMAN L. MUSLIN

INTRODUCTION

This chapter represents an attempt to spell out developmental processes concerning the self of the father. Clearly there are many differences in the final self-organization of fathers, but there are also certain qualities of the self-that-can father that are essential.

In recorded history, the father has been described frequently as the tyrant preoccupied with his destiny, driven to suppression of all around him, including his sons and daughters (Campbell, 1964). Freud's assumption, it will be recalled, was that the primordial father was a tyrant who owned all the women and drove away his sons (Freud, 1913). The Greek cosmogony and theogony revealed that the world of the gods began with Uranus who was created by Gaea, the earth mother who became his wife. Uranus, the primordial father of the gods, also hated and persecuted his children. Cronus the youngest son of Uranus, who castrated and dethroned Uranus, was a more sadistic tyrant who initiated infanticide as soon as his children were born. Zeus, the youngest son of Cronus, who overthrew him, continued the pattern of the tyrannical father in Greek legends and myths. It reached its height in that most moving of the legends, the pathetic figure of Oedipus who could not control his destiny and had to participate in yet another tragic filioparental drama. Some of the most moving myths or historical accounts relate to the tragic acts performed by fathers toward their daughters. The aborted sacrifice of Iphigenia by Agamemnon, the killing of Othman, the Caliph's daughter, all these tragedies come to mind revealing the image of the brutal patriarch in the time of his need (Graves, 1955).

Hyman L. Muslin. Department of Psychiatry, University of Illinois College of Medicine, Chicago, Illinois.

However, the relationship between father and son, particularly infanticide of the first-born son, has always commanded considerable attention in mythologies and in organized religious teachings. A variety of motivations including the fear of being usurped, killed, and stripped of possessions, including wives, were manifested; and, as Frazer reported, perhaps being reborn in the son. Frazer (1959) noted that male Hindus in some parts of the Punjab performed funeral rites in the 5th month of their wives' pregnancies. The stories of infanticide appear throughout all national and racial histories, from the ancient Mexicans who sacrificed to their sun god, to the stories of Odin, the King of Sweden in the 12th century, who slaughtered nine of his sons to prolong his life (Wellisch, 1954).

The transformation of the original father–child infanticide is expressed in the many legends of exposure, including those of Oedipus and Moses. The attempted but averted sacrifice of Isaac by Abraham called the Akedah (the binding) celebrated in Genesis XXII is yet another manifestation of the father-to-son sacrificial motif. This time, however, we can observe what may have been a transformation of the self—specifically a firming of the values of Abraham which caused him to turn away from the egress of instinct to solve problems (*New English Bible*, 1970).

The psychoanalytic contribution on fathering has its inception in Freud's well-known notions of the primordial father as castrator, the inhibiting force for both male and female children and, of course, the rival to the male child and his emerging sexuality (Freud, 1905, 1909, 1913, 1921, 1923, 1930, 1939).

In recent years, beginning with Freud's comments and observations on the pre-Oedipal, nonhostile relationship between fathers and sons in 1921 (Freud, 1921), various psychoanalytic authors have discussed the father's input in the developing child from a perspective different from the earlier version of the harsh, punitive father. Many authors have stressed the father's role as important in extricating the child from the maternal orbit (Loewald, 1951; Greenacre, 1966; Ross, 1975, 1977, 1979b), while others have stressed the role of the father in resolving the rapprochement crisis by facilitating a sense of reality and self-constancy (Abelin, 1971, 1975; Gurwitt, 1976; Mahler, Pine, & Bergman, 1975). Still other psychoanalysts have discussed the fathers who can mother (Burlingham, 1973; Benedek, 1970a, 1970b). Ross, one of the most prolific contributors to the literature on the role of father, stated:

> Rarely, if ever, can fathers rival the encompassing presence of the mother. And yet, notwithstanding his seemingly diminished developmental importance, this perspective on earliest individuation and the power of identification also implies a new "positive" notion of the father. No longer is his primary impact on children that of an ihibitor; now he is seen to invite self-articulation and independent expression. It is father who first offers ways out of a child's arresting entanglement with the mother.
>
> During the pre-oedipal phase, a father has been seen as the first representation of masculinity and, more fundamentally, as the first significant other, apart from siblings perhaps, outside the orbit of mother and child. His impor-

tance is as a purveyor of triangulation and the Oedipus complex, which in turn structure the child's personality in ways that consolidate gender identity and object choice making a child a complex person with inner wishes, fantasies restraints and outer actions that are his or her own. (1979a, p. 321)

Thus the psychoanalytic notion of the father and his impact on the child's development has gone from the initial discussion of the Oedipal father of the primal horde to a version of the father as facilitator of reality, self and object constancy, and gender identity. The focus of these works has been in the context of the notion of the essential shaping of the character coming about as a result of the resolution of the Oedipus complex, albeit stressing the paternal influence on the pre-Oedipal phases, including the rapprochement crisis and its relation to object constancy. In the psychoanalytic literature, however, there has been an absence of focus on the self of the father.

What then is the content of the *self* in order to be a father? The self of the father must have arrived at a developmental level in which there exist optimal *capacities* for nurturance of the child (i.e., mirroring) as well as the capacities that permit idealization (i.e., to allow the child to form an idealized parent imago). Another way of stating this notion is that the self of the father must be sufficiently developed so that he can empathize with the child, and thus, comprehend what is needed in the way of building and maintaining the cohesiveness of the child. Of course, it is not sufficient to possess the capacities to be the confirming parental presence of the target for idealization—one must be able to experience these functions as abiding self-pleasures—the joy of being the provider of worth to another. There does, however, exist in some males the restraints or resistances that so interfere with the empathy needed or the development required so that one can speak of a resistance in the self to fathering.

As Kohut has pointed out, the development of the cohesive nuclear self requires sufficient mirroring on the part of the parent, so that an abiding quality of worth is added once transmuting internalizations have taken place (Kohut, 1977). Further, the child's second source of esteem building is established (particularly important if there is inadequate mirroring), when sufficient internalization of the idealized parent is added to the strength of the self. At this point, a cohesive bipolar self of the child becomes a reality, and the assertiveness of the self is carried out by living up to the internalized ideals through the talents and skills of the self. Input into this self through its selfobjects which lend structure is a life-giving charge of the parents throughout the entirety of the development of the child, adolescent, and young adult—indeed throughout life. Who, then, can perform these selfobject functions—the male or female parent? Mirroring and idealized parent functions have no gender. Certainly, in the infant there seems to be no special reaction to a woman or male parent who is performing parenting functions, granted that familiarity is not an issue (i.e., that the experience with the woman or man is not time-limited).

In considering the male as performing the parental function of the selfobject, the crucial issue is not gender in terms of a biologic "mothering" quality, but rather in terms of the parent's self development. The parent who has a self that can nurture, and allow for idealization has a self which has sufficient mergers and internalizations. With this self, he can empathize with the structural needs of children and not use them to repair his own self-failures.

This ideal male parent, in empathizing with the neonate or the young infant, revives memories of the infancy he experienced and the joy of having been mirrored, calmed, and soothed. Further on in development, the male parent—in empathizing with the child during the times when "civilization and its discontents" are imposed to assist the child in phase-appropriate assertiveness—encourages the formation of adaptive channels and supports the accomplishments of his progeny. During the transformation of the self in adolescence when the ambition and ideals of childhood must be altered to accommodate to the impact of drive maturation and changing social expectations, the adolescent needs the empathic understanding and cohesive maintaining boosts from the parents, as well as support from peers.

Throughout the apprenticeship with our own parents, we can identify a responsiveness, an empathic reaching-out, and can contrast this with an unresponsive, unempathic self-absorption which constitutes the *resistance* to the self-object function of parenting. Selfobject confirmations are vital for the child's development of self-esteem, skills, and knowledge. These are necessary in all developmental phases from acquisition of language, motility, interpersonal relatedness, and the ability to receive and give love.

In summary, the male parent, depending on his unique experience in his self–selfobject development, may be the parent who can mirror effectively, even more effectively than the female parent. Mirroring, per se, the human capacity to confirm and admire—whether it involves support of verbal skills or admiration for the child's ability to skip or jump—is not a function specific to any gender. Thus, it falls into the realm of either male or female parent. The parents who can mirror are the parents whose selfobject needs are stabilized and therefore can empathize with their children's need for admiration with little tension and/or rage, and/or emptiness. The capacity to function as the selfobject who can nurture, is present, it is to be hoped, at many developmental levels. Of course, this is ideal since each parent, reflecting his/her ontongeny, will be more or less effective at different developmental levels of children. Some parents, reflecting their backgrounds, will perform well as mirrors for infants, some only as parents of adolescents. The parent who can allow herself/himself to be the idealized parent—the target of the child's need to put the mother or father on a pedestal to derive borrowed strength in a potentially frightening world—is the parent who has had appropriate idealizing selfobject relations in his/her life. These parents can empathize with the wishes of their progeny, can calm, soothe, lead, and allow the needed aggrandizing to take place.

CASE EXAMPLE

Mr. L came to analysis for relief of a psychological state characterized by pervasive sadness and feelings of futility which to him were unexplicable since he was a successful engineer. He had his own business, his wife had recently given birth to a son, he had moved within the last year into his new home—all on the surface was well.

In the initial months of his analytic work, while his complaints of ennui ranged over many areas of his life, he focused on one area that was his particular source of unhappiness—being at home. Immediately on finishing his day's activities, he became depressed, in anticipation of being with his wife and son. Riding home, he experienced the feeling state of a great unexplained loss, regardless of the day's achievements which were impressive. On arriving at home, his characteristic experience was the inner feeling of agitation. He could not find a comfortable place to sit or to lie down. Nothing was pleasing—not in his relationship with wife and child, in diversions; nothing worked. He was most aware of his tensions and emptiness in his interactions with his son. From the beginning of his wife's pregnancy, he was apprehensive, concerned without being able to identify the source of his concerns. Although he attempted to minister to the infant, it was always by a self-admonition that he should spend time or play games, but never feeling a spontaneous warmth, never feeling a longing to be with his child. As the son grew, he became more aware of anger mixed with emptiness in the child's presence. Along with these experiences, he was aware of deeper barriers in his relations with his wife. It seemed to him that as his relations with his son became more stifled, so also did those with his wife. He experienced her as distant, even foreboding. He found her touch "like sandpaper," her voice "shrewish." His feelings of inadequacy at home pushed him into a flurry of activities of all kinds—athletic, social, business—by which he could escape from his painful home situation and regain some measure of esteem. Thus, he could not parent. Painfully aware of his lack of loving and caring for his child, he became more diminished in his self view.

During one session, late in the first year of the analysis, after a lengthy period of self-abuse for his poor fathering and husbanding, he became quiet and suddenly revealed that the loneliness he felt at home with his family reminded him of the loneliness he had experienced when he had to be hospitalized at 10 years of age for a severe gastrointestinal distress. He recalled that the hospital stay was probably 10 days, and that his family rarely visited, and that he cried himself to sleep. Now, in association to this memory, he described for the first time another traumatic set of circumstances. Apparently his younger brother had developed spinal poliomyelitis during the same summer when he had to be hospitalized. His memory was of hearing his brother cry out with pain each night during that summer and in conjunction with this, his mother and father were constantly frightened and preoccupied with the welfare of the brother. He, too, was caught up in the family trauma and remembers that he had many difficulties during this time. He had frequent gastrointestinal upsets, he was known in school and at home as an unhappy youngster who could not be pleased. From his earliest recollection, his mother was always a haughty, critical person whom he could never please. Since he had one younger brother (1 year younger) and a sister

2 years his junior, he was never without siblings. His mother, however, in his view, had only one child—the polio-ridden brother whom she always praised. The patient always "kept his guard up" around his mother, always feared her criticisms, always anticipated her "put downs." Thus, there was a major interference with the evolution of his confidence; he experienced a paradoxical sense of diminished worth and emptiness when he wanted support, as if he was always aware of his brother's greater need.

His father, unfortunately, while an adequate provider, was a man of no status in the family. His wife apparently commonly derided his occupation, his lack of formal education, and above all, his indecisiveness. To our patient, he was a disappointment. He, too, was ashamed of his father's occupation and his lack of assertiveness, which was manifest in his servile attitude to his wife and children. The father successfully resisted attempts at idealizing so that the patient was constantly frustrated when he turned to him for advice, money, or alliance against his mother. He could not complain to his father about his mother's favoritism toward his brother without being reminded not to speak ill of her. On the other hand, the patient's father could be gentle with his children, although secretively lest the mother become aware of these activities and rail against him.

A mixture of strivings for mirroring maintained in silent, ordinarily repressed fashion, together with strivings for an ideal to follow, to fuse with operated in the patient's self. Both poles of his self were at once incompletely elaborated and hidden from view. Thus, his aspiration for forming selfobject idealizing transferences, which emerged, rarely, and with apprehension of being led by business associates, was countered, that is, disavowed, by hypomanic activities. Throughout his adolescence and adulthood as he learned the "tricks," none was more daring, extravagant, or hard driving. His aspirations for forming mirroring or alter ego self–selfobject relationships were ordinarily out of awareness (although they emerged at times) and so he exhibited diminished self–selfobject relatedness with people. His investment in his work and his financial status, from which he experienced a sense of enhanced regard, became substitute mirroring selfobjects. Thus, while his talents and skills and other constitutional endowments permitted him to stave off many of his ordinary human selfobject strivings for acclaim and for leadership, they were never sufficient to provide escape from the life-long lesion of emptiness along with the fear (which would repeat the experience of abandonment) of succumbing to a potentially destructive mirroring object or a painfully disappointing parent-who-can't-be idealized.

The entry into parenthood found him experiencing his son as the stimulus for his fragilely repressed strivings for selfobject rewards, strivings which he associated with rebuke, strivings which he remembered with apprehension. Once again, he felt shabby.

Although there were suggestions from the material that the patient would establish a hostile brother-transference, in the course of the analysis he developed, in the main, a selfobject transference of the idealizing type. The need for structure to fill out his self in the area of a sense of direction and standards to live up to were manifest in the anamnesis as he described his directionless childhood and youth and the disappointments with his parents, neither of whom he could address as idealized figures. However, the resistances that emerged shortly after the beginning of analysis were profound. He questioned every detail of the analytic procedure, he wondered whether analysis was the correct treatment for him, he could not understand how he was going to be helped. He stated frequently that he could not be exploited by me or anyone, he had to be in charge of every activity in which he participated—business, games, the marriage. This resistance to establishing me as an important figure in his life was diminished finally to be replaced by a reenactment in the analysis of the attempts to obtain leadership from his father. Out of this transference, he could stress his confusion, his ignorance on how to parent or be a husband, and how in his fantasies I was never missing for the proper word, gesture, or action with children or wife. The establishment of me as a major figure in his life was not a simple or consistent process—after an interruption (e.g., holiday) either by myself or him, the challenging, questioning, depreciating process began anew. The interventions on my part that seemed to be of service were to acknowledge that his burning needs for direction were legitimate and based on his many serious disappointments which rendered his ability to make decisions (choices, direction), in his mind, fraudulent or vulnerable to criticism. These interventions ushered in the accounts of the actual disappointments with his father and worries that his analyst might also not be firm and constant. The acknowledgment of the painful experiences permitted him to reveal with lessened shame his sad lonely experience in "getting the day to move."

He went over and over a memory of his father, a small businessman in men's wear, deciding to expand and open another store in a fashionable location. This expansion led to a depression that required hospitalization and ECT. The patient, then 16, recalled the apprehension and rage toward his regressed parent who seemed permanently unavailable to him. A time came when his esteem seemed clearly enhanced and his idealizing transference seemed about to become firmly established (i.e., become cohesive), when, again, his resistance emerged. This time it took form in an affair with a woman who seemed to be an exact duplicate of his description of his mother—a demanding, self-centered person (in his view) who demanded all of his time and a great deal of his money. This regression from an idealizing transference was made accessible to him by the efforts we made to reconstruct the very early similarities in this relationship to his relationship with his mother. Mother did acknowledge, that is, did give him some "gleams" in proportion to his being subservient to her and to his sick brother. Clinging to whatever morsels of confirming behavior—even at the expense of his growth—was clearly a necessity in childhood and now reenacted by attempts to rid himself of me.

Other hurdles similar to this one, such as two clearly destructive business ventures, presented themselves for analytic work before a securely cohesive transference, mainly of the idealizing type, was established. The recognition of the validity of his needs to experience me as a helpful and idealized persona, it seems, elevated his self-regard in an area that he had always felt was shameful—his wish for direction and calming and soothing. Subsequently, a phase of gross identification followed, with a burgeoning interest in music and novels; however this was short-lived. Concurrently, there was awareness on his part that Sunday became a relaxed part of the week and he was beginning to enjoy his son's presence; he actually started planning a day's activities with his son in mind. It went from, "It's not so bad" to, "Sunday was fun." In the analysis, growing evidence of transmuting internalizations were apparent, that is, evidence of the patient experiencing himself with a heightened sense of regard. His frenetic pace in business and athletics had slowed down, his ability to participate in his family without inner experience of emptiness had grown. There was a growing calmness and cohesiveness even during weekends and short separations, for example, during short holidays.

In sum, this man's resistance to parenthood stemmed from his inability to empathize with a child's selfobject needs without fear. His selfobject deprivation resulted in his perpetual struggle to unconsciously reenact his search for structure to fill his empty self. The child he helped bring into the world evoked the reliving of the emptiest time of his life. Thus, he could only view his child as a stimulus to his fear of abandonment. The empathy required to initiate parenting was blocked by an unconscious insistence that the child, like Laius's Oedipus, like Abraham's Isaac, or any of the sons of Odin, would usher in once again fear of abandonment. The initiation of parenting by vicarious introspection demands that the infant and child be experienced in his/her own right without evoking fear of abandonment, displacement—that is, without evoking fantasies of being suddenly dropped, left without sources of esteem. A revival of intense memories of disappointments in mirroring, or the memory of disappointments in merging with idealizing parents permits only the evocation of disintegration anxiety and fragmentation. The capacity to parent, therefore, devolves on relative freedom to empathize with the self of the infant and child. Indeed, parenting is initiated by the ability to introspect one's own self of the early years—thus, there must have been enough confirming, nurturing experiencing in one's life for one to be able to parent spontaneously.

CONCLUSIONS

The self of the father represents a self that has evolved beyond the needs for mirroring and forming idealized transferences. The self is no longer vulnerable to intense urges to attach to selfobjects for cohesion. Although needs for selfobject relationships are ubiquitous throughout life, it is not, ordinarily, with the intensity or immediacy of the child, or of the person suffering a narcissistic deficit, or in a crisis situation. This self will, of course, be more or less assertive (or even charismatic), more or less filled with the thrust to express high-mindedness. This self, when parenthood enters into its life, will experience the needs of the beginning self of the infant and either enter into the parental mirroring functions or find himself in the main performing the calming work of the idealized parent, *or* shift from the nurturing to the protecting functions—the result of the valences of identifications with parents who provided experiences in mirroring or idealizing that established these functions with their special intensities (i.e., quantities). Thus, the male parent, depending on his unique capacities and development, may function as mirror, as idealized parent, as both—depending on those functions that have been established through his development. The functions of mirroring and of being the idealized parent do not reside in the gender of the individual parent. They reflect the unique experiences of the parent as they had been mirrored adequately or having had adequate selfobjects for idealization purposes.

In Western societies since the advent of the agrarian movement, women have been the more available parents for infants for a variety of rational and irrational reasons. Thus, the woman has been identified, until recently, as the sole agent to provide cohesion through mirroring in *infancy*. Likewise, as a result of societal modeling, the female parent has been an important target in the idealizing process. However, these models are evanescent so that in modern times (as in many other previous cultural patterns) the selfobject functions of parents are not assigned exclusively to either parent as in past times. It is becoming clearer that parental functions are not assigned regularly along gender lines; the notion of mothering or fathering may become passé and be replaced by the more important emphasis on mirroring or the idealized functions executed by the most available and the most endowed parent—the man or the woman.

The patient described in these pages was not able to parent—to share the inner mental life of his child, to witness his child's growth with joy. The father is not only that person who has passed through certain psychological developments unscathed. He is someone who can give to his progeny with joy, the joy of gift giving, the joy of vicariously experiencing what he has or has not had, the joy of being witness to the beauty of the unfolding maturation of his children. That is the unique experience of having been witness to the events of the maturation of children under one's guidance without self-absorption, without the intrusion of one's own needs; this represents the transformed self of the parent. Thus becoming a parent, psychologically speaking, implies that a process of transformation of the self has taken place, and that self revels in the unfolding of his/her charges. The transformed self of the parent is not without needs for mirroring of the self by the selfobject aspects of his love objects and, of course, continues to need targets for idealization; selfobject relations occur on all developmental levels and do not imply immaturity (Kohut, 1977, p. 188).

In concluding this chapter, I will add that I attempted to find a model, in literature, of a father–son relationship that would demonstrate the features of the self of the parent with the requisite transformations of narcissism that has been described. However, I found this search quite difficult. Why this was so difficult a task is of special interest. Perhaps it is because the great man celebrated in literature, or in biblical works, has rarely demonstrated optimal parental attitudes and is not able to "experience the growth of the next generation with unforced nondefensive joy" (Kohut, 1977, p. 237). The transformations of the self of the parents consist of the alterations in the ideals of the self, and the determination (assertiveness) and skills necessary to promote and maintain the development of the child. In my view, the heroes of the great books have not experienced sufficient self transformations to encompass the pleasurable aspects of parenting. In the Yiddish vernacular, the term "kvell" approximates the affect contained in the intended self state to be achieved. The term implies an experience of unbridled joy at being witness to an activity of the child. It is differentiated from the term "nachas" which implies the gift of achievement from child to parent. Parents should and can "kvell."

REFERENCES

Abelin, E. The role of the father in the separation–individuation process. In J. B. McDevitt & C. F. Settlage (Eds.), *Separation–individuation*. New York: International Universities Press, 1971.

Abelin, E. Some further observations and comments on the earliest role of the father. *International Journal of Psycho-Analysis*, 1975, *56*, 293–302.

Benedek, T. Fatherhood and providing. In E. J. Anthony & T. Benedek (Eds.), *Parenthood: Its psychology and psychopathology*. Boston: Little, Brown, 1970. (a)

Benedek, T. Parenthood during the life cycle. In E. J. Anthony & T. Benedek (Eds.), *Parenthood: Its psychology and psychopathology*. Boston: Little, Brown, 1970. (b)

Burlingham, D. The preoedipal infant–father relationship. *Psychoanalytic Study of the Child*, 1973, *28*, 23–47.

Campbell, J. The masks of God: Occidental mythology. New York: Viking Press, 1964.

Frazer, J. G. *The golden bough*. New York: Criterion Books, 1959.

Freud, S. The interpretation of dreams (1900). *Standard Edition, 4*. London: Hogarth Press, 1953.

Freud, S. Three essays on the theory of sexuality (1905). *Standard Edition, 7*. London: Hogarth Press, 1953.

Freud, S. The family romances (1909). *Standard Edition, 9*. London: Hogarth Press, 1955.

Freud, S. Totem and taboo (1913). *Standard Edition, 13*. London: Hogarth Press, 1964.

Freud, S. Group psychology and the analysis of the ego (1921). *Standard Edition, 18*. London: Hogarth Press, 1957.

Freud, S. The ego and the id (1923). *Standard Edition, 19*. London: Hogarth Press, 1961.

Freud, S. The dissolution of the Oedipus complex (1924). *Standard Edition, 19*. London: Hogarth Press, 1961.

Freud, S. Civilization and its discontents (1930). *Standard Edition, 21*. London: Hogarth Press, 1961.

Freud, S. Moses and monotheism (1939). *Standard Edition, 23*. London: Hogarth Press, 1964.

Graves, R. *The Greek myths* (Vols. I & II) (1955). Baltimore: Penguin Books, 1970.

Greenacre, P. Problems of overidealization of the analyst and analysis: Their manifestations in the transference and countertransference relationship (1966). In *Emotional growth*. New York: International Universities Press, 1971.

Gurwitt, A. R. Aspects of prospective fatherhood. *Psychoanalytic Study of the Child*, 1976, *31*, 237–270.

Kohut, H. *The analysis of the self*. New York: International Universities Press, 1971.

Kohut, H. *The restoration of the self*. New York: International Universities Press, 1977.

Loewald, H. Ego and reality. *International Journal of Psycho-Analysis*, 1951, *32*, 10–18.

Mahler, M. S., Pine, F., & Bergman, A. *The psychological birth of the human infant*. New York: Basic Books, 1975.

New English bible. London: Oxford University Press, 1970.

Ross, J. M. The development of paternal identity: A critical review of the literature on nurturance and generativity in boys and men. *Journal of American Psychoanalytic Association*, 1975, *23*, 783–817.

Ross, J. M. Toward fatherhood: The epigenesis of paternal identity during a boy's first decade. *International Review of Psycho-Analysis*, 1977, *4*, 327–348.

Ross, J. M. Fathering: A review of some psychoanalytic contributions on paternity. *International Journal of Psycho-Analysis*, 1979, *60*, 317–327. (a)

Ross, J. M. Paternal identity: The equation of fatherhood and manhood. In T. B. Karasu & C. W. Socarides (Eds.), *On sexuality: Psychoanalytic observations*. New York: International Universities Press, 1979. (b)

Wellisch, E. *Isaac and Oedipus*. London: Routledge & Kegan Paul, 1954.

22

AFFECT AND PARENTHOOD: THE IMPACT OF THE PAST UPON THE PRESENT

DAVID M. TERMAN

The attempt to elucidate the origin and shape of parenting inevitably requires the reconsideration of basic issues of structure formation. My attention has been drawn to these issues by my psychoanalytic work especially as it has been informed by the theories of self psychology. These theories focus the analyst's attention more systematically on the patient's experience of the interface between himself/herself and the analyst and on the inner meaning of that interface. In this context, the how and why of the perception of the analyst's responsiveness illuminates the perceptions and experiences of parental responsiveness. As these phenomena are explored in ever greater depth, specificity, and subtlety, their role in the formation of psychological structure assumes greater importance than previously credited to them. The wide range and great variety of such phenomena at the interface necessitate revision and expansion of our notions of psychic structure formation.

One can classify classical psychoanalytic theories of structure creation into two categories; the vicissitudes of energy and the processes of identification. From the perspective of energy transformation, structure arises from the frustration and/or delay of impulse discharge. Delay forces a detour which embraces reality. The later necessity to modulate instinctual discharge is partially responsible for the erection of countercathexes (i.e., defenses) which also constitute structure.

Processes of identification, the second category, are equally, if not more important sources of psychological structure. Freud described two kinds of identifications. One was related to object loss; the other, less well understood, was said to precede that related to object loss. The former, most elaborated and familiar, was first suggested in *Mourning and Melancholia* (1917). Freud had

David M. Terman. Department of Psychiatry, Michael Reese Hospital and Medical Center, Department of Psychiatry, University of Chicago, and Faculty, The Institute for Psychoanalysis, Chicago, Illinois.

postulated that in the process of melancholia, "an object cathexis had been replaced by an identification." Later, in *The Ego and the Id* (1923), he generalized this mechanism. By virtue of the abandonment of object cathexes in development, he suggested, that "the character of the ego was a precipitate of abandoned object cathexes and that it contains the history of those object choices."

The other, earlier form of identification was said to be the individual's "first and most important identification, his identification with the [parents] in his own personal pre-history" (Freud, 1923, p. 31). Freud stated that this "is a direct and immediate identification and takes place earlier than any object cathexis" (1923, p. 31). However, it was difficult for him to "give a clear metapsychological representation of the distinction" (1921b, p. 106), he said.

Edith Jacobson (1964) tried to clarify the nature of these earlier identifications further. She distinguished between very early identifications born of fusions, and pre-Oedipal identifications which grew out of wishes for likeness and imitation. The fusions were conceptualized as the "fusion of self and object images" and were associated with the early experiences of libidinal gratification. And though the fusions were seen as the "foundation on which all object relations are built," Jacobson implied that a breakdown of a previously established boundary between self and object images could occur and that this always connoted a functional regression. Such fusions, for Jacobson (and others), became refuges of magic and omnipotence—a temporary haven of calm for the mature or maturing ego—but a trap of chaos and disorganization—the basis for psychosis—for the fixated. For Jacobson, the maintenance of the boundaries was one of the all-important tasks of development, and such fusions always represented a danger or obstacle to growth.

Kohut (1971) has thrown a new light on the nature and role of such fusions. Where Jacobson, and others, have stressed the illusory nature of this experience, and the importance of yielding this mode of experience to more discrete, boundary defined interactions, Kohut has explored and elucidates a variety of functions that can occur *only* in this psychological mode. Kohut has come to call this experience or mode a selfobject experience. Its essential characteristic is that in some respect two bodies are functioning for one party, as a psychological unit. Certain essential psychological functions in one member of the dyad are being performed by the "other." The functions range from the cohesion of the self via the experience of total oneness with a powerful other to an accretion of self confidence by virtue of the experience of an approving nod from the other. Kohut elaborated on the establishment and development of the inner organizations of wholeness, cohesion, continuity, goals, and values—the development of a self—which are the consequences of the variety of selfobject experiences. Many important patterns are established in the experience of unity and as one looks more closely at the nature of these emerging patterns, one can observe that many attitudes and behaviors—many aspects of character—resemble those of the "organizing" member of the dyad, that is, the parent who must perform the many functions the child requires.

The lack of psychological boundary at the time of functional unity creates a kind of mold. The experience is partially dependent on the behavior, attitude, or affect of the selfobject, and the residua, consequently, are not the outcome of an active molding of oneself to resemble a discretely perceived, separate other, but the memory of experience of how one is defined. This definition of the self includes characteristics an observer could attribute to the "other." To the extent that the response is both self defining yet the product of the "other," one cannot be said to mold oneself. Rather, one is molded.

This is not to imply that the child is passive in the creation of his/her own experience, nor that other mechanisms of identification are not important. However, there are many points in the developmental process where the experience of response is intrinsic to the creation of the ultimate structure. These experiences of response establish the core of the inner experience of wholeness and oneness. But, later discrete phases of development must also be met with discrete responses which are equally essential and which form an intrinsic part of the structure. With our increasing awareness of the shaping effects of the interactive interface which is simultaneously experienced as functionally a part of the self, we can make more sense of a wider range of data that have up to now not been fully integrated in our theories of development and structure formation. I think this gives a more precise explanation of the way in which "a clear metapsychological distinction" can be made between the forms of identification Freud was attempting to distinguish. This explanation differs, however, from that offered by both Freud and Jacobson; for the mechanism is not confined to the earliest years, and it is not simply a fusion of self and object images associated with libidinal gratification. The shaping goes beyond and includes much more than gratification or frustration of tension—as important as that may be. The experience of parents' perceptions and responses functions more like an auxiliary perceptual and evaluative apparatus. Such functions may apply to the real world issues. Is this step too high? Can I cross this space? Is it safe? Is it dangerous? It may relate to the experience of affects—is one comforted in sadness or will sadness cause even more sadness, or anger? Is joy met with pleasure, or disapproval? The wishes and interactions of which these affects are indicators and mediators are all given meaning and set in relation to each other and the world in the context of the parent–child dialogue. The elaborate apparatus for affect expression and communication (noted by Basch, 1975) is no accident. The shaping of function which these affects constitute is not yet sufficiently appreciated.

The affective component of the responses are prime organizers of the child's experience. Though Kohut (1971) has explicitly elaborated the effect of the presence or absence of positive affect, especially in the mirroring phases of selfobject experience, we can consider a wide variety of affects (and the attitudes they indicate) which can structuralize. Theoretically, any affect in the parent could define any aspect of the child's self experience any time it was brought into juxtaposition with the leading edge of this self development. Anger, shame, disgust, guilt, excitement, and depression can become as shaping as pleasure or withdrawal.

Some examples will illustrate this phenomenon. These three following vignettes show the effects of several affects at different developmental phases. In each example the experience of the parental affect was a prime ingredient in the patient's experience of himself/herself. Though it was not the *only* ingredient, for all these deformations had numerous secondary and defensive functions, and it was important to understand them and work them through. Nonetheless, it was no less essential to permit the full flowering of the transference experience of the affective response of the parent and work *that* through as well.

A young woman with a severe drinking problem would become silent and withdrawn on the couch. Long periods of silence were unbearable to her, yet she could not break them herself, and needed me to do it. Her inner feeling of deadness, lethargy, and immobility arose if she experienced any sadness in herself, but especially if she felt I was somehow unresponsive or inattentive. This state was soon linked with her mother's serious clinical depression which occurred when she was around 2 years old and again in late adolescence. Memories of her mother's staring unresponsiveness or dull preoccupation were frequently associated with her own dull, unresponsive state. The experience of me as depressed and unresponsive corresponded to her mother's affective state. Her own boundless lethargy and immobility was her experience of herself as it formed in her mother's affect. What was most difficult for her to endure was a kind of exponential depression in which she would experience her self as depressed and then experience me as depressed in response to her depression. Such states were one of the determinants of her drinking. Though obviously the perception of me as depressed was a projection of her own affect, it was only possible to work through that state by understanding its origins in the crucial, overwhelming, self-defining experience of her mother's depression. In other words, understanding of the genetic experience, which was equally "internal" had to include the experience of the maternal affect. The exclusive focus on her affect in isolation—as *only* a function of her own wishes, conflicts, etc.—to which of course it did also relate, would have precluded understanding and working through and would have reduplicated a variety of unresponsiveness.

A young married man with problems in self-assertion who also experienced periods of anxious silence on the couch was not immobile or lethargic, but was aware of wanting some kind of stimulation or response from me. He, too, associated to his mother's depressive feelings. These were not bland muteness, but rather they were manifested by diffuse apprehension and vagueness. His mother reacted to him with a vaguely anxious benignity that focused on food, denied unpleasantness, and seemed unengaged with much else. He experienced himself as uninteresting and unstimulating; and at such times, he experienced me as unable to understand and as ineffectual. In reexperiencing the mother's distracted depressions, he, too, felt unstimulated and depressed. This affective state was also a structural part of his experience of his self assertion. He felt ineffective, unreliable, and inconsequential. In the transference, he felt helpless to affect me, for I would be unable to even register the fact of his helplessness; and later, if I could, I would collapse. There were clearly defensive aspects to this kind of experience of himself, which involved anxieties concerning the effect of his wishes. But the feeling of his ineffectiveness as determined by his mother's affective state had to be worked through in its own right.

For this patient, as for the next one, the structural impact, the selfobject function of the affect, seemed to occur after the first 2 years of childhood. I have found that the selfobject experience of parental affect is an important component of every developmental phase. As I have reported earlier (1975), and as Kohut (1977) has also suggested, even understanding of the Oedipal period requires the elucidation of the continuing self development characteristic of the phase and the concomitant selfobject functions which help determine its character. Affective responses structuralize there, too.

The third example is a male artist with homosexual problems who experienced intense shame over any wish to show any part of his body. He kept his jacket on for a long time when he lay on the couch. He was equally ashamed of a wide variety of sexual—especially heterosexual—thoughts and feelings. One important determinant of his feelings was the experience of his mother's disgust with and aversion to his physical maturation. As he began to grow body hair, she vocalized her repugnance, and suggested that he shave it off! Her attitude toward his pubescent changes was paradigmatic of her attitude toward any expression of "manliness" whether it was physical or psychological, throughout his development—both early and late; and this attitude and affect was totally imbricated in the patient's experience of and attitude toward his own masculinity. His changing this inner structure depended on his reexperience of his childhood feelings toward such displays of maleness, understanding its origin within the maternal affect, and his gradual ability to distinguish between the conditions of its origin and the nature of the rest of the world.

It was important to later work through the need to see himself as defective to avoid the overstimulation and burden of the woman's total dependence on him as well. The mother's psychological parasitism was another powerful factor in his aversion to closeness with a woman. But this later state, too, was not only a function of sexual overstimulation, but also arose as part of the experience of unbearable disappointment and burden that the mother's psychological fragility imposed.

In each of these patients, the parental affect structured an aspect of inner experience in the selfobject mode. The affect was an essential constituent of the inner state—depression, ineffectiveness, shame over masculine wishes. Any of those states, those modes of organization of aspects of self, could not arise (or dissolve) autochthonously. However, the patients experienced them as the conditions of being, as givens. And, in fact, it is when they could begin to be viewed as particular, individual, even idiosyncratic, that we knew that change was occurring.

Granting, for the moment then, that such selfobject affect structures inner experience, what bearing does that have on parenting? How does that shape the parenting function? It is a commonplace observation that one repeats with one's children what was done to oneself. Usually this has a negative connotation. Recent accounts of a local trial of an especially depraved homosexual murderer offer a dramatic example of that principle if our own literature were not sufficient.

This man's heinous murders seemed to be at least partially understandable as one learned of his own childhood exposure to murderous physical abuse from his alcoholic father. The father often spent his nights drinking in the basement, and in uncontrolled rages, frequently beat the child on the head. Brandt Steele's account of the history of parents who are child abusers documents the invariable incidence of severe emotional or physical abuse in their own childhoods (1970). The abuse especially seems to center around the expression of dependent needs. The parents of the abusing parents angrily refuse to care for their children while they demand, in effect, that the children care for them.

It was Freud, of course, who first offered an explanation for these apparent reversals of role (1921a). He described a toddler who had just experienced separation from his mother and who then threw a spool under a bed and "lost" it from sight, only to retrieve it and make it reappear. The child was active in causing a separation, which he controlled, since he had been passive in suffering the separation from his mother. Freud focused on the repetition of the painful aspect of the experience and explained it as something "beyond the pleasure principle"—that is, the operation of the repetition compulsion which was a derivative of the death instinct. He was loath to explain the apparent gain in mastery as the motivation or the cause of the reversal.

Anna Freud (1937) later labeled this phenomenon of turning painful passively experienced traumata into active aggressive acts toward others as "identification with the aggressor." In response to threatening or anxiety-provoking "others"—usually parents—the child identifies with the aggressive attitude or action, but, at first, instead of turning it toward himself/herself, the child turns it against the world. More recently (1959), George Klein had made the intriguing reformulation of this phenomenon in terms of "self syntonicity." He had suggested that "reversal behaviors concern experiences that threaten self-continuity (1959, p. 265). And it is only by turning passive to active—by reversing the voice—that self syntonicity could be achieved.

Benedek (1959), however, in her classic paper on parenting (the parent of parenting papers) has called attention to nontraumatic, essential positive experiences of parents' childhoods which are the very foundation of parenting and which, descriptively at least, can also be characterized by the reversal of passive to active. She noted, "The mother's ability to receive from her child (and to mother) is strongly affected by the confidence which the mother herself has incorporated into her mental structure while receiving from her own mother. Her giving, her patience, and her motherliness derived from the developmental vicissitudes of the primary identification with her mother."

Hence, though our attention is dramatically called to the traumatic antecedents of reversals, this kind of relationship—the relationship between the "passive" experience and "active" repetition—characterizes both traumatic and nontraumatic experience. Perhaps Freud's hesitancy in accepting mastery, or the wish for mastery, as the motivation for these apparent reversals is well founded. The experience of the child who is patiently and calmly soothed is, of course, no less "passive" than the child who is traumatically raged at, yet each may and does repeat his/her experience actively in play and when he/she becomes a parent. Each of these kinds of experiences becomes structural; and if we can extend the selfobject position of parental affect beyond the earliest phases, we can explain the subsequent "reversals" as the outcome of a process of structuralization. Reversals, then, would not necessarily imply a wish for mastery, but would simply occur as the outcome of the way the world and oneself is organized. As with identification the "reversal" is less the product of a conscious—or unconscious—"willing" or imitation than the outcome of the only knowable pattern available. There is no choosing of one mode of perception or reaction over another. The most deeply engrained patterns are most absolute and do not admit of alternatives.

When the parent is confronted by the needs and affects of the child, he/she will process, understand, and react to them, in part, as his/her own parent had responded to similarly expressed needs and affects. Those grandparental responses are as much a part of the parent as the individual's own creation. The structuring and patterning includes not only "superego" functions—that is, evaluative, judgmental attitudes—but many "ego" regulatory processes as well—for example, affect control and expression and the intensity or selection of certain affect patterns. The origins of these patterns in grandparental responses are revealed only in the psychoanalytic exploration as they are reenacted in the transference. Hence, the shape of subsequent parental function and its resemblance to the parents' experience in childhood would be an outgrowth of the intrinsic structure of the parent and the fact that an integral part of that structure was the grandparental affect. A case report will help illustrate this thesis.

A 30-year-old suburban housewife, whom I shall call Mrs. Smith, mother of two young children, sought analysis when she experienced periods of acute anxiety, phobias, and uncertainties around the management of her younger child. She was reasonably happily married to a caring, thoughtful man, who, though somewhat prone to depressions, was quite an adequate and sensitive husband. And the adequacy and stability of her marriage reflected her adequacy in other aspects of her life as well. She was warmly involved with her friends and responsibly involved in her community, etc. Her inner suffering, however, was intense, and had been made more acute by the move of a good friend, and by a minor surgical procedure which stimulated both increased anxiety and moderate hypochondriasis.

Mrs. Smith came from an upper-middle-class home and was the oldest of three girls. Her mother was also a warm, dynamic woman who was quite demonstrative, but equally overstimulating. She felt very close to the patient, and did not hesitate to respond enthusiastically to her. Mother was enchanted with the patient's strengths and never failed to note them. However, Mother could seldom stop. She suffered from frequent migraines, and though in considerable discomfort, she would not "give in." She would describe her feelings in some detail to the patient while pushing herself, usually successfully, to complete the

activity she had initiated. She was, of course, equally unrelenting when it came
to the patient's needs for calm or rest. She would schedule many activities on
a trip, for example, and would proceed to complete them at a whirlwind pace.
Mrs. Smith, herself, had no recognition at the time that she either might need
or want rest. She only was aware of anxiety surrounding such excursions, the
reason for which was unknown. The siblings were even less amenable to the
states of overexcitement and were subject to tantrums.

Mrs. Smith's father was a much quieter, passive man who removed himself
from her mother's intense involvement with the children. He, however, was
very worshipful of the mother, whom he considered beautiful and lively, and
was somewhat impatient and awkward with his children. His wife alternately
depreciated him for his practical weaknesses, and revered him for his intelligence
and education. When he did try to relate more actively to his children it was
often at mother's prompting, and his attempts were correspondingly inept.

With all this, the patient had a reasonably normal development. She did
not do as well in school as she would have wished for herself—or as well as she
felt her mother would have wished, but she had an active involvement with
friends and a better than expectable social life. Her adolescence was stormy and
marked by considerable family turmoil. She was disrespectful to both
parents—especially to her father whom she once angrily called a "mouse." And
with mother's sophisticated values that expressing anger was "good," patient
had no help in controlling her inner tensions and rages. A timely psychotherapy
with a skilled social worker helped restore some inner equilibrium, but not
without a sojourn in a boarding school for her last high-school year.

The patient went on to college and obtained a graduate degree in education
without further difficulty. She met and married her husband, a skilled and am-
bitious surgeon, and settled into her active and sometimes hectic suburban life.
Her first pregnancy and first child were the source of unambivalent pleasure.
Her second, 2 years later, was felt to be troublesome from the start. She felt
unwell during the pregnancy, and when the young son was born she found him
"colicky" and difficult to soothe. She, herself, became tense and frustrated in
her attempts to do so.

By the time the patient came for analysis, this child, then 2 years old, had
severe tantrums that would make mother extremely tense and rageful herself and
fearful of her own loss of control.

The analytic process revealed difficulties at several developmental levels.
Her anxiety attacks were overdetermined symptoms. And numerous facets of
both a mother and father transference appeared and were worked through. We
will focus on one aspect of what we came to recognize as the selfobject experience
of her mother throughout her development, which is her overstimulated, excited
state.

This was manifested in numerous ways. She spoke rapidly and with ani-
mation. She often had to have her hands in motion doing something. She filed
her nails, played with pieces of paper, etc. Most striking, however, was her

periodic need to rise from her recumbent position and sit up on the couch—her back facing me. At first she had no idea why she did that—only that she felt she had to. She felt that she could not lie still. She would sometimes remain sitting until the end of the hour; other times she would resume recumbency after a few minutes. This behavior occurred periodically in the course of the analysis; it was not a daily or even weekly event.

Gradually she was able to associate to her experience, and we were able to observe its context. At first it seemed related to a recital of especially taxing series of tasks which she felt both great pressure to complete and insufficient time, skill, cooperation, etc., to do so. Slowly, the transference elements began to emerge. She realized that she might evoke a response of pleasure or approval in me—to her activities or to some piece of analytic work. If, in fact, she evoked such a response—such as a chuckle in reaction to an amusingly told story—she would soon rise. As we then would understand her unbearable overexcitement, she would lie down and feel calmer. Her associations always led to one or another aspect of her mother's intense reactions to her. Mother was always ready to praise her performance and exclaim over her. But, while praising her for her competence, goodness, and consideration, she also involved her in her own concerns. Mrs. Smith gradually became aware of her discomfort in her and her mother's intense feelings. Mother exclaimed over her beauty, but then anxiously would wonder aloud if she were a lesbian. Mother expressed her admiration, but also voiced anxiety about losing her daughter. Some of the mother's appreciation of her competence was somehow associated with patient's sensitivity to her mother's illnesses and discomforts. The sense of burden and anger emerged more clearly and was worked through, but there remained a sense of pleasurable–painful experience of herself which, because of its intensity, would quickly lead to hypochondriacal anxiety. The experience of my comparative calm and systematic understanding of her tensions and her pleasure with herself without demeaning such pleasure, helped her integrate such self experience more comfortably and reliably into her personality structure.

This aspect of analytic work continued intermittently through the course of the analysis. For the first few years, Mrs. Smith was unaware that she was frequently hyperactive—in spite of the overexcitement in the analysis. As she became more aware of it, she would note it in passing—as a given. Later still, observing herself, she saw it as a positive value. She liked to "be up"—she could get so much done; she hated the idea of being depressed; one shouldn't "give in"; etc.

As one might guess, such attitudes toward herself also affected her parenting. The most salient feature of the early analytic years was her son's tendency to react to her increased tension and excitement with tantrums. She would become frantic in response, as noted above, and become preoccupied with her fear of losing control, but she had no awareness that her overstimulating pace of activity had anything at all to do with the onset of the tantrums. And, though I made the inference to myself, I did not share it with her. It seemed to me that it would have detracted from my elucidation of the inner transference experience. Further, I did not think that at that point she could do anything differently. For her to be able to calm herself sufficiently to change the level of stimulation and be able to effectively soothe this child I knew would be the product of additional analytic work, and to have pointed that out would only have increased her helplessness as well as demanding that *she* control the tension when she needed to experience a selfobject calm in the face of her tension. As the analytic work proceeded, she realized, first, that the child needed her to be calm in order to calm himself. Much later she also understood that her activity might stimulate a state of excited tension in her son which he could tolerate much less well than the older daughter.

Thus, as a function of her changing inner state, she began to perceive her children's needs differently and interact with them differently. *Her* changing perspective validated my early inferences about the nature of the overstimulation. As she realized more about her own state, she could see how she had been too excited and intense with her children. She realized, for example, that they needed to go to bed in pajamas even when they were only moderately ill with a fever, and they should not have to dress in street clothes while staying at home. She could see that the presence of playmates all day might overtax a child, that many children at a birthday party might be more difficult than a few, etc. She did not feel that she had to stimulate their interest continually, etc.

As she continued to work through her experience of herself in my eyes, she came to experience her excited state as related to her now decreasing symptoms of anxiety. She was afraid of not feeling special and worthwhile to me or to herself if she were not so stimulating. Together with an increasing calm, the working through of her unexcited meaning to me permitted her to feel differently, and begin to grasp the negative aspects of her overexcitement. She found she could think things through and concentrate in a way that had been unavailable to her before.

There were further changes in her parenting as well. With her increased calm, and the son's maturation, the tantrums ceased, but paradoxically her daughter slowly began to show symptoms. Mrs. Smith had seen this daughter as the good child who could tolerate her tension and excitement. As this child began to have difficulty going to sleep and she became more aware of herself, Mrs. Smith realized that she, too, felt burdened by the excitement and intensity and needed yet further attention to her level of stimulation as well.

I should underscore that in spite of the children's difficulties, Mrs. Smith's narrative revealed them to be talented, basically well-functioning children. Each performed extremely well in school. Each had a variety of friends and was well liked, and each pursued a variety of interests. Both patient and children continued their growth, and the analysis terminated uneventfully.

This case illustrates that it is precisely the experience of pleasure, excitement and engagement which was the basis of *both* Mrs. Smith's strengths and symptoms and became the basis of strengths in her offspring as well. This sense and/or experience of herself was directly derived from her mother's excited appraisal of her. This appraisal was too intense and surrounded by anxiety. It seemed primarily to be the intensity itself which was most troublesome for the patient. But each of those affects created an inner structure which was, to say the least, overheating. Though elaborated and integrated out of both defensive and identificatory mechanisms, the primary origin of the self excitement and overexcitement was within the experience of the mother's responsiveness to her. The transference perception of my excitement permitted the elucidation of the origins of her inner excitement, and these understandings together with the experience of calmer perception of her, permitted the restructuring of her self experience.

The mother's excitement with her became her excitement of herself and her perception of the world and her mode of structuring and interacting with others. The passively created shape was actively reproduced in the world and in response to her own children. What was passive became active, but not chiefly in a self-willed, imitative way, but as an outgrowth of an organization.

One could argue justly that I have still not shown that such active repetitions of passive experience are not chiefly motivated by traumatic factors. After all, the intensity of both Mrs. Smith's and her mother's responses were quite traumatic to their children. Yet it was equally true that each had intense investments in themselves, their relationships, and the world which were deeply rewarding and were also the product of the passive experience of the parental excitement.

SUMMARY

Parental affect is an essential component of inner experience. It helps define inner experience for, as selfobject function, it *has been* an intrinsic part of inner experience. Hence parental affect in the selfobject position is an important determinant of subsequent structure.

Aspects of structure are reenacted in the subsequent parenting functions. These functions—when linked with their antecedents in the parent's childhood—look like reversals, identifications with the aggressor. Though our attention has been drawn to the negative and traumatic aspects of such apparent reversals, I have suggested that such apparent reversals occur as a result of both traumatic and benign experience. The repetitions, then, are not as much willed or intended as they are functions of the way the psyche is organized. Important aspects of that organization were the experiences of the parental affect and that is why subsequent functions resemble the grandparental affect.

A case was presented which illustrated three points: (1) the origin of the patient's structure—her positive self-experience and her overstimulated state—was in the experience of her mother's affect; (2) the positive and problematic nature of that experience; and (3) its reenactment (and change) in her own parenting function.

REFERENCES

Basch, M. Toward a theory of depression. In E. J. Anthony & T. Benedek (Eds.), *Depression and human existence*. Boston: Little, Brown, 1975.

Benedek, T. Parenthood as a developmental phase: A contribution to libido theory. *Journal of the American Psychoanalytic Association*, 1959, *7*, 389–417.

Freud, A. *The ego and the mechanisms of defense*. London: Hogarth Press, 1937.

Freud, S. (1917). Mourning and melancholia. *Standard Edition, 14*. London: Hogarth Press, 1957.

Freud, S. Beyond the pleasure principle (1921a). *Standard Edition, 18*. London: Hogarth Press, 1957.

Freud, S. Group psychology and the analysis of the ego (1921b). *Standard Edition, 18*. London: Hogarth Press, 1957.

Freud, S. The ego and the id (1923). *Standard Edition, 19*. London: Hogarth Press, 1957.

Jacobson, E. *The self and the object world*. New York: International Universities Press, 1964.

Klein, G. The principle of self-initiated active reversal of passive experience (1959). In *Psychoanalytic theory*. New York: International Universities Press, 1976.

Kohut, H. *The analysis of the self*. New York: International Universities Press, 1971.

Kohut, H. *The restoration of the self*. New York: International Universities Press, 1977.

Steele, B. Parental abuse of infants and small children. In E. J. Anthony & T. Benedek (Eds.), *Parenthood: Its psychology and psychopathology*. Boston: Little, Brown, 1970.

Terman, D. *The self and the Oedipus complex*. Unpublished paper delivered to Chicago Psychoanalytic Society, May 1975.

23

PARENTHOOD AND
THE THERAPEUTIC ALLIANCE

JAMES FISCH

In this chapter I will present the thesis that a relationship exists between the parenthood experience and the capacity to form a therapeutic alliance in psychoanalysis. I will use illustrative case material to show that parenting and the unique experiences associated with the parent–child relationship may lead to the expansion of the parent's ego including cognitive advances, a deepening awareness and tolerance of affects, and new self representations. These ego advances connected with parenthood promote the self-observing function and facilitate the establishment of a therapeutic alliance. I will also show the utility of this thesis by demonstrating that when the analyst focuses on parenthood as a specific technical intervention, the ego expansion and therapeutic alliance is enhanced.

Support for the above thesis may be found in discussions promoting the view of psychoanalysis as a developmental process within which structural development may occur, and where the establishment of a therapeutic alliance is viewed as a major therapeutic goal. Settlage (in Panel, 1979), citing the work of Loewald, Zetzel, Fleming, and Greenacre, articulated this when he stated, "Our increased efforts at analyzing dyadic-stage pathology have brought the therapeutic alliance within the compass of analytic process rather than having it remain a prerequisite capacity for analyzability" (p. 632). Along with this emphasis on the therapeutic alliance there is a broader view of the nature of the therapeutic action of psychoanalysis, with questions raised as to whether significant parts of the therapeutic action of psychoanalysis are seen to lie "outside of the technique of analysis" (Ritvo, in Panel, 1979, p. 629). I understand "outside of the technique of analysis" to include technical interventions other than interpretation, and transference objects other than the analyst. Further support for this position may be found in Valenstein (1979, p. 151) in his examination of the concept "classical" analysis. He states:

James Fisch. Department of Psychiatry, Michael Reese Hospital and Medical Center, and Department of Psychiatry, University of Chicago, Chicago, Illinois.

My impression is that most patients who are borderline, like those who are severely narcissistic, are also relatively inaccessible to interpretation and to the insight that correct interpretation intends, during at least a prolonged earlier phase of treatment. The treatment of such conditions during a lengthy preanalytic phase has to be paramountly experiential and developmentally reparative insofar as possible.

If we accept the reality that our primary analytic technique, the mutative interpretation, is at times rendered ineffectual, then at those times we must look for help wherever it can be found. I submit that the object world outside the analytic relationship during the initial preanalytic phase referred to by Valenstein, assumes great importance with regard to facilitating or obstructing analytic progress. I would argue, also, that if these extra-analytic experiences help to restore a patient's sense of confidence in his/her ego functions, they also increase his/her tolerance for the analytic experience and the capacity to form a therapeutic alliance. I believe the unique nature of the parent–child relationship, and especially the "developmentally reparative" effects of the parenting experience can have just such a positive extra-analytic influence.

The psychoanalytic literature dealing specifically with the relationship between parenthood and psychoanalysis is limited to Hal Hurn's (1969) paper, "Synergic Relations between the Processes of Fatherhood and Psychoanalysis." Hurn commented on the lack of interest in the subject at that time, which surprised him, since there were striking parallels between the structural changes occurring in the adult parent's ego associated with parenthood and the changes in the analysand's ego as a result of psychoanalytic treatment. In both instances, he states, there is a powerful motive force, the basic transference in the case of analysis, and the parent's love for the child in the case of parenthood, that counteracts defensive–resistance forces and enables unacceptable tendencies to enter into the matrix of preconscious derivatives (p. 446). He reported the analysis of a patient with a narcissistic personality disorder with whom he was unable to establish a therapeutic alliance or transference neurosis. The patient's exaggerated narcissistic demands and imperious behavior precluded any analytic process, although the patient received therapeutic relief and discontinued treatment after a 2½-year period. When the patient returned a year later, Hurn reported:

Although there was no change in the steady analytic posture of the analyst, in a few months there began to appear, at first infrequently, but shortly thereafter with mounting regularity, a strikingly new and different kind of response to the analyst's interventions. Instead of responding as though he had hardly heard the analyst, and there being no subsequent evidence of any impact on him as in the previous period, the patient now began to employ a special form of rejoinder that indicated unambiguously an interested understanding of the analyst's communications and a willingness to test conjointly the hypothesis presented. These rejoinders were in the nature of spontaneous, associative memories of interactions between his son and himself or between his son and various family members. (1969, p. 441)

Hurn goes on to cite examples of how his patient would immediately associate to some relevant observation of the son's behavior when the analyst made an interpretive comment about the patient. The associations to the son were used by the patient as a device to objectify and understand the interpretation, were nondefensive at this stage of the analysis, and were decisive in helping to cement a therapeutic alliance. Hurn discusses the synergic relationship between fatherhood and psychoanalysis and his case material indicated an improvement in the therapeutic alliance, but he did not specifically explore the relationship between parenthood and the therapeutic alliance.

A recent experience with a young woman in analysis who suffered from a severe depression resulting from early developmental fixations, and who was unable to utilize interpretations or affective recollections, enabled me to observe the relationship between her mothering experience and the psychoanalytic process—particularly the establishment of a therapeutic alliance.

CASE EXAMPLE

Mrs. N, a woman in her early 30s, was in analytic treatment three to four times weekly for 3 years, which was terminated at the patient's request. She was the mother of two latency-age children, and when she began treatment she was engaged in full-time homemaking functions.

Presenting Illness

Mrs. N sought treatment following a sudden attack of incapacitating depression manifested by symptoms of insomnia, anorexia, obsessive rumination, and a state of total physical and emotional collapse. She was unable to get out of bed and could not care for her children or perform minimal household duties. This episode had lasted for about 1 week, during which her husband had been solicitous, remained home from work to care for her, and with gentle nurturing she regained a good deal of her former strength. At the time, neither she nor her husband considered psychiatric consultation. After there had been sufficient functional recovery, and with the support and advice of friends, she sought treatment and was referred by her family physician.

When I saw Mrs. N, she was an attractive, intelligent, articulate, and reflective person who seemed eager for help. She was no longer immobilized, but she slept poorly, brooded constantly about her problems, and felt little pleasure in any aspect of her life. She was obviously still clinically depressed. She felt her current symptoms made it impossible to properly relate to her children, which was her most serious complaint, and the concern that finally brought her to therapy. There was no history of therapy prior to the present illness.

The focus of her obsessional thoughts was that she had made irreversibly wrong decisions in the past by choosing marriage and raising children; that she had thereby abandoned her earlier strivings for a professional career, and now when women her age were finishing their training and entering gratifying careers she was left out and would never catch up. Her husband had his work, her children were growing up and would eventually leave her, and she would be left with nothing. These issues of conflict between personal and family goals were very serious, and led to feelings of hopelessness and endless self-reproach.

I was able to piece together the following sequence of events which were the precipitants leading to the acute illness: Mrs. N is the youngest of two children, with a sister 4 years older who is married, has two children, and lives in another city. As children they were never close, but as they became older, and particularly since having children, they found more in common. During this particular year, her sister had nowhere to go in the summer and wanted to get out of the city where she lived, so Mrs. N invited her sister and the children to stay with her for a month. Conditions were crowded and uncomfortable, but she took great pains to make her sister and the children happy. During the month, she and her sister talked frequently about their early years at home. Mrs. N offered support and understanding which helped her sister deal with various resentments she had toward their parents. They talked about her sister's perfectionistic traits and her need to live up to exaggerated self expectations. Her sister had been in therapy off and on, and had been the family problem child, in contrast to Mrs. N, who had been self-sufficient, mature, and never a source of worry to her parents. During these talks with her sister they never discussed Mrs. N's problems or anything about her childhood recollections. At the end of the summer, Mrs. N's mother, a widow since the father's death 8 years earlier, underwent a mammoplasty operation and Mrs. N flew to her mother's home to care for her postoperatively. It was after this sequence of events that Mrs. N's mysterious breakdown occurred. The one significant introspective observation she reported from her breakdown was the recollection that during her acute illness she had the wish that her mother were there to take care of her.

Past History

Mrs. N initially described a happy, secure, uneventful childhood. During the initial diagnostic interview, when I asked questions which related to childhood dependency needs, she responded as if I were speaking a foreign language. Need help from parents? What for? Her portrayal of her own childhood was of herself as independent, providing help to others, and always knowing what she was doing. She made all her own decisions and went to her parents with issues that required their approval only after working over all the alternatives in her own mind and deciding on a course of action. Problems with her sister, peers, authority figures, or her medical needs were all taken care of without parental help. She had no recollection of any relationship or interactions with her sister—they never fought, talked, or helped one another. She recalled her sister as just being there and frequently worrying her parents.

Mrs. N's mother was raised in an orphanage following the death of her own mother within a year after Mrs. N's mother's birth. The mother's entire childhood was spent in the orphanage until age 18. The maternal grandfather was alive, but unable to care for the children. The mother had two older sisters who also spent time in the orphanage. One went to live, as a teenager, with the father to keep house for him. When Mrs. N's mother left the orphanage her father insisted she also keep house for him, which she refused, and went to live, instead, with the family of a friend from the orphanage. The orphanage friends were the mother's social community and remained so throughout her life. When mother and her friends eventually married, they remained in close proximity to one another and served as an extended family to their children. Mrs. N recalls her mother's devotion and attachment to her friends' children, which was greater than her own attachment to her mother's friends.

Mrs. N's father, an insurance agent, emigrated from Russia when he was 15. He was the oldest of four children. His father had left the family behind in Russia for 10 years, from the time the father was 5, until age 15, in order to establish himself in America. The father was recalled as extremely quiet, reliable, and a man who rarely expressed his feelings or thoughts. Mrs. N had no recollection of childhood interactions with him except for occasional nonverbal moments, such as sitting on his lap as he read the paper, or being together early in the morning, since they were the only early risers in the family. She felt estranged from him. When father became terminally ill, she flew home alone from overseas where her husband was stationed with the army, and moved in to help care for him. At the time, she was aware of a desperate desire to get information from him, hoping to finally know him as a person. Unfortunately, he was no more verbal than when he was well, and his death left her with intense feelings of loss and disappointment. She always felt love for him and that he loved her, but she felt also, that he died a stranger.

Mrs. N viewed her father as the dominant figure in the family, and although her own relationship with him was distant and nonverbal, she recalled watching with wonderment as he served as advisor to several male cousins. Father was a favorite and active participant in the development of these cousins, who sought him out regularly and toward whom he responded with warmth and interest. Her explanation for this was that father would have treated her that same way had she been a boy. She never saw that side of him in her own home.

Mrs. N recalled having the strong wish throughout her childhood that she had been born a boy. She recalled as a young adolescent hoping her body would not change, particularly that her breasts would not grow. For as long as she could remember, she had employed a particular masturbatory fantasy in order to achieve orgasm. A typical version of the fantasy was as follows: She arrives at the apartment of a cold, distant man, wearing a coat with nothing on underneath. He orders her to lie down on the couch and coldly uses her sexually, after which she is dismissed. She had never had an orgasm without employing this fantasy, including to the present. She reported that the fantasy had never bothered her, since she was able to separate it clearly from reality. She gave a history of gratifying sexual experiences beginning in high school, without guilt or inhibition, and considered sexual satisfaction to be an important part of her life. This continued to be true even during her most acute periods of depression.

Mrs. N viewed her mother as strong and adaptive, having made the best of such a deprived childhood. To her knowledge, her mother had never been depressed. She took what life gave her and made the best of it, achieving all she ever really wanted—marriage, security, and a family of her own. Mrs. N recalled the many times mother had told her how fortunate she was in getting a better start in life than she had had. Mother never spoke with bitterness, nor did she acknowledge feelings of deprivation connected with her early childhood spent in an orphanage—it was just a fact. It was Mrs. N who supplied the feelings for her mother. She felt a great sadness whenever she thought of her mother growing up without a mother, and recalled even as a young child feeling identified with her mother's pain. But, she was very careful to suppress her own feelings, particularly anger or unhappiness. She was, thus, on the one hand separate and independent from her mother in her actions, but in her affective life she assumed the affects of her mother rather than her own. The effect of this was to leave her feeling that she never had a childhood. She felt a deep responsibility to compensate for her mother what she had missed. This fantasy was implicit with Mrs. N but at times explicit with her mother. For example: after Mrs. N gave birth to her first child, her mother came to help out during the postpartum period. After being with her for a few days, the mother became angry that Mrs. N hadn't made coffee for her in the morning. She left abruptly, without explanation, and flew home. Mrs. N never learned directly of her mother's dissatisfaction, but only heard about it, later, from her sister.

For many years, beginning when Mrs. N was age 10, mother worked as a receptionist for a local dentist. He was probably an important transference figure and provided a type of therapeutic support, although this was never acknowledged. The myth of mother's strength and self-sufficiency was always maintained. The main point regarding mother's life adjustment and its effect on Mrs. N is that mother's early parent loss was the central psychological determinant of her life. It influenced all her parental attitudes and actions, but no one knew it. When Mrs. N started kindergarten at age 5, she felt frightened and unhappy being left alone the first day of school. Her mother's response was to keep her home the rest of the year. When she started the following year, she had no trouble at all. Mrs. N was raised in an atmosphere where separation anxiety, fears of abandonment, and the explicit anxiety about parent loss were in the forefront of everyone's mind, without the source ever being identified. Mrs. N suffered, through identification, from her mother's separation anxiety which was evident to her, despite her mother's denial. But, because she had a living mother, she had no recognition of her extreme sensitivity to separation experience until these feelings emerged in analysis.

In addition to making her own decisions and assuming a general attitude of self-sufficiency, there was another area of autonomous function that was evident throughout Mrs. N's life. She loved going to school and the whole process of learning. She could not recall ever experiencing difficulty associated with academic learning and always grasped new material easily. This was true at elementary and at higher levels of education, including college and graduate school. Her particular strength and interest was in science and mathematics, and she had little interest in the humanities. Along with her facility for mastery, she had no comprehension of examination anxiety, since she had always mastered the material and felt confident in her ability to perform.

When Mrs. N graduated from high school she chose a college (without the help of her parents) in another region of the country, preferring to be as far removed from her family as possible. She was happy at school, did well academically as usual, and rarely visited her family during semester breaks or summer vacations. Even when she required medical treatment, she made all arrangements independently, and her parents were never informed. She did not want to worry them and felt she had everything under control. She met a young man at college who graduated during her freshman year and she formed a strong attachment to him during her second year at school. She had numerous boyfriends before, but this was the first man upon whom she allowed herself to become dependent. He was a reliable, supportive person who enjoyed being needed and was neither demanding nor intrusive. When time came for her own graduation, he was moving to another city and she did not want to lose him. Previously, she had been seriously considering a career in medicine, but under the threat of separation, she married and attached herself completely to her husband's ambitions in place of her own. She worked to support her husband's passage through law school and setting up practice. When she became pregnant, she quit her job, and with her husband occupied in his professional work and no job of her own, she completely immersed herself in early child care. When the children were infants, she never left the home, nor did she want to do so. She looked back on those years as the happiest period of her life. Her desire was to be a perfect mother and create an ideal environment for her children. During the early years, she felt successful in her goal of perfect mothering and fulfilled as a woman. As the children grew, her frustration mounted as she responded to their need for separation. She was particularly frustrated with any expression of dissatisfaction or anger on their part. Her contentment depended on providing contentment for her children. Their greediness and demandingness bothered her, and she would give just a little more and try to please them. However, their sibling rivalry was a problem of a different sort. When the children fought with each other, she began to feel the first twinges of incompetence as a mother. She was unable to tolerate their hostility toward her, or one another, and when she occasionally reacted with rage, she became frightened, guilty, and mortified. At such times, she wished she had no children, a thought she could not imagine her mother ever having had. The frustration connected with the loss of the perfect mother fantasy, along with her guilt and anxiety associated with her "unacceptable" hostile feelings toward her children were the issues that eventually led to her depression. They were the major contributing factors which related to her core pathology, with the episodes of cartaking of her mother and sister serving as the final precipitants for the acute breakdown.

Clinical Course

Mrs. N perceived herself as having been a vigorous, healthy individual until, one day, she awoke sick. To her, this was all a mystery, some sort of visitation from an external source. She did not perceive her obsessional thoughts as symptomatic of depression. To her, hopelessness was a reality, and her depressed affect was the logical consequence of that reality. She was, in effect, untreatable as long as she held to this perception of her illness. She answered my questions faithfully. Her descriptions of the events and people in her life were sensitive, coherent, and perceptive. When she touched upon her current life situation and prospects for the future, the rigid depressive syndrome took over. Over the course of several sessions, as I was learning more about her, I actively challenged her concept of her illness, as to what was symptom and what was reality. I had no understanding of the source of her symptoms at that point, so my arguments appeared weak. Nonetheless, I saw no hope for any form of psychological intervention as long as she believed her illness was a response to hopeless reality, namely, being a married woman with children. Although she was stubborn and argumentative, she listened to every word I said, carried my comments away with her, and struggled to understand my point of view. There was a quality of intellectual openness which I sensed in her, despite the obvious rigidity. Her orientation was that of a student, and she could be attracted by a challenging idea. Gradually, with my persistence, her greater receptivity, and some fortuitous events, she came around.

An incident at the time comes to mind: She went to a dinner party with her husband, feeling better than usual and somewhat optimistic. At the party she was introduced to a female physician. Just the introduction was enough to remind her of what she wasn't, throw her into an acute depression, and ruin the rest of the evening. The incident "proved" to her satisfaction the irrational nature of her overreaction to minimal stimuli, and she was becoming convinced that her illness was in her way of thinking. It was this kind of movement and the possibility of engaging her intellect in self-understanding that encouraged me to pursue psychological treatment and eventually suggest analysis. It also threw me off guard, in that I did not fully appreciate the extent of her difficulty in handling affects, which I will describe later.

Although in her depressive obsessional thoughts Mrs. N communicated hopelessness, I was impressed by the intensity with which she grasped every comment I made and tried to use it as a clue to understanding her illness. She was clinging to life despite her protestations of hopelessness and was desperately anxious to recover. We had established enough rapport so that she saw me as a potentially helpful person, although she was far from satisfied with what I had accomplished so far. She was no longer in acute distress and was managing her life, albeit in a grim fashion. From what I knew at the time, she had a number of unresolved areas of conflict and unfinished development, including ambivalence about her sexual identity, conflict between self and family goals, perfectionistic self-expectations, and exaggerated defenses against dependency needs. She had maintained herself for many years utilizing adequate compulsive defenses along with denial and avoidance of conflict. Her avoidance techniques had been successful in helping her to maintain a sense of control over her emotional life. In recent years, however, those defenses had been less successful and her current illness was testimony to her need for more self-understanding and the development of broader mechanisms of adaptation. The quality of her relationship with me, which included a certain degree of transference readiness, and the use she made of the therapeutic contacts, along with her obviously high level of intelligence, encouraged me to go deeper with her.

She knew practically nothing about herself, which was striking and perplexing, particularly since she seemed to use psychological awareness in her understanding of others. She was apparently cut off from her own affective life and lacked any viable frame of reference for understanding her own regressive reactions. These were some of the considerations that entered my mind as I embarked on analytic treatment with her. Her schedule was compulsively organized around child-care responsibilities and commitments, so we were only able to work out three sessions per week in the beginning. As we had discussed the idea of analysis she was receptive if not thrilled, and felt quite strongly that "some things seemed to have gotten opened up that I'm not able to put back."

When she began using the couch, the alliance and perspective we had achieved was difficult to maintain. Whereas we had felt that a reasonably cooperative rapport had been established, she now complained that I had never helped her and she was just getting worse. It was hard for her to remember ever having had positive feelings toward me or her treatment. She reverted to concrete thought processes, was unable to consider her feelings as reactive or meaningful, and insisted on symptomatic relief. She believed I had the magical power to provide relief, but was withholding out of perverse meanness. She revealed her sadomasochistic masturbatory fantasies for the first time during the couch sessions. The revelation did not bring relief, since she was experiencing her sessions as an enactment, in reality, of her fantasy of sexual exploitation by a cold, distant man. Whereas before, these fantasies were under her control and brought sexual pleasure, in analysis the experience was erotically overpowering and frightening.

Previously, I had been able to talk to her and address an observing ego, even in the midst of anxiety and depression, but that possibility was vanishing rapidly. I directed my attention to her ego state on the couch, and tried to communicate my empathic awareness of her feelings of helplessness and her anxiety about loss of control, with the hope of helping her regain a sense of equilibrium. She sought only magical relief from me, so even my empathic comments which she confirmed were in tune with her feelings, were frustrating, since they failed to bring about immediate cure. A "holding environment" (Modell, 1976) did not provide sufficient relief of tension, since she needed my active presence so as not to feel abandoned. Silence was even more intolerable than my making useless comments. Comments of any sort were invariably perceived as accusations or criticisms. She wanted, desperately, to please me so that I might cure her. She assumed that if I wasn't curing her, she obviously wasn't pleasing me. Her thinking was so concrete and confined to the phenomenology of depression, that I had practically nothing to go on that might add to her understanding. Throughout all this she complained that analysis was making her feel "weird," and that she was losing confidence in her mind. During many sessions she would curl up in a fetal position, weep uncontrollably, and feel worse when she left. My countertransference reactions were becoming oppressive, since at that point I was feeling responsible for her suffering, which seemed to have been precipitated by my initiating analysis. I was shocked by her apparent loss of reality testing and severe ego regression, and along with her, I felt helpless in the situation.

She was angry all the time and reacted to any frustration as a personal injury, such as the end of a session, my being several minutes late, or my having to cancel an appointment. She resented my other patients and openly admitted her wish for an exclusive possessive relationship with me. These feelings, which she perceived as clearly infantile, mortified her and added to her despair. Her reactions, which derived from archaic levels of experience, could only be understood as derivatives of childhood experience and early ego states. However, she had no image of herself as a child, could not associate affects of any sort with childhood experience, and she lacked any concept of her own development. These critical defects, which represented her core pathology, I learned later were the result of her having been a parent substitute for her mother and the container for her mother's feelings rather than her own. This was a dynamic I did not understand at the time.

She had always been a star student, the first to understand the material, but now she was feeling like a retarded child. She knew there was some system for being a patient and getting analyzed, but couldn't figure it out. This was essentially true. Her cognitive regression in analysis led to concrete thinking which then precluded the search for meaning; her affective flooding left her feeling confused and disoriented, and she lost all sense of self awareness. In this state of mind all her reactions to me were dominated by extreme transference regression and could not be used therapeutically. As I was a primary nurturing object with whom she sought primitive merger and loss of boundaries, she had to defend herself by using paranoid defenses and withdrawal mechanisms. And, as a sexual object, I had become the literal representation of her sadomasochistic fantasies, which were also unmanageable.

The lack of communication in analysis had reached a point of serious impasse. All object relationships were caretaking ones, and were not available as subjects for discussion. Her feelings about the caretaker analyst, as I have described, were dominated by rage and anxiety; the other caretakers (such as her husband and friends) were rarely mentioned for fear I would interfere with her network of support. Relationships from the past were also unavailable, because of a lack of recall and her resentment of bringing up things that "only make me unhappy and can't be changed, anyway."

There was one subject that was different. When she spoke about her children, her tone was different and it was possible for me to listen and respond differently. She wanted to be a good mother and she loved her children. She revealed a wide range of affective responses to her children, including affection, pride, anxiety, confusion, frustration, and anger. The wish to be a better mother motivated her to discuss conflicts regarding her handling of situations with the children and she looked to me for help in understanding their needs. She knew I had five children and she viewed me as an authority on the subject. In addition, she told me I enjoyed my children, since every time I mentioned them I smiled. I was relieved to find a "neutral" subject we could discuss, and it became one parent talking with another, rather than a doctor with a sick patient. Whereas previously I had been unable to discuss her childhood experiences as a way of understanding her transference regression, discussion of her children's experiences was productive. It should be emphasized that I did not use the material she reported about her children in an interpretive manner, bringing the focus back to her. My comments were confined to the children themselves. I began to teach her about child development, and she was an eager and apt student. Previously her communication had been inhibited and secretive, but now she described in detail the subtle and complex problems that arose with her children. She seemed intrigued by the complexity of the issues, whereas when she had talked about herself she wanted simple answers and showed no curiosity whatsoever. She utilized whatever she learned about child development to feel more competent as a mother, which reduced her feelings of guilt and frustration.

The analytic atmosphere began to lighten, noticeably, and we were able to use the same concepts derived from direct child observation to understand her reactions in the analytic situation. The data were now within the framework of normality and infinitely more acceptable. Now she was able to employ her intellectual curiosity in understanding the workings of her mind and the vicissitudes of her emotions. I believe she began to perceive the child within her for the first time as she learned to understand her children, and she began to perceive herself as a multidimensional individual. Her tolerance of affect was much greater, and the affects themselves were more neutralized. In addition, for the first time she believed that analysis could help her.

The use of Mrs. N's parenthood experiences in the analysis was a spontaneous and fortuitous development which arose from her desperate need to find a way out of her intractable regression. Her attachment to her children was the way she found. Within the analysis, I picked up on what she found useful and used it to further the analysis. Therefore, although I had not intended to do so, discussing her parenting experiences and explaining what I knew about child development became a technical intervention.

The establishment of a working alliance by the route I've described took about 18 months. We were able subsequently to work on the core problems of her primitive identification with her mother and all the anxiety associated with merger, loss of boundaries, separation, and the numerous associated defenses and aggressive phenomena. Her reactions of transference rage and self-condemnation were reduced to the signal level and we could work on them productively. Material emerged which was connected to childhood feelings of emotional isolation, recollections of her fantasies of merger, loss of boundaries, and ambivalence about her female body. Also a history was revealed of prolonged, inappropriate physical intimacy between her and her mother. Oedipal issues never emerged, nor did the father ever develop as a significant object beyond the presenting information. My impression is that Mrs. N accomplished a successful analysis of one sector of her personality, the sector associated with deep maternal issues, and the other sectors remained unanalyzed. At the end of 3 years, she achieved what she had come for and it was clear that she wanted to terminate. She had regained a sense of control and momentum in her life, was no longer clinically depressed, nor were her defenses quite as brittle as before. She had established a professional career of her own in the insurance industry, an apparent identification with her father, although the deeper meaning of that choice had never been discussed.

DISCUSSION

I have tried to illustrate through the clinical material the nature and extent of the patient's ego impairment and its manifestation in the analytic situation as an intractable regression. Also discussed were the significance of parenthood as a stimulus leading to symptomatic breakdown and as a restitutive force; and the value of an educative technical intervention in breaking through the analytic impasse.

The primary ego impairment from which the patient suffered was in the area of self and object differentiation. Her impairment must be considered as partial, rather than a complete failure to achieve self–object differentiation. She had achieved separateness, in fact, was precociously detached from her mother in her actions and intellectual functions, while arrested at a preindividuated developmental level in her affects. The genetic determinant for this developmental arrest can be found in her mother's childhood marked by early parent loss and institutional dependency with a massive use of denial regarding her (mother's) own emotional vulnerability. The patient's childhood defenses and her lack of affective individuation served a narcissistic function for her mother, who attached herself to the image of a strong, wise child and thereby creating in fantasy the mother she never had. I would speculate that the lack of affective individuation served even a more primary function for the mother. Her daughter's deep identification with her affective experience might have satisfied early childhood longings for merger with an idealized parent. I am describing powerful narcissistic strivings within the mother's personality resulting from her early childhood deprivation; again, providing a fantasy of restitution of the lost maternal object. In addition, by identifying with mother's pain which was never verbalized, the patient performed the narcissistic function of supporting mother's defenses of denial and self-sufficiency. For all these reasons, the patient functioned as a narcissistic extension of her mother and was fixated at an earlier undifferentiated level of development. Thus, narcissistic vulnerability was a prominent feature of her personality along with anxiety about merger and loss of control.

The patient had grown dependent on the maintenance of a rigid self-representation of self-sufficiency and control. Her self-sufficiency was an illusion she required to maintain her self-esteem, and her ego paid a price for this illusion (Modell, 1975). The price paid was a brittle character structure dependent on grandiose self-representations. She was intolerant of her own dependency needs or infantile wishes. Just as the affective merger had interfered with individuation and self-development, the rigid repression of all hostile aggressive impulses had impaired her capacity to tolerate conflict. Hostile feelings evoked intense anxiety at the level of fear of abandonment and fear of destroying the object. Thus in the area of drive and ego development, neutralization of hostile aggressive impulses was impaired and was defended against by primitive defenses of avoidance and denial, along with the illusion of control. Her superego was consequently primitive and harsh, as was evidenced by her depressive disorder. I regard her use of the sadomasochistic masturbatory fantasy, although certainly an overdetermined phenomenon with multiple functions, as a primitive control mechanism which protected her from the threat of merger during sexual intercourse.

The analytic transference opened up her repressed childhood dependency longings as well as her archaic merger fantasies, and provoked a severe ego regression. Her ego was overwhelmed by the intensity of primary process fantasies and her anxiety was diffuse, traumatic, and at the paranoid level. I believe the threat to her ego was perceived in exaggerated terms as loss of boundaries and annihilation. Her reality testing function was overwhelmed by the regression and her fantasies were indistinguishable from reality. The transference situation could no longer be perceived as if it were the revival of archaic fantasies, but became the realization of those fantasies. Her ego regression also mobilized magical thinking, which further deepened her inaccessibility to therapeutic intervention or interpretation. Her only wish was for immediate relief from an omnipotent controlling object. Her reflective, observing functions vanished, and as an omnipotent primary object, the analyst either provided magical relief or he did not. If he failed, her frustration and rage only intensified her regression and the further need for exaggerated paranoid defenses. In summary, the core problem of developmental arrest associated with poor self–object differentiation, the intolerance of affects related to dependency and aggression, the dependency on grandiose self-representations, along with her loss of reality testing and the self-observing function, made analytic intervention impossible. All experiences were focused in the immediate analytic transference, the analyst had become a persecutor, and the analytic relationship had become a psychotic transference.

In the light of the patient's areas of ego impairment, what did the parenthood experience mean to her, what functions did it serve, and what effect did it have on her life adjustment? The patient's character structure, as previously discussed, was organized around defenses against merger, which was associated with anxiety about loss of boundaries. The early relationship with the mother had been overstimulating with regard to merger type of feelings. The material which eventually emerged in analysis revealed evidence of excessively close physical contact between mother and child, with cuddling and huddling together for warmth. This had continued well into adolescence and was a perpetuation of mother's relationship with the other girls in the orphanage. The patient feared the merger as a threat to individuation, while craving physical intimacy as a source of warmth. The clinical findings suggested that her Oedipal development was arrested and that men, who were important objects for her, were perceived primarily as nonthreatening mothers. There was no evidence in the analytic material of meaningful Oedipal issues—triadic conflicts with sexually differentiated objects. A man served an important function as tension regulator, source of security, and the vehicle for her becoming a mother. Marriage did not pose a threat to her in that arrangements were possible in the marital relationship between two adults that enabled her to satisfy basic needs while maintaining emotional distance and control. Childbirth introduced the element of loss of control.

The drives and affects stimulated by the early mothering experiences were at the deepest level of psychological experience (Benedek, 1959). If we assume that primitive merger experience was a powerful motive force in the patient's psychic structure, and that defenses had to be rigidly maintained against the merger, then we must view childbirth and early infant mothering as an equally powerful event which mobilized her deepest longings. The fact that she enjoyed the period of "perfect mothering" and experienced it as the fulfillment of her deepest fantasies, reflects an identification with her mother's basic values, a revival of her own early childhood experience, and the satisfaction of her wish for merger without the problem of anxiety. All other object relationships that offered the potential for merger threatened her with loss of ego boundaries. Only merger with her infant children allowed for deep gratification of self and object needs without threat to either. The early mothering experience was a restitution of an earlier ego state and deeply gratifying. With the onset of her children's moves toward separation, the stage was set for her mounting feelings of frustration and eventual symptomatic breakdown. One can speculate as to what the patient might have been like had she never given birth to children. Would she have been protected against the frustration, guilt feelings, and threat to self-fulfillment she eventually associated with motherhood? That is certainly possible, although admittedly, a moot point, since she had such strong maternal drives and was unlikely to deprive herself of the gratification of having children. If she had protected herself from the dangers associated with parenthood, one can imagine her as stable, technologically oriented, and emotionally cold.

The parenthood experiences clearly opened her up to frustration and feelings she had never before felt. Having been so dissociated from her own childhood affects and needs, she had no available childhood self representation. Lacking an image of herself as a child, and concomitantly cut off from childhood memories, she had no comprehension of her own children's feelings of rivalry, greediness, or any behavior associated with regression. She understood separation, although before analysis she had no recognition of her own sensitivity in this area, and she conceptualized good mothering almost exclusively in terms of protection and gratification. When optimal frustration became more appropriate she was at a loss. She was also at a loss to understand feelings of anger toward her children, and the comparison with the image of her mother's total devotedness evoked profound guilt feelings and depression. In this precarious state of balance, even had the precipitating events (the caretaking of her mother and sister) not occurred, it was just a matter of time until some event stimulated her own repressed dependency needs and caused a symptomatic breakdown.

Turning now to parenthood as a restitutive force and the use of an educative technical intervention, the first point to consider is the profound relief associated with talking about her children rather than herself. It is not unusual for patients in analysis to focus away from themselves when they feel threatened by the intensity of transference feelings. In addition to their children, analysands dwell on their spouses, lovers, parents, businesses, hobbies, and patients, to name just a few. The motivation is often primarily defensive, as an avoidance of the transference, but not always. The extra-analytic objects may be associated with significant conflicts, drive derivatives, and reparative tendencies. Often there is much of value that is learned from understanding of extra-analytic transference and real experiences, and the more impaired the patient's ego, the more the focus is likely to remain on these extra-analytic objects for a long time. It is implicit in the thesis I am presenting that because of the close association of parenthood with libidinal and developmental issues, discussion of child-related issues and parenting experiences is among the most valuable of all extra-analytic material, particularly in helping to form a therapeutic alliance.

When the patient talked about her children instead of herself she was able to distance herself from her hostile feelings toward the analyst and toward her children. When she was away from the intensity of their demands and her frustration, she could think about them, which helped restore her sense of intellectual mastery. She was, at the time, suffering from her parenthood, so there was strong motivation to bring them into analysis, in contrast to bringing in her husband or mother, who were not central concerns. I think it was also significant that the focus of her thoughts about the children was her own frustration and guilt feelings, rather than feeling there was something wrong with them. It was crucial to her self-esteem that she be the normal mother of normal children. She was not obsessed with her children's normality, but seemed to take it for granted. Had she, for whatever reason, perceived her children to be defective, that would have made her own recovery near impossible. It was the perception of herself as defective for the first time, which made the treatment experience so narcissistically damaging. Therefore, focusing on her children in the analysis helped the patient recover her equilibrium by distancing her from transference rage and rage toward her children, by restoring her intellectual defenses, and by opening up a line of communication in an area vital to her self-esteem.

Once the patient was no longer in a state of trauma and was able to use her primary ego resource, her intellect, she talked about her children as separate objects, and was receptive to learning more about them. When she had perceived herself as the sick, retarded analytic patient, understanding was out of the question; but with the issues now objectified, she could accept her need for more information as she had always accepted learning new ideas at school. She wasn't ashamed of not knowing more about childhood, since she always knew her mother had no model and was unable to really teach her. She was grateful for the opportunity to discuss "real" problems with me and seemed to incorporate every useful new idea. This led to many cognitive advances in her understanding of regression, childhood perceptions of reality, fantasy life, transference displacements, the expression of affect, ambivalence, and the role of the parent in the ongoing process of development.

What emerged from this educative process was a frame of reference for thinking about childhood experiences. Without that frame of reference she had been unable to tolerate her own transference reactions which were literal and immediate. The self-observing function of the ego is the essential ego function related to the establishment of a therapeutic alliance (Greenson, 1965). For the self-observing function to be useful in the analytic situation, a patient has to be able to observe his/her own transference reactions, and the understanding of the transference ultimately depends on the capacity to cathect childhood self-representations. We take this capacity for granted in more differentiated patients, but where there has been interference with the normal internalization of a childhood self-representation, which would apply to many cases of premature self-sufficiency, the ego is impaired in a critical function that prevents the establishment of a therapeutic alliance.

There is precedence in the literature for conceptualizing the technical approach to therapeutic alliance as an educative process. Greenson's (1965, p. 157) definition of the working alliance (therapeutic alliance) is, "the relatively non-neurotic, rational rapport which the patient has with his analyst. It is this reasonable and purposeful part of the feelings the patient has for the analyst that makes for the working alliance." Later on (p. 161), in one of his case illustrations, he describes a patient with a passive–compliant attitude toward the analysis: "He did not know what he was supposed to do in the analytic situation." And again, regarding the same patient, "I carefully explained, whenever it seemed appropriate, the different tasks that psychoanalytic therapy requires of the patient." Greenson is describing a need to educate his patient about psychoanalysis, what it requires of the patient, and why. Granted, he was not conducting an introductory course in child development, but neither was he writing within the context of the widening scope of indications for psychoanalysis. When he confirmed after 6 months of analysis that his patient suffered from "insatiable infantile hunger and a terrible rage" (p. 162), he diagnosed schizoid "as if" character and referred him for psychotherapy.

If a preanalytic patient is ever to become analyzable, the capacity to form a therapeutic alliance has to be nurtured and facilitated by technical means. The patient will need to learn a great deal about the source of the frightening and literal reactions he/she has in the transference situation in order to relax rigid automatic defenses and begin to view the treatment situation in more symbolic, "as if" terms. The patient will learn from his/her experience with the analyst, and whatever techniques the analyst is able to employ that facilitate the learning process can only be helpful.

It would be hard to imagine talking to a patient in an explicitly educative manner who was engaged in an analytic process, since the intervention would be so loaded with transference meaning that it would probably never be successfully analyzed. However, with a patient in a preanalytic phase, who is not yet able to tolerate interpretation or transference exploration, what is there to lose? It might also hold that the educative intervention would never be analyzed, but then again, it might not be necessary to do so. What I am suggesting is that for a patient who is so ego impaired that the transference becomes literal and unmanageable, and where a prolonged preanalytic phase is necessary, an explicitly educative technical approach that helps to organize primary process experience in a cognitive developmental framework is bound to have a developmentally reparative effect.

SUMMARY

The thesis was presented that a relationship exists between the parenthood experience and the establishment of a therapeutic alliance in analysis. Illustrative case material was presented of a patient with severe ego deficits in self-perception and affective recall whose childhood self-representation had been undeveloped due to lack of differentiation. The technical use of observations of the patient's children as reported in analysis to explain child development helped to bring about cognitive advances, the integration of affect, new self-representations, and the restitution of healthy defenses. These changes in ego structure enabled the patient to establish a therapeutic alliance.

REFERENCES

Benedek, T. Parenthood as a developmental phase: A contribution to the libido theory. *Journal of the American Psychoanalytic Association*, 1959, *7*, 389–417.

Greenson, R. R. The working alliance and the transference neurosis. *Psychoanalytic Quarterly*, 1965, *34*, 155–181.

Hurn, H. Synergic relations between the processes of fatherhood and psychoanalysis. *Journal of the American Psychoanalytic Association*, 1969, *17*, 437–451.

Kohut, H. *The analysis of the self*. New York: International Universities Press, 1971.

Modell, A. A narcissistic defense against affects and the illusion of self-sufficiency. *International Journal of Psycho-Analysis*, 1975, *56*, 275–282.

Modell, A. The holding environment and the therapeutic action of psychoanalysis. *Journal of the American Psychoanalytic Association*, 1976, *24*, 285–308.

Panel. Conceptualizing the nature of the therapeutic action of psychoanalysis (reported by M. Scharfman). *Journal of the American Psychoanalytic Association*, 1979, *27*, 627–642.

Valenstein, A. F. The concept of classical psychoanalysis. *Journal of the American Psychoanalytic Association*, 1979, *27*, 113–136.

24

PSYCHOANALYTIC DEVELOPMENTAL
PERSPECTIVES
ON PARENTHOOD

DONALD D. SCHWARTZ

Good childhood or bad, happy or unhappy, if for some reason the adult can
allow himself to live with the sufferings of his childhood and reach a degree
of reconciliation with them as a part of his development; if he is able to "reflect"
or relive the same emotions he had as a small child on this or another occasion;
if he has managed to work through his early experiences (not necessarily in
analysis) and come to find it natural in retrospect and remoteness that he did
once have infantile needs; if he considers those needs of the past as much a part
of himself as his history is a part of himself; if in the course of growing up,
and perhaps with the aid of his sense of humor, he has gained some perspective
towards those needs—then he can begin to take for granted the child's primitive
behavior. Then he will not feel seduced or endangered by being confronted with
the manifestation of primary process. Then he can permit himself to gradually
live in the strange fantasy world of children and, by the way of sublimation,
to be their guide and enjoy their growth.

In this relatively simple statement, Christine Olden (1953, p. 125) presents
something of the essence of being a parent. An elaboration and refinement of
her descriptive comments within a psychoanalytic conceptualization of parenthood will serve as the background against which to focus on the psychopathology
of mothers and fathers in the process of raising their children.

A parent is defined as a person who has gotten or borne a child; a father
or mother; and parenthood as the state or position of being a parent (*Oxford
Universal Dictionary*, 1955). Parent derives from the Latin *parere*, to procure,
hence to produce young; and is akin to the Latin *parare*, to procure, to prepare;
and is related to the English parturition, childbirth (Partridge, 1959). With the
possible exception of prepare (to make ready, to fit, or put in order beforehand),

Donald D. Schwartz. Faculty and Committee on Child and Adolescent Analysis, The Institute for
Psychoanalysis, Chicago, Illinois.

the definitions and etymological roots are biological, without reference to the psychological or sociological parent as caretaker which is usually referred to in discussions of parenthood.

In the evolution of life from lower forms to mammals, primates, and man, there is increased and prolonged parental care of the young after birth. Nursing in mammals results in greater safety for the young and with increased closeness, contact, and intimacy, a unique, durable bond is established between infant and mother which allows for a slower rate of growth and development (Kaufman, 1970). It is Kaufman's contention that the loss of estrus in humans enabled the woman to rear each child over a longer period of time without the loss of sexual activity or the capability of reproduction, and for the establishment of a relatively permanent male–female relationship without the intensity of sexual competitiveness. The family, formed out of the adaptation to social and economic needs and permanent sexual relations, was ultimately involved in divisions of roles. Kaufman views the evolution of parents as caretakers and the organization of cultural institutions to be based on man's biological adaptability and capacity for learning which permitted slow maturation and development as the child remained with the parents for a long time.

In their introduction to a volume devoted to the study of parenthood, Anthony and Benedek (1970) note that parenthood while a function of biology is also a "tool of civilization" and, in their view, the universality of the biological processes are markedly influenced by the social, cultural, and ontogenetic experiences of individual parents in regard to the more specific manifestations of parental attitudes and behaviors. The biological universal, the individual variations, the family, and society are interrelated and mutually influencing forces in the development of a man and woman as a father and mother. Progressively, the psychology of parenthood becomes dominant and it is to the psychosexual, object-related developmental motivations for parenthood and its psychopathology that I will direct my attention.

Parenthood may be considered as a developmental continuity which begins at birth with the coming together of the infant's innate characteristics and the maternal surround, and proceeds with increasing complexity throughout an individual's personal development to be actualized in the experiences of being a parent to one's child. The mother and father of a newborn infant each have a history of parent–child relationships with their own parents, grandparents, and others, including older siblings. They have had innumerable opportunities to carry out caretaking functions; as young children playing at being parents (both mother and father), doing what parents do, in acting as a "parent" to younger brothers and sisters, or other younger children, in behaving as they believe (consciously and unconsciously) their parent would in certain circumstances with friends, and at times in taking care of their own parents. Thus, the biological parent engages his child in the process of becoming a psychological parent with an established conscious and unconscious network of images and configurations (influenced as much by the psychic reality as the actuality of the parent) of what it is to be a parent.

Complex in itself, parenthood cannot be understood in isolation from the total personality with its various lines of development. Parenthood is an integral part of a parent's personality, influencing and influenced by all aspects of the parent as a person. Concomitant with continuing individual development as an adult, a parent in the course of interactions with a child as the child progresses through his development may be able to achieve more satisfying resolutions of conflicts remaining from the parent's own previous passage through these same developmental stages. For many parents there may be an exacerbation of those neurotically resolved maturational issues with pathological consequences regarding the capability of implementing their parental responsibilities to their growing child.

The crucible of evolving parenthood is the parent–child relationship with its intrapsychic and interpersonal referents; the interpersonal behavior being a manifestation of the mainly unconscious intrapsychic meanings and motivations. It is in these transactional experiences with his child that the individual becomes a psychological parent. The child is important in the affirmation of the appropriateness of a parent's efforts to be a good father or mother and every parent knows the satisfactions and disappointments, the sense of confidence or doubt that depend upon the reflection from his child. On the other hand, a parent also strengthens and coalesces his sense of himself as a parent during those times in which the parent, wiser than the child, stands fast on what he regards to be in the best interests of the child, in some instances in spite of intense negative reactions by the child. The following is an example of this latter circumstance related by a woman during her own analysis.

Her 13-year-old daughter told my patient, her mother, that she had been invited to a party, and while she was asking for her mother's permission her manner was demanding and indicated she considered this a formality. The woman listened to her daughter's request, and in the course of their discussion discovered that most of the adolescents who would be at the party were 16 and 17 years old. (From previous experiences with an older daughter and the generally known behavior of teenagers in that area, she also was reasonably certain there would be liquor available at the party.) The mother explained reasonably and patiently why she believed it was not appropriate nor in her daughter's best interests for her to attend this party and they were soon joined by her husband who concurred with his wife's opinion. When it was clear to the girl that her parents would not give their permission, all hell broke loose. While earlier she had tried to convince them to allow her to go, now she became furious and resentful. She accused them of being bad parents who didn't want her to grow up, of not trusting her, of interfering with her social relationships, her freedom and independence. Unsuccessful efforts to gain her father as an ally were replaced by disparaging remarks about her parents, especially her mother's lack of understanding of teenagers, reminders that times had changed since they were her age, and odious comparisons with the parents of her friends. This confrontation continued over several days during which the mother experienced surges of self-doubt and ambivalence. In our analytic work the mother and I were already aware of conflicts in relation to her own unreasonably strict and restrictive fundamentalist mother which were now stimulated by her daughter. We were able to understand that the major source of the interference with her appropriate empathically based response to her daughter was her sympathetic identification of herself as an adolescent with her daughter in the present (which was unconscious), as well as a concurrent identification with the mother of her adolescence. (I will discuss empathy in relation to parenthood and psychopathological parenthood more fully later.) The latter, because it was more conscious, was rejected by the mother; however the unconscious identification with her daughter caused her anxiety, conflict, and uncertainty. In regard to an older daughter, my patient's behavior as a parent had at times been such that from an interpersonal view she would probably have been considered "permissive." From a psychoanalytic intrapsychic perspective we understood that when she determined she would not be like her mother she had at the same time identified with her daughter's ostensible wishes and vicariously achieved gratification via her daughter's acting on (out) her mother's unconscious desires. It was possible in her analysis to reconstruct the unconscious communication between my patient and her mother during her adolescence when she had also identified with her mother in regard to the mother's severely repressed sexual wishes and fantasies. In her relation with this older daughter, the same unconscious projection and identification had occurred; and with her mother's permission the girl had acted out to a certain extent. It was these same identifications in regard to her 13-year-old daughter which became conscious, and with analysis enabled her to empathically realize her daughter's underlying anxiety and hope that her mother would not allow her to place herself in a social situation for which she was not yet emotionally ready. Both parents were able to maintain firmly their belief in the correctness of their parental action in the face of their child's intense negative reactions and insistence (corresponding to the unconscious conflicts, impulses, and related identifications of the mother). The girl finally accepted, ungraciously, the decision of her parents and subsequently indicated indirectly her relief and appreciation of her parents for their understanding of what was best for her.

This vignette demonstrates a not unusual form of pathological parent–child interaction with my emphasis being on the psychodynamics of the interference with a mother's conscious intention to be a good parent when unconscious conflicts involving autonomy and sexuality intruded.

The child from infancy on, with his idiosyncratic rhythms—for example, regarding sleep and hunger—preferences, traits, and characteristic modes of gratification and interaction, profoundly influences the evolving parenthood of his mother and father. Generally the literature on mother–infant, mother–toddler relations indicates that via mutual cueing between them the infant and young child adapt to maternal (and paternal) attitudes and expectations; that the child shapes himself to the human environment, and becomes the child of his mother (Mahler, 1968). There is an expanding literature related to early development (Emde, 1981; Lewis & Rosenblum, 1974) which emphasizes the parents' responses to their child's individuality and the parents' adaptation to the infant's requirements and preferences, that is, the influence of the infant on the mother. An empathic mother (and often enough an unempathic mother) also becomes the mother of her particular infant. This can be readily extrapolated to apply to children and adolescents as well. It is in this mutual reciprocating cueing, conscious and unconscious, that the development of a parent in conjunction with the unfolding development of the child occurs with the infinite varieties of healthy and pathological outcomes. One area of personality which may be expanded or succumb to psychopathological reaction in the process of becoming a parent is that which involves the mother's coming in touch with her "fatherliness" and the father with his "motherliness" (Benedek, 1970b). As this includes identification with one's own parent of the opposite gender, ensuing anxiety, conflict, and defense may disturb a parent's ability to respond appropriately to the child's developmental needs. I will present such an occurrence which is exemplified by the reactions of a man to the birth of his second child, a boy.

The man whose "mothering" care during the infancy of his first child, now 3½, was a willing and pleasurable experience, reported his awareness of difficulty after the birth of his second child, also a son. He realized he was ignoring the baby, felt uncomfortable, and avoided the caretaking he had enjoyed with his first child. In analyzing this, the most readily accessible unconscious significance of the baby was the identification by the father of this son with his own brother (about 3½ years younger) and the accompanying feelings of displacement (which was conscious) and hostility toward the infant (which was preconscious). Further analysis revealed a more serious motivation for this father's discomfort. He had identified himself with his mother which was first manifest in the form of anxiety about a "feminine identification," with some not especially prominent references to castration anxiety. The dominant cause of the interference with his "maternal" parental relationship was the identification with his mother as she was at the time of the birth of her second child, his younger brother. From family information and transference in the analysis, we understood that his mother had not wanted a second child and took care of him only reluctantly. At the time of his brother's birth and infancy, this man's childhood phase of development included as a major component his identification with his mother as an active caretaker of children. It was the intensification of this identification (with a mother who wanted to ignore the baby, though she didn't) after the birth of his second child which motivated his behavior; that is, his behavior was in accordance with his mother's conscious and unconscious feelings toward her second child. For this man such an attitude was not in accord with his image of himself as a parent, yet the unconscious identification compelled him to behavior which represented a neurotic parental interaction.

This illustration of a parental psychopathology, as was the one involving the mother and her daughter, is taken from an analysis where the complexities could be made conscious, clarified, and differentiated as well as interrelated. I present it to demonstrate under close scrutiny what may be involved in a parent's inappropriate reactions to his child at a particular time in the child's life. Not only are there the more ubiquitous reactions, such as hostility toward a child unconsciously perceived as a sibling, or anxiety and conflicts related to a sense of masculinity or femininity, but there are parental responses which are determined by idiosyncratic aspects of the parent's personal ontogenetic development.

Therese Benedek (1959), in a paper which was to become a cornerstone of psychoanalytic investigations of parenthood, stated, "In the process of striving toward this goal [of being a good parent], through the continued alternations between success and threatening failures of parenthood, the parent's personality undergoes changes which under normal circumstances seem to justify our assumptions that *parenthood is a developmental phase*" (p. 416). In a 1974 panel (Parens, 1975), Benedek, in agreement with Brody and contrary to Kestenberg's view, said she regretted having conceptualized parenthood as a developmental phase, and that she had for some time considered that developmental *process* was a more appropriate designation. (This change in view is evident throughout her contributions to the study of the psychology and psychopathology of parenthood; Anthony & Benedek, 1970.) From a psychoanalytic frame of reference, parenthood does not involve predominant phase specific developmental tasks resulting in higher levels of psychic organization. In a developmental perspective on the psychopathology of parenthood, development is more meaningfully considered as a process than as a phase of development and the suggestions of Colarusso and Nemiroff (1979) are applicable to that issue. They offer five psychoanalytic hypotheses regarding the developmental process in adults, among which they include the proposition that in childhood development the focus is "primarily on the 'formation' of psychic structure" and development in adulthood is "concerned with the continuing 'evolution' of existing psychic structure and with its use" (p. 62). This accords with the standard definition of development and evolution as a gradual unfolding, a fuller working out of the details of anything; to bring out what exists implicitly or potentially. A corollary question is when does parenthood end?

Throughout the Michael Reese Hospital Conference on Parenthood held in Chicago in March 1980, there was general agreement (including mine) with the thesis of parenthood as a developmental phase which extended throughout the adult life cycle and included becoming a parent to one's aging parents. Upon further reflection, I think it to be otherwise. I find it unlikely that a phase of development can extend over some 40 to 50 years, nor does it seem to me valid to consider the inevitable regression and deterioration which accompanies aging as developmental, assuming that development implies progressive maturation. The regression (which is certainly not total) in aging parents does not permit us to equate them with children in the process of growing and developing, and to thus designate the care for elderly parents by their children now adults as parental and the caretakers as parents to the parents. In my view, parenthood as an aspect of adult life during which a mother or father acts in relation to his/her child as a facilitator of that child's development ends when the child enters upon young adulthood after traversing his/her adolescence. E. J. Anthony (1970), writing about parental reactions to adolescence, states, "[Optimally, the parent helps] the process of separation and individuation to its completion and culmination in the adult child. A new relationship becomes possible in which two adults linked by mutual happy memories, find to their surprise (not knowing the strength of the identification process) that they have many interests in common and discover a new mature pleasure in each other as people. This pleasure is no longer derived from the old anaclitic model but depends upon the rediscovery of the child as adult object, the parent having gracefully relinquished the child at the start of adolescence" (p. 320).

Aside from the use of this quotation in support of my contention that parenthood gradually comes to an end as the relationship of parent to child and vice versa gives way to one of mature adult to maturing adult, the preceding comments refer to an important aspect of parent–child experiences with implications for understanding parenthood and its pathological manifestations. While Anthony's observation centers on separation and individuation in adolescence, the principle involved is applicable to parental involvement in every phase of a child's development. A twofold task of parenthood is the management of a balance between the parent's identification with the child which tends to blur the distinction between the psychic representations of the parent and child on one hand, and on the other to maintain a representation of the child as separate and individualistic (Kestenberg, 1975). Both occur simultaneously, thus enabling the parent to act upon an empathic appreciation of the needs and wants of the child. Intrapsychically the child is differentiated from the parent and other children, although the psychic representations of the child change over time. The parent integrates the representations of the child of the past with the child of the present and those images of the potential and wished for child, "unless the parent's mental health fails, the process which integrates the past and present never ceases; the child is never alien, never a stranger" (Benedek, 1970a, p. 190). These obviously involve more than representations relating to separation—individuation and self and object differentiation, and what can be inferred about the influences of parental psychopathology in the area of object relations must be applied to libidinal and aggressive aspects of personality development. Such strivings and their vicissitudes, with the associated inevitable conflicts, are vital in the formation of ego and superego.

Parents may interfere selectively with their child's natural developmental processes. A parent who encourages a child appropriately toward independence in general may impose serious restrictions on the same child in regard to sexuality. The result, for example, can be a child who is physiologically pubertal, and chronologically teenaged, but psychologically entrenched in latency. This circumstance is not unfamiliar to therapists who work with children and adolescents. Another frequently observed configuration is that of a child who acts out the unconscious wishes of a parent who is upset consciously by the child's behavior (Johnson & Szurek, 1952). The father of a young boy, referred to me because of repeated fighting, was outspoken in his condemnation of his son's seemingly unbridled aggression but unaware of how he glowed with pride as he enthusiastically recounted the details of his son's altercations.

I have presented examples illustrating attitudes of parents toward a child which speaking broadly are causative in effecting inhibition on the one hand and a lack of self control on the other. The parent may be conscious or unconscious of his attitude of encouragement or discouragement and identification is an important constituent in the psychic processes involved, as is whether the psychopathology of the parent is chronic throughout the child's development or is evoked during one phase of the child's life. These will be discussed more fully later. The degree to which the parent's wishes and conflicts and the communication of these to the child are conscious or unconscious and the behavior is obvious or subtle, is a determinant of the nature of the parental influence on the child.

The illustrative value of the examples and clinical vignettes presented thus far is predicated on a view of psychopathology of parents in relation to development. The evolution of parenthood is inextricably bound to the epigenetically unfolding development of the child. The term "psychopathology of parenthood" is somewhat inaccurate for the phenomena under discussion, which would more precisely be referred to as the psychopathology of a man or woman which interferes with the capability of functioning as a good-enough father or mother in relation to a particular child at any particular age and phase of development. An understanding of parental psychopathology will be clarified with some discussion of the question of what is a good-enough parent, and a brief overview of development which I will take up later in this chapter.

Parenthood as consciously perceived and intentioned is unique to human beings. As a developmental process which takes place in a psychological field involving the mutual interactions between parent and child, it is a human psychological experience which evolves in concert with biological, phylogenetically determined potentials for parental behavior. Human beings are not bound by the innate instinctual-like predispositions. The evolutionary underpinnings of parenthood which initiate the process of becoming a parent are most prominent in the mother in the early months of her infant's life. Because of this, a parent is able to initiate and respond, delay, prolong, and vary the parental part of parent–child experiences according to the needs and preferences of the infant, child, or adolescent (and at times according to the need and preference of the parent). With increasing complexity, the psychologically motivated basis for parent–child interactions becomes predominant; and within a relatively stable character structure, the already present identifications and representations making up the psychic configuration of parent are activated in the actual experiences of these interactions. Transactional experiences between parent and child are not simply action and reaction and often involve simultaneous communication and effects between both participants; and the multiplicity of motivations involved include influences of the other parent, siblings, social mores and cultural traditions. Empathy is essential in determining whether the parent interacts with the child in ways that are growth inducing and disturbances in empathy (manifestations of underlying psychopathological reactions) may result in inappropriate responses which interfere with development. However the capacity for empathy is not itself synonymous with being a parent, nor is every failure in empathy indicative of parental psychopathology.

Empathy is a complex psychological experience by which one may comprehend the inner life of another person and thus be able to use that understanding to respond in a manner that is in the best interests of that other person. Empathy in a parent entails a temporary trial identification (Fleiss, 1953) by which the parent puts himself in the child's emotional place while remaining himself at a higher, more integrated level of psychic organization. When the latter does not happen, the parent may sympathize with the child, that is, identify with the child, and be unable to do other than experience himself just as the child feels or the parent imagines the child feels: triumphant, enraged, humiliated, anxious, helpless, confused. Empathy is closely correlative with being a good-enough parent.

Good-enough parent is a term obviously derived from the "good-enough mother" of Winnicott (1965) and represents the human parents in a child's average expectable environment. A good-enough parent is not self-consciously preoccupied with being the perfect mother or father. Good-enough parenthood is imperfect, a condition which is inherent, inevitable, and indeed a psychological necessity in the developmentally elicited parent–child relationships. A good-enough parent (sometimes both parents acting together) is just that, good-enough for his child; good-enough in taking into account that child's personal individualistic nature at every stage of development, and providing what is required —protection, modulation, stimulation, acceptance, criticism, encouragement — when appropriate and in an appropriate manner. A good-enough parent facilitates the child's evolving maturation at each developmental level and the most effective and satisfying experience occurs when, for example, a mother can simultaneously and harmoniously be herself in the act of being a parent to her child. Such parents will spontaneously and thoughtfully "know" the multiple factors (narcissistic, sexual, aggressive, self-regulation, guilt, shame, anxiety, peer group values and pressures) involved in any experience and situation and respond to what is most relevant for that child at that time. The mother who must modulate excessive tension in her child will behave differently in doing so if the child is an infant, a toddler, or a pubertal boy. Similarly, the father of an early adolescent daughter can optimally respond to her with recognition of her age and phase appropriate physical and social sexuality while not becoming overstimulating nor ignoring her psychosexual development. Before continuing with the psychopathology of parenthood, I will present an overview of psychic development from a psychoanalytic point of view.

The essential premise upon which the psychoanalytic theory of psychic development is based is the mutually influencing effects of nature and nurture; the innate and the ontogenetic. Initially and over a long period of time the most important persons in the nurturing human surround are the child's mother and father. Out of innumerable and repeated experiences between them, the child gradually evolves ontogenetically into a psychological being whose thoughts, motivations, affects, and behavior are the resultants of the interrelationship of psychic systems. Through progressive sequential developmental stages the child becomes an individual who is relatively stable and autonomous from, though still influenced by, internal motivations as well as significant persons in his life.

Throughout the epigenetic unfolding of human development as a child traverses the psychosexual phases, nature (libidinal and aggressive drives, the inborn primary autonomous ego functions, self representations) and nurture (mother and father and the child's psychic object representations of them) are united from the beginning of postpartum existence. As a consequence of an infinite number of reciprocal transactions between child and parents, and the establishment of psychological constellations of increasing complexity, differentiation, and integration, a developmental progression of hierarchically ordered levels of psychic organization and motivation occurs. Evolving through narcissism, the formation of psychic structure culminates in the cohesive psychic systems id, ego, and superego with their attendant psychological functions. The process of identification is essential in the psychoanalytic conceptualization of the creation of psychic structure out of the interactions of self and object representations referent to actual interpersonal experiences and the influence of the existing psychic reality (Freud, 1905, 1914, 1917, 1923, 1926, 1930). Associated with these developments are the institution of psychological defenses and the gradual advance through separation and individuation to self and object constancy and a coherent sense of self identity manifest as an individual's character or personality.

Therese Benedek (1959), referring to mother and infant, contends that through reciprocal introjection and projection structural change occurs in each participant and states "in each 'critical period' [of development] the child revives in the parent his related developmental conflicts. This brings about either pathological manifestations in the parent, or by resolution of the conflict it achieves a new level of integration in the parent. In turn, the child reaches each 'critical period' with a repetition of the transactional processes which lead anew to the integration of the drive experience with the related object and self representations" (p. 397). In her conceptualization of the family as a psychological field, she iterates this view of psychic changes as a result of reciprocal processes in regard to the marital partners and the child and concludes that the psychopathology of parenthood is comprised of "the manifestations and the intrapsychic and interpersonal spirals that evolve in such critical phases of parenthood which leave transient or permanent scars in the parent and the child" (Benedek, 1970b, p. 130). The development of parenthood is an ongoing process in interaction with the child's sequential developmental phases, and it is those psychodynamic constellations which interfere with empathy and result in at least partial failure of a parent's efforts to facilitate the child's unfolding development which I will now consider.

Development in every phase is multidetermined involving narcissistic, object-related, and drive motivations in mutual and conflictual interaction along various lines of development (A. Freud, 1965). In each phase specific issues will be most dominant (Freud, 1909; Erikson, 1950; Blos, 1962) and the hierarchically ordered levels of psychic organization are evidenced in sublimated forms as well as neurotic and characterological psychopathology. A child in the immediacy of living through a phase of development acts as a powerful stimulus in evoking in his parents the parents' past experiences and conflicts in regard to that phase. Where there has been pathological resolution for the parent, the effect of the child's experiences will be to intensify these conflicts with inappropriate interactions by the parent in response to the child. The manifestations of such underlying psychopathology is already evident in the parent's interpersonal relationships, for example, within his/her marriage, in work, with friends and enemies, and the unconscious repetition of the pathological object relations and conflicts of the parent's personal history is inevitable and of special importance in relation to his/her child. There are reasons for this. For one, a parent always maintains a narcissistic investment in a son or daughter which tends to blur the distiction between psychic representations of the self and the child. In the psychoanalytic theory of structure formation, identification has a central role, and developmental arrests or fixations involve sexual and aggressive impulses in relation to self and object representations; and regressive experiences in the present involve these psychopathological constellations of the past (Sandler & Rosenblatt, 1962). The ongoing developmental processes in the child which entail dynamic interactions between representations of self and object (the most vital of which are the parents) are actualized in interpersonal exchanges between child and parent, while in the parent the regressively elicited imagos of his past are in psychodynamic exchange with mental representations of the child in the present. The parent in response to real encounters with his child will remain unconscious of the pathological fixations which impel his behavior toward the child, that is, the confluence of psychic representations of the child with self or object representations that belong to the parent's ontogenetic development. In clinical terms the parent's response to the child is an identification of himself with the child or a transference reaction in which the child is reacted to as if he were someone from the parent's personal past. The expression of unconscious motivations in the parent's conduct toward the child may be overt and obvious, or it may be covert and subtle, in communicating the parent's psychopathology to the child, who is also unconscious of the influence on his/her resolution of relevant developmental conflicts (Hellman, 1978). An adolescent boy in the course of his analysis was aware of the rivalry and competitiveness of his father which was openly, though not maliciously, manifest in his relationship with the son, and which the father admitted to when confronted about it by the boy. Its appearance in the positive Oedipal transference was easily interpreted because the boy and the analyst were both readily conscious of his belief that certain behavior by the analyst was a competitive reaction to the boy. There was much greater resistance to the transference involving negative Oedipal issues which included the father's homosexual attraction to his son which was unconscious to both father and son. "An analysis of transactions between parents and adolescents around a covertly sexual conflict can illustrate how both sides play out their conscious and unconscious roles in response to wishes and fears that are implied but seldom verbalized'' (Anthony, 1970, p. 316). The preceding clinical example demonstrates the results of a pathological parental interaction which in this case interfered with a healthier resolution of the Oedipus complex, in part because of the child's unconscious identification with his father's unconscious conflictual wishes and fantasies.

Parenthood evolves in direct relationship to a child and without a child there can be no parent. Of primary importance in the experiences of becoming a parent are identifications with the parent's parents established throughout the parent's psychosexual development from infancy to young adulthood. The reactivation of psychopathologically motivated psychodynamic relations on an unconscious level occur in response to the child's development and these needs and conflict which are most specific for a given phase as is amply demonstrated in Parts III, IV, and V of their volume on parenthood by Anthony and Benedek (1970) and also by Nagera (1966). Regressive identifications in the parent annul the conscious good intentions toward the child and the consequences for the child (and parent) are disturbances in self identity, self and object differentiation, and object relations in regard to dyadic or triadic levels of psychic organization, as well as neurotic solutions in regard to sexuality, aggression, guilt, and shame. The parent's major identifications are an identification with the child, identification of the child with the parent as he experienced himself at the same stage of development, and identifications by the parent with his own parents; and all of these are interrelated.

Non-development-facilitating parental relations with a child transpire when such identifications distort the parent's empathy and the parent's involvement is not reciprocal and in accordance with the state of the child physically or emotionally. The earlier example of the mother and her adolescent daughter is relevant to this as is the following one.

A woman during her analysis brought up her concerns about her 3½-year-old son's regression in regard to defecation. She was perplexed about his behavior which indicated conflicts centered around autonomy and control because she felt that she had not been overly concerned about toilet training. I asked her to tell me about her son's toilet training and her account revealed that the boy's toilet training had been accomplished by an older woman who regularly cared for him while his mother was away from home, and that she had taken it on herself to teach the boy to use the toilet without the mother telling her to do so. (It was obvious that this was in accordance with the mother's unverbalized wishes.) Furthermore, the toilet training had been forced on the boy without consideration of his readiness, at a time when he was struggling with his reactions to separation (physical and psychological) from his mother to whom he was especially close; and when the related developmental conflicts involving autonomy, which were manifest as oppositional behavior, were intense. My patient associated to what she knew of her own toilet training and remembered that her own mother was not like this woman, "She wasn't concerned about toilet training," and she proceeded to add that her mother was working at that time and her toilet training had been done by a housekeeper, apparently without her mother specifically directing the housekeeper to do so. Until I brought it to her attention, she was unaware that the memory of her mother's unconcern about toilet training coincided with her statement about herself; and that the circumstances of her son's toilet training were essentially the same as her own.

In this instance of pathological parenthood the mother, at the time her son was engaged interpersonally and intrapsychically in conflicts relevant to the anal psychosexual phase of development, had unconsciously identified with her own mother. Simultaneously she identified her son with herself at that developmental phase (represented by her toilet training experience) and was unable to empathically identify herself with her son's state of mind, his psychological needs and capabilities. (While it did not come up at this time in her analysis, it seems probable that an additional source of interference was the mother's identification of her son with her father, who in her childhood was considered uncontrollable in regard to doing what he wanted, when he wanted.)

I have used this vignette as representative of parental interactions at all levels of development in which identification enables us to understand the phase-related disturbances in the parent's response to the child.

Via regressive identification with the aggressor, the parent may identify with his own parent and the child is treated the way the parent as a child was treated; or the parent now inflicts on the child what he as a child fantasized doing to his own parent. Similarly, a commonly observed basis for failures in empathy is the identification of the child with a sibling of the parent.

A psychopathological response to a child involving projection and identification and which is particularly confusing for the child and parent is one in which a parent acts out on the child the unconscious wishes, impulses, and fantasies of the other parent. At such times the parent's behavior can be very intense or impulsive, the sense of its irrationality devastating for the parent and child, and often there is further bewilderment when the parent who enacts the wish feels guilty and is chastised by his/her spouse. Even worse is the situation in which, for example, an acting-out mother who, in the aftermath might begin to question her behavior, is told by her husband that she was absolutely justified. Not unusual is a vague feeling of resentment toward the parent who is the unconscious instigator. Closely related to this type of parental psychopathology is the involvement of a child in the complex psychodynamics and identifications of a neurotic marital relationship which becomes more acutely disturbed as a result of effects on the parents of the developmental stage of the child. While these preceding forms of aberrant parental interactions may ensue during a child's infancy and preoedipal phase, I think they are more apt to occur after an Oedipal stage of development has been achieved by the child because of the triadic nature of that phase in which reverberations are set off not only between the child and a parent but between the parents who are both actively involved in the child's Oedipus complex.

Painful for the parent, if they become conscious, are the identifications by the child with aspects of the parent which he dislikes in himself; and the frustration of his attempts to eliminate them in the child can lead to distressing parent–child relationships. When the parent must remain unconscious of such negative characteristics, he may deny its presence in the child; or while not recognizing himself in the child, the parent will find it necessary to exorcize the devil in the child by severe disapproval and punishment. Of course certain identifications by the child with traits or defenses which are detrimental for the child but ego syntonic for the parent are more pleasurable for the parent than being faced with his unacceptable aspects. Nevertheless, the pathological effect on the child's development may be even more serious as the parent and child unconsciously enter into a collusion and mutual reinforcement without even the conscious disapproval which accompanies the confrontation of the parent with his ego dystonic self.

Similar to this is the well-known identification by a parent of himself with the child and the projection onto the child of the parent's unfulfilled ambition, for example, the father in regard to his son as an athlete, usually in a particular sport, or the mother in regard to her daughter as a dancer or lawyer. When the child accepts this narcissistic investment in himself and has the talent and intellect to attain success, the overt relationship between parent and child may appear to be gratifying to both, but even superficial observation will reveal the pathological effects on the child. When the child does not respond to the parent's projected wish, the parent's disappointment or continued demands will develop into pernicious parent–child transactions distorting the child's development. This distortion may affect the child's development generally or in more specific ways, in part depending upon the unconscious meaning to the parent and the phase of the child at which this becomes a critical issue. Even more devastating for child and parent is the situation in which the child as a narcissistic extension of the parent does not possess the aptitude or mental endowment necessary to attempt to fulfill the dreams of the parent.

I have discussed in this chapter the psychopathology of parenthood from a developmental perspective, with emphasis on identification as the psychic process which is the cause of disturbances in empathy and resultant interpersonal relationships by which the parent interferes with a child's unfolding ontogenesis. I have suggested transference as a useful concept for understanding these transactions when the parent unconsciously perceives and reacts to the child as some significant person from the parent's past, most notably the parents of the parent's childhood and the parent as he experienced himself as a child. The child as he progresses through sequential though overlapping phases of development is also subject to transference reactions in which his parent of the present (phase) is experienced and responded to, or acted on, as if the mother or father were the parent of the child's past, that is, at the preceding developmental phase. This will take place during the transition to a succeeding phase with the transference behavior due to a carryover of the psychologically represented parent, which includes actual parental behavior and attitudes as well as the child's psychic reality of the previous phase of development.

Transference reactions to the parent occur as a consequence of the normal and typical temporary regressions during any stage of development and transference repetitions in the present can be the result of pathological fixations and object relations of the preceding phase. A child moving from a pre-Oedipal position to the Oedipal phase with its increasing triadic level of psychic organization and object relations may persist in an intense dyadic involvement with the parent who is the primary libidinal object. In latency, because of relatively unresolved Oedipal conflicts, the child will continue the (unconsciously) incestuous and rivalrous (transference) relationship with his/her parents; or as a manifestation of regression to pre-Oedipal concerns, the child will engage a parent in struggles related to autonomy, control, neatness, and schedules. The parent who is unable to empathically understand these transference repetitions will respond in what may be considered a countertransference reaction which is nonfacilitating of the child's development in the phase in which it transpires. For example, the parent who does not comprehend the regressive transference attitudes of the child in the course of his/her progressive maturation will reengage the child as if both of them were again in that earlier, and for the most part, superseded phase. The results will be a transference–countertransference transaction which will pathologically influence the child's (and parent's) resolution of developmental issues and conflicts pertaining to the present ongoing phase.

In considering the psychopathology of parenthood, I have taken the generally accepted position that such parental psychopathology exists only in relation to the phasic development of one's child; and I have viewed the parent as the facilitator of the child's natural unfolding development and pathological parental influence as that which interferes with that progressive development. Such behavior of the parent is an interpersonal manifestation of intrapsychic disturbance and it is not possible to understand parental psychopathology except from the psychoanalytic perspective of the internal world of the parent. I have not attempted to discuss the varieties of psychopathology which are integrally related to each phase specific constellation of developmental processes and conflicts. (The same is so in regard to parental interactions with children which are particular for motherhood and fatherhood.) These are well represented in the literature, including some of the references in this chapter, for example, the Anthony and Benedek (1970) volume on parenthood. Instead I focused my discussion on the intrapsychic basis of psychopathological parenthood, presenting vignettes from the analyses of parents to illustrate it more directly. Recognizing that it is not an exclusive frame of reference, I have given particular attention to identification—in its clinical and theoretical usages—and correlated it with the well-established concept of transference to explain the meanings and motivations of the responses of parents to their children relevant to every phase of a child's ontogenesis and a parent's development as a psychological parent.

REFERENCES

Anthony, E. J., The reactions of parents to adolescents and to their behavior. In E. J. Anthony & T. Benedek (Eds.), *Parenthood: Its psychology and psychopathology*. Boston: Little, Brown, 1970.

Anthony, E. J., & Benedek, T. (Eds.). *Parenthood: Its psychology and psychopathology*. Boston: Little, Brown, 1970.

Benedek, T. Parenthood as a developmental phase: A contribution to libido theory. *Journal of the American Psychoanalytic Association*, 1959, *7*, 389–417.

Benedek, T. Parenthood during the life cycle. In E. J. Anthony & T. Benedek (Eds.), *Parenthood: Its psychology and psychopathology*. Boston: Little, Brown, 1970. (a)

Benedek, T. The family as a psychological field. In E. J. Anthony & T. Benedek (Eds.), *Parenthood: Its psychology and psychopathology*. Boston: Little, Brown, 1970. (b)

Blos, P. *On adolescence*. Glencoe, Ill.: Free Press, 1962.

Colarusso, C. A., & Nemiroff, R. A. Some observations and hypotheses about the psychoanalytic theory of adult development. *International Journal of Psycho-Analysis*, 1979, *60*, 59–71.

Emde, R. N. Changing models of infancy and the nature of early development: Remodeling the foundation. *Journal of the American Psychoanalytic Association*, 1981, *1*, 179–220.

Erikson, E. *Childhood and society*. New York: Norton, 1950.

Fleiss, R. Counter-transference and counter-identification. *Journal of the American Psychoanalytic Association*, 1953, *1*, 268–283.

Freud, A. *Normality and pathology in childhood*. New York: International Universities Press, 1965.

Freud, S. Three essays on the theory of sexuality (1905). *Standard Edition, 7*, 125–243. London: Hogarth Press, 1953.

Freud, S. Analysis of a phobia in a five-year-old boy (1909). *Standard Edition, 10*, 3–149. London: Hogarth Press, 1955.

Freud, S. On narcissism: An introduction (1914). *Standard Edition, 14*, 67–104. London: Hogarth Press, 1957.

Freud, S. Mourning and melancholia (1917). *Standard Edition, 14*, 237–258. London: Hogarth Press, 1957.

Freud, S. The ego and the id (1923). *Standard Edition, 19*, 3–66. London: Hogarth Press, 1961.

Freud, S. Inhibitions, symptoms and anxiety (1926). *Standard Edition, 20*, 77–175. London: Hogarth Press, 1959.

Freud, S. Civilization and its discontents (1930). *Standard Edition, 21*, 59–145. London: Hogarth Press, 1961.

Hellman, I. Simultaneous analysis of parent and child. In J. Glenn, L. M. Sabot, & I. Bernstein (Eds.), *Child analysis and therapy*. New York: Aronson, 1978.

Johnson, A., & Szurek, S. The genesis of antisocial acting out in children and adults. *Psychoanalytic Quarterly*, 1952, *21*, 323–343.

Kaufman, I. C. Biological considerations of parenthood. In E. J. Anthony & T. Benedek (Eds.), *Parenthood: Its psychology and psychopathology*. Boston: Little, Brown, 1970.

Kestenberg, J. *Children and their parents: Psychoanalytic studies in development*. New York: Aronson, 1975.

Lewis, M., & Rosenblum, L. A. (Eds.). *The effect of the infant on the caregiver*. New York: Wiley, 1974.

Mahler, M. *On human symbiosis and the vicissitudes of individuation*. New York: International Universities Press, 1968.

Nagera, H. *Early childhood disturbances, the infantile neurosis, and the adulthood disturbances*. New York: International Universities Press, 1966.

Olden, C. On adult empathy with children. In R. Eissler, A. Freud, H. Hartmann, & E. Kris (Eds.), *The psychoanalytic study of the child* (Vol. 8). New York: International Universities Press, 1953.

Oxford Universal Dictionary. London: Oxford University Press, 1955.

Parens, H. (Reporter). Parenthood as a developmental phase (Panel). *Journal of the American Psychoanalytic Association*, 1975, *23*, 154–165.

Partridge, E. *Origins: A short etymological dictionary of English usage*. New York: Macmillan, 1959.

Sandler, J., & Rosenblatt, B. The concept of the representational world. In R. Eissler, A. Freud, H. Hartmann, & E. Kris (Eds.), *The psychoanalytic study of the child* (Vol. 17). New York: International Universities Press, 1962.

Winnicott, D. W. Ego distortion in terms of true and false self. In *The maturational processes and the facilitating environment*. New York: International Universities Press, 1965.

25

FATHERS IN DEVELOPMENT: AN OVERVIEW OF RECENT CONTRIBUTIONS

JOHN MUNDER ROSS

Cognizance of the importance of fathers in the lives of young children is a relatively recent development in psychology, psychiatry, and psychoanalysis. Before 1970 (a watershed year, it seems), these and related fields revealed a dearth of literature on the subject of fatherhood (Lynn, 1974; Biller & Meredith, 1974). When they did study fathers, empirical researchers (Biller, 1968a, 1968b, 1969, 1970, 1971a, 1971b; Hetherington, 1966; Santrock, 1970a, 1970b, 1972; Barclay & Cusumano, 1967; Nelson & Vangen, 1971; Nelson & Maccoby, 1966; Herzog & Sudia, 1973) tended to focus mostly on the unfortunate corollaries of *father absence*: disturbances in sex-role identity (especially so for boys); poor school performance; compromised controls; and rather deep-seated cognitive deficits. But few of these studies brought into relief the specific impact, positive or negative, of fathers when present. And they failed to explore the interpersonal, intrapsychic precipitants of father absence itself (Sprey, 1967).

Theirs remained the era of the suburban commuter. The "momism" of the '50s was still very much in the air. And so perhaps it was only natural that researchers should tend to find in fathering a void, dwelling, as they basically did, on one of the saddest trends of the times—the removal of men from the home. "Paternal deprivation," Henry Biller once called it (1974).

Our clinical literature and practice were for many years even more remiss as far as fathers were concerned. Conceptual oversights were mirrored by the pervasive and abiding failures of most clinicians and clinics to include fathers systematically in their treatment plans (see Ferholt & Gurwitt, 1982, and Staver, 1944; Stephens, 1961; Sternberg, 1951). Implicitly relegating responsibility for

John Munder Ross. Division of Child and Adolescent Psychiatry, Department of Psychiatry, Downstate Medical Center, and Department of Psychology in Psychiatry, Cornell Medical College, New York, New York.

children to "women's work," theorists as well as practitioners succumbed to the cultural limitations of their era. And at times, one cannot help musing, they further seemed to fall unconscious prey to those covert archaic myths, explicit in both young children and simple societies, whereby women remain sole agents of procreation. Their nurturance and fertility treated as incidental matters, or equated with some austere, remote authority, fathers were tacitly exempted from the responsibilities and excluded from the prerogatives of biological parenthood. Their children suffered in turn, in ideology and reality, denied a vital birthright. Profound, long-standing inner resistances diverted attention from the actuality of father–child relations (Jacobson, 1950).

Certainly, the father of Freud's early *theory* was hardly a fatherly father at all. Stepchild of Freud's own romanticized patriarchal legacy and of a surrounding Victorianism in which adult men loosed their libidinal selves in bedrooms hidden from the home, he loomed as the fantastical father–tyrant of the primal horde and the disciplinarian of the Oedipus complex. Rarely gentle, only fleetingly available, and never sensuous, the father was portrayed as the stark personification of aggressivity, of threats to his son's genitals and to his daughter's desirability and future self-worth (Freud, 1924, 1925). As such, this theoretical persona was depicted as the agent of, and model for, his children's unfolding morality, the predecessor of conscience.

Meanwhile, ironically enough, the real-life fathers described in Freud's case histories (Freud, 1905, 1909a, 1909c, 1911, 1918) proved to be distressingly sensual and corruptible—self-serving, seductive, perverse, and duplicitous. Freud's chronicles of their indiscretions and cruelties were often apologetic and obscure. Yet he could not help presenting the pathology of his subjects as *lament*—a protracted, agonized, most often sexualized appeal to a foresaking, uncaring father. For the most part, Freud merely mentioned mothers. Lacking in character, they colluded or seemed to have simply left the children to their husbands' tyrannies or inconsistencies. Their offspring thus became emotional orphans, like Oedipus the infant, victims of a psychic infanticide, unconsciously recoiling in turn from their own unwitting acts of parricide. Only occasionally in his cases and theoretical excursions did Freud isolate the generative dimensions of paternity, of "good-enough fathering": the concern and insight proferred by 5-year-old Little Hans's father (Freud, 1909a); the identificatory longing implicit in the rebellious son's patricide and ritual cannibalism (Freud, 1921); the central imperative of a dependent childhood, namely the need for a father's protection (Freud, 1927, 1930). "Protection," we modern-day observers would add, from what reigns without and within—that is, from the drives and from deneutralization.

This Oedipal father of classical analysis was destined to be dethroned during the 1950s and 1960s by ego psychology's pre-Oedipal mother. Infant observers like Bowlby (1958, 1969), Escalona (1968), Spitz (1965), and, most of all, Mahler (Mahler, Pine, & Bergman, 1975), studied the first 2 to 3 years of development, emphasizing interchanges within the dyad of baby and mother.

In part, their emphasis was an inevitable outcome of the facts themselves. During these years, a typical mother is indeed ascendant in her baby's experience. Working with the forces of maturation, she serves as chief midwife to the birth of the "self" and its sustaining executive functions.

But other factors extrinsic to the subject matter also seem to have led to this preemptive focus on mothering. For one thing, because of complex psychological reasons, as well as workaday realities, men were hard to get into observational settings with any regularity. They could be observed with their children in the lab only incidentally, or second hand—through a mother's eyes. Then, too, there was the continuing impact of the psychosocial tendencies noted earlier. But, above all, it seems to me, with increasing numbers of women rising to prominence within the field, observers and developmental theorists like Edith Jacobson (1964) were moved to counter what Ernest Jones once dubbed the "phallocentric bias" of psychoanalysis (1927, 1933). If women were to be cast as passive, receptive, somewhat masochistic pawns within the *Oedipal* drama, they were as the mothers of *infancy* supremely active and potent. Indeed, with babies, no mere man could hope to rival them. These innocuous queens, Jocasta of the Oedipal myth or Hamlet's mother, Gertrude, so easily led, receded to reveal the guardians, earth goddesses, huntresses, and she-demons noted, but not dwelled upon, by Freud.

But what had become of fathers in all of this? Had analysts and observers gone too far?

FATHERS IN PSYCHOANALYTIC THEORY AND DEVELOPMENTAL ISSUES

From the outset Mahler had highlighted the importance of the father in facilitating individuation (Mahler & Gosliner, 1955; Mahler, 1966). Other analysts, like Hans Loewald (1951) or Phyllis Greenacre (1966) (who found her general views congenial and who reconstructed their adult patients' histories accordingly), also remarked on the place of a father in providing an alternative to mother. They emphasized his early incarnation as an emerging figure for identification and as an object of awe, excitement, and attraction—a sort of pure hero. No longer were fathers to be seen initially or primarily as despots threatening castration. Outside the mainstream of American psychoanalytic thought, too, Fairbairn (1954), Lacan (1966), and Chassaguet-Smirgel (1975, 1976), among others, highlighted the part of fathers in the unfolding of early object relations, the crystallization of the symbolic function, language development, identificatory processes, and self-replenishing idealization.

In all of these efforts, however, the authors' interest in fathers was subsumed by their preoccupation with seemingly more general psychological issues. Nor did they substantially revise the male parent's basic representation in developmental theory. Less aggressivized, to be sure, nonetheless the father remained, as social theorist Talcott Parsons once articulated (Parsons & Bales, 1955; Parsons, 1954, 1958), the purveyor of the instrumental universe and *social reality* outside the pre-Oedipal orbit of mother and child and the widening family circle of the Oedipal era. True enough; but still this portrayal remained, two-dimensional and static, omitting, as it did, to encompass a father's gender-specific *parenting* capacities, much less the dynamic evolution of his psychological parenthood.

A number of developments permitted the emergence of a broader perspective on fatherhood during the last decade:

First, feminism took hold of the *zeitgeist*, demanding a reevaluation in theory of our existing notions of sexual identity, male as well as female (Ross, 1975). And, in reality, partly as a result of the women's movement, more and more men became confronted with the concrete, everyday aspects of child care (Levine, 1976). No longer could real-life fathers recede so readily and conveniently into the background of the theory's fictions—its "average expectable" environment or so-called "traditional nuclear" family.

Second, Erikson's overview of the life cycle (1959) and attention to mature generativity and caretaking spawned systematic studies of *adult development*, and of *parenthood* in particular. Therese Benedek was a pioneer in this area and, with E. James Anthony, brought out in 1970 a groundbreaking volume on parenthood (see Benedek, 1959, 1970a, 1970b). In it they, along with analytic authors like Kestenberg, Rangell, Steele, Mahler, and others, underscored the reciprocal influences and dynamic interactions of children and their mothers and fathers throughout the life cycle.

Finally, the use of videotape, frame-by-frame film analysis, and systematic quantification enhanced and refined observational *techniques* in the study of infant development. The seminal efforts of researchers like T. Berry Brazelton (Brazelton, Tronick, Adamson, *et al.*, 1975; Brazelton, Yogman, Als, & Tronick, 1978) and Dan Stern (1974) on the extraordinary social responsiveness and interpersonal repertoire of the infant—even the neonate—called into question the discrete developmental sequence and timetables postulated by Spitz (1965) and others on the basis of their inevitably cruder methodologies (see also Lewis & Rosenblum, 1974). Among other things, these devices enabled observers to isolate the behavioral interactions of infants with significant adults other than the mother (Brazelton *et al.*, 1978).

Drawing on these instruments, a number of researchers began to look at the behavior of babies with mothers, fathers, and strangers (e.g., Lamb, 1975, 1976a, 1976b, 1976c; Pedersen, Rubinstein, & Yarrow, 1973, 1978; Pedersen, Anderson, & Cain, 1977; Pedersen, Yarrow, Anderson, *et al.*, 1978; Parke, 1978; Parke, O'Leary, & West, 1972; Parke & Sawin, 1975; Parke & O'Leary, 1976; Yogman, 1977, 1982; Yogman, Dixon, Tronick, Als, & Brazelton, 1977; Yogman, Dixon, Tronick, Adamson, Als, & Brazelton, 1977). Michael Lamb, in particular, examined the attachment and affiliation behaviors of babies and toddlers with fathers in contrast to mothers at different ages and under different circumstances (home/laboratory). According to Lamb, fathers figure as prominent at.d stimulating beings in a baby's world, easily as much as mothers do—perhaps even more so he and others assert, at least in some respects.

In collaboration with Brazelton, Michael Yogman at Harvard has arrived at similar conclusions on the basis of videotapes contrasting the impact of mothers, fathers, and strangers on the behavior of a baby during the first months of life—from 2 weeks to 6 months. He noted that infants attune to both parents more than to strangers, revealing almost as much "conjoint" or synchronous behavior with fathers as mothers—again, quite early on. Differences are to be discerned essentially in the greater excitement provided by fathers. Whereas mothers tend rhythmically to envelop and enfold their infants, reestablishing homeostasis, fathers arouse them, providing what Yogman terms "a base for play."

Much of this and other recent work remains controversial. Thus the psychoanalytic theorist would question the inferences drawn by these behaviorally oriented researchers to the effect that fathers and mothers are of equal importance to the baby. There is no sure way of determining the correspondence between what is shown in *action* by an infant and what the representational or "intrapsychic" *underpinnings* of this behavior may be. When a baby is brought "into alert" by a father, for instance, does it mean that it attunes to an entity which is recognized and remembered? What, if any, are the memory traces being activated? Or, is it rather the *father's* recognition of and active response to the child, his high-keyedness and intrusive style, which momentarily motivate the vivacity of their encounter? And, if the father rather than the baby's nascent impression of him *is* the central determinant, what about the *performance artifacts* of the laboratory situation where parent and offspring are on display? Do fathers interact with children as much, or as intensely, at home?

The statistics indicate quite the contrary. For example, conservative estimates have it that fathers spend about 9.7 hours weekly tending home and family. Pedersen and Robson (1969), who have a stake in emphasizing the importance of fathers to babies, believe fathers play with 9-month-olds a mere 8 hours a week. More dramatic are the findings of Ban and Lewis (1976), who conclude that the average play time of their interviewed fathers of 1-year-olds was only 15 minutes per day. Finally, there are the distressing results of Rebelsky and Hanks (1971), whose subjects spent an average of *37.5 seconds daily* interacting with infants 3 months and younger—the age range focused on by Yogman (1977, 1982) (see also Atkins, 1981, 1982). And, what about *socioeconomic* variables? The fathers studied are mostly middle-class, white professionals, academics and the like.

Notwithstanding the differences, research such as this does find a correspondence in the more "ethological," longitudinal efforts of analytic observers. Most notable is Ernst Abelin, a collaborator of Mahler, who has scrutinized the father's role in development in a series of evolving and increasingly speculative papers over the past decade (1971, 1975, 1977). In agreement with other psychoanalytic authors, Abelin suggests that fathers first figure distinctly in a baby's world around the time of "hatching," at 4 to 5 months, when the symbiotic phase peaks and begins to give way to differentiation—the first subphase of separation–individuation. He then becomes an increasing source of what Abelin refers to as "specific refueling." (Where, for example, mother is typically turned to for solace or comfort, fathers provide stimulation.) By the 1-year-old toddler's practicing subphase, he has come to represent "non-mother space," inviting the now ambulatory child into an exhilarating environment outside the safer but quieter maternal sphere.

It is at this point, rather than earlier, during the first year, that the father serves many vital, gender-specific developmental functions, and here the analysts tend to differ with these behavioral developmentalists who are bent on minimizing sex differences in parenting. Abelin speaks of a "father thirst" and James Herzog, another psychoanalytic student of father–infant interaction, of "father hunger." Even previously oblivious little boys and girls now become totally excited, and aroused, in the presence of their father and other males. At times they may imitate or flirt with him in surprisingly precocious ways.

Husband and wife, the differences between them, and their relationship begin to provide what Abelin terms a "double mirror" for the reflection of the self—and its protean forms of trial expression. Around 18 months, according to Abelin, during the child's problematic *rapprochement crisis* with the mother and at the inception of representational thinking, the father becomes an essential participant in *early triangulation*. This is especially true when the child is a *boy*, Abelin asserts, postulating marked sex differences in the toddler's relation with his/her parents and, consequently, in a male's and female's basic sense of self. The boy now identifies himself with his father, his perceived masculine attributes, and his wishes for mother. The rivalrous words " 'I' [like Daddy] want Mommy" indicate the existence of a representational triad and, further, a greater degree of *individuation*. The toddler draws more and more affective, instinctual, semantic, and cognitive distinctions between his/her primary objects. It is at this point that Abelin's formulations become abstruse and thus more open to empirical doubt. To simplify:

For a boy, sex differences and the maleness which he shares with father become particularly important during the second year of life. This period is critical in determining his male gender identity and later sexual orientation. For the girl, generational relations are seen to be more salient. Hers is a *Madonna complex*, Abelin believes, in which she would interpose herself somehow between mother and baby, identifying herself now with the one generation, now with the next. The father's presence at this juncture is less crucial for the consolidation of a girl's sexual identity than for the boy's—becoming more pivotal later, during the Oedipal years. The further implication is that her self-representation is often less clearly defined and her self-esteem more vulnerable than is his, a finding corroborated by Galenson and Roiphe (1971, 1976), among others (Greenacre, 1950, 1958; Kestenberg, 1968, 1975; Mahler *et al.,* 1975; Parens, Pollock, Stern, & Kramer, 1976).

This brief sketch cannot do justice to the theroretical complexities of Abelin's scheme, which draws directly on complex Piagetian notions—for instance, the vertical decalage whereby representations of interactions ensue upon a clash of sensorimotor schemas—and, implicitly, on Lacanian psychoanalytic semantics: *le mot, la parole*. At the simplest level, however, two sets of conclusions are open to doubt. First, given the primacy of splitting phenomena at 18 months, together with the child's as yet tenuous capacity for psychic representation, the kind of elaborate triangulation postulated by Abelin seems unlikely except perhaps as a rather fleeting, state-specific phenomenon. It is doubtful whether it serves as a major developmental organizer.

Second, observational and clinical data suggest that the father serves a vital mirroring function for female as well as male toddlers. As Galenson and Roiphe (1971, 1976, 1978, 1982) demonstrate, his appreciative presence is quickly enough internalized to affect a little girl's esteem for her body and the sexual anatomy of which she is becoming more aware. Thus, for example, the work of Parens and his associates has suggested that by 2½ years what Stoller (1976) terms "primary femininity" may become linked to a heterosexual love for father and to procreative or maternal ambitions with regard to him. For some girls, these wishes may prefigure and help usher in their Oedipus complex proper. Boys, in their turn, unmistakably male though they may be, nonetheless exhibit a significant interest in babies, as well as selective identifications with mothering. (This is demonstrated in Kestenberg's [1975] work on inner genitality and in my own earlier studies [Ross, 1974, 1977] of parental identity in early boyhood.)

Notwithstanding these caveats and questions, other implications of Abelin's views are inescapable. Even if the first year of life serves mainly as a rehearsal for what emerges later on as a most important relationship, by bonding and attuning the father to his child (Ross, 1979), during the second and third years a father's presence is clearly felt by the child as such and is crucial for his/her personality development. For example, his importance during rapprochement is vividly demonstrated in a study of labeling by Brooks-Gunn and Lewis (1975). At 15 months, only 25% of the infants studied labeled the pictures of their fathers correctly. But by 18 months, 100% of the toddlers identified the pictures of their fathers and, further, began to generalize his designation to include other male adults. Representations of mother lagged behind, and it was not until 2 years that all infants labeled her without errors.

Core gender identity is determined during this period, and must be properly consolidated before a child reaches his/her third birthday. A father's physical being and active, empathic involvement with children of both sexes seem to be *the* critical elements in this process, as the research and clinical data of such diverging theorists as Stoller (1968, 1975) and Socarides (1978, 1982) demonstrate. As noted earlier, father absence, actual or emotional, is inescapably associated with severe disturbances in *gender identity* or, at the very least, in sexual *orientation*.

Along with his impact on psychosexual development, a father also acts as a container of instinctual impulses in general. He is a disciplinarian, an external source of control, and a wedge between child and mother. He thus aids in the neutralization of *aggression*. Corroborating earlier empirical investigations, Herzog's poignant studies of 2-year-olds bereft of fathers through divorce *in vivo* captures the child's longing for protection from his/her projected *destructiveness*, from the undeflected urges of the remaining parent, and from the real dangers of the unknown environment (Herzog, 1982a). Once more, boys seem most vulnerable during this period.

The father figures as an alternative object to mother. The toddler can turn to him with split-off or otherwise inadmissible and inchoate feelings and desires. And he/she can identify with him as an *object related to mother but not fused with her*—an identification which thereby helps buttress, demarcate, and stabilize the self-representation, consolidating the foundations of primary self-identity. Empirical research has suggested that a father's comings and goings further help stimulate and solidify object constancy. Talking with mother, he also facilitates the language development so vital in the representational process itself (see Gunsberg, 1982; Brooks-Gunn & Lewis, 1975; and Clarke-Stewart, 1977).

Finally, as family theorists have noted (Lidz, Fleck, & Cornelison, 1965; Forrest, 1969; Anderson, 1968), fathers serve as alternatives to the child for the *mother*, helping her anchor her adult womanhood and parental identity in the midst of the regressive currents stirred by the child's infantile object world, pregenital demands, and primitive modes of communication.

I have just considered a few of a father's unique contributions during toddlerhood. Thereafter, the relations of father and child deepen and expand, both in fantasy and reality. The Oedipal era and the manner in which fathers serve to imbue sons and daughters with an "ego ideal" and a sense of "purpose," to borrow from Erikson, have already been elaborated upon in the literature (see Erikson, 1950, 1959, 1964). Here, I would only underscore the importance of a child's representation of father as a *nurturer and procreator* during this period, a representation which helps counter sadomasochistic notions of intercourse and which thereby helps resolve residual conflicts and ambivalences in the sexual identity of both boys and girls (Ross, 1977, 1982a, 1982c).

During latency, ideally, the father functions as a mentor, although this is less a matter of course in our culture than in others. His instruction and expressed appreciation can enable girls to reconcile autonomy and competence with femininity. Thus, Lora Tessman (1982) speaks of melding sexual excitement and endeavor excitement (see also Leonard, 1966). With boys, his ideally benign presence and facilitating care tend to prevent a son's industry and curiosity from becoming subject to excessive competition or submission (see Ross, 1979b, 1979c). And, of course, there are the generational dialectics between fathers and children in adolescence which, even as Freud noted (1909b), ensure the culture's historical continuity while they promote progress (Esman, 1982).

THE FATHERHOOD EXPERIENCE

As a boy grows into a man and actually becomes a father, he may reach the climax of a developmental progression. A number of researchers—including Kestenberg (1975) and myself (Ross, 1977)—have traced the evolution of paternal identity to a man's earliest childhood. In this perspective, a baby's primitive efforts at reversal of voice soon become organized in terms of increasingly selective identifications with a mother's creative and life-sustaining powers. These are subsequently linked to *maternal* wishes and may be manifest in more or less transparent childbearing and child-rearing fantasies. The essentially bisexual or feminine cast of these wishes quickly becomes troublesome for a typical boy, however, conflicting with his phallic strivings and the realites of his male gender. Ideally, they are reorganized and subsumed by a specifically *paternal identification* at the close of the Oedipal phase, fostered by a boy's inklings about intercourse, procreation, and the life cycle, as well as by the father's discernible involvement with family and children.

Because it is the climax of a developmental line, fatherhood can revive a variety of primitive identifications and conflicts from childhood. Producing a child, especially the first, represents for a father an actual Oedipal triumph and tends to reawaken old guilts even as it augurs *his* death. Destructive urges toward the child (and until this century infanticide was a common enough reality in many societies) enter as essential ingredients of the grown father's "Laius complex" (Ross, 1982d). In assuming the functions of his mother and father, a man must renounce his longings to be tended himself by beneficient, omnipotent parents. He must mourn them in this guise as well as himself as a child. Ambivalences and ambiguities in sexual identity, compensated until now, are also exposed once more, especially to the extent a man takes part in child rearing (Brody, 1978). The child poses many competing narcissistic problems. Incorporative yearnings, with their libidinal and aggressive components and thus sadomasochistic derivatives, are excited by the child—the "Kronos" or "Tantalus" motif wherein "children are good enough to eat." There is a search for a representation of the "good father"—an image derived from fantasy, real experience, and displaced impressions of mother, with which a new father can identify. These and other conflicts and desires converge on a man's adoption and practice of fatherhood (Ross 1979a, 1979c).

The adult father, before and after the child's birth, thus recapitulates and reworks early development in an age-specific progression. In his ground-breaking clinical analytic study of a prospective father, Alan Gurwitt (1976, 1982) postulated a specific sequence for paternity: "getting ready, impregnation, conception, bridging, midpregnancy, coming-to-term" (see also Herzog, 1982b). Other authors—for example, Esman (1982) and Colarusso and Nemiroff (1982) —underscore a father's need to adapt to a child at *each successive developmental juncture*, well into adolescence and even beyond. One impression conveyed by

382 CLINICAL AND THEORETICAL PERSPECTIVES

all these authors is that a man's procreative ambitions and active nurturance constitute deep-seated, long-standing aspects of his libidinal makeup and character. These are activated by a paternity which both derives from and reverberates with the innermost reaches of his psychic organization.

In response to their growing child and to their own inner struggles, then, fathers themselves *change*. They assimilate images of their children and of themselves as parents with the available structures of their existing personality and in turn accommodate to the repeated novelties occasioned by parenthood. In the face of these inner and outer demands, fathers may be thrust toward higher levels of identity organization. Or else they may capitulate, regress, or simply retreat from their newfound generational status. Indeed, the birth and the first years of fatherhood seem to be a time of heightened risk for a man, as Jarvis (1962) and Wainright (1966) have pointed out. And just as he has adjusted to his child at one point in development—the incontinent newborn or negativistic toddler, for instance—a man has then to contend with him/her in a dramatic new guise—Oedipal rival, for example. Even adult fatherhood cannot be treated as a discrete, static psychological event or state.

Thus, the child itself does much to shape a father's *paternal identity*. A reciprocity exists between father and child, an ongoing *paternal* "dialogue." From the start, the nature of the child (male or female, damaged or especially endowed, active or quiet) affects a man's identity as a father as well as the self-identity and masculinity bound up with his paternity.

The already complex father–child dyad is further informed by context. It is embedded within a family system, a sociocultural ethos, a daily routine, and a father's personal and collective history. Mothers, siblings, societal prescriptions and proscriptions, the constraints of work, compelling identifications with a man's own parents—all these further impede or facilitate his evolving interaction with his offspring (see Atkins, 1981, 1982). These and other factors help determine his attunement to, pleasure in, and, above all, respect for his child as a growing, if as yet immature, person who must traverse the rough terrain of development.

Thus, children enter into predetermined roles in the drama of a man's life. Thereafter, they rewrite the plot—future, present, and past—and even recast some of the characters, notably the chief protagonist. These subtle psychological changes within the adult resonate with the more visible upheavals in a child's momentous emotional growth. Thus, in order to comprehend the child's and father's relation to each other, one must glimpse at least the dialectical nature of their multifaceted, ongoing interaction. In the process, we may deepen our understanding of the life historical sources of both cultural continuity and the changes evolving through the generations.

CONCLUSION

John Demos, in a study of the history of fatherhood in America (1982), has demonstrated the but gradual disengagement of men from home and family.

Images of the father's role with children have changed over the past 300 years with the advent and elaboration of industrialization, and, I would add, the mushrooming, in the mid-20th century, of a technological and corporate society. Prior to these developments, when men worked at or near the home, often in a family business, fathers were held to be a child's primary caretaker, responsible for his/her emotional and, above all, moral development. Women, mothers, were regarded as the ancillary figures, serving basically to help implement a father's guidance. Only as a man's hours away from the family increased did he become essentially only an external protector and material provider, with the mother becoming more exclusively involved with their offspring's upbringing.

More recently, the advancing technology, occupational specialization, and the vastness and complexity of the current economy have dealt successive death blows to the viability of the family as an essential socioeconomic unit. With this, a man's loyalties have shifted to his corporation or institution as the owner of his life, well-being, and energies, indeed as his real family. And these various employers have responded by demanding more and more time from him, ever more work for its own sake. The impact on women has been various.

Their vital child-rearing functions minimized or ignored, many wives may respond to the aggression implicit in their husband's abandonment by leaving themselves. In what is probably a distortion of feminism, an acquiescence to a tacit bribery on the part of the extrafamilial power structures governing our lives, they, too, have come to vow work achievement as more fulfilling and creative than the production and nurturing of human life itself. Like men, they have immersed themselves in their jobs, relegating the sustenance of sons and daughters to hired housekeepers and custodial centers, which have no deep commitment to and certainly no special love for them. Real financial factors further impel these centrifugal forces and their dissolution of family bonds. Freed from the onus of exclusive economic responsibility and in possession of women less invested in children, and thus more in them, men have gradually come to support their wives in their enterprising, long and hard hours of work where, in the past, they recoiled in protection of their hitherto masculine prerogative. Significantly, with exceptions here and there (Levine, 1976), husbands of working wives have not opted for "co-equal homemaking" or "child rearing." Like Oedipus on the mountain, their children have been left to the capricious kindness of servants and surrogates. Indeed, the result, it seems to me, is less equality of the sexes and a real valuing of women's identities than a neglect of and loss of love for children whose development is shortchanged at the very beginnings of their lives.

When they are left at home, and choose to stay there, many women, embittered at the misogyny they have suffered, may avenge themselves on sons who recoil from their grip at the same time that they are deprived of any model of masculine nurturance. An underlying homosexuality and postures of bravado propel such children out of the home, further compromising the future of the family. An atmosphere of selfishness, indifference, and sadistic pretensions to power envelops the lives of all within the unfathered family, compounded by a lack of clear moral teachings and consequent values. Such myths as the story of the House of Atreus and the Agamemnon trilogy, Medea's filicide, and the Oedipus legend might all be read as family tragedies deriving from failures in fatherliness (see Ross, 1982d).

When fathers are present and active within the family, they bring with them a number of virtues which serve all of its members and endow them with a sense of unity and direction. I have touched upon some of those earlier. They provide mothers with mothering and fathering, replenishing their resources as nurturers while they fulfill and stimulate their genital longings, securing their functioning as adults. They lend utterance to the preverbal longings and strains to which her parenthood makes a mother vulnerable. To their sons and daughters, fathers offer, at their best, the kind of warmth and discipline which lends coherence to their lives and establishes a basis for love and purpose. Girls, whose sexual and self-identity is very much dependent on a father's appreciation, feel worthy as women and aspire to be wives and mothers. A boy's almost inherent terror of, and rage at, male authority is modulated by way of familiarity and a mutuality of love while he further learns that an essential dimension of masculinity is parenthood.

If fathers are to be fathers, concerted efforts must be made to lobby for the time necessary to do so. Quality is at least partly a function of quantity. Paternity leave, as practiced in Sweden, the adjustment of work schedules and travel and relocation priorities to meet the sort of ''personal'' needs all too easily dismissed, custody rights—all these and other institutional and policy issues require commitments on the part of the men involved. And professionals, in projects like the Bank Street Fatherhood Study now underway, must penetrate resistances of all kinds and reach out to the core of vast numbers of men to help them discover the psychological, ethical meaning of their biological paternity. Such efforts may or may not be successful, and we may simply have to accede to a more or less loveless world with a stress on money, competence, and efficiency—a world characterized by middle-class parental and thus emotional deprivation.

REFERENCES

Abelin, E. The role of the father in the separation–individuation process. In J. B. McDevitt & C. F. Settlage (Eds.), *Separation–individuation*. New York: International Universities Press, 1971.

Abelin, E. Some further comments and observations on the earliest role of the father. *International Journal of Psycho-Analysis*, 1975, *56*, 293–302.

Abelin, E. *Panel contribution on the role of the father in the preoedipal years.* Presented at 66th Annual Meeting of the American Psychoanalytic Association, Quebec, Canada, April 1977.

Anderson, R. Where's Dad? Paternal deprivation and delinquency. *Archives of General Psychiatry*, 1968, *18*, 641–649.

Anthony, E. J., & Benedek, T. (Eds.). *Parenthood: Its psychology and psychopathology.* Boston: Little, Brown, 1970.

Atkins, R. Finding one's father: The mother's contribution to the early representation of the father. *Journal of the American Academy of Psychoanalysis*, 1981, *9*, 539–559.

Atkins, R. Discovering daddy: The mother's role in the representation of the father. In S. Cath, A. Gurwitt, & J. Ross (Eds.), *Father and child: developmental and clinical perspectives*. Boston: Little, Brown, 1982.

Ban, P., & Lewis, M. Mothers and fathers, girls and boys: Attachment behavior in the one-year old. *Merrill-Palmer Quarterly*, 1976, *20*, 195–204.

Barclay, A., & Cusumano, D. Father absence, cross-sex identity, and field dependent behavior in male adolescents. *Child Development*, 1967, *38*, 243–250.

Benedek, T. Parenthood as a development phase. *Journal of the American Psychoanalytic Association*, 1959, *7*, 389–417.

Benedek, T. Fatherhood and providing. In E. J. Anthony & T. Benedek (Eds.), *Parenthood: Its psychology and psychopathology*. Boston: Little Brown, 1970. (a)

Benedek, T. Parenthood during the life cycle. In E. J. Anthony & T. Benedek (Eds.), *Parenthood: Its psychology and psychopathology*. Boston: Little, Brown, 1970. (b)

Bettelheim, B. *Symbolic wounds*. Glencoe, Ill.: Free Press, 1954.

Biller, H. A multiaspect investigation of masculine development in kindergarten-age boys. *Genetic Psychology Monographs*, 1968, *76*, 89–139. (a)

Biller, H. A note on father absence and masculine development in young lower class Negro and white boys. *Child Development*, 1968, *39*, 10003–10006. (b)

Biller, H. Father absence, maternal encouragement and sex role development in kindergarten age boys. *Child Development*, 1969, *40*, 539–546.

Biller, H. Father absence and the personality development of the male child. *Developmental Psychology*, 1970, *2*, 181–201.

Biller, H. The mother–child relationship and the father-absent boy's personality development. *Merrill-Palmer Quarterly*, 1971, *17*, 227–241. (a)

Biller, H. *Father, child, and sex role*. Lexington, Mass.: D. C. Heath, 1971. (b)

Biller, H. Paternal deprivation, cognitive functioning and the feminized classroom. In A. Davids (Ed.), *Child personality and psychopathology*. New York: Wiley, 1974.

Biller, H., & Balm, R. Father absence, perceived maternal behavior and masculinity of self concept among jr. high school boys. *Developmental Psychology*, 1971, *4*, 178–181.

Biller, H., & Meredith, D. *Father power*. New York: David McKay, 1974.

Biller, H., & Weiss, S. The father–daughter relationship and the personality development of the female. *Journal of Genetic Psychology*, 1970, *116*, 79–93.

Bowlby, J. The nature of the child's tie to its mother. *International Journal of Psycho-Analysis*, 1958, *39*(V), 1–23.

Bowlby, J. *Attachment and loss*. New York: Basic Books, 1969.

Brody, S. *Fathers*. Symposium on fatherhood presented at the Denver Psychoanalytic and Clinical Social Work Societies, 1978.

Brazelton, T., Tronick, E., Adamson, L., *et al.* Early mother–infant reciprocity. In R. Hinde (Ed.), *Parent–infant interaction*. Amsterdam: Elsevier, 1975.

Brazelton, T., Yogman, M., Als, H., & Tronick, E. The infant as a focus in family reciprocity. In M. Lewis & L. Rosenblum (Eds.), *The social network of the developing infant*. New York: Plenum, 1978.

Brooks-Gunn, J., & Lewis, N. *Person perception and verbal labeling: The development of social labels*. Paper presented to the Society for Research in Child Development and the Eastern Psychological Association, New York, 1975.

Chassaguet-Smirgel, J. A propos du délire transsexuel du Président Schreber. *Revue Française de la Psychoanalyse*, 1975, *5–6*, 1013–1025.

Chassaguet-Smirgel, J. Some thoughts on the ego ideal. *Psychoanalytic Quarterly*, 1976, *45*, 345–373.

Clarke-Stewart, K. A. *The father's impact on mother and child*. Paper presented at the Society for Research in Child Development, New Orleans, 1977.

Colarusso, C., & Nemiroff, R. Father in mid-life: Crisis and the growth of paternal identity. In S. Cath, A. Gurwitt, & J. Ross (Eds.) *Father and child: Developmental and clinical perspectives.* Boston: Little, Brown, 1982.

Demos, J. The changing face of fatherhood. In S. Cath, A. Gurwitt, & J. Ross (Eds.), *Father and child: Developmental and clinical perspectives.* Boston: Little, Brown, 1982.

Erikson, E. H. *Childhood and society* (1950). Nw York: Norton, 1963.

Erikson, E. H. *Identity and the life cycle* (Psychological Issues, Monograph 1). New York: International Universities Press, 1959.

Erikson, E. H. *Insight and responsibility.* New York: Norton, 1964.

Escalona, S. K. *The roots of individuality: Normal patterns of development in infancy.* Chicago: Aldine, 1968.

Esman, A. Fathers and adolescent sons. In S. Cath, A. Gurwitt, & J. Ross (Eds.), *Father and child: Developmental and clinical perspectives.* Boston: Little, Brown, 1982.

Fairbairn, W. F. *An object relations theory of the personality.* New York: Basic Books, 1954.

Ferholt, J., & Gurwitt, A. Involving the father in treatment: The dilemma. In S. Cath, A. Gurwitt, & J. Ross (Eds.), *Father and child: Developmental and clinical perspectives.* Boston: Little, Brown, 1982.

Forrest, T. The paternal roots of male character development. *Psychoanalytic Review,* 1967, *54,* 81–89.

Forrest, T. Treatment of the father in family therapy. *Family Process,* 1969, *8,* 106–117.

Freud, S. Fragment of an analysis of a case of hysteria (1905). *Standard Edition, 7,* 3–122. London: Hogarth Press, 1953.

Freud, S. Analysis of a phobia in a five-year old boy (1909a). *Standard Edition, 10,* 3–129. London: Hogarth Press, 1955.

Freud, S. The family romance (1909b). *Standard Edition, 9,* 236–241. London: Hogarth Press, 1955.

Freud, S. Notes upon a case of obsessional neurosis (1909c). *Standard Edition, 10,* 153–230. London: Hogarth Press, 1955.

Freud, S. Psychoanalytic notes upon an autobiographical account of a case of paranoia (1911). *Standard Edition, 12,* 3–82. London: Hogarth Press, 1958.

Freud, S. Totem and taboo (1912). *Standard Edition, 13,* 1–161. London: Hogarth Press, 1955.

Freud, S. From the history of an infantile neurosis (1918). *Standard Edition, 17,* 3–122. London: Hogarth Press, 1955.

Freud, S. Group psychology and the analysis of the ego (1921). *Standard Edition, 18,* 67–143. London: Hogarth Press, 1955.

Freud, S. The ego and the id (1923). *Standard Edition, 19,* 3–66. London: Hogarth Press, 1961.

Freud, S. The dissolution of the Oedipus complex (1924). *Standard Edition, 19,* 173–179. London: Hogarth Press, 1961.

Freud, S. Some psychical consequences of the anatomical distinction between the sexes (1925). *Standard Edition, 19,* 243–258. London: Hogarth Press.

Freud, S. The future of an illusion (1927). *Standard Edition, 21,* 3–58. London: Hogarth Press.

Freud, S. Civilization and its discontents (1930). *Standard Edition, 21,* 59–145. London: Hogarth Press, 1961.

Galenson, E., & Roiphe, H. The impact of early sexual discovery on mood, defensive organization and symbolization. *Psychoanalytic Study of the Child,* 1971, *26,* 195–216.

Galenson, E., & Roiphe, H. Early female development. *Journal of the American Psychoanalytic Association, Supplement: Female psychology,* 1976, *24* (5), 29–58.

Galenson, E., & Roiphe, H. The emergence of genital awareness during the second year of life. In R. C. Freidman, R. M. Richart, & R. L. Vande Wiele (Eds.), *Sex differences and behavior.* New York: Wiley, 1978.

Galenson, E., & Roiphe, H. Fathers and the preoedipal development of the girl. In S. Cath, A. Gurwitt, & J. Ross (Eds.), *Father and child: Developmental and clinical perspectives.* Boston: Little, Brown, 1982.

Greenacre, P. Special problems of early female sexual development. In *Trauma, growth and personality*. New York: International Universities Press, 1950.

Greenacre, P. Early physical determinants of identity (1958). In *Emotional growth*. New York: International Universities Press, 1971.

Greenacre, P. Problems of overidealization of the analyst and analysis: Their manifestations in the transference and countertransference relationship (1966). In *Emotional growth* (Vol. 1). New York: International Universities Press, 1971.

Gunsberg, L. A selected critical review of psychological investigations of the father–infant relationship from six months through the first three years of life. In S. Cath, A. Gurwitt, & J. Ross (Eds.), *Father and child: Developmental and clinical perspectives*. Boston: Little, Brown, 1982.

Gurwitt, A. Aspects of prospective fatherhood: A case report. *Psychoanalytic Study of the Child*, 1976, *31*, 237–270.

Gurwitt, A. Prospective fatherhood. In S. Cath, A. Gurwitt, & J. Ross (Eds.), *Father and child: Developmental and clinical perspectives*. Boston: Little, Brown, 1982.

Herzog, J. On father hunger. In S. Cath, A. Gurwitt, & J. Ross (Eds.) *Fathers and child: Developmental and clinical perspectives*. Boston: Little, Brown, 1982. (a)

Herzog, J. Patterns of expectant fatherhood. In S. Cath, A. Gurwitt, & J. Ross (Eds.), *Father and child: Developmental and clinical perspectives*. Boston: Little, Brown, 1982. (b)

Herzog, E., & Sudia, C. Children in fatherless families. In M. Caldwell (Ed.), *Review of child development research*. Chicago: University of Chicago Press, 1973.

Hetherington, E. The effects of paternal absence on sex-typed behaviors in Negro and white adolescent males. *Journal of Personality and Social Psychology*, 1966, *4*, 87–91.

Hetherington, E. Effects of father absence on personality development in adolescent daughters. *Developmental Psychology*, 1972, *7*, 313–326.

Jacobson, E. The wish for a child in the man. *Psychoanalytic Study of the Child*, 1950, *5*, 523–538.

Jacobson, E. *The self and the object world*. New York: International Universities Press, 1964.

Jarvis, W. Some effects of pregnancy and childbirth on men. *Journal of the American Psychoanalytic Association*, 1962, *10*, 689–700.

Jones, E. The early development of female sexuality (1927). In *Papers on psychoanalysis*. Boston: Beacon Press, 1961.

Jones, E. The phallic phase (1933). In *Papers on psychoanalysis*. Boston: Beacon Press, 1961.

Kestenberg, J. On the development of maternal feelings in early childhood. *Psychoanalytic Study of the Child*, 1956, *11*, 257–291. (a)

Kestenberg, J. Vicissitudes of female sexuality. *Journal of the American Psychoanalytic Association*, 1956, *4*, 453–476. (b)

Kestenberg, J. Outside and inside, male and female. *Journal of the American Psychoanalytic Association*, 1968, *16*, 457–520.

Kestenberg, J. A developmental approach to disturbances of sex-specific identity. *International Journal of Psycho-Analysis*, 1971, *52*, 99–102.

Kestenberg, J. *Children and parents*. New York: Aronson, 1975.

Lacan, J. *Écrits*. Paris: Editions du Seuil, 1966.

Lamb, M. Fathers: Forgotten contributors to child development. *Human Development*, 1975, *18*, 245–266.

Lamb, M. The role of the father: An overview. In M. Lamb (Ed.), *The role of the father in child development*. New York: Wiley, 1976. (a)

Lamb, M. Interactions between two-year-olds and their mothers and fathers. *Psychological Reports*, 1976, *38*, 447–450. (b)

Lamb, M. Effects of stress and cohort on mother– and father–infant interaction. *Developmental Psychology*, 1976, *13*, 637. (c)

Leonard, M. Fathers and daughters: The significance of "fathering" in the psychosexual development of the girl. *International Journal of Psycho-Analysis*, 1966, *47*, 325–334.

Levine, J. *Who will raise the children? New options for fathers.* Philadelphia: Lippincott, 1976.

Lewis, M., & Rosenblum, L. *The effect of the infant on its caregiver.* New York: Wiley, 1974.

Lidz, T. *The origin and treatment of schizophrenic disorders.* New York: Basic Books, 1973.

Lidz, T., Fleck, S., & Cornelison, A. *Schizophrenia and the family.* New York: International Universities Press, 1965.

Liebenberg, B. Expectant fathers. *American Journal of Orthopsychiatry*, 1967, *37*, 358–359.

Loewald, H. Ego and reality. *International Journal of Psycho-Analysis*, 1951, *32*, 10–18.

Lynn, D. *The father: His role in child development.* Monterey, Calif.: Brooks/Cole, 1974.

Mahler, M. S. Discussion of P. Greenacre's problems of overidealization of the analyst and analysis. *Psychoanalytic Quarterly*, 1966, *36*, 637.

Mahler, M. S., & Furer, M. *On human symbiosis and the vicissitudes of individuation.* New York: International Universities Press, 1968.

Mahler, M. S., & Gosliner, B. On symbiotic child psychosis: Genetic, dynamic and restitutive aspects. *Psychoanalytic Study of the Child*, 1955, *10*, 195–212.

Mahler, M. S., Pine, F., & Bergman, A. *The psychological birth of the human infant.* New York: Basic Books, 1975.

Nelson, E., & Maccoby, E. The relationship between social development and differential abilities on the Scholastic Aptitude Test. *Merrill-Palmer Quarterly*, 1966, *12*, 269–284.

Nelson, E., & Vangen, P. *The impact of father absence upon heterosexual behaviors and social development of preadolescent girls in ghetto environment.* Proceedings of the Annual Convention of American Psychological Association, 1971, *27*, 46–49.

Parens, H., Pollock, L., Stern, J., & Kramer, S. On the girl's entry into the Oedipus complex. *Journal of American Psychoanalytic Association*, 1976, *24* (Supplement 5), 79–108.

Parke, R. Perspectives on father–infant interaction. In J. D. Osofsky (Ed.), *Handbook of infancy.* New York: Wiley, 1978.

Parke, R., & O'Leary, S. Father–mother–infant interaction in the newborn period. In K. Riegel & J. Meacham (Eds.), *The developing individual in a changing world* (Vol. 2). The Hague: Mouton, 1976.

Parke, R., O'Leary, S., & West, S. Mother–father–newborn interaction: Effects of maternal medication, labor, and sex of infant. *Proceedings of the American Psychological Association*, 1972, 85–86.

Parke, R., & Sawin, D. *Infant characteristics and behavior as eliciters of maternal and paternal responsibility in the newborn period.* Paper presented to the Society for Research in Child Development, Denver, Colo., 1975.

Parke, R., & Sawin, D. *The family in early infancy: Social interactional and attitudinal analyses.* Paper presented to the Society for Research in Child Development, New Orleans, 1977.

Parsons, T. The father symbol: An appraisal in the light of psychoanalytic and sociological theory. In L. Bryson, L. Kinkelstein, R. MacIver, & R. McKeon (Eds.), *Symbols and values.* New York: Harper & Row, 1954.

Parsons, T. Social structure and the development of personality: Freud's contribution to the integration of psychology and sociology. *Psychiatry*, 1958, *21*, 321–340.

Parsons, T., & Bales, R. *Family, socialization and interaction process.* Glencoe, Ill.: Free Press, 1955.

Payne, E., & Mussen, P. Parent–child relations and father identification among adolescent boys. *Journal of Abnormal and Social Psychology*, 1956, *52*, 358–362.

Pedersen, F., Anderson, P., & Cain, R. *An approach to understanding linkages between the parent–infant and spouse relationships.* Paper presented at the Biennial Meeting of the Society for Research in Child Development, New Orleans, 1977.

Pedersen, F., & Robson, K. Father participation in infancy. *American Journal of Orthopsychiatry*, 1969, *39*, 466–472.

Pedersen, F., Rubinstein, J., & Yarrow, L. *Father absence in infancy.* Paper presented at the meeting of the Society for Research in Child Development, Philadelphia, 1973.

Pedersen, F., Rubinstein, J., & Yarrow, L. Infant development in father-absent families. *Journal of Genetic Psychology*, 1978, *135*, 51–61.

Pedersen, F., Yarrow, L., Anderson, B., *et al.* Conceptualization of father influences in the infancy period. In M. Lewis & L. Rosenblum (Eds.), *Social network of the developing child*. New York: Plenum, 1978.

Prall, R. C. Panel Report: The role of the father in preoedipal development. *Journal of the American Psychoanalytic Association*, 1978, *26*, 143–162.

Rebelsky, F., & Hanks, C. Father's verbal interaction with infants in the first three months of life. *Child Development*, 1971, *42*, 63–68.

Ross, J. *The children's children: A psychoanalytic study of generativity and nurturance in boys*. Doctoral dissertation, New York University, 1974. (University Microfilms, Ann Arbor)

Ross, J. M. The development of paternal identity: A critical review of the literature on nurturance and generativity in boys and men. *Journal of the American Psychoanalytic Association*, 1975, *23*, 783–817.

Ross, J. M. Toward fatherhood: The epigenesis of paternal identity during a boy's first decade. *International Journal of Psycho-Analysis*, 1977, *4*, 327–347.

Ross, J. M. Fathering: A review of some psychoanalytic contributions on paternity. *International Journal of Psycho-Analysis*, 1979, *60*, 317–327. (a)

Ross, J. M. The forgotten father. In M. C. Nelson & J. Ibenberry (Eds.), *Psychosexual imperatives: Their impact on identity formation*. New York: Human Sciences Press, 1979. (b)

Ross, J. M. Paternal identity: The equations of fatherhood and manhood. In T. B. Karasu & C. W. Socarides (Eds.), *On sexuality: Psychoanalytic observations*. New York: International Universities Press, 1979. (c)

Ross, J. M. From mother to father: The boy's search for a generative identity and the oedipal era. In S. Cath, A. Gurwitt, & J. Ross (Eds.), *Father and child: Developmental and clinical perspectives*. Boston: Little Brown, 1982. (a)

Ross. J. M. In search of fathering. In S. Cath, A. Gurwitt, & J. Ross (Eds.), *Father and child: Developmental and clinical perspectives*. Boston: Little, Brown, 1982. (b)

Ross, J. M. Mentorship in middle childhood. In S. Cath, A. Gurwitt, & J. Ross (Eds.), *Father and child: Developmental and clinical perspectives*. Boston: Little, Brown, 1982. (c)

Ross, J. M. Oedipus revisited: Laius and the Laius complex. *Psychoanalytic Study of the Child*, 1982, *37*, 169–200. (d)

Ross, J. M. The roots of fatherhood: Excursions into a lost literature. In S. Cath, A. Gurwitt, & J. Ross (Eds.), *Father and child: Developmental and clinical perspectives*. Boston: Little, Brown, 1982. (e)

Santrock, J. Paternal absence, sex-typing and identification. *Developmental Psychology*, 1970, *2*, 264–272. (a)

Santrock, J. Influence of onset and type of paternal absence on the first four Eriksonian developmental crises. *Developmental Psychology*, 1970, *3*, 273–274. (b)

Santrock, J. The relation of type and onset of father absence to cognitive development. *Child Development*, 1972, *43*, 455–469.

Socarides, C. *Homosexuality*. New York: Aronson, 1978.

Socarides, C. Abdicating fathers, homosexual sons. In S. Cath, A. Gurwitt, & J. Ross (Eds.), *Father and child: Developmental and clinical perspectives*. Boston: Little, Brown, 1982.

Spitz, R. *The first year of life*. New York: International Universities Press, 1965.

Sprey, J. The study of single parenthood. *Family Life Coordinator*, 1967, *16*, 29–35.

Staver, N. The use of a child guidance clinic by mother-dominant families. *Smith College Studies in Social Work*, 1944, *14*, 367–388.

Stephens, W. Judgments by social workers on boys and mothers in fatherless families. *Journal of Genetic Psychology*, 1961, *99*, 59–64.

Stern, D. The goal and structure of mother–infant play. *Journal of American Academy of Child Psychiatry*, 1974, *13*, 402.

Sternberg, H. Fathers who apply for child guidance. *Smith College Studies in Social Work*, 1951, *22*, 53–68.

Stoller, R. *Sex and gender*. New York: Science House, 1968.

Stoller, R. Healthiest parental influences on the earliest development of masculinity in baby boys. *Psychoanalytic Forum*, 1975, *5*, 232–262.

Stoller, R. Primary femininity. *Journal of the American Psychoanalytic Association*, 1976, *24* (5) (Supplement), 59–78.

Tessman, L. A note on the father's contribution to his daughter's ways of working and loving. In S. Cath, A. Gurwitt, & J. Ross (Eds.), *Father and child: Developmental and clinical perspectives*. Boston: Little, Brown, 1982.

Van der Leeuw, P. The preoedipal phase of the male. *Psychoanalytic Study of the Child*, 1958, *13*, 352–374.

Wainwright, W. H. Fatherhood as a precipitant of mental illness. *American Journal of Psychiatry*, 1966, *123*, 40–44.

Wallerstein, J., & Kelly, J. Divorcing fathers. In S. Cath, A. Gurwitt, & J. Ross (Eds.), *Father and child: Developmental and clinical perspectives*. Boston: Little, Brown, 1982.

Yogman, M. *The goals and structure of face-to-face interaction between infants and fathers*. Paper presented to the Biennial Meeting of the Society for Research in Child Development. New Orleans, 1977.

Yogman, M. Observations on the father–infant relationship. In S. Cath, A. Gurwitt, & J. Ross (Eds.), *Father and child: Developmental and clinical perspectives*. Boston: Little, Brown, 1982.

Yogman, M., Dixon, S., Tronick, E., Adamson, L., Als, H., & Brazelton, T. *Development of social interaction of infants with fathers*. Paper presented at Eastern Psychological Association, New York, 1977.

Yogman, M., Dixon, S., Tronick, E., Als, H., & Brazelton, T. *Parent–infant interaction under stress: The study of a temperamentally difficult infant*. Paper presented to the American Academy of Child Psychiatry, Toronto, 1977.

Zelazo, P., Kotelchuk, M., Barber, L., et al. (1977). *Fathers and sons: An experimental facilitation of attachment behaviors*. Paper presented at the Biennial Meeting of the Society for Research in Child Development, New Orleans, 1977.

Zilboorg, G. Depressive reactions related to parenthood. *American Journal of Psychiatry*, 1931, *10*, 927–962.

IV

FUTURE PERSPECTIVES

This volume represents a significant shift in the study of personality development, once focused in the early years of childhood, to a broader view of continuing development across the life cycle. This expanded vista is firmly affixed in our psychodynamic exploration of the parenthood experience. This perspective was developed initially by Benedek (1959) and Anthony and Benedek (1970) in their seminal works wherein parenthood is conceptualized as a developmental process. Benedek and Anthony contended that the parenthood experience creates shifts in the intrapsychic systems of the parents. They conceptualized parenthood within the psychoanalytic framework of the processes of identification and introjection of early drive experiences. In this view of development, early templates are laid down in the child for his/her future parenthood. The later experience of parenthood permits the reworking of earlier inner developmental experiences within the context of the interactions with the child whose development is in process. This reworking leads to the intrapsychic shifts which accompany the multifarious adaptations parents make as they help children achieve their own goals and destinies.

Benedek's theory utilizes a drive or conflict psychology. Nevertheless, in her later work (1970), she deals with the significance of the experiential parental self and issues of self-esteem and self equilibrium. She alludes, also, to the importance of the connection or attachment of the child to the parent. Seemingly, additional theoretical framework is necessary to more adequately explain the parenting process. The object relations theorists (both British and American) provide a possible framework in their view that the attachment of the child to the parent is the stimulating force that motivates and directs the course of development. Psychoanalytic self psychology theory provides a more potentially useful framework for the psychological origins of parenthood. In this theory, parenthood develops out of the earliest proclivities of children and parents to form a bond made up of selfobject relationships. These become transformed, over time, into intrapsychic and transactional connections among adults. These connections are experienced within the individual as a cohesive sense of self.

In the adult life course, parenthood is the most likely experience to forbode discomfort or anxiety, the content of which is often a fear of experiencing developmental derailment. In each of the child's developmental phases, parents confront concerns which emanate from a reexperiencing of earlier unpleasurable affects or the fear of losing structural stability. In classical psychoanalytic theory, this phenomenon is considered to be a partial regression in drive organization to an earlier period of developmental fixation or arrest. It must be noted that drive theory does not regard regression as necessarily pathological. Rather, it maintains that parents master the fear of regression because of the power of the attachment to and love of the child and the efficacy of their identifications with their own parents. Psychoanalytic self psychology theory explains this experience of potential discomfort within the context of the superordinate structure of the self, which under stress, may require self-selfobject relationships in order to sustain self cohesion. Whatever the theoretical stance, the seminal issue is that parents fear reencounter with their childhood selves.

A significant issue for adults in the parenthood experience is to remain effective and stable during the child-rearing process which creates great risk for maintenance of self-esteem and self-regulation of affects. It seems to us that the concept of the self–selfobject relationship provides an added dimension to understand this risk in the self–selfobject relationship of child and parent. The process is not simply one of identification with the child but a reencounter with painful experiences in childhood and adolescence which created unpleasurable affects. Terman points up the essential function of the parental selfobject as that of a regulator of excitation. If as children, their own parents had not been able to provide for this, adults cannot approach parenthood with an inner experience of a stable or whole structure. Furthermore, the continuous interactions among parents and children (intrapsychically and interpersonally) as development proceeds present ongoing needs for affect regulation. For the parents, the possibility of a reexperience of noxious affects is ubiquitous in any of the child's developmental phases. Conceptualized thus, as Terman demonstrates, the study of parenthood as a stimulus for reencountering earlier affective experiences opens up many possibilities for investigation. Certainly for clinicians, we see great advantage in shifting from an essentially drive conceptualization to that of affects and the experiential components of development. We consider, also, that the self–selfobject relationship construct has significance in explanatory power and for further investigation of adult development with parenting and the parenting alliance as paradigms. Perhaps the mastery of parenting tasks, including its disorganizing potential, may be paradigmatic for understanding how adults acquire professional training and learn other adult tasks (Weissman, 1980).

In looking to the future we can divide our concerns in the broad category of psychosocial issues into a number of areas. First, we must be prepared to address the future impact of changing role models as they effect both men and women. Clearly, however, the most significant changes will continue to affect women. Since World War II we have progressed from the woman's position of being "at home" with her children and working only because of a mandated national emergency. The large number of women who went into the labor market performed essentially in defense related work. Women of that era were socialized to perform as mothers and wives. Paid work was performed only because of national or domestic crisis. At the end of the war women returned to their roles of wives and mothers.

Recent social changes have presented to women new options. The expansion of the middle class created opportunities for larger groups of women to acquire advanced education. Particularly among these middle-class women, a virtual revolution was brought about by the women's rights movement. New expectations brought old role models into conflict with new ones. The place of a career and the family became a significant issue for many middle-class American women. Other American women have had to face this issue not because of changed understandings of significant social roles but as a result of economic necessity. In fact, Altmann's work indicates that from a biological time-line, work among mothers is certainly not a new historical event. Most primate females have "dual careers" as mothers and workers in providing for themselves and their infants. Inflation across the past two decades has made it necessary in many American families for the wife to perform both as paid worker and to function as housewife and mother. For these women, economics, not the women's movement dictated the assumption of new roles.

In the next decade we need to determine the effect of such changes upon the lives of these wives and mothers as well as the impact of these changes upon the children of the 1980s, across social strata. The middle-class male lawyer married to a physician-wife and the steel worker whose wife must work to support the family during a layoff both present challenges for future study.

Social changes and economic necessities of the next decade may create a natural experiment. We will be able to compare women who enter the paid labor force when finishing school but delay becoming mothers until their mid- and late 30s with women who marry early, bear children, and enter the labor force in their 30s or 40s. The impact of social timing on these women's subsequent adult lives, as they follow different routes through a critical experience of adult parenthood must be explored. Additionally, we must investigate what effects delayed parenthood has on men and the experience of fatherhood.

Our future work must carefully assess the impact on the parent and child of the single-parent family. Although there is some increase in the number of single family households headed by men, we can anticipate that single parent families will continue predominantly to be headed by women. What are the long-term effects both on children, and the single parent, when the single parent family is established by divorce or death, or when the mother never married? Burland suggests that among the poor, where there are an increasing number of single-parent families, the outlook for this family type is potentially disastrous for both mother and child. We must develop new more effective interventions with these families.

An interesting developmental issue emerges out of our consideration of parenthood as a developmental and psychosocial experience. From Benedek to

Hagestad, we recognize that the parenthood experience moves across life to its completion and disruptions such as divorce and death create intergenerational dislocations. We have moved from the restricted focus on parental pathology as it affects the character of the child to recognition that both the characters of children and parents evolve overtime and interact upon each other. Elson's concept of the double helix in which both generations are actively engaging in characterological shifts and changes introduces issues similar to those which emerge out of Cohen and Weissman's concept of the parenting alliance. Are we to consider that adults who do not become parents are deprived of a significant developmental experience? Can single parenthood provide parent and child with the necessary psychological nutrients which bring forth flourishing self-esteem, joy in relationships, and pleasure in other aspects of private and public living? Here, we see the confluence of psychosocial and developmental issues which must be confronted in the future study of the inner life of human beings, their cultural milieu, and how the resources of the social surround can be mobilized in behalf of a sturdy outcome for the many problems which emerge from our theoretical stance.

Additionally, we must look to a number of issues which affect parenting brought about by the significant lengthening of the life cycle. It has always been the case that there have been numbers of people in our society over age 65. Today, however, even larger numbers of persons reach this age. We can look forward to a large population of middle-aged parents caring for their children as well as addressing the needs of their aging parents. The profound inflation in the cost of higher education will further tax middle-aged parents who must educate children at a time when their parents may also make economic demands. We will have a new group of adults who will live much of their lives along with their own living parents. Further work will be required of the sort addressed in this volume by Hagestad *et al.*, regarding the role of the parent–child relationship when the child enters middle age or later when both parent and child are retired. Can or does one ever psychologically stop being a parent to one's child or a child to one's parent?

The reduction of the fertility rate, such that the aging parent will have fewer children upon whom to rely in his/her old age, may in turn bring further pressure on governmental agencies to provide support for the aged with limited family resources. The chapters in this book which have addressed psychosocial issues have suggested the means for addressing these and other crucial concerns in the last years of this century.

The collegiality (or selfobject relationships) which developed as we pursued our endeavor to push further the investigation of parenthood grew out the commonly shared values of the three mental health professions we represent. However, each of us brought to the task the riches and elegance of his/her own discipline and cherished commitment to it. We hope, therefore, that this work can serve as a model for future collaboration among various mental health scholars and practitioners to broaden the boundaries of our knowledge and competence. Each of us brought vitality to our work because of our human and clinical commitment to our patients from whom we learned much about the meaning of the parenthood experience in the adult as a person. To them, we express our gratitude. A commonly held value among us is the appreciation for the abundance of resources in the evolving nature of psychoanalysis which has been of great emotional and intellectual significance as we pursued our personal lives and our professional courses. Certainly, it informed us greatly about parenthood and made us humble as our deliberations called forth the great internal tensions which tend to militate against the study of the inner life during the child-rearing years. Our final commentary will focus on psychoanalytic directions with a perspective toward integration with other behavioral science inquiry.

The chapters in this volume have implications both for the study of parenthood, and also for psychoanalytic inquiry itself. As already noted, across the past two decades there has been a dramatic shift in psychoanalytic perspectives on personality development, from a theoretical approach based primarily on a 19th century understanding of neurology and behavior, emphasizing so-called drives, to contemporary understanding concerned with the uniqueness of individual experiences.

As Bowlby has noted in his chapter, traditional psychoanalytic formulations portrayed the infant as existing in an world devoid of satisfying human contact. In this view, relationships were established largely as a consequence of satisfaction of needs essential to survival. With the realization that the capacity for relationships is inherent, and increased appreciation of the competence of the infant, there has been a shift to study of the determinants both within the child, and within the parent, which together fosters the development of a particular interpersonal tie. The quality of this first tie between parent and child should not be viewed as solely responsible for the later relationship between parent and child. Changes of place in the life course affect the current quality of the parent–child tie, and also the experience which parents and children each have of their relationship.

Again, as noted, with increased realization of the inadequacies of the drive approach in psychoanalysis, represented by the distinction currently being made between the clinical and metapsychological contributions of Freud's own work, psychoanalytic formulations increasingly emphasize the importance of subjective experiences of relationships based on memories of the past, shaped by present life situations which continually alter the context in which past memories are recalled. The experience of parenthood is codetermined by the manner in which parents were, themselves, cared for as children, and also by experience of caregiving itself. Changing understandings both of the determinants of parenthood, and of the course of the parent–child relationship lead to an understanding of parenthood as a process of mutual accommodation between child and caretaker, each of whom make independent contributions to the relationship.

Even as an infant, the child seeks satisfying social relations, the quality of which are but one of the influences both on the child's later experience of relationships with others as more or less satisfying in particular ways, and as a source of regulation of self-esteem, including both capacity for modulating inner tensions, and sustaining the quest for desired values and goals. Emphasis is upon the child's experience of parenting as more or less satisfying at a particular time, which leads to internalization of the capacity for regulation of self-esteem and for the establishment of representation of the caretaking process as the earliest source of the child's later capacity to respond empathically to the needs of his or her own children.

From the perspective of the parent, it is assumed that the quality of the parenting is generally satisfying for the infant's needs, and that the parent accommodates early his/her own needs and interests with the particular qualities of child. As Schwartz has suggested in reviewing Benedek's own pioneering contributions, parenthood is less a developmental phase than a process or developmental line. While, in some sense, active parenting may end when the child becomes an adult and establishes his/her own family, there is another sense in which parenting continues through the very oldest stages. Parents continue to think of themselves as parents for their now adult offspring. The experience of parenthood is not merely unresolved unconscious conflicts, but contains contributions from all life experiences, from earliest childhood, to the present.

Culture and particular social–historical circumstances are interwoven with the parent's experience of the course of life both in the actual relationship between parent and offspring, and in the parent's present experience of parenthood. Individual experience of parenthood takes place in a particular social context, influenced both by present and past. As Glen Elder (1974) has noted in his work on parenting and child care during the Great Depression of the 1930s, economic privation was a common experience which permanently altered the perceptions of those persons, now middle-aged, who were children at that time. These created a commonly recognized conservative, saving orientation, reflecting the belief that hard times may come again. However, there is considerable variation in responses to this event: some persons reacted to this economic privation as adversity to be overcome, and are proud of having been able to succeed in making their way and raising a family even in the midst of such difficulties. Others regarded their adversity as an excuse for not having been able to be more successful. Parenthood for some of these children of the depression was made more difficult as a result of such privation, while seen by others as a training ground in having been enhanced by the necessity for sharing and for increased working together as a family unit.

Particularly striking in reports such as those of Elder and his colleagues is the apparent discontinuity between parents own understandings and those of their offspring. While there is considerable evidence in the social science literature that values and attitudes of offspring are similar to those of their parents, discontinuity in values and attitudes may be introduced both by unexpressed as well as expressed parental views, and also by social change itself. Many of the children of depression reared parents are much less conservative and pessimistic than their parents. Indeed, these children may not be able to understand their parents' more conservative and pessimistic attitudes. Such findings raise questions about the development and transmission of identifications. Particular life experiences of both parents and offspring, as well as social and historical contexts, shape the transmission of values and attitudes across the generations, and of the role of intrapersonal and interpersonal processes in determining identifications.

Study of parenthood provides a unique opportunity for collaboration between psychoanalysis and the social sciences in understanding a complex social role and developmental process which is essential to the maintenance of personal identity and the perpetuation of the social order. Recognition that parenthood as an adult experience continues among two and, increasingly, three adult generations, further enhances such collaboration. At the same time, study of the relationship between adult offspring and their parents challenges fundamental assumptions of psychoanalysis, including that of the developmental line from dependence to independence.

All too often, it has been assumed that maturity represents not just the abandonment of an anaclitic tie to the caregiver, but that it requires a degree of insulation from ties to other family members which is consonant neither with the reality of family life, or with the continued affection and concern which family members feel toward each other. Realization of the necessity of caring for an older, widowed parent, as a part of adult responsibilities, is expected among middle-aged men and women in our society. While earlier wishes and needs may contribute to a heightened concern with this issue, including unusually rigid demands upon self for visiting and providing care, more often such care is provided in an appropriate manner which further enhances a life-long caring relationship between parents and offspring. Increased sense of concern for the welfare of others, and enjoyment in helping one's parents, just as they had earlier been of help, is characteristic of parent-caring in much of contemporary society.

Findings both from psychoanalytic inquiry and from empirical study of intergenerational ties suggest that the developmental line from dependence might better be understood as interdependence than an independence. Much of the psychological significance of this interdependence has been portrayed in other terms by self psychology in describing the psychological phenomenon of the self–selfobject. Not just in earliest childhood but, across the life course, parents and offspring continue to assist each other, serving as a source of soothing and caring in times of distress, and as a means for confirmation of self-worth. While, in early childhood, it is primarily the offspring who, characteristically, uses the parent as a source of self-confirmation, with attainment of adulthood, and increased congruence of the lives of each generation, mutual self-confirmation becomes a fundamental aspect of the interdependent relationship of parent and adult offspring, which contributes positively to the mental health of each generation.

To date, there has been much less study of these so-called self–selfobject ties among adult family members than of such ties in early childhood. Further, most such discussion has been on the continuing tie between women and their mothers, rather than men and their fathers and, for both men and women, parents of the other sex. Recognition of the father's role in development has been until recently a major unstudied problem in psychoanalytic inquiry. A groundbreaking work edited by Cath, Gurwitt, and Ross (1982) challenges an earlier view of the father as a source of conflict and of fatherhood as a problematic, rather than a positive, role in the family.

Fathers, too, care for their offspring, and provide a means for acquiring both self-regulation and also skills and interests, among both boys and girls. Pioneer investigations, such as that reported by Ross in this book, have begun to address this issue. At least in the childhood years, issues of time spent with children, and the quality of the relationship, have been addressed. Muslin's chapter focuses on the psychological significance of fathering, noting the importance of the father as a selfobject, and of the restorative contributions realized by the advent of parenthood for fathers. Across adulthood, fathers and sons continue to provide comfort and support in ways seldom discussed in the literature. Interdependence among fathers and both adult sons and daughters is far more important than has been realized. Once again, developmental study of parenthood has informed psychoanalysis, just as psychoanalysis has informed the study of adult development; however necessary the father–son conflict may be for the young boy's consolidation of identifications, and motivation for mastery in the world beyond the family, there is a much more important, supportive element to the father's care of his children across the life course, which is seldom considered.

Finally, it should be noted that psychoanalytic study of parenthood has implications not only for understanding of the life course, but for intervention as well, both in psychoanalysis and in psychotherapy. Adults are not just patients, but also parents, and parenthood may become an important avenue for the development of a therapeutic alliance, or a facilitating idealizing selfobject transference. Indeed, as a consequence of bringing the patient's experiences as parent into the therapeutic process, psychotherapy may both foster the parenting alliance, and benefit from enhancement of the therapeutic alliance. Particularly for adults with developmental deficits, the recognition of the child as a selfobject puts into proper locus the pain experienced by the patient–parent. Perhaps this understanding will better equip dynamic therapists to treat patients whose early disordered affective lives make transference experiences foreboding, and psychotherapy unlikely. Failures of personal integration, unconscious fantasies, and exploration of previously unacceptable wishes both to give and to receive care may all be expressed through analysis of the significance of parenthood for the patient. Parenthood represents the central most significant role in adult lives, and provides the connection of past experiences, present sources of satisfaction and dissatisfaction, and future intentions, hopes, and fears. It is an irony that, to date, so little has been written about the place of parenthood in psychoanalysis and psychotherapy. It is hoped that the present book has highlighted the significance of this as a clinical issue which is so little discussed in considering factors leading to effective treatment.

Few life experiences as clearly as parenthood combine the biopsychosocial forces that direct our lives. The foundation and critical concerns, be they theoretical or clinical, which we have covered can promote the further study of parenthood in an evolving psychosocial universe. Perhaps out of this a richer developmental understanding of adulthood will emerge which will synthetize the biological, the psychological, and the sociological contributions—both discretely and in their intrasystemic interactions.

REFERENCES

Anthony, E. J., & Benedek, T. (Eds.). *Parenthood: Its psychology and psychopathology*. Little, Brown, 1970.

Benedek, T. Parenthood as a developmental phase. *Journal of the American Psychoanalytic Association*, 1959, 7, 389–417.

Cath, S. H., Gurwitt, A. R., & Ross, J. M. (Eds.). *Father and child: Developmental and clinical perspectives*. Boston: Little, Brown, 1982.

Elder, G. *Children of the Great Depression*. Chicago: University of Chicago Press, 1974.

Weissman, S. H. *The process of becoming a parent—A paradigm for becoming a psychiatrist*. Paper presented to the Conference on Parenthood as an Adult Experience, Chicago, March 8, 1980.

AUTHOR INDEX

SUBJECT INDEX

Abortion, 93, 162
  for minors, legal aspects, 220–222
Abraham, 285, 316, 322
Abuse, physical, 253 (*see also* Child abuse)
Adaptation, psychosocial, and developmental
  tasks, 2, 3
Adolescent mothers (*see* Mothers, adolescent)
Adolescent pregnancy (*see* Pregnancy, adolescent)
Adolescents
  attitudes toward parents, 71–75
  career orientation, 79
  egocentrism, 88–90
  gender intensification, 74
  hospitalization, 39–42
  identity confusion, and adoption, 215
  imaginary audience, 88–90
  narcissim, 310, 311
  promiscuity in a girl, 45–47
  pubertal changes, 69, 70, 78, 80
  school, concern with, 71, 73, 74, 79
  self-image, xv
  selfobjects, 311
  substance abuse, 43–47
  suicide attempts, 245
Adolescents, parents of, 65–79
  age-related changes, 65, 77
  agreement with in dyads, 73
  competition, 311
  difficulties, 64
  disciplining and chores, 71
  employement, 68, 69
  marital satisfaction, effect on, 65
  parenting alliance, 38, 45–47
  and parents' own adolescence, 5, 6, 75–78,
    80
  perceptions, 67, 69–72, 75, 76
  self psychology, 310, 311
  sex, 66, 72–74, 78, 79

sexual component, 77, 78
  suburban middle class, 67
Adoption, 214, 302
  adolescent identity confusion, 215
  versus delivery, postpartum stress, 122, 123
Adult development (*see* Development, adult)
Advocacy
  Child (*see* Child advocacy)
  function of parenthood, 229*n*.
Affective disorders, 131, 132
Affects (*see also* Depression)
  assuming mother's, 343
  in development, 328–330
    case illustrations, 329, 330, 332–336
    structuralizing role, 328, 329
  difficulty in handling, 345–347
  fear of, in parents, 168
  selfobject function, 330–337
  self-regulation in parents, 392
Agamemnon, 315
Aggression, auto-, in chldren, 154, 155 (*see also*
  Anger; Hostility; Rage)
Aging and parenthood, 103–111, 361, 394, 397
  caretaking, 110
  case illustrations, 104–108
  depression, 104, 105
  loss of own siblings, 104, 105
  Oedipal situation, 108
  paranoia, 107, 110, 111
  regression, 103, 104, 106, 107, 110
  and self-esteem, 105
  self psychology, 108, 109
  widowerhood, 106, 107
Alcoholism, 253, 329, 331
Alliance, parenting (*see* Parenting alliance)
Alliance, therapeutic (*see* Therapeutic [working]
  alliance)
Amenorrhea, postpartum, 12
Anal phase, 368

411